THE OLD TESTAMENT SINCE THE REFORMATION

Lutterworth Library Vol. XLVII

THE OLD TESTAMENT
SINCE
THE REFORMATION

by

EMIL G. KRAELING

Formerly Associate Professor of Old Testament
in the Union Theological Seminary, New York

LUTTERWORTH PRESS
LONDON

First published 1955

To

Professor H. H. ROWLEY

honoured and beloved

by Old Testament scholars

of all lands

374 50

PRINTED IN GREAT BRITAIN
BY EBENEZER BAYLIS AND SON, LTD., THE
TRINITY PRESS, WORCESTER, AND LONDON

CONTENTS

INTRODUCTION

THE first book on the Old Testament to arouse my curiosity
was that of James Orr,[1] which stood on the shelves of the
library in the manse in which I grew up. I was attracted by
the bright red colour and gold lettering to finger this volume
and dip into its contents from which, though they were far
above my head, I gathered this much, that there were some
people in the world who chopped up the books of Moses and the
prophets and considered much of Old Testament history as
composed of myth and legend. It was evident that Dr. Orr was
worried about the truth of such critical theories and recoiled
from the consequences they had for the Christian faith. He
sought to discredit them by showing how they cancelled each
other, and he held that archæology was providing wonderful
confirmation for a more conservative view. The subject
troubled me enough, however, to wish to get to the bottom
of it.

A vast change has come over the world since Orr's book was
written. There no longer is any great excitement about the
"higher criticism". The barriers he and others sought to raise
up against it have been abandoned. Universally it is conceded
that Old Testament scholarship has given us a new, realistic
and dependable picture of the way in which the literary
materials of the Old Testament arose and of what they mean
historically.[2] While the future may bring many corrections,
nothing that could be adduced along critical lines could change
the situation very much in principle. The passing of the debate
over the higher criticism still leaves us with the real problem
of the Old Testament: *should it have any authority in the
Christian Church and if so how is that authority to be defined?*

Once one has awakened to the commanding importance of
this question one will be able to see that it runs through the
whole of Christian history like a scarlet thread.[3] Yea, more:
one can see that much of the difference in theologies springs
from the extent to which they build Old Testament ideas or
impulses into the primitive Christian patterns. And the latter,

7

one may discover, differ in themselves already because of the degree of Old Testament influence received. The Old Testament problem, therefore, is not just one of many. It is the master problem of theology. And even for those who regard the first half of the question, as formulated above, beyond debate, the second half still remains in force. All theology that operates in any way with biblical heritage hangs in the air until it is settled.

Informed discussion of the Old Testament problem requires some insight into its history. A particular importance attaches to the genesis of the problem in early Christianity and to the diversity of attitudes and viewpoints concerning it that are revealed there. The relation of the Testaments is commonly studied from the angle: "the Old Testament in the New." The question is not: does early Christianity have strong links with the Old Testament? It is rather: do these links with the Old Testament merely represent the egg-shell out of which Christianity emerged, and which therefore may be discounted? Or, if one refuses to accept that question, then it is this: what part of the Old Testament heritage received by the early Christians is permanently binding for Christianity? We hope to deal with the beginnings of the problem in another volume[4] and can only stress their importance in passing here.

Our concern in the present book is with the thought on the subject of Christianity and the Old Testament since the Reformation. These studies were undertaken in the desire of garnering the fruits of modern theological history for our subject. Only passing attention can be given to the history of Old Testament scholarship, for we seek something more fundamental: the thought concerning the authority and meaning of the Old Testament for the Christian. Matters of purely antiquarian interest must, therefore, fall by the wayside. The views of many who have dealt in some way with our theme are rehearsed in detail. Our desire has been to make the full weight and range of the standpoints reported discernible. That of course necessitated selectivity. But the information here assembled should give the reader an adequate picture of the more recent phases of what may well be called "the greatest inner-Christian debate".

Chapter One

LUTHER AND THE OLD TESTAMENT

IN Roman Catholic Europe of the Middle Ages Scripture had not enjoyed as influential a role as it had in the Church of the first six centuries. Theoretically, the Bible was the supreme authority (especially for Duns Scotus and Occam), but in practice it did not function as such. Even the guardianship of the Canon was not exercised very rigorously,[1] for apocryphal pieces like the Epistle to the Laodiceans and Fourth Ezra could be carried along in the Latin New Testament without compunction, and the Old Testament contained materials later rejected by Catholicism at Trent. The Church, furthermore, had come to set up an accumulating "tradition" as a second principle of authority, and by means of it neutralized Scripture authority wherever it chose. As a devout son of the Catholic Church, Luther did not at first deny the authority of tradition. As late as the Leipzig disputation with Eck in 1519, he still held fast to it. But soon afterwards he took the fatal step and set aside a tradition that put to nought the Word of God (Mark 7: 13 f.). The Protestant Church now became a necessity and a reality, and this Church apparently had the principle of the Bible as sole authority put right into its cradle.

Influenced as he was in his early years by the scholastic belief in a fourfold sense of Scripture,[2] Luther did not at first see the problem of the unity of the contents of Scripture, which would at once have raised the Old Testament problem. At the time when he gave his first exegetical course at the University of Wittenberg, he had already devoted much effort to biblical study. In his grasp of the Bible as a whole, as revealed in his early lectures on the Psalms, he had, according to Holl,[3] only been equalled by men like Tertullian or Origen. But he had never doubted that the Bible in all its parts has the same meaning, for the Holy Spirit, who, as Catholic doctrine that he did not question taught, stands behind the Bible, naturally must

9

be consistent in the intention of making known God's redemptive purpose. Hence, Luther in those days could read Paul's
doctrine of justification and Christological interpretations into
the Psalms without observing that he was doing violence to
their plain meaning.

The assumption of a definite, clear and consistent meaning of
Scripture as a whole then becomes for Luther a cardinal point
when he begins to teach that the Bible is the sole authority.[4]
If there were any doubt as to what the Bible meant to teach,
how could faith have a firm foundation, and how could man
turn to the Bible?[5] In the disputation with Eck, Luther pointed
out that it was not enough to have the immediate context of
a biblical passage in mind in interpreting it; one must have the
totality of the Bible before one's eyes to appraise properly the
sense and bearing of a given passage. He once advised Spalatin
to read the whole Bible from beginning to end—then only, he
asserts, can one interpret with success.[6] "If one pauses at some
individual passage and seeks help for its interpretation in the
patristic books, one has nothing but sorry patchwork in one's
hands." In the controversy over indulgences Luther was forced
to maintain the right of individual Scripture interpretation over
against the collective authority of the Church. He did this not
by affirming his personal qualifications, but rather by teaching
the clarity of Scripture; "no clearer book has ever been
written." By that he did not mean that it was devoid of obscurities. He himself had often enough spoken of its profundity
and of the need of gradually growing in the understanding of it.
What he meant was that in the things that mattered for man's
salvation the Bible was absolutely clear. The principle of using
clear passages to explain obscure ones (which he followed, e.g.,
in his dispute with Zwingli over the words "This is My body",
giving heed to I Cor. 10: 16f.) naturally flowed from this.

But after Luther had emancipated himself from the scholastic
doctrine of the fourfold sense of Scripture and had begun to
apply his principle of literal interpretation more consistently,
he became increasingly conscious of the diversity of the contents of the Bible.[7] He saw that even within the New Testament there was not the full unanimity that, in view of the
doctrine of inspiration, really ought to be there. Catholic
theologians were not slow in pointing out the passages that dis-

agreed with his understanding of the message of Paul and which, in the light of the principle that the Bible cannot contradict itself, had somehow to be harmonized with Paul's statements. But Luther was unable to accept such sophistries. When pressed, he chose the alternative of differentiating between elements of the Bible having greater and lesser authority, or such having an importance for all time, and such having an importance only for a time that is past.[8] "The question is," he once says—

"What is the Word of God for me?" One must deal carefully with Scripture. The Word of God came about in diverse ways from the beginning and one must not only see whether it is God's Word and whether God spoke it, but, much more, to whom it is spoken and whether it is intended for thee or for another. Then there is a partition as between summer and winter. God spoke a great deal to David and told him to do this and that. But it is no concern of mine. Nor is it spoken to me. He can speak to me if He wishes to have it so. You must look at the Word that concerns you, that is spoken to you and does not concern another. There are two kinds of "Word" in the Scripture. One does not concern me or have aught to do with me. The other has to do with me, and following that which has to do with me I may boldly go forward and rely on it as on a strong rock. If it does not deal with me, I must stand still. The false prophets rush in and say, dear people, this is God's Word. It is true, we cannot deny it, but we are not the people to whom He speaks.

It is apparent, then, that Luther, in his own spontaneous and original thinking, shies away from unilateral biblicism. Not "the letter that killeth" is supreme, but the message of salvation through Jesus Christ that Paul preached is his principle of authority. The Bible as a whole is only the Word of God when and to the extent that he can view it as in harmony with or expressive of that message. At the time of the writing of his prefaces to his translations of the biblical books he seems to have realized more clearly than before that the gospel is not originally a book but an oral message. The writing down of it was already an ailing in the spirit of the early Church; it became necessary because of the perversions of it that were being spread abroad at that time. The Bible as a whole is not an end in itself—it is merely the vehicle of a certain content. And the thing with which the Bible is concerned is to make evident "the great fire of God's love for us".[9] This love, of course, is expressed in the gospel of Jesus Christ. He once refutes an opponent who harps on Scripture: "You base your claim on the slave, i.e., Scripture, and not on the whole of it or its most excellent portion. I leave this slave to you. I invoke the Lord who is the King of Scripture." Yea, Luther would undertake to draw on the Psalms, Isaiah, and the same Holy Spirit and fashion as good a New Testament as the apostles have written.[10]

He finds that all the proper sacred books agree in this respect, "that they all preach and treat of Christ (*Christum treiben*). Furthermore, this is the right yardstick wherewith to criticize all books—whether they treat of Christ or not. For all Scripture exhibits Christ (Rom. 3: 21), and Paul will know nothing but Christ (I Cor. 2: 2)."[11] This emphasis on the contents makes Luther supremely indifferent with respect to formal matters such as the authorship of the biblical books. "That which does not treat of Christ is not yet apostolic though Peter or Paul taught it. And again, that which preaches Christ would be apostolic though Judas, Annas, Pilate or Herod taught it. Christ alone and nothing but the Crucified and none other do we recognize for our Master. Paul would not have us believe him or believe an angel (Gal. 1: 8, 12), unless Christ dwell in him."[12]

It is important to discern that Luther is forced to discriminate between more and less authoritative areas even in the New Testament. From the immutably fixed centre of the gospel as preached by Paul (who, it must not be forgotten, affirms the unity of his faith with that of the Jerusalem Church), he came to evaluate the various writings in a surprisingly free manner. His observations were so shocking to subsequent Lutheran orthodoxy that they were consigned to oblivion until Semler (following Wetstein) again called attention to them in 1764.[13]

In effect, Luther puts certain New Testament writings into a primary and others into a secondary position. Paul, with his Epistles to the Romans, Galatians, and Ephesians, naturally stands in the foreground. The Gospel of John and I John, I Peter and Acts also meet with his favour. In the latter book

he overlooks the "Catholic" leaven and finds a demonstration
of the manner in which the Holy Spirit came to men through
the hearing of the gospel and not of the law. He did not
esteem the Synoptic Gospels so highly because he finds them
dealing more with Christ's miracles and with the works and
fruits of faith than with the real Christian message. His
strictures against the Epistle of James[14] are well known—he
regards it as late owing to its dependence on Pauline and
Petrine sayings. Jude he considers secondary and based on
II Peter; the author of Hebrews, too, speaks like a later disciple
of the apostles (2: 3), and was not Paul, as the ecclesiastical
tradition claimed. Revelation seemed to him rather close to
II Esdras (where the Vulgate, indeed, puts it), and not truly
apostolic or even prophetic. In his Bible translation he even
puts Hebrews, James and Jude at the end of the Epistles and
before Revelation, thus in effect establishing a group of books
of secondary authority. We can therefore see that Luther not
only disregards the doctrine of Scripture-inspiration (at least
for a portion of the New Testament), but is in effect, though not
in method, verging rather close to one of the positions of
Marcion, who had set up ten Epistles of Paul and Luke's
Gospel as authoritative.

It seemed essential to us to set forth Luther's general attitude
on Scripture before entering upon the problem that is our particular concern. We may now turn to the latter and ask, Where
does this leave the Old Testament?

We have seen that Luther, at the very beginning of his career
and so long as he still held to the scholastic idea of the fourfold
sense of Scripture, was full of the thought that the gospel was
to be found in the Old Testament. Under the influence of his
new principle of exclusively literal interpretation, he later modified that as evidenced by the preface to the Psalms in his Bible
translation. Nevertheless, the problem of how to relate the Old
Testament to the gospel and thus give the Old Testament a
value for the Christian occupied him. Following the New
Testament writers and the Church Fathers from Justin Martyr
on, he believed that the Old Testament contained individual
utterances or sections in which there is anticipation of the
Christian message. How could this be otherwise when the same
Holy Ghost who had given the New Testament had also given

the Old Testament? One could not, of course, expect the Holy Ghost to impart the full truth to men on the Old Testament stage of existence; pedagogical considerations made it possible or even necessary for Him to give teachings not yet up to the evangelical level. But here and there the evangelical element breaks forth like the sun through the clouds. These passages of the Old Testament have a high importance. Luther can, on occasion, demand that the whole Old Testament is to be interpreted in the light of the gospel; he can compare it to a testamentary letter of Christ that is only to be understood properly from the standpoint attained after the death of Christ. In speaking of Matthew 22: 40, he says:

> The Lord therewith shows us the right technique to interpret Moses and the prophets and gives us to understand that Moses with all his stories and parables points to him, pertains to Christ and means him—namely, Christ is the point in the circle about which the whole circle is drawn, and whoever faces toward him belongs in it. For he is the point in the middle of the circle and all the stories of Holy Writ, if they are rightly regarded, refer to Christ.[14]

From a psychological angle, one feels that Luther is really setting up a defence-mechanism. Behind this reasoning stands the fear that the Old Testament interpreted alone—without regard to the gospel—has a natural drift leading in another direction. Since he cannot emancipate himself from the New Testament Scripture proof, he is forced to emulate early Christian example in resolutely seizing the Old Testament and subjecting it to Christian purpose. But it is one thing to set up such a principle and another thing to carry it out in detailed exegesis. In his early study of the Psalms he could do it on the basis of a sincere false assumption and with the help of the scholastic doctrine of interpretation. Can it be done on the theory of an alone legitimate literal interpretation?

Since Luther was entirely dominated by Paul's understanding of the difference between the way of the law and the gospel of grace,[15] he naturally looked at the Old Testament by and large as representing the way of the law. The late Jewish view of the Old Testament, it must be recalled, had put the emphasis on

Moses and the law, and Paul had imbibed and shared that view. In thinking about the law Luther yields to highly enlightened viewpoints. The early Church had emphasized the moral law of the Old Testament as distinct from the bygone ceremonial law also found in that work. Luther found it difficult to disengage the moral from the ceremonial element in Old Testament law. Even in the Decalogue there is a ceremonial ordinance—the Sabbath commandment, and a commandment that is no longer important in Christian countries: the prohibition of graven images. It becomes clear to him that the entire Mosaic law is an indivisible whole, intended for a definite nation of a definite time. He conceives of it as essentially parallel to other bodies of national law, such as the *Sachsenspiegel* (a collection of laws in vogue among the Saxons, made about A.D. 1200 and widely quoted in Luther's time). Hence, Moses is the "*Sachsenspiegel* of the Jews". Non-Jewish people can simply substitute their own laws for the Mosaic law.

He makes an interesting distinction, however, between what he calls "natural laws" that forbid sins we understand as such and the "Levitic laws" that are without a discernible moral basis. As the designation "natural" shows, he does not consider this moral law as requiring supernatural revelation, but rather looks upon it as "written in everybody's heart". The significance of the Decalogue he finds in this—that these "natural laws are nowhere so finely and properly stated". But even this moral law has lost its importance as a way of salvation (cf. Romans 3: 28). It can, however, serve the useful purpose of a yardstick with which one may gratefully determine "how far the Holy Spirit has brought us with his sanctification, and in how far we are still deficient, so that we do not become too self-confident and think that we now have done everything, and that we may thus continually grow in sanctification and increasingly become a new creature in Christ".[16] The office of Moses, he argues, was to make the Jewish people conscious of sin and thereby to pave the way for redemption. Essentially he looks at the remainder of the Old Testament as merely continuing that function.

What now are the other books of the prophets and the narratives? Answer: nothing else than what Moses is. For they all carry on Moses' office and ward off the false prophets so that they don't lead the people to (rely on) works(!) but let them stay in the right office of Moses and knowledge of the law. And hold fast to this, that by the right meaning of the law they keep the people in (the consciousness of) their own unworthiness and drive toward Christ as Moses does. And they exhibit a twofold example, of those who have Moses right and who don't have him right, and the reward and punishment of both. Thus the prophets are nothing else than handlers and witnesses of Moses and his office that through the law they may bring everyone to Christ.[17]

We likewise find Luther affirming his rejection of the applicability of the Mosaic law as a whole over against the enthusiasts who claimed that Christians must obey the Old Testament also.

Therefore say to these same enthusiasts: Leave Moses and his people together. They are a thing of the past and none of my business. I hear the word that concerns me. We have the gospel. Christ says: "Go ye and preach the gospel, not only to the Jews . . . but to all creatures" . . . These words include me . . . for I am one of all creatures. If Christ had not added: "preach to all creatures", I would not bother about it and would take the same attitude toward it I now take toward Moses. I pay no attention to him, he does not concern me.[18]

It is quite obvious, if one views the Old Testament primarily as preaching the law and views its law as being primarily a Jewish national concern, or an illustration of what reason can produce without the aid of revelation, that one is very close to robbing it of most of its value for the Christian.[19] While Luther in the Antinomian controversy shrank back from the consequences of his earlier position, this was due more to practical considerations than to better theological insight, and both he and his opponent Agricola may well be accused of veering away from the true evangelical idea of faith in this debate.[20]

If Luther felt free to evaluate the New Testament canon on the basis of his central principle, it is to be expected that he would feel even more free to express independent opinions on the Old Testament writings. He valued Genesis highly and, because it praised faith and because of the use Paul makes of it,

he considered it an almost evangelical book.[21] The rest of the
Pentateuch is, of course, so much concerned with the law that
it could not have much appeal for him. He makes little use of
the historical books. In Judges he finds excellent heroes and
deliverers portrayed. He once refers to the Books of the Kings
as the Gazetteer of the Jews, in which the Jews are well described,
and places its credibility above that of Chronicles. Essentially,
therefore, he looks upon this as patriotic historiography rather
than as sacred literature. Esther is offensive to him as a
Judaizing document, and of Ezra-Nehemiah he says that it
"Estherizes and Mordecaizes" in like manner.

He valued the prophets chiefly for their Messianic prophecy,
but in the latter he saw primarily the special activity of the
Holy Ghost. Isaiah 53 is a witness of Christ that stands so
bright that even in the New Testament, apart from Paul, there
is hardly a passage to equal it. He puts Daniel among the
prophets and considers him the most excellent one next to
Isaiah because of his supposed prophecies of the death of Christ.
But otherwise he does not have much use for the prophets.
Their prophesying of future things he considers of no benefit to
faith; indeed, such prophesying "is almost one of the least of
gifts; yea, occasionally it comes from the devil". He finds them
prophesying concerning kings and worldly events, wherein, he
says, they often erred. He recognized the fact of literary
dependence when he says the earlier prophets studied Moses,
and the later prophets previous ones, and implies that occasionally hay, straw and wood got into their teachings along with
silver and gold. This amounts to saying that there is a great deal
of material in the prophets which is of no value for us. Concerning the prophetic books he was willing to assume redactional
activity by other hands in arrangement of material—expressly
so in the case of Hosea, Isaiah and Jeremiah.

Luther had a particular fondness for the Psalter.[22] He had
given his first exegetical course on that book, and its phraseology (notably Psalm 31: 2) had helped him to discover the true
meaning of the New Testament gospel as expressed in Romans
1: 17.[23] He gave utterance to his affection for it in classic
fashion in his preface to his translation of it in the edition of
1531 (partially quoted below). But it is to be noted how far he
has progressed in his understanding of that book since his early

2

grappling with it.   There is little left of the "Christological" interpretation or of any supernaturalism.   His view of it seems to be entirely human, for he now looks upon the Psalms as expressing the living reactions of the Old Testament saints in the concrete situations of life.   Over against the Catholic fondness for hagiography, he points out that the Psalter does not tell of the works of the saints but reports their *words*—how they spoke with God and prayed to God.   "Yea, it enables us to look into their hearts and see what thoughts they had and how their hearts reacted to all the happenings, exigencies and necessities of existence."   He compares the human heart to a ship at sea driven by winds blowing at different times from all four directions:

Fear and worry over that which is to come, sorrow and sadness over present evil, hope and pride of future happiness, assurance and joy of things presently enjoyed—such are the winds that blow and teach the tongue to speak and open the heart to pour out its contents.   In the Psalms the chief thing is such a speaking in all manner of stormy winds.   Where does one find a finer word of gladness than the psalms of praise and thanksgiving have? There you look into the heart of all the saints as into lovely, blessed gardens, yea as into heaven; you perceive fine, lovely flowers grow therein in the shape of all manner of beautiful happy thoughts toward God and His kindness.   Again, where do you find more profound, more sorrowful, more miserable words of sadness, than in the psalms of lamentation?   There you again look into the heart of all saints, as into death, yea as into hell. How black and dark it is there from all manner of sorrowful seeing of the wrath of God.   And so also where they speak of fear and hope they use such words that no artist could paint the fear and hope, and no Cicero or other orator form them in such a way. And as already said the best thing is that they speak such words to God and with God, which has the result that a twofold seriousness and life are in the words.   For where one merely speaks to men of such things, it does not come out of the heart so deeply, does not burn, live and penetrate to such an extent.   Hence it comes about that the Psalter is the booklet of all saints and everybody in whatsoever situation he may be finds Psalms and sayings in it that rhyme with his affairs, and seem to him as though they were thus formulated just for his sake.   So that he himself could not formulate them better or find them or wish for them.

This is almost a modern psychological understanding of the Psalter, though coupled with a belief in the validity and authority of its words which does not accord well with such a point of view.

The Book of Job is linked by Luther with those Psalms which deal with the trials of the pious.[24] The pious sufferer is an example of that trial which Christ later was to endure—that of extreme forsakenness of God. He does not consider it strictly historical, but rather a poetic creation. The three books ascribed to Solomon stand apart from the main stream. Proverbs is chiefly concerned with the individual and his private existence and is a *liber oeconomicus*. Ecclesiastes, whose direct authorship by Solomon he doubts, (in one instance even conceding the possibility of its being edited and assembled by Sirach), Luther first viewed as inculcating the lesson of Matthew 6: 34 (take no thought for the morrow, learn the uselessness of all human undertaking and leave everything to God). Later he looked upon it as chiefly addressed to those in authority, counselling them to fear God and endure bravely amid the trials of their position; it is a sort of *liber politicus*. In Song of Songs, which he also derives from Solomon only in a secondary way, he allegorizes the bride as referring to Solomon's kingdom. Where there is obedience and good government God dwells and kisses His beloved bride with the kiss of His mouth, viz., His Word. A poem of Luther's own time by the poet Theuerdank, in which a bride symbolizing his kingdom is brought to the Emperor Maximilian, seems to have influenced his interpretation here.

In his arrangement of the Old Testament books in his Bible translation, Luther, as in the case of the New Testament, follows a literary classification. He has three divisions: (1) historical books, under which heading he put "the law" and the "former prophets" (with Ruth after Judges), the Chronicler's work (I and II Chronicles, Ezra, Nehemiah), and Esther; (2) the didactic books (Job, Psalms and the three Solomonic books); (3) the prophetic books (i.e., the "latter Prophets" of the Hebrew arrangement, but with each of the twelve "Minor" Prophets counted separately, and with Lamentations put after Jeremiah, and Daniel put after Ezekiel). Luther heeded the Jewish tradition, however, in eliminating those books which were not found in the collection of the synagogue. Since in the

Vulgate I and II Maccabees stand after Malachi, he put the other rejected books (except I and II Esdras which he discarded entirely) with them, thus setting up a whole division which, taking a cue from Jerome, he called The Apocrypha.

That the arrangement of books in the Protestant Old Testament translations thus inaugurated (for the Authorized Version followed suit) possesses certain advantages is undeniable. But one might wish that Luther had accepted Carlstadt's suggestion and had gone back to the Palestinian Jewish arrangement which graded the books in three groups of decreasing authority.[25] This would have put troublesome books like Daniel, Chronicles, Ezra, Nehemiah, Esther, Song of Songs and Ecclesiastes in the third division and hence on a distinctly lower level than others.

Luther is a whole cosmos of thought and impulses. Ecclesiastical responsibility, combat with extremists, reluctance to depart very far from the common ground established in the early Christian creeds, the impossibility of thinking through all Christian problems, prevented him from following up his many original insights and personal leanings. Indeed, many statements can be adduced from his works in which he emphasizes Scripture authority in a manner that seems inconsistent with the knowledge he had attained. One definitely feels that if it were not for the use of the Old Testament made in the New Testament Luther might have veered farther in the Marcionitic direction.[26] If he had realized as clearly as we are able to do to-day that the Messianic prophecy of the Old Testament does not actually predict the life of Christ or the redemption brought by Him in as clear and direct a manner as the New Testament writers and the early Fathers believed, the revelation of the Old Testament would probably have shrunk to purely historical significance in his eyes. Human values of a spiritual or moral sort alone would have remained. The epochal thing about Luther and the Scriptures is really that he subordinated them to what he conceived to be the Christian gospel.[27]

Chapter Two

ZWINGLI AND CALVIN AND THE OLD TESTAMENT

UNLIKE Luther, who was concerned with the individual's certainty of salvation, the Reformed theologians placed their emphasis on the Christian life flowing forth from such certainty. They appreciated the importance of creating a social and political environment favourable for Christian nurture. A Christian state run according to Christian principles was to them an objective worth striving for. The New Testament did not provide a sufficient background for their ecclesiastical and political practice,[1] for the early Christians had been a minority group in a hostile world. One had to go back to the Old Testament to find a community run on such a basis as they envisioned, and hence the Reformed leaders had a particular interest in stressing the authority of the older portion of the Canon.

This already becomes vivid in the work and thought of Zwingli. For the Swiss Reformer, the Holy Spirit is the overriding factor in religion. He looks on Scripture not as teaching us what God did in the past to redeem man, but rather as teaching what He now does and what we must do to serve Him.[2] Christ is not so much the heart and centre of Scripture, as He is one of a series of biblical personages revealing the will of God to man. Zwingli's humanistic background, which had given him a rich appreciation of Greek and Roman thought, led him to broaden the concept of revelation and to esteem noble sayings of a Plato or Seneca as manifestations of the working of the same Holy Spirit who inspired the biblical writers. The difference is that Scripture is inspired throughout. In interpreting Scripture Zwingli shows a most remarkable ability to discount the local and temporal elements; only after that is properly done is it authoritative. The Old Testament to him has the same dignity as the New, and where the latter does not prescribe afresh the Old Testament regulation is still in force. The external revelation of Scripture must, however, be brought to appreciation and understanding by the Holy Spirit working in us. Interpretation of Scripture must be free from any curbs or restraints. The only limitations he recognizes are a few simple hermeneutic rules: (1) Every passage has a plain meaning. (2) Allegorical interpretation is without validity, but, especially in the Old Testament, is permissible. (3) Scripture is fully consistent in itself. In case of doubt as to how to interpret, that meaning which is most in line with God's glory is to be preferred.

In building a Protestant political as well as religious community the Swiss Reformer was faced by the fact that the Anabaptists, who were seeking to translate the ideals of the Sermon on the Mount into local group life, were an obstacle. Since the Old Testament alone provided the justification for a national religious ideal the Anabaptists were driven to reject that book as given only to the Jews and no longer authoritative for the Christian. Other arguments against it were also adduced by them, notably that the Old Testament did not have a belief in individual immortality and thus was not on the level of Christian faith; but they were of secondary importance. In his *Refutation of the Wiles of the Anabaptists*, 1527, Zwingli dealt with their claims in the following manner. He insisted that there was only one covenant and one people of God (thereby affirming the relevance of the Old Testament for the Christian), but went so far as to concede the following differences between the two parts of the Canon: (1) Christ was given to the Christians and only promised to the Jews. (2) Christians go to heaven after death while the Jews go to Abraham's bosom. (3) For Christians, the Old Testament types and shadows are done away with. (4) The understanding of religion in the New Testament is clearer than in the Old Testament, because in the latter religion is impaired by ceremonialism. (5) The universalism of the New Testament religion stands on a higher plane than that of the Old Testament.[3]

Zwingli's position on this matter was followed at first by Bucer, but the latter subsequently made a sharp about-face in his commentary on the Gospels, and particularly in his commentary on Romans. Here he denied that there was any difference between the Old Testament and the New Testament and read the whole Christology and doctrine of the Atonement back into the former.   This seemingly cut the very ground away from under the feet of the Anabaptists.[4]

Bucer's line of thought was taken up and developed further by John Calvin in his *Institutes* of 1536, a work which was expanded and improved in subsequent editions.   Since Calvin became the dominant teacher of a great segment of Protestantism, it is worth while to take up his views in some detail.

Unlike Zwingli, whose humanistic and philosophic bent inclined him to so broad ideas, Calvin was purely a Biblicist. He had little use for secular wisdom, but looked exclusively to the Bible as the source of all religious insight.   But a basis had to be found for the belief that the Bible is the Word of God.   The Catholic believed it on the authority of the Church. In a book on the *Central Doctrines of St. Paul*, (1539) Calvin attempts to controvert that position on the basis of Eph. 2: 20, according to which the Church rests on the foundation of the prophets and apostles (erroneously taking this to mean the prophetic and apostolic writings!).   But he then adduces arguments to buttress the revealed character of Scripture—first, the consideration that Scripture provokes our reverence by its power, and second, that the witness of the Holy Spirit convinces us of its divine origin.   In the latter particular he had been anticipated by Luther, though Luther did not raise the thought to such high prominence.[5]   In the *Institutes* of 1550 Calvin not only added these reflections but increased his emphasis on the authority of the Bible.[6]   The famous saying of Augustine, "I would not believe the gospel if the authority of the Catholic Church had not impressed me", is controverted by him on the basis of Augustine's own words, for he finds that Augustine actually has other and better reasons for believing, viz., the inner illumination by the Spirit, and that the Church has only a preparatory role in connection with the origin of faith.   In the final edition of 1559 Calvin first discusses the witness of the Spirit, which he now regards as principal proof for the authority of Scripture, and then adds other auxiliary proofs, viz., the dignity of the subjects treated, the diction of the prophets, the antiquity of the writings, the attending miracles, the miraculous preservation through the ages, the obedience

Scripture has received through many generations, and the witness of the martyrs who died for its truth.

Calvin did not follow Luther in the point of feeling free to evaluate and even criticize the canon. He viewed the Bible as the book in which God had set forth His will officially and definitely for all time. The biblical authors were to him only the amanuenses of the Holy Spirit and their writings were therefore oracles from on high. Every part of Scripture is equal to the other in authority. Supremely logical, he drew every consequence from this doctrine of inspiration, which he presupposes, though he does not develop it. Presumably his legal training influenced him in the direction of imagining the Bible as a sort of ideal *corpus juris*.

Without realizing it, Calvin, while elevating the Bible to the rank of sole principle, was actually governed by a second principle—a doctrinal slant that grew out of a subjective choice of biblical materials which suited his type of mind and his interest. With the help of this slant and these materials he mastered everything else in the Bible that stood in his way. The thing in Scripture that appealed most to Calvin was the idea of a God bent on his own "glory". We have seen that Zwingli had made that thought central for biblical interpretation, though not for doctrine, as Calvin now proceeded to do. "What is man that thou art mindful of him and the son of man that thou visitest him?" These words of Psalm 8 have been aptly said to describe the spirit of Calvin's theology. Whatever happens in the world may serve some useful purpose, but that is not the ultimate reason why it happens: God has primarily His own glory in mind and founded the whole world to the end that it might be the scene of that glory. Thus Calvin takes man out of the centre of the stage—an achievement in itself—and puts God there instead. The idea of the glory of God is raised to the nth degree by being combined with an absolute determinism.[7] The corollary to that is that certain people, the "elect", are predestined to be saved and all the others predestined to be lost. The Church is the society of the elect. Some may, indeed, have got into this society who are not of the really "elect", but the Church has an obligation to exercise strict discipline and to expel such persons as soon as it becomes certain of their status. The idea of the chosen people is thus reconstituted, though on non-national lines, in the spirit of certain Old Testament writings like Deuteronomy.

It is quite surprising in view of such presuppositions to find Calvin as an exegete showing a far-reaching insight into the historical conditioning of Scripture.[8] He interprets Scripture literally with a lawyer's precision and usually resists the temptation to impute to the author of an Old Testament passage a deeper meaning than the words themselves warrant. Even the New Testament interpretation of Old Testament passages does not deter him from first taking the latter in the plain meaning which the context in his opinion demands. But since, for him, one and the same Holy Ghost is the author of Scripture, there is a tendency on his part to view ideas and thoughts of Scripture that are on a distinctly lower level as an accommodation of the Holy Ghost to the plane of the time when such utterances were made, and to look for elements tending toward a nobler insight such as is attained in passages that are on a higher level. The particular biblical passage thus is to be interpreted in the light of the great connection of the whole process of scriptural revelation.   Calvin's biblically-derived philosophy of revelation, which views all history as under the aegis of an eschatological promise, with Christ's appearance on earth as the pledge of a final fulfilment, gives him an opportunity to put everything in its proper place. Interestingly enough, he is able to view that philosophy of revelation itself as one that emerges gradually and thus to appraise its earlier and cruder forms of expression as only preparatory.

Turning now to the problem of the "law", let us see how Calvin dealt with it in the successive editions of his great work. In his treatment of it in the first part of the *Institutes* of 1536[9] his purpose is the strictly evangelical one to show that the law, by revealing the will of God, makes us conscious of our inability to fulfil it and thus prepares us for the message of the gospel of grace. But in carrying it out, Calvin Christianizes the Old Testament law to an extent that we would not consider historically permissible. In fact, he practically closes his eyes to the new moral values in the preaching of Jesus and reduces Him to the level of a correct interpreter of Moses; for Jesus, he holds, did not add anything to the law—He merely did away with Pharisaic misinterpretation of it. If the Catholic Church asserted that Jesus had added "special counsels" to the law, but that these were only applicable to monks, Calvin insists that these special counsels are already implied in the eternal law of the Old Testament. He denies the double moral standard of Catholicism and asserts that everything in the law is too difficult for us to fulfil unless God gives us the strength to do so. The *pièce de résistance* of his whole section on the law is an interpretation of the Ten Commandments, after the manner of Luther's catechism. But Calvin's strict biblicism does not permit him to accept Luther's arbitrary elimination of the second commandment and his partition of the tenth commandment into two commandments; the former gives Calvin a welcome weapon against Catholic "idolatry". Interesting is his partial spiritualization of the Sabbath ordinance in this early phase of his thinking; its "ceremonial" aspect, he holds, is merely a shadow of things to come, and is no longer binding. The commandment now signifies that we should desist from our evil works and find rest in God. Since there is no qualitative difference between one day and another, the Christian Sunday serves just as well as Saturday as a day of rest from labour and for the assembly of Christian congregations.

In the *Institutes* of 1539, Calvin made significant revisions and alterations in the direction of Christianizing the Old Testament law still further and of watering down Christian principles with Old Testament ideas. In his revised interpretation of the Decalogue he now is bent on showing that it is a perfect code of morals. He assumes that each commandment contains a great deal more than the mere words express, and his way of discovering its full range is to inquire into the Lawgiver's intent. After Christianizing the Decalogue all along the line, he can affirm that the law is by no means abrogated, but is in full force for the Christian. In contrast to his earlier exposition of the first commandment, in which, like Luther, he had emphasized faith combined with love and hope as of cardinal importance, he now placed these things in a cultic framework, making them subsidiary, as it were, to divine *worship*.[10] This cultic orientation of religion affords an easy transition to the discussion of images, of the hallowing of the name of God, of the Sabbath and of the oath. With respect to the Sabbath he now—after three years!—acknowledges the divine institution of a special rest day, though arbitrarily substituting the first day for the seventh, and thus takes a first step in the direction of later Calvinistic Sabbatarianism that played such a great role in England and America. In his discussion of the oath, his "watering down" of the New Testament ethic becomes particularly apparent. If the Anabaptists based their refusal to swear on Matt. 5: 34, Calvin rejects that because the oath is commanded in the Old Testament (Deut. 6: 13). To interpret the words of Jesus as the Anabaptists do, he asserts, is to make Christ contradict the Father. The intention of Jesus, he argues, was merely to curb the misuse of the oath. So he proceeds to justify the oath and set forth its permissible varieties, interpreting Jesus on the basis of Moses, the New Testament on the basis of the Old Testament.

In the second edition of the *Institutes* Calvin added an appendix of a general character to this discussion and exposition of the law.[11] It was evidently provoked by the attacks of the Anabaptists on the Old Testament. He accuses them of thinking of the Hebrew people much as one might think of a herd of swine that was being fattened on earth by God without any hope of eternal life. Calvin asserts that "all persons from the beginning of the world, whom God has adopted into the society of His people, have been federally connected with Him by the same law and the same doctrine which are in force among us". He thus emphasizes the point that there was only one covenant, so that those of the days before Christ and ourselves are in an uninterrupted religious sequence. It should be noted, too, that he sets up a concept of a "society of God's people" into which men are "adopted". He thus substitutes the Church for the Jewish racial and national community. Having prepared the ground in this manner he states that he is now going to show the similarity and the differences between the Old and the New Testaments. He narrows the discussion down unduly, however, by confining himself to setting forth what kind of a covenant the Lord made with the Israelites before Christ and what it is that He has entered into (note avoidance of the word covenant here!) since Christ. He finds the one and the same covenant enduring;[12] that of the Christian period varies only in administration. He maintains (1) that the Jews of the Old Testament were

adopted into the hope of immortality; (2) that their covenant
was not founded on their merits, but purely on the mercy of the
God who had called them; (3) that they possessed and knew
Christ as the Mediator, through whom they were united to God,
and so became partakers of His promises. We and they thus are
one in the hope of immortality, in the character of the covenant
as covenant of grace and in the knowledge of the Mediator Jesus
Christ.

In undertaking to substantiate these claims in detail Calvin
had his difficulties. The first point, in particular, that the hope
of immortality was the same in the Old Testament as in the
New Testament, posed a considerable hurdle. His starting-
point was the Christianizing and spiritualizing interpretation of
the Old Testament found in the New Testament. Paul's line in
I Corinthians 10, stressing the essential identity of the Hebrew
and Christian religions, and finding the Christian sacraments
present with Moses in the desert, provides the key. If in
John 6: 49 Christ establishes a contrast between the manna of
the desert that could not keep the fathers from dying and
Christ's own flesh that gives eternal life, Calvin explains this as a
concession to the low mentality of His listeners, who could not
penetrate to the deeper mystery that Paul had in view. But
Calvin also seeks to demonstrate the actual presence of a hope
of immortality in the Old Testament itself. He adduces some
rather subtle arguments to the effect that this is implied in
God's communicating Himself to the saints in His Word of life—
notably in the covenant formula, "I will be your God and ye
shall be my people", and connects herewith also the argument
of Jesus over against the Sadducees (Matt. 22: 32). But he also
seeks to demonstrate more directly that some pious Israelites
had received the assurance of immortality. Does not the
eleventh chapter of the Epistle to the Hebrews suggest that it
was only this hope that gave the fathers, from Adam on,
strength to endure in the midst of this miserable existence?[13]

Various subsidiary thoughts support the position. Why the
struggle for the right of the first-born in the patriarchal history,
if a higher blessing is not implied? What but eternal life can be
meant when Jacob, dying, anticipates the salvation of God
(Gen. 49: 18)? Without lingering further in the Law, Calvin
then turns to the Psalms. The utterances dealing with the

transitory nature of our earthly pilgrimage, such as Ps. 39: 13 and 103: 15, he claims, must be seen against the background of the hope of everlasting life. Psalms 49 and 73 are naturally stressed also. From here he passes to Job 19: 25, in which he at least finds this hope reflected, even though he concedes that Job is primarily referring to the day when God will show His grace to him here on earth.

Proceeding to the prophets, he finds that all the descriptions of future blessedness, with their earthly colours, are but suggestions of supernal realities. Thus, while he concedes that Ezek. 37 applies primarily to the national restoration of the Hebrew people, he thinks it simultaneously has the purpose of teaching the Jews the resurrection of the flesh as such. A comparison with Isa. 26: 19 is employed to make this reasonable. Isa. 66: 22 and Dan. 12: 1 f. are naturally also utilized by Calvin to re-enforce his thesis. In reality, this is meagre proof for his sweeping assertion that the hope of eternal life is found *throughout* the prophets. In the light of our modern critical insight these intimations of immortality appear on the scene only in very late Old Testament passages, and are not characteristic of the Old Testament religion.

In developing the second point that the Old Testament and New Testament are one in the character of the covenant of grace, i.e., that there was only one covenant and one people of God, Calvin, like Zwingli, is willing to grant that some differences between the Old and New Testaments do exist.[14] He devotes a special section to these differences. In the New Testament the hope of immortality appears with much greater clarity. While establishing this fact he concedes, what he had not admitted previously, that the Old Testament saints valued the life this side of the grave much more than is befitting for Christians, who should meditate on the future life.[15] But he sees a process of purification and clarification going on within the Old Testament itself. A second difference is suggested by the Epistle to the Hebrews, with its typology of the Old Testament cult and priesthood as prophetic of Christ and the Atonement. The proof of the correspondence between particular prophetic passages and their fulfilment, as attempted in the Gospels, is not prominently taken up by Calvin at all. In dealing with Jesus' saying on the new covenant (Matt. 26: 28), Calvin twists it to fit his theory of only one covenant; the old covenant, he argues, became new and eternal in its truth through the blood of Christ. In the third place, Calvin, proceeding from Jer. 31: 31 and its interpretation in II Cor. 3: 6, grants a difference between the law of the letter and the gospel of the spirit. He finds Paul speaking with more hatred of the law than Jeremiah, but he excuses this on the ground of his opposition to the Judaizers (a point Melanchthon had also made). In the central position that the law can tell man what to do but that man is powerless to do it, Calvin maintains Paul's standpoint, though in concluding the discussion he obscures Paul's position by again contrasting the gospel and the *ceremonies* of the law. In the fourth place, Calvin contrasts Old Testament and New Testament as bondage and freedom, in accord with Paul's teachings in Galatians and Romans. Even so, he finds traces of the spirit of faith and its freedom already present among the Old Testament saints. Finally, Calvin contrasts the universalism of the New Testament with the particularism of the Old. But Christian universalism, prophesied by the prophets, is fulfilled in Christ only gradually—primarily after His resurrection. Such sayings as Matt. 10: 5, 15: 24 (which modern scholars by and large incline to regard as Judaizing) suggest the idea of a development.

In his edition of 1543, Calvin was moved to append a paragraph defending the idea of the immutability of God against doubts arising from the impression that God had changed His own original arrangements. For it could be argued that in the New Testament God rejects what He had previously commanded, and even abhors that which He had previously delighted in—e.g. the animal sacrifices and all the arrangements of the Levitic priesthood. Can God take back what He has said? Here Paul's idea of a divine pedagogy is utilized by Calvin as a means of escape from the difficulty.

The third point that the Old Testament and the New Testament are one in the knowledge of the Mediator Jesus Christ is also taken up in the second edition of the *Institutes*, but finds its most elaborate development in Book II, chapter 6, in the final edition of 1559, to which we shall here confine ourselves. Genesis 1–3 and speculations based thereon now loom large. Calvin put the Christian ideal of religion in the pre-lapsarian state. The Fall made redemption necessary. The whole history of Israel, including the Mosaic legislation, is viewed as a revelation of the redeeming God through the pre-existent Mediator, Christ. Wherever God showed His grace to Israel, everything depended on Christ. In justifying this position, Calvin stresses Messianic prophecy. These predictions, he holds, were intended to draw men's eyes toward the Redeemer. After such a Christianization of the Old Testament and its history, he subordinates the whole Old Testament legislation to Christology in chapter 7. The law was given to nourish the hope of salvation in Christ until He should come. All the seemingly absurd sacrifices and rites had a spiritual sense that becomes revealed in Christ. The Davidic kingship and the priesthood, too, pointed to Christ. As for the moral law of the Old Testament, Calvin stresses its perfection and the utter impossibility of fulfilling it; its purpose is to awaken the longing for forgiveness through the Mediator Christ. All this spelled such a Christianization of the Old Testament, and notably of the law, that the newness of the gospel was almost lost sight of. The latter is merely the fuller revelation of the mystery of Christ. The difference between the two revelations is only one of degree of clarity. And so in the ninth chapter of Book II Calvin really abandons Paul's (and Luther's) antithesis of law and gospel. This is largely due to his yielding to the influence of the Epistle to the Hebrews and its Christianizing allegorical use of Old Testament law and institutions. In connection with Christology Calvin affirms that Christ came as priest to effect atonement made necessary by the Fall and its consequences, but he also stresses His prophetic and regal office. It is significant that this whole Christological pattern of the *munus triplex*, the threefold office of Christ as Prophet, Priest and King, that still survives in numerous works on Christian doctrine, is based on the Old Testament!

Here a strong-willed, sober and clear-headed man set forth the characteristic Reformed position in a thorough and powerful way. Providence willed that Calvin should become the most influential teacher for a large segment of Protestantism. Thus a form of Christianity that was full of Old Testament spirit moulded the ideas and ideals of generations—just at the time when a new promised land had opened up to receive another chosen people.

The question is: can that which Calvin taught about the relation of the Testaments be regarded as valid? In recent years some have turned to him for light, as others have turned to Luther. Thus, even such a critic as Albertz can remark that "theology and the Church would have been spared the following of many erroneous paths if with respect to the unity of and the differences between the Old Testament and the New Testament they had borne in mind what Calvin is able to say on that question in so careful and circumspect a manner in his *Institutes*."[16] It will have become obvious, however, from our critical account of what Calvin himself has to say that many of his positions are untenable.

The plain fact is that Calvin has Christianized the Old Testament and Judaized the New Testament in his efforts to make the two appear as one. He was able to Christianize the Old Testament largely because he viewed it through the coloured glasses of the author of the Epistle to the Hebrews. We, however, must view the Old Testament through the clear lenses of realistic observation and interpretation. The philosophy of history offered in the Epistle to the Hebrews is an interesting attempt from the time of the early Church to cope with the problem of the relation of the earlier dispensation to the Christian order, but it was intended for Hellenistic Jews and is highly speculative in character. The history of the New Testament canon shows, furthermore, that the Epistle to the Hebrews is among the New Testament writings carrying the least weight for Christian doctrine.[17] The really crucial question then is: can one, discounting its support, in fact maintain Calvin's position that there is only one covenant and one people of God? Other early Christian thinkers, notably Paul, saw contrast rather than continuity in the relation of the two orders, and the early Church in calling the two Testaments "Old" and "New" clearly differentiated them. It may be, however, that Paul's view is too one-sided and due to his involvement in sharp controversy with Judaism. There is a real problem here which cannot be settled in an external manner by appeal to authority, but which requires a fundamental approach in the full freedom of Christian reflection.

Chapter Three

THE OLD TESTAMENT FROM THE REFORMATION TO THE MIDDLE OF THE SEVENTEENTH CENTURY

IN the great creative period of the Reformation the opportunity existed to place a new construction upon the Bible as a whole and the Old Testament in particular. But great decisions had to be made and stands had to be taken before there was a sufficient development of unfettered biblical scholarship. Essentially the Catholic doctrine of inspiration remained in force. There was no attempt to develop further the liberal insights of Luther or the thoughts of Carlstadt. Nevertheless, the extreme restraint shown in the Augsburg Confession of 1531 with respect to the Scriptures (there are only passing allusions in prologue and epilogue that the teaching is being set forth "out of the Holy Scriptures and the pure Word of God") may largely be due to a realization on Luther's part of the complexity of the problem. The Lutherans subsequently clung to one element of their founder's heritage: the overriding importance of the doctrine of justification by faith. They made the latter the "material principle" which was to stand side by side with the "formal principle" (Scripture authority).[1] Scripture was to be interpreted after the analogy of faith, i.e., the material principle (justification) was to govern the interpretation of Scripture. Thus biblical statements were, if necessary, brought forcibly into line with the basic Pauline gospel and a seeming harmony of Scripture established. The Reformed theologians, on the other hand, held fast to the formal principle without any qualification. They thus could strive to use the whole biblical heritage more freely. Since they, too, regarded Scripture as inspired by the Holy Ghost and then argued that the Holy Ghost could not have contradicted Himself, their interpretation likewise became harmonistic.

It is interesting to see how the Roman Church reacted to Protestant biblicism. On April 8, 1546, in its fourth session, the Council of Trent declared:[2] (1) That the Church accepted all the writings of both Testaments *and* the unwritten traditions going back to Christ and the apostles with equal reverence. (2) The Council set up a list of the authoritative books. In it not only the books acknowledged by the Palestinian Synagogue, but the so-called Apocrypha of the Old Testament, were accepted as canonical. In the New Testament the Epistle of the Hebrews was declared Pauline and that of James apostolic, but II Esdras, which the Vulgate puts after Revelation, was quietly omitted, following Luther's example. (3) An anathema was pronounced upon all who did not consider these books in all their parts as found in the Latin Vulgate sacred and canonical. (4) The Vulgate was declared authoritative for all public lectures, disputes, sermons and interpretations. (5) Since the text of the Vulgate was often carelessly or arbitrarily given in manuscripts and printed books, it was moved that an official edition of the Vulgate be made (this edition appeared forty-six years later in Rome under Pope Clement VIII). (6) All biblical books, it was asserted, have equal authority, for they are all divinely inspired. (7) The Church is the final, because infallible, judge of the true sense of the Sacred Scriptures. The last mentioned point is not taken to mean that scholarly research in the sphere of Scripture interpretation is forbidden, but rather that the interpreter must not contradict the consensus of the Fathers, or an exegesis officially accepted by the Church in the past, and must be ready to retract a new interpretation if the Church condemns it. Such individualism as that shown by Luther was thus declared out of order.

The repercussions of the western debate over the Scriptures were not felt until much later in the Eastern Catholic Church. By way of rounding out our picture of the attitude of Christendom toward the Bible and notably toward the Old Testament, we may, however, make brief reference to it here. In the eastern area the authority of the articles of faith set up by the ancient ecumenical councils was regarded as resting partly on Scripture and partly on oral tradition. The latter proceeded from the apostles, was handed down in the Church, and was fixed by the councils and the holy Fathers. Scripture is inspired throughout and the Church is the guardian of its integrity and interpretation. In the Confession of the Synod convoked

at Jerusalem in 1672 the Old Testament was declared to include
also the Apocrypha.[3] Since Scripture is clear in its meaning as
to central dogmas, but not readily understandable in all its
parts, it is not meet that all people should have the privilege of
reading the Bible, but only those with the proper understanding.
Notably, some books of the Old Testament are to be kept from
the layman. A certain fear of the consequences of reading
the Old Testament is evident in this attitude of the eastern
Church, and this is comprehensible since it did not have an
infallible tribunal to govern biblical interpretation, as Rome
did.

Reverting again to sixteenth-century Europe we note that
Trent left its impress on Protestantism, too. The Reformed
theologians were induced by Roman example to enter in more
detail into the matter of the Scripture doctrine than the
Lutherans had done. Two basic thoughts about Holy Writ reappear with ever-increasing sharpness in their Confessions:[4]
(1) that the Scripture canon is forever definitely fixed; (2) that
its authority is not from man, nor from the Church, but from
God. The Second Helvetic Confession[5] of 1566 interprets
Deuteronomy 4: 2 ("ye shall not add unto the word which
I command you") and Revelation 22: 18 f. ("if any man shall
add unto these things") as commandments of God with
reference to the canonical writings of both Testaments. It also
declares its loathing of all the heretics of former times who
either did not recognize the inspiration of these writings, or
rejected some and changed others with interpolations. With
respect to the Apocrypha, the view of the early Church that
they are not to be used for Scripture proof, and hence not to be
regarded as canonical, but that they may be read in the
churches, is upheld. On the second point, viz., that Scripture
has received its authority from God rather than from the
Church, the clash is more sharp. The Second Helvetic Confession insists that Scripture has this authority inherently, in
so far as God himself spoke to the prophets and apostles and
continues to speak to Christendom through their writings. The
question how we know that this is so and whence we derive
the right to declare these particular writings inspired and
authoritative in contrast to others, is answered in this Confession by a collection of biblical quotations which really relate

partly to Old Testament writings (under the presupposition of their inspiration), partly to the oral preaching of the gospel by the apostles, and partly to the ecclesiastical arrangements made by the apostles.

Other Reformed Confessions, however, go so far as to make declarations of the extent of the canon—the 39 Articles of 1562, the Confession of the Anglican Church, designate those books of the Old Testament and of the New Testament as canonical whose authority has never been doubted in the Church (a statement rather interesting in the light of the debates in the history of the canon). More explicit still are the French Confession of 1559, the Belgian (based on the French) of 1566, and ultimately the Westminster of 1648, all of which list the writings considered canonical. These Confessions declare, "We recognize these Scriptures as canonical and as the absolutely certain rule of our faith, not so much because of the agreement and assent of the Church as because of the testimony and inner persuasion of the Holy Spirit who teaches us to differentiate them from other ecclesiastical writings."[6] Some influence is thus conceded to the tradition of the Church, in the matter of canonicity, but the decisive thing is the witness of the Holy Spirit, in accordance with the doctrine put forth so forcefully by Calvin.

In claiming that the Holy Spirit testified to them that all these books were inspired and canonical, the Reformed theologians ignored the fact that other men and groups of men likewise claiming the Holy Spirit for their guide had arrived at other judgments. The prelates at Trent in the introduction to their decree on the Scriptures declare themselves as a "synod lawfully assembled in the Holy Spirit", and yet were induced to recognize the Apocrypha as canonical. Luther evidently did not hear the witness of the Holy Spirit for quite a number of writings; the Church Father Irenaeus uses *The Shepherd of Hermas* as canonical; Athanasius does not count the Book of Esther as canonical, but includes Baruch and the Epistle of Jeremiah in the Book of Jeremiah. Did the Holy Spirit not testify to these leaders? The Calvinistic theory really ignores the fact that the canon has evolved gradually and in a process of compromise. In the light of the knowledge that was even then available to those who had patristic learning, Zahn declares, the theory that God had fixed the canon was "as much a fiction as any fable of the Papal Church".[7] And equally fictitious, he asserts, is the idea that the witness of the Spirit could enlighten one to know that exactly the twenty-seven New Testament books accepted by the Church in the fourth century and exactly the twenty-four Old Testament books accepted by the Jews were inspired and authoritative. One may safely say that what these men took to be the witness of the Spirit is no new revelation at all but only an echo of that which is traditional in the Church. It is difficult to see what prompting of the Holy Spirit could have convinced a seventeenth-century Protestant that the Books of Ecclesiastes, Esther, or Jude's Epistle are canonical, but that Sirach, I Maccabees and the Epistle to the Laodiceans are not worthy of that esteem. Calvin himself could adduce no other ground for the canonicity of the Epistle of James in the Preface to his Commentary on it than that he sees no reason for rejecting it and feels able to harmonize its teachings with Paul's. The witness of the Spirit in this case amounts to nothing but an acceptance of the traditional canonicity of the Epistle, without any real investigation into the question of how well it was attested and how it came to be received.

With respect to the relation of the Old Testament to the New the 39 Articles of the Church of England were more liberal than other Reformed Confessions. The Seventh Article states:

> The Old Testament is not contrary to the New: for both in the Old and New Testament everlasting life is offered to mankind by Christ, who is the only mediator between God and man, being both God and Man. Wherefore they are not to be heard, which feign that the Old Fathers did look only for transitory promises. Although the law given from God by Moses, as touching ceremonies and rites, do not bind Christian men, nor the civil precepts thereof ought of necessity to be received in any commonwealth; yet notwithstanding, no Christian man whatsoever is free from the obedience of the commandments which are called moral.[8]

The belief that Christ speaks in the Old Testament and that the Old Testament saints hoped for eternal life is expressed in the first part of this statement. This is evidently the Calvinistic line, whereas the emphasis on the non-binding character of the

ceremonial and civil law that follows suggests the influence of
Zwingli or Luther.

With Confessions sprouting up on all sides the Lutherans,
too, felt the need of going beyond their Augsburg Confession.
True, the latter was regarded as possessing symbolical authority
by considerable sections of the Reformed group; no less a man
than Calvin had subscribed to it (in 1541). But in the *Formula
of Concord* of 1580 there now was set forth a fresh and more
comprehensive statement of the Lutheran position.[9] So far as
the Scriptures are concerned, its restraint is remarkable. It
simply states, in its opening paragraph, "We believe, teach and
confess that the only rule and norm according to which all
teachings and teachers are to be judged and appraised are alone
the prophetic and apostolic writings of the Old and New
Testaments." The primary point here is the elimination of the
Catholic principle of tradition. No reasons are given for the
normative significance of the Bible, no doctrine of inspiration is
taught, and the prophetic and apostolic writings are not identified in detail. There is not even an attempt to insist on the
authority of the Hebrew and Greek texts over against the
Vulgate. The extremely reticent position taken by this the most
elaborate Lutheran Confession suggests that Luther's insights
and the lessons of Carlstadt's treatise were not yet forgotten.
This paragraph gave a considerable advantage to modern
German and Scandinavian theology, because of its very general
terms. The rise of biblical criticism was much more difficult in
the Reformed Churches, because their Confessions were more
specific in the matter of the Scripture doctrine.

Looking at the Lutheran theological rather than the purely
ecclesiastical and confessional scene, it is of interest to note how
Martin Chemnitz (one of the authors of the *Formula of Concord*)
dealt with the Catholic doctrine of Scripture.[10] The great
problem at issue for a Protestant theologian, of course, was how
to escape the logic of the Catholic claim that the Church is the
source of the canonical authority of Scripture. Chemnitz asserts
that the present Church is bound by the testimony of the early
Church, but even the early Church had no other function in this
respect than to declare authority that is inherent in the biblical
writings: i.e., they merely recognized the reality that existed
but did not create it, as already taught by Zwingli and others.

But he then goes so far as to differentiate between proto-canonical and deutero-canonical writings in the New Testament. Only those can be regarded as proto-canonical and be authoritative for doctrine which (1) are derived from the authors from whom they claim to come and (2) are recommended by the sure and unanimous testimony of the ancient Church. This position is astonishingly liberal. If the first rule were applied to-day to the New Testament in the light of modern historical insight only eight or nine Pauline Epistles could be regarded as proto-canonical. For the Old Testament the consequences would be even more serious. In Chemnitz's day, of course, the authenticity of most biblical writings was still taken for granted. It is not surprising that subsequent Lutheran theologians did not maintain the distinction of proto- and deutero-canonical.[11]

The emphasis on the inspiration of the whole received Bible, making its supposed supernatural origin the self-sufficient basis of its authority, remained characteristic of the Reformed approach. The Westminster Confession of 1647 states that the "authority of Holy Scripture for which it ought to be believed and obeyed dependeth not upon the testimony of any man or Church but wholly upon God (who is truth itself) the author thereof; and therefore it is to be received because it is the word of God". The sacred books are "given by inspiration of God to be the rule of faith".[12] But in introducing the discussion of the Scripture doctrine this Confession betrays some qualms over the emphasis on biblicism, when it concedes that God had originally given His revelation to men in other ways, but that He had then decided "for the more sure establishment and comfort of the Church against the corruption of the flesh and the malice of Satan and the world to commit the same wholly unto writing, which maketh the Holy Scripture to be most necessary; these former ways of God's revealing His will unto His people now being ceased".

Other Reformed Confessions put the emphasis on Scripture even more sharply. Thus the Helvetic Consensus of 1675, which was accepted by most of the Swiss Churches, claims in its first article that God watched over His written word in so fatherly a manner that no jot or tittle ever was or ever could be lost. From this it was inferred that even the vocalization and accentuation of the Hebrew text of the Old Testament was inspired and that all attempts to set up a purer text with the help of Greek and Latin translations or the Samaritan Pentateuch were an undermining of religion.[13]

The unanimity and resoluteness with which the Reformed Churches emphasized their Scripture doctrine impressed the Lutherans to such a degree that they yielded to an increasing extent to its influence. The doctrine of the witness of the Holy Spirit gained practically unanimous consent among them. Hollazius, for example, in objecting to such a position as that of Chemnitz, taught that external witness could only produce human convictions, not true faith in Scripture—such faith rested in the last instance on the internal testimony of the Holy Spirit. But there was some disposition to doubt that such witness could support the canonicity of all received books. Thus Quenstedt (c. 1685) denies that this can be an article of faith, and concedes that there are true believers who do not accept a number of the books of the traditional Canon.[14]

With respect to the relation of the Old Testament to the New Testament Calvin's ideas also had a powerful influence upon the Lutherans. In the debates with Catholics on the one hand and Protestant sectarians on the other hand they were constantly invoked. Thus Gerhard[15] in his polemic against the Catholic Bellarmin rejects the latter's claim that the Old Testament doctrine is "inchoate" while that of the New Testament is "perfect", and that the Old Testament only teaches obscurely and imperfectly such mysteries of the faith as the Trinity; he asserts to the contrary that the Old Testament too, is perfect, since it teaches the same fundamental articles of faith which Christ and the apostles state in the New Testament.

The Socinians, who were banished from their main centre in Poland in 1658 but whose émigrés in Holland and England exercised a considerable activity, soon became an object of orthodox polemic, in part because of their stand on the Old Testament. These Protestants, though conceding the divine character of the Old Testament, claimed that it now had only a historical interest and was not essential for Christian doctrine. True, both Testaments had certain mandates—the moral ones— in common, but otherwise there was a great difference between the perfect mandates and promises of the New Testament and the imperfect ones of the Old; and the latter book, furthermore, taught such inadequate doctrines as that of retribution. The orthodox theologians countered by asserting that both Testaments were one in the covenant of grace and insisted that the belief in eternal life was already found in the Old Testament. The doctrine of the single covenant is espoused by the Lutheran Carpzov so wholeheartedly that he would even do away with the terms Old and New Testament and replace them with Old and New Instrument,[16] thus Christianizing the Old Testament and making a sort of *corpus juris* out of the Bible. In fine, for orthodoxy, Lutheran as well as Reformed, the Bible became a single book, and passages of both parts were used indiscriminately in scholastic fashion to supply proof-texts for doctrines.

Nowhere in the Christian world did the Old Testament receive such a warm reception or penetrate so deeply into the lives of men as in England.[17] This cannot be attributed entirely to the fact that the Anglican Church from about 1550 on became increasingly influenced by Calvinism. For one would then expect the Old Testament emphasis to have been even greater at Geneva, where Calvinism was to be found in undiluted purity. The amazing phenomenon of the permeation of English life by Old Testament ideas is due rather to the dissenters.

The free Churches, established in the seventeenth century in opposition to the state Church, found in the Old Testament, in which prophets denounce and oppose kings and priests, a marvellous weapon for their own cause of freedom. A curious sympton of this love of the Old Testament is the use among the dissenters of Old Testament names as baptismal names in a degree not found elsewhere. Another symptom is the way in which the Sabbath legislation was foisted on England and the reluctant Anglican Church after long agitation and pressure by the dissenters. We need not speak here of the extremes of a "lunatic fringe" which demanded adherence to Jewish dietary laws and the acceptance of circumcision, or of British Israelitism which regarded the Anglo-Saxons (or some other group in the British Isles) as descendants of the Lost Tribes.[18] Even apart from such extremes, the Old Testament character of English life became ever stronger. Nowhere else, not even in Switzerland or Holland, with their Calvinistic populations, was there any such surrender to Old Testament influence. Doubtless the almost complete absence of Jews in the English scene, from their expulsion in 1291 to their re-admission in 1655, made it much easier than elsewhere for Christian people to consider "Israel" a synonym for "people of God", rather than a national designation, and then, with complete *naïveté*, the membership of one's own sect. The Old Testament influence that got into the very bones of the English people through the dissenters and was carried to America by the Puritans and others was a leaven that helped to make the Anglo-Saxon mentality different from any other Western European mentality.

One may well accuse Protestant orthodoxy of having placed a heavy yoke on men's shoulders with its biblicism in place of the light yoke that Jesus Christ proclaimed. Harnack points out that modern conservatives who still insert such items as inspiration, infallibility, clarity and sufficiency of Scripture into doctrinal systems in a few spots, but ignore them in a hundred other places, have no idea how terribly realistically these things were taken at one time. But even the generations that still knew and understood the implications of this terminology, he says, were not consistent. They allowed themselves to dilute the meaning of Scripture, or in innumerable instances simply did not draw the consequences that the doctrine really required. "A sacred document, a thousand pages long, written by the finger of God," he observes wrily, "is an intolerable burden for the weak human race, whether one reads it or not." The orthodox dogma of the Scriptures, he thinks, has only been taken seriously in books on Doctrine, or generally speaking, "on paper".[19] But it must not be forgotten that where scientific thought endangered the Scripture doctrine at any point the latter was quickly invoked. Above all it was the insistence on the authority of the Old Testament that blocked progress in almost every sphere of knowledge. The story of that struggle makes melancholy reading.[20]

Chapter Four

THE REACTION AGAINST THE ORTHODOX VIEW
OF THE OLD TESTAMENT

A NUMBER of factors, however, were tending to break down orthodox biblicism. The first and most important was the rise of philological and historical scholarship of a new order. One presupposition of orthodoxy had been the conviction that the words of Scripture were very words of the Holy Ghost. That implied the perfect dependability of the received text of Scripture, for it was held that the Holy Ghost had been active in its preservation as well as in its creation. But the new art of the critical evaluation of ancient texts, evolved in the study of the Greek and Roman classics, showed that the text of Scripture was by no means as certain as had been believed. The French Protestant Capellus demonstrated that the vocalization of the Hebrew consonant text—which at the same time is an interpretation, without which other translations were possible in obscure connections—was of relatively recent origin, and that even the consonant text itself was by no means perfectly preserved.[1] The French Catholic Morinus next discerned that the old Greek translation, the Septuagint, often had readings better than those of the Hebrew text, and therewith laid the basis for what we call "textual criticism".[2] A Protestant who had reverted to Catholicism, Richard Simon, advocated the right to deal with the Old Testament according to principles of historical investigation, thereby inaugurating what we call "higher criticism".[3] In the same year Spencer in England sought to link the cult of the Mosaic law with other ancient Oriental cults, thus prophetically paving the way for the application of a comparative religious method to the religion found in the Old Testament.[4]

At the end of the century an *émigré* from Geneva to Holland, Clericus, produced a great work of critical scholarship, in which, among other things, he pointed out that the Old Testament canon was by no means produced according to a blue print from heaven, but had had a historical growth and development[5]—a thought that was to become important in the following century through the labours of Semler.

A second factor tending to disrupt orthodox biblicism with its unilateral treatment of the Bible as Word of God from cover to cover, was the federal theology[6] that was inaugurated in the Reformed Church in the era of the Thirty Years' War by J. Cocceius of Bremen, who subsequently went to the Netherlands (1669). He held that there was a twofold covenant of God—one of nature and good works, concluded with man before the fall, and the second of grace and faith concluded after the fall. The latter has three stages—before the law, under the law, and under the gospel. This thought suggested a development in revelation, thus making relative the earlier stages of the record, and was antecedent to the "progressive revelation" philosophy that came up in the conservative theology of the nineteenth century.[7] Cocceius recognized the defects and limitations of Old Testament piety in comparison with the New Testament, though this led to violent attacks on him since it was contrary to the Reformed idea of the identity of the Testaments. A distinctive feature of his approach was his fondness for typological interpretation, which found much following. He regarded it as permissible to put as much mystical meaning into biblical verbiage as seemed possible. If it had not been for this defect his thinking might have carried much farther in the modern direction.

But a third factor working against Biblicism was secular thinking, now beginning to emancipate itself from ecclesiastical control. A man like Hugo Grotius, famed as the founder of International Law, espoused a Christian tolerance in an age of intolerance and favoured a single Christian Church for all confessions. As biblical exegete he showed an objective, matter-of-fact approach and an ability to interpret ancient texts out of their own time.[8] Hobbes, in his *Leviathan*, brought extremely radical ideas to the fore in England.[9] He sought a secular state, emancipated from all ecclesiastical influence, and held that whatever the state sanctions is good. Religion, he taught, is fear of invisible powers whose existence is invented, or just accepted on the basis of tradition. In biblical criticism he advocated the principle that the time of origin of biblical books must be inferred from the books themselves, rather than from traditions about them, and put forward critical views of his own concerning the Pentateuch and Daniel.

But even more significant of this trend was the reliance on reason that came up through the philosophy of Descartes. Its application to the biblical problem appeared on the scene in Spinoza's famous Theologico-political Tract.[10] Such was the terrorism practised by Protestant orthodoxy that he found it wise to publish it anonymously and with a false place of publication on the title page (Hamburg, rather than Amsterdam). Spinoza desired a non-dogmatic kind of religion, focused on practical conduct. Over against the orthodox claim that the Bible is the revealed book, absolutely reliable and consistent in every respect and the proper yardstick by which all truth is to be judged, Spinoza set forth that the Bible is no such system of revealed truth, and urged that its stranglehold on philosophy and on the state be abolished.[11] He denies the doctrine of inspiration which provided the basis for this view. The biblical books, he says, must be understood as historical documents of their own time and place, and not as a set of supernaturally given, timeless teachings. He distinguishes, too, between the sphere of knowledge and that of obedience. The latter is the proper sphere of the sacred writings, which then were not intended to convey theoretical truth, but must be interpreted as providing what is for our moral improvement. Consequently, they have their authority and meaning in the realm of morality alone. He then proceeds to develop a historico-critical view of the origin and character of these writings, which, though it cannot satisfy us to-day and hence need not detain us, was far in advance of his time. He even asserted that the Pentateuch was not written by Moses and thus is the precursor of the great critical movement that was to come long afterward. But greater than any single insight on the Old Testament that he contributed is the fact that he built into the whole future development the belief that religion must not contradict reason, and that where they clash the representatives of religion should not have the power of suppression of reason that they were claiming as a matter of divine right. It was a century or more, however, before this principle was to prevail.

There is one further element in Spinoza's discussion which deserves special mention, as fraught with future significance. Observing that the supposed Mosaic revelation rests on the idea of the election of Israel, he subjects the latter tenet to criticism. The belief of having been elected, or shown favouritism, he asserts, is basically not religious. The advantages of one are the disadvantages of another. He who rejoices in his advantages really finds a satisfaction in the fact that others do not have them. Thus the proud and self-satisfied feeling of "election" belongs to the sphere of a self-love, envy, and wickedness that have nothing in common with piety and the love of God. The Hebrew belief of having been elected among all peoples as the people of God, therefore, is not religious but selfish in its roots. To what end did the Jews believe themselves elected by God? Obviously only to obtain something that human nature could not achieve without His help. This desired end was not true knowledge, or virtue, or piety, for these things are attained only by the help of God within us. There is thus no election with respect to them. The object of election for Israel was the attainment of external things "that thy days may be prolonged and that it may go well with thee". This is the goal of the Jewish faith—to be blessed and rich and powerful! Obedience to the law was a means to that end, because it was supposedly the condition for God's granting their desires, while disobedience meant punishment, misfortune. This Jewish belief in election and in the law, he insists, is not religious but political. Thus the Jew Spinoza challenges the religion of his own people at its very foundations, and in this respect also throws a searchlight far into the future. For this materialistic and nationalistic philosophy of the Old Testament to which he opened men's eyes has in recent times become a great source of offence. From Spinoza the line leads via Kant to Schopenhauer.

There now came into existence a peculiarly divided situation —a continued, entrenched orthodoxy, and opposed to it an enlightenment, prevailing primarily among intellectuals. In France, Bayle proclaimed the rule of reason in morality and denied religion's right of interference; Church and state were to be separated, atheism to be tolerated.[12] In England, conditions were particularly favourable for the reign of reason, for here as nowhere else religion was ruled out of philosophy. On the other hand the unsatisfactory religious situation led to a movement aspiring to set up a purer and more enlightened form of Christianity. Deism, beginning in that spirit, soon got involved more and more in polemic against existing Christianity and, favouring a natural theology, assailed the theology based on revelation.

The Old Testament provided a convenient object for such attack. In the third decade of the eighteenth century we find Morgan publishing an imaginary dialogue between a Christian and a Jew.[13] He has some sound principles of biblical criticism and makes intelligent observations on the authorship and antiquity of various biblical writings. To some extent he is led astray by inferring from St. Paul's use of the Old Testament that that work contains things incomprehensible to its contemporaries because of their blindness and obduracy but capable of being understood by those who have good sense and reason. This is exegetical backsliding, when viewed in the light of such principles as those of Luther and Calvin, and tends toward theosophy. In other respects Morgan wants to subject Scripture to the judgment of "sense and reason", to see whether it be coherent with all other reasonable knowledge. It is no wonder that one who wants everything to be reasonable should dislike the Old Testament and the people whose life it reflects. Miracles and revelation, of course, had to be denied. The immoralities of the Old Testament were another thing at which he took offence.

Morgan's work elicited much theological discussion, but since Deism in England was about to pass into general decline it did not exert any widespread popular influence. Methodism was now coming to the fore in that country and influencing people's minds. On the apologetic side, Warburton defended the Old Testament against deistic attacks.[14] He conceded the absence of a doctrine of immortality in the Old Testament, but held that this did not detract from the weight of the Mosaic law, for which, therein influenced by John Locke, he had a high esteem. He even ventured to take the position that God had so ordered things in individual as well as collective life in the time from Moses to Christ that the doctrine of retribution was actually operative during that period!

Stimulated by Voltaire and the English Deists, a German,

Reimarus (really an Oriental philologist), author of some popular books of a philosophical nature, wrote a voluminous work of sceptical character about the year 1747. Desiring to avoid persecution by the heresy hunters, he wrote this treatise only for private circulation. Portions of it were published thirty years later by Lessing, without revealing the author's identity.[15] To shield the family from opprobrium Lessing called the excerpts the *Wolfenbüttel Fragments*. Actually he had been shown the manuscript in the author's house at Hamburg. In these "fragments" the reality of the biblical revelation was denied; the revelation of God in nature was regarded as the only true revelation.

It cannot be said that the published "fragments" added much to what the other Deists had already said about the Old Testament, though for the New Testament they did put forth original ideas that subsequently were to have an influence on Strauss' *Life of Christ*. The significance of the publication lies primarily in the fact that it involved Lessing in a discussion with the champions of orthodoxy, in which he expressed significant ideas of his own, and that this debate had an effect on the moulding of his famous drama *Nathan der Weise*. In a brief paper of 1777 Lessing, while not denying that Christ had performed miracles or had risen from the dead, emphasized the fact that no historical certainty was obtainable on these matters and that therefore beliefs could not be built on them.[16] He noted that an Origen saw in present evidences of the activity of the Spirit and in contemporary miracles done by holy men a proof more powerful than any that dialectics could provide; but he complains that nowadays we no longer see such evidences, and that the proof for that sort of thing has sunk to the level of mere human testimonies about such phenomena in the remote past. If it is asserted that such testimonies are guaranteed by the inspiration of the sacred writers, that claim, too, unfortunately is historically uncertain. Lessing finds the only support for Christian belief in the teachings of Christ, which carry conviction by their own weight.

Lessing was now attacked by Goeze, a Hamburg divine,[17] and replied to that attack in his *Anti-Goeze* (1778), which has been described as "the most important polemical writing in the struggle between Philosophy and Theology".[18] The chief issue between the contestants is that of the relation of Christianity to the Bible. According to Lessing, the author of the *Wolfenbüttel Fragments* (Reimarus) and Goeze have one thing in common: both say the Christian religion depends on the credibility of the Bible—for the former that book is incredible, while for Goeze it is infallible. Lessing, in contrast to both, tries to differentiate the Bible and religion. Religion was there prior to the Bible, he asserts. It consists of eternal truths (therein showing himself to be a true son of the age of enlightenment), that can never be demonstrated by particular facts. He asserts that the set of truths that existed before the New Testament and that form the basis of Christian belief, the rock on which the Church was founded, was the *regula fidei*, the confession of fundamental tenets exemplified by the Apostles' Creed. The value of the apostolic writings lies not in their being the source but only the oldest expression of this rule of faith.

In his discussion of this controversy Harnack declares Lessing to have done more than anyone else in breaking the terrible stranglehold which the dogma of the authority of the Bible had upon Protestantism. While some of the theses Lessing put forward in his *Anti-Goeze* are not tenable and were undermined by the learned Walch, his main contention was unshakeable and forever robbed of intellectual respectability a biblicism operating with the idea of an infallible, authoritative book.[19]

In the essay (1780), of which Lessing claimed to be merely the editor (perhaps to escape being held accountable by the heresy hunters), he views the revelation of God as the "upbringing" of the human race. The divine pedagogy accounts for the vicissitudes of history—notably of that of the chosen Hebrew people—and for the gradual progress in this people's religious and moral insight as reflected in the books of the Old Testament. The comparison is even employed at a point where a side-glance is directed at other nations. While God was leading Israel through the various stages of training, other nations went their way by the light of reason with which the Creator had endowed all mankind. Some of them remained very backward, but a few, such as Greeks and Romans, even advanced beyond Israel. But just as the few who progress by their own initiative do not disprove the value or necessity of education, so the Gentile nations that exceeded Israel in the knowledge of God up to a certain point prove nothing against revelation. The properly trained child eventually catches up with the more fortunately organized child of nature and surpasses him permanently. Lessing then compares the Old Testament to an elementary school book, given to the Jewish people. Its lack of a doctrine of immortality with reward and punishment in a life after death is no proof against the divine origin of this book. An elementary book must be suited to the actual stage of life for which it is intended. It cannot and need not give information unsuited to the age of those it is to instruct. All that can be required of it is that it does not block the road to knowledge temporarily withheld. The doctrine of retribution, he holds, tended to drive men in the direction of a belief in immortality; the latter solves the difficulty raised by the clash between reality and the divine justice experienced in individual life. The Jewish people was sent into Babylonian captivity, as a child is sent to a foreign land. Here they saw that other people knew more than they did, and under Persian ægis attained a nobler idea of God, and the idea of the immortality of the soul. Ashamed of themselves, they turned to their discarded elementary school book, the Old Testament, in order to place the blame on it for their previous backwardness. But they realized that the guilt was their own, not the book's. The latter had all the qualifications of a good elementary book—if they had only heeded it!

But an elementary book is only for a definite age. It is harmful for a child to linger longer over it than he is intended to do. Such a procedure has a bad effect on the mind and character, and this is discernible in the Jewish people. A better pedagogue must come and take this elementary book out of the child's hands and give it a new book. This happened when Christ came. He was the first dependable and practical teacher of the immortality of the soul, and His disciples who handed this truth on to other nations and gave them the new second-book— the New Testament—are thus among the benefactors of mankind. Let us not criticize them too much for mingling other less convincing teachings with this main one, but let us rather investigate whether a new impulse was not thereby given to human reason. Certain it is that the New Testament in comparison to the Old Testament is the more advanced schoolbook. But it is not the final book. As we can now dispense with the

Old Testament for the doctrine of the unity of God, so some of us can even begin to dispense with the New Testament for the doctrine of the immortality of the soul. In some of the more difficult doctrines of the New Testament Lessing finds indications of a higher stage of the divine pedagogy still to come, in which a new, eternal gospel will be given, and thinks the enthusiasts of the thirteenth and fourteenth centuries were not so far wrong when they asserted that the New Covenant must become antiquated just like the Old; they erred chiefly in thinking of being able to make their contemporaries, who were still on the childhood level, worthy of being citizens of that third world age. The ideas thus set forth represent a bold, speculative attempt to set up a popularly understandable philosophy of revelation. Its chief weakness is the rationalistic outlook—the emphasis on "truths" as the essence both of Old Testament and New Testament religion.

But the most important thinker of the time, the man who toppled reason from its pedestal, Immanuel Kant, also put forth weighty thoughts on the matters that concern us. In the *Critique of Pure Reason* (1781) he at one point makes an interesting observation on the idea of Sacred History; speaking of the antinomies he points out that both the statement that the world had no beginning and the opposite that it had a beginning in time can be proved as well as disproved, but that the second finds greater favour with mankind, for man flees the endless and desires a point where he can rest. "Thus there rises amid the miserable huts of men the cathedral with the everlasting peace of God." And then he adds, "So also religion in the endless flood of happenings has a Sacred History, where God works immediately and reveals himself directly to men."[20] While Kant does not state that this idea of a Sacred History is an illusion, a product of wishful thinking, that conclusion could readily be drawn, and doubtless represents Kant's opinion.

In his treatise *Religion within the Boundaries of Pure Reason* (1793), Kant has occasion to speak of biblicism in general and Christianity's relation to the Old Testament in particular. Religious faith, Kant held, was reasonable and exclusively based on the moral law written in the heart. The belief in a special divine revelation is rejected because it assumes the existence of statutory laws which are not based on the law written in the heart and thus are accidental and contrary to the true nature of man. It is our duty to hold fast to the moral religion and to hope that it will eventually prevail over the so-called revealed religion. The latter is of and for the senses and it is conceded that it serves a useful purpose in the present order of things. If the conflict between this illusory revealed religion and moral religion is to be reconciled at some future stage the former must have something in common with the latter. It is to be found, Kant held, in the predisposition to a moral religion which lay hidden in human reason from the outset and was partly operative in the formation of the belief in a special revelation.

This position already contains the nucleus of a philosophy of the history of religion. Religion, Kant taught, originally introduced humanity to moral teachings in the course of a historical process. Reason could have done the job, too, but humanity was not yet on the level where that was feasible. Since the history of the religion of individuals cannot be written, one can speak of religion only in terms of ecclesiastical history—the history of that (Christian) Church which from its beginning possessed the germ and the principles that could lead to true religion (in the Kantian sense; i.e., ethics). At this point Kant denies that the Jewish faith stands in any essential connection (i.e., exhibiting unity with respect to concepts) with Christianity, even though it immediately preceded and gave the physical occasion for the founding of the Church.

In explaining why he thus cuts the cord between Judaism and Christianity, Kant declares that the Hebrew faith is an aggregate of merely statutory laws on which a state constitution was founded. Whatever moral elements were added thereto at first or later do not belong to Judaism as such. The latter is no religion at all, but just a union of people of the same tribal origin for the purpose of attaining a common life under political laws. It was not projected to be a Church, but rather a worldly state, and if it were destroyed by accident there would still survive the political faith in its restoration (at the coming of a Messiah). That this state organization supposedly is theocratically governed (actually this only means a domination by priests or leaders, who claim to have received instructions directly from God), and shows reverence to the name of God (who here is imagined chiefly in terms of a sovereign and does not address himself primarily to the conscience of man) does not make it a religious organization. It is clear from the following reasons that it did not intend to be that at all:

(1) The Old Testament laws are of the sort valued and imposed by a political organization because they only concern external actions. Even the ten commandments, though they might be considered ethical before the forum of reason except for the fact that they were publicly promulgated, are not in that legislation associated with the requirement of a moral attitude in connection with obedience but are only directed to external observance. (2) All consequences of obedience or disobedience are innerworldly, and even these are not in accord with ethical concepts, as when children are to be punished for the sins of the fathers. Since (in the view of that rationalistic age) no religion worthy of the name can be conceived of without belief in eternal life, Judaism is no religion. Whatever genuinely religious ideas the Jews may have had, they were not included in this political programme which has come down in the Old Testament law. (3) Far from being the universal Church, Judaism excluded humanity from its fellowship; declared itself the chosen people, viewing all others with hostility and receiving hostility in return. Its imageless worship is not to be valued too highly, for among most other nations, too, there was a trend in the same direction. A God, furthermore, who only demands external obedience to such commandments as this Hebrew law contains and does not require an improvement in fundamental moral attitude of his devotees is not the truly moral Supreme Being that we need for a religion. Conceivably a polytheism in which people thought of their gods as approving only of him who adhered to virtue with his whole heart would even be preferable to a monotheism of the Jewish sort.

Moral religion, then, according to Kant, began with Christianity. It was an abandonment of Judaism and the introduction of a new principle. If the first teachers strove to connect the two and represented Christianity as a continuation of the old order, which in its types and shadows had contained all that later flowered forth, this must be regarded as an effort on their part to introduce religion to people of Jewish extraction without too much offence to their prejudices. The subsequent abolition of circumcision shows that the new faith was not bound to the statutes of the old, nor to any statutes at all, but was a religion valid not only for one people but for the world.

Much as he dislikes the fact, Kant perceives the religion of Protestantism as existing in his time in the form of faith in a book. Religious and moral instruction must therefore operate with the Bible, and so Kant recommends expounding the biblical writings by moral reason. The method may be arbitrary and unscientific but it is necessary, for a literal interpretation such as is alone admissible for scholars and their students can contribute nothing to the improvement and redemption of men. One must not interpret morals according to the Bible, but the Bible according to morals. If, for example, God is asked by a Psalmist to destroy his people's enemies, this refers actually to the enemies of the Jewish people. But that literal sense is contrary to morals. One should, therefore, re-interpret the passage and give it a moral meaning by making the "enemies" of the Psalmist symbolical of our own evil inclinations. Kant sees that taken literally, in its true meaning, the Old Testament is at many points an intolerable burden. Only allegorization provides an escape from the consequences of the canonical authority of this collection.

Kant's foray into the theological field brought him a letter from the Prussian king, Frederick William II, reprimanding him for having spoken in a derogatory manner concerning some fundamental teachings of Holy Scripture and Christianity. The philosopher preserved a loyal silence until under the next ruler. The official climate then having changed to one of "tolerance" he reverted to the topic in his *War of the Faculties*, wherein he made public the exchange of letters between himself and the new king's father, and restated his position in a fresh and interesting way.[21] A striking example of Kant's Old Testament study is furnished by his discussion of the theodicy problem which leads him to speak in detail of the Book of Job.[22]

The Old Testament question also attracted the attention of the two men who were to attain great influence in philosophy after Kant. The young Fichte, in his first philosophical treatise, attempted to show that revelation, too, was a postulate of practical reason.[23] Assuming that the moral law which had been revealed to men before the Flood had lost its earlier influence on mankind, he held it conceivable that God should have inaugurated anew a revelatory process imparting moral impulses to men by way of the senses. He could well have chosen to manifest Himself to them as lawgiver by some such visible and audible arrangement as tradition presupposes. Since the doctrines of God, liberty and immortality are all we need to know about the world of the Divine, these teachings must have formed the contents of such a revelation. All in all a naïve acceptance of Old Testament history undergirded by a parallel speculation! The young Schelling, on the other hand, in the course of his theological studies had attained the important insight that it was not enough to have grammatical interpretation, such as had been advocated; it was necessary to understand the biblical writings and their ideas historically-genetically. He rejected, too, the belief of Kant and others that "philosophical" interpretation of Scripture was legitimate; that, he rightly held, could only result in perversion of the real sense of those writings and was damaging to true philosophy.[24] In his dissertation on *The Third Chapter of Genesis* and a related paper on ancient myths Schelling set forth the theory that religious ideas initially had to take on mythological form. The story of the fall of man was utilized by him in the former production to apply this theory. In this tale, as in all myths, there is an underlying philosophy, and he ably sets forth its deeply pessimistic view. Schelling thus became the precursor of those who were later to use comparative mythology for the illumination of Scripture in a more external, historical manner than that which he here demonstrated.

Meanwhile biblical studies had been receiving impulses to progress. In 1753 the French physician, Jean Astruc,[25] rediscovered the key to Pentateuchal criticism that a German cleric, Witter, had found in 1711.[26] Astruc's views would probably have been forgotten like Witter's, the more since the leading Old Testament scholar of the day, Michaelis, found them unacceptable. It was their espousal by Eichhorn a generation later which gave them an epochal significance for Old Testament criticism. Of more immediate importance for late eighteenth century thought was Ernesti's introduction into German theology of the grammatical-historical exegesis[27] which had been pioneered by Dutch scholars like Grotius, and Semler's great work on the canon.[28]

Semler insisted that the early Church did not consider Scripture a fixed norm of doctrine for all time but rather a list of the books publicly read in Christian gatherings, and that purely external reasons had governed the selection. The idea of a canon is virtually abandoned or hollowed out, and the New Testament is viewed simply as a collection of early Christian documents. He claimed full freedom on the Christian's part to criticize them. Under the influence of Spinoza's thought he set up the principle that only those biblical books which serve man's moral improvement can be considered authoritative. On the basis of this rule he rejects Song of Songs, Ezra-Nehemiah-Chronicles, and less emphatically, Joshua, Judges, Samuel. In the case of the Gospels, he concedes some interpolations and claims that they were written for Jewish Christians and were permeated by Jewish phraseology and ideology which the Christian must first of all discount. The Book of Revelation he condemned as the product of an enthusiast. The line begun by Semler leads straight over to modern historical criticism.

Since Semler and in consequence of his work the idea came up with increasing force that ecclesiastical doctrine and Biblical teaching were at variance, and this brought about a more methodical analysis of Biblical teaching. Rationalists as well as some supernaturalists shared in this undertaking, though with very different results. Zachariae's work was written from the supernaturalist standpoint.[29] The rationalistic attitude, on the other hand, underlies that of Bauer.[30] The rationalists held that one must make allowances for local and temporal "disguises" of scriptural truth; this done, they tried to get at the pure underlying truth of the scriptural documents. At that point, however, their exegesis often passed into absurdity, for the truths they found were those of the "common sense" mind of their day. That limitation was soon to pass with the changing spirit of the times. Gabler's discourse of 1787[31] is regarded as the starting-point for the critical differentiation of the "theologies" of the various biblical writers, a subject thereafter called Biblical theology. With a sound higher criticism developing under the pioneering leadership of Eichhorn[32] and de Wette,[33] Biblical theology, utilizing criticism's results, was able to become truly historical in character.

Over against all this array of intellectual forces on the one hand and a stubborn orthodoxy on the other hand there stood that movement commonly called Pietism in the continental scene, and akin to Methodism in the English scene. In addition to nurturing a deeply religious spirit and showing great mission- ary zeal, Pietism produced theologians[34] and exercised a great influence on some who cannot be labelled as of that class. A theosophic current ran through this pietist theology and appears notably in men like Bengel, Oetinger and Crusius, whose thought was to affect the standpoints of various conservative scholars in the nineteenth century as well.[35] With these men we may mention one whose place is rather in the philosophical current, Hamann, an opponent of rationalism and exponent of the importance of emotion.[36] For all of those referred to, Old Testament prophecy had a great authority and attrac- tion.

The days of the "reign of reason" were about over. Sympto- matic of the changing outlook was the interest in nature and in the life of unspoiled children of nature that arose through Jean Jacques Rousseau. Attention was now also directed to folk- ways, folktales, folk-poetry and folk-song. In Germany Herder for the first time studied some of the materials of the Old Testa- ment in the light of folk-literature, and found it a rich repository of that sort of thing, on which the educated taste may dwell with infinite delight.[37]

Influenced by Herder's example, the most versatile mind of the time, Goethe, also gave attention to the Old Testament from a secular angle and even contributed to biblical criticism.[38] Instructive as revealing his general position are several little papers in which he took the role of a country parson. In one he writes that when he was a student the Bible was explained too universally, as though everything said in it was for the whole world and for all time. His son, the Master of Arts, has the opposite foolish notion of twisting all passages that do not fit into his system of ideas into "local bagatelles". He thinks he has struck a middle of the road-course, and sets up a sign post showing the direction. This is done in the form of an allegory, reminding one of that of Lessing (p. 49 f.). The Jewish people was a wild unfruitful trunk in a circle of similarly wild, un- fruitful trees. But on this trunk the celestial gardener grafted that noble branch Jesus Christ, that it might improve the nature of the tree and that from it new scions might be obtained for the grafting and ennobling of all the other trees. The history and teachings of this people, from the first germ to the time of grafting, was particularistic, and the little of universalism that may have occurred in it, in view of the impending divine intervention, is difficult and perhaps unnecessary to seek out. After the grafting, however, the whole thing took a different turn. Teaching and development now become universalistic. Although each tree that was grafted from that one source has its special history and its special teachings, according to circumstances, it is nevertheless the parson's opinion that there is as little that is particularistic here as there is universalistic yonder. This line of thought indicates that Goethe, however much he may have loved the Old Testament, saw the centre of things in the new order that began with Christ.

But through Herder a rich stimulus was also given toward appreciating other religions. If Spencer a century before had discerned the affinity existing between Hebrew ritual laws and the laws of other peoples, this was now carried further into the field of mythological ideas and theological concepts and perspectives of a universal history of religions arose before the mind. Biblical theology was bound to become enriched with comparative religious observation—a process that was destined to assume rising importance once the recovery of ancient Oriental civilizations provided first-hand testimony about the beliefs of Israel's contemporaries. This whole literary-historical and comparative-religious approach was, in spite of Herder's own theological slant, destined to become purely secular, and, purified of the romantic idealizations of Herder's time, is still bearing rich fruit in Old Testament research.[39]

Chapter Five

SCHLEIERMACHER AND THE OLD TESTAMENT

THE orthodox doctrine of Scripture had been toppled from its pedestal in the eyes of all those amenable to reason. It might take a long time before the Churches were driven to acknowledge the fact, but an unfettered theology could not do otherwise than to concede it. The problem now arose what was the right way to regard Scripture, and implicit in it was also that of the degree of authority to be accorded to the Old Testament. The greatest mind in Protestant theology since the Reformation, Schleiermacher, grappled with this, as with many other things, and set forth views that in retrospect carry forward the problem from the point where the advanced line in Luther's thinking had left it.[1]

For Schleiermacher, revelation does not stand at the centre of theology. He is closely linked with German Idealism, which had occupied itself with the ontological problem of the idea of God.[2] It had realized that God cannot be treated theoretically as a conditioned innerworldly entity, for He is the unconditioned. It posed the question for theology: how can we speak of God's Being in such a way as to do justice to His absoluteness? Idealism, furthermore, had an understanding for the practical nature of religion; it is not a theoretical certainty, but one that bears and governs our lives. Schleiermacher, therefore, sought its true sphere in the feelings and gave his famous religious-philosophical definition of (higher) religion as "feeling of absolute dependence on God".[3] Revelation for him thus could be no communication of knowledge, as for the supernaturalists, but only the rise of a new religious experience. He defines revelation as something new in the sphere of religious feelings that is basic for a certain religious community's life and is not understandable from the historical nexus preceding.[4] He makes no assertion about the new being divinely caused, for that would be dualistic. Thus theology through Schleiermacher, after searching for God in vain in the objective sphere, came to look for him in the subjective.

It is obvious that Schleiermacher has absorbed the lesson of Lessing's researches. In his general doctrine of Scripture[5] he teaches (1) that Holy Scripture cannot provide the basis for faith in Christ and only receives a special distinction where such faith is already present; (2) that the Holy Scriptures of the New Covenant are the first of an ever-since continued series of presentations of Christian faith and that they are normative for all subsequent presentations; (3) that the New Testament writings are "authentic" in their origin, (which term he dilutes to mean productions of the circles influenced by the Holy Spirit that went forth from Jesus, but not necessarily written by the authors to whom tradition attributes them), and that they are sufficient as norm for Christian teaching. The question is, Where does this leave the Old Testament?

Since Schleiermacher is bent on analysing the living Christian consciousness and extracting from it the beliefs that are a real expression of Christian convictions and spirit (for that is his new approach to doctrine), he naturally saw more clearly than those who operated in external fashion with Scripture authority that a gulf exists between the Hebrew and the Christian consciousness. He comes to grips with the matter of the Old Testament already when he discusses the relation of Christianity to Judaism on the one hand and to heathenism on the other.[6] It is not enough to quote his general proposition and then dismiss it as is so often done. The discussion with which he attempts to substantiate his proposition deserves careful attention.

By "Judaism", Schleiermacher says he means "the Mosaic institutions" and anything earlier that influenced the Jewish people in the direction of separatism. He concedes that Christianity has a historical connection with Judaism in so far as Jesus was born a Jew. But one must not imagine this connection as too exclusive, for at the time of Christ this people's manner of thinking was no longer centred entirely on Moses and the prophets, but had been refashioned in many respects by non-Jewish ideas absorbed in the captivity and dispersion.[7] On the other hand, Græco-Roman heathenism had also been prepared for monotheistic developments and was filled with the expectation of a new shape of things to come, while among the Jews the

Messianic promises were partly abandoned and partly misunderstood. If one views the entire historical situation comprehensively the differences between the two areas—Jewish and Græco-Roman—are less than would appear at the first glance. And the Jewish origin of Jesus is counterbalanced by two facts: first, that many more Gentiles than Jews went over to Christianity, and second, that Christianity would not have found as much acceptance among Jews as it did if Judaism had not itself been permeated by extraneous Græco-Roman influences.[8]

In so far as Christianity represents a transition from both Judaism and heathenism to another entity, its relation to both is the same. The transition from heathenism to Christianity appears more difficult, since the heathen had first to become monotheistic in order to become Christian; but in reality the two things were not so far apart, for monotheism was now given to the Gentiles in the form of Christianity, as previously in the form of Judaism. By contrast, the requirement made of the Jew not to rely on the law and to interpret the promises to Abraham otherwise than he was in the habit of doing was no less of a hurdle. Since we, therefore, must infer that Christian piety, as it was constituted from the very beginning, cannot simply be derived from the Judaism either of that time or of an earlier time, Christianity cannot in any way be regarded as a mere revised form of Judaism. If Paul in the third chapter of Galatians regards the faith of Abraham as the prototype of Christian faith and represents the Mosaic law as a temporary departure, one might infer that he wants to portray Christianity as a renewal of the original and pure Judaism of Abraham. But his real idea was only that Abraham's *faith* was related to the promise as ours is to the fulfilment, and not that the promise was the same to Abraham as the fulfilment is to us. And where he speaks specifically of the relation of Jews and Gentiles to Christ, he portrays Christ as the same for both, and both as equally far removed from God and therefore in need of Christ.

If Christianity bears the same relation to Judaism as it does to heathenism, it cannot be a continuation of Judaism any more than it is of heathenism. Whether the individual hails from the one area or the other, so far as his piety is concerned, he becomes a new man. The promise to Abraham, in so far as it is fulfilled in Christ, is only portrayed as having a relation to Christ in the divine plan and not in the pious consciousness of Abraham and his people. And since we can only concede the sameness of a pious fellowship where the consciousness is formed in the same way, we cannot recognize an identity of Christianity and the Judaism of Abraham any more than an identity of Christianity and later Judaism or heathenism. Nor can one say that a purer, original Judaism bore the germ of Christianity in itself in such a manner that in a natural progression, without intervention of something new, Christianity would have evolved out of it, or that Christ Himself was so involved in this Jewish progression that a new common life and existence could not have begun with Him.

The widespread belief that there is a single Church of God which has existed from the beginning of the human race and will continue to the end, does not, Schleiermacher urges, contradict his statement as much as would appear. For if the Mosaic law has a place in this unified divine order of salvation, the same is also true of the Greek wisdom of the world, notably that tending toward monotheism, according to acknowledged Christian teachers.[9] One cannot assert, of course, that the teaching of Christianity forms one whole with pagan wisdom without entirely cancelling the distinctiveness of Christianity. But if by this doctrine of the single Church one wishes to express the absolute relevance of Christ to all that is human, and make it extend even to the sphere of the past, then this is a purpose concerning which he cannot as yet express a judgment at this point in his doctrinal system, but with which his statement can well be harmonized. And so in Old Testament prophecy itself there is ascribed a different character to the New Covenant than to the Old (Jer. 31: 31–34). The juxtaposition in terminology already expresses the intrinsic separateness of the two quite definitely. Therefore, the rule is to be set up that for Christian use almost everything else found in the Old Testament is only a container for this particular prophecy, and that whatever is most definitely Jewish in its pages has the least value for the Christian. We can, accordingly, only find those of our Christian sentiments which are of a more general nature and not developed very peculiarly, reproduced with any exactitude in Old Testament passages; for those Christian sentiments that are distinctively developed, however, the Old Testament sayings will not be a suitable expression if we do not mentally subtract something or add something. Taking that into account we shall doubtless find in the utterances of the nobler and purer sort of heathenism many things relatively just as close and conformable to our point of view. Hence, apologists were formerly quite fond of referring to certain prophecies of Gentile origin that they regarded as "Messianic" and so recognized in that quarter a tendency of human nature toward Christianity.[10] The classic proposition in which Schleiermacher sums up this discussion is —"Christianity, it is true, stands in a special historical connection with Judaism, but with respect to its historical existence and its purpose, it has the same relation to Judaism as to heathenism."[11]

After setting forth his doctrine of Scripture as summarized above, Schleiermacher adds an appendix on the Old Testament.[12] This material, he says, stands outside the pale of doctrinal exposition because it is polemical, and thus will be superfluous as soon as the difference between the two groups of writings is recognized. He concedes, however, that the time when this will be the case is still remote. It would be audacious, furthermore, he grants, to set this up as the "Christian" teaching, since, in some quarters so much use is made of Old Testament passages for Christian edification that the New Testament only seems to play a minor role. And this takes place for opposite reasons both at the hands of those who place less value on that which is distinctive in Christianity and those who recognize that distinctive element as all-important for the salvation of man. Schleiermacher addresses himself only to the latter group because with them alone could he reach an understanding.

Turning to the Old Testament writings he distinguishes law and prophets. Concerning the law he says that if Paul is right in saying that the law, though divinely ordained, is something which came in between the promise to Abraham and its fulfilment (Gal. 3: 19), and that it is lacking in the power of the Spirit out of which Christian life proceeds (Rom. 7: 6 f. and 8: 3), then one cannot assert that the law was given by that same Spirit of which the apostle says that He is not communicated through the law and its works (Gal. 3: 2), but that God only sends Him into the heart in view of our connection with Christ.

Nor does Christ represent the Spirit that is sent (and with whose testimony He associates that of the disciples—John 14: 26, 15: 26, 27) as the return of one that was formerly present and had only disappeared for a time. But all the historical books from the giving of the law on hang together with the law.[13] And if we contrast Messianic prophecy as that most related to Christianity with the law as that most foreign to it, nobody will dare to assert that the Jewish historical books contain more of the history of Messianic prophecy than that of the law. Yes, even in the prophetic writings the bulk of the material refers to the legal constitution and the affairs of the nation as such, and the spirit out of which these things have come is none other than the spirit of the group, and therefore has nothing to do with the Christian Spirit which as the One should remove the wall separating this people from other peoples. Hence Messianic prophecy alone is left which could be due to inspiration in the sense in which we use the term. But if we recall that the prophets only rise to such heights on rare occasions and that only with respect to this is the spirit that animated them called "Holy" (II Peter 1: 21), then we must conclude that such prophesying only occurred infrequently. The spirit of the group combined with the consciousness of a need of redemption expressed itself in the form of intimation of a more spiritual divine sovereignty. This intimation bore in itself the highest receptivity for the Holy Spirit, and was also able to kindle and maintain it outside of itself.

Next Schleiermacher inquires into the matter of the authority of the Old Testament. It cannot be denied on the whole, he thinks, that pious Christians recognize that a considerable difference exists between the two portions of Holy Scripture. Even the noblest psalms always contain something that Christian piety cannot regard as a pure expression of itself, so that one must first deceive oneself by unconscious addition and subtraction if one thinks that one can set up a Christian doctrine of God out of prophets and psalms. On the other hand, he finds that the great fondness of Christians for availing themselves of individual Old Testament sayings as expressions of piety is almost always combined with a legalistic mode of thinking or a bondage to the letter of Scripture.

Turning to the use of the Old Testament for theological purposes, he grants that there are few Christian doctrines for which one has not attempted to adduce Old Testament passages as proof. But how, he asks, should it be possible that anything belonging to the doctrine of redemption through Christ should have been presented so clearly in the period of mere divinatory anticipation that it could still be usefully employed alongside of that which Christ Himself said, and that which His disciples said after His completion of the work of redemption?[14] Or, if one wishes to imagine this as possible through inspiration, would not an entirely different recognition have had to be accorded the Redeemer and the manner in which He announced the Kingdom of God by that part of the Jewish people that was learned in the Scriptures, so that the effect would in no way be commensurate with the cause to which one would ascribe it? Furthermore, the history of Christian theology shows plainly how this effort to find our Christian faith in the Old Testament has partly had a baneful influence on our application of the art of interpretation, and partly heaped upon the development of doctrine and the debate concerning its more exact definitions a lot of useless complications; so that an improvement is only to be expected when one entirely abandons the Old Testament Scripture proof for Christian teaching and leaves aside supposed doctrines that are primarily based upon it.

But if something that has long been in vogue in the Church is to be reformed, it is necessary to show how this practice arose. There are two grounds upon which the external co-ordination of the two collections rest. First, that not only Christ and the apostles based teachings on Old Testament Scripture lessons but that this was continued in the early Church before the New Testament canon was formed. But it is impossible to conclude from this that a similar homiletic use of the Old Testament should even now continue, or that we would have to reckon it a disaster for the Church if the Old Testament were no longer as well known to Christians as the New. Indeed, the gradual recession of the Old Testament, in so far as its ecclesiastical validity stems from this historical connection, is in the nature of the case, and least of all can that historical connection guarantee the normativeness or the inspiration of these books. The Pauline passages which testify to the usefulness of the Old Testament writings primarily relate to this customary homiletical mode of using them, and the free manner in which the apostle himself employs them agrees entirely with that which we have said, so that he would testify for us that we have no further need of these proofs.

The second reason is that Christ and the apostles themselves refer to the Old Testament writings as to divine authorities favourable to Christianity. But from this it does not by any means follow that we shall have need of these adumbrations for our faith, since we have the experience—and the New Testament Scripture (John 4: 42) approves of it—that one ceases to believe for the sake of such testimonies once one has more direct and immediate certainty. He concedes, however, that it belongs to historical fidelity and completeness that that to which Christ and His first witnesses appealed as authority should be preserved. This applies almost exclusively to the prophetic writings and the Psalms; on this basis the practice of appending the Psalms to the New Testament seems justified. But since these writings had no separate existence at the time of Christ but only existed as parts of the holy collection, and are often only cited in this manner; and since, furthermore, occasional quotations from other books occur, one cannot object to it that the Old Testament (even though it cannot possibly form an indivisible whole for us in the same sense as for the Jewish people) be linked with the New Testament. Only the true state of affairs would be better expressed if the Old Testament were put after the New as an appendix, since the present order seemingly sets up the requirement that one must first go through the whole Old Testament in order to get to the New in the right way.

The greatest theologian of nineteenth-century Protestantism was thus in favour of putting the Old Testament in an extremely subordinate position. But he hesitates to draw the full consequences of his standpoint by joining the Marcionitic group. Elsewhere he asserts that from the arguments against conceding equal authority to the Old Testament it does not follow that the Bible should be cut in two. The latter is a resultant historical entity. That the Church has put the two parts together is a fact of such antiquity that no cause exists to change this, for the disadvantageous consequences that can arise from this circumstance can be obviated by other means.

This is all religious thinking of a high order. It should, perhaps, be mentioned that modern Old Testament scholarship
cannot concede to Messianic Prophecy the weight that Schleiermacher gave it. But it is true historically, at least, that Jewish
Christianity arose out of the sphere of Jewish Messianism, and
so his point can stand with some modification. More controversial is his thesis that Christianity is as much a continuation of
"heathenism" (in the sense noted above) as of Judaism. I have
encountered no endorsement of it, unless it be the somewhat
related, yet different view of De Lagarde (p. 93f.). But there is
more to be said for Schleiermacher's view than is commonly
realized.[15] In the light of to-day's insight the Greek element
in early Christianity was a very important factor in its survival
and success. A mere Jewish messianic movement had no prospect of becoming a world religion. It was its metamorphosis
into a religion of redemption, its employment of Greek mysticism and thought forms that set it aloft among the nations and
permitted the properly denationalized Semitic element in it to
become operative.[16] Schleiermacher could not yet have seen
this as clearly as we can. But apart from these historical considerations, a mere appraisal of the Hebraic and Greek heritage
in Christianity, when properly carried out, will show that the
latter is both considerable and essential. It seems to me that
Schleiermacher's position in this matter deserves consideration.

Chapter Six

THE OLD TESTAMENT IN NINETEENTH-CENTURY
THEOLOGICAL THOUGHT BEFORE RITSCHL

DOMINANT though the influence of Schleiermacher was on the subsequent theological development in so many respects, his views on the Old Testament were soon discounted. Even those who were his most immediate followers accorded them no defence. The unilateral treatment of both Testaments as the source of authority in the age of orthodoxy had impressed itself so deeply on the Christian mind that men were disposed to speak with regret about Schleiermacher's limitations in this matter and were quick to restore the Old Testament to a more exalted place.[1] We therefore need not linger over the successors of that master.

Some attention should, however, be bestowed on De Wette, who in certain respects continues the enlightenment, while in others he belongs to the new era. As biblical scholar he ranks with Eichhorn—above him, in fact, in originality of contribution. At this point, however, we are concerned with his theological views.[2] He was greatly influenced by the philosophy of Fries, who over against the scepticism of Kant in metaphysical matters held that the human mind could apprehend transcendent reality through feeling or intuition.[3] De Wette viewed all dogmas from the angle of discovering their underlying religious content, after abstracting their thought-forms as antiquated shell. Everything in the Bible which is not capable of appealing to this intuitive feeling is thus of no significance for us. The Old Testament is to be sharply differentiated from the New, but at the same time they are to be diligently compared. The process of life and thought in the Old Testament, he thinks, is strange to us in great measure; he sees it as "a great, wide territory of the unconscious or immediate in which the Spirit of God is operative in a mysterious way, filling the hearts of the

enthusiastic and the pious with intimations which they themselves cannot control or express clearly and purely, but which
His creative breath constantly fashions according to archetypes
unknown to them; using men as the unconscious agents of his
activity and as exhibitions of a divine-human life that develops
in the conflict with the world in stage after stage until it reaches
its consummation with Christ." De Wette defines the Unconscious as something general and indefinite, which lies at the
bottom of the particular; it is partly the universally human and
partly that which links the Old Testament with the New and
composes the life element in which the former moves on toward
the latter. It cannot be circumscribed intellectually, but only
apprehended by the feelings.

De Wette seeks to present the Christian faith in terms of
Biblical Dogmatics (therein a representative of an earlier age).
In handling the Old Testament materials he differentiates
between Hebraism and Judaism, with the Babylonian exile as
the dividing line.

In one of his later works[4] De Wette describes the Old Testament as containing the history of the founding and development
of that distinctive life of the Hebrew people which is commonly
called "theocracy". He distinguishes between the original
revelation of the Mosaic era and the further development of that
revelation, and finds a similar situation in the Christian order;
for there, too, the original revelation in Jesus Christ had a
further development after His time. The significance of the Old
Testament books for the Christian rests on the relation of the
new order to the old. The latter was imperfect and preparatory.
He finds that the Old Testament is only canonical in a certain
sense. The canon lies in the New Testament and only that which
accords with it in the Old is canonical.

In speaking of Christian use of the Old Testament De Wette
demands strict historical interpretation in complete independence of the New Testament. He finds intelligent handling of
some Old Testament teachings, such as those on retribution,
necessary and asserts that the layman cannot penetrate the
darkness and dusk of the Old Testament unless a teacher who is
filled with Christian truth carries the light ahead for him. He
would avoid preaching from Old Testament texts and finds the
Old Testament useful chiefly for such teachings as are not

covered, but only presupposed, in the New Testament, or for the purpose of projecting oneself back into the pre-Christian situation—a thing that he believes may be edifying.

But a reactionary current, continuing the line of eighteenth-century supernaturalism, now came to the fore and busied itself with battling against the dying enlightenment. It had the support of conservative political forces in Prussia and its chief leader was Hengstenberg, who began editing an influential Christian journal in 1827 and was forced upon the faculty of Berlin in 1828, thereby becoming the colleague of celebrities like Schleiermacher and Neander, the church historian. This current, being primarily ecclesiastical, did not at first affect the whole realm of scientific theology to any marked extent. Only in the field of Old Testament scholarship "in which the difficulty of language and the remoteness of the times with which it deals particularly favoured arbitrary play of fancy, where rabbinic theology and the allegorizing method of the church fathers and of the scholastic theologians had done advance service, was this influence immediately felt". Hengstenberg himself,[5] and kindred minds, carried on an orthodox interpretation of the Old Testament, condemning the higher critical views that had come up through Eichhorn and De Wette. "The Old Testament remained the favourite science of this new Judaism, even after its influence had spread to other fields and had captured important theological faculties." But Old Testament research of this stamp was not "to the taste of the times, which regarded such pettifogging, rabbinical interpretation of the Messianic passages of the Old Testament, such proofs for the Mosaicity of the Pentateuch, etc., with astonishment and amusement."[6]

Vast stimulation on the further development of all theological thinking, including that on the biblical problem, went forth from German philosophical Idealism. If the criticism of Kant trained the mind to operate more cautiously the teachings of Fichte, Hegel, Schelling gave it new goals and powerful inspiration. All the great German philosophers, beginning with Kant, branched out from the study of theology and in their writings show an understanding of its problems and a desire to deal with them. Schelling in the course of his development reaches a point where he views the religious question as paramount for philosophy.[7] The Hebraic heritage as well as the mystical-pantheistic are both strong in him and it is fascinating to observe their relative influence.[8] We shall confine ourselves here, however, to those thoughts which he developed in the final phase of his reflections, in which he dwelt on the philosophy of revelation. A preview of his thought on the matter appeared as early as 1815 and he lectured on it in Berlin in 1844–46.[9]

He brought forward the stone which the Rationalists had rejected—the idea of the eternal Incarnation of God and of His revelation—and made it the corner-stone of his final philosophical system. Lessing had described revelation as a progressive divine pedagogy and the Old Testament and New Testament as successive schoolbooks suited to the different stages. In so doing he had viewed the divine pedagogy rationalistically as consisting in the communication of important salutary truths. Schelling asserts that something can only be "revealed" which we could never know without revelation—something which transcends reason. The revelation that constitutes the content of Christianity is a *fact*—an act of the divine will which we can only understand and become convinced of by experiencing it. The fact of revelation consists in this: that a humanity fallen away from God is brought back to Him and reconciled with Him. This reconciliation was through Christ and therefore the person of Christ is the content of Christianity. He is not only the end and goal but the beginning and sole cause of revelation, and hence revelation in its full scope is embraced in Him. But this revelation which is completed in Christianity also passed through earlier pagan and Jewish stages; mythology, which is the essence of paganism and also is inherent in Judaism, forms the necessary presupposition of Christianity and is related to it as the abrogated is to the abrogator. It is apparent that for the biblical problem Schelling's position here is similar in its effect to that of Schleiermacher: emphasis on the Christian order; the Old Testament abrogated and on a par with pagan mythology.

The philosophical current reached its climax in Hegel. He touches on the theme that concerns us in his posthumously published *Philosophy of Religion*, when he surveys the religions of mankind.[10] We need not linger over his general theory except to note that he puts the Jewish, Greek and Roman religions together in one group as the three "religions of spiritual individuality"; the first is the religion of Exaltedness (*Erhabenheit*), the second that of Beauty (*Schönheit*). the third that of Purposefulness (*Zweckmässigheit*). Christianity then is discussed in a final section and labelled "the absolute religion". Hegel—like Schleiermacher—does not view Christianity as an offshoot of the Hebrew religion. Its immediate predecessor, he holds, is the Roman state religion, which prepared the soil for Christianity by the destruction and levelling down of all independent religious life. Hegel, furthermore, disapproves of representing Christianity as a "revealed religion" (*geoffenbarte Religion*), which looks for proof to miracles, signs, outward testimonies, documents and biblical quotations. He considers it rather "the manifest religion" (*offenbare Religion*), and would have the power of its own inherent truth as apprehended by the mind be its sole demonstration.[11] Obviously his position leaves little room for the authority of a sacred book, and must have extremely negative consequences for the Old Testament in particular, owing to his views on the Jewish religion that we have already referred to.

The close link with theology found in Hegel is snapped asunder in his follower Feuerbach.[12] For him religion is an illusion, and theology nothing but anthropology. The Old Testament religion, he held (therein an apt pupil of the British and French Deists of an earlier day), is entirely immoral; even the highest idea produced by "Hebraism", that of the love of God, is merely a form of human selfishness that puts the self in the place of God. In the doctrine of Creation the human will projects itself into ultimate power. The God of the Old Testament is one who satisfies all the wishes and desires of the human heart. Thus man has created God in his own image. Feuerbach believes Græco-Roman paganism was superior to the religion of the Old Testament; it is rooted in nature and that for him is the only reality.

While speaking of the philosophical development we may mention at this point also the thought of Schopenhauer[13] which was destined to attain a great importance in its effect on the German masses in the succeeding decades. He is a Kantian, but develops Kant's position further by making the will antecedent to reason instead of leaving the two side by side; thought, he held, must serve the will. Therein a change in the view of man and the world was indicated more fundamental than any since the days of the Greeks, for Descartes, Spinoza, Kant all basically continued Greek rationalism.   Schopenhauer's basic starting-point could have led to an association with the Christian religious heritage. But his pessimism led him to deny the will to live and therewith to anti-Christian tendencies. Viewing Christianity as derived from Judaism, Schopenhauer made the latter an especial object of his hate, and indeed it may well be said that he paved the way for the anti-Semitic crisis of our century by the publicity he gave to his viewpoint.

The theistic idea of God, he thinks, was made impossible by the Copernican astronomy. He explains the rise of theism with a psychological theory somewhat after the manner of Feuerbach: monotheism arose out of polytheism in a process of reduction of many gods to one, while polytheism arose out of the human desire for agencies able to aid men to get what they want or to ward off what they fear. True philosophical religion for Schopenhauer has two criteria—the belief in the moral significance of human actions and the belief in life after death. The moral significance of our actions consists in self-denial and a virtuous state of mind that excludes all selfish motives. The Old Testament religion is destructive of morality because it awakens selfish motives, making the desire to obtain rewards or to escape punishment fundamental. That religion, furthermore, knows no immortality; where the belief appears on the periphery, as in the twelfth chapter of Daniel, it is of foreign origin. Ecclesiastes 3: 19–21 expresses the real Hebrew view.

In the theological development, however, Hegelianism was the order of the day. Notably the evolutionistic approach that Hegel had applied was having its effect on all historical thinking. Biblical studies now took on a fresh hue, and particularly all efforts to deal with the story of the religious development of Israel and early Christianity. Utilizing the results of the criticism pioneered by Eichhorn and De Wette but proceeding evolutionistically in the spirit of Hegel, Vatke now gave a brilliant presentation of the development of the Old Testament religion,[14] on which a Wellhausen fifty years later still bestowed the praise that it was the most important contribution ever made to the historical understanding of ancient Israel. Fully Hegelian was Bauer's book on the Old Testament revelation.[15] He paves the way for his study by a whole philosophy of religion rooted in Hegelian idealism. Religion is the self-consciousness of the absolute mind (God). This self-consciousness is in the process of evolution and is confronted by limitations which it must overcome in order to attain its full growth. That process constitutes the history of revelation. The contents of revelation are apprehended by the subjective mind (man) in the thought of a divine purpose. Their recording leads to the origin of Scripture. While the initiative in revelation is entirely that of the absolute mind, the subjective mind takes the initiative in the recording (Scripture), but moving the while within the growing self-consciousness of the absolute mind. Limitations and errors of the subjective mind unavoidably creep into the Scripture record, but are corrected and outgrown in the general process.

In describing the history of revelation Bauer sets forth how the true idea of religion is gradually realized in it. Being historical, religion passes through various stages which by themselves are in antithesis to the very concept of religion on its highest plane. The presentation of its history is thus necessarily critical, and involves discernment of the degree of antithesis in which a particular stage stands in relation to the ultimate goal, as well as of the way in which this situation sets up a drive toward attaining a higher synthesis. There is thus an upward progression in the Old Testament revelation. So far as the authority of the Old Testament is concerned little could be left of it under such a view.

In the wake of Hegel, however, the theological interest soon shifted to a more crucial area than the Old Testament—to that of the New Testament revelation. Here Strauss' book on Jesus, in which he dissolved the gospel story into mythology, was a blazing beacon casting its rays far into the future.[16] And then came the great criticism of the New Testament literature and the study of the evolution of Christian dogma by the Tübingen school, shaking all Christendom. What Schleiermacher was to Systematic theology, F. C. Baur was to Historical theology.[17] Generations have laboured at the problems he posed and some of the answers he gave are more nearly right than many were willing to believe.

But theological conservatism, too, produced its important

figures whose positions were to sway many. Out of German Pietism and its fidelity to a biblical study coupled with mysticism, which had flowered so markedly in the work of a Bengel a century earlier, there now arose Beck.[18] He stressed the idea that the Bible is the source of all religious truth, and urged that one must go back to it directly—disregarding all the confessions of the Churches. He viewed the Bible as an organic whole in which nothing is accidental, but each part is planned to serve a function, like the pieces of a picture puzzle. The theologian must extract the essential things from the Bible and restate them in reflective thinking. The Bible contains, as it were, a whole system of truth. Beck does not consider the inspiration of the Bible as verbal, but rather thinks of the persons behind the Bible as inspired men of God. Hence to understand the Bible properly one must have personal religious experience. For Beck, Love is the basis and goal of all revelation. In interpreting Scripture he believes one must first determine the individual physiognomy of a given document and then take the further step of seeking the traits of a Messianic theological character that lie hidden in it (considering the totality of the Scriptural revelation), and in this way discover the significance such a document has in the plan of the Holy Spirit. Apocalypticism, as it lives on in part of the New Testament, had a great attraction for Beck. The coming Kingdom of God as preached by Jesus (and having nothing to do with any ecclesiastical organization) was a vivid reality to him. Since this is really Old Testament heritage in the New Testament it is apparent that an important strand of Old Testament belief exercised a strong effect on him.

Within the current of Hengstenberg which had come to the fore at the University of Erlangen a scholar arose who, next to Calvin, provided the most useful viewpoints for the defence and proper utilization of the Old Testament on a conservative basis: J. C. K. von Hofmann. He realized that mere dogmatic assertion of biblical authority and inspiration was not enough; it was his ambition to justify them by historical means. While his major efforts were devoted to the New Testament, he also gave considerable attention to the Old Testament. His work in the latter field[19] was of basic importance for the development of his whole theological position. He sees the Old Testament against the background of a "history of redemption" or

Heilsgeschichte—a word that he hammered into the more conservative strain of German theology. He imagines this as a real historical development (albeit of a stained-glass window variety) with progressive stages. In this development, he holds, Messianic prophecy played a considerable role. The true significance of any particular prophecy was not discernible at the time it was given, but only becomes clear in the light of the standpoint of redemption, which reached a preliminary completion in the work of Christ and will not be entirely completed until history shall have ended. The full import of some prophecies, therefore, cannot be understood even now. Holding Christ to be preexistent, he finds his redemptive influence operative in the area of Old Testament thought and experience. He even believes that this pre-existent Christ influenced Gentile trends toward a hope of redemption.

In a second major work[20] von Hofmann then attempted to determine the significance of the biblical materials for Systematic theology. The important point to him is that we Christians are in a relation with God that is a part of a great divine-human relationship extending through history. This larger history is reflected in the Bible in such a way that the divine-human relationship is mediated through Christ. This is the case throughout the entire Bible; at each point, however, we see it in a different stage of its development. A system of theology is demonstrated when all of its tenets are in accord with Scripture, every part of the latter having been studied in such a way that it is seen in its correct position and integral relation to the whole of that development.

To undertake the task of examining all Scripture—at least that of the New Testament—in such a manner in detail was the tremendous project to which von Hofmann next addressed himself.[21] Starting with the Epistle to the Galatians, he hoped to show how the individual stages of the development of the literature of the New Testament fit into the historical process of the earliest history of the Church, and what their relation is to the whole. The growth of the New Testament canon as such was also to be viewed in teleological terms. The final step was to be the investigation of the relation of the Old Testament Scripture to New Testament Scripture in order to determine by what right the Church considers the former a part of its Holy Writ. By striving to show that every part of Scripture served an end and had a necessary place in the scheme of the whole, he hoped to prove its divine origin and inspiration—at least to the satisfaction of the Christian believer. This approach, he thought, would render it unimportant whether any particular New Testament document was really "apostolic" in authorship or not.

Hofmann's project remained incomplete for the New Testament, with its continuation for the Old Testament not even in sight. But his ideas had a powerfully stimulating and enduring effect in conservative quarters. Various scholars of more recent times have called for a resumption of Hofmann's approach in more modern form (e.g., Procksch). His influence survives also in the work of Vischer. Consonant to some extent with Hofmann's *Heilsgeschichte* was the emphasis that A. Vilmar placed on the theology of God's saving acts in history (*Heilstatsachen*),[22] over against rationalistic emphasis on truths or Schleiermacher's emphasis on feeling.

In the continuation of the theological current that stemmed from Schleiermacher various shades of opinion, liberal and conservative, had their share. In connection with the problem of the Bible, Rothe deserves particular mention,[23] for his doctrine on this matter powerfully influenced all subsequent conservative theology. He follows Schleiermacher in differentiating sharply between revelation and Scripture. Since he was more of a believer in the supernatural than Schleiermacher, he placed a much stronger emphasis on revelation than his great predecessor. There are two sides to revelation according to Rothe: manifestation and inspiration. God manifests Himself by His actions in the historical process. Sinful man, however, would not be able to interpret God's action aright if it were not for the fact that God had inspired certain men to do this for Him by their spoken word. As authoritative interpreters these individuals had an active part in the historical process of revelation. But in order that this process of revelation might become a factor in subsequent history, when the living voices of these interpreters were hushed, it had to be reliably recorded. This recording was achieved through the execution and preservation of a series of writings in which the facts of the sacred history and their authoritative interpretations were made available for future generations. These writings have the character of "records" or

official documents and this gives them a permanent authority—
they too have become a part of the extension of the process of
revelation. But they are not inspired as such. They are not
infallible in the sphere of that which does not pertain to revelation, but only in that which does pertain thereto. They form an
instrument that suffices for the necessary knowledge of the
divine revelation because it contains within itself the means to
correct errors contained in any of its parts taken by themselves.
Rothe finds that it was a great weakness of the orthodox period
that it could not differentiate between religion and theology.[24]
The Protestant Scripture-principle must be understood as meaning that one should use the Bible not as a source of doctrines
but of daily companionship, inhaling its sacred atmosphere, as
it were, seeking a living view of its revelation. But important as
the Bible is for the individual Christian, it must be remembered
that it is primarily the book of Christendom as a whole, not of
one day, but of all ages, lands and peoples. This reminder was
particularly important and cannot be stressed too often.

In this connection we may cite the views of another speculative theologian, who, however, belongs to the ecclesiastical
current: Frank.[25] He inaugurated the approach of investigating the grounds of Christian certainty (1870) as a form of
Christian apologetics. On what grounds, he inquires, is the
Christian convinced of the truth of the Christian religion? This
is something very different from attempting to persuade non-
believers. According to Frank, all certainty is based on experience, and the experience of regeneration gives one certainty as
to a considerable number of "objects of faith". He divides these
into three classes: immanent, transcendent and transeunt. In
the last mentioned category belongs "the Word of God". The
latter, he argues, is by no means identical with Scripture, but
since it is laid down in Scripture in its initial and documentary
form, a certainty concerning the Word of God includes also a
certainty concerning Scripture. This certainty in no wise proceeds from our becoming convinced first that various portions of
Scripture are Word of God and then proceeding to embrace the
whole, nor does it exclude doubts as to the divine character or
relevance of some of its parts. Nevertheless, Scripture is a sort
of living organism of many members in which any particular
member is only understood or appropriated in relation to the

whole and receives its vital force from the centre. In regeneration the individual may only have experienced the Word of God
as it came to him in the living oral message of the Church. If he
turns to the Scriptures and finds portions of them bearing no
discernible relation to salvation, he will set them aside, but will
all the more firmly embrace those portions which confirm his
possession of that salvation and open his eyes as to their content
and origin. But in this case the individual really can only be
arbitrarily differentiated from the Church, for the Bible (notably
the New Testament) is the book of the Church, having arisen
out of its own life, and being the expression of its faith in the
very days of its crystallization. The faith thus expressed has
continued to nourish the life of the Church ever since. Historical
criticism has its place and must deal with the matter of the
integrity and authenticity of the individual writings. While
faith must believe that those who first proclaimed the Word had
a special authority owing to the position given them by Christ,
this does not preclude the possibility of doubting that every one
of those whose writings the Church accepted into its canon
really was one of those possessing such authority. However,
it is difficult for the individual to isolate himself from the Church
or set up his judgment against that of the Church. Furthermore,
the spiritual experience which the Church has had with these
writings is even more important than such critical considerations of the individual. The original words, handed down in
writing and spoken in relation to definite historical situations
and concrete problems and experienced as saving Word of God
either at the time or subsequently in retrospect, are experienced ever anew by the Church in similar or divergent situations
and perhaps with a much richer and fuller understanding.

While certainty as to the Word of the New Testament is the
first thing to be embraced as one proceeds backward from the
present living Word of God in the Church, Frank holds that the
Word of the Old Testament also has a claim upon the Christian
because it is the preparation for and the presupposition of the
Word of the New Testament. But certainty of the pre-
Christian Word is not to be had for the Christian except as
mediated through the Christian Church. Our situation was
fixed by the early Church when it took Old Testament Scripture
to its bosom and read it in the light of Christian fulfilment. And

with the Church of that time and all ages, we can discern how God dealt with the people of the Old Covenant in a manner not unlike that with which He dealt with the community under the New Covenant. Born out of the womb of the Old Testament Church, the Church of the New Testament has ever been and still is capable of apprehending the preparatory Word that was given under the earlier Covenant, not indeed without the historical record of the Old Testament, and yet not merely through it, but rather through a spiritual response, confirmed as that is by all the historical threads that tie the two orders together. Naturally the Old Testament Word must recede into the background—not because it was to a lesser degree Word of God, but because it points beyond itself to a fulfilment without which it would lose its significance. There is no Psalm that the Christian can pray without infusing into it elements drawn from the Christian consciousness, and in doing so he does not corrupt the Old Testament Word of God, but takes it to his heart in just the sense in which it is and remains Word of God for him. The preparatory character of the Old Testament order has of necessity antiquated certain of its arrangements which were once in full force and possessed a divine validity for that order. We can discern in them, in spite of human imperfections attending their mediation, the hand of God ordering the life of the Old Testament community with a view to the coming realization of salvation. Even books like Esther or Ecclesiastes can be understood as not entirely unrelated to the Old Testament Word of God in so far as the former testifies to a particular deliverance of the people of God, and the latter to an experience of an Old Testament believer which has points of contact with phases through which Christian experience of life may also pass. Even so, there can be no Christian certainty that must necessarily embrace every book of the Old Testament. The Church itself, as in the case of the New Testament, is in a continuous, never completed process of trying to understand and becoming certain of the Word of the Old Testament.

Careful attention will disclose that this conservative Lutheran thinker has granted (1) that the process of fixing the canon is by no means definitely completed and that doubts concerning individual books are permissible; (2) that the Old Testament belongs primarily to a pre-Christian order; (3) that our acceptance of the Old Testament is chiefly due to its use in the early Church, as reflected in the writings comprising its New Testament. Obviously the liberal views have captured a conservative stronghold, and one may infer that only the feeling for the historical continuity of the Hebrew and Christian orders and loyalty to ecclesiastical tradition make him hold fast to the Old Testament at all. It is not our function here to examine Frank's general theological presuppositions, but we may at least point out this much, that his emphasis on the subjective factor of regeneration *per se* tends to subordinate the idea of the Word of God. This gives his whole theology an anthropocentric tinge and lays it open to criticism at the hands of those who desire a theocentric approach.

We may before terminating this account of the period between Schleiermacher and Ritschl glance at how some leading Old Testament scholars saw the biblical problem. It will suffice to single out Oehler, Diestel, and Ewald.

In his able historical survey of 1845, which was preparatory to his *Theology of the Old Testament* (published after his death), Oehler already sets forth his basic ideas.[26] He rejects all Christianization of the Old Testament, but at the same time views it as preparatory for the New and organically connected with it. Since in every sphere of organic life the earlier stages can be understood only from the final stage, so too the key to the Old Testament is given us by the New. For Oehler the Incarnation and Reconciliation of the world with God are the essence of Christianity. He therefore views the Old Testament as reflecting the movement leading up to the attainment of this reconciliation. The Old Testament presupposes: (1) The differentiation of God and the world—the Holy One versus sinful humanity; (2) The realization that God is for the world and desires to reveal Himself to it and fulfil His purpose in it, and that as the world is of God so it is for God, as place of His revelation and scene of His glory, and especially that man is created unto God. Hence the Old Testament shows on the one hand a progressive manifestation of God to the world and in the world toward the goal of union with man, and on the other hand a striving of man to enter into this fellowship and so become partaker of life. The attempt must then be made to find a meaningfulness in the historical and intellectual develop-

6

ments mirrored in the Old Testament. No thoughts are to be imputed to the ancient writers not warranted by sound historical interpretation, but at the same time that which was in their minds is to be viewed in its nexus with the whole organic development from the Christian standpoint. The ancient writers themselves, he concedes, could not yet have this understanding. In practice this must lead to considerable speculation if one is to discern and explain such connections.

A generation later there appeared Diestel's great study—a vast inventory of our whole subject in all its antiquarian aspects.[27] In a concluding chapter, however, the author discusses what he calls "the solution of the theological problem". The latter, according to him, is that of the "correct discernment of the religious content of the Old Testament". To our present-day way of thinking this would limit him to the purely historical. But Diestel has more than the merely historical in mind. He asserts that the various lines of thought concerning the Old Testament problem that have appeared in the course of time follow diverse principles and main viewpoints which are one-sided and can only do partial justice to the task in hand. He rules out entirely any doctrinal approach (because he regards that as tackling the problem with a ready-made solution in one's pocket), as well as any theosophical viewpoint (because that represents a false fusion of the philosophico-historical and the religious principles), and finds three lines of inquiry hitherto pursued alone legitimate:

(1) The purely historical (Diestel says "national") which stresses the full objective understanding of the Hebrew nation, of its literary remains, and of its religion in the light of its Oriental character and background. He finds this approach unsatisfactory in that it points beyond itself, crying out for an evaluation of Israel—of its place in the world and the relative quality and worth of its literature and religion. Where that task is undertaken at all on this standpoint, it results in what Diestel calls "ethnicism", which he defines as the undue emphasizing of the similarities and the overlooking or slighting of the differences between Israel and the nations. (2) The philosophic-historizing line. By this he means attempts to approach the Old Testament from the angle of a philosophy of religion in such a way as to construe the Hebrew development

in accordance with certain ideas or principles. This approach is particularly exposed to error when, instead of proceeding from the standpoint of Christianity, it takes a standpoint in pre-Christian "ethnic" viewpoints (dualism, deism, pantheism). On all sides it threatens to fall into a more or less humanistically fashioned naturalism.   (3) The purely religious line.   This emphasizes primarily the eternal truths of Israel's religion or its kinship with Christianity, as well as those historical aspects of the Old Testament religion that are important from the point of view of a history of redemption. Presupposing that history is not merely a work of accident or a product of the human mind, it sees in these factors the hand of a divinity and thus regards them as products of revelation. But this view can also become artificial when it fails to give due heed to realistic knowledge. The Hebrew records are then looked upon merely as revelations of God and everything that is not pleasing to ourselves in them is set aside; as a result the distance existing between this religion and Christianity at various points is not gauged with exactitude and the purely human and historical factors opera-tive in the whole Hebrew situation are overlooked. Indeed, the approach can become so one-sided that it results in a new Judaism (by neglecting criticism from the Christian angle), or a sort of Docetism (by denial of the co-operation of any human factors). Actually the Bible does not content itself with giving us God's Word, but shows how the latter became the possession of men, and thus provides us with documents of human piety as well. Providence, Diestel holds, shows itself most glorious when it does not put out of action the natural conditions under which human documents are wont to arise, but when it permits these to operate undisturbed.   If imperfections and errors necessarily creep into such records, the spirit of Christ, that will not be lacking in any honest searcher of the Scriptures, will illuminate the reader so that his eye is not blinded by them, but rather becomes sharpened and accustomed to proper dif-ferentiation.

Diestel then recommends a combination of all three principles, hitherto used only in a one-sided manner, in their essentially correct and justified aspects. The really religious approach, he asserts, must take its standpoint within Christianity and the Christian idea of God as He revealed Himself in Christ, and thus must consider the Old Testament phenomena in the light of their approximation to or distance from Christianity. Before Christianity came there could not be any adequate idea of the divine truth. As for the human side of Israel's life, there could be no full understanding or appraisal of its meaning and worth before the coming of Christianity. Just because divinely given possibilities and values work themselves out in that human element, the exact study of the latter must be demanded of Old Testament scholarship in the name of religion itself. To understand the self-revelation of Israel in its religious documents, as they hang together with their ancient environment, must be the object of strenuous effort. Our belief that God is operative in history and that the totality of that ancient history prepared the way for Christianity requires an interest in that history itself. It also justifies our applying the comparative study of religions to the religion of Israel, and gives us the task of discovering and setting forth this religion's exact place among all the others. In such a fusion of three hitherto separate and legitimate approaches, Diestel sees a programme in accordance with which ever new attempts to study the subject must be made. For as long as there is human development and the depths of Christianity remain inexhaustible, our knowledge of it can never be final.

In essence, Diestel here set forth the procedure with which Christian biblical scholarship is now coming to operate. We are inclined to tone down the second principle (though we cannot do without the unifying activity of the mind or evolutionary considerations) because of our modern distrust of all speculative constructions. But the third principle, except for the emphasis on "truths" or on "providence" is now being invoked more fully by Old Testament scholars, in so far as they are Christian churchmen. That the trail thus blazed by Diestel was not followed sooner was partly due to the fact that men's minds became focused on the objective and material side of life, beginning with the 'seventies, and that this spirit, carried over into the field of biblical studies, resulted in their increasing historization and secularization. Graf's great critical work which had already appeared[28] and Kuenen's book now being issued[29] were harbingers of the Old Testament scholarship of the immediate future.

A particularly significant figure is Ewald. He is the first among German scholars to follow the example set in England by Milman's *History of the Jews*, 1829, of treating the history of Israel in secular spirit. His work on that subject is on a large scale[30] and contrasts markedly with the "stained-glass window" presentation (in von Hofmann's vein) given by the noted Church historian Kurtz.[31] Ewald also did yeoman service in awakening literary appreciation for Hebrew prophecy and poetry. The main effect of his labours was thus of a secularizing nature. Nevertheless he wanted to be a theologian, and his theological position on the Bible and the Old Testament in particular was set forth in a Biblico-theological work of 1871.[32]

Ewald recognizes the Bible as only one of three agencies by means of which modern man can come to the knowledge of the true revelation and to the fear of God—the other two being sufficient by themselves to that same end: they are the Christian fellowship which embraces us from cradle to grave with its wealth of impulses, and our own practice and experience of the fear of God whereby we alone attain an actual religious life. But alongside of these two other factors, the Bible nevertheless remains the sole unchangeable mirror of this revelation and fear of God, by means of which we can alone discern for certain whether the other agencies are as pure and undefiled as they should be. Its supreme position for the Church is thus assured, even though it may not be the agency that chiefly touches us as individuals. But high as the Bible stands, it is only a means to an end—a passageway through which we pass. Let us not over-estimate this mere passageway and imagine that in this or that word of the Bible we hear the Word of God without considering what the Word of God which we ought to follow really is, and let us not take offence at this or that word and stumble over a book that is meant to elevate and help us.

Ewald differentiates three strata of material pertaining to revelation in the Bible: (1) a stratum of earlier religious ideas no longer fully alive in the days of the authors themselves, e.g., ideas like Cherubim and Seraphim, or of God as Lord of Hosts; (2) the middle stratum lying in the sunlight of full contemporary experience on the part of the people for whom these books were written, e.g., the great truths about God, the Kingdom, and the Messiah, or in the New Testament, Jesus

Christ; (3) a stratum dealing with mysteries such as the secrets of the divine wisdom or purpose of God in the life of individuals and of mankind, and with the remote historical mysteries of the beginnings of the world and of history.—It is our duty to bring these three stages together into a higher unity, taking our starting point *from the middle stage* that lies before us in full clarity, and always following the materials of the other stages in such a way that we ask ourselves whether these things can still have the same significance for us as for the ancients. We must not allow ourselves to be disturbed by former or present errors, no matter how influential they may have become. If the Jews, since the wars of annihilation under Titus and Hadrian, discarded all Hellenistic writings and broke with Christianity as well, how can that obligate us *not* to see the great historical truth? And if many learned Christians would hold only to the New Testament and reject the Old, that is an even graver error and soon leads to the discarding of the New Testament too. Therewith the true and necessary connectedness of the whole great history is overlooked, just as was done by the Jews, and with worse consequences. The Old Testament contains such a host of basic truths, so well and perfectly stated, that they cannot be more profoundly established or more adequately defended in the New Testament, but are simply presupposed there, as standing fixed since of old. If in other respects the Old Testament does not reach the highest perfection, it nevertheless strives toward that goal most valiantly and at least in some of its most advanced areas comes close to it. No greater praise can be accorded the Old Testament than this, Ewald holds, that without it the New Testament with all its fruits which it provides for us would not have been possible.

In this attempt to deal with the problem Ewald practically subordinates the Bible to the Church and individual experience, though theoretically maintaining its supremacy in the long range view. The Scripture problem is thus made less acute than when everything is staked on Scripture. His defence of the Old Testament is less satisfactory. Basically, we are on rationalistic ground when we emphasize ideas or truths. In that respect Ewald's doctrine of revelation is really only a modification of orthodoxy and subject to some of the same criticisms as its progenitor.

A brief glance at the state of affairs in the Anglo-Saxon countries reveals a continuance of orthodoxy on the one hand and the spread of a deep Christian revivalism on the other hand. Theologically speaking the most significant figures in England were Pusey and Newman. The former was a believer in the literal inspiration of the Bible. He reacted strongly against the higher critical movement because he saw in it an underlying "disbelief" in supernatural revelation. This comes to the surface, e.g., in the polemical preface to his commentary on Daniel,[33] where he discerns the uselessness of argument with those imbued with the prejudice that there cannot be such a thing as supernatural prophecy. Newman had less reason than the biblical scholar Pusey to concern himself with nineteenth-century criticism. He stands committed to the inspiration and literal truth of the Bible. This does not prevent him from speaking disparagingly on occasion of the "Jewish Scriptures" as delivering to us only those attributes of God already known to "natural religion",[34] or of acknowledging that some writings like Esther, Ecclesiastes and Song of Songs hold a weak position in the canon. The latter, he believes, depends for its authority on the Church, since Scripture contains no "internal mark" of its canonicity. He held that the gospel was contained in the Old Testament in a hidden way; that it was not on the surface had proved to be a stumbling-block for the Jews and had ultimately become their undoing.[35] He adopted the method (ultimately rooted in Calvin) of establishing a doctrine by working backwards from its clear statement in the New Testament to its hidden formulation in the Old. As an example of his procedure one may take his treatment of Justification.[36] He contends that Scripture in its various portions conspires together as a whole to this doctrine, but he limits himself to showing how several Psalms pray for forgiveness and renewal of life and how a few prophetic passages predict the granting of these things in the Messianic future, and then swiftly passes over to the New Testament teachings.

In the American scene Calvinism prevailed, with some inner dissensions that we need not dwell on. The influence of the Old Testament was large and there was little thought of questioning its authority, though there were Christian men, led by such a vastly influential preacher as Henry Ward Beecher, who put the God of Love and the teachings of Christ at the heart of Christianity and recoiled from the "spiritual barbarism" of Calvinism and of some elements of Old Testament teaching. But they had no clear idea of the consequences for the status of the Old Testament to which such a position was bound to lead. But German higher criticism had entered the American scene in 1843 through Theodore Parker's translation of De Wette's *Einleitung*,[37] and Moses Stuart, though an orthodox scholar,[38] had translated Gesenius' Hebrew Grammar and furthered Hebrew studies, as well as interest in German Old Testament contributions (of the conservative variety). The fires of the higher criticism were thus beginning to smoulder, and as more and more young men were attracted to the German Universities and introduced to the rapidly moving intellectual life that was going on there a dissatisfaction with the tyranny of dogma arose. It needed only the wind of definite occasions to fan the fire into flames. The fact that in the great debate over slavery, prior to the outbreak of the Civil War of the 'sixties, the Old Testament had been much used to defend the supposed divine endorsement of that institution was doubtless a factor making for greater readiness on the part of New Englanders to examine the earlier portion of the canon with a critical mind.

Chapter Seven

THE TRANSITION TO THE MODERN SITUATION

THE enlightenment which went forth from eighteenth-century England to France and reached Germany last returned in metamorphosed form since 1860 from Germany to the tight little isle. The latter had been powerfully influenced by the evangelical movement led by the Wesleys, and now the Oxford Movement led by Pusey and Newman was revitalizing the Church of England. Orthodox biblicism was deeply entrenched once more and it seemed unlikely that biblical criticism of the sort being carried on in Germany could find admission there. But it was overlooked that biblical criticism had arisen on the Continent in emulation of the critical method developed in the study of the Greek and Roman classics. Homeric criticism found a hearing in England and thus paved the way for the application of similar principles to the biblical literature. A series of incidents now occurred which, through the publicity they received, helped to bring about a change.

A situation of pressure demanding some reasonable adjustment of the Scripture doctrine had been created in England by natural science. A nation taught to believe that the world was created in 4004 B.C. was naturally shocked when Smith and Lyell laid the foundations for Geology and made clear that large periods of time were necessary to account for the stratification of rock, and when the historicity of the Flood became very doubtful.[1] Instructed by Moses that man was a product of special creation, it was horrified to have Darwin talk of the *Origin of Species* (1859) and proclaim an evolution of man from lower forms of life.[2] Hardly had the first excitement over Darwin passed when there occurred the *Essays and Reviews* incident of 1860.[3] Seven scholars, six of them Anglican Churchmen, were contributors to this volume, in which were to be found such modern ideas as that the Bible must be interpreted

like any other book or that the Mosaic account of the creation
of man was not to be taken as accurate history. Under the lead
of Bishop Wilberforce of Oxford, who had already played a role
in the ecclesiastical excitement over Darwin, the essayists
were assailed as "guilty of criminal levity". The Christian
public vociferously demanded that they be ousted from the
Church. When two of the authors were suspended by their
local authorities they appealed to the Queen in Council. Even
a man of such lofty character as Pusey favoured their condemnation. But the Court, over the protest of its two Arch-
bishop members, but with the approval of the Bishop of
London, Tait, found the suspension unwarranted. After the
excitement had subsided some of the things that had been said
on the liberal side found response in many quarters and continued to simmer there.

Another incident capturing public attention arose through
the publication by Colenso of a work on the Pentateuch.[4] Here
for the first time the Anglican fold was actually invaded by the
continental type of higher criticism. Pushed off into the African
mission field as "bishop of Natal", the scholarly Colenso had
through experience in teaching the Africans come to doubt the
inspiration of the Old Testament. When making a translation
of the Bible into Zulu he sometimes found himself in a tight
spot with his flock in certain Old Testament passages. Thus
when rendering Exodus 21 : 21 (where a master is held blameless,
if the slave whom he has chastised dies from the effect, "for it
is his money"), a Zulu aide asked Colenso "Did God really say
that?" Colenso in that moment realized what it meant to make
God responsible for everything that is said in the Old Testament and answered negatively. He now began to study the
Hexateuch with a critical mind, and his keen observations in
the publications mentioned had their effect on the thought of
Continental scholarship, notably on that of Kuenen. But for
Colenso himself his venture brought on trouble akin to that
experienced by the essayists two years before. He was excom-
municated, but appealed to the British courts, which twice
rendered a verdict in his favour despite all the influence and
power arrayed against him and the public clamour that he be
condemned.

But Modernism did not confine itself to invading the Church

of England; it also got a foothold even a little earlier, though less spectacularly, among the Congregationalists, when S. Davidson contributed a chapter on *The Text of the Old Testament* to a revised edition of Horne's *Introduction*. As a result of the protest that arose over it he was forced to resign his chair in Manchester. In 1862, however, he brought out a three-volume *Introduction to the Old Testament* in which that collection was treated like other literature and the presence of myth and legend in it acknowledged. In the same year A. B. Davidson published the initial part of his never completed *Commentary on Job*, generally recognized as the first modern Old Testament Commentary in the English language. But, though affected by modernity, he kept clear of the more controversial matters and filled the role of apologist against Continental critical extremes. His influence on Hebrew studies was considerable, however, and some of his pupils were to attain great eminence as Old Testament critics, *e.g.*, W. R. Smith, G. Adam Smith and J. Skinner.

Meanwhile a new great science was emerging that was bound to have a tremendous impact on Old Testament study— Assyriology. British and French explorers had stirred the imagination by their archæological discoveries of the 'forties. In 1857 occurred the famous incident proving to the numerous sceptics of the time that the decipherment of the Assyro-Babylonian language was indeed accomplished, when five scholars, headed by the master of them all, Sir Henry Rawlinson, separately deciphered a new cuneiform text (a cylinder of the Assyrian ruler Tiglathpileser I of 1100 B.C.) in substantially the same way. And as the vast treasure of the library of King Ashurbanipal of Nineveh was studied a whole literature contemporary with Old Testament times was exhibited to the world, thus creating an opportunity to institute comparisons. In 1876 occurred the startling incident of the publication of Adam Smith's *Chaldean Account of Genesis*, in which that indefatigable decipherer and explorer published for the first time the Babylonian version of the flood story from the cuneiform tablets found by Layard at Nineveh. All the long dispute with science over the Mosaic account of the Deluge now became pointless. To their amazement men learned that the biblical account of the flood was virtually identical with the cuneiform one, with the chances of the borrowing being done by "Moses" being better than even. Apologists of the veracity of the primal history reported in the Old Testament now were confronted with a serious problem. What was illumined here in a momentary flash was to become in cumulative measure a terrible dead weight on the shoulders of any form of supernaturalist belief— viz., the historical conditioning of the Hebrew records, their inextricable entanglement in event, word and thought with the events, words and thoughts of dead civilizations and all the limitations thereby implied.

Under the cumulative effect of all the new learning the resistance to biblical criticism in England was weakened. When W. Robertson Smith published his article on the Bible in the 9th edition of the *Encyclopedia Britannica* in 1875, and in the ensuing years had to undergo heresy trials, the change of atmosphere from that which had marked the trial of a Colenso was curious. Though he was suspended in 1880 from teaching in the Aberdeen Free Church College, the charge of heresy was not sustained and he was merely admonished for having made unguarded statements. His removal from his chair in 1881 in consequence of a further Encyclopedia article on *Hebrew Language and Literature* even aroused a mass meeting on his behalf and led to his being invited to give lectures in Edinburgh and Glasgow.[5]

Meanwhile the vast upward surge of the sciences was taking place and a radically changed spirit was arising. The philosophy of Comte in France had heralded this modern age by proclaiming a total rejection of metaphysics and therewith of the whole philosophical development from Descartes to Hegel, and favouring a "positive" philosophy, based only on the insights obtained by science. The study of Sociology which he inaugurated was destined to have an increasing significance for that of religion. Parallel therewith went the rise of the science of Psychology, the pertinence of which for religion likewise was bound to be great. The importance of Economics was highlighted by Karl Marx's *Das Kapital*, 1867, and a new materialism was permeating life in the wake of the industrial expansion. If Schopenhauer had proclaimed the will supreme and Spencer had raised evolution to a cosmic principle, Nietzsche preached the will to power and drew the consequences of the doctrine of evolution by foreseeing man's rise to a higher and better estate after the hindrance of Christian conditioning was cast off. Finally, nationalism raised its head, as the new possibilities of national self-assertion arose through improved means of communication and increase of military striking power.

A prophetic incident that looms much larger now in retrospect than it did a few decades ago occurred in Germany in 1878, when De Lagarde published his essay on the *Religion of the Future*.[6] Here Christianity is looked at in a critical manner by a man to whom patriotism is paramount. Historically, he regards Christianity not merely as the individual creation of Jesus of Nazareth but as the product of many contributing forces and influences and, with a more or less "political" slant, as essentially a creation of the Roman Empire and the nations united under its sway. It is doomed to perish, he holds, because of the Jewish element which it has carried along through the centuries as part of its heritage. The national consciousness of modern peoples simply cannot tolerate this. A new religion must be constructed by synthesizing genuine Christianity with the natural attributes of the modern nation. Obviously there can be no place for the Old Testament with its Jewish nationalism and racialism in this religion of the future. While De Lagarde seems to think exclusively in terms of his own national scene, he would presumably expect the same judgment to apply for other nations as well, so that the universal religion that Christianity aspires to be would be split up into, or be replaced by, various national religions. (This is indeed what happens temporarily to Christianity in times of war.)

This predominance of a national outlook puts De Lagarde, who regarded himself as a theologian, somewhat outside the theological horizon, and yet it seems necessary to mention him because he brought to light in principle thoughts that cropped out anew in the German scene in terrible realism from 1932–1939, in fusion with absolute political power. The liquidation of that power in the late war by no means puts an end to the significance of De Lagarde's thought, for it is quite conceivable that eventually the same process will repeat itself in other countries and times, wherever or whenever nationalism becomes ascendant. It must be conceded, too, that there is something artificial and incongruous in one's glorifying the past of an ancient Semitic people instead of one's own national past, or the cities and hamlets of Palestine instead of those of one's own land. The hymnology of the Church is particularly vulnerable to this criticism.

Within the process of professional Old Testament study a more immediately influential event occurred in Germany in that same year, 1878—the publication of Julius Wellhausen's great work.[7] It marked the beginning of a completely secular and evolutionistic study of the Old Testament sources. Wellhausen gave convincing demonstration to the thesis, put forward a decade earlier by Graf but not well established by that scholar, that the Old Testament legislation was post-prophetic. By setting up a convincing theory of the structure of the Pentateuch and determining the relative age and succession of its main strata J.E.D.P., he therewith found the key also to the main stages of Israel's religious development. It was now possible to fit all the other materials of the Old Testament into their proper place in that sequence and to obtain the criteria wherewith to differentiate between older elements and accretions in all the other books. The prophets of Israel suddenly assumed a much greater importance. A host of able scholars quickly followed Wellhausen's lead. The outcome of all this tremendous activity, carried on through several decades and with increasing participation of scholars everywhere, was the creation of an entirely different picture of the Old Testament literary and religious history from that held formerly.

The new Old Testament science inaugurated by the movement symbolized by Wellhausen sought to be and was scientifically respectable. It applied methods that had been productive of great results in the study of classical and other literatures to the Old Testament literature. As a result, there came into being an insight into the fact that the Hebrew religion had undergone a historical development.[8] It matters little, as we now see it, that the development is not one of such steady upward evolution as was first thought. It is enough to say that there was flux and change, and that it was affected by historical circumstances, spiritual movements, as well as by the actions and influence of individuals. This history has not yet been adequately written up and probably never can be because of the fragmentary information at our disposal. We must divine more than we can see. The materials we have all fit somewhere into a picture puzzle, but the trouble is that a great number of pieces are missing which, if we had them, would make the picture clear and meaningful. But the mere circumstance that scholarship, from Wellhausen on, established the fact of religious *change* in Hebrew history and discerned important aspects of it, made forever impossible the belief on the part of the intelligent portion of humanity that the Old Testament writings were a supernatural communication of the Holy Spirit.

An awareness of the secular forces operative in modern theological trends was shown by Delitzsch,[9] a man who deserves to be remembered when the roll of Old Testament scholars is called, because of the great usefulness of his Old Testament Commentaries and the inspiring role he played as a teacher. He was a supernaturalist, strongly influenced by the pietist school. But at the same time he preserved a somewhat open mind in critical matters. When he gave in to such results of higher criticism as the existence of a Deutero-Isaiah, the lateness of the Priestly Code, and the Maccabaean origin of Daniel, the fact had a powerful influence in giving criticism an entry into conservative quarters.

In England the higher criticism soon began to make further inroads. W. Robertson Smith, driven out of Scotland, found Cambridge willing to listen. Keble College at Oxford, which had been founded as a haven of orthodoxy after the *Essays and Reviews* incident, produced out of its midst a book of essays entitled *Lux Mundi*, 1889, in which the idea that the Genesis narratives are a historical record was given up and numerous critical views of German and Dutch scholars were espoused. But there was no heresy trial. When a Driver went over to the Wellhausen theory and a Sanday endorsed it in the *Bampton Lectures* (so long regarded as a province of orthodoxy), it began to take on the appearance of respectability, and so English scholarship was set free to participate in the great critical movement.[10]

In the United States, sound philological and historical Old Testament study, but remaining on neutral ground, had been carried forward by Edward Robinson.[11] The higher criticism, however, only invaded America successfully after Wellhausen's demonstration of it. The Baptist C. H. Toy was driven out of his post at Louisville for endorsing it in 1879.[12] But the Briggs heresy trial before the Presbytery of New York did more than anything else to break down the dykes hindering its entry. Briggs was assailed for his 1891 inaugural lecture at the Union Theological Seminary in New York on the *Authority of Scripture*. After proceedings lasting several years he was suspended from the Presbyterian ministry.[13] He was fully supported, however, by his colleague Francis Brown,[14] and Union Seminary severed its bond with the Presbyterian Church rather than drop him. Another able American scholar who suffered a heresy trial was H. P. Smith.[15] In consequence of such events the interest in Wellhausenism was heightened.

While there was still powerful opposition to higher criticism, best represented by W. H. Green,[16] it became increasingly unable to stem the tide. The new University of Chicago, under the ægis of W. R. Harper, cultivated the link with progressive Old Testament study (as with German research in general);[17] in a seat of old congregational orthodoxy such as Yale's Divinity School a Bacon could contribute to Pentateuchal criticism;[18] while in the Andover of Moses Stuart a Moore could arise and wield the higher critical scalpel with the skill of the best.[19] Soon the mighty contenders of orthodoxy were only a memory.

While criticism and historical research were engaged in showing up the Old Testament in its true light against the background of the Hebrew historical process, that process as a whole, with all its intellectual and spiritual content, was being illuminated by Oriental science. The prophetic incident of George Smith's Chaldean Genesis rapidly attained a larger fulfilment than he could foresee. Through the labours of excavators, archæologists, philologists and interpreters of ancient texts and objects, the Oriental cultures were being resurrected, and therewith also knowledge of the literatures and religions of a world contemporary with the Old Testament.[20] It was impossible not to make comparisons between these cultures and that represented by the Old Testament. Yet it came once more as a terrific shock to popular, orthodox supernaturalism when the younger Delitzsch delivered his "Bible and Babel" lectures in 1903 and declared the biblical and Babylonian world views identical and claimed the dependence of the former on the latter.[21] People all over the world felt that Christianity was basically threatened.[22] In reality, the only thing that was threatened—though really not more so than it had been all along—was orthodox theology.

The moderate Delitzsch was soon followed by others who carried their claims to greater extremes. Thus Winckler and Jeremias indulged in the dream of a great Babylonian *Weltanschauung* that was basic for the whole Near Eastern culture including Israel's,[23] and Jensen saw in the Babylonian Epic of Gilgamesh the source of innumerable motifs in the biblical and other ancient literatures.[24] They furnished good targets for the Apologists. But Oriental exploration was vastly stimulated by his publicity, and historical research was in any case making it clear that the Hebrews shared in the ideas, legends and myths of pagan Oriental peoples—something so self-evident that men should have known it anyway.[25]

Chapter Eight

THE OLD TESTAMENT IN SYSTEMATIC THEOLOGY
SINCE RITSCHL

THE Protestant Church of the 'seventies and 'eighties confronted the biblical and notably the Old Testament scholarship of the time with a feeling akin to that which must afflict the hen that has hatched out ducklings and sees them go swimming off whither she cannot follow. The Reformation's setting up of the Bible as sole principle of authority, in the belief that its accurate and impartial interpretation was all that was necessary, had had the unforeseen consequence of proving that it is impossible to use this book as authority in the sense in which this was contemplated. The historical-genetic view of its contents, worked out in co-operation with the higher critical determination of the antiquity and extent of its separate units, was providing a (fragmentary) picture of a great religious history of the past—no exhibition of a single, unified, planned product such as seemed requisite for an authoritative book dictated by the Holy Ghost.

There was abroad an uneasy awareness of the seriousness of the loss for the Protestant Church. The former generations had slept peacefully within the citadel of the Church's ancient biblical doctrine. With an infallible revealed book they had guaranteed information on sin and salvation, heaven and hell, world history and natural science. One had only to quote chapter and verse, rely implicitly on what was written, and the affairs of the universe were comfortably settled. The preacher, learned in Hebrew and Greek, had inherited St. Peter's power of the keys. There was always, of course, a minority of sceptics, agnostics and scoffers, but they stood outside the pale of respectability. The Scriptures were a bulwark from which the fiery arrows of unbelief recoiled harmlessly. In England and America, and in reactionary quarters on the Continent as well, this had still been the situation a few generations earlier. But now this bulwark had fallen.

But providence had ready a man and a new theology for this exigency—at least for all those who could not close their minds to the truth—in the person and work of Albrecht Ritschl. His theology provided the tools for a presentation of Christianity able to weather the troubles caused by philosophy and biblical criticism. If philosophy had on the one hand caused confusion by seeking to dominate theology and on the other hand peril by trying to destroy it, Ritschl, by casting metaphysics out of the theological temple, greatly simplified the theological task. Over against historical criticism he set up the idea of faith, as taught by Martin Luther.[1]

The Reformers' conception of it had, indeed, survived in the consciousness of German Protestantism in theological quarters, but Ritschl saw that for the common man faith meant two things: (1) that one admits that everything in the Bible is the Word of God; (2) that faith at the same time was firm reliance on what is taught and reported in the Bible. This amounted to forcing oneself to accept that of which one was not honestly convinced, and made swallowing of the incredible a merit. The uncomfortable fact remained that this was just the same thing as the Catholic idea of faith. Hand in hand with this went the sham of the pulpit—preachers moving on an artificial plane and delivering biblical sentiments and ideas that were not an expression of their personal convictions. Over against this sort of thing Ritschl stressed faith as something vital and real.

In spite of Ritschl's opposition to philosophy he was governed by one—a dualism. The ultimate terrestrial realities are nature, conceived of as a mechanism, and an aggregate of intelligent personalities whose distinctive quality is ethical autonomy. Ritschl attained a higher unity by use of the teleological idea, in dependence on the philosophy of Lotze. God, imagined as moral will, thus establishes unity by governing the natural order according to the purpose of the moral order. In Christ, Ritschl held, God has revealed that He is governing the world in such a way that a moral goal, in which the individual and community may participate, is attained.[2]

Ritschl's principles were greater than Ritschl's theological system. Once he raised the flag of his principles—and he only did it near the end of his career—he gained a great following. The converts did not follow him in detail but in full freedom. They all concurred in what mattered most: the independence of theology, the true nature of faith and the necessity of relating all Christian teachings integrally with such faith. That meant an enormous simplification of theology and involved relegating many things to the background that had no close connection with living faith. Theology was sent forth courageously into the modern world to win it for Christ (though from the angle of present-day thinking with only a wooden sword). The conservatives and the radicals alike were aroused against Ritschl and his school, and for years there was a tempest over Ritschlianism. But it was the theology of the immediate future, had a standing in the eyes of the intellectuals and even found following in England and America.

Ritschl was deeply imbued with the historical attitude. He had begun as a pupil of the great Baur and wrote at least one historical work of long-time significance. In his systematic thinking he retained something of this historical attitude—a thing not quite consistent with his principle of faith. His views on Scripture and notably on the Old Testament impress one as born out of his historicism.

Ritschl taught that authentic knowledge of the Christian religion and revelation can only be derived from documents close to the founding of this religion.[3] He sees this conceded already in the early Church, for the writings of the succeeding Christian generations are dependent on the thought of the apostolic writings. But instead of asserting that what makes these writings so distinctive and peculiar is their inspiration, Ritschl advances a natural criterion for their worth. The chief difference between the post-apostolic literature and the canonical New Testament writings he holds to be this, that the former authors are incapable of properly utilizing the Old Testament presuppositions of the thought of Christ and the apostles. He believes, furthermore, that the insights of the apostles and New Testament authors into the content, purpose and divine basis of Christianity, as well as Christ's own sphere of thinking, are mediated by an understanding of the Hebrew religion different from that of contemporary Judaism (whether Pharisaic, Sadducaic or Essene). He concedes that in one respect the way was already prepared for the thoughts of Jesus and the New Testament writers in Judaism, viz., by the emergence of the belief in a final judgment, but even here he does not think that the Jewish ideas were merely taken over, but rather that Jesus produced them anew out of His own unique position over against human history. This genuine Old Testament conditioning of the classic writings of the period of Christian origins binds them all together into a group. Discerning their superiority in this respect over other books, he holds, one can refrain from all attempts at justifying their segregation such as that given by the doctrine of Inspiration.

The New Testament writings, then, are the authoritative source of Christian religious ideas for Ritschl. But that does not mean that all the ideas found in them are to be counted valid Christian tenets! He links up with Luther's principle that Scripture is authoritative only in so far as it "treats of Christ", i.e., in the sphere of the direct portrayal of man's redemption. He points out that therein lies a difference between the true Lutheran position and some others. Calvin, for example, took the doctrine of twofold predestination into his system, even though he finds it impractical, just because he thought it was taught by Paul, and he regarded certain ecclesiastical arrangements existing in the early Church and found in the New Testament writings as binding for us. Other Christian leaders have claimed that the communism of the primitive Church of Jerusalem should be regarded as normative for us. Still others, stressing the apocalypticism of the New Testament, have made millennialism important. Ritschl has no use for such biblicism. He holds that the subject of Biblical theology, which must be developed historically and be free from dogmatic interests, is one thing, while Christian Doctrine is another thing. The latter must reach out from the central point of New Testament Christianity and then take in such other elements as hang together with it essentially and integrally. The central point for Ritschl lies in Justification and Reconciliation.

In proceeding to study the New Testament source material that is important for these Christian doctrines, Ritschl everywhere goes back to the Old Testament to set forth the relation between the idea in the two parts of the canon. Since he denies the doctrine of the witness of the Holy Spirit in any form, his touchstone for the authority of the New Testament writings remains this Old Testament background. That makes the task of convincing oneself of the validity of the New Testament teachings a rather complicated one. It seems, too, that he takes the authority of the Old Testament very much for granted. One may well argue that the Hebraic derivation of a concept does not in itself prove its superior value, but may even form an obstacle to our appreciation of it. One must also point out a fact of which Ritschl could not yet be fully aware but which research carried on since his day has made clear, that Hellenism and contemporary Judaism permeate the New Testament writings to a very large degree. Nevertheless, one must see in his approach an interesting effort to find an abiding significance for the Old Testament, and one that has by no means been fully exploited or tried out.

Progress beyond Ritschl was possible in several directions. One was to stress the historical Jesus as bringer to man of the true knowledge of God and as embodiment of an ideal requiring our emulation.[4] Another possibility was to stress the present experience of God in faith, by the Christian individual through contact with the Jesus of history. That was the road taken by Herrmann,[5] whose thought found a considerable echo in both England and America.

Religion for Herrmann is an experience given only to those with a capacity for it, and is authentic only when it has a moral effect. Over against a traditionalist idea which conceives of revelation as a tradition of how the faith of pious men of the past expressed itself, and over against a rationalistic idea which regards reason as the source of religion or as revelation, and over against mysticism which—though it rightly sees that religion must be personally experienced—falsely finds the source of revelation in an excitation of the feelings apart from the realities of our situation, Herrmann sees in revelation an experience that forces itself upon some of us and convinces us of the reality of God. This experience is not only—as Schleiermacher thought—that of becoming conscious of our absolute dependence (though that is included), but also of our becoming conscious of our inner freedom and independence. We have this experience when we know ourselves seized by a spiritual power which works upon us as a manifestation of pure goodness and to which we joyously submit. This experience is given to us, in our living together with other men, when the feelings of awe and trust are awakened in us.

The fundamental thing in Christianity as we see it about us, Herrmann asserts, is the way in which all Christians ultimately derive their spiritual resources from Jesus Christ. We are thus compelled to study the New Testament and to observe how the disciples of Jesus and the early Christians experienced the power unto life that went forth from Him. But we should have an entirely different brand of Christianity from that of the early Christians if we could not ourselves experience Jesus. The New Testament mediates this experience. In defending his position against the alleged results of modern higher criticism, Herrmann argues that, if every fact of the external life of Jesus were uncertain, yet the power that goes forth from His inner or spiritual life, as that shines forth from the record, is so great that we are brought to true faith in God through Him and thus experience redemption.

With such concentration on the Christian experience and on the influence proceeding from Jesus Christ one cannot expect Herrmann to have much use for the Old Testament.[6] While he does not take up this problem of the authority of the Old Testament specifically, he sometimes expresses his reverence for the books of both the Old and New Testaments as the sole tradition in which we can find Christ.[7] He sees in the knowledge of these books a means by which we may come nearer to the historical Jesus, and asserts that for this reason we desire no other kind of preaching than that which interprets the Word of God to us from Holy Scripture.

But for Herrmann, God alone and not a book is the authority to which we subject ourselves. Scripture has authority only where and in so far as a man by virtue of his faith already understands the God who is speaking to him.[8] Hence Herrmann can use the Bible where it suits him and set it aside where it does not. Thus, in his discussion of the doctrine of man, he contrasts the idea of the image of God in man found in the Old Testament with that found in the New Testament, and, after adopting the New Testament idea, adds that the rest of the "anthropological" ideas found in the Bible have no place in Christian doctrine because we cannot see how they can be made to arise in our minds anew through the faith that the inner life of Jesus creates within us.[9] His ethical emphasis, primarily Kantian, does give him a friendly attitude toward the ethical insights of the Old Testament prophets, and, of course, he clearly perceives the Old Testament heritage in the mind and soul of Jesus.

In Herrmann, the historical is first abandoned, and then brought back by a new route. He attempts to make Christianity independent of the results of the most radical historical criticism. Revelation has its reality only in the framework of the practical, ethical existence of man and therefore cannot be theoretically studied but only recognized in ethical decision, in a surrender to it. But the reflection of the spiritual (Herrmann says "inner") life of Christ in the New Testament (which is thus accepted as providentially provided and substantially dependable, in spite of the inaccuracies of the reporting of the external circumstances of His history), is the saving factor in our situation. In reality, therefore, a faint supernaturalism still stands in the background of his thought.

But while the Ritschlian theology enjoyed the greatest amount of esteem, notably because it commanded the allegiance (in principle) of so many scholars who did great work in the area of New Testament and other early Christian literature, other theological trends, too, remained in the field.

Among the conservatives of that period Martin Kaehler looms up as a particularly significant figure.[10] He attempted to grapple with the difficulties created for supernaturalism by the modern world-view on the one hand and by historical criticism on the other. Relating the divine activity to history rather than to nature, he understood it (in analogy to contacts between persons), as a contact of God and man. The decisive category for the history of revelation in this ontology is *Das Uebergeschichtliche* or "the transcendent"—a thought later seized upon by Karl Barth. Here is an attempt to get outside of the natural process—to take the "nature" out of supernaturalism. The "transcendent" in history differs from the historical in the ordinary sense in that it is due to the immediate activity of God, has a universal significance as work of His saving purpose and is always presently influential in God's dealings with men. Historical facts therefore are not as such revelation but only in so far as they have such a transcendent character. The Bible becomes the interpretative witness of the divine activity and performs its living function in the present as it has performed it in the history of the Church in the past.

The biblical problem was particularly alarming in Kaehler's time. He was deeply influenced in his youth by J. T. C. Beck, for whom Systematic theology was still "biblical dogmatics". But though his mind was steeped in the Bible, Kaehler had a very clear conception (gained during prolonged activity as New Testament exegete) of how criticism must deal with the Bible, and what rather radical results inevitably flow from a rigorous application of scientific method. In a series of important lectures he sought to persuade laymen, who were deeply shocked by much-publicized developments in biblical research, that criticism had its place and function, and tried to set up guide-posts for them in their perplexity. He distinguished rather sharply between the empirical, inductive method applied by research (usually culminating in a welter of conflicting opinions and hypotheses) and a theological approach which puts a transcendent Word of God at the centre of everything and proceeds to illuminate Scripture from that angle. He recommended this latter method to those who would really serve the interest of the Church.

In his chief work he reveals a strong predilection for Old Testament ideas. Justification by faith is considered the true ecumenical starting-point for the theology of Protestantism. In the light of this, Christianity must be understood as faith in the Messiah, in so far as He sets up a new covenant in place of the old. For in Jesus the Messiah or "Christ" the final and conclusive "Word" of God's self-revelation was given, and man's deliverance from the state of separation from God as well as the assured founding of a divine kingdom embracing humanity were provided. These biblical ideas, Kaehler asserts, well describe the nature of Christianity in such a way that the first, faith in Christ, gives content to all the others, but so that this content is only properly and completely expressed in the others.

It is obvious that from this basic position Kaehler does not view Christianity as something totally new, but rather sees it in its continuity with the Old Testament order. His is a conservative adherence to the terms "Messiah", "Old" and "New Covenant", in the manner of Von Hofmann and of the "federal" school. From this angle the Messianic expectations and predictions of the previous order are important. The Bible of two Testaments is a witness of the abiding significance of this historical connection between the two orders. The Judaizing and paganizing aberrations that have arisen in the life and teachings of the Church in the course of the centuries show how necessary it is to take the preparation and the fulfilment together to do justice to the whole Messiah.

Kaehler occupied himself with the problem of the Old Testament in a special paper. Since he holds that Jesus Christ came into the world and did His work within the framework of a divinely-willed historical plan, it is not enough to conceive of this in terms of causality and evolution. Christian faith requires the belief that God guided this history to prepare the way for Him through whom He desired fully to reveal Himself. All that is known about that preparation appears in the collection called the Old Testament. The only adequate light on the meaning of Christ was found by the New Testament writers in the Old Testament—not in contemporary Judaism which did not understand or recognize Jesus.[11] Through Jesus and Christianity this Old Testament collection of books became a mighty factor in the history of mankind. The moral insight of man was nurtured by the Decalogue; the Psalms taught men to pray; the figures of Old Testament narrative replaced the old heroes of the national sagas; the prophetic sayings of judgment, reassurance or consolation have, since Jesus, stood like the stars over the beds of the sick and dying. "We are all Semitized, and we would have to dissolve our religious thinking, and our Esthetics, as formed by our greatest artists, as well, if we wanted to pull out these fibres of Semitic thinking."[12] Can we imagine Jesus taking a serious interest in the Agora at Athens or in the Forum at Rome? It was only possible for His message to be appreciated where the ground had been prepared for it by Old Testament history! Through Jesus and Christianity the Old Testament is continuously serving to lay a similar foundation in our present life.

Kaehler stresses the authority of the Old Testament as a *whole*, which according to him implies no compulsion to concede great importance to every book (e.g. Esther) or of claiming equal value or perfect comprehensibility for all its varied contents. The Old Testament element in Christianity—and it continues into the New Testament (cf. the Sermon on the Mount)—is, he declares, the pedagogical element in it, which continuously does its service to those still in need of tutelage (Gal. 3: 24). While the interpretation of the Old Testament in the New Testament is not "historical" in the sense of repro-ducing the exact meaning of the Old Testament writers, it is nevertheless "historical" in the larger sense. Who to-day would wish to write the history of the Napoleonic wars accord-ing to the horizons of the contemporaries?[13] The New Testa-ment writers, too, could not ignore the fact that something very tremendous had occurred since these books had been written, and could not but view the ancient history and writings in a new light. If we were not so curious to know what *really* happened in the centuries before Christ (on the empirical plane Kaehler is a sceptic, who holds we can only know very little of the real facts!) but were concerned about the great creative purposes of God, we would not be so disturbed by the use of the Old Testament made in the New Testament.

Kaehler then declares that the Old Testament collection has the dignity of being part of the Christian canon solely as a *whole* in which the pre-Christian revelation is handed down. Studied in modern historical fashion (*zeitgeschichtlich*) the Old Testament is not canonical, i.e. normative for our own thought and action. Nor is it of any particular importance for us that we should satisfy our historical curiosity by discerning how this or that thought arose and developed in Israel. The Old Testa-ment is important only in its totality, and if we read it as Jesus and His apostles read it—bearing in mind the "but I say unto you" of the Master. No one should be so foolish as to attempt to apply aspects of Old Testament law conditioned by local, national, and historical circumstances to ourselves. Let them read the exemplary discussion of ceremonialism in the Augs-burg Confession (Art. 26) and learn with the Reformers how to deal with such matters! Kaehler even goes so far as to assert that the Old Testament collection only has canonical validity for us when interpreted in Christian fashion. In its original meaning it has no relevance for us! It will be seen that these admissions of a great conservative are not really far removed from the claims of the radicals.

Kaehler, however, has a rather unique tenet with which he counterbalances this liberalism. It is a really new and peculiar principle of biblical interpretation, arising out of his category of the transcendent happening, and he emphasizes it over against the purely historical approach. He believes that a deeper insight into the real significance of many a portion of Scripture may be gained from heeding its *effect* in the history of the Church than by vainly trying to recover irrevocably submerged situations of the past. Thus he finds that two great episodes of Christian history illuminate the Epistle to the Galatians better than antiquarian exegesis ever can do: the role it played in Luther's criticism of Catholicism and the place it held in the gigantic Hegelian effort of F. C. Baur and the Tübingen school to interpret the early Christian scene.

In a valuable study on the history of the Bible in its effect on the Church, Kaehler has a section on the "Old Testament and the Church" in which he applies this principle.[14] The significance attained by the Old Testament in Christian life and history is, he claims, ecclesiastically speaking, far more important than what it meant originally to the Jews and how it came into existence. If one considers the lessons of this history of the Old Testament, the following points stand out. While the covenant of God with Israel was superseded by the new covenant established by Jesus, this does not mean that the earlier arrangement has lost all its meaning. Even where "law" and "gospel" are used as characteristic designations for the old and new orders, it must be recognized that there are elements of law in the New Testament and of gospel in the Old Testament. The Protestant Reformers rejected the Antinomian position out of a realization that one cannot appreciate the gospel without being aware of the demands of the law. Out of this insight into the difference as well as the similarity between the two orders there follows the inference that they belong together. They do not merely stand in a historical relationship of past and present; together they form the unified heritage of the Church of Christ. One cannot understand the biblical gospel without the Old Testament, for the content of that gospel is the Son of God, the Messiah of the Jews and the goal of the law. But one also cannot understand law and promise without the fulfilment effected by Him who was put under the law. As He has been set over the House of God, so He has also been set over Scriptures and rules over them. Henceforth the important thing about the Old Testament is not the temporal, but the eternal, not the letter or flesh but the spirit. Still, since the eternal element was clothed in the temporal shell of the letter or flesh for pedagogical purposes, this shell, too, continues to have a pedagogical value. Under the Christian dispensation the Old Testament is in a continuous process of becoming antiquated, but at the same time continuously serves Christianity by preparing the way for it, as well as by illustrating and showing up the basis of various errors into which Christianity may readily fall.

Kaehler finds abundant traces of the Old Testament heritage in Christian history, many of them none too praiseworthy. He points out how Protestantism from the beginning assailed the "Judaism" of the hierarchical Churches. Already the Christian development after Paul illustrates this trend back toward a mere religion of the law. Everywhere the pagan impulse of man—and that is the natural human one—adapts itself more readily to the external order of the Old Testament than to the gospel. The Roman bishop becomes a high priest after the manner of the Jewish high priests; sacerdotalism, the sacrifice of the mass, vows, good works, etc., all represent a renaissance of Judaism within the Church. The Reformation at first was a rebirth of New Testament Christianity, but a similar relapse into Old Testament mentality shortly took place, when Bible and Confessions were treated like codes of law. The Old Testament element in Calvinism and Puritanism also comes to mind in that connection. Kaehler is inclined to view all this rather philosophically, however, and to regard the Old Testament as continuing to do yeoman service in repeating the ancient function of the whole Old Testament order of being a "tutor unto Christ". He finds that there is a radical difference between the early Christian community, composed as that was of people who had become Christians by personal decision, and an institutional Church into which ever new generations are born without having made such personal decision; this institutional Church is in a role much more like that of the Jewish Church, and the Old Testament heritage performs a valuable preparatory function in training this humanity and preparing it for the gospel of Christian freedom.

Kaehler, of course, does not wish to excuse too obviously Judaizing aberrations, but he maintains that they are not the fault of the Bible of the two Testaments. This unified Bible corrects itself where necessary, and when properly handled— with due attention to all the self-criticism found in it—will do no harm at all, but rather provide the most valuable guidance. But he warns that Protestant Christians are all too prone to make the Bible the vicar of Christ on earth. The Bible is not the only form in which the Word of God comes to us, and it is wrong to put demands on it that it cannot possibly fulfil.

Kaehler's position on the Old Testament is inseparably entwined with a theology that leans rather close to the conservative line in Paul. If one is willing to stress the radical line in Paul and is not quite so philosophical as to the rather preliminary character of the Church or the tolerability of sub-Christian viewpoints and horizons on pedagogical grounds, one will immediately come to a different conclusion.[15]

But the Erlangen school, too, retained a following and received a new leader in Ihmels, who sought to modify the position of Frank on Christian certainty in order to meet the criticism of subjectivism levelled against it.[16] In connection therewith his thought on the Scripture problem is of interest.

Christian certainty, Ihmels says, rests on personal experience, which he defines as present communion with God, rather than as that of regeneration (as Frank had taught). He thus veers rather close to Kaehler for whom everything flows from the experience of justification. In granting His fellowship to men, God strives to elicit faith on the part of man. In this act of faith, certainty concerning the reality of the divine revelation, in and through which God seeks us out, is implicit. Revelation and faith are correlatives.

Christian certainty embraces three things: (1) It is a certainty of the historical revelation of God. (2) It is a certainty of the Word of God, which for Ihmels is the living Word of God embracing both "law" and "gospel" and by no means identical with Scripture. (3) It is a certainty about Scripture. The latter testifies to that revelation of God which comes to us in the living Word of God. The Christian attains a growing certainty about Scripture in a threefold manner; firstly he becomes convinced that the present Word of God has its source in an original revelation. Secondly, all insight that comes to him in the living Word of the Church is clarified and even mediated in a unique way through Scripture, so that this progressive growth in certainty includes also a certainty concerning the testimony of the original witness of revelation. Thirdly, while a formal certainty about Scripture is not obtained in this purely religious way it must be remembered that Scripture as a canon is primarily given to the Church. But since it also is to serve the individual to encounter God, a certainty concerning the testimony of Scripture emerges to the extent that this purpose is realized.

The last point in this general theological background is naturally the one from which Ihmels' evaluation of the canon as a whole and of the Old Testament in particular must stem forth. His previous definition of the Word of God as both law and gospel augurs a relatively favourable attitude toward the Old Testament (on which, however, he does not elaborate). But Ihmels cannot attain certainty concerning the canon as a whole for either Testament. In affirming that the Bible is given to the Church he has some protection for the traditional canon, but he concedes that the Church's attitude is nothing that is fixed with absolute finality and hence grants that criticism of the canon on theological grounds is certainly admissible.

A unique figure among the pre-war theologians was Schlatter.[17] He deserves some attention here, in spite of the fact that he neither founded nor continued a school of theology. Of Swiss birth, he exhibited leanings toward the Reformed type of Christianity more than the Lutheran, and also betrayed the strong influence of the Pietism and Biblicism of Beck. He was strongly anti-Kantian and willing to trust reason much more than those deeply impressed by that philosopher's teachings. He virtually re-establishes a sort of Natural theology and deduces much insight concerning God from nature, notably in his theological anthropology, which for him is the basic starting-point. This would seem to put Christ and therewith the revelation in History in a supplementary position. He defends himself against attacks on that score by saying that this arrangement of material is due to the intellectual objective of Dogmatics: to set forth the knowledge of God. In other writings, when not governed by that special interest, he proceeds from the vantage point of New Testament Christianity, stressing the Christian community or congregation.

For Schlatter, the authority of the New Testament is greater than that of the Church because Christ is irreplaceable and Scripture alone brings us into relation with Him. This does not mean that no thought or act is justified which is not found in the New Testament; Christ rules to-day and His grace is alive in our midst. Nevertheless the radius within which the Church may move is governed from one point—the Word of Jesus and the apostles. The authority of Scripture is thus a derived one. The authority really resides in Christ and His apostles. "Authority" is a word that in human relations often spells tyranny; but the authority of Scripture is based on the divine grace—it should not oppress us but rather strengthen us. Wherever Scripture is used as a substitute for our own knowledge of God or where an unreasonable obedience to it is demanded, there we have a relapse into the carnal idea of authority. The orthodox Protestant Scripture-doctrine treated Scripture as though it were timeless. In that way Scripture becomes a burden instead of a help. It no longer influences knowledge or the will. Since the higher criticism was a serious menace to that kind of Scripture authority, orthodoxy developed an opposition to Criticism. But Scripture must be subjected to criticism—not only historical but "dogmatic". For every biblical writer or personage (including Jesus) is a part of the web and woof of his time and we who are part of our time cannot just take over as normative any biblical statement. We are constantly called upon to differentiate between what we can accept and what we must reject in the light of all the other truth that God gives us to-day. Even the richest words of Scripture are historically conditioned.

But Schlatter takes no offence at this close fusion of the eternal and the transitory. To him the human element is ever undergirded by the divine grace, and with all his obscurities the biblical writer remains the servant of God. The false judgments concerning Scripture that have been rampant so long are due to the intellectualistic approach to which the western world is so prone. We are apt to be disturbed by the "poetic element" of Scripture (as Schlatter, rather euphemistically, describes what other scholars call myth and legend) or by the fact that it leaves so many questions unanswered. The infallibility of God does not transmit itself to man or to what men write. There is no use in constructing a revelation apart from men or one that makes the human element disappear. Scripture puts us in relation to God, not primarily in the sphere of thinking but in that of the *will*.

Schlatter holds to an inspiration of the apostolic (and prophetic) personalities. As every personal relation with God is mediated by the Spirit, so the apostolic and prophetic work has the same presupposition. Only in this way does a Word of God to man result. But inspiration is misunderstood if thought to bring about intellectual correctness or to produce timeless truth. It affects the entire life and makes a man able to speak the Word of God. It is not a case of passive receptivity. The individual consciousness is not destroyed but is utilized.

Schlatter stresses Messianism, therein continuing the line of J. T. C. Beck. The Christ, he asserts, was preceded by the long series of Hebrew prophets. He points out that there is objection to that statement from several standpoints. Those who see nothing new in Jesus but regard Him merely as another Jewish prophet or teacher object to giving Him an independent position and putting Him in juxtaposition to the prophets. On the other hand, those who are embarrassed by Jesus' connection with Judaism, and who prefer not to see Christianity burdened with the difficulties arising from the Old Testament and with the objectionable elements of the Jewish character, also dislike the statement. Both objections sacrifice the Messianic idea. As the Christ, Jesus is set apart from all His predecessors as well as from His successors by the uniqueness of His office. At the same time Messianism is inseparable from Israel. Christ was not only prophesied—His work was made possible by what went before.

Schlatter then rejects as false several ways of describing the religious change wrought by Jesus; He did not, as is sometimes asserted, reject the national community and replace that by "religious individualism"; He did not set up a religion of the gospel as opposed to the religion of the law; He did not concentrate on the purely spiritual. The difficulties of the Old

Testament cannot obscure the fact of the indissoluble fellowship of Jesus with Israel. Our historical and ethical insight does indeed transcend that of the Old Testament; but this is a result of the coming of the Christ. With Him, religion ascends to a new level. Jesus' own attitude, he holds, gives us the directives for the right use of the Old Testament—to be bound and at the same time free, the eye fixed upon God.

Schlatter believes in the unity of Scripture, which, he says, does not mean uniformity. This unity results from the fact that the history which created Scripture and to which it testifies has its unity in Christ. He accepts Luther's formula of "whatever treats of Christ" as an excellent yardstick, when taken properly, in the sense of considering how a given section hangs together with central Christian positions. He recognizes that there are parts of lesser and of greater importance in the Old Testament. But on the basis of Paul's argument concerning the different parts of the body and their functions (Rom. 12), he finds a value even in the lesser members of the scriptural organism. The nineteenth psalm may not be as important as the eighth chapter of the Epistle to the Romans, or Ecclesiastes as important as the First Epistle of John, and yet they have their value within the scriptural body. For from every point of Scripture we are led forth into the whole. In individual life this may be a slow process, but the life of the Church vindicates the fact.

Schlatter thus succeeds in maintaining the importance of the Old Testament canon, but his assumption that Scripture is an "organism" is a survival of Beck's idealizing view. He actually devaluates the older order by viewing it as preparatory to the new. He avoids speaking of revelation, since his conception of the latter is very broad. If Schlatter had not been so conservative in his literary criticism of the New Testament, or so deeply imbued with pietism, his thinking might have carried farther in the radical direction.

In sharp contrast to the approach of Schlatter stands that of Schaeder.[18] Indeed, he criticizes all theology since Schleiermacher for being anthropocentric, and seeks to set up a theocentric viewpoint, therein being a forerunner of Barth. An impact on him from the Old Testament side is particularly noticeable in the use he makes of the 139th Psalm at the begin-

ning of one of his books. We shall here, however, confine ourselves to analysing a study of his which chronologically belongs
to the post-war period and shows him reacting to the situation
created by Barth, but which on the whole remains within the
orbit of his own earlier thought.[19] He has a particular interest
in the doctrine of the Holy Spirit, but he links the Spirit entirely
with "the Word of God". The Spirit begets faith in the Word
and thereby creates the Church of the Word, and in so far as He
prevails in the Church He makes it the place in which the divine
sovereignty dwells. That is the starting-point of his cogitations.

The Word of God is not, however, identical with Scripture for
Schaeder. The Word is the oral message that deals with God
as the Lord of the world and of man. Everything communicated
in that Word concerning God, Christ and the Holy Spirit
stands under this unifying principle of the divine sovereignty.
Schaeder's idea of God is primarily that of a majestic, voluntaristic deity who carries out his purpose irresistibly. Even
justification of the sinner through faith is seen as an act of the
majestic grace, rather than of the love of the deity. There is thus
a Calvinistic sternness, ultimately resting on Old Testament
influence, in his approach.

The Scriptures for Schaeder are no external principle of
authority. Faith bound to the Word of God (in the above
described sense of the message of the sovereignty of God) sets
up its own articles of belief, and contemplates Scripture in full
freedom, judging it in accordance with its relation to the Word
of God as defined above. But in the last analysis, he concedes,
his freedom from Scripture is at the same time also a tie with
Scripture, for ultimately the Word of God is mediated to us
through Scripture. The judging of Scripture is a continuous
process, in which the individual, the congregation and the
Church as a whole—not merely of the present but of all generations—take an active part, simultaneously bound and free in
the sense indicated.

For the Christian, Schaeder holds, the normative portion of
Scripture is the New Testament. Faith is for us faith in the God
who is in Christ. We only have an interest in the Old Testament
in so far as the New Testament compels us to have it. Scripture
throughout is a series of documents testifying to God's relations
with the world, as manifested in certain actions. Directly or

indirectly it is the book of divine works, or divinely wrought circumstances which have a more or less immediate significance for the congregation that hears about them. The divine actions necessarily occur in space and time. The knowledge of them is mediated by, or associated with, historical circumstances and personages. So close is the fusion between the eternal and the temporal that it is impossible to disengage the former from the latter. The actions of God, such as those described with relation to Greeks and Jews in Rom. 1-2, 9-11, do not hover, like ideas, above the earth, but are deeply woven into a concrete historical process. Nevertheless, for faith, the eternal side of that which took place in this history is the thing that is paramount. The Spirit of God, though He leads us into His living creation with all its details and in all its concreteness, nevertheless makes us free from all this in view of God and His Christ. In this sense Schaeder favours a "spiritual" type of exegesis—but not in what he believes to be the impossible sense of separating the temporal from the eternal (cf. p. 174).

While the New Testament is gospel, since it preaches the Christ who Himself is the Word incarnate, in whom and through whom the goal of history—God's sovereignty—becomes a reality, the Old Testament does not attain to this rank. It is the first duty of any consideration of the canon to make this difference between the two Testaments clear. But the Old Testament writings, too, are testimonies of faith; they affirm God to be the Creator, the Lawgiver and Judge, and the one who is going to bring to a realization the goal that He has set for history of man—that state of affairs in which His reign will become complete. All these elements of the Old Testament message are not gospel, but they form the inseparable presupposition of it. If God were not Creator and Lord of the world, He could not mould history in sovereign grace. If He were not the Lawgiver, He could not free us from the effect of the curse of the law and from its external, formal authority, as he actually does in His justifying grace. If He were not Judge, the abolition of His judgment over us in the atoning death of Christ would be incomprehensible and impossible. If, finally, the God of the Old Testament witness points both in preparatory actions and words to the goal of history—the establishment of His sovereignty over the world—then that sovereignty is on the way. It has not arrived yet, since Christ is not here, but it is coming. Thus, the New Testament gospel draws the afore-mentioned elements of the Old Testament to itself. Even though these elements reappear in the New Testament in a purified form, the Old Testament cannot be dispensed with. For the elements described do not stand alone in the Old Testament but form the basis for the preparatory process leading to the gospel. It is one and the same God who is operative both in the prepara-tion and in the gospel itself.

In short, the Christian theologian who chooses the Word of the New Testament as his standpoint is driven by that very standpoint to take the Old Testament in its main, dominant lines (creation, law, judgment, and promise) into consideration in determining the contents of the Word of God. Attempts to set aside one or more of these elements as below the evangelical level must have their repercussions on the attitude toward the New Testament which likewise contains them.

Realizing the connection between the Old Testament heritage and Christianity, one must concede to the former an inalienable significance for faith in the Word of God. But this significance is not to be set forth on the basis of any external, biblicistic, authoritarian approach. It is reached only by a faith that seizes intuitively upon the main lines of the organic connection exist-ing between the order of the gospel and the order that prepares the way for it in the form of the promise, and of setting up the abiding basis of both orders, viz., knowledge of the reality of God and of His relation to the world that is implicit in the order of creation.

But is that in the Old Testament which we may call the Word of God so pure in content and so unobjectionable that Christian faith is not contaminated by taking this Old Testament element to its bosom? This question subdivides into two separate ones: (1) Does this Old Testament Word of God in any way mis-represent the divine reality or the will of God as focused on us? (2) Does it represent a lower stage in the self-revelation of God which is superseded in certain respects by the revelation in Christ?

In examining the first of these questions Schaeder dwells on the idea of God as the Creator. From the Christian standpoint we can only be satisfied with a purely theistic view. If it should actually be the case that the writer of the Creation story holds matter to be co-eternal with God (exegetically it is by no means absolutely sure that the "created" of Gen. 1: 1 is a *creatio ex nihilo*) we would have to reject that aspect of its presentation as sub-Christian. When the Old Testament from its first to its last page proclaims the God of the law, who asserts Himself over against both the sinful group and individual, does He always at the same time appear as the God of Love who accepts the repentant sinner? Is the wrath of God in the Old Testament always the expression of an eternally pure will, bent on warding off the evil, or conceived of as analogous to human passion, jealousy and other impure human attitudes? Does the Old Testament idea of righteousness always exclude the thought of merits? Does it reveal an insight into the corruption of the human will? Does it leave room for the sole validity of repentance and faith in the sight of God? And when we turn to the large area of the Old Testament future expectations must one not above all ask whether the destiny of Israel as chosen people is always seen as due to the free grace of God, irrespective of any national virtues of this people?

Schaeder concedes that lapses into lower moral levels occur in the Old Testament all along the line. Faith thus has every reason to use the critical plumb-line in dealing with that book. He realizes that an improperly used Old Testament can have a confusing and baneful effect on Christendom. Faith must eliminate these elements in constant effort. To determine what elements in the Old Testament are authoritative for us is a never-ending task both of the individual believer and the Church.

The second question to be considered is whether the Old Testament does not represent a lower stage of the self-revelation of God than the Christian revelation and how it is to be related to the latter. One must, for instance, recall that Old Testament law makes certain concessions, which are transcended in the New Testament—so in the marriage question, or that as to who is one's neighbour. Furthermore, there is the whole cultic-ritualistic legislation which we regard as having lost its importance with the coming of Christ. So far as Old Testament prophecy is concerned the question arises to what extent it really prepares the way for the Christ of the New

Testament. In particular there is the matter of Messianic Prophecy, or the question of what elements of the Old Testament witness actually have been fulfilled in Christ. This can be stressed in such a way that the preparation sheds light on the fulfilment, or, *vice versa*, that the preparation receives light from the fulfilment. The Christianizing and sublimating of Old Testament passages after the manner of the New Testament writers, however, should be abandoned. Finally, there is the subjective piety, notably in the Psalter, the expressions of which belong to the Word that is valid, wherever they grow out of a "pneumatic" and godly understanding of the Israelitic prerogatives, and dwell on the line of penitential faith in God's elective love.

Thus the relation of faith to the Old Testament canon is one of being bound to the Word of God in that work, but mediated and conditioned by adherence to the New Testament and, therefore, one of selectivity. No one can make a final statement as to how we are bound by the Old Testament "Word". But the living process of faith in the individual and in the Church of Christ will always combine, in ever new decisions, the link with the God of the Old Testament who is the God and Father of Jesus Christ and the rejection of that which is erroneous or exaggerated in the preparatory order.

The culmination of the pre-war Liberal theological development is to be found in Ernst Troeltsch.[20] More than any other Christian thinker he has yielded to the impact of modern scientific method and insight. It will be of interest to see what standpoint he takes on the matter of Scripture doctrine in general and the Old Testament in particular.

Of fundamental concern, of course, is the question of revelation. There are three points at which the Christian claim to revelation, as hitherto formulated, clashes with reason, and Troeltsch thinks that reason here has the better of the argument. In the first place, reason asserts that the whole of reality is subject to its arbitrament; it cannot grant that there is any special area which is unattainable to reason and which can only be apprehended with the help of revelation. In the second place, modern reason with its relativistic view of nature asserts that there are no isolated facts, no islands of unreality in the historical process; it is impossible to see the special presence or activity of God in certain facts of history.   In the third place, recent philosophical thought convincingly asserts that there is no unity and no teleology in the historical process and therewith undermines the assumption that a historical entity (Jesus Christ) can be a valid revelation for all mankind.

In seeking for new positions that will not be exposed to a direct clash with modern insight Troeltsch does not cling to compromises like the Ritschlians but goes to the end of the road marked out by the modern world-view, courageously sacrificing various Christian beliefs that most people would regard as essential. He uses the term revelation to describe the apprehending of the unified nature of things (i.e. God) through religious feeling.   That which is thus apprehended is beyond rational understanding and can only be believed, and the term "revelation" expresses this aspect.   It is rational only in so far as it has the striving toward totality and final values and thus can serve reason in the solution of its ultimate difficulties. It can be experienced by all those who are capable of harbouring religious feeling.

A link not only with Fries and his emphasis on intuition but with Schleiermacher, who stressed feeling so prominently, seems to appear in this line of thought, but Troeltsch broadens the base by not limiting the feeling to dependence, or the object toward which it is directed to a personal God.   He also has more use for the historical than Schleiermacher.   The productive power of the average religious person, he argues, is very slight and requires stimulation from without.   The strongest stimulus is afforded by a religious tradition which unites in itself the religious impression left by certain favoured individuals and the aggregate of the religious forces of whole generations.   The prophetic individuals, who are the starting-point and centre of the great world religions and about whom the whole heritage of their religious sphere centres, naturally furnish the very strongest stimulus.   The belief in a revelation in the narrower sense is most strongly developed and most clearly exhibited in this area.

From this angle it can be seen that Troeltsch will take a friendly attitude toward the Old Testament, since it increases the range of our knowledge of religious experience.   At the same time it is clear that he cannot stop there, but must see a value in religious experience outside of Judaism and Christianity. For contact with rival religions and their equally exclusive faith in their own revelations creates the necessity of comparison. This, he says, soon leads on the one hand to the assertion that revelation was laid down in a particular institution or book and, on the other hand, to a denial of or attack upon the validity of alien revelations. Better knowledge and understanding eventually produce the realization that all religions partake of the character of revelation. Comparative evaluation of their religious and moral ideas results in the conviction that Christianity is superior to all the others, but not to a certainty that it is the absolute religion.

Troeltsch's approach to the Old Testament is highly modern.[21] He points out that in the popular mind undue stress is laid on the untenable narratives of Genesis and on the Messianic predictions, as though these things were the most important elements of the Old Testament. That, he declares, is entirely unhistorical. He takes up the problem from a more organic, sociologically oriented angle. The history of Israel, he declares, has a deep significance for our whole historical sphere —both for Islam and Christianity. He formulates his views as follows:

(1) The recognition of Christianity as the supreme revelation includes also the recognition of the religion of Israel as preparation for and presupposition of this revelation. Without it Christianity is incomprehensible; it must constantly be taken together with its rich Old Testament background. (2) The function of the religion of Israel, historically considered, was to break through the area of nature-religion in every sense of the word and to establish ethical monotheism. In that respect it is absolutely unique. The religion of Israel through the mediation of the prophets marks the release of the Deity from the bondage of nature and the placing of Him above all the world as creative will.

Troeltsch then develops this along three lines: (a) This signifies that the Deity is conceived of in anti-rationalistic and anti-naturalistic manner as "living will"—incomprehensible and not to be measured by man—and thus involves the idea of Creation; (b) This will, furthermore, is directed toward obtaining the recognition and worship of the divine holiness in active moral obedience, in contrast to all cult and ceremonial religion, and over against all worldly, eudaemonistic conceptions of human destiny, or all pantheistic or unworldly and passive mysticism; (c) Since the idea of God is governed by that of a morally conceived purpose set for man, there results a trend in the direction of its illustration by history and its vicissitudes in the personal life of the prophets and in the great national destinies, while the illustration by nature and abstract regularities recedes entirely.

(3) In these three respects prophetic monotheism is an original religious creation, entirely in contrast to the rest of the world, and hence there lie in it the germs of the finally humanized ethical religion of a personal Christianity. The limitations of the religion of Israel lie in its nationalism, never entirely overcome, in the legalistic shell in which the ethical religion of mankind here is encased, and finally in the narrowness of its religious view of history, with its small horizon, its nationalistic and apocalyptic goals, its crude belief in the miraculous and its trend toward eudaemonism in the ethical sphere. But the great thing about this religion is the one-sidedly voluntaristic idea of God. It feels no need of including the unity and connectedness of the life of the world in its idea of God, and therein differs strongly from all Indo-European religions.

(4) This abiding significance of prophetism, which must be recognized despite all limitations, finds expression in the fact that its precipitate (the so-called Old Testament) has become a Christian document and that Christianity designates the prophetic religion as the "Old Covenant", "Old Testament" or "old dispensation" of God which prepared the way for the "New Covenant" or "new dispensation" of grace. This estimate remains permanently valid. It involves at the same time an elimination of the nationalistic elements of the Old Testament and emphasis on the prophetic elements. The latter in their simplicity and strength have the abiding function of holding Christianity firmly down to its basic, ethical moorings, and to keep it from falling into sentimentality, subjective mysticism or intellectual dogmatism.

Troeltsch's essay on the Old Testament prophets shows him deeply influenced by Max Weber's sociological thinking, though carrying it further in theological reflection, but otherwise does not add much to the fundamental aspects of his position. Its importance lies primarily in the field of the historical understanding of the spirit and motives of prophecy and the influences it exerted on Hebrew life. Those who would make the prophets of Israel exponents of democracy or social justice will get little comfort from it. He argues that the message of the prophets has absolutely nothing to do with law deduced from reason, and is no proclamation of social morality.[22] With humanity or liberty or even democracy and socialism in the modern sense, this ethic does not have a single thread in common. The ultimate fact about prophetic religion is that it is the religion of a passionate, transcendent, voluntaristic God and of the human personality that is formed in the fellowship with Him. Because of this the prophetic ethic is full of activism and of an exertion of the will analogous to that of the Creator. But in spite of this activism and voluntarism, it is indifferent toward the world and civilization in the occidental sense,[23] as well as toward all moral values that lie outside the sphere of the personal orientation of the individual toward God and the mutual, divinely oriented fellowship of the group. This trend attains an even sharper and purer expression in Jesus (cf. Matt. 16: 26). The effects of His attitude flow through the whole of Christian history. It is the struggle between the radicalism of faith and the inclination also present in religion to fuse and compromise with cultural trends.

In a manuscript note, posthumously published,[24] Troeltsch set down the thought that the manner in which the prophetic idea of the Old Testament was disengaged from its sociological ties (including nationalism) and became a religious-ethical principle in Christianity is particularly noteworthy. The difficulties which this principle encountered and still encounters, when applied to other and more developed social situations of life, are due to its origin and constantly compel an increasing spiritualization. All these obstacles, however, have not hindered it from becoming the most powerful religious principle in the world, as the religion of theistic reverence, ethical purity, humane love of man, repentance and pious interpretation of nature and destiny. Contact with all concrete relations of social life has been wiped out or become peripheral. The very difficulty of applying it has elevated it to a radical requirement, which confronts the secular life with an alternative and which the world, under the curse of sin (which in Christian re-interpretation no longer signifies Israel's apostasy and worldliness but rather general human selfishness and inertia) does not seem to be able to meet. The necessity of choosing between God and the world has become basic for this whole ethic and its necessary consequence is the doctrine of an involvement of all men in the sins of self-love and love of the world. But at the same time this faith appears as a summons to repentance, as an appeal to the free will to choose between two ways. "Repent" was already the call of the prophets; choice and decision remain the high point of all Jewish ethics; repentance and change of heart are the theme of the initial message of Jesus. It is the religion of those that choose, the religion of decision, of the radical "either—or".

Within these two poles—the ethical-personal idea of God and the fateful, world-encompassing idea of sin—the faith of the prophets, after its general human content had taken on a new form in the preaching of Jesus and of Mohammed (but in a fully humanized form only in that of Jesus), became a spiritual power of the first magnitude in the occident and in the Islamic world, even where men are unaware of it. True, Christianity has within itself a large number of other forces beside "Hebraism" and enjoys its eternal influence just because of its combination of these diverse elements into a new spiritual world, superimposed upon Hebraism but not identical with it. While it must be conceded that European religion, activism and wealth of contrasts did not spring directly from the Hebrew religion, they nevertheless show themselves led, dominated, nurtured and regulated by it.

Since Christianity is no mere refurbishing or further development of Hebraism, it follows that the latter, in spite of its fusion with Christianity, also has played and continues to play a separate role. The Old Testament never merely remained an earlier stage and means of interpreting the New Testament. The hard, strict virility, the reverence and ethical simplicity of its religion of humanity, the poetical nature-piety, the kinship with stoicism (a movement that also has extended its influence through the centuries), finally the fusions with neo-platonic mysticism and pantheistic interpretation of radical monotheism

—all this has given the Old Testament an independent influence as well. It is especially discernible at the very beginning of the modern intellectual life.[25] Troeltsch sees a trend in the world of religious ideas of his day toward eliminating the gnostic, supernatural, mystical-sacramental elements from Christianity and reverting to a Hebraism with Christian modifications. The attempts of theologians to go back to a simple gospel of Jesus,[26] usually resulting in a more or less rationalized Hebraism, are significant of this. He concedes that a simplification of Christianity is not possible in this "historical" form. The need is not for a reversion to an earlier form of Christianity with some modernization, but for a great synthesis in which its basic theistic-personalistic trend is fully expressed, without petty anthropomorphism and anthropocentrism.

Troeltsch obviously has seen the character and significance of Old Testament religion against a larger background than any one since the days of German Idealism. His thoughts on the matter, however, can only appeal to those who have emancipated themselves from biblicism. His emphasis on religious individualism, furthermore, is strongly tied up with the intellectual climate prevailing before the First World War, and fails to satisfy us entirely to-day. He fittingly marks the end of an era.

Chapter Nine

THE APOLOGETIC OF BIBLICAL SCHOLARS

WITH the passing years the differences between conservatives and liberals in the Old Testament field became more and more meaningless. There was scant comfort in the fact that a staunch exponent of supernaturalism like E. Koenig[1] dated the Pentateuchal sources differently (E before J) and earlier than the liberals, and defended the substantial historical reliability of the Old Testament narratives. He had accepted the documentary hypothesis in principle and the consequences of that were inescapable, no matter how obstinately he might refuse to draw them. The dividing line between conservatives and liberals was partly this: that the former were disposed to haggle about how much had to be conceded to criticism, while the latter went blithely from one destructive result to another; partly it was also in an underlying religious attitude. The liberals were content to view the Old Testament in a more or less humanistic light, with some mild emphasis on its literary excellences, moral and religious values, but full and frank admission of all its backwardness and defects. The conservatives, while compelled to agree with most of this, took refuge in the doctrinal position which the theology of a von Hofmann and others had created for them, viz. that the revelation of God was one that had taken place in history, that the Old Testament literature gives us knowledge of that history and of that revelation, and that this literature itself, in its full reality, belongs to the revelatory process.[2] In the course of the latter, backward or primitive elements were gradually overcome. Their survival in the record is instructive. From the citadel of this position they could participate freely in Old Testament criticism, believing that truer historical insight achieved by the best available scientific means was bound to be helpful in giving us a better understanding of the history of the revelation in question.

It may be useful to consider a few instances of what might be called the professional apologetic for the Old Testament on the part of leading scholars, from the period succeeding the triumph of criticism to 1914. We will first glance at a lecture Marti gave to clergymen in Switzerland in 1893.[3]

The lecture had received considerable publicity. Marti finds that in some quarters there was excitement over it; the more benevolent critics were concerned about the salvation of the author's soul and the others lamented about this horrible example of infidel scholarship. At the occasion of its delivery, he finds, there was either baffled silence or outright unwillingness to accept such views. But he holds that the new insights are far too well established to be set aside on emotional grounds or with an appeal to the faith of the Church. He hopes for a better response from a larger public; may it remind timid souls how often the doom of Christian faith has been foreseen by theologians, if this or that position were true. He emphasizes the Reformed position that the Bible itself holds first place, and that its realistic study, therefore, and the truth concerning it are not to be judged by faith. Even if scholarship proves some traditional ideas to be untenable, that does not matter; faith in the grace of God awakened through Jesus Christ is immune to any danger. The Church can rather rejoice at the growth of insight; the ever-increasing knowledge of revelation must serve to put Christ as basis of our faith in a clearer light than ever before. He rejects the idea that such discussions as the present one should be kept secret on account of the weaker brethren; silence has done more harm than the truth could have done, which could before this have helped people to a right understanding of Scripture.

Marti rejoices that Old Testament study has ceased being an innocuous pursuit. Time was when men were encouraged to undertake it in order to render them harmless; thus in 1818 Monod's thesis on the *Divinity of Christ* and another on *Prayer* were rejected by the Geneva faculty, but one on the *Authenticity of the Pentateuch* proved quite acceptable. To-day, Old Testament study touches vital matters.

After describing the view of Old Testament religion now developed by biblical scholarship, Marti sets forth how it affects the study of the History of Religions. The latter subject has all along been hampered by the claims, based on the Old Testament, of a monotheism at the beginning of things, from which a degeneration supposedly took place. This has now been done away with and the evolution of the Hebrew religion itself out of primitive beginnings discerned. Therewith the comparison of the biblical religion with other religions takes on a fresh significance. It will result in establishing the superiority of that religion. Finally, the intensive study of the development of the Old Testament religion that has been carried on recently will sharpen the eyes of men in studying the phenomena of other religions also and thus greatly fructify the subject of History of Religions as such.

For one who has occupied himself with this Old Testament religion in the modern manner it is clear that in describing a religious development one should not merely consider what ideas of God a people had or what teachings it held to be true, but rather discern above all what influence a religion had on morality, whether the two became joined and to what degree such union was demanded. For the right conception of God only becomes valuable as it represents an ethical force. Hence he would not join a Jewish apologist's claim that the monotheism achieved by the Jews was their supreme glory. The Old Testament development exhibits monotheists whose belief had little effect on their morals; Ecclesiastes is a case in point, and so are the ritualists who emphasize the Kosher or certain ceremonies. The Old Testament teaches us not to be impressed by zeal for cult or a refined scholasticism, since they do not prove that a religion is in flower, but are rather symptoms of its decadence. The value of a religious life is demonstrated only in moral conduct.

If the History of Religions has obtained an increased significance through modern Old Testament criticism, Dogmatic theology can be said to have declined in importance as a result of it. In addition to the complete revision of the doctrine of Scripture that such criticism has necessitated, it has brought about a decrease in emphasis on exact formulation of Christian teaching. Like cultic or liturgical forms, the intellectual formulæ mean little in comparison to the proof of faith in living deeds and trust in God as exemplified by Israel's prophets. Next, Old Testament study had shown the futility of Natural

theology and of efforts to prove the existence of God, such as
were so long a feature of the *Prolegomena* of Dogmatics. The
prophets would have regarded that sort of thing as unbelief.
They were overpowered by God and then saw His activity in
history and finally also in nature. This points the way for
Dogmatic theology, too. Furthermore, Old Testament study
has relieved Dogmatic theology of all the fruitless discussions
about a history of redemption, based on the idea of repairing
the damage done by Adam's fall, or all speculations about the
origin of sin, or debates on supra- and infra-lapsarianism.
Then, too, God is no longer to be considered as governed by the
laws of the Priestly Code in His dealing with man. The doctrine
of the atonement, in particular, is thereby relieved of all
juridical elements.

For real knowledge of God's ways one must turn to the
prophets, who teach one to understand Jesus and His message
of the love of God. All dogmatic concepts need to be examined
in the light of whether they have been unduly affected by
extraneous ideas, foreign to or not on a level with prophetic
thought. Even in using New Testament concepts like Kingdom
of God, Marti thinks, we should not just accept New Testament
usage, which in this case has been influenced by contemporary
Jewish eschatology, but rather go back to the genuine ideas of
the great prophets, who expected a kingdom that would come
through moral and spiritual regeneration, such as Jesus then
brought about in those who believed in Him. Finally, Marti
claims that the prophets give us the best means to understand
Jesus. Standing in the counsel of Yahweh and trusting in Him
they were free from all traditionalism and fear of men, discerning the falsity of the things on which men relied, and pointing
them to Him who alone can save. If we view Jesus in similar
manner we will, he thinks, have a higher and better appreciation of Him than by having recourse to lower stages of the
earlier religion in which "sons of God" played a role (Gen.6:1f.).

In this manner, Marti thinks, Old Testament criticism
vindicates its value for theology. By showing the line that
leads from the great prophets to Christ it replaces the purely
external juxtaposition of the two Testaments that has hitherto
prevailed with the far better one of an organic connection
existing between them.

9

Equally interesting are the thoughts of a more conservatively minded scholar like Dalman.[4] He is fully aware of the inescapable necessity of historical research and of the consequences it must have when applied to the Old Testament sources. Christianity, he reasons, comes to us in the form of a teaching that belongs to the living tradition of the Church; this teaching bases its certainty on a collection of writings received from the past. The Old Testament portion of this collection is the sacred collection of the Jewish Church of the time just preceding the rise of Pharisaic-Sadducaic rivalry. It gives information (1) concerning the origin and nature of this Church and its divine services—from Genesis to Esther; (2) concerning words of God that were given to it—the Prophets and Daniel; (3) concerning the religious feeling prevailing in its midst— Psalms and Lamentations; and the thinking done in it— Proverbs, Job, Ecclesiastes; (4) concerning the way in which it ordered the natural relations of life—Song of Songs, Ruth.

This scholar would thus seem to stress the intellectual aspect of Christianity and see the importance of the Old Testament in the historical information it gives us about the background out of which Christianity came. Dalman is of the opinion that the Christian Church should not have taken over Old Testament books like Esther, Ecclesiastes and Song of Songs that were of doubtful canonical authority at the time of Christ. He is not particularly disturbed by the fact that criticism has shown that we cannot depend absolutely on biblical history as reported. "It has not pleased God to inform us about that ancient era in the form of completely indubitable historical documents. Hence the external particulars cannot be the important thing for us here." He admits that materials that *per se* are non-religious are to be found in the Old Testament and holds that the prophetic light shed on them by editors and revisers is ofttimes the only religiously significant thing about them. That is the case with the Book of Judges: only the framework, into which the older elements have been put, gives the book the character of revelation, and only because of this framework did it become part of the canon. In some other instances, too, the canonical claim of a book and of its contents hangs close together with the position and significance that redaction gave to the individual entity. Historical and canonical evaluation have divergent laws and go different ways.

Dalman is not troubled by such a matter as the historicity of the patriarchs. He believes that our sources are not of sufficient antiquity to prove anything one way or the other. The real question is merely whether the early Hebrew story is dependable when it asserts: (1) that Israel's special place came about through divine election; (2) that human conduct counted only in so far as Israel endorsed this election in faith. Dalman thinks it is. He finds the Holy Spirit active in a three-fold manner in the bringing forth of Old Testament Scripture collection; first, as decisive force in individual personalities whose word becomes the vehicle of divine revelation; second, as decisive force within the congregation whose spiritual life became capable of expressing in a literary manner the revelation given by word and to judge it in literary productions; third, as decisive force causing the origin of a whole collection that is suited to serve in the further course of the history of the congregation as record of its founding. In this sense, Dalman thinks, we can still hold fast to inspiration to-day. The Old Testament for him is a document of a divine revelation that is still *en route* to its goal. As such it is an important object of theological study, though not without the New Testament. To discern the individual thing in the Old Testament in relation to the whole and the whole in its relation to Christ, and in this way to apprehend the consensus of Holy Scripture progressively and in accordance with the current needs of the Church—that he described as the true task of Old Testamant theology.

It is apparent that Dalman has here combined a conservative loyalty to the Old Testament heritage with all the concessions that criticism demands. Realistically minded, he does not believe in saying what God should have done, but accepts that which actually has taken place in the historical process as divinely willed. But that a modified supernaturalism stands in the background is nevertheless clearly discernible.

Of similar spirit is Kittel's inaugural lecture of 1899.[5] It begins by describing the crystallization of the modern theological situation. The question is whether by drawing the Bible down into the historical process the very basis of faith and the future of the Church are not being menaced. The theological attitude must proceed from the fundamental principle of the Reformation and of the Protestantism that has been built on it. The cardinal principle of Protestantism, he asserts, is the freedom of the Christian man, who is responsible to God and his conscience but is no slave of an institution or tradition. On this principle is based the right of free research in pursuit of the truth. Wherever historical problems arise they must be dealt with in a scientific manner. But at the same time all freedom has its limitation at some point. That point for the Christian is the gospel of Jesus Christ: our standpoint can only be within its radius. He concedes that one who approaches the Old Testament materials with non-Christian presuppositions will deal with the larger aspects of any problem they present in a different way. But then it is merely a case of one dogma standing against another. Divergences in result already appear where one proceeds on an inner-Christian basis, depending on the standpoint taken. But this is inevitable. Convinced of our faith in Christ, it will be possible for us to discern the traces of God's gracious will and activity in history and therewith to see and recognize in the development mirrored in the Old Testament the revelation of our God. Kittel thus concedes as much as possible to criticism, while at the same time holding to a belief in a modified supernaturalism.

Soon after the turn of the century Kautzsch dealt with our subject.[6] His essay was aimed against various kinds of agitation intended to do away entirely with the Old Testament. He demands that the defenders of the Old Testament must first of all refrain from resorting to untenable kinds of argument. Such, for instance, is any doctrine of inspiration which claims infallibility and equal authority for every letter of Scripture. In practice, most people are sensible enough to differentiate between what is of greater or of lesser importance, but dogma has not yet arrived at that point. Over against the unfortunate Christian habit of treating all Scripture as of equal rank, we must remind ourselves that even the Jews who gave us the Old Testament canon did not do this. Such differentiation as is practised by the Synagogue in ascribing different degrees of authority to the three divisions of their collection, shows that it is by no means out of place for Christians to differentiate between more and less authoritative portions of the Old Testament. Another foolish thing is to defend the Old Testament ethic at every point. He points out how Jesus discriminated between things in the Old Testament of which He approved and others which He found morally or religiously insufficient. It is doing the Old Testament a disservice to defend things in it that belong to a lower level of moral insight. A similarly foolish thing is to defend the religious level of the Old Testament at every point. On the basis of the old doctrine of inspiration it was claimed that no imperfect or erroneous ideas could be attributed to the Holy Spirit. The zeal to prove the correctness of the Bible in such matters as the harmony between science and the first chapter of Genesis is something utterly useless. False in the third place is the spiritualization of Old Testament ideas in the interest of their better utilization for religious purposes. Old Testament Messianic prophecy provides much temptation along this line. Not only is it used to demonstrate the exact correspondence between prophecy and fulfilment, but the allusions of the former to Jerusalem and Zion are even transmuted into descriptions of the kingdom of heaven. Kautzsch thinks such procedure unwarranted and finds that the Templars, who urged the emigration of converts to Palestine to help prophecy to become fulfilled at the place to which it refers, or those Jews who travel to Jerusalem to die in order to be close to the scene where the resurrection is to take place, are at least obedient to the literal meaning of Scripture. But these instances show how impossible it is to stick to the letter of the Old Testament. We must not, however, twist and change the meaning of the Old Testament surreptitiously. It behoves us to recognize the limitations and inapplicability of certain passages in order that we may admire all the more those in which such limitations are overcome.

Kautzsch is not opposed to lines of thought stressing the value of the Old Testament from a purely historical or æsthetic point of view. But he rightly realizes that the mere fact that the Old Testament has had a large influence, and contains admirable and stimulating literary material, does not really prove that it has a living relevance for to-day or to-morrow. These are only the outer works of the citadel. Its actual invulnerability can only be demonstrated if it is irreplaceable for morals and religion.

In trying to demonstrate the moral irreplaceability of the Old Testament, Kautzsch insists that in spite of all the defects found in the book, which make it impossible to defend everything contained in it, there still remains a large amount of material that is valuable for the moral education of man. Here he dwells on the Old Testament expression of moral law and on certain of the more impressive Old Testament stories. But the thing he stresses most is the fact that all moral conduct in the Old Testament order is religiously permeated and grounded. This in his opinion is entirely unique and hence gives the Old Testament everlasting significance.

For the religious irreplaceability he points first to the purity of the Old Testament ideas of God. Of course he recognizes that there are outgrown stages, both primitive and mythical, in many an Old Testament passage. But they only serve to make the more remarkable those areas in which the Old Testament idea of God rises to the full stature of monotheism. The great thing about this monotheism is that the world-God does not become a mere abstraction but remains a living God. He contrasts the scholastic discussions about the eternity of God with Psalm 90 and those about the omniscience and omnipresence of God with Psalm 139. He finds it quite understandable that the proof-texts for a great many religious concepts formerly used by theologians in elaborating on the idea of God were chiefly drawn from the Old Testament. The New Testament really did not have much to add to the idea of God as expressed in these basic passages and itself continually reverts to Old Testament quotations. Opponents of the Old Testament argue that such use of classic Old Testament passages should continue, but that there is no necessity for burdening oneself with the whole apparatus of Old Testament viewpoints and phraseology. This Kautzsch rejects—claiming that the outstanding statements in such Psalms as 90, 103, 139 can only be appreciated out of the totality of those psalms. He points out how the same thing applies also in Psalms 37: 25 and 73: 26.

Secondly, Kautzsch emphasizes the abiding significance of Old Testament prayer. All the theories about prayer and its effectiveness are overshadowed by the demonstrations the Old Testament gives of how piety expressed itself in prayer in the lives of the Old Testament saints. But even these prayers cannot be isolated from the source from which they flowed—the whole Old Testament religion. But the third and decisive thing for Kautzsch is that the Old Testament proves for us the existence of a divine plan of salvation which then finds its perfection and consummation in the person and work of Jesus Christ. He rejects the counter-claim that this is purely a matter of faith. He sees the phenomenon of prophecy as proving that we are not dealing merely with an evolution of human ideas in Israel. In prophecy we can study divine revelation better than anywhere else except in Jesus Christ. To give up the heritage of Old Testament prophecy would be to close up a well of inexhaustible religious knowledge and certainty of faith. Hebrew prophecy, it is true, has its links with allied pagan phenomena, but the important thing is that in Israel this institution stands in the service of a divine plan of salvation from which it cannot be disengaged. Could one imagine Greek seers like Teiresias or Cassandra serving a plan of salvation of Zeus or Apollo? The Old Testament prophet is under the compulsion to speak the Word of God even against his own will. This irresistibility of the divine commission is illustrated in the much misunderstood Book of Jonah, in Amos 3: 8 and, above all, in Jeremiah 20: 7 f.

In setting forth the goal of prophecy, and the reasons for God's having employed it, Kautzsch would not stress Messianic prediction. In its personal form the latter occurs only sporadically and is conspicuously absent in long sections of Old Testament prophecy. It always is something conditional that can only be fulfilled after certain presuppositions have been met. The presuppositions themselves form the real burden of Old Testament prophecy: the recognition of sin and guilt, the yearning for redemption. These are the foundations on which the New Testament messages of John the Baptist and Jesus, with their call to repentance, are built. In this way the New Testament message links up with prophecy and bears witness that the God now revealing Himself is the same as the one who revealed Himself in the earlier order.

It is thus a modified supernaturalism that comes to the surface here at the very end of Kautzsch's line of thought. In the main, however, he develops the religious and moral "values" of the Old Testament literature—a secular line of reasoning which can be applied to any literature equally well.

Representative of the emphasis on the saving events of history (*Heilsgeschichte*) is the study of Koeberle.[7] He steers his ship into the channel marked by two guide-posts—the special significance of the Old Testament for the Church as affirmed by Christ and the apostles, on the one hand, and the merely preparatory character of the Old Testament on the other. For him the problem is to find a definition of the Old Testament that will stay within this groove. In attacking the problem of the authority of the Old Testament he says that this is tantamount to investigating the question whether it partakes of the character of divine revelation at all. He recognizes that there is a considerable difficulty in defining revelation and quotes Schleiermacher who, unwilling to concede any theological usefulness to this term because of its haziness, says: "Not only do some consciously play hide and seek with revelation, but even those who use the term in good faith can only with difficulty come to an agreement as to what they mean with it." Without going into the question of principle thus raised, Koeberle proceeds to describe the present crisis. On the one hand, the school of comparative religion, by considering the Old Testament religion as one of many manifestations of human piety, is undermining the belief in revelation as such, and on the other hand, historical criticism has destroyed the orthodox view of the Old Testament. In the face of this situation, is the Church's procedure of continuing to use the Old Testament as Word of God in doctrine, preaching, and religious education at all tenable?

Koeberle thinks that even on the basis of the comparative religious approach it can be shown objectively: (1) that the Old Testament is unique and far superior to any other collection of religious documents, and (2) that it has a unique importance as preparatory to Christianity. It then only remains to show that God was operative in bringing about these situations and the revealed character of the Old Testament is proven. He realizes, however, that this third thing is not objectively demonstrable. Yet it is the decisive thing on which the use of the Old Testament in the Church, as it has continued in practice to this day, depends. We must take the position that this God who speaks in the Old Testament is our God and that the history which He gave this people concerns us religiously more than the history of any other people; the plan of salvation which God has for humanity according to the Old Testament is not merely a lofty religious notion but a reality. The words that he spoke through the prophets were not idle fancy, but were actually divinely inspired. The self-revelation of God of which the Old Testament testifies is real; the salvation which he promised His people is not an illusion; it has partly been realized in Christ and is partly still on the way to fulfilment. These positions, he admits, do not permit scientific proof—they are articles of faith, but they are the certainties for which the Church must fight in connection with the Old Testament. He defends this position, on the one hand, against those who would speak disparagingly of scholarship and foolishly hide behind outworn defences of external "proofs" for Scripture authority, and, on the other hand, against those who think that by scientific means they can disprove such tenets of Christian faith, or that the Church could content itself with a comparative-religious demonstration of the superiority of the Old Testament over other documents of human piety.

The important thing for Christianity is that the Christian Church accept the history to which the Old Testament testifies as preparatory history of salvation. This history concerns us immediately and personally as the presupposition of the salvation that appeared in Christ. Everything that God did for the preparation of this salvation, anything whatsoever that affected this development in any way, belongs to this history. The completed Old Testament partakes of the character of revelation too because it mediates the knowledge of this history that is essential for our salvation. In particular, we recognize the divine working (as a result of which we ascribe to the Old Testament the character of revelation) in the following facts:

(1) God is operative in a peculiar way in the historical experiences of mankind and in those of His people. While we realize that the total historical process cannot be embraced in this framework, the religious side of it can be. The Old Testament story-tellers recognize that there are areas of additional interest which are not their immediate concern when they refer to sources of purely historical information that they did not choose to take over (e.g. II Kings 10: 34). (2) The appearance of religious personalities within the web of the history of the people is the work of God. The prophets and the interpreters of past and present who speak to us in the writings of the Old Testa-

ment were among them. (3) Out of the interaction of historical experience and religious personalities the nation, under divine guidance, attained the status where the situation was ripe for the coming of Christ.

Since the Old Testament gives us knowledge of these things in such a manner that we recognize this history of redemption for what it is, and in such a way as is necessary to grasp it as the divinely wrought preparation for Jesus Christ, it partakes of the character of revelation, and that is why we consider it as belonging to sacred Scripture. Everything, of course, depends on one's attitude toward the salvation of which the New Testament testifies. With that New Testament salvation stands and falls the preparatory history of redemption in the Old Testament. The proof of its revealed character cannot be formal, but must be developed on the basis of content. It applies, first of all, to the Old Testament as a whole; the individual component part partakes of the character of the whole, but the character of the whole does not rest upon the equal value of the individual parts. Everything that does not stand in a close connection with the divine redemptive plan belongs to the contemporary shell (basically Luther's principle). In essence, the Old Testament revelation is to be described as preparatory to Christ; its limitations are its national character, its legalistic form and its application more to a future than present salvation.

But as every age must take its special message from the Word of God, so the Old Testament has a special one for our own time. How mightily it preaches of the significance of the moral forces in the lives of nations! That God governs justly in history and punishes wrong, that deceit and untruth, no matter how successful they may appear, finally perish of themselves, that social injustice, oppression of the weak, violation of law and immorality bring about the ruin of nations, that belief in God's just government makes peoples and individuals strong, and that faith is the most powerful force—all that is expressed in the Old Testament in classic manner for all time. And the same thing applies even more to the purely religious content of the book, from Genesis 1 to Isaiah 53, from the story of Abraham and Joseph to the prophecy of Malachi; everywhere the Christian finds new confirmation of what Jesus said of the Old Testament writings: "They are they which testify of me" (John 5: 39).[8]

We may cite here one more German attempt to deal with the problem. It reflects full realization of the situation created by modern historical study and is from the pen of Gunkel—a man who carried the purely secular study of the Old Testament to new heights by giving heed to the literary techniques and forms employed in the Old Testament story-telling, poetry and prophecy, thus taking up the century-old legacy of Herder.[9]

He grants at the outset that the Old Testament appears to us in a different light than it did to former generations. Modern biblical science has virtually destroyed the belief that it is the inerrant Word of God and a safe guide to true religion and morality. The respect it formerly enjoyed was shaken by the disproof of the traditional authorship of numerous writings, by the casting of doubt on biblical narrative, whether on grounds of natural science, or contradictory statements in the record itself, or criticism of its religion and morals. But merely to discard the Old Testament is not the correct thing either. What is needed is an intelligent use of the Old Testament based on the knowledge provided by modern Old Testament science. The latter has studied this book as one produced by human means and in human ways. By this approach, he believes, it has rediscovered its true significance for the history of the world. Actually, he asserts, we have a very great treasure in the Old Testament!

The line he then follows carries forward the principles of Herder in a modern form. He sees in the Old Testament an almost illimitable wealth of artistic stimulation. He dwells on the charm of the Old Testament stories, on the power of Old Testament prophecy, on the marvellous production of Old Testament lyric poetry, on the titanic character of its one extensive poem (Job), and on the amazing objectivity and simplicity of Old Testament historiography. After thus pointing out the excellencies of the various types of literary material found in the Old Testament, he contemplates what a loss it would be if people no longer were to become acquainted with all this glamour.

Then he comes to the matter of the religious value of the Old Testament. In general, he holds that we cannot dispense with it. The fact that the Old Testament is necessary for the understanding of the New Testament and that Jesus and His apostles held the Old Testament to be sacred Scripture carries great weight with him. He also stresses the thought that the decision of the Church on the Old Testament was rendered at the time of Marcion and that it is improbable that history will retrace its steps in this regard. "The Christian Church—a mighty structure—will unfold its nature in the course of its growth, but will only change it at the cost of serious convulsions; and one of the foundations of the Church is the Old Testament." When it comes to particulars, however, he concedes that the Old Testament is inadequate in many respects and insists that this must not be covered up by artificial interpretation but be honestly admitted. He grants, furthermore, that some things formerly held to have a religious value can no longer be so regarded. In addition to mentioning sections or books that have no discernible religious bearing, he points to the close connection of the Jewish religion with the Jewish nationality, and the intolerance of the Hebrew religion toward all other religions, as things that are indefensible.

Gunkel sees, on the other hand, in the Old Testament things that can never become obsolete, for they lie at the root of all modern thinking, whatever attitude men may take toward Church and religion. They are expressed in characteristic simplicity of thought and are rammed like posts into the soil of our civilization. The principles of morality taught in the Ten Commandments, the tenets of monotheism and of the divine retribution of good and evil are of this sort. But he also stresses the new conception of the relation of morals and religion that is emphasized by the prophets, and points out how all modern social legislation is an outcome of Old Testament prophetic spirit. He sees the prophetic eschatology, with its hope of a better day in store for God's people, living on in the forward-looking attitude of modern man. He furthermore finds certain aspects of Old Testament belief valuably supplementing the New Testament. In the latter, God's activity in the realm of nature has receded very much into the background. The re-awakened modern feeling for nature, which can become an ante-chamber to the temple of religion, finds notes struck in the nature-hymns of the Old Testament which awaken an echo in our hearts. Even in the national religion of the Old Testament —*per se* on a lower level than the New Testament religion of individual salvation—thoughts were born which are still of value for our time. That an interest in politics and patriotism on the one hand, and piety on the other hand, belong together, that there is such a thing as a universal history (an insight given to mankind by the Book of Daniel), and that God's sovereignty is its goal, are thoughts of this character possessing an unforgettable value.

Gunkel then lists other virtues of the Old Testament such as the sheer simplicity of Hebrew thought, which is good for us whose spiritual world has become so complex, and the magnificent utterances of religious emotion. What he has to say on the latter score about the extremes of passion or even fanaticism to which that emotion often grew is not entirely a recommendation from the point of view of religion and morals, though it may be enlightening from the angle of knowledge of human life, or be highly pleasurable or stirring. He takes recourse here to Nietzsche's oft quoted remarks about the great men and things in the Old Testament—a quotation that in our opinion should not be used, for what that philosopher considered great in the Old Testament were things a Christian consciousness regards as shocking and even horrible.

Gunkel describes certain aspects of the idea of God in the Old Testament. He dwells notably on the sterner side of that idea such as the connection of the deity with volcanic phenomena and His being a God of War. He speaks of the dreadful deeds done for this dread God and of the greatness of some of His representatives from Moses and Elijah down, and shows the power of moral passion that dwelt in them. He next speaks of the grandeur of the Hebrew conception of God as illustrated in the sublime narrative of creation in Genesis I and in the disdain of the use of images in the Hebrew worship. The profound feeling for the greatness of God accounts for the prominent role hymnody played in practical religion. The fear of the Holy God is another valuable element, Gunkel feels. "The Old Testament in its rugged strength would be as iron in the blood for our time which has become so soft, so irresolute, and so out of joint." But he also sees gentler and more tender notes expressed in the Old Testament religion. One thing he finds common to all these writings and utterances—absolute religious certitude. To these men of Israel God is no mere postulate of reason, but a living and real God. That is why the religious heart of all ages has loved the Psalms, for we find here something we long for and lack. The great achievement of Israel, realized through the influence of prophecy, is that it produced human personality living its own life in the presence of God. What a rich and varied gallery of such personalities the Old Testament contains! Other Oriental nations had nothing comparable, and we of the machine age are coming to the point where great personalities are no longer being produced. After some practical counsel on how knowledge of the Old Testament should be taught in various stages of education, Gunkel concludes by asserting that history has made the Bible (both Old Testament and New Testament) and the Greek civilization the two pillars supporting the civilization of the Christian nations, and that it would be a revolution the effect of which no one living can estimate if either of these pillars were to fall.

We hear nothing in Gunkel of supernaturalism. The Old Testament merely has great aesthetic, moral and religious "values" which mankind for cultural reasons cannot afford to do without. But no divine authority is invoked to buttress these values, which must stand entirely on their own merit or generate their own power. This type of Old Testament study has put aside the sun-glasses of theological reflection and views the Old Testament with the naked eye—in full realism, though with wonder and admiration over the religious capacities of the human mind and soul, and with a mild belief in a divine providence standing in the background.

The logical outcome of the scholarly study of the Scriptures of both Testaments under the German liberal theology was that proclaimed in the title of a lecture by a master of historical-critical exegesis in the New Testament field, von Dobschütz: the abandonment of the canonical idea.[10] These writings bear witness to the religious life of Hebrews and early Christians, and as such are permanently valuable and stimulating, but not normative.

In England George Adam Smith's book fitly leads the parade of twentieth-century reflections on the Old Testament.[11] In the main it is of an informative nature, seeking to present the results of modern critical study and to show how with their help the Old Testament comes alive. His own enthusiasm for the new approach is so great and his personal piety so serene and unshakeable that the problem of our present concern plays no great role in it. But it deserves a permanent place in the library of books about the Old Testament.

The disturbing aspects of the new knowledge come to the surface more vividly in McFadyen's work.[12] He sought to bridge the gulf existing between the modern critical viewpoint and the Church, by putting criticism within its proper bounds and discouraging any irreverence on its part, and by showing the Church the necessity, and even the advantage, of criticism. He believed that criticism leaves the religious message of the various sections of Scripture intact. When it comes to the decisive question: "Standing, as we do, in the full brightness of the revelation of Christ, holding as we do that the truth which He teaches is final, are we in a position to dispense with the Old Testament, or have those Churches been right which have sought to reinforce their faith and hope through psalm and prophecy no less than through epistle and evangel?" he asserts that history has decided in favour of the Old Testament.

In particular, he claims for the Old Testament a twofold value—absolute and relative. It lives both because of what it is in itself and of that for which it prepared the way and which without it would have been impossible. There is no part of the Old Testament in which we cannot see the finger of God, shaping the institutions which were largely to determine the practice of the Christian Church. Were there no New Testament with its perfect revelation of God in Christ, the Old Testament might yet in its own way bring us into the presence of God.

McFadyen stresses what it meant to Jesus. He even finds that in certain directions the Old Testament has been able to help men more than the New. We see in it the history of a people unfolded in a wonderful way, with the divine purpose working through it. There is no history like Israel's for convincing us of the transcendence of God, and no book like the Old Testament for teaching the inner meaning of history. He finds the prophets standing nearer to modern needs and meaning more for our time than the apostles, because they teach us to relate religion to public life. He finds the Psalmists teaching us how to enter into the sanctuary of our hearts and commune with God better than the New Testament does. Speaking of its relative value, he views it as preparing the way for Christ and the New Testament order. The New Testament is practically a dead letter to one who chooses to ignore its historical relations. Over against those who would have the Church become "contemporary", he insists that she must also continue to be historic.

Another significant British production, and perhaps the most massive and thorough attempt to deal with all aspects of the problem raised by the higher criticism, was the book by James Orr,[13] to which reference was made in our Introduction. He lays it down as axiomatic that, whatever they may be for others, these ancient Scriptures can never have less value for the Christian Church than they had for the Church's Master— Christ himself. Believing scholars of all standpoints, he boldly asserts, may be trusted to agree in this. He has a deep realization of the gravity of the situation created for supernaturalism by Old Testament research. The great problem of the Old Testament, as he sees it, is, "How are we to conceive of the religion which the Old Testament embodies and presents to us in its successive stages, as respects its nature and origin? Is it a natural product . . . or a result of special supernatural revelation to Israel?" Orr condemns Old Testament critics from Eichhorn and De Wette on to Wellhausen and Kuenen for operating in a manner discounting the supernatural. He wants to prove that the Old Testament's claim to be the record of revelation is not affected by higher criticism when the latter is reduced to conservative limits. His book is largely concerned with discrediting the more radical theories which seem to him inimical to maintaining that claim for the Old Testament. But Orr also has valuable chapters of a positive nature. His discussion, in his second chapter, of the Old Testament from its own point of view, where he deals with such matters as its organic unity, the fulfilment of the Old Testament in the New, the teleological character of the history it mirrors, the unique ideas of the religion it contains, and the revelation it represents and reflects, are all worthy of attention to-day. Particularly significant, too, is the third part of the final chapter in which he discusses the progressiveness of revelation. He holds: (1) that revelation at whatever point it is to begin must take man up at the stage at which it finds him; (2) that revelation can only be held responsible for the new element which it introduces—not for the basis on which it works, or for everything in the state of mind or limited outlook of the recipient with which it happens to be associated; (3) that it is the function of revelation to lay hold on whatever better elements there may be in that state of mind in order by their means to overcome the imperfections and create something higher. Orr, then, views revelation as an organic process, with adaptation at every point to the stage of development of its recipients. "Its higher stages criticize its lower; shed off temporary elements; disengage principles from the imperfect forms in which they are embodied, and give them more perfect expression, yet unfailingly conserve and take up into the new form every element of permanent value in the old."

Turning to the American scene we find that Old Testament scholars, when they wrote about Old Testament criticism, were chiefly engaged in justifying it, or in imparting some knowledge of its results. Perhaps the best known book of this kind was that of Kent,[14] which in its title echoed that of Kautzsch's contribution already outlined. Kent enjoyed a large audience and so this book passed through several editions. Like Smith of Glasgow he had enthusiasm for the Old Testament and gave little heed to the theological problem connected with it.

We shall content ourselves with mentioning but one further book from the American quarter—that of Fullerton.[15] His concern is not with the Old Testament as a whole, but only with the prophets. But what he has to say on the subject is of general significance. He sees the Protestant Church enmeshed in an untenable dualism—adhering to the dogmatic view of Scripture established in the Reformation, and at the same time appropriating the results of modern research in every other field. Protestantism, he holds, must come to terms with itself, as to its own fundamental principle—the Scripture principle— and must frankly adopt the results of modern scientifically pursued biblical scholarship. Over against millennarianism, which operates with the orthodox Scripture doctrine and dwells particularly on biblical prophecy and apocalyptic, Fullerton seeks to show that the belief that the Bible tells what is happening now or what will happen at some point in the future has been maintained only by means of false principles of exegesis, and that the adoption and recognition of correct principles will automatically eliminate it. Accordingly he discusses the change that has taken place in the interpretation of predictive prophecy from the patristic to the modern periods and ends by showing that a purely historical interpretation is alone legitimate.

But Fullerton does not make clear to himself the full consequences of a complete surrender to the modern scientific method for all forms of Protestantism; the theological problem involved has not entered his field of vision. Hence the value of his book lies chiefly in its historical studies on the history of interpretation.

In retrospect, then, the apologetic of biblical scholars of the period covered in this chapter shows a widespread acceptance of critical results and a desire to make them palatable to a larger public. Whether the credit should be given to such apologetic or to some other factor, it is clear that a vast change took place in the attitude of the average Christian during these decades. The phrase "higher criticism" virtually passed out of existence, while the thing for which it stands was accepted in all but the most orthodox quarters as something self-evident—and quite boring.

While biblical scholarship did little in America to show to men any positive meaningfulness of the Old Testament, a movement arose from the side of practical application of Christian ethical thinking which was of considerable importance in that direction. Fully aware of the social crisis brought about in capitalist America by the rise of modern industrialism, Rauschenbusch,[16] with prophetic zeal and fervour, demanded that Christianity furnish its contribution of moral and religious power in the struggle for social improvement. And here, quite naturally, not only the ethics of Jesus but also those of the prophets of Israel, so much emphasized by the modern critical school, were invoked to furnish directives. This social gospel had a wide appeal and gave fresh impetus to the Churches to come out of the shell of passive orthodoxy into active participation in the great current of life. Its influence abides to this day, and one still finds leaders of liberal religious thought in America stressing the social message of the prophets, when there would not appear to be any warrant for according them any authority under the Scripture doctrine presupposed.

Chapter Ten

HARNACK AND DELITZSCH

IN the situation immediately after the First World War the problem of the Old Testament lifted its head very noticeably in the German scene. While it may seem out of place to couple the names of the two men who aroused so much debate on the subject, because the first addressed himself to theologians and theological students while the second, though a distinguished scholar, sought the limelight of publicity and poured grist into the mill of the anti-Semitic agitators, they do supplement each other. For Delitzsch gives the detailed indictment of the Old Testament that Harnack only hints at, and both in effect desire the same thing and for the same reason.

The problem of Christianity and the Old Testament had occupied Harnack throughout his long career. He reverts to it time and again in his studies and treatises dealing with early Christian literature, quite often in a manner that suggests a vacillation in his own attitude. While the main tenor of his remarks is negative, he occasionally pulls in the opposite direction. Even a friend of the Old Testament can take no issue with such a statement as this:

> The Church is younger and older than Jesus. It existed in a certain sense long before Him. It was founded by the prophets, at first within Israel, but already at that time it pointed beyond itself. All the developments that took place later are refashionings. It was present at the moment when a fellowship tending toward universality was formed within Israel, striving out of darkness into the light, out of national and legalistic religion to a religion of the spirit and saw itself led to a higher level of humanity on which God and His holy moral law exercise sway.[1]

Harnack thus clearly discerns Christianity's connection with Israel. But that evidently did not compel him to believe that

Christians needed the Old Testament. In his work on Marcion he came out with a completely negative declaration on the problem.[2] In appraising the significance of the great heretic he claims that what Marcion had wanted was basically right: the Old Testament should be deposed from canonical rank. He concedes that Marcion went too far in considering the Creator God and the Christian God two entirely different gods, and grants that the Christian will want to preserve the belief in their identity. But that, he argues, cannot save the Old Testament. The intellectual history of the eighteenth and nineteenth centuries has made it evident that the Old Testament simply cannot be a part of the Christian rule of faith and life. The trouble with the Churches is that they are too timorous to admit the truth. Let them consider the harm the Old Testament does their cause. Much of the opposition to Christianity in the modern world is based on the Old Testament which affords so much opportunity to people to attack and ridicule the Bible, and thereby to justify their standoffishness toward the Church. The heroic action demanded of Protestantism to-day is to acknowledge this situation and do something about it. He warns that it is almost too late (and for the German scene, as events soon showed, his warning would seem to have been well-founded). He rejects the excuse of the clever ecclesiastical politicians who say that since the authority of the New Testament in the old sense of the word has also been dissolved, one may as well leave Old Testament and New Testament together. Granting that the idea of the authority of the New Testament has undergone a change, he, nevertheless, considers it to be the true canon of the Church, "because a better collection of documents to set forth what is Christian cannot be made."

He concedes no weight to the argument that because Jesus recognized the Old Testament as Holy Scripture we, too, must do so, and that it is the great document for the history leading up to Christianity. Jesus Himself dismissed the idea of the continued importance of earlier stages of revelation when he said in a most solemn saying that henceforth all knowledge of God is given through Him (Matthew 11: 27). The idea, furthermore, of combining the document for the preparatory history of Christianity with its own original documents on one level is not a religious idea but a secular one. The trouble with Marcion was that he had to portray the Old Testament as a false and ungodly book in order to preserve the gospel. This difficulty no longer plagues us. We are not bound by certain Gnostic limitations at which the Church rightly took offence. The Old Testament, Harnack believes, will receive its full significance and appreciation only when put at the head of the books which are useful to read but not authoritative (i.e., the Apocrypha). These were impressive words, spoken by one of the most widely known scholars of Christendom.

The chief weakness in Harnack's presentation was the fact that it was put forward only incidentally in speaking of a figure of a remote past. He did not—and could not in that connection—restate in full the arguments against the Old Testament that arise in men's minds to-day. Delitzsch, however, had, several years earlier, made himself a spokesman of the present and had carried forward the attack against the Old Testament in a two volume work.[3] We have already referred to the stir previously caused by this author in his "Babel-Bible" lectures in 1902–05. His new venture did not have such far-flung repercussions, but nevertheless received large publicity in Germany, where it coincided with a mounting wave of anti-Semitism. Delitzsch, himself the son of a convert from Judaism, Frank Delitzsch, who had been one of the foremost Old Testament scholars of his day, disclaims anti-Semitic intentions and points to his friendship for numerous high-minded Jews and to the help he had given to Jewish students as indications of his true position. We may well believe that his opinions on the Old Testament could have arisen apart from any anti-Semitic bias, and, in the cases where it would seem to appear, discount that element as a post-war accretion (or a part of Schopenhauer's legacy?) that has no integral connection with his main argument. A detailed review of his position will be given, because he strives to show in some detail and with strong arguments why the Old Testament is unfit to be used as normative Scripture by the Christian Church.

Delitzsch puts himself on the plane of the intelligent layman who is reading the Old Testament connectedly with a critical mind. He assumes that this layman has been taught, as he himself was in his orthodox home, that the Old Testament is the Word of God, and his book reflects all the reactions of com-

plete disillusionme   at score. Delitzsch's critics quickly
attacked him as incompetent in Old Testament science. We
would hesitate to join in such condemnation, for Delitzsch's
contributions to Old Testament study, notably to its philological side, are substantial. That in publishing this new work
he did not think it necessary to occupy himself very fully with
modern Old Testament criticism is comprehensible enough,
because the standpoint chosen by him seemingly made that unnecessary. He wanted to point out what anyone could see
without taking recourse to the technical literature of critical
interpretation. In the Preface he tells what a shock it was to
him as a student when he took a course on Old Testament
Introduction and heard his teacher admit that Deuteronomy
was not written by Moses, in spite of all its pretensions to that
effect. "Then Deuteronomy is a falsification?" he asked the
professor. The reply was: "For God's sake! That may be true
but one mustn't say such a thing." Since German biblical
scholars of those days were by no means safe from being investigated by heresy-hunting ecclesiastical authorities, the professor's caution is quite comprehensible. But it had an unfortunate effect on this particular pupil. He makes the words
"For God's sake" the motto of his book, believing that the truth
and nothing but the truth should be told "for God's sake". The
incident, among other things, reveals Delitzsch's fine feeling for
that which is ethical. And herein lies the explanation of his
whole attack on the Old Testament. In a nutshell, he considers
it a book full of fraud and immorality, that has damaged the
moral fibre of Christendom and should be no longer read as
sacred literature by Christians.

In the first volume Delitzsch tries to elaborate on this by
dwelling in some detail on three sets of Old Testament narratives
—the accounts of the conquest of Palestine, of the revelation at
Mount Sinai, and more briefly the stories of the early prophets.
It is obvious that he has chosen areas of Scripture which present
great difficulties to most people and for that reason are not read
or studied anywhere with unmixed delight. As to the first
theme, he mercilessly shows up the falsity, self-contradictori-
ness, yea monstrosity of the conquest narratives when read as
though they formed a single continuous account (as the untutored reader might naturally do). In some instances Delitzsch

places undue historical reliance on some aspect of a particular story, as well as on his own imaginative reconstructions of what happened. Thus he utilizes the incident of the scarlet thread of Joshua 2:18 to insinuate that Jericho fell through betrayal by a *bribed* harlot who admitted the Israelites to the city. He treats that fanciful reconstruction of what happened as a proven fact and considers it a terrible indictment of the morals of the Israelites that the spies went to a harlot's house! More convincing is the way in which he sets forth the absurdity of the narrative of the march around the walls of Jericho. He reasons that since the walls of the ancient city have an actual circumference of only 750 metres, as measured by modern excavators, it would have taken 15 hours and 10 minutes for the 531,150 men allegedly composing the invasion host to march around them if they went 5 deep; how then, he asks, could they march around Jericho seven times in one day? As a matter of fact, 1300 men would completely ring Jericho at a bowshot's distance from the walls! But a person of any insight knows that this absurdity of the present narrative has merely resulted from combining the fantastic figure of the number of Hebrews that went out of Egypt, as given in the P source, with the older narratives that presupposed no such numbers. Would it not be better to provide the layman with the key to the understanding of the narrative than to ridicule the effect of the compilation? These matters have long been recognized and are among the things that show the need for biblical criticism. If Delitzsch is merely arguing to convince naïve literalists of the impossibility of numerous statements made in the Old Testament narratives as they now stand, this is really gratuitous.

Weightier than this is his revulsion of feeling at the murderous mentality reflected in the Book of Joshua. The God of the Hebrews commands the extermination of the Canaanites—the horrible, callous murdering of captive men, women and children. Why did He not send a merciful plague to destroy them instead of ordaining this ghastly carnage? (Here Delitzsch might well have compared the more mercifully-minded Babylonian deity that rebukes Enlil at the conclusion of the Babylonian flood story.) Delitzsch then dwells on the inconsistency between the divinely given prediction that Israel was to possess a realm extending to the Euphrates and the historical fact that it did not obtain even the present limits of Palestine. The Old Testament scholar who does not consider the prophecy as actually focused on the conquest, but rather on a future to which the authors writing much later were still looking forward, does not feel as shocked over that as Delitzsch. He then points out that the extermination command is given its basis in the supposed immorality of the Canaanites. But Melchizedek (Gen. 14) and Ephron the Hittite (Gen. 23) show on the contrary that the Canaanites were good people, while the record of the Book of Judges reveals the moral depravity of whole Hebrew tribes (Benjamin, chapters 19–21; Dan, chapters 17–18). The divine command to exterminate the Canaanites could not even be carried out, as Judges 1 and the taking over of Baal worship by the Israelites clearly show. The God Jehovah who has been unable to make good His promises thus supposedly stands convicted of impotence—He is an *ellil* (a "nothingness") just like all the other Oriental gods!

Turning to the Sinaitic revelation, Delitzsch first dwells on the picture given in Exodus 25–27, 35–40, of the Tabernacle. He shows that it is a purely imaginary projection of the Jerusalem temple into the Mosaic era. The whole Priestly Code is a forgery attributed to Moses but written 900 years later. Deuteronomy is another forgery written 680 years after Moses, and the Book of the Covenant (Ex. 20: 23–23: 19) a still earlier similar forgery. This is a very harsh judgment and overlooks the ancient fondness for literary masquerade, of which even Christians still made use without much sign of scruple. Coming to the Decalogue, Delitzsch points out how monstrous it is that its text as given the second time in Exodus 34 does not agree with that given the first time in Exodus 20 on the tables broken by Moses. He dwells on the crudity of the theophany situation —the elders of Israel "saw God, ate and drank!" And after all the experience of the theophany and while Moses was on the mountain with God, the people could make a golden calf and worship it! How totally absurd everything is. Why, there is not even a mountain in the Sinaitic peninsula around the foot of which a million people (once more a naïve acceptance of the Priestly source's imaginary figures) could have congregated!

After so many "deceptions", Delitzsch comes to the supreme

one—originally a self-deception of the narrators—that this
divinity Jehovah (he refuses to accept the pointing "Yahweh"
that is customary in literature on the Old Testament and uses
the form Yaho which appears in so many Hebrew names, e.g.,
Jehoiada, instead) is identical with our God. He grants that it
was consistent enough for Israel to elevate its own god to the
rank of God of gods, just as other people, like the Babylonians
and Assyrians, did with some of their gods. But the fact remains that Jehovah is always and exclusively the God of
Israel. The finest passages of the Old Testament speak of this
God's care and love for His people and have no relevance for
the Christian reader. All non-Israelites are excluded from the
benefits of this religion, or are only dragged along if they attach
themselves to Jewish coat-tails (cf. Zech. 8: 23). How incredible that the God in whom we Christians believe, who
knows no partiality and is Father over all that are called children
in heaven and on earth, should have elected one people as His
own, and condemned all others to perdition (cf. Spinoza)!
Delitzsch is shocked by such a statement as Amos 3:2: "You
only have I known of all the families of the earth", the naked
meaning of which is that God has only concerned Himself
about the Hebrews and no others. This election is grotesque
already on Old Testament grounds, since that book in hundreds
of passages shows that the Hebrew people did not even want to
have Jehovah for a God or be loyal to Him. Who can believe
that God could have chosen one people and conferred idolatry—
a thing punished in Israel with death (Deut. 17: 3 f.)—on all the
rest of mankind, as Deuteronomy 4: 19 claims? He then points
out that the God Jehovah moves on a low moral plane—giving
unethical or inhuman commands in the matter of robbing the
Egyptians (Ex. 3: 22) and of chastising a slave with im-
punity to the point of causing his death (cf. above, p. 90). Particularly objectionable and ethically inferior to the Babylonian
law which Delitzsch knows so well are the supposedly divinely
given Hebrew marriage laws, which left a wife without rights
and made divorce at the whim of the husband possible.

To the religious and moral grounds that rule out the identification of Jehovah with our Christian God must be added the
cultic manner of His worship, fixed most strictly by the
Priestly Code, and involving bloody sacrifices, exactly like

those brought to the idols of Western Asia, and, above all, the narrowest of all narrow ideas—the Deuteronomistic centralization of worship at Jerusalem! Delitzsch finds the Canaanite cults on every hill and under every green tree, that the prophets condemn, "poetic" by contrast—an absurd, romantic idealization that he might better have omitted.

This deception, that Jehovah has anything to do with our Christian God, is an unheard-of fraud perpetrated on all humanity, says Delitzsch.[4] The way for it was already prepared in pre-Christian Judaism and was greatly furthered by the use of the word *Kyrios* (lord) in place of the name Jehovah in the Greek translation of the Bible. Jewish Christians like Paul espoused the idea. Identifying the Church with a "spiritual" Israel—a purely allegorical, unjustified interpretation!—they arbitrarily appropriated the Old Testament for Christianity. In Ephesians 2: 11 f. the apostle reveals himself enmeshed in the horrible Jewish philosophy that God left the Gentiles "strangers from the covenants of promise, having no hope and without God in the world". How unworthy this is of the Almighty who looketh only on the heart of man (here Delitzsch forgets that he is quoting the Old Testament (I Sam. 16: 7), and who loves all peoples equally.

Delitzsch then turns to the narratives of the early prophets. These men are exponents of a fanatical Hebrew racialism, and have infused their excessive nationalism into supposedly divine oracles and predictions. At the same time they were skilful politicians who understood how to dominate the people and the kings—sometimes, in fact, demagogues of the worst sort. Their interference helped to undermine the authority of the kingship, which alone could have preserved the state. He points to the role of an Ahijah of Shiloh (I Kings 11: 29 f.) in provoking a revolution that destroyed the unity of the kingdom and produced bloody civil war (I Kings 14: 30, 15: 7), and to that of an Elisha, who in the name of Jehovah incites a revolution and lets the terrible murderer Jehu loose on his own people; the latter exterminates the whole house of his master Ahab, and is then even praised and rewarded by Jehovah for his foul deed (II Kings 10: 30)! To add to one's confusion the same Jehovah inspires the prophet Hosea to threaten Jehu's house with punishment for the crimes of "Jezreel" (Hos. 1: 4). Is not the presence of such contradictions in the records an indication of the abuse that the prophets carried on with the assertion of their inspiration? After a few kind words for the prophets as preachers of social justice, Delitzsch gives instances of crude and absurd miracle stories about the prophets from Kings and Chronicles, and points out that these stories have had a warping effect on people's ideas of the divine ways, giving encouragement to fantastic hopes of miraculous divine interpositions, and have stultified the intelligence of a humanity that is supposed to accept this preposterous stuff as gospel truth.

This sketch of Hebrew prophecy is supplemented in his second volume, where Delitzsch shows that the prophets are all bound by one and the same dogma: there is no higher God than Jehovah and Israel is Jehovah's people.[5] He rejects the idea that Isa. 56:7—"Mine house shall be called a house of prayer for all peoples" (which, he had been told, is engraved above the door of many a synagogue) is in any way an expression of liberal sentiments; these Gentiles, he points out, all have to accept circumcision, i.e., become Jews, and he reminds of the comment of Duhm that in spite of the promise of verse six the foreign born were not admitted to the great day of prayer after the first correctly celebrated Feast of the Tabernacles (Neh. 9: 2). Actually, the idea that Gentiles should join in their national worship is an abomination to the prophets. O that Christian leaders would be able to discern this clearly and acknowledge the truth! If Isa. 2: 2–4 speaks of the peoples streaming to Jerusalem for instruction, the parallel, Mic. 4: 1–5, puts a damper on it by adding "For all people will walk everyone in the name of his god, but we will walk in the name of Jehovah our God for ever and ever"! He finds a callous indifference to the fate of other peoples vividly reflected in these words. The prophets, he claims, were not "inspired"— they were speakers of the Hebrew national genius as embodied in the supposed god Jehovah! Their sayings are composed of purely human combinations, inferences, hopes and fears. He cites Jeremiah's idea that the proof of the inspiration of a prophecy is its coming true (28: 9). What a lot of prophecy falls to the ground when judged by that principle! He gives three examples of unfulfilled prophecy.

(1) The predictions of the fall of Babylon. In Jeremiah 50–51

and in Isaiah 13–14: 23, 46: 1 f., 47: 9, 11 the catastrophe befalling Babylon is described in lurid colours. Nothing of this
kind ever came to pass. These prophets were completely mistaken as to the divine plan, for Babylon opened its gate to
Cyrus and was absolutely untouched to the time of the Seleu-
cids; it just died a natural death. Its ruins remained till to-day
a veritable mine for building stones for the inhabitants of the
neighbourhood, putting to shame Jehovah's alleged saying in
Jeremiah 51: 26. (2) The prediction of the fall of Tyre. Ezekiel
was so firmly convinced of the fall of Tyre at the hands of
Nebuchadnezzar and foresaw in it such a display of Jehovah's
power that he revelled in the idea (26–28: 19). Obviously his
god had not taken him into his confidence, for that which he
expected did not happen. Nebuchadnezzar's siege was un-
successful. (3) The return of Israel to Zion. How vividly the
prophecies, notably those of Deutero-Isaiah, speak of the
glorious return of Jehovah's people, and what promises of
future prosperity they make! They remained unfulfilled. When
the opportunity came to return, Israelites and Jews, in cool
calculation, stayed where they were better off materially.

Delitzsch then takes up what he considers to be the lack of
any real value in the prophetic books of the Old Testament.
He asserts that the speeches of a Jeremiah or an Ezekiel are
entirely ephemeral and have not the least religious interest for
those living to-day. All of their hymns of hate against neighbouring nations, with their predictions of doom, have already
been proven valueless by history, since these nations outlived
the Kingdoms of Israel and Judah. He has sharp and not
entirely unjustified words for the prophetic misrepresentation
of idolatry, notably in Deutero-Isaiah. The Babylonians, he
asserts, did not pray to the idols of wood and stone; they
prayed to celestial divinities of which the idols were mere
artistic portrayals.

The Psalms, too, come in for a discussion.[6] From the first
to the last, Delitzsch holds, they are full of the particularistic
Jewish view of God. The Gentiles are only called to praise
Jehovah because He has blessed Israel, and must become Jews
to share in any way in Israel's blessedness. Historically he has
great respect for the Jewish element that returned from the
exile and rebuilt its destroyed national home, passing through

a fire of trials. But that has nothing to do with the question whether the Psalter is a book fit to serve Christian religious needs. That imputation must be entirely rejected.

In the first place, the Psalter rests on the Torah. The Torah, as Jewish law, is a thing of the past so far as we are concerned. If the Psalter divides people into two classes, the godly and the ungodly, depending on whether they observe this Torah or not, that is a totally remote situation for us who enjoy the glorious freedom of the children of God through the new message of Jesus Christ. Still less are the references in the Psalms to past events, such as that of the exodus from Egypt, of any use to us. The Psalms even justify the low cunning practised by the patriarchs and later by the departing Israelites (cf. Ps. 105: 13–15, 37). In other respects, too, he finds the Psalms defective— he stresses their materialism and their melancholy view of life after death. Only two or three references to the immortality idea are found in them, and in these it is confined entirely to the pious, leaving the rest of mankind to a dismal Hades. Not a single Psalm is devoted to the theme of the love of one's neighbour (limited at best in the Old Testament to one's fellow national). Everywhere there are thoughts of hatred for the personal enemies of the psalmists. How few are the Psalms that have any value at all! He concedes that Ps. 73: 25–26 is indeed, a fine utterance but asserts that the Old Testament scholars who praise it to high heaven are thereby tacitly condemning the whole previous history in which they can find no such expressions of religious sentiment. It is an isolated saying, expressed at the very end of the Old Testament development, and occurs only in a Psalm influenced by the imported (Delitzsch erroneously says: Sumerian) immortality idea.

In passing, Delitzsch ridicules the Catholic priests who are obliged to pray the whole Psalter once a week in Latin, and gives examples of Vulgate renderings which are so obscure that they can convey no intelligible idea to the reader's mind. He speaks of the inappropriate use made in thousands of Christian homes of Psalm 90 when read as a Lesson for New Year's Eve; its cheerless melancholy sentiments should not be those of the Christian at that season! He mentions the impudence with which in the last decade before Christ so many obviously late Psalms were ascribed to David (cf. Ps. 138 f.) and even linked to certain definite situations in his life. The tendency to put a halo around the head of that king may be understandable, but a man whose ruthless acts, crimes and immorality are a matter of record does not deserve a place of honour in the Christian Church and is not worthy of being considered the ancestor of Jesus.

The summary of his indictment that Delitzsch gives, after reviewing the favourable reactions his first volume had elicited from various quarters, may be quoted here:

> That the Old Testament is full of deceptions of all kinds: a veritable hodge-podge of erroneous, incredible, undependable figures, including those of biblical chronology; a veritable labyrinth of false portrayals, misleading reworkings, revisions and transpositions, therefore also of anachronisms, a constant inter-mixture of contradictory particulars and whole stories, un-historical inventions, legends and folktales—in short, a book full of intentional and unintentional deceptions, in part self-decep-tions, a very dangerous book, in the use of which the greatest care is necessary. I repeat: the Old Testament in all its books is full of linguistic beauties, of archæological information, and retains its value as a historical document in spite of its defects, but it is in all directions a relatively late and very cloudy source, a propa-gandistic document from the first chapter of Genesis to the last of Chronicles.[7]

There is little in this recapitulation with which the Old Testa-ment scholar needs to take issue except with his over-emphasis on "deception". As though conscious of a weakness in his argu-ment, he adds the words "and unintentional" to "intentional". Self-deception is, indeed, a great element in narratives far removed from the times of which they speak. Historical memory fades very quickly. In the crystallization of stories about things past that bubble up anew out of the wellspring of the popular thought and life the facts are often distorted beyond recognition. It seems to us that wilful deception, though perhaps present in some instances, is not as prominent a factor as wishful thinking. Delitzsch gives Old Testament scholars a sorely needed lesson on at least one biblical narrative in which few had hitherto realized how much it distorted the actual

events—that of Sennacherib and Hezekiah (II Kings 18–19).[8]
To what extent this is an instance of an intent to deceive remains debatable. The natural tendency to forget what is
painful and unpleasant, the upsurging of a nationalistic-
prophetic attitude which accepted the dogma that Jehovah
protects Zion, could have produced gradually a form of narrative concerning that episode tending to be more satisfactory to
Hebrew religious and patriotic feeling than the transmission of
naked and shameful truth. There is an unconscious "drift" in
the development of popular narrative of which the scholar
should be aware. For this Delitzsch seemingly has no understanding at any point—he thinks it was malice aforethought
that produced the result.

In his presentation of Jesus and Christianity as differing
radically from Judaism, Delitzsch has some interesting things to
say. He argues that Jesus was no Jew, but a Galilean, in whose
veins may have rolled blood of the "Cuthaeans" who had come
from the Sumerian plain. The real Jews had all been removed
from Galilee. His ancestors can only have been people of
Ituraea (cf. Luke 3: 1), whose inhabitants were compelled to
accept circumcision and Jewish law by Aristobulus I, one
hundred years before Christ.[9] As a member of this Galilean
group of mixed derivation, Jesus could, on occasion, be defamed
as "Samaritan" (John 8: 48)! If that be rather unconvincing
Delitzsch finds further proof for Jesus' supposed non-Jewish
origin in His unique mental attitude. His broad universalism
and humanitarian outlook are in the sharpest possible contrast
to the exclusive particularism of the Jews (which Delitzsch
apparently regards as a congenital trait of the Hebrew people).
Hence in His use of the Old Testament Jesus saw things that
had not entered the consciousness of the original story-tellers at
all; thus when He makes a peculiar observation on the widow
of Zarephath and Naaman (Luke 4: 25 f.), His statements were
so un-Jewish that the men of the synagogue at Nazareth cast
Him out of the city. His setting up of a Samaritan as an
example of mercy (Luke 10: 33 f.), and of gratitude (17: 15 f.),
His association with publicans and sinners in utter disregard of
Psalm 1, are all un-Jewish. There is no bridge at all, he thinks,
from the Old Testament to the mentality of Jesus. *Christianity*,
he says, *is an absolutely independent, new religion—no mere*

higher stage in the development of Judaism. Here one feels
reminded of the position of Schleiermacher.

What Delitzsch says about a possible Aryan origin of Jesus
is not without interest. But we know too little about the Jewish
element in Galilee to say that Jesus was not of Jewish extraction. His broader attitude toward the Gentiles might, for
instance, be like that of the Jews of Beth Shean in Maccabean
times, whom their non-Jewish fellow citizens protected in an
era of persecution—doubtless because they had conducted
themselves blamelessly.[10] Certainly some late books of the Old
Testament like Jonah and Ruth show the existence among the
Jews (albeit in pre-Maccabean days) of kindly humanitarian
attitudes. Could not Jesus have been an outflow of a stream
of this type within Judaism? We cannot set up an *a priori*
picture of what the Jew must have been like and then, when we
find one who was not like that, deny that he was a Jew! As
nearly as we can judge, Jesus does not act as He does because
of a non-Jewish background, but because of what He (rightly
or wrongly) felt was in accord with the noblest strain of the
religion of the Old Testament. That the intellectual and moral
sides of His environment contained numerous stimuli of non-
Jewish origin need not be denied.

Delitzsch casts ridicule on the "medieval paper dogma"
found in so many books on Old Testament theology, according
to which God supposedly elected Abraham's descendants that
they should observe justice and righteousness, and that later
on all nations should share in this blessing. What a clumsy
pedagogue this Jehovah must be! he exclaims. The pages of the
Old Testament show that this people, instead of serving such
an end, were the breeding ground of the worship of the golden
calf and of a lawlessness and immorality that its own prophets
had to condemn. How monstrous from the standpoint of
Christianity that the all-wise God should have chosen as His
favourite people one that was to crucify the Son of God and
entertain for Him and for Christianity as such a deadly hate
through all the centuries. Thanks to this hate with which the
Jews of Arabia defamed Jesus as "Esau" and Christianity as
"Edom" (by way of wishing Old Testament curses on them),
Mohammed got to know Him as "Isa", with the result that
250,000,000 Moslems are unwittingly continuing this Jewish

defamation of Christ.[11] If some liberals claim that there has been an upward progression in Israel from an original particularism to a universalism leading to the idea of Christ, this would, if true, prove that the greater part of the Old Testament ought to be eliminated anyhow; but he sees no such universalism—prophets and psalms prove the very opposite. Everywhere there is nothing but Jewish nationalism.

Delitzsch concedes that certain passages of the Old Testament can, indeed, be utilized by Christians. He doubts, however, whether they are numerous enough to compose a whole devotional book such as a popular author had suggested. He thinks such a collection would have to be supplemented by the many beautiful sayings of Gentile poets and thinkers. However, he lays the foundation for such a collection by listing a number of outstanding Old Testament passages.

Delitzsch thinks that study of the Old Testament as a theological subject should be abolished. It should be handed over entirely to the secular sphere of Oriental studies and History of Religions.[12] He believes it an absolute waste of time for the average Christian theological student to learn Hebrew.[13] The expenditure of effort necessary for that purpose, he thinks, might better be utilized in acquiring some knowledge of the social sciences, along with some History of Religions. A brief general course in Hebrew history, literature and religion should give the theological student all the Old Testament background he needs.[14] He recommends studying the use of the Old Testament in the New Testament with the help of books by capable scholars; the student will then discern how the unfortunate effort of Jewish evangelists and apostles to find the teachings and the history of Jesus indicated or foretold in the Old Testament, by means of false translation and interpretations, drew the New Testament into a dependence on the Old Testament that is no longer bearable. In short, the New Testament must be freed from its artificial embrace by the Old Testament; the teachings of Jesus must be worked out in their purity for the blessing of every Christian and especially every future servant of Christ, and therewith of the whole Christian Church. Above all, the theological student should begin as soon as possible to become a practical follower of Jesus by being the embodiment of loving, kindly service to his fellow men. That Delitzsch, like

Harnack, has the welfare of Christianity at heart and is fully sincere in his belief that the Old Testament influence does irreparable harm is quite obvious.

If we take Delitzsch's books at their face value (disregarding the unfortunate way in which anti-Semitism capitalized upon them and for which his emphasis on "deception" is partly responsible), we do not find them as worthless as is commonly claimed. He has made his readers conscious of the limitations of the Old Testament. Christians have been too prone to read the terrible and shocking things contained in that book in a sort of pious daze. This has doubtless been seriously detrimental to the moral sense of Christendom. The constant uncritical acceptance of the most monstrous contradictions in the record, furthermore, has helped to lull people's critical faculties. If the Church was shaken by having this said, it well deserved to be. Delitzsch has shown how necessary it is for theology to find a better basis for its retention of the Old Testament than antiquated constructions of philosophy of history, or a mere reliance on the Jewish traditionalism on the part of certain New Testament writings.

But while Delitzsch's attack illustrates the impossibility of certain orthodox views of the Old Testament which no enlightened admirer of that book has any desire to defend, it leaves out of consideration the benefits which the Old Testament properly understood may be able to confer, and hence is too one-sided. The question can only be whether it is possible to get into the popular mind an idea of the place of the Bible as a whole, and the Old Testament in particular, in our religion which will be more tenable than that which Delitzsch takes to be the self-evident and accepted one and which alone makes such attacks as his possible. The flood of literature by Old Testament scholars in reply to Delitzsch did not come to grips sufficiently with this theological issue, but was primarily focused on giving the scholarly slant on the Old Testament to the public. But in this scholarly slant the doctrine fixed in the popular Protestant mind was sacrificed by implication. These men were not fighting on the same front with the churchmen. Thus Delitzsch's results seemed at least partly vindicated in the eyes of the impartial observer.

Harnack had expressed the wish that Marcionites should

again be found in the Christian chorus of to-day. Delitzsch fulfilled that hope before the utterance of it saw print. Marcion's church did not survive any more than did the opposite extreme of Judaistic Christianity. Harnack himself, in a vacillating moment, infers from this that possibly neither alternative can be carried through.

Chapter Eleven

SYSTEMATIC THEOLOGY AND THE
OLD TESTAMENT AFTER 1918

IN the disintegration and despair of continental post-war Europe the entire range of human values and beliefs was shaken. New philosophies arose seeking to probe life and reality in a new manner. Behind them stood a great scepticism as to all previously accepted truth. We are like the blind man who has to grope his way and try to comprehend the mysterious character of things in gradual and circumstantial approach; and beyond those immediate things lies the great world of the unknown. The phenomenology of Husserl was particularly important here; his method was to get at the "meaning" of a given entity by determining its place and approaching it intuitively from various angles. Soon there arose the existential philosophy of a Heidegger and Jaspers. Under impulses deriving from the gloomy Dane, Kierkegaard,[1] a view putting personal existence before all compulsion of ideas or abstract concepts was promulgated. Existential thinking, therefore, is concrete thinking. Every thought-form is dependent on the form of existence represented by the thinker; the axis of philosophizing is the illumination of the existence of the inquirer. From this angle belief in the objectivity of most social sciences and of philosophy as well became dubious.

Out of the same Kierkegaardian roots emerged also the theological movement of Karl Barth, who prefers that it be called the "Dialectic theology".[2] Dialectic is the art of dialogue, be it with another person or with the self. The designation "Dialectic theology" is derived from the conviction, shared by Barth and the circle about him, that theological statements can be made only in the form of human speech and response, in full consciousness of the impossibility of drawing near to the divine reality. In the Hegelian dialectic, thesis is followed by antithesis, and then by synthesis, in which the contrast is dissolved.

In the new theology the thesis is God, the original given entity. The antithesis is: God is unapproachable. The synthesis is the paradox that the unapproachable one has made himself approachable. Since a metaphysical entity, God, is involved here the dialectic is merely "analytic": i.e., the "thesis" is not changed, but only limited in the antithesis, and defined as to content in the synthesis.

Behind this theology stands an experience of the sovereignty and unapproachability of God, and of our human limitations; it holds that we cannot draw near to Him, either theoretically or practically, unless He Himself draws near to us first. All speaking of God, therefore, must be positive, in the full consciousness of our being under God—God cannot be dealt with as an object of debatable reality. Another significant fact about this theological attitude is its dependence on the basic doctrine of the Reformation—*justification* with the emphasis on God's declaring sinful human beings just. This puts the concept of God's "speaking", or his "Word", or "revelation", in the very centre of things.[3] On the surface at least this linked up with the basic Reformed position.

For the Dialectic theology, revelation is not a mere divine communication of teachings as for orthodoxy, or a limited portion of a historical process in which God revealed Himself in events and in inspired interpretations of these events, as for the modified supernaturalism of the nineteenth century. The teaching of Herrmann that revelation is a *present* reality, encountered when the individual meets God in personal, ethical experience of the saving power of Jesus Christ, was adapted by Barth to suit his new starting-point. The question that concerns Barth is the crisis of human existence (for which reason his theology is sometimes called the "Theology of Crisis"). What is this crisis? Man, thirsting for life, is delivered over to mortality; yearning for goodness he is unable not to sin, etc.

This crisis is increased and becomes an acute one where man is conscious of standing before God. God speaks to man in this situation; such speaking is revelation. It is the answer to man's question as to how he can bring his existence to its desired realization. God is veritably in His Word (not at all identical with Scripture), and His Word is to be heard by the human heart. The Word thus cannot be adjudged by man as Word of

God on the basis of various characteristics or of its content but confronts man with absolute and unquestionable authority. Barth recaptures something of that complete certainty concerning the divine Word that one finds in Luther. Since God answers our existential question in His Word, this speaking is not ended so long as our existence endures; we can never talk about His Word as though it were a completed product. It is a reality not given to us like the objects of the world about us. If we speak of it in positive statements as orthodoxy does, we make it a part of the world, "forgetting that as a solution of our existential need it stands absolutely beyond our existence with its physical and metaphysical realities."[4] If we speak of it in negative statements, we still remain in the area of that which is in our own control and do not establish a bridge to the unattainable positivity of God. The only thing remaining is to point to the impossibility of exercising any control over God's Word either in substance or by concept. Positive and negative thus stand dialectically side by side; we speak positively of the positivity of the Word of God, but put alongside of it the negative statement that this positivity does not belong to the series of positivities under the control of man. But this dialectic is only the form in which we must speak of God. Revelation itself completely transcends reason and is entirely under God's control.

The Word of God which is so completely transcendent to reason and of which one can only speak dialectically is for short "Jesus Christ". But the Dialectic theology here faces a dilemma: If taken as the answer to the existential question, revelation or the Word of God cannot be a historical fact in the ordinary sense, for man can control, or attempt to control, historical facts but not the Word of God. And yet, at the same time, this theology does not wish to give up the Christian claim that revelation occurred at a point in time and thus must be reported by a tradition subject to critical control. It asserts paradoxically both that it is historical and not historical. History is a predicate of revelation but revelation is not for that reason a predicate of history. God acts in history, but history is not itself the revealing action of God. Revelation, therefore, is no category of the general concept of history. Indeed, history as such is never revelatory. "In history *per se*, as far as the eye reaches, there is nothing that could provide a basis for faith." "In history *per se* everything could always be regarded in a different light."[5] Revelation is an historical event, but only in so far as the event transcends the historical is it revelation.

The Dialectic theology denies that one can speak of the "being" of God in revelation on the basis of general philosophical presuppositions. No ontological concept can be found in advance to provide a niche for revelation. It is something completely apart and above the process attainable to natural reason. What revelation is can only be determined through revelation itself. The necessity for a theological ontology which then will spread light also on the reality around us, thus looms up on the horizon. Over against historical relativism, the Dialectic theology asserts that the Christian claim of the revelation through Christ as central for humanity is not to be defended with a unified teleological philosophy of history that is subject to the attacks of reason, but with a "theology of history" that understands history in other terms than that of a progressing dotted line. The nature of history and the place of Christ, as well as the relation of revelation and Scripture to each other, are to be interpreted from the vantage point of faith in revelation.

If Herrmann had emphasized the present nature of revelation, Kaehler had provided the idea of the transcendent or suprahistorical (*das Übergeschichtliche*), which likewise proved stimulating here. The fact that God speaks with *us*, who are bound by space and time, makes His speaking historical; but the fact that it is *God* who thus speaks, makes the speaking more than historical; something eternal enters the here and now and this bit of history takes a transcendent aspect. Barth unhappily coins a term for the higher unity of the historical and transcendent—"primal history" (*Urgeschichte*), a word ordinarily used for the prehistoric era of human life on earth.

Barth considers the Incarnation the real "primal-historical event". The deepest meaning of history is revealed here: the victory of God in man's clash with God (which Christian insight sees as going on through the ages). No other point in the historical process takes on the same character of "primal history", except one in the future—the final redemption.

It is at this point that the attitude of Barth toward Scripture in general (and the Old Testament in particular) becomes

understandable.   Scripture has a revelatory authority only
because it is witness of the "primal revelation". It is set apart
by the fact that its authors had an immediate relation to the
divine revelation—a relation very different from that of other
men, even the greatest teachers of the Church. "The circumstance that revelation begat the witness of Scripture and speaks
for itself in Scripture, makes Scripture the Word of God, without its ceasing for that reason to be simply and historically the
word of the prophets and apostles, sharing in the relativity, the
ambiguity and the remoteness, which pertain to all that is
historical."[6]

Barth holds that the Word of God in Scripture is by no means
confined to that which impresses *us* as the Word of God. God
Himself and not our ever-limited insight determines what is His
Word. According to the testimony of the Church, the Bible as
a whole is the Word of God. This statement does not require
us to believe all Scripture to be the Word of God, but says to
everyone, no matter how much or little of this may actually be
recognizable to him, that over against this literature *as a whole*
we are confronted with the task of the discernment of that
reality.

Barth regards the whole of Scripture, both Old Testament
and New Testament, as witness of this "primal history" in
Christ. Unlike the historical process, "primal history" is not
bound to historical succession. The Old Testament testifies to
the coming "primal history"—not to the when, where and how
of its temporal appearances (for the prophets were no clair-
voyants and self-evidently thought and spoke in their own
historical sphere), but to its reality. Messianic prophecies are
not the main thing in the Old Testament, but are only the
exponents of the basic and decisive thing that they proclaim:
the God who speaks in Christ; the Word that becomes flesh;
the *deus absconditus*, who as such is the *deus revelatus*. For just
this God, the inscrutable, strong, powerful God of Moses,
Jeremiah, Job, the 39th and 139th Psalms is also the God of
Capernaum and Nazareth, of Gethsemane and Golgotha. The
New Testament takes its place alongside the Old Testament as
witness to the "primal history"—not as a second and higher
stage but as a witness of the succeeding one alongside of the
preceding.

Barth thus proclaims the singleness and continuity of revelation in such a way as to put the Old Testament on a level with the New Testament. He views the New Testament Christianity as looking forward to a consummation, like that foreseen by the Old Testament saints.[7] With Christ present in the Old Testament (he stresses Christ's pre-existence) and the men of the Old Testament still with us as a cloud of witnesses (Heb. 12: 1), the two Testaments are merely testimonies of before and after the Incarnation. He asserts that only a secular thinking, which confuses the Incarnation with the so-called origin of Christianity, can attribute a lower dignity to the Old Testament.

Barth wants to maintain the designation of the Bible as the Word of God.[8] It makes clear that which is the object dealt with in this literature: the Word, heard—not spoken or written —by its authors. Since the Church knows the Word only through this medium it can call the medium itself the Word of God. But he rejects the Roman position that it is the authority of the Church which established the authority of Scripture; the canon was merely *declared* by the Church after these writings had *proved* themselves to be the Word of God. Barth recedes, however, from the older Reformed position that the canon is definitely fixed for all time. He theoretically concedes the possibility of widening or narrowing it, but holds that only the Church can act in this matter.[9] In individual experience, he admits, other things may be more important than the Bible, but for the Church the priority belongs to the latter. He dismisses the doctrine of verbal inspiration as unknown to the great leaders of the Reformation, and contents himself with the position of merely affirming that "God speaks to us in the Bible". This conviction is not one to be demonstrated, but is axiomatic (though of course not immediately acceptable to reason like an axiom in mathematics). It is implied in the Christian faith from the outset, for Barth holds with Calvin that a believer is one who subjects himself to Scripture.[10] God Himself speaks to us in and through the Word and thereby gives evidence of Himself (the so-called internal testimony of the Holy Spirit).

Serious dangers, Barth warns, beset all efforts to be more precise. If one stresses the objective reality of God's speaking in the words of the prophets and apostles, one gets the conception of a mysterious book, out of which one vainly tries to hear the Word of God. Or if one stresses the fact that the Spirit testifies in us to the reality of the revelation given to the prophets and apostles, then there is a tendency to exalt mystical experiences on the part of the individual. Barth affirms that both things are true: God speaks in the Word and God (the Spirit) speaks within us. But the light that goes forth from the Bible and the eye that sees this light cannot be separated. Both factors together constitute the single voice of God.[11]

Dialectic theology thus tacitly accepts the validity of the objections reason had advanced against supernaturalism and tries to find an unassailable position for revelation.[12] It concedes that the assertion of an absolute revelation in Jesus Christ is impossible according to reason, but paradoxically asserts that it is a reality none the less; it grants that a historical event can have no universal significance, but asserts the universal significance of this one. Over against the claim of reason that there is no special exempt area in which revelation imparts truth rather than reason, it radicalizes revelation, as something apart from knowledge and as a mystery and paradox even to the believer.

Here Kierkegaard's thought on the paradoxical was influential. The paradox, according to the Danish thinker, is present whenever one thinks that things are other than they appear to reason. In philosophy one speaks of antinomies—truths that seem mutually exclusive and yet are valid; behind them stands a paradox. There is an irritating border-line for reason in every paradox—reality asks reason to take a step which reason according to its own laws is unable to take. To live in the face of this border-line becomes a practical attitude, in which theoretical considerations are no longer decisive.

In this new manner, then, revelation is upheld over against reason. And at the same time theology shows up the inadequacy of the modern world-view; it points out that it disregards the very heart of all reality—human existence—and necessarily so, because, since one stands within it, one cannot see it from the outside, objectively. One can only speak of existence in terms of one's own concrete existence and only in a confessional manner. Revelation, it is claimed, addresses itself to and operates in this centre of reality. The Dialectic theology thus could claim that it had given revelation a deeper and more genuinely theological form. Over against the "heteronomy" of Supernaturalism and the "autonomy" of a liberalism that was in league with philosophical Idealism it had created a "theonomy", a god-centred approach. The impact of this thinking on all fields of theological study, including that of the Old Testament, was bound to be great.

In the early twenties the Dialectic theology, while important, was not yet dominant; there were other lines which also had their dignity and following. Perhaps the leading systematic theologians of that period were Heim and Otto. We need not enter particularly into Heim's theology, for in spite of his links with Pietism and love of the Bible he is primarily concerned with problems arising in Christianity from the angle of the natural sciences.[13] When he steers toward a positive presentation of the Christian message he goes directly to the experience of the forgiveness of sins through Jesus Christ. Old Testament categories thus do not basically affect his position, and there is no occasion for the problem of the Old Testament to come into view. In such an essay as that on the Biblical World-View,[14] however, his affection for the Old Testament is revealed, and he looks for insights of abiding value in much that others consider purely mythological.

Of greater interest for our theme is the work of Otto, whose viewpoint may be described as a combination of historicism and mysticism. Here are world-wide horizons with attempts to understand and interpret appreciatively the non-Christian religions, and a feeling of ecumenical Christian unity together with practical concern with the modernization and enrichment of the worship of the Church. Here is interest for the tie-ups with philosophy (notably the Kantian as modified by Fries) and a psychological approach to the study of religious experience in the whole great sphere of the History of Religions.

Limited by the task in hand it cannot be our function here to dwell on all aspects of Otto's theology. It is obvious that one so deeply and reverently concerned with religious phenomena everywhere will have a very great partiality for the Old Testament. In his *Idea of the Holy*,[15] which had a vogue comparable to Schleiermacher's *Reden*, the strain of Old Testament influence is very marked. Indeed, one may doubt whether Otto would have been led to describe the experience of the Holy as the basic thing in religion without that collection of Sacred Writings. We must differentiate sharply, however, between a religious philosophical observation, viz., that in empirical religion the idea of Holiness is basic, and a theological-normative statement that it *ought to be* basic. Where the latter standpoint is taken the Old Testament strain in Christianity will be very large and will veer toward Calvinism. Otto's ideas seem to have run along that line—as his efforts to enrich the liturgical element in the Church service reveal—but he did not give any systematic presentation of that viewpoint. That the atmosphere he created with his emphasis on the non-rational and the awesome in the experience of God helped pave the way for an increased success by the Dialectic theology, which similarly stressed these aspects of the idea of God, seems patent.

But modern individual psychology, which under the leadership of William James had interested itself in the religious experience of the present-day individual, also found favour with certain theologians. Thus Wobbermin produced a Systematic Theology written from this angle.[16] He holds analysis of the psychical as well as the logical structure of the religious consciousness to be the fundamental preliminary task that needs to be performed before any theological statements can be developed. The basic religious conviction is viewed as taking root in the individual experience of faith. Through consideration of the latter the attempt is made to fathom the meaningfulness of the content (*Sinngehalt*) of religious faith on the basis of its own motives and to the exclusion of all motives, ideas, and concepts of an extraneous origin. This transcendental-psychological manner of inquiry stands close to that of the phenomenological school in Philosophy (cf. below on Tillich). The effort is to do justice both to the object and subject side of the faith-relation. The object, God, not being directly controllable, it is necessary to consider the historical objectivation of religious conviction and relate that to subjective conviction going back to personal experience. This historical objectivation is found primarily in Holy Scripture as the historical document of the divine revelation culminating in Jesus Christ—His life and teaching, death and resurrection. The primacy of Holy Scripture is recognized because there is no Christian experience that does not depend on it directly or indirectly. Indeed, Scripture is viewed as the sole source of evangelical teaching. It is apparent that in such an approach room can be found for the pre-Christian revelation, though there is no need for especial emphasis on it.

Individual-psychological interest also governed the theology of Karl Girgensohn. He undergirds his outline of Christian doctrine with Psychology and Philosophy of Religion.[17] Stressing the non-rationality of Christianity, he rejects Troeltsch's demotion of it to one religion among many and tries to develop the distinctive character of Christianity by means of partly contrasting and partly harmonizing thought. He distances himself from the Erlangen theologians by making subjective experience only one of the sources of doctrine—the other two being Scripture and the Confessions (in broadminded manner he welcomes use of the Reformed Confessions as supplementary to his own Lutheran). His views concerning Scripture are those of a moderate. He stresses revelation and inspiration of the men behind Scripture, but limits the infallibility of Scripture to the sphere of that which concerns the preaching of the saving purpose of God and the manner of its realization. That smacks somewhat of the same artificiality as the Catholic doctrine that the Pope is only infallible when he speaks *ex cathedra*.

Girgensohn's views on the Old Testament may be inferred from the way in which he discusses the Jewish religion of the law. He restates Christian criticism of the latter, in the light of Paul's contribution, and hence must regard the Old Testament as a partially outgrown stage of the biblical religion.

To Girgensohn the theology of that decade owed a renewal of the plea for an improvement in the method of Scripture interpretation.[18] Since that was bound to affect the Old Testament problem, we may dwell on it here. The post-world-war generation of theological students, which had seen life at its grimmest on the battlefield, had little equipment for or patience with the scholarly type of biblical exegesis, which sought to set forth the meaning of the biblical writings in their true ancient colour with the aid of the tools of philology, and of antiquarian research. Those who went into the ministry complained that the biblical exegesis which they had been taught, or which was available in critical commentaries, did not enable them to preach on the Bible, or even hindered their preaching. Girgensohn was particularly impressed by the fact that professional exegesis of Scripture failed to raise the question of the abiding worth and significance of a Scriptural thought. It was becoming increasingly useless for Systematic theology, for though the theologian cannot be indifferent as to the original historical sense of Scripture, he is really always seeking for the normative element in it. Paul's remark, "the natural man receiveth not the things of the Spirit of God . . . but he that is spiritual judgeth all things" (I Cor. 2: 14–15), suggested to him that there are two ways of interpreting Scripture: the historical-critical type of interpretation which belongs to the horizon of the natural man, and a spiritual or "pneumatic" exegesis, which he holds is the thing that is needed to-day. The term was not new—it had been used, e.g., by J. T. Beck, half a century before. But churchmen hailed the revival of the idea by a responsible scholar with great joy.

Girgensohn's untimely death prevented his publishing a demonstration of the method he had in mind. His idea, however, was that the exegete should extract the timeless element in Scripture from its historical shell and transpose it to a higher plane; and he conceived of this as a service to be done by and for Systematic theology. His much discussed programme was soon crowded off the scene, however, by the rival idea of "theological exegesis", which Karl Barth had introduced and demonstrated so effectively in his *Commentary on Romans*. But Girgensohn's ideas did stimulate biblical scholars to enrich their exegesis somewhat with religious reflection in order to meet the needs of theological students and pastors, without sacrificing critical insight. A comparison of Gunkel's and Weiser's expositions of selected Psalms will vividly reveal the shift made in this direction.[19]

Another important theologian of this period was Tillich. He links up with the phenomenological method of Husserl. As already indicated, the aim of this method is to describe the "meaning" of a given entity in intuitive approach, before deciding to accept or reject it. An interesting example of his treatment of Christian teachings is his lecture on revelation.[20] To him revelation is an idea. An idea cannot be demonstrated— only the place where it appears can be pointed out; whether one sees it depends on one's inner inclination. The idea of revelation is as old as religion; but the concept of revelation was created by late Greek philosophy at the time when there was a complete collapse of existence. In that age of scepticism men turned to the eastern religions, which had revelations in abundance. The concept of revelation is the correlate of late scepticism and the supernaturalism of revelation the correlate of the collapse of the belief in reason. Christianity took over the concept of revelation and focused it on Christ; in Him supernatural revelation was held perfect. Insights obtainable by reason were held to be natural revelation. Both ideas have come down through the ages. Where natural revelation is stressed the supernatural revelation is dissolved into an immanent process— a history of religion. Where the supernatural revelation is stressed, the connectedness of the process is interrupted. In the former case culture becomes hollowed out, in the latter case religion is put in a compartment. Tillich sees a need for a fresh start in examining revelation as well as all other "symbols" of religious knowledge.

Only that can be revealed which is by nature concealed, and revelation pertains to the absolutely concealed. If that be revealed it must be revealed in its quality as absolute and it must furthermore be fully revealed. This absolutely concealed is the utterly strange to which no way can be found out of our reality, but it is also our very own, present whenever a way begins. If that which is revealed is my own it absolutely concerns me. There is no revelation that does not put an absolute requirement on him to whom it is given. Hence it is not possible to receive it neutrally. Only what concerns me is revelation; hence we cannot think of other religions as revelation. How can the absolute enter the connectedness of the conditioned? It must appear in the conditioned, then the connectedness is not broken. The possibility exists *in* the conditioned to experience revelation. An object or being that has become an area in which revelation takes place is holy. Not through itself or its own excellence does a being take on holiness, but only through its character of bearer of revelation. Therewith Tillich believes he has overcome the contrast of natural and supernatural revelation. The idea of "natural revelation", he asserts, is at best an echo of original revelation, but is inadequate. "Supernatural revelation", on the other hand, is either revelation itself or a poor concept, identifying revelation and the bearer and doing violence to the connectedness of the conditioned.

Revelation for Tillich is not confined to the sphere we call religion. It points both civilization and religion back to their ultimate origin in which both are one.[21] Revelation is perfect only in so far as it can again be troubled. When a finite such as Bible, Church, Christianity is put in the place of the concealed absolute then Tillich sees a "demonic" seizure of revelation taking place.[22] A Church, secure in dogma and cult, is "demonizing" the revelation on which it rests.

Tillich aroused special attention with his "Kairos" teaching (Kairos being "the right, the favourable moment") which he made central in his religious philosophy, thereby designating the moment in which man experiences the irruption of the eternal into the present.[23] He regards numerous Christian doctrines as symbols which are produced by the basic forms of being. Thus the "Eschaton", as he calls the sphere of the "eschatological", is a symbol based on being, in so far as it is historical, for the Eschaton is the transcendent meaning of happenings. In this manner Tillich seeks to find the ultimate ground of the various assertions of religious experience or conviction by regarding their traditional form or description as merely symbolical. Some doctrines are undergirded by this procedure while others are devalued.[24] Since Tillich preserves an Old Testament element, stressing sin and the consciousness of guilt as well as the thought of the divine holiness (though at the same time incorporating elements of mysticism derived from Schelling), his attitude toward the Old Testament heritage is by no means hostile. He can afford religious selectivity, and it enables him to stress the elements of it that suit his purpose, without being handicapped by the elements of the Old Testament religion for which he can have no use.

It is of interest to note that the aged Ferdinand Kattenbusch in his valuable survey of contemporary theological trends (1934) saw good reason to stick to the Ritschlian appreciation for the Old Testament.[25] He counselled Old Testament theology not to continue to view the Old Testament in too detached a fashion—without regard for the New Testament. The same thing, however, applies to New Testament theology—it must not continue to view the New Testament without taking account of the prophetic literature of the Old Testament and the mentality that lies behind it. The "pneumatic" Old Testament substratum in the consciousness of the men of the New Testament, notably of Jesus, has not, he thinks, been sufficiently heeded. That the early Church lost its appreciation for this under the dominance of Paul's teaching about the law is a fact. But, he asserts, we here touch on the inability of the ancient Church to create durable formations of dogma. Jesus as the "Christ", Paul and John as those who proclaim Him in this unique exaltedness of person, are only to be rightly understood and theologically evaluated in their true canonicity if one makes clear to oneself that they lived in the old prophetic "pneumatic" atmosphere of an Isaiah or Jeremiah, which was later choked by Hellenism. This programme which, however, is not developed in detail would seem to place on theologians a heavy burden of historicism, especially in the requirement of stressing the Old Testament background of the men of the New Testament. The danger is that by that procedure we shall make them more remote than they already are.

This sampling of significant theological thought between the two world wars must suffice to indicate the range of new stimuli thrusting themselves upon the common mind and thus bound to affect Old Testament study in diverse ways.

Chapter Twelve

APOLOGETIC OF THE 'TWENTIES AND 'THIRTIES

GERMAN Apologetic on the Old Testament theme was of a varied nature in the two decades between the two great wars. It was at first strongly concerned with the situation created by Harnack and Delitzsch. Then the Dialectic theology and its interpretation of the Old Testament, notably by Vischer (see p. 219 f.), entered the picture. Next followed the rise of National Socialism, with an attendant anti-Semitism, bent on eliminating the Old Testament influence from national life. Finally, there was the doctrine of Hirsch representing a compromise between retention and rejection of the Old Testament (see p. 239 f.). Some of the writers dealing with our subject may be found fighting on several fronts at the same time. In England and America the Old Testament theme found increasing attention, but was detached from any special situation. It was merely a case of its being in the air as a result, probably, of the dust it was raising in Germany.

In the German debate over Harnack and Delitzsch two of the leading contributions were those of Eissfeldt[1] and Sellin.[2] The latter in part re-echoes the former, but since Eissfeldt's general position will be reviewed later we will confine ourselves here to some account of Sellin. He held that Old Testament scholarship was at fault for not having properly disseminated its new knowledge and having left the Christian public bound in the untenable beliefs of the older orthodoxy. Hence the shock given Christian people by the publicity over his two colleagues. He found it necessary to demonstrate to his readers that the Old Testament is no infallible revealed book; it is human literature pure and simple, which, however, testifies to a divine revelation that took place in the history of a people. Revelation he defines as self-communication of the living God for the purpose of granting personal, living fellowship with Himself. Such revelation cannot take place in a manner dissociated from human presuppositions, but takes place in the historical process—in and through the medium of events, personalities and human utterances. It is only recognized in faith—only he who already has a relationship with God will discern His activity and presence in all these circumstances; the others will see only an immanent development. That would seem to leave the decision as to whether there is divine revelation in the Old Testament an entirely subjective one. But Sellin does not wish to grant that— instead he adduces arguments supporting the belief that there was actual revelation in Old Testament history.

The first is based on Comparative Religion; in the light of that subject, he thinks, it can be demonstrated that the Hebrew religion is so vastly superior to other religions in its spiritual insight, purpose and attainments that one cannot explain it on a purely historical basis, but must sense the Spirit of a living, personal God as operative in it. In this way we can lead anyone who is willing to use his eyes to the point where he can at least divine the existence of revelation in Israel. Here he evidently is following in the wake of Troeltsch. The second argument is that since Jesus and the apostles recognized the divine revelation in the Old Testament all those who see a divine revelation in Jesus cannot be indifferent to that book.

After setting forth that the Old Testament exhibits a struggle that went on in Israel and Judah between higher and lower forms of religion, and that Christians, following Jesus and the apostles, can only regard the former strain in it as normative, Sellin turns to Delitzsch's and Harnack's books. He accuses the latter, whom he takes more seriously, of employing a double standard in his treatment of the two Testaments. When referring to the Old Testament, Harnack implies that it must be "holy and therefore infallible Scripture" in order to be retained in the canon, while in speaking of the New Testament he contents himself with the more moderate estimate that it is "a collection of documents for determining that which is Christian". Harnack's criticism of the Old Testament, he believes, would fall to the ground if he gave the earlier collection the same leeway. He rejects, too, the idea that the Old Testament is primarily "law" and therewith the law-gospel contrast.

Sellin then raises the question whether the Church would not suffer serious loss in dropping the Old Testament. Not the

New Testament alone but the Bible of the two Testaments won over the nations for Christianity. While he does not feel capable of setting forth in detail just how the substance of Christianity would be affected by depriving it of a part of its equipment wherewith it has hitherto fulfilled its mission in the world, he makes the following observations:

(1) The Person of Jesus would lose something if no longer regarded as the culmination of a historical development leading up to Him. Even Schleiermacher, with good reason, conceded some importance to Messianic prophecy. (2) Christian piety easily becomes one-sided if it exclusively relies on the New Testament. The latter everywhere presupposes the earlier revelation and the idea of God as Creator and Provider, which finds little emphasis in the New Testament. (3) The Old Testament establishes a bridge between Christianity and the world. Without it an ascetic tendency is apt to prevail, for New Testament Christianity stands under the impression of the imminent return of Christ. (4) In the Old Testament the faith in a righteous but merciful God proved itself in a long history. There are admonitions, impulses, and consolations in this which are of positive value for the nations to-day. Christianity cannot do without this heritage. The New Testament alone is of little help for the historical process, because it is not oriented in the direction of a continuation of history, but looked on the end of the world as at hand. (5) In foreign mission work, especially, the Old Testament serves a useful purpose of drawing people gradually upward to Christ. (6) The Old Testament contains "law". Law and gospel belong together and the grace of God is only appreciated where the divine imperative has first been heard.

In a concluding section of his treatise Sellin makes a powerful appeal to all those who with the best of intentions urge a revision in the relationship of the Church to the Old Testament. He urges them to make clear to themselves what a loss it would be to do without this book. He reminds of the impulses that have gone forth from it on art and civilization, and of the way in which people in the midst of the trials of life have found strength in its utterances. He sees the Church partly responsible for the present crisis. He points to its unfortunate handling of the Old Testament—its inability to teach people to differentiate between what is bygone and eternal in that collection,

its failure to make clear the difference in the religious levels of
the Old Testament and New Testament and its leaving people
under the false impression that it is infallible and verbally
inspired Holy Writ   thus giving monstrous offence to reason.
The slogan for the Church must be "forward to the right understanding and evaluation of the Old Testament".[3]

Turning to the British scene in the mid-'twenties, we may
take from the shelf an important volume of essays by Members
of the Society for Old Testament Study which contains two
contributions relevant to our theme. The first, that of R. H.
Kennett, seeks to appraise the contribution of the Old Testament.[4]

The more we subject that book to critical investigation, he
says, the more we find it to contain passages at variance with
what Christians believe to be true and right, not merely in
regard to history and science, but also in connection with
morality and theology. Hence he finds it inevitable that the
question should be asked "What has the Old Testament to do
with Christian faith?" He would approach the Old Testament
critically—scrutinizing every part of its teaching in the light of
what our Lord has taught. The result will be that we shall find
ourselves compelled to classify these teachings under various
categories. Some of its elements are mere pagan survivals, not
suited to the needs of higher religion; others, though of pagan
origin, are capable of being made subservient to genuine
spirituality through allegorization, or may be shown to possess
some practical utility. Finally, we must recognize the presence
of teaching of an infinitely higher order, which has to a great
extent transformed those heathenish elements of which it was
unable wholly to get rid.

Kennett finds in the Old Testament survivals of the same
primitive, folkloristic thinking that existed outside of Israel,
and is not so sure of the superiority of Hebrew religious and
moral ideas over those of their pagan neighbours in every
respect. It may well be asked, therefore, why the race that
produced the Old Testament should have been chosen to prepare
the way for Christ. He finds the answer in the resolute monotheism of Israel, and in the combination in its idea of God of
qualities such as justice and mercy, which in men might seem

incompatible one with another. From these ideas great influences flowed forth. No relationship or activity of life remained unaffected.

But the Old Testament is more than a compendium of moral rules, it is a record of God's revelation (apparently understood as higher religious insight) to Israel. That revelation possesses a unity and completeness not found elsewhere. We cannot imagine any other nation in which our Lord Jesus Christ could have proclaimed His gospel with equal immediate effect. This revelation was a continuous one. It is impossible, however, to understand the Old Testament without studying the history of the people among whom it took shape; for the members of Israel were interpreters of the national history in the light of their belief in Jehovah. If, as they believed, God's mind could be known from what was then happening, it was evident that it must also have been revealed in the events of the past. That gave the history of the past a very great interest.

Kennett then describes various ways in which the teachers and prophets of Israel reflected on the events of the past. He points out, too, that universalism and individualism are attained in the high-water marks of their thinking; and individualism has produced a faith which can move mountains and suffer martyrdom. Though the immortality idea was not fully attained in the Old Testament, Jesus drew the natural inference from the highest teaching of that book when He deduced from Ex. 3: 2 "He is not the God of the dead but of the living". (Mark 12: 27). Finally, the Christian Church owes a great debt to Israel for providing a pattern of worship for us in the hymns and prayers of the Old Testament.

In the last paper of the same collection of essays, G. H. Box deals with the indebtedness of the New Testament to the Old Testament.[5] He finds it necessary to protest against a misguided policy, urged by some, of eliminating the Old Testament from popular religious teaching. He admits that there is much that is fresh and novel in the New Testament, but insists that much that is old is inextricably interwoven with the new elements. The influence, he grants, came via the Septuagint. In speaking of Paul he holds that his thought "was fundamentally Jewish—not Hellenic or Hellenized in any deep sense—and his great ideas go back to the Old Testament. He does, it is true, use Stoic terms and, to some extent, the terminology of the mystery religions; but in all such cases the language is charged with new meaning and content. The determinative element is Jewish." In fine, he sees the New Testament standing in a single line of development with the Old. And here he stresses the fact that it continues Old Testament prophecy, instead of linking up with contemporary Rabbinic Judaism. The criticism of the Old Testament, he acknowledges, by rediscovering that great literature for us, has enabled us to see more clearly than was possible formerly how the New Testament really expresses and emphasizes at their true value the most vital elements of the religion of Israel.

In another British symposium arranged by Jewish scholars, the emphasis is not so much on the Old Testament as on the Jewish nationality. Nevertheless the Old Testament stands in the background all the time. The essay of G. Adam Smith on "The Hebrew Genius as exhibited in the Old Testament" cannot do more than point out the literary and religious heights attained in that literature.[6] Burkitt's contribution on the debt of Christianity to Judaism strives to approach its theme by first clarifying what parts of Christianity are derived from other than Jewish sources.[7] He finds that English Christianity evolved in a Judaizing direction after separation from Catholicism. In the latter, the hierarchy, the creeds, the sacraments are linked with the imperial Roman and the Greek heritages. But there is still much left that was of Jewish descent—notably Jesus and the Bible. This was, and is, an ineradicable and inseparable element. Burkitt finds Reformed Protestantism to have been most deeply influenced by the Old Testament by virtue of a conscious antiquarianism. But there is one point in which all forms of Christianity have been influenced—the view dominating Judaism of a divine purpose manifested in time. Reality, in this view, is a grand drama. Right or wrong, wise or foolish, it is part of the debt of Christianity to Judaism (really to the Old Testament). The noble epilogue of the Jewish scholar, Montefiore,[8] points out that for these Christian contributors "Israel" might as well be dead—their detachment is complete. Asserting, then, that Israel is still alive, he asks whether its contribution to humanity is totally a thing of the past or whether it is still capable of giving. He finds the Jewish conception of God and His relation to man, and the Jewish conception of the relation of religion to morality, akin to but not quite identical with the Christian, and able to complement the latter to the benefit of mankind. Indirectly this becomes a plea for the value of the Old Testament heritage for Christianity and to that extent deserves mention here.

Prominent among those in England who thought much about the biblical question was A. S. Peake.[9] He discussed its "permanent value" in lectures of exemplary clarity. He sees it is a real problem why the Old Testament, the book of an earlier order, should stand side by side with the religious book of Christianity. The expedients used by former generations to meet the difficulty are no longer possible for us. We cannot use the Old Testament and the New Testament to make a composite amalgam of doctrine. We must take the Old Testament for what it is and must see whether we can vindicate for it its position alongside the New. He concedes that it is no easy task, but thinks that if we will only put ourselves at the proper point of view we will accord the Old Testament an inalienable right to be considered part of our Christian Scripture.

With a surprising paradox Peake then argues that the fact that the Old Testament is imperfect is the very reason why we want to keep it in the Bible. Before pursuing that point, however, he speaks of other things that make the Old Testament seem valuable. The social reformer, for instance, finds it precious —the more because the New Testament dwells very little on problems of that kind. "Principles are expressed in the New Testament more universal and deeper and more inward than the principles which were expressed in the Old; but the application to the social and economic conditions, to question of politics, are not made in the New Testament in the same way in which they are made in the Old." Then he dwells on the literary excellencies of the Old Testament. To that class of readers who think the Old Testament primarily gives us the revelation of truths which we could not otherwise have discovered he points out that there are other values besides the intellectual. There is the emotional value which gives the Bible much of its power over the hearts of men. Illustrating with a church hymn how we are stirred by words that *per se* are mythological, he states that the Old Testament moves us in the

same way when we find language in it that we may not be able
to work into our scheme of theology and which does not lend
itself to the scientific statement of doctrine, but that touches us
at the elemental bases of our being. Just as Jesus Christ was
greater than anything He said, so the religious experience of the
Old Testament is greater than any verbal expression of it could
be.

Peake then speaks disapprovingly of the older attitude towards the Bible and the Old Testament in particular as being
"too atomistic". We must radically break with this way of
looking at Scripture. When we are talking about the Old
Testament as revelation it is the Old Testament as a whole that
is meant. It is true that this view has its difficulties. While
there are many passages that have a self-evidencing divine
quality to anyone with spiritual insight, there are also long
passages which do not speak to our soul at all. The tendency
then is to say that these things should not be there. And the
matter is even worsened when we find sections that are a contradiction and a negation of what is dearest to us in the gospel,
and indeed of much which we find in the Old Testament itself.
Nevertheless, Peake wants to form a theory that will accept the
whole Old Testament as it stands, for what it is and what it
really means to be.

He holds that we must look at the Old Testament as the
record of an exceptional movement of the Divine Spirit upon a
chosen and a guided people, taking them at a low level and
gradually leading them to a higher level until it becomes
possible for them to receive the supreme revelation in God's
only begotten Son. When we see this, we no longer come to the
Old Testament with illegitimate demands on it. If revelation
is a process which comes through history we can understand
revelation only as we know the history, and in this we find the
meaning for very much in the Old Testament that in our first
impatience we might have been tempted to cast aside as
irrelevant. Even the imperfect or definitely false things found
there are not useless. For it was necessary for us that we should
see not only the light side but also the dark. Unless we have
them all and can paint them all into the single picture of the
history of revelation we have not rightly understood the Old
Testament. In this way Peake vindicates the paradox state-

ment referred to above. The objection of those who say that, when all is said and done, the Old Testament represents a stage of religion that is superseded, is answered by the arguments that it gives us the only key to the understanding of the New Testament and that Jesus appealed to its authority.

The arrival of the 'thirties brought a fresh outpouring of literature on our subject in Germany. Among those who spoke up was Meinhold.[10] After portraying the situation of the time in which rising anti-Semitism went hand in hand with demands for abolition of the Old Testament from Christian use the author addresses himself to the question: can the Old Testament be taken away from Christianity without its suffering harm from the loss, or is the harm greater if it adheres to the Old Testament? If we would keep the Old Testament must not the use be selective and must not even that which is selected frequently be reinterpreted along Christian lines?

Meinhold then paves the way for further discussion by showing how Old Testament scholarship has liberated us from the nightmare of verbal inspiration, which a false theory of the origin of the canon first laid upon the Synagogue and then upon the Christian Church. Describing the origin of the Old Testament sacred collection, he concludes that the historical process is entirely a matter for scholarly study. The viewpoints which led the synagogue to accept or reject this or that document, in so far as we can determine them, are not binding for us. One may well hold with Luther that some rejected writings might with more justice have been taken into the canon than some which were accepted and are now included—that is if one still cares at all about a term such as "canonical", which originated in dogmatic thinking, and will not simply use it as a designation for the collection made by the Synagogue and Church.

Meinhold then discusses the limitations of the Old Testament. Rejecting all *a priori* dogmatic assertions about inspiration, he urges that the Protestant Christian must follow his conscience and first discern the real nature of the Hebrew religion. He describes it as a national religion and gives an account of various phases of it in the light of modern Old Testament scholarship.

In the final part of the book, however, Meinhold tackles the question of whether one can still speak of a significance of the Old Testament for theology and the Church in the light of such a historical study of the materials. He gives an affirmative answer and then proceeds to justify it with the progressive revelation philosophy (revelation understood as addressed to the intellect). If there is a God for us it can only be one who revealed Himself. It is difficult to see how else He could have revealed Himself except in a national religion. Israel claims that God revealed Himself to it and that it received Him into its heart and soul. The Old Testament is the record of this revelation of God. History seems to prove that this was no illusion, for we still are experiencing the after-effects of this consciousness of Israel through the medium of Christianity; and history knows of hardly any illusions that are operative for millennia.

He then traces the current of ethical religion, as represented in the prophetic and wisdom movements, through the Old Testament and up to Jesus of Nazareth. In Him he finds the conclusion and therewith the end of the religion of Israel. He combined the roles of prophet and sage perfectly and finally in His person. If the Primitive Church sought to prove Jesus the Messiah, this need not greatly concern us—it is merely a token of its inability to get away from Jewish presuppositions. For us Jesus is rather the "saviour" and "redeemer", as the Gentiles, taking terms offered by their own tradition, preferred to view Him. The religious mission of Israel ended with the rise of Christianity, so that it no longer makes sense to regard the Jews to-day as the chosen people. But the Old Testament as well as the New Testament remain documents reflecting the history of the divine self-revelation. They are not the Word of God as such, but they contain it and we have it through them.

In his concluding pages Meinhold discusses the problem whether the plain and unlearned Christian can still use the Old Testament as Holy Scripture. He who has been educated in the study of the Hebrew Scriptures in their original tongue and in accordance with modern scholarship can be expected to use the Old Testament with discretion. It is different with those who have not had this advantage. That the unlearned have in the past derived great stimulation from the Old Testament is revealed by the story of Pietism. But at the same time this use of it by the unenlightened causes all manner of confusion. It is quite true that we must bear with the weaker brethren, as Paul says (Rom. 14: 1), but at the same time we cannot suffer them to rule us with their pretensions. Of such a nature is insistence by the untutored on the whole of Scripture as gospel truth. Here Paul's admonition to his converts not to become entangled again in the yoke of bondage which the Judaizers would foist upon them (Gal. 5: 1), is apropos. Meinhold's thought is that the selective attitude toward the Old Testament taken by Jesus —about which he had already written in 1896 in a manner to provoke ecclesiastical protest—should be a model for us. He finds the Primitive Church sometimes failing to live up to that example; thus, if a series of sayings of Jesus was put together redactionally into a "Sermon on the Mount" (Matt. 5–7), with the implication that He was a new law-giver like Moses, this was contrary to the spirit of Christ, who was not the bringer of a new yoke and who even replaced the Decalogue with the twin commandments of Deut. 6: 5 and Lev. 19: 18 (which really are no commandments at all, since love cannot be commanded), thereby giving us a yardstick for the right use of the Old Testament. Jesus was not so much concerned with the correction of external actions, as with improving the inward attitude, from which right actions then will flow forth. The God He found in the Old Testament was the one whose voice He heard in his own heart. And so we, too, can find the God and Father of our Lord Jesus Christ in the Old Testament, if we read it with Christian eyes and use it in a Christian sense. Jesus and the Old Testament on its higher levels are in concord in many things. The Old Testament, he notes, affords a protection against a false asceticsm, such as crept into Christianity at a very early date, and has an appreciation of nature and of natural things that is most excellent. Recalling the way in which Paul emancipated Christianity from the Jewish nationality Meinhold emphasizes the universality of Christianity as a way of redemption for all men, and rejects slogans arising from the lunatic anti-Semitic fringe that was becoming so vociferous during the years in which he was writing.

But alongside the apologetic directed against the detractors of the Old Testament in the German scene there was also the problem of the theological position of the Old Testament as raised by the Dialectic theology. While among Old Testament scholars there was as yet no one to participate directly in this approach, a need for some positive attitude on the subject was felt even by those who had been wont to think of this literature chiefly in historical terms.

Thus we find Hempel touching on the problem in the conclusion of a fine study on the Old Testament and History.[11] After describing the distinctive nature of Old Testament piety he raises the question: can a religion of such characteristic stamp, bound with a thousand threads to earlier and contemporary Near Eastern religions, claim to be the religion of revelation? How can a temporal entity be something of eternal value, the beginning of a kingdom of God?

After dwelling on the nature of history, which never repeats itself, and viewing it theistically as governed by God, he sees divine revelation as the working of God in a particular, concrete situation with human beings of peculiar sociological and cultural structure and with all the limitations of mind and outlook that that implies. It is thus not to be expected that Old Testament prophecy should be infallibly true as to coming events, or that Old Testament ideas of the past history should be absolutely reliable. The legalistic character of the Old Testament in its contrast to the New Testament order of grace is not as insurmountable an obstacle as is sometimes thought, for every revelation of the divine will, being an attempt to win man, in the last analysis partakes of the character of grace. So the law, too, has an aspect of grace. The real difficulty lies in the assertion that the Old Testament testifies to a portion of a history of redemption as such. If the actual facts of the divine revelation are often submerged beyond recovery, then the document purporting to tell of such divine action has a value only in so far as it can claim to be a paradigm of how God acts again and again. But since the action of God is not primarily symbolical but rather directed toward a particular situation, this necessary imperfection of the record cannot refute the fact of the divine action itself. He finds that the latter, whatever its true nature may have been, remains tangible in its effects.

But here the doubts from a comparative religious angle claim Hempel's attention. We find similar ideas and conceptions outside of Israel: have we divine influence in the one case and not in the other? Hempel sides with a liberal view here, basing it on the ancient ecclesiastical doctrine of the *logos spermatikos*. But that does not annul the claim of the Old Testament to be the record of a special revelatory activity and history of redemption. He finds that claim seriously threatened, however, where the Old Testament ideas of faith cannot be ours and do not have the internal testimony of the Holy Spirit in their favour. He hesitates to make limited individual experience the measuring-rod, but he concedes that portions of Scripture have lost their ability to convince us of their being actually a Word of God. We have no yardstick for judging whether a thing was *once* the Word of God, if it is not Word of God for us *now*. A certain amount of help is afforded by the thought of a divine pedagogy, but only as an intellectual possibility—not as a certainty of special revelation. One of the great theological tasks of the future, he holds, in conclusion, is to establish a theological basis for the scriptural canon. In connection there-with the question of the relation of the Old Testament to the New Testament will have to play a special role. One will have seriously to apply the idea of the actuality of the divine activity, and avoid all softening up of exact, historical exegesis by Christianizing procedures. But we have no other criterion validating a Word of the past than the testimony of the Holy Spirit. Since we can experience it as Jesus did, we have a right to hold to the unity of the history of redemption and to the belief that God's dealing with Israel forms a part of that history and to sense in it the secret stirring of the spirit of Jesus Christ.

In 1933 Hempel discussed the religious value of the Old Testament.[12] According to him our task to-day in connection with the Old Testament is fixed by the fact that we have such a vast increase of comparative religious material on the one hand and new tools of psychological analysis on the other hand. Our first duty is to find the place of the Old Testament in the development of the religious life of mankind. The second, to understand the special character of Old Testament piety in its finest emotions. He confines himself in this connection to the second of these objectives. The peculiarity of Old Testament piety, he asserts, consists in the realism of its faith. It knows a real God who is active in a real world with its differences and troubles. He then elaborates on the Old Testament idea of God and on the faith which the people of the Old Testament placed in Him. The last word in this Old Testament realism of faith, embracing as it does a realistic view of God, of the world and of sin, is the word "forgiveness". God rules over His own anger, while man is inclined to vengeance (Ps. 103: 9). The Old Testament shows God to be one to whom we can pray: "Forgive us our trespasses."

But we may interrupt here the parade of biblical scholars to let a leading representative of the Dialectic theology, Brunner, tell us how he regards the Old Testament problem.[13] He asserts boldly that the understanding of the Word of God of the Old Testament is decisive for the understanding of the Word of God of the New Testament. In elaborating on that thesis—which reminds one of the teaching of Ritschl—he first shows that the New Testament alone provides a dangerous temptation in the direction of Hellenizing religion. We can see the peril of a conflation of the gospel with Greek abstract thinking illustrated in the case of the great idealistic philosophy, for instance when Fichte makes the Son of God an eternal idea on the basis of the *logos* of John's Gospel.

The normal road for the right understanding of the New Testament, according to Brunner, leads through the Old Testament. He then lists a number of ideas that occur in that manner only in the Old Testament but without which the New Testament is not comprehensible.

(1) There is the idea of Creation and the Creator. The New Testament hardly refers to this at all; it takes it for granted. But we must note how the Old Testament speaks of the Creator. The Creator is He who revealed Himself as Lord of His people Israel. Theology is revealed theology, not Natural theology. Outside of this revelation God is unknown to His people. The world is not like Him and He is not like the world. Hence "thou shalt make thee no image or likeness". God and the world are to be absolutely differentiated. One must come from Isaiah in order to understand the harshness of the statement that God became man.[14] One only knows this God through revelation, not from the world. And one only has this God through election and grace, not by nature. Israel had Him only because God chose to reveal Himself. He is, furthermore, a God who can reject His chosen instrument. He has revealed

Himself in a particular area of history and through persons who proclaim His Word. Therein He is recognized as personal God. For revelation is always given to definite persons at a definite moment.

(2) There is the role of the divine law. God is a voluntaristic God. He wants to take my will captive and bind my existence to Himself. His call can only be answered by life and action. Brunner at this point engages in a polemic against those who find the Old Testament prophets emphasizing an abstract moral law. He points out that they know nothing of a moral law based on reason. They know only of the divine commands, which on occasion may go contrary to what the moral law that proceeds from reason seems to require. He thinks that Luther fell into a grievous error when he identified Old Testament law and general moral law—Calvin adhered more closely to the Old Testament spirit here. Nevertheless, he credits Luther with having made an important contribution in differentiating between legalism and faith. God is not first of all a God who makes demands on man. He gives before He asks. His requirement is that one permit Him to give what He chooses. The very meaning of the law is expressed in the command: "Ye shall be My people"—words that imply a privilege given by God to man. Thus God's holiness can not be separated from His love and mercy. In the Old Testament alone this fusion is found.

(3) The covenant of God with Israel is focused on a goal. It is no stabilization of a *status quo*. The Old Testament is eschatological. God is going to come to His people in a different manner. The message of judgment is an essential presupposition for the understanding of the New Testament religion. One must first know the fear of being lost before one is receptive for redemption. The Old Testament performs an indispensable service here; without it the idea of the love of God is in danger of becoming mere sentimentality. Hebrew eschatology stands in a sharp contrast to Greek thinking for which redemption is apt to become a denial of the world and to lead to asceticism. In eschatology God chooses to bring the world closer to Himself again. The Old Testament is full of the idea of the coming kingdom. The present receives a vast importance in the light of the End. And this Old Testament eschatology is one that takes a positive attitude toward the world. It is so realistic

that at times it seems as though it were an inner, worldly goal that is envisioned. But one must approach the New Testament hope from that Old Testament background, he says, and understand that for Christianity, too, the world is not to be dissolved but rendered perfect.

(4) With this eschatological realism is associated the social viewpoint. God is concerned with the group and with the individuals in so far as they are members of this people. His will is directed toward a fellowship. Old Testament ethic is social ethics. One sins not against oneself but against one's neighbour. The highest good is not ascetic purity but correct conduct toward one's brother. Hence, the Old Testament has an unparalleled drive in its idea of the religious community: that the righteousness of God is to be realized in such a community is paramount. God and one's neighbour belong together. The Old Testament knows of no private relationship with God; there are no individual lone spirits that stand forth in solitary greatness. The prophets are not to be classed as such; their concern is not for their own salvation. That which the God of the Old Testament wishes to bring about is a public thing. It is from this Old Testament angle that we must see the New Testament eschatology.

In all these particulars, Brunner concludes, the Old Testament is the beginning of the New. It is not replaced but fulfilled; through Jesus Christ prophecy begins to become fulfilment.[14]

The spirit of von Hofmann and his *Heilsgeschichte* comes up again in the thought of Procksch. Of his impressive book on Old Testament theology we shall make some mention later. In an essay of 1931 he dealt with the significance of the Old Testament for the Church.[15] He correlates the two entities—both are born out of the Spirit of God and are thus "pneumatic organisms"; the one is the Word of God congealed into Scripture, the other the people of God born in history. But the Word of God is the cause, the people of God or the Church the effect. Procksch first sets forth the dependence of the Church on the Old Testament in the very roots of its existence. Jesus, he says, by being bound to Old Testament thinking forces the Old Testament upon the Church. He does not stand apart from the

Church, but is its Prophet, Priest and King. Procksch sees Jerusalem as the symbolic centre of the history of the Church. The latter must always keep its eyes turned in that direction if it would not lose sight of its goal. This implies a connection with Israel. The Church must never forget that in worshipping the Father of Jesus Christ it is at the same time invoking the God of Abraham and Moses. In its prayers it will never be able to emancipate itself from the language of the Psalms. The history of Israel and the history of the Church are undergirded by the same forces of revelation that manifested themselves in the great heroes of the faith of the Old and New Covenants.

Procksch then discusses the dependence of the Church on the Old Testament in its social relations. The Church has a relation to the nation, but the theme of king and prophet in the Old Testament shows what stresses and strains may occur in this relationship. The question of the relation of the Church to the Jewish people and religion, too, comes up; he thinks that it is only soluble for the Church on an Old Testament basis.

In the third part of his article Procksch describes the Church's dependence on the Old Testament in theology. Every theological concept, he declares, (in apparent agreement with Ritschl), must have a Hebrew basis or it is none. Dame Theology is a Hebrew, not only in vocabulary but in spirit. He then proceeds to illustrate this by examining a number of such concepts. In fine, to pull Christianity away from the Old Testament is to drag it from its historical moorings and can lead only to gnosticism or rationalism. The Old Testament is the regulator of the historical nature of Christian thought and the thing upon which the latter's health and fruitfulness depend.

Procksch was much taken with Girgensohn's idea of the desirability of having a more spiritual type of exegesis developed to supplement the historical critical.[16] He saw, however, that it would be virtually impossible to carry this through for large sections of the Old Testament and so suggested particular emphasis on those areas in which the spiritual element actually comes to the surface.

Another scholar who was prone to think theologically about the Old Testament was Hänel.[17]

He starts with the assertion that the faith of the Church holds that we have the Word of God in the Old Testament as in the

New Testament. But he sees a real need for re-examining this belief in view of the fact that modern interpretation is forced to apply a method to Scripture study which has nothing to do with its normative use and even relegates the latter to the background. The handmaiden, historical criticism, nowadays has usurped the place of the mistress, theology. The Church must regard that situation as unsatisfactory. Furthermore, certain valid results have been attained by this scientific method which are extremely disquieting. For one thing the belief in verbal inspiration, on which our forefathers primarily based their doctrine of Scripture authority, has been made impossible. For another thing, the identity of the two Testaments, which seemed so vital a prop for maintaining the authority of the Old Testament, is not easy to defend. The latter work cannot be viewed as on one religious and moral plane, but exhibits different strata, higher and lower. The widespread realization of this special situation is reflected in the fact that nobody to-day undertakes to present the theology of the Old Testament in a systematized form, but that the usual thing is to describe the religion of the Old Testament in its historical development.

Hänel then inquires whether the fall of the doctrine of inspiration actually makes it impossible to believe in the divine character of Scripture. He points out that when this doctrine was at its height it came to be overshadowed by another that really made it superfluous and that remained as a firm support when the other fell: that of the internal testimony of the Holy Spirit. Notably Lutheranism, which combined the material principle (justification by faith) with the formal principle (Scripture authority), was able to employ this doctrine of the internal testimony of the Holy Spirit in such a way as to uphold the authority of the central element of scriptural content. But Hänel holds that revelation has a larger scope than the belief in Justification. The thing common to all revelation, he argues, is the manifestation of the holiness of God and of the absolute contrast between the divine and the human, which reaches its high-water mark at the point where God does the seemingly impossible and regards the sinner as righteous for the sake of Christ. With respect to God's holiness, Hänel feels that he is utilizing the Reformed emphasis on the majesty of God which amounts to the same thing. It is for the sake of the testimony of the Spirit, given in the revelation of the holiness of God, that Scripture which mediates this revelation proves itself to be the Word of God. The Church, he thinks, has rightly held fast to this truth brought forward by orthodoxy.

But Hänel finds it desirable, owing to the fact that many other religions beside Christianity have entered our field of vision, to attempt to reach this same certainty by another route. While reason has been sorely discredited, owing to the speculative excesses of a former era, he regards it as not out of place to reflect rationally on this matter after the manner suggested by the dictum of Anselm, *credo ut intelligam*, "I believe that I may know." His starting-point is the definition of the nature of the Old Testament. While this work is a complex product of various groups of materials, these all have this in common that they are governed by the idea of the divine holiness, though in various shades of import. The most primitive stratum looks on this holiness primarily as unapproachability (I Sam. 6: 20). Another, perhaps representative of the patriarchal era, looks upon it as exaltedness (cf. Gen. 28: 17). A third, perhaps beginning in the Mosaic era, regards it as zealousness (Josh. 24: 19). The climax is attained in prophecy, where Yahweh's holiness is glory (Is. 6: 3) or perfection. Jesus links up with this stage, directly substituting the perfection concept for the holiness concept (Lev. 19: 2; Matt. 5: 48). Post-exilic Judaism viewed the divine holiness primarily as transcendence, as remoteness from this profane sphere (cf. Ps. 11: 4).

Hänel then points out that the concept of holiness is not confined to the Old and New Testaments but occurs in all religions, yea, (in dependence on Otto's famous book), is the very essence of religion; it is the *logos spermatikos* that is embedded in every religion. At the same time, however, this idea is very much corrupted in religions outside of the Old and New Testament sphere. The emphasis on the unholy or unclean is almost as important in the extra-biblical religions as that of the holy, and the latter is applied more to men and things than to deities. Mysticism, too, in its original form, disregards the contrast between human and divine; it therein reflects a lack of appreciation for the holiness of God and reveals its pagan origin. The moral decadence so commonly associated with heathen cults is a proof of a low status of the experience of holiness. From this angle of its higher conception of holiness, Hänel argues for the uniqueness of the Old Testament religion over against all others, and takes that for a proof, sufficiently satisfying to the mind of the believer, that in this religion alone of all pre-Christian ones God truly revealed Himself. In pursuing this line of reasoning Hänel is following the course recommended by Troeltsch, of setting forth the superiority of Christianity over all other religions by comparative analysis.

From the point thus reached Hänel proceeds to inquire how we can imagine the divine influence to have brought it about that the books of the Old Testament became Word of God. He makes light of the importance of any theory on that subject— the character of the Old Testament as belonging to revelation is fixed for us without any such theory. We can either stress the idea of the inspiration of persons, with the Holy Spirit awakening important religious thoughts in them, or we can imagine the Spirit as so organizing the individual religious constitution that it will guide the religious author aright in whatever he has to do for God's purposes. Such a theory must also take due consideration of the fact that the books of the Old Testament have a complicated history, and must regard their evolution to final shape as also having taken place under the workings of the Spirit of God.

Going back to the revelation that precedes the literary process, as experienced by the personalities of prophets and others, Hänel asserts that this, too, is a matter of secondary importance —that the Old Testament is Word of God is fixed for us without any results of such investigation. He concedes that not all of the numerous ideas of revelation found in the Old Testament can be utilized. Who would wish to employ the theophany idea found in the primeval and patriarchal histories, or the notion of obtaining divine oracles through use of the Urim and Thummim? More importance may be attached to prophetic visions and auditions, and the thought of actual inspiration may have to be given more weight in that connection. But we stand on even firmer ground, he thinks, where faith and history meet. We can see how the whole Old Testament religion is dominated by the revelation experienced at the Exodus, and how other historical events are understood as having been brought about by God's government. Revelation comes into being here in that God offers His manifestation of Himself in the extraordinary events of history, on the one hand, and on the other hand in creating the prophetic interpreter who understands and gives the authoritative interpretation of these events (Rothe's manifestation and inspiration). In this interpenetration of divinely wrought history, in which God speaks, and of mightiest faith, which He Himself awakens, the foundations of the temple of the Old Testament, in which God's Word is proclaimed to us, were reared.

Hänel next discusses the topic of the unity of the Word of God in the two Testaments, for he asserts it is a desideratum that such unity exist, if the Old Testament is to be considered Word of God. As an Old Testament scholar of rank, he cannot endorse attempts to Christianize the Old Testament by artificial devices. Even though the God of the Old Testament is our God, it does not follow that He already gave the salvation that was to come through Christ to the Hebrew people. His pedagogy could envision other temporary goals. Nevertheless, Hänel would equally reject the over-emphasis on the differences between the two orders. In spite of all that is bygone in the older one there is an identity of the Testaments which cannot be explained away. It is not true that the Old Testament is only law and the New Testament only gospel. Nor is the Old Testament only prophecy and the New Testament only fulfilment. It is not enough to think of the Old Testament in terms of the clues it gives for the understanding of the New Testament concepts.

Before setting forth the relationship of the two Testaments more precisely one must duly appreciate the majesty of the New Testament revelation. It may be measured first of all by the contrast with the inadequate and primitive ideas found in the Old Testament; but it can also be seen over against those very elements of the Old Testament which represent the latter's high-water mark and for the sake of which one must speak of the unity of the Testaments. We may, for instance, consider the basic shift in emphasis on certain ideas in the two areas. In the New Testament the idea of divine love, as the most exalted expression of the divine holiness, moves into the centre. The Old Testament, too, has penetrated to a knowledge of the divine love, but it is only one insight alongside of others there, and does not hold the centre of the stage. The difference between the two Testaments culminates in the person and work of Christ; for in the Old Testament Messianism is confined to prophetic insights and thoughts, whereas in the New Testament there is the living experience of Jesus the Christ. But in spite of all changes in emphases Hänel would hold fast to the idea of a unity of the Testaments.

There is one sphere in the Old Testament that is a worthy counterpart of the New Testament—that of prophetic religion— or, if one chose to abide by differentiation on the basis of ideas, the area in which the divine holiness is understood as perfection. Here the ideas of prevenient grace and of the failure of the law as way of salvation, as well as the belief in free grace and in vicarious sacrifice, are to be found. Notably Deutero-Isaiah, Jeremiah, Ezekiel, and the Psalms provide material for this insight. If one proceeds from a New Testament basis to consider sin and grace, righteousness and faith in the Old Testament, one can likewise illustrate the approximation of many Old Testament passages to the New Testament level. Indeed, Hänel declares that there is no insight of a basic nature in the New Testament for which an Old Testament counterpart cannot be found. The connection between the two Testaments is not merely genetic. With all due concessions to the distinctive position to be accorded the New Testament we must assert that within the Old Testament there is a world that is substantially identical with that of the New Testament.

In his final section Hänel discusses the unity of the Word of God in the Old Testament. The Old Testament as a whole claims to be authoritative. How can this claim be reconciled with the fact that it contains in itself higher and lower levels of religion? The author rejects the idea of smoothing this over by allegorization. Historical-critical exegesis alone can tell us what a passage means. But he believes that one must proceed from the historico-critical basis to further reflections in the light of a belief in the fundamental unity. One way would be to seek at every point the relationship of a passage to what Hänel believes to be the basic motif of Old Testament religion—the idea of holiness of God. Another way would be always to bear in mind the goal toward which revelation tended and to illuminate every step of the path it took in the light of that goal. He thinks the interpretative method used by Jesus in the Sermon on the Mount stands close to such a procedure, and even sees a value in the New Testament typological interpretation which is to be differentiated from allegorization. To view the Old Testament from a New Testament angle is the culminating function of Old Testament exegesis. We can only do justice to the task, however, if we see it from the angle of the whole Christ—not merely in the light of His person and work, but also of His words and ideas within which they are centred.

The fateful year 1933 saw the ascendancy of National Socialism in Germany.

The crisis that arose for the Church under the pressure of the new political régime from without and the elements from within disposed to co-operate in the idea of creating a truly national type of Christianity that was purged of the Semitic ideas, is well reflected in the contribution of Herntrich, who took his stand with the conservative churchmen.[18]

He insists that religions are born, not made. To manufacture a national religion by setting up some collection of Nordic religious texts to replace the Old Testament, as had been suggested, is not feasible; the old Teutonic religion is little known, remote and dismal. Analysing the motives behind the opposition to the Old Testament he finds that at their root lies an idolatry, a setting up of the nation as an idol. A belief in the idea that man can redeem himself by his own efforts is likewise operative. These things constitute rebellion against the sovereignty of God. The message of the Old Testament God, who demands our submission to His will in consciousness of our guilt, is the one we need to hear. There is nothing Jewish about that message, because the Old Testament shows that the Hebrew people were in constant opposition to this God whom the prophets proclaimed. To attempt to set up a new national religion to-day would involve doing away with final moral standards and leaving the peoples of the earth to follow their lower impulses unchecked. Of what help could national gods be, whose power ends at the boundary lines? All ethical experience of God depends on the idea that He is present and active everywhere and that all men are responsible to Him. Differentiating between faith and piety, Herntrich asserted that while there can be various national types of the latter there can only be one Christian faith, because there is only one Christ. Influenced by the Dialectic theology at this point he stresses the Incarnation; this belief implies that God revealed Himself in a definite nationality at a definite moment; there is no getting away from it—Jesus was a Jew according to the flesh. But at the same time he was conceived by the Holy Ghost, and that signifies that He is not just a Jewish man, but transcends that nationality, and brings salvation to all men. With Barthian eyes he sees the Incarnation idea basically operative in the Old Testament order; there, too, the Word (in the sense of revelation) became flesh. It was incarnate in the history and life of the Hebrew people, amid all the limitations their condition and circumstances imply.

After rejecting the doctrine of verbal inspiration which the opponents subtly fasten on the Church and then make the basis for ridiculing this or that biblical statement, Herntrich asks why the link between the Church and the Old Testament must be held inseparable? He concedes that if Jesus Christ is the full and perfect revelation of God that would seem to obviate the necessity of our clinging to that older order. But he finds a basis for it in the thought that there was a history of redemption and that Christ is not separable from the divine plan of which He was the culmination. However, we must carefully differentiate between the various stages of development in this history. Even the earlier stages are not without their lessons. Once we realize that God acted in history and revealed Himself in a particular time and place we can read the Old Testament with eyes opened to its importance. He stresses what the modern nationalists could learn from an Isaiah or a Jeremiah. The awareness of human depravity that these prophets had shows that they were realists, while those who ridicule this attitude are blind to reality. Nations to-day do not want to hear the truth any more than the Jews of old did, but God rudely breaks into our history with His Word—His promise as well as His threat.

In closing, Herntrich stresses the need of properly relating the idea of the nation as a divinely willed entity to a Christian universalism that knows no race or colour. The misunderstandings that arise between the nations are to be viewed as due to sin and in their consequences partake of the nature of divine punishments. The old story of the Tower of Babel already reflects this insight, but the sequel to that also shows how God prepared a way of salvation leading out of that situation through a particular line of His choice. The Christian Church is the continuation of that line into the present and future.

Soon afterward we find three Old Testament scholars of high rank, Alt, Begrich and von Rad, publishing lectures given by them, in which they sought to show how the Old Testament tended to lead men to Christianity—a service it had always performed and could continue to perform.[19]

Alt's introductory general discussion first defends the Old Testament against the virulent anti-Semitic book of Th. Fritsch, which at that time was receiving renewed attention, and then goes over to a positive presentation of the uniqueness of the Hebrew religion, culminating with the philosophy of history in which the Yahwistic writer of Genesis views Israel's destiny as bringing blessing to all peoples and thus as not an end in itself but bound up with the greater purposes of God.

Begrich discusses the prophets. After developing matters of an essentially historical nature opening the proper perspective on these figures, he asks whether the words of the prophets that grip us do not really confront us with the living God. He then stresses Jesus' approval of the prophets and their being an inalienable part of His message. The prophetic line of the Old Testament thought, he says, only reaches its fulfilment and fruition in the New Testament. But it remains the presupposition without which the message of the God of love and reconciliation is not comprehensible. We must avail ourselves of the Old Testament anew as living Word of the God and Father of the Lord Jesus Christ.

Von Rad, in conclusion, then sketches the Hebrew religious development in such a way as to show how there was an advance in insight, in the course of time, involving correction of earlier Hebrew dogmas, and how the whole heritage, preserved in the canon, was available for Jews and Christians in the first century A.D. Each group now claimed that this heritage belonged to itself alone. The rival claims still endure to the present, as the example of Martin Buber on the Jewish side, who denies that Christians have any right to the Old Testament, shows. Von

Rad finds this question decided by the answer given to the other: whether Jesus was the Christ. If the Church were mistaken in this its assertion, then all Christian claim on the Old Testament would fall to the ground. In the measure that we take offence at Jesus the Christ we also take offence at the Old Testament. While we cannot see God in the Old Testament or anywhere else, as the instance of Moses in Ex. 33: 18 f. reveals, we can hear in it the Word of God's grace, and in studying its pages we can see "His back parts" in that unique road on which he led His people Israel through history. This is all professional apologetic on a high level with slants and sidelights that will refresh the Old Testament student.

In 1934 there also appeared a book which in many respects crowned the whole German literary critical movement that began with Wellhausen—Eissfeldt's *Einleitung*.[20] Since the author in a concluding section speaks of the effect the Old Testament has had on mankind we may here develop his standpoint, not only in the light of what he says in that chapter but of other utterances.

Already in 1921, in a study in honour of Harnack, he had registered his opinion that the Old Testament is too deeply ingrown in Christendom to be uprooted and had pointed to certain values that the Old Testament has contributed to our religion. In the book mentioned he speaks of it as having been an object of the most intensive study on the part of both Jewish and Christian scholarship, due to the fact that it is a source of religious life to both communities and—however that may be justified or qualified—a norm for faith and conduct. Scholarship, however, not only receives its interest in it from this circumstance, it in turn helps these Faiths to understand the Old Testament in a more realistic manner. Christian and Jewish scholars can co-operate, learning from each other, up to the point where the ultimate spiritual content of this book comes up for consideration. Here there is a parting of the ways. We thus continue the struggle that began when early Christianity appropriated the Old Testament, and asserted that its promises were for the Church and no longer for the Hebrew people. The influence of the Old Testament will continue in the future in spite of all opposition of the present. Through the fact that Christianity appropriated it the Old Testament was elevated to the rank of a purely spiritual entity, no longer concerned with a particular people and its members, but with nations and men in their relation to God. The way in which those elements in the Old Testament that militate against such spiritualization and generalization were neutralized or brought into line did not remain the same at all times. The New Testament and early ecclesiastical writers used allegory or typology to that end. For us, the historical way of looking at this literature serves the same purpose. In all epochs of its history Christianity has experienced formative influences from the Old Testament, and this is bound to be the case also in the future. The Old Testament played a great role when Christianity came to realize that the end of the world was not as near as the first generations thought and that it was necessary to understand and evaluate properly, from the angle of religion, institutions such as the family and the state which play an essential part in the world of men. For the Old Testament was closely linked with the business of man's living in the world and could show the Christian how he could integrate his higher spiritual existence with life in a human society. Notably the close connection of Old Testament religion with nationality and the state opens the way for Christian appreciation of these entities; at the same time Hebrew prophecy prevents exaggeration of their importance by the polemic of its prophets against that sort of thing. Christian Ethics, furthermore, though it receives its ultimate impulses from the gospel, has up till to-day enjoyed much guidance from the Old Testament and will not be able to dispense with it in the future, least of all in an age when we must rethink the Christian's relation to the world in which he lives. Eissfeldt believes that the influence of the Old Testament is not at an end but rather that a new phase of such influence is beginning.

During the war years Eissfeldt gave utterance to his opinion on the question sometimes asked: whether the God of the Old Testament and the God of the New are the same.[21] While the New Testament writers regard that as a fact, they could have been mistaken. We must discount some of their convictions, e.g., their ideas of cosmology and historical chronology. We cannot, therefore, just accept their belief in this matter either, but must test it in direct approach. He then resolves the question into a twofold one, viz., whether the same idea of God is found in the Old Testament as in the New, and whether the two revelations coincide. The former question can be answered objectively, but the latter involves an inner participation. For revelation and faith are correlates and no generally valid proof can be substituted for faith.

Eissfeldt then compares the ideas of God in the two Testaments. The Old Testament idea represents a long history and may be divided into four stages: the pre-Mosaic, the pre-prophetic (to Elijah), the prophetic and the post-prophetic. He finds that the New Testament idea of God has little kinship with the pre-prophetic (to say nothing of the pre-Mosaic religion about which so little is known), though there is still some survival even in the New Testament of the "numinous" element, as Otto had pointed out. But the prophetic and post-prophetic ideas of God have much more relationship with the New Testament idea. One must take the high-water mark line of Old Testament thinking and compare that with the New Testament thought to perceive their relationship.

Eissfeldt then turns to the second question, as to the two revelations. He sees various answers possible according to the standpoint. He notes that many things that earlier generations found very meaningful in the Old Testament have no appeal for us. He cites as example that of a beloved clergyman whose assistant he once was, who placed a very great valuation on the theme of the Holiness Code of Leviticus: "Ye shall be holy: for I the Lord your God am holy,"—a thing impossible for him. In the days of the First World War, he hints, certain Old Testament passages were greatly appreciated by German people, but now stir them no longer. But then he asks: are there still things in the Old Testament which we can find valuable to-day? This he affirms, and specifies three things: (1) The attitude of individual Old Testament personages towards thoughts about God. (2) Monotheism. (3) Religious poetry and prayers. There is certainly, he believes, a continuity between the Old and New Testament revelations, but there is also tension between them. This leaves him untroubled. He makes an interesting point in the matter of the hurdle we have to take in proceeding from the Old Testament revelation to that of the New, by recalling Alt's thesis that in the Hebrew religion itself there was one

such sharp shift, when the God Yahweh was adopted by those
who had hitherto revered a God of the fathers. In the new stage
of religion it was asserted that the two were the same, and in
the narrative accordingly Yahweh says "I am the God of thy
father, the God of Abraham", etc. (Ex. 3: 6). This is a bridge
thrown across a gulf separating two stages of religion. In the
same way the New Testament identification of the Christian
God with the God of Israel is such a bridge. He sees an organic
growth going on in religion, and in each stage something useless
is cast off and something that is useful conserved. The inference
is that we must be selective in our use of the Old Testament and
employ that which is of value for us to-day. Eissfeldt, therefore,
is no biblicist, and the monastic aisles of the history of revela-
tion-philosophy have no charm for him. When he uses the word
revelation it is obviously not weighted on the supernatural side.

The theological problem comes into particularly sharp focus
in an article by a clergyman, Press.[22] He argues that æsthetic
and utilitarian considerations are of no avail for the problem of
whether we are to keep the Old Testament. The decisive thing
is its religious significance, and even here one cannot be content
with general religious "values"; the question must be whether
the Old Testament is Word of God, in other words whether there
is a special revelation in the Old Testament. If the Old Testament only contained valuable religious documents it could not
differ in principle from any other collection of religious texts.
The position of the Old Testament must be established theologically or the Old Testament must be given up. It is insufficient to say that it is of decisive weight for us that Jesus saw the
Word of God in the Old Testament. This could be taken over
from the ideas of His contemporaries and be part of a heritage
that must be discounted. One must prove directly from the
Old Testament that it contains the Word of God.

Press then shows that it is impossible to understand the
whole Old Testament as Word of God. There are large sections
which are of no religious value, e.g., the legal codes. It is of no
use to defend the law in general with the alleged necessity for a
preaching of law alongside of the gospel. The New Testament
contains more effective preaching of law. The cultic law of the
Old Testament cannot even be understood as expression of the
will of God addressed to a certain people at a certain time;

for how then could the prophets have indulged in polemic against it? The thought of a divine pedagogy, too, is not without its weaknesses. The requirements of God must be the same from age to age. We can only do justice to the law if we look at it as a manifestation of the fact that Israel heard God's claim on itself but had not yet attained a clear realization of what constitutes the true service of the Lord. There are two currents in the Old Testament which struggle with each other; one leads to the New Testament and the other to the Talmud.

A sharp line of demarcation, Press says, also goes through the Old Testament between that for which the prophets stand and a false popular conduct and piety that they oppose. And it is here that the Old Testament takes on a real significance for us. The prophets, like Jesus, demand a new life of repentance and faith. The sins that the prophets assail are found among us as well. It is the mind of the old Adam. Over against it stands the ideal of the new man. Is that message not Word of God for us and in full conformity with the New Testament?

Press then sets forth a series of Old Testament thoughts that stand in contrast to the thought of later Judaism, but in principle are on one plane with the New Testament. The purpose of God is to draw men to Himself. All the contrast between the sinner and the holy God in the Old Testament cannot obscure that. Even the prophetic predictions of doom have this for their background, and in eschatology the belief in the realization of this fellowship of man and God is maintained. But the divine purpose rests on God's free grace, not on human initiative. The gracious will of God is recognized in such passages as Hos. 11: 9, Mic. 7: 18, Ps. 103: 3, 8 f. The covenant of God results in the setting up of covenant-statutes. The belief in divine election is the basis of a new morality (Am. 3: 2). The Old Testament does not preach good works, but the life that flows from faith alone. This thought in the Old Testament belongs to the "special revelation" contained in it.

One truth is proclaimed in the Old Testament as in the New Testament, and yet the Old Testament is only realized in Christ. It is not accidental that Jesus grew up in Jewry, where a long spiritual struggle was tending toward its conclusion. Since Jesus and the prophets stand together in a common front, over against sinful man, the Old Testament in its prophetic strata is not antiquated. Though the preaching of the prophets is not in the power of Christ there is an inner unity in both. However, it is only for faith that the Old Testament contains a Word of God. Even though we have the whole Word of God in the New Testament, we cannot give up the Old Testament. It stands in God's choice through which portion of the Bible He first works upon our hearts. Ofttimes the Old Testament serves His purpose before the New. We would lose something of the wealth of form in which the Word of God took shape, if we gave up the Old Testament.

Another scholar who touched on our subject in those years was Volz.[23] He has his eyes focused notably on the preacher's use of the Old Testament and is concerned not only with foes of the Old Testament but with Vischer (see p. 219 f.). Over against the former he sets up the demand that more use of the Old Testament heritage is needed in private study, devotions, preaching and above all regular lectionary use in the service. The Old Testament era was an era of gigantic battle in the religious sphere and the prophets were the great protagonists of God against humanism, against reliance on good works and against rule by priesthoods. They emphasized the moral independence of the individual, and put the Word of God rather than ritual in the centre of things. Prophecy is the Protestantism of antiquity and with its help one can illuminate what Protestanism is and should be to-day.

Volz then discusses the difficulties involved in accepting the Old Testament as normative. Undoubtedly there are things in it which are sub-Christian; we should not be honest if we did not, e.g., see a difference in the level of Ps. 103 and of Gen. 19: 30–38. But study enables us to discern how God's Spirit unveils the divine truth gradually, and how even some of His greatest servants gradually attained a deeper understanding of it than they had at first. Thus if we had I Kings 19: 1–13 among our stated lessons (customary in German Protestant Churches) we could show how God brings Elijah to realize that fanatic zeal and violence in the cause of religion are not in accordance with His will. The instances where prophets used violence in God's cause are to be read in the light of the correction given at that occasion; the danger of a vindictive spirit associating itself with religion is ever present (cf. Luke 9: 54 f.). Other difficulties in connection with the Old Testament arise from the national character of the Hebrew Religion. And yet Jer. 29: 7 shows how these were transcended. Thus the Old Testament contains within its pages the necessary correctives against its own lower elements.

Volz then takes up the idea of the election of Israel, which was particularly offensive to those being influenced by National Socialist doctrines. He finds that this difficulty is easily obviated, if we recall (1) that not the world-rule of Israel but rather of God is the thing the Old Testament emphasizes, (2) that such election is stressed primarily in times of despondency and not without reference to the spiritual calling of the nation, (3) Israel is not just considered a favourite of the deity, but as having an increased responsibility because of its election (Am. 3: 2).

Another difficulty arises for us from primitive ideas of God surviving in the Old Testament. Volz finds these instructive rather than disturbing. We must realize that monotheism had to struggle upward against all manner of opposition, and passages of a backward religious character show how arduous that struggle was. On the whole, he finds, the historical books of the Old Testament provide the chief hurdles. This to him highlights the fact that religious and moral progress came about chiefly through prophecy. The best way to fight for the Old Testament is to set forth prophecy's greatness and divine power.

Volz then turns to the question of the unity of the two Testaments. The idea that the essence of the Old Testament is law is only an echo of the late Jewish view of it. As soon as we emancipate ourselves from that standpoint and look at the Old Testament with our own eyes we find it full of gospel. Its words of consolation simply cannot be spared. In its very nature the Old Testament is gospel and even its law is embedded in the grace and redemption of God. The mission of the prophets reflects the saving will of God. The goal of history is the divine kingdom, the salvation of Israel and the nations. Even the national catastrophes are viewed in the light of a constructive divine purpose that is to be realized through them. As it speaks of redemption and of the love of God, so the Old Testament speaks of the perfect forgiveness of God (Is. 1: 18, Ps. 103, etc.) and is aware of His pedagogical activity (Gen. 22, Jer. 15: 19, Is. 49: 4–6). It teaches the prevenient grace of God, holding

14

that man can only be converted after God redeems him (Deut. 6: 4–5). If we had Ps. 130 as a stated lesson we could set forth the unity of the Bible by means of it; it is an exultant celebration of the forgiveness and redemption of God.

Volz then dwells on aspects of the Old Testament that are by no means superseded. In part their influence continues in the New Testament, but they are more clearly discernible in the Old Testament and must be recaptured by the Church. (1) There is the feeling of God's presence and activity in the larger historical process; thus Jerusalem receives its fate from the hand of God (Is. 40: 2); kings are only the agents of God (Is. 10: 5, Jer. 27: 6, Is. 45: 1) and prophets are his heralds. (2) There is the idea of responsibility to God in public affairs. The divine message permeates all areas of public life—law, commerce, culture, politics; no secular department of life is acknowledged. The people as a whole must receive the divine imperatives. Whether God's requirements are practicable does not trouble the prophet any more than it troubles Jesus in the Sermon on the Mount. The messengers of God set forth the goal and point out the sources of strength that make it attainable. (3) There is the idea of God's universal presence and his interest in men's small, everyday affairs. How vividly I Sam. 1 and Gen. 24 exhibit this! Everyone of us has his own problems, and the Old Testament illuminates a considerable range of these in the light of religion. (4) There is the idea of the judgment of God. Our own pride rebels against the pricks of our conscience. The Old Testament supports conscience by laying low the pride of man, and emphasizing the totality of God's requirement of us. Much of the wrath men are venting against the Old Testament is because it tells us the truth about this. (5) There is the idea of the inscrutability of God. While the New Testament in its message of the Cross shows that God moves in a mysterious way, to accomplish His ends in the larger sphere, the Old Testament makes this vivid in more ordinary human concerns. Gen. 22, which speaks so powerfully of this, combining the divine inscrutability with His nearness and mercy, should be a stated lesson in Christian services. (6) There is the Old Testament consciousness of corporate personality; the individual is a member of the group representing the cause of God. The "thou" of the decalogue is the congregation and yet at the same time the individual. We to-day particularly need this feeling of solidarity with our fellow Christians and of a united responsibility. All this wealth of special material in the Old Testament, Volz thinks, needs to be utilized more in the Church than is the case to-day.

The final topic of which he speaks is that of the Christological interpretation of the Old Testament. Here Volz (who once wrote a quite negative critical work on Messianism) is willing to concede that we can, indeed, say of a few Old Testament prophecies that they were fulfilled in Christ (so Is. 42: 1–4, or Is. 53). But we are not in the situation of the Primitive Church and cannot just utilize its mode of Scripture-proof. There is a danger of exaggeration in the Christological interpretation of the Old Testament on the part of Vischer and others. The *richesse* of the Old Testament is lost sight of when everything is studied from the narrow angle of Christological prediction. It is more important to see how the Old Testament *as a whole* prepares the way for Christ, and how the word of the prophets and psalmists lives on in Him. For testimony concerning Christ the New Testament witness is fully sufficient! This new Christocentrism is a veritable dethronement of God, and contrary to the New Testament, which stresses theocentrism most at the very points where it dwells on Christ's exaltedness (I Cor. 15: 22 f.; Phil. 2: 5 f.; Heb. 1; 1 f.). In closing he quotes John 14: 6: God is the goal, Christ the way and the truth, and holds that we only understand the Old Testament aright when we are under Christ.

Turning now to the American scene, we may first consider an address by G. R. Berry.[24] This scholar first speaks of the harm that has resulted to Christian life and thought from the Old Testament, owing to its use as authoritative Word of God. The idea of God has been grievously corrupted by the immorality, injustice, arbitrariness and vindictiveness of the God of the Old Testament narratives. The dogmas of election, and especially of hell and damnation, embody some of the worst features of Old Testament belief. The idea of man, too, has been affected. The dogma of total depravity is based on Gen. 3 and what New Testament writers read out of that passage. Where religion affects society, the Old Testament influence has likewise been harmful. Militarism, slavery, persecution of witches, polygamy, capital punishment, and religious persecution are all justified and demonstrated in its pages. These results, he grants, need to be estimated in connection with other results of a beneficial nature which it has also without doubt produced. But he does not elaborate that part of the picture. All in all, he considers it a real question whether in the past the Old Testament has not been more a liability than an asset to Christianity.

But Berry thinks that whatever harm the Old Testament may have done is due more to the wrong use of it than to its essential nature. It is inconsistent to treat it dogmatically as the infallible Word of God and then evade the consequences by allegorizing interpretation or other expedients. The right view of the Old Testament is that of modern criticism which is inductive, in contrast to the conservative view which is deductive. It asks not what the Old Testament must be, but what it really is. He rejects a mediating position which is often taken, viz., that the Old Testament does not intend to teach history, politics or science, but only religion. In this way many wish to shake off the liabilities of the Old Testament and keep its advantages; so far as this is reading the mind of God it is a matter difficult to prove, and so far as it is reading the intention of the human authors of the Old Testament it may be challenged by the contrary assertion that they were really trying to write history, science, etc. The interest of the Old Testament writers is by no means confined to religion. Whole books like Esther, Song of Songs, and Ecclesiastes are devoid of it.

The historical approach to the Old Testament teaches us that there is an evolution in Old Testament thought and enables us to differentiate between higher and lower stages. Accurately discerning the meaning of given portions of the Old Testament, we can see its lack of unity and appreciate what sections have no helpful message for general use at the present time. Berry then points out in what ways the Old Testament thus studied may and should be an asset for present day use. (1) All the documents, of course, have importance from a historical standpoint, but that use "belongs to the study much more than to the pulpit". (2) The Old Testament is an asset in so far as it expresses religious truth which is universal and permanent. Here he stresses ethical monotheism and the teaching concerning the redemptive power of vicarious suffering (Is. 53). (3) The literary quality of the Old Testament. (4) Those portions which express feeling—notably the Psalms. While they are largely a restatement of familiar ideas, coming particularly from the prophets, and often ordinary or even platitudinous in thought, their feeling gives them an appeal to the human heart at all times. (5) The biographical element in the Old Testament. (6) The element of personal experience. This expression of personal experience and conviction reaches the heart. The heroes of the faith lived in a very real sense in a fellowship with God.

Another American Old Testament scholar who was stirred to speak about this problem was J. A. Bewer.[25] After conceding all the difficulties the Old Testament has caused Christianity, he argues that it is nevertheless too valuable for the Christian to discard. We need it for the true understanding of Jesus and the early Christian writers, especially Paul, who were all rooted in the Old Testament. Furthermore, next to the New Testament, it is our greatest source for the enlarging and deepening of our spiritual life and thought. It is great literature; parts of it belong to the greatest literature of the world, e.g., some of its stories and Psalms, some of its prophets and the Book of Job.

> In it we find the record of the experience of the great men of the spirit, the original geniuses of religion, the pioneers in the moral and spiritual realm. It is a book of power. Here we may nourish our spiritual life by fellowship with the prophets, deepen our sense of the reality of the spiritual world, refine our moral and spiritual perception. Here we may learn from Amos penetrating insight into social conditions, from Isaiah tenderness, forgiveness, and moral redemption, from Ezekiel pastoral fidelity. Here are the sources of the social side of religion, the social ideal of the prophets, the kingdom of God, reformed and deepened by Jesus. Here are the great teachers of prayer, the psalmists who give us the words of worship which we use when we are inarticulate and dumb. Can we afford to forgo all this? Need I mention the wealth of material the Old Testament presents not only for sermons and for religious education, but also for theology, especially for ethical monotheism? One has but to think a little of all that is involved in neglecting or discarding the Old Testament to see how impossible it is for the Christian minister.

The evil consequences of the Old Testament can all be avoided, Bewer thinks, by the truer understanding and use of the Old Testament we owe modern criticism. As significant points in the new view, he lists: (1) We use the methods of literary study to find out what the authors actually mean or say. (2) There is a development from lower to higher religious and moral ideas and ideals, "a progressive revelation" as it has been called. (3) The norm by which every step in the marvellous development is tested: the spirit of Christ. (4) The necessity of distinguishing between the truth and the manner in which it is presented—taking poetry as poetry, etc. (5) Going on to the spiritual appreciation of the truth in the Old Testament.

In a later paper,[26] Bewer sets forth how impossible the former idea of the Old Testament is for the Christian but how the new view has made it fascinating and inspiring. But he discerns a reluctance of the Christian Church to acknowledge this. The danger of which it is afraid is that, in this eager study of the human side of the Old Testament, the reality of the truth and revelation of God in these pages will be forgotten, and the authority of the Old Testament entirely lost. Bewer warns that nothing can restore the authority of the Old Testament in the former sense of the word, once a modern man has read it in the new way. He asks: Is there anything in the Old Testament of such authoritative character that we may say "While indeed the Old Testament as a whole is not the Word of God, it nevertheless contains the Word of God"? But where, he continues, is the distinguishing principle that will enable us to separate the imperishable divine from the ephemeral human? The only norm and standard is the Spirit of God as revealed in Jesus. Those things contrary to it or without spiritual meaning to us are for us without authority and not canonical. If, however, this is to have real meaning the external authority must become internal authority: the Word of God in the Old Testament must become Word of God to me in my own heart and conscience.

He sees the Word of God in the Old Testament finding us, striking home, touching our hearts, justifying itself to our minds, commanding our consciences along three lines: (1) That of its moral teachings and precepts. (2) In the spiritual experiences of the prophets. (3) Its illustration of the search of the human heart for God in Old Testament prayer. All this is authoritative only to him who believes himself directly confronted and addressed by God. Many read the Old Testament professionally, with unconcerned hearts, and so do not hear its message, and others read it with hearts and consciences only and without discriminating intellect, with equally unfortunate results. Jesus read it with a warm and eager heart, and yet also with discrimination, and His example should be followed.

In a valuable symposium of Old Testament articles that appeared in England in 1938, Lofthouse gave a discussion of our theme.[27] He finds that it is with the New Testament, rather than with Christian theology, that the Hebrew Scriptures can be usefully compared. He begins by pointing out that from the point of view of *form*, the religion of the Old Testament is the religion of promise. For the best of the Hebrews the object of their vision is what is out of sight. They dauntlessly look forward to the coming intervention of God that will bring salvation. The religion of the New Testament, on the other hand, looks from the future to the past. The promise is fulfilled, the deliverance has appeared; though there is still more to come, faith conceives of it as almost realized.

Taking up the comparison from the point of view of *contents* of the two Testaments, Lofthouse first dwells on the two great pioneers of the Christian faith, Paul and John. While they have different slants they both turn away from the old dispensation, even while they breathe its air. They both look to one who is felt completely to transcend what the older writings would suggest—to Jesus.

Turning to Jesus he finds that if the vocabulary of His sayings is that of the Old Testament, the spirit is fresh. He veers especially toward the line of the anti-sacrificial utterances of Prophets and Psalmists. But He did not remove the law to establish the gospel. Properly speaking there is no opposition between the two, for the law was more than a catalogue of burdensome duties—it was God's instruction to men, revealing to them how they could enjoy His favour, and even more it was a promise, though a conditional one. The gospel is a second and this time unconditional promise. It is a triumphant present, though it passes into the future—therein linking up with the Old Testament mood once more. Discussing the New Testament eschatology he says its heart is the approach to God by faith in Christ (itself God's gift), and the welding of all who believe into one great redeemed community; he finds this no mere legacy from Jewish apocalyptic but outgrowth of the work of Jesus.

Lofthouse then discusses another aspect of the Hebrew religion that he considers essential in thinking about the Old Testament promise, as well as about the relation of the Testaments—the Covenant idea. While the word occurs but seldom in the Old Testament, the idea is present constantly. Nowhere is it clearer than in Is. 53, which chapter forms a kind of bridge between the Testaments, and though rarely quoted in the New Testament is, as it were, the *leitmotiv* of the Gospel story. Turning to Christian doctrine and concepts, Lofthouse finds the Old Testament a kind of acid test for the consonance of a doctrine with the spirit of the New Testament. Properly used it could have protected Christendom from the misconceptions of a thousand years of Christian speculation, and he then illustrates this in the matter of the doctrines of God, Sin, Atonement, and the Church.

In closing, he speaks of record and revelation. The Old Testament is a double record, how God dealt with men and how men have felt about Him, and knows a double revelation—a revelation through the world of nature and history, and a revelation given through inspired men. The New Testament is also a record and revelation, but in it the final veil which had remained in the Old Testament is also a revelation of priceless worth, for it brings men to the place where they stand before the last veil that awaits removal.

In the same volume the editor, H. Wheeler Robinson, has a contribution on Old Testament theology.[28] He prefaces his delineation of the characteristic doctrines (God, Man, Sin and Grace, the Judgment of History) with a section on the Philosophy of Revelation. He finds the Hebrews realists, who continually adjusted their ideas of God to the events of life. The strong sense of corporate personality among them, combining ancestors and descendants with the present generation into a single unity, helped to make history the supreme revelation of God. The philosophy of history for the Hebrews thus becomes the philosophy of revelation. The record as given in the Old Testament is dominated by particular theories evolved in the course of the development of the religion, e.g., the doctrine of retribution, or the idea that Moses gave the law in all completeness. The task of critical scholarship is *to get behind these theories to the original history of both the events and the ideas*. This actual history, so far as we can reach it, must be the basis for a modern philosophy of revelation. Only when we have decided on a probable series of events and a parallel series of human reactions to these events can we usefully begin to ask how far and in what way they both in their blended unity really serve to reveal God.

But Robinson does not follow this out. Instead he deals with the "record", speaking of that as "revelation". While Old Testament criticism has removed many former difficulties with which that book confronted us, new intellectual difficulties have arisen for those who believe it to be divine revelation. The very phrase "historical revelation" is a paradox (when revelation is understood as static and permanent truth), for history implies dynamic movement of some kind, whether or not it can be called progress. And how can absolute truth be relative to each of a series of generations? The answer of the Hebrew to the difficulty is a *solvitur vivendo*: he says, "God knows me and I know God in the experience of living."

Robinson finds that this leaves us with the theological problem of the canon. While its precise boundaries have no more than a historic interest this does not diminish the authority of the Old Testament. Both Judaism and Christianity really only made *selective* use of this literature, the one emphasizing the Law, the other the Prophets and Psalms. The authority of the Old Testament thus rested from the beginning on what we call value judgments. No Tridentine decree can eliminate that historic fact and its theological significance. But Robinson insists that this does not entangle us in the slough of subjectivity. Revelation has always been and still remains the unity of the subjective and objective. As the word of the prophet only became revelation when it found obedient and intelligent response from his hearers, so the objective fact of the Old Testament as literary record still awaits the response of the reader through the internal testimony of the Holy Spirit. Such authority is in no way inferior to the authority of truth, goodness and beauty wherever they are found. Secondary authority may rightly belong to the living tradition of the Church, or to the written record of the life that went before it, but only as guides to a goal—that goal being the direct and individual knowledge of God. The authority of the Old Testament depends on the penetrating character of the intuition of the prophets, the rich variety of religious experience, the vocabulary of worship, the picturesque character of the language and thoughts and the dynamic quality of the idea of God behind the record.

In the same year there appeared a book by the present writer[29] which, though it did not deal with the authority of the Old Testament, attempted to interpret a single Old Testament book, that of Job, in a new way. After first approaching it in historical-critical manner, in which form-criticism played an important role, he "stood off" to view the meaning of the whole. For he held that a literary product may in reality have a meaning and message of greater range than its creator realizes at the time of writing, and that this is even more the case with a book like Job, which was taken to be a social product. The meaning Job now conveys was held to be that of the greatest of all theodicies, in which all the important viewpoints that can be adduced are brought in and powerfully presented in poetic form. Whether this approach could be used as readily in the case of other Old Testament writings the author does not know, but he believes it deserves further trial. For there are times when we prefer to read ancient books with an eye to appreciating and enjoying them, instead of getting wrought up over "decisions", "time and eternity" and other deadly serious matters. Such a search for "meaning" of an entity suggests a link with phenomenology and evidently would conform best to theologies of the kind advocated by Tillich or by Otto.

Chapter Thirteen

THE REVIVAL OF THE NEW TESTAMENT APPROACH

UNDER the influence of Barth a trend toward a Christianizing interpretation of the Old Testament arose in the outer fringes of German and Swiss Old Testament study. It was chiefly promulgated by theologically interested clergymen[1] and found great favour with all those who were deeply dissatisfied with what the professionals had to offer. For the scholar's approach demanded toil, critical analysis, and in the end there was no religious profit in it. The Church, bereft of its ancient support by a paternalistic, aristocratic state, was now the prey of the nihilistic forces that were let loose when the thrones sank into the dust. In this situation a liberal was a man with a wooden sword. The crying need was for a more effective weapon. In the Reformation era Protestantism had found the Bible of the two Testaments a sword of the Spirit. The idea arose: we must recapture that standpoint. Barth had provided a great stimulus in this direction and indicated the possibilities. Among the clergymen who came forward with such sentiments Vischer took a leading role.

In an article of 1931[2] he gave an outline of the views he was promulgating and in a work that began to appear in 1934[3] he has been applying them exegetically to the three parts of the Hebrew Canon (taken in their Hebrew arrangement rather than the one accepted in the Protestant Bible translations). We shall deal here with his thought on the basis of his early article, since that gives his standpoint in principle, without encumbrance by exegetical details. By one's surprise at his exegesis one may too easily lose sight of his central positions, and be too hasty in one's condemnation of his approach.

Vischer first raises the question: Is the Christian message of to-day bound to the Old Testament? He begins with the assertion that there is no getting away from it that Christianity is bound to a fact of the past: namely that God became incarnate in Christ

1–30 A.D. All the lines of a relationship between God and any man at any time intersect this particular point in history. There is no salvation apart from Christ (Acts 4: 10, 12). Christianity, furthermore, he says, is bound to the literary testimony of this fact of Christ. The New Testament bears its own witness, but, at the same time, it brings its proof for Christ from the Old Testament. Vischer does not believe it possible to reject the Old Testament and keep the New Testament. They hang together inseparably. With Calvin and Barth, he holds to the basic identity of the two Testaments.

The chief ground of objection to the authority of the Old Testament, Vischer asserts, is to be found in the fact that there is so much in the Old Testament that is low and immoral. But those who read the Bible as a document of human piety are not reading it aright. The theme of that book is—as Barth has said —the piety of God, not that of man; the morality of God, not the morals of man. The modern individual is motivated at every turn by the Greek ideal—he is looking for the glorification of man; but the Bible seeks only the glorification of God (I Peter 2: 9). God's condescension to sinners, His acts of grace whereby He chooses sinful men for His ends—these are the things of which the Bible speaks.

The Church, Vischer asserts, (and it is a most debatable assertion), *rests on Holy Scripture*, which is composed of two halves—an Old Testament and a New Testament. It is the task of an Old Testament study carried on by the Church to inquire into this given relationship. This task prevents Old Testament scholarship from becoming a mere branch of the study of Semitic languages and literatures. That the latter fields of study also have a legitimate interest in the Old Testament is fully conceded. The Semitists may tear the Old Testament down and build it up again to suit themselves; they may evolve a "history of the Hebrew religion" on the basis of such critical study. But that sort of thing does not do justice to the needs of the Church with respect to the Old Testament.

The task of an ecclesiastical study of the Old Testament is to understand the Old Testament as a whole (as we now have it) and the relation of every part of which it is composed to the whole. This task is not merely an æsthetic one—as for instance

the appreciation of the artistic character of a composite building
like San Marco in Venice—but a theological one. Every generation anew must make a fresh attempt to understand the Old
Testament and New Testament as a unified structure.

For Vischer the Old Testament is like an arch of which the
keystone is the Messiah—a thing which he infers from the
testimony of the New Testament. If it were not for this inclusion
of the witness of the apostles into the arch of prophecy, the Old
Testament would still be an open question concerning one yet to
come (John 1: 41, 45; Acts 4: 11). One can deny this, but then
one does not read the Old Testament as Old Testament—part of
the sacred book of the Christian Church. On a purely historical
basis, such as a non-ecclesiastical scholarship may pursue, only
hypothetical judgments are attainable concerning this matter.
Highly important Old Testament passages like Is. 53 cannot
be understood at all, or only hypothetically, without the New
Testament. The Old Testament as a whole becomes fully clear
only when it is related to Christ, and critical scholarship without
wishing to do so has made that increasingly apparent.

The Old Testament could not be authoritative witness of
Christ for the Church of all times if the Messiah had not been
actually present as head of the Church of the Old Testament
and if the saints had not seized upon salvation through hope
and faith in him (cf. John 8: 56–8, 12: 41, 1: 30; I Cor. 10).
Vischer thus stresses the pre-existence of Christ as the thing
that makes the continuity reasonable. But the fact of historical
progression has a full reality. The incarnation of the *logos* was
the event through which the Old Testament became the *Old*
Testament. "He came unto his own, and his own received him
not" (John 1: 11). If that had not occurred, the Old Testament
would not have become *old*. In that it became *old*, it must now
bear witness that this unheard-of thing (the crucifixion of the
Messiah) took place, and that this turning-point from the Old
Testament to the New Testament is also the turning-point of
the world and of the individual life.

Real history does not repeat itself. The genuine Christian
message based on the Old Testament summons us to let ourselves be drawn by that which the Bible tells of the people of
the Old Testament, into the presence of the same God who
commands and promises, and not to harden our hearts (Heb.

4: 7). In order to become servants of the same master, we must hear Moses and the prophets (Luke 16: 29).

Vischer then proceeds to inquire into the meaning that "the Law", i.e., the Pentateuch, has for us.[4] The absolute claim that God has on us comes to us in the Bible through relative, historically and individually conditioned commands. Every word of the Torah draws us into the presence of this sovereign God, who is the same to-day as He was for Moses or Habakkuk. The question, then, is whether a particular commandment also applies to me in every concrete situation.

Here Vischer is highly modern; he asserts every commandment was spoken in and for a concrete situation of its own which may by no means be identical with mine. As such they all testify to concrete commandments which Israel received. They concern us only as witness of what God once commanded. He quotes Barth to the effect that no Biblical commandment or prohibition is a rule or moral generality, but that it comes to us rather as a testimony of the absolute, concrete, real commandment, that is behind and above all recorded commandments.

Vischer then tries to define more closely what "law" really means. He considers it to be the most definite expression of the deity's will for the right. It is an expression of the fact that the address and claim of the gospel are meant existentially. "I am the Lord thy God" (Ex. 20: 2)—that is not only the presupposition but also the content of the divine legislation; it is that which expresses itself in its totality as well as in its particular decrees.

The self-revelation of God is the source of this law. God only says "thou shalt" to him to whom He has said "thou art mine". I cannot existentially hear the gospel "thou art mine" if I do not in the obedience of faith also hear the commandment "then be mine". Vischer thinks it a mistake to believe that the law was given as a preparatory condition for entering into the covenant relation. The law flows out of the covenant. "You are my people—therefore really be my people." The indicative is turned into an imperative. Man's obedience to the law is man's answer in the obedience of faith to the promise of the gospel; it is gratitude for grace shown, not an attempt to earn grace.

Judaism, Vischer finds, misunderstood this basic theological situation. How was that possible? Did not the cultic law even show in what sense it was meant? In rather speculative fashion Vischer then presents a teleology of the law of sacrifice, explaining what the purpose of God was in establishing such an arrangement. How was it possible for the Holy One to dwell in Israel's midst when His requirement was "You shall be holy, for I am holy" (Lev. 19: 2) without the dispensing of daily forgiveness through daily sacrifice? Since knowledge of the moral law could produce nothing but consciousness of sin (Rom. 3: 20) and resultant despair, God gave His people the cultic law as a sign that they might live before Him and with Him, in spite of their sin. Every sacrifice points beyond itself. It would be nothing if it were not for that one sacrifice of which all other sacrifices are but the symbol and prophecy. Here Vischer avails himself of a thought of Luther: the *obtaining* of forgiveness took place only once, but the *distribution* of it took place often, both before Christ and after Christ. For since God had decided upon forgiveness, it mattered not whether He dispensed it previously or subsequently through His Word: as He subsequently dispensed it in the sacrament through the Word, so He previously dispensed it in the Old Testament sacrifices through the Word.

At this point the reader will have his doubts. The manner in which Vischer explains "sacrifice" shows him as understanding the cultic law of the Old Testament in the light of the Epistle to the Hebrews. But the thought of the author of Hebrews hangs together at that point with an ancient philosophy of typology that is in itself of debatable value. Can we, furthermore, naïvely assume that the sacrificial law was revealed by God, as the Jews did, when we know that its whole procedure and terminology are closely related to what we find among Israel's heathen neighbours?[4] Surely there is no use in resolutely ignoring what modern knowledge teaches us and proceeding along an orthodox line as though nothing had happened in the last hundred years. Fine religious dicta of Calvin or Luther, valuable as utterances of their piety, but "pre-scientific" in their use of the Old Testament, can only becloud the situation.

Vischer's view of the prophets[5] and of the prophecy element in the Old Testament is similarly governed by New Testament viewpoints. God has elected Israel to a living history in order that His will may be done on earth and in heaven. His will, however, is never a fully revealed entity, but only present in the history of revelation, as it unfolds. "I shall be that I shall be"—that, rather than "I am that I am", as the familiar translations render, is the real meaning of the divine name of Ex. 3 and it expresses perfectly how God reveals Himself in different moments. Again and again we hear in the Old Testament that "the Word of the Lord came". God does not reign as rigid law but as a free sovereign. Hence, in the Old Testament the law is woven together with history, and bound to the books of the prophets.

God is present in the word of the prophets, and His Word given through them makes history. Prophets and history belong together—that is why (a purely speculative assertion) the historical books Joshua—II Kings are called the "former prophets". The Old Testament history, furthermore, is written in prophetic spirit, with an eye to the eschatologically oriented chronological scheme of the Priestly writer. It is evident, too, in the way in which contemporary history is interpreted in the prophets. If we say that all this prophecy is fulfilled in the New Testament, then that is true in the sense that it is confirmed. All promises of God find their confirmation in Jesus Christ, but not necessarily their complete realization. The goal of prophecy is not yet attained at the stage of the Incarnation. We, too, live in faith in the promise like the Old Testament saints, except that we see more clearly than they.

As for the third part of the Hebrew Canon, the Writings,[6] Vischer looks on this division as "the congregational echo" to the speaking of God in law and prophets. They cover the whole breadth of human life—health and sickness, love and hate, prosperity and adversity. This would seem to imply a lower rank for this portion of the canon—unless one regards the Old Testament congregation as so fully inspired by the Holy Ghost that the "echo" is given back in absolute purity.

In his elaboration of his programme in his *Witness of the Old Testament to Christ*, Vol. I, Vischer argues that Christianity must regard as normative for its reading and understanding of the Old Testament the New Testament assertion John 5: 39. "Ye search the Scripture because ye think that in them ye have eternal life; and these are they which bear witness of me." Christological exegesis of the Old Testament is the slogan.

The very humanity of the Scripture is seen as comparable to our Lord's humanity in the Incarnation. God willed that these imperfect human and fallible words should testify concerning his Son, the incarnate Word, and be attested to by the Holy Spirit. Vischer finds the Old Testament fully on a par with the New in principle—Jesus is only the Christ if the unity of the Bible is preserved. The Christian Church, he declares, stands and falls with the acceptance or rejection of the Old Testament. He spurns the idea of a "pneumatic" exegesis—thinks of it as leading over to a theosophy. But he then has recourse to the Holy Spirit as the one that gives us proof out of the Old Testament that Jesus is the Christ. He quotes Augustine's saying: "Read the prophetic books without reading of Christ and what can you find that is more insipid and flat? But read Christ here, then that which thou readest not only tastes good but will intoxicate thee."

Writing of the literature on the Old Testament from the period of the German church struggle, a reviewer who was not inexperienced in biblical criticism, Abramowski, described Vischer's book as "both necessary and correct".[7] It is "necessary" because the theological and political situation of the hour required a Christian witness on the basis of the Old Testament— not merely an opinion about the Old Testament—and it was impossible to wait until modern Old Testament science should arrive at the point where it would produce it. The book is "correct", furthermore, because the New Testament and the Protestant Reformers declare in unison that the Old Testament gives witness to Christ. He agrees with Vischer that no mere humanistic approach, augmented with æsthetic and religious considerations, will find Christ in the Old Testament. Since, furthermore, the attack is being carried forward by the anti-Christian forces to Christ Himself, it is necessary to hold the Old Testament from the vantage point of Christ and for Him.

Such an utterance highlights the fact that Vischer's book arose out of a special situation and met the acclaim it did on that account. There is a definite principle behind Vischer's thought—it was heard much earlier from the lips of the great liberal, Stade (p. 267)—that for Christian use the Old Testament must be Christianized. But Stade conceived of that task as part of the preacher's role. Vischer's exegesis is essentially a preacher's and that of one sharing the dogma that is basic for all Calvinism, viz., that the whole Bible is sole authority. From this doctrine flows the need of fusing the Testaments to create unity, and the view of Messianic prophecy found in the New Testament provides the means of mastering the Old. Vischer manages in this way to give the Old Testament a present significance, just as the apocalyptically minded are able to do in their way for both Old and New Testament prophecy.

The advantages of this are clear. But have we a moral right to attempt to read the mind of God and assert that something about Christ is foretold or foreshadowed in the Old Testament, when that is only our own guesswork? For Vischer indulges in typological interpretations beyond those found in the New Testament. And do we have the obligation to accept New Testament assertions of a similar nature about this or that Old Testament passage? The assumption that we have that obligation governs Vischer and all who are of his colour. Behind this attitude stands the fear that without such Christianization the Old Testament loses all living importance. That explains much, but it can hardly justify the approach taken. For to force oneself to believe something that is contrary to reason is hardly the evangelical idea of faith. To take such a view is to lose sight of the great lesson taught by Ritschl (p. 99). The Old Testament, furthermore, is too rich to be compressed into the prophecy and fulfilment formula. Some better way must be found to make it meaningful than Vischer's, whatever may be the benefits that have accrued from his approach.[8]

Chapter Fourteen

THE OLD TESTAMENT AND THE EXISTENTIAL QUESTION

A LINE of Dialectic theology differing considerably from Karl Barth's is that represented by Gogarten and Bultmann. Instead of assuming a direct relationship of man and God, they hold that our relation to God is indirect and is only realized in our relation to our fellow man or the world.[1] For these theologians, therefore, a theological anthropology was of basic importance. Necessarily, then, they had to seek a link with contemporary philosophical thought—the approach of Gogarten being influenced by E. Grisebach,[2] and that of Bultmann by Heidegger.[3]

These philosophies attempted a new ontology, describing human existence in its fatefulness, its bondage and contradictoriness, and in particular stressed the idea that this life is not to be regarded in a neutral manner as from the outside, but is to be understood only by actively participating in it. Our responsibility is not to the individual self, as Idealism presupposes, but to *being* as such, which we did not create and over which we have no control. Therein these philosophies provide a starting-point for thought about revelation as an existential reality that claims us.

We may now inquire how this affects the standing of the Old Testament.

For Gogarten, then, our fellow man is the decisive existential reality, and it is toward him that our responsible action is directed.[4] Where the relation of man to man is fully realized it is as the work of the creating and redeeming God. Speech or word being the channel of contact between the self and the other, revelation must take place through "Word". There being no direct relation between us and God, revelation can only come to us in this roundabout manner. But Gogarten does not limit the "other" to our contemporary. He sees us holding a relation also to men of the past. History is decision and can only be understood in participating action. While history, therefore, is something that happens in the present, it is incessant contact of a past with the present. Where this contact is not experienced there is no real history. From this angle Gogarten accepts the idea that God has also revealed Himself to men of the past, in other words, he posits a history of revelation. This history occurs within total-history, it is the history of the people of God, through which God desires to show Himself as Creator and through which He would accomplish His history of redemption. But to believe in this history is to participate in it. The history of revelation consists in this—that the word of men of the past speaks to me as present "thou", exercising a divine claim upon me. Christian faith confesses this of the men of biblical history, and that includes also the Word of the Old Testament.

But the Old Testament, according to Gogarten, only speaks to us of God as Creator and of His order of Creation. It is revelation of the law, not as a timeless idea, but rather as a concrete claim. It is but the requirement of a responsible "I-and-thou-relation", not its fulfilment; but at the same time it is a prediction of fulfilment. The implication is that in this history of the people of God, with which we become associated through our hearing the Old Testament Word, the relation will be fulfilled. Contact with the Word of the Old Testament is thus not yet revelation in the full sense. The latter is experienced only in contact with the Word of the New Testament—the message of Jesus Christ, who vicariously fulfilled the law and gives Himself to man in His Word. In so far as Christ's love of man is the work of God and obedience to God, His love is revelation of the love of God and His Word the Word of God.

It is thus apparent that for Gogarten, as for Luther, the Old Testament is primarily "law". In later essays he dealt in more detail with this supposed primary aspect of it.[5] The only revealed commandment of the decalogue, he declares, is the first "that we permit God really to be our God as He, in revealing Himself to us, wishes to be our God".[6] The legal materials of the Old Testament, or in other words, the whole law apart from this one commandment, he takes to be derived from reason and experience.

Bultmann, to whom we must now turn, is impressed by the

fact of our mortality, which would make life meaningless if it were the ultimate thing.[7] Revelation, he holds, can only consist in the gift from on high of a life that overcomes death. As such it is not a phenomenon of the present order, but a future entity that is ever drawing near and to that extent is already present. This "life", however, is not revealed to us as something objective, but as a mode of being that we comprehend only in faith. Revelation is the new understanding of the self and the boundaries fixed for us, as ordained by the Creator and opening the way from death to life.

History is another important category for Bultmann. He regards it as involving decision. The decision is a choice between oncoming possibilities: death or life, God or the world. The possibility of life or God is not a tangible actuality but something potential. I can only know it if I know the possibilities of being, and I can know these only when I seize one of them and in the moment of seizing it. But the past, too, reaches into the present situation, because in the latter a possibility that occurred in the past is merely being repeated. Only in the present existential encounter with the claim that the past places on us is there any history. This is true of all history, including the history mirrored in the Bible.

For Bultmann the person of the historical Jesus is of no particular concern. He stresses the Christ who is God's Word to man as bringer of divine forgiveness. The Word is bound to its bearer and does not count except as spoken by him who is its authorized messenger. On the other hand, Jesus has no revelatory authority apart from his central "Word" and mission. Like Kaehler, Bultmann hands the "historical" Jesus over to the critics (of whom he himself was one of the most radical) to do with Him as they please, and stresses the Christ of faith. For we encounter the revelatory Word only through the biblical testimony, as it is brought home to us in the living preaching of the Church.

The problem of the Old Testament engaged Bultmann in a special essay.

He first of all rejects certain ways of approaching the problem of the relation of the Old Testament to Christianity as outside of the pale of specifically theological interest. These other ways are legitimate in themselves on neutral or more or less anti-Christian standpoints, but must be ruled out where the discussion is truly theological. He even discards an approach that would ask in a detached manner whether the Old Testament has a significance for a faith that sees in Christ the revelation of God; this mode of questioning, he asserts, is still an asking from the *outside*—in which one surveys everything from the historical perspective. Theological questioning can only be from *within*—from the vantage point of faith. Can the Old Testament Word of God be heard by me as intended for myself? That he says, is how the question must be formulated.

In dealing with the Old Testament, Bultmann asserts, one must ask what basic possibility of understanding human existence finds expression in it? And this is not to be regarded as an inquiry out of idle curiosity; it is to be undertaken from the point of view of one who is convinced in faith that the Christian understanding of existence is the only correct one, but who is compelled to measure it and compare it with other possible views of existence. It takes the Old Testament seriously, not asking what it had to say to the men of 2000 years ago, but what, if anything, it continues to say to us here and now.

Bultmann finds that in the days when men really were aware of the understanding of existence that speaks forth from the Old Testament and sought to contrast or relate it to that which is truly Christian, they expressed it in the antithesis "law and gospel". For Paul, as for Luther, the Old Testament as a whole was an expression of the law, or the requiring will of God. In the new order, represented by the New Testament, man stands under the grace of God that accepts him, though a sinner. But only he who is aware of the law and of his inability ever to fulfil its requirements can understand the message of the gospel. Hence the law remains the presupposition of the gospel. Man must continue to hear what God requires of him, for though the Christian is free from the law and stands under the Spirit, his status in that respect must be a constant experience of the renewal of such a liberation. Yea more, the Christian may be free from the law as a "must" for the sake of obtaining grace, but not in so far as it is reconstituted through grace.

But the question arises: If the Old Testament remains the presupposition of the New—namely, as expression of the requirement of God that constantly encompasses man—does it retain its specifically Old Testament character? This Bultmann denies. The concrete legislation of the Old Testament, in so far as it is cultic or ritualistic, had a significance only for particular stages of Hebrew history. The ethical requirements of the Old Testament, however (as well as those of Jesus), in so far as they grow out of the basic relationships of life and not merely some concrete, transient form of such life, have not fallen to the ground. But for that very reason they are not specifically Old Testament requirements—even if they had by any chance first been formulated there. Their validity depends on their universal acceptability, and actually they were not first or exclusively laid down in the Old Testament. One can see how even Paul recognizes this. For he assumes that Gentiles who have not had Old Testament indoctrination know of themselves what God requires of them (Rom. 1: 32). Their consciences testify that the Word of God is written in their hearts (Rom. 2: 14 f.).

Thus, while the gospel presupposes the law, the latter is not necessarily identical with the concrete legislation of the Old Testament. Some other historical embodiment of the law may conceivably serve equally well for such a presupposition. The zeal for God that Paul concedes Israel possesses but calls a zeal "not according to knowledge" (Rom. 10: 2), and to which the message of the Cross is particularly addressed, is possible in principle everywhere. Hence the reasons for using the Old Testament in the Christian Church are purely pedagogical. It is a useful instrument to bring home to man that he is under the requirements of God. Bultmann thinks that in the Decalogue and in the words of the prophets these requirements are expressed with a force and a clarity found nowhere else except in the preaching of Jesus. But the law of the Old Testament, he concedes, is not actually addressed to us but to a definite people, living a definite history that is not ours. If we understand it as an expression of the law of God as such, we simply do so by virtue of the fact that in the Christian history out of which we have come this Old Testament element has happened to have played a considerable role.

Bultmann then takes up the Old Testament understanding of existence in direct approach. He points out that we are subject to a variety of influences, not only collectively but individually, so that various possibilities of understanding of the self are intermingled in our present situation. In striving to obtain clarity and to appropriate the fruits of our own history, we are forced to give consideration also to the Old Testament and its distinctive view of existence. For here a very important human possibility becomes clarified in all its consequences.

Bultmann, thereupon, tries to set forth the peculiarities of this Old Testament view in contrast to that which comes to us from the Greeks and likewise forms so potent a factor in our heritage. In the Old Testament, he asserts, the divine imperative governs man's entire existence in the most radical fashion. It makes no concession to an idealistic or utilitarian interpretation of the moral requirement. When you read the Old Testament you have to be conscious of the fact that there is a parting of the ways between the striving to attain some ideal of excellence or perfection, and that of serving one's neighbour in obedience to God and in perpetual consciousness of inadequacy and guilt. The real Old Testament understanding of man finds expression notably in the consciousness that we have been created by a higher power. It implies that man cannot in his thinking deal arbitrarily with the world, but in his capacity as a creature is delivered up to the Lord of the world. And since man primarily has his destiny in history, the Old Testament understands history not as the result of human activity but as the work of God, which assigns to man his fate and comforts him with tasks conferred. Man knows himself to be put in a definite place by the divine will and facing the possibility of judgment or grace, according as he does that which God demands of him.

This peculiar understanding of existence found in the Old Testament is basically identical with that of the New Testament and stands in sharp contrast to the idealistic or humanistic view of the Greeks. Only in a fundamental, critical grappling with this Old Testament position, whether its result be negative or positive, can we attain clarity for the understanding of existence that we would make our own. Only in such grappling can the question whether Christianity has any significance for the present be clarified. In view of this similarity of the Old Testament and New Testament view of existence it would appear senseless, Bultmann says, for anyone to want to hold fast to Christianity and discard the Old Testament! Such a one can be sure that the Christianity he wants to hold fast to is no longer

Christianity. The alternative is neither or both. Our whole history gives the Old Testament a claim on us—the claim to be heard and to make us come to grips with its idea of existence and thereby to grasp our own present situation.

But after thus insisting on the place of the Old Testament in a manner that seems almost too strong in the light of what he said previously and develops subsequently, Bultmann hastens to point out that what he means is something very different from that which the New Testament and the Christian Church mean, when they describe the Old Testament as revelation or Word of God. The critical consideration that he has just characterized is no listening to the Word of God, and not faith. The question whether Christian preaching can refer to the Old Testament as the revelation of God, and if so, to what extent, is one yet to be considered. He approaches it via a further discussion of the relation of the Old Testament to the New Testament. If the understanding of existence is the same in the New Testament as in the Old Testament, if faith, righteousness and grace, sin and forgiveness are essentially the same in the Old Testament and New Testament, as already stated, where, then, is the difference? What is the new in the New Testament over against the Old?

Bultmann now inquires whether the difference between Old Testament and New Testament is correctly described as that between law and gospel. Just as existence under grace always refers back to that under the law, so likewise the Old Testament knows no existence under the law that is not at the same time an existence under grace. He then tries to show how the grace of God underlies the entire Old Testament order. The prevenient grace of God establishes the Old Testament relation of God and man, and provides the basis for man's obedience.[8] It was an act of divine grace that God chose Israel and bestowed His law upon it and gave His people a task to be realized in a definite history. Furthermore, in the Old Testament the grace of God is understood as forgiveness. Amid all the unfaithfulness of His people, God's faithfulness remains unchanged: He is the God who forgives and has mercy upon His children (Ps. 103: 8–13). Hence the Christian Church can directly take over sayings in the Psalms and Prophets which pray for forgiveness or which promise God's grace.

In so far as gospel is the preaching of the grace of God for the sinner, one cannot assert that the gospel element is lacking in the Old Testament. One can, of course, say that this gospel is not found everywhere in its purity, and that the ideas of sin and the forgiveness of God are not always understood radically. A symptom of this, for instance, is the manner in which a Psalmist appeals for God's grace by pointing to the frailty of man as a mere mortal creature (103: 14–16); so long as man thinks there is something about himself that is deserving of grace, even though it be only his own frailty, he has not yet understood God's grace radically. But in Psalm 90: 8 f. this human frailty itself is considered the result of God's wrath, whereby it is put in a different light. Sometimes the appeal for divine mercy is uttered in absolute humility, as in Psalms 51 and 130. In the Old Testament the typical idea of sin is not one of moral transgression, but of injury done the divine honour, of distrust of God's grace, of human rebellion—in short, of unbelief. For the thing required of man above all is faith, waiting on God (Ps. 147: 10 f.). It is finding one's help in the Lord and boasting only of Him. It is hoping and experiencing the grace of God in the vicissitudes of collective and individual life. In all this the men of Israel experienced the forgiveness of their God. And if the Old Testament saints did not always experience it, they looked forward to it. Here lie the roots of the eschatological hope. On the basis of the radical knowledge of collective sin that has deserved nothing but judgment, prophecy reaches out to the last things. The future of hope that looms up behind the judgment is purely one of grace (Is. 48: 11; cf. Ezek. 36: 22). There is no continuity between past and present; Israel may be dead but God's grace can and will restore it (Ezek. 36: 26 f.; 37: 1–14). He will make a new covenant with the people thus re-established (Jer. 31: 33 f.).

In so far as both the idea of God and the ideas of sin and grace are radically understood in the Old Testament, its faith is at the same time a hope. Over against it there stands the faith of the New Testament, as the faith that has the fulfilment. For this is the decisive thing in the New Testament and in Christian faith, that God has carried out an eschatological act in Jesus Christ; that in Christ he has forgiven sin, called the new Israel and given it His Spirit. If in Christianity our relation to God is bound to the person of Jesus, this means that we believe in a God who has reconciled the world with Himself through Christ (II Cor. 5: 19). Such an assertion is no mere supplementing of Jewish belief in the one God by a belief in a second divine person. Nor is faith asked to assent to speculation about the deity of Christ and His alleged two natures. Faith in Christ is faith in what God does through Christ.

If in Christ we have the eschatological act of God's forgiveness, then the idea of the grace of God is understood radically. This means that knowledge of forgiveness is not tied to the experience of external, collective or individual destinies. God's grace is pure forgiveness, and this alone makes man new and strong (II Cor. 12: 9). The judgment has transpired, the new æon has begun, all speculation concerning future final events is cut off in principle. God's grace and forgiveness are present exclusively in the message that God has established in the world through Jesus Christ (II Cor. 5: 18 f.). The Word is the light that has come into the world and Jesus is the Word (John 1: 1 f.).

If Jesus is understood in this manner then the demonstration of God's grace given in Him is quite different from the proofs of such grace of which the Old Testament speaks. The latter expects that this grace is to be manifested in the destinies of the Jewish nation. In the grace shown to the nation of the past the individual shares because this history lives on in the present life of the people. Similarly in the future, the individual will share as a member of the nation. But the act of God in Christ is not to be understood as similar to an historical event of Hebrew history from which succeeding generations derive profit. One cannot think of Jesus as of Abraham or Moses, or as the passage through the Red Sea or the Sinaitic legislation. For He is the eschatological act of God which makes an end to all national history as the sphere of God's dealing with man. The message of the forgiving grace of God in Jesus Christ is not a historical report about an event of a distant past, but is the Word of the Church spoken now to each one as God's Word, in which Jesus Christ is present. In this Word God and His forgiving grace encounter man directly. Man is not asked to look at the proofs of God's grace in a past history and then draw the inference that God is gracious and hence will probably also be gracious to him now, but rather God's grace comes to him directly in the Word that is preached. The Church of Christ is not a mere sociological entity that has a history like any other group. It is constituted through the Word of God's forgiveness in Christ and is the fellowship of those who receive the message in faith. It is the eschatological congregation that stands at the end of history, for Jesus Christ is the end of the old æon—He is the final word that God has spoken and speaks. The preaching of the Word is not just another link in the process of universal history, but proceeds, as it were, on a plane outside of or above it. "Old things are passed away; behold, all things are become new" (II Cor. 5: 17).

This means that for the Christian faith the Old Testament no longer is revelation in the sense that it was and still is for the Jews; and the history of Israel is not for us the history of revelation. The events that had a significance for Israel and were a Word of God to Israel cannot be that to us. Of course, one can say that certain happenings like the Exodus, or the giving of the Sinaitic law, or the building of the temple of Solomon, are of some interest to historical reflection, since they have had an influence on our Occidental history. But in the same sense one can say that the Spartans who fell at Thermopylae fell for us, or that Socrates drank the cup for us. Furthermore, whatever is discernible in any effort to grapple with history, in so far as it shows us the possibilities of human self-understanding, can be seen by the eye of unbelief as well as by that of faith. It therefore does not belong exclusively to the province of faith.

If Israel's history is not a history of revelation for Christian faith we may still ask, however, whether the Old Testament entirely divorced from its history—not as it spoke to Israel but as it speaks immediately to us—can be revelation for Christian faith. It is true that Christian faith can appropriate the Old Testament and can assert that that which is said there, though it was originally only said in a preliminary and limited sense, now has a much fuller and clearer meaning. But this in itself implies that, in so far as the Church proclaims the Old Testament as Word of God, it is merely finding in it what it already knows from the fuller revelation in Christ. This was, indeed, the procedure of the New Testament and primitive Christianity.

It interprets the Old Testament from the eschatological consciousness that all that has gone before was preliminary and limited, and only now receives its deepest meaning.

The form in which the New Testament and early Christianity used the Old Testament was that of Scripture-proof. The understanding of the significance of the fate of Jesus was based on the assertion that it was prophesied and interpreted in advance in the Old Testament. Such Scripture-proof, however, is actually impossible. The supposed prophecies of the Old Testament are partly no prophecies at all and partly contain merely expressions of the Hebrew hope of the future. Most of the relevant passages were understood by the early Christians in a way contrary to their real meaning, in an allegorical manner, to provide the supposed predictions. This shows that faith existed before and without the Scripture-proof: it only discovered and seized upon such proof secondarily. This Scripture-proof played its historical role in the first and second centuries, but it cannot and should not convince anybody today. A faith resting on such proofs is no true faith at all.

But is there any other sense in which the Old Testament can be understood as Word of God? One thing is clear: the Old Testament must not be interpreted contrary to its original sense, as historical research can alone determine it. For then it would no longer be the Old Testament that is speaking. All allegorization is mere trifling and nonsense.

If Jesus Christ is God's Word to man, as the eschatological act of forgiveness, then one can say that all words that help to make this Word understandable (in that they bring man into the situation in which he can understand it and unfold the understanding of existence contained therein) are God's Word in an intermediate fashion. In this sense one can still consider the Old Testament, too, to be the Word of God. In it is found the understanding of the law and gospel in their correlation, that is normative for the Christian understanding of existence. In it we have the understanding of man as a lord of creation, as well as the consciousness of sinfulness and the hope of God's grace—all of which are highly important elements of the Christian consciousness as well. We therefore can see ourselves reflected in the Old Testament, just as Paul (I Cor. 10: 11) holds up the generation of the desert wanderings for our instruction.

Faith thus dares to take words not spoken for us and to address them to ourselves in order that we may get an understanding of our own situation and of the Word of Christ that is addressed to it. In this sense one can call the Old Testament "prophecy" and the New Testament "fulfilment".

This *may* be done and is, perhaps, the normal thing to do. But it does not *have* to be done. Even in the New Testament there are differences in this respect. Some writings utilize the Old Testament prominently and others do not. It depends on the particular situation of teacher and hearer. Similarly to-day, the use of the Old Testament cannot be regarded as absolutely essential. But if the Old Testament is still to be given a place in the preaching of the Church as Word of God, then two conditions must be laid down for its use. First, the Old Testament must be taken in its original sense, without any allegorization, though it is permissible to detach it from its original exclusive pertinence to the Hebrew people and its history. Second, the Old Testament must be utilized only in so far as it really prepares the way for the Christian understanding of existence. To the extent that it can be made to do this, one may say that Christ speaks already in the Old Testament.

It seems clear that this approach has enabled Bultmann to discern the human situation in the Old Testament and to compare it with the Christian situation in a more fundamental way than has ever been done. The result is that one realizes both the similarities and the differences in the Hebrew and Christian religion more clearly. In spite of the statements already noted pointing in the conservative direction, his main line of argument is negative in its consequences. The value of the Old Testament lies in the sphere of the intellect—in the insight it gives us into existence, but what insight we really need we can have without it. From the angle of making the Old Testament essential for the Church this view is not as effective as Vischer's. But it has the virtue of requiring no *credo quia absurdum*.

Chapter Fifteen

THE OLD TESTAMENT AS ANTITHESIS TO CHRISTIANITY

IF Vischer, carrying Barth's approach further, attempted to give the Old Testament the immediate value and authority of Word of God that it had for the early Christians; if Bultmann sought to make it meaningful by pointing out that its understanding of human existence was substantially the same as that of the New Testament and that, with proper allowance for the transitory elements, it was still valuable (though not absolutely essential) for Christianity; Hirsch, basically following the radical line in Paul's thinking, views the Old Testament as the very antithesis of Christianity, but instead of rejecting it on that ground holds it to be of value for us because we can only appreciate the meaning of the gospel fully in the light of the contrast it provides.[1] And Hirsch does not merely present this as historical enlightenment but in terms of individual human experience.

For the better understanding of Hirsch's position it should be said that like Herrmann he regards revelation as a thing of the present, not of the past.[2] It is God's speaking to us as apprehended by faith and is in principle of twofold character— law and gospel. The revelation of law confronts us in the reality of human-historical existence. There is an external law and also a deeper law,[3] of the existence of which man is not at first aware. Divine revelation by means of the law is experienced in our passing through both of these spheres. *Per se* the deeper law is present in the external law, but man in his rebellion against God seeks to use the power and responsibility given him by the external law for his own vain purposes, therewith making this law a wall shutting man off from God. But in so doing he gets out of harmony with the deeper law. God in His goodness then reveals the latter to man and forces him to perceive the reality of his life before God. The passage from the one sphere to the other has a negative result in that it leads to the realization that we are under the divine wrath, and can only be considered "revelation" in conjunction with the gospel-revelation, for which it prepares the way.   The aforesaid transition is the ultimate secret of all non-Christian religions and at the same time the abiding part of the Christian's sharing in human-historical existence.   The Old Testament revelation does not concern us in so far as it is external law (for the latter differs in its expression according to national character and historical circumstances) except in so far as there is a kinship and similarity above all differences between all such legislations. The relation of the Christian to the Old Testament rests on this, that since it also preaches the deeper law it is an instrument endowed with effectiveness by God and operative in Christian history.

In frank fashion Hirsch describes how he arrived at his position on the Old Testament. As a theological student he came in contact with modern critical scholarship and realized to what extent the Old Testament is an Oriental book. He found Old Testament science a rather chaotic thing. It seemed doubtful to him whether it deserved to be included in theology at all.   In the instruction he received at the hands of such scholars as Gunkel, Gressmann and von Baudissin he felt that the one thing lacking, from a theological point of view, was any real grappling with the significance of the Old Testament for the Christian. Old Testament study had therefore left him disappointed.   It came as a shock to him when, following German graduation requirements, he was directed to prepare for the ecclesiastical authorities a thesis on the question whether one could justly accuse certain Psalmists of self-righteousness and carnal vindictiveness. In investigating this theme he realized that the relevant utterances of the Psalmists were not mere individual aberrations, but flowed from the central idea of the religion of the Old Testament as such. His conclusions opened his eyes all the more to the basic difference existing between Christianity and Judaism on the one hand, and Judaism and the pagan religions on the other hand. Subsequently, incidents of pastoral experience and homiletical exercises conducted with theological students forced him to come to grips with the matter of the Christian religious use of the Old Testament. He found some of Luther's thinking along these lines particularly suggestive. In a controversy with advocates of Bible revision he defended Luther's occasionally Christianizing translation of the Old Testament over against all modern attempts at correction for the purpose of rendering the Hebrew more accurately; such activity, he warned, would bring about either a Judaizing of Christianity or the casting out of the Old Testament from the Christian Bible.[4] Subsequently he was driven to even more extreme conclusions by certain utterances of Kierkegaard, which we shall cite later.[5]

Finally, in the fierce anti-Semitic agitation that arose in the Third Reich after 1933, Hirsch saw that the Old Testament was a serious liability for Christianity and took that situation for an indication that the Church must clarify its position concerning that book. He set forth his views first in a rather incidental manner in a commentary on the Gospel of John,[6] and then more elaborately in the treatise already mentioned.

Hirsch points out that the Old Testament owes its place in the Bible of the Christian Church to three presuppositions: (1) False Christianizing understanding of the Old Testament by the Church; (2) Infiltration of Jewish and pagan ideas into Christianity, corrupting the original purity of the gospel and thus making the toleration of the Old Testament easier; (3) The belief in the permissibility of symbolic, spiritualizing interpretation of such a mysterious book. All of these presuppositions, he asserts, have fallen to the ground to-day. Biblical scholarship makes it impossible for us to read the Old Testament in Christianizing or spiritualizing fashion. Read in its full Hebrew realism, as it must be, the book no longer seems close to us at all.

According to Hirsch, the early Christians really took away the sacred book from the Jews and turned it into a witness for Jesus against Judaism. A worse injury could hardly have been inflicted on the Jews than that. But no honest person to-day can accept the evangelists' proof from prophecy for the Messiahship of Jesus as carrying any weight, or regard the allegories of Old Testament stories which a Paul develops as having any validity. The anti-Semitic agitators sometimes represent Christianity as having perpetrated a fraud in such matters. But that inference is doing the early Christians an injustice. They used the Old Testament as it was customary to use ancient writings in their time—reading more profound meaning into sayings than the context warranted. The Greeks did this with Homer and other writings, and the Jews themselves did it with their canon. If the Christians outdid all others in this procedure, they acted simply as children of their time. But now that we recognize it as false and untenable, we cannot allow it to be continued. Should we not rather give this book back to the Jews and let them keep it exclusively for their own use?

Hirsch then sets forth that the Old Testament can be understood in four different ways. *First*, there is the plain historical meaning. Read in this manner the Old Testament is not a unity, but a book containing a considerable diversity of viewpoints. It is a compilation of a variety of documents from a thousand years of Hebrew history, in which minds great and small, narrow and broad, have left some record of their faith. Even the underlying religion is not a unity but exhibits a process of struggle in which various ways of serving God remain in constant clash. *Secondly*, there is the sense in which it was understood by the Jewish Church from Ezra to the destruction of the second temple in A.D. 70. Here the whole Hebrew religion is conceived of as built on the Mosaic law, though a certain open-mindedness for the elements of divine grace and the humane viewpoints inherent in the Old Testament faith, as well as for the prophetic and apocalyptic possibilities, still remains. This Jewish view of the Old Testament religion is really the only unified one—and, be it noted, it is that of the period that created the Old Testament canon, and hence has a special importance.

The *third* meaning is that which early Christianity gave the Old Testament in its polemic against Judaizing influences. It does not accept the view that the five books of Moses, understood as "law", are the heart and soul of the Old Testament. It takes chiefly three books, Genesis, Isaiah and Psalms, and understands them, in accordance with the artificial scheme of prophecy and fulfilment, as pointing to something above and beyond the religion of the law. So far as the other elements of the Old Testament religion are concerned, there is a vacillation between two different attitudes. In part, there is a rejection of them as belonging to a strange order and mode of worship— an old covenant abrogated by Jesus—and in part acceptance of them as symbols of something not yet realized in the Old Testament, but attained in Jesus. *Fourthly*, there is the meaning given to the Old Testament by late Judaism which has lost its temple and has rejected Jesus. It represents a deterioration of the earlier Jewish viewpoint (the second described above)—a hardening of the legalistic outlook together with a polemical attitude toward all the elements in the Old Testament heritage that rise above and beyond the national and legalistic. "It is the Jewish religion debased toward the demonic[7] by the negation of Christ." The fourth interpretation may be dismissed as decadent, but the first and the second seem legitimate in their sphere. The third, or Christian interpretation, has ceased to be the solely valid one —in fact it has become extremely difficult to maintain it at all. Wherever the Christian Church fails to admit this and gives the Old Testament out as a Christian book, this amounts to a lack of honesty which rightly draws wrath down upon its own head.

The impossibility of holding to the Christian interpretation of the Old Testament has become clear not only because of the destruction of the early Christian proof of the correspondence between prophecy and fulfilment, but also because of a better historical understanding of the Old Testament hope. We discern quite clearly what elements were included in this hope and though we see that a Christian continuity with it is quite possible at some points, we realize that Judaism of the time of Christ could well take the position that Jesus was not the Messiah whom its sacred books had foretold, and that the kingdom He brought was not that for which Israel was waiting. The Christian "fulfilment" of the Old Testament expectations is in reality their disappointment. Christianity has not been able to take over a single word or thought from the Old Testament religion without filling it with a different meaning. We can no longer read the Old Testament to-day without becoming conscious of this essential remodelling, of this constant doing of violence to the Old Testament, of this destruction of the religion of the law by the freedom of the gospel, this steady breaking down of a faith and worship basically bound to racialism by a religion which recognizes only those as God's children that are His in spirit and in truth. We are therefore forced to ask ourselves whether the Old Testament is revelation for us at all. In the Yahweh of the Old Testament there is as yet an unclarified fusion of a Jewish national God who grants His people a kingdom, and the Creator of heaven and earth whose living voice comes to all men. The Jewish national God is as much a thing of the past for us as Odin and other Nordic gods. Only when we understand the Old Testament out of an idea of God that is not really the one meant in its own pages does it speak to us of *our* God.

The right of the early Church to use the Old Testament in a Christian re-interpretation that is not in accord with its real meaning rested on the fact that the Old Testament religion is something unclarified, contradictory in itself and having no possibility of further vitality after Jesus had come. In its ultimate aspect, as faith in the living God, it either had to burst through the historical shell to which it was bound (Judaism)—or die and be mummified in those fetters. The former possibility was realized where the first and second type of interpretation were dissolved or metamorphosed into the third—the Christianizing one—while the latter eventuality occurred where the first two types of interpretation passed over into the fourth—the late Jewish. It was Jesus who ushered in this fateful crisis for the Old Testament religion by partly adopting and partly rejecting it. He adopted it in so far as He regarded Himself as the promised Messiah and found the eternal life that the children of God have through Him expressed in the Old Testament hope of the kingdom. He rejected it in so far as He denied the political Jewish Messianism and divorced the kingdom of God from all national hopes of the Jewish people. In other words, Jesus brought the inner contradiction that was inherent in the Old Testament religion out into the open. With the authority of the Son who knows the Father, He took the ultimate, hidden idea of God that was contained in that religion and revitalized it, and thereby turned it against the whole historical shell that held it. Thus He liberated the grace that lies in man's encounter with the living God from the bonds of servitude to Mosaic Yahwism, when He reached beyond the Jewish national and religious community with His gospel. And this received absolute finality by the cross to which the Jews delivered Him.

The coming of Christianity is thus a revolutionary event within the Jewish religion. And when the Church, in the light of its faith in Jesus, re-interpreted the Old Testament in Christian fashion, it only did again in the sphere of theological reflection what Jesus had already done in the living historical process: it burst through the historical limitations of the Old Testament by availing itself of an eternal and transcendent element that was in it. Nothing remained now for the Jews who had rejected Jesus but to destroy or abandon this eternal and transcendent element of the Old Testament that had been turned against them, and hold fast to the dismal remnants. Of their own volition they thus condemned themselves to a miserable existence as a community that has really died off to the hidden Holy that was theirs.

For a constructive attitude toward the Old Testament, Hirsch thinks that we must have a picture of the Old Testament religion as a whole from another of the aforementioned standpoints.[8] He considers it impossible to create such a picture purely on the basis of the Old Testament understood as modern criticism reads it, or the first standpoint; he believes that it can only be done from the second standpoint, i.e., that of the Jewish community of the Persian and Hellenistic eras, for it was this community that created the canon and thus had a standpoint into which all these books could fit. Neither the presence in the Old Testament of barbaric elements which this community rejected, nor the greater possibilities of earlier prophetic religion which it did not wish to realize, can be decisive when we seek to establish a relation between the Old Testament and the New. Only when we regard the Old Testament as a whole from that Jewish standpoint are these demonic trends and these nobler possibilities seen in their correct perspective.

Hirsch then sketches the main characteristics of this Old Testament Jewish religion as follows. Its most obvious earmark is the fact of its being bound to a cult in which laws of clean and unclean, sacrifice and other observances, and emphasis on a specific holy place are dominant. In this respect this religion does not basically differ from any pagan religion of the old world. Through the cross of Christ this whole cultic theory of religion has been cancelled. There is only one way in which God manifests His presence: in Jesus Christ, raised to be Lord through the cross, and there is only one thing with which God is pleased: with the faith in a gospel that makes us free. There is only one service of God: the living realization of this faith in the service of one's neighbour, out of the strength of the Holy Spirit. We are thus radically cut off from the entire range of religious experience of the people of the Old Testament, and are simply unable, if we are clear as to the implications, to share the outlook of even Isaiah 6 or Psalm 23 or Psalms 42 and 43 without subtracting much of what is basic there.

The second earmark of the Old Testament Jewish religion, according to Hirsch, is the fact that its very heart and soul is an indissoluble relation between the God Yahweh and the Hebrew people. This people is the chosen, and God's glory is manifested in its destiny. Congregation and nation are a unity. This belief is cancelled in the New Testament idea of the kingdom and redeemer. Nation and congregation, civil law and will of God have become separated; the relation of the individual to God is based only on faith. This really makes a large part of the Old Testament entirely useless for us. We cannot identify nationality and kingdom of God, as the Jew could, without becoming unfaithful to the gospel. To apply the Old Testament promises given to Israel to the Church involves spiritualizing and allegorizing them in a manner doing violence to their real meaning. It is obvious, therefore, that the New Testament history is fulfilment of the Old Testament order only in a paradoxical sense really involving the disappointment of the actual expectations.

A third earmark of the Old Testament Jewish religion is its lack of knowledge of the Christian belief in eternal life. It is purely a religion of this life, even though at some high points it does get beyond a mere eudaemonistic approach. The thought of a resurrection which comes to the surface in a few late passages does not change this in principle, but is only a fantastic broadening of the Old Testament position—even the dead are to share in the glory promised Israel. It signified a radical change of outlook when Christianity, by virtue of the death and resurrection of Christ, saw the goal of man in an eternal life that comes to us through death and that transcends this earthly existence. At once the idea of God, as well as the idea of human life, and every thought connected with the divine-human relationship completely changed their meaning. The more fully we appreciate this, the more clearly must we realize how radically different, how unsatisfactory the Old Testament religion really is, but the more we will also see how in some of its utterances this religion is vainly seeking to break through the bars of its cage.

The fourth main trait of the Old Testament Jewish religion is that it is the religion of the law. This does not mean that it has no knowledge of grace and forgiveness, but rather that grace and forgiveness are legally conditioned. Forgiveness is granted the sinner who purifies himself and returns to the state of obedience through penitence; the grace of God is a grace that is zealous to reinstate man in the legal relation. In Christianity this is totally changed. God freely gives the sinner sonship and eternal life. Repentance is simply the reception of forgiveness in faith and is not the work of man but of God. The relation to God in which we are placed by forgiveness, faith and repentance is not that of being bound under a law, but one of freedom from the law in that love which faith begets in the heart. According to the Old Testament, the law and the divine judgments reveal the glory and holiness of God, and forgiveness and grace are related to this glory and holiness; according to the New Testament, the law and the divine judgments are the "strange work" of God (Isa. 28: 21) in which He is concealed, while He is truly revealed in that work which is clearly expressive of Him, in grace and love. Under the influence of Old Testament ideas this true Christian idea of God is usually corrupted and distorted in Christian preaching.

In view of this situation, it is by no means self-evident that the Old Testament should continue to be used by Christianity. If at every point along the line we must be conscious of the sharp divergence of that religion from all we hold dear, why plague ourselves with it at all? Protestant theology has only two reasons to offer for the continuance of the use of the Old Testament. The first is that the Old Testament has not its equal as a document of the History of religion as such, that nowhere in any literature outside of Christianity do we find such clear and powerful expression of the belief in a deity. It is thus held to be useful for religious training, as an auxiliary source. Secondly, the historical connection between the Old Testament and the New Testament is such that the latter cannot really be understood without the former. Hirsch concedes that both of these points rest on correct observation, but holds that they must be brought into relation with the insights previously emphasized. When this is done, it is realized that nowhere is there an alternative to Christianity.

The proper Christian use of the Old Testament, Hirsch thinks, depends on a full realization of the revolutionary character of the situation involved in the coming of Christianity. In the first place, there must be constant and conscious renewal of this grappling with the Old Testament, appropriation of that which is eternal in it, and polemic against that which is intolerable. We must realize that a Christian faith which does not maintain a polemical attitude toward the Old Testament religion actually is unfaithful to Jesus and is drawn into Judaism—putting grace captive beneath the law. In the second place, Christianity must cease putting the Old Testament on a level with the New. For us, the former is definitely of a lower order. The Old Testament has no message for the disciples of Jesus; there is merely a Christian freedom on the part of the disciple of Jesus to illuminate with the word of the New Testament the difficult and mysterious history whereby God prepared the way for the coming of His Son. Of that history the Old Testament is indeed a witness. But there is no possibility for us to proceed from the Old Testament basis to faith in Jesus. From the basis of faith in Jesus, however, we can have a Christian glimpse into the dark mystery of the Old Testament that is both opponent and preparer of the way for the gospel.

In this final line of thought a stimulation by Kierkegaard's viewpoints, of which Hirsch had made mention in connection with the narrative of his own development, becomes apparent. Kierkegaard had experienced a crisis in July 1843 in which his faith in a divine justice in life, as based on the Bible stories of Abraham and Job, broke down completely; from that time on he had had no use for the Old Testament. Hirsch quotes the following:

> It cannot be made sufficiently clear or be repeated often enough that Christianity, indeed, does have a relation to Judaism, but, be it noted, of this sort, viz., that Judaism is for Christianity the thing with the help of which the latter makes itself negatively recognizable—that it is its absolute opposite. . . .
> This cannot be emphasized enough. For one will find in Christendom, that almost all (if you will) of the 'more pious'

aberrations hang together with the circumstance that the Old Testament has been put on the same level with the New Testament instead of this, that the New Testament constantly presupposes the Old in such a way as to make that which is truly its own negatively known. In this sense the New Testament can not be rightly understood without the Old, for this, its absolute opposite, is its (the New Testament's) dialectic criterion and the indication of its spiritual altitude. . . .

But people would much rather be Jews, and sensually cleave to this life—and that, furthermore, with (apparent) divine sanction—than be Christians, that is to say, spirit. . . .[9]

Christianity could not have had any other religion as foreground, for no other makes so definitely, so decisively known by means of negation, what Christianity is, as does Judaism.[10]

Only when it is understood in this fashion, Hirsch claims, does the Old Testament have anything to say to the followers of Jesus Christ. But that is still important enough. For the history of the struggle between a religion of the law and the sonship of God according to the gospel is an everlasting history that is repeated in every life. The moment we think of it as closed, the gospel becomes a new law and the relapse into Judaism is complete. The history of Jesus is the coming of the truth and freedom of the gospel in the destruction of the Old Testament religion and of every other religion of the law, through which the expectation of God on the part of the human heart that cannot live or die out of captive grace, is fulfilled.

Hirsch concerns himself in particular with the use of the Old Testament in preaching, and a large part of his book is devoted to showing what theological reflections should occupy the mind of the preacher in dealing with the Old Testament. He discusses three selected biblical stories: the Sacrifice of Isaac, David and Goliath, and the tale of Jonah, to illustrate how this should be done. In each case the divergence of the Old Testament religious ideas and ideals from Christian ideas and ideals is carefully considered.

Hirsch's points did not find much favour, though they elicited a considerable amount of critical discussion, for his view was too moderate for those who wanted to get rid of the Old Testament and too radical for those who were determined to hold the Old Testament as present Word of God to the Church. His position is a half-way station on the road from Paul to Marcion and can hardly be put outside of the pale of Christian possibilities. If it fails to appeal, Kierkegaard's remark that people would rather be Jews than Christians could well occasion some searching of soul. One must concede to Hirsch, as to Harnack and Delitzsch, a sincere desire to see Christianity attain the full purity inherent in its nature.

From the angle of Old Testament scholarship Hirsch's position is unsatisfactory, of course, in that he views the Old Testament in terms of the Judaism that set up the canon. We prefer to interpret the documents in their full historical reality. If one follows the high-water mark line in the Old Testament there is no such sharp contrast between it and Christianity as is established by Hirsch.[11] But one must concede that on this basis the entire Old Testament cannot be given immediate importance for us. For Hirsch the whole of it has the abiding significance of total contrast.

Chapter Sixteen

RECENT DISCUSSIONS

DURING the years of the Second World War German discussion of our subject was limited by the internal situation and was sealed off from the attention of those in other lands. The desire to use the Old Testament, and therewith also the necessity of justifying its use, came forward prominently in England and in America in this period, as was but natural, since cataclysmic events always make people turn to a book so full of that sort of thing.

Two notable works by American scholars that appeared at the beginning of the fourth decade are not only significant for their learned material, but also because they reveal the urge to bring into focus some sort of positive relationship to the Old Testament. This is the more surprising since both authors are primarily identified with Semitic philology and historical inquiry. Yet W. F. Albright[1] injects into an account of Biblical and Oriental research, as that illuminates Hebrew history, a chapter of discussion of Philosophy of History and dignifies the succeeding chapters with such religious titles as: "*Praeparatio*", "When Israel was a Child", "Charisma and Catharsis", "In the Fulness of Time". He sees civilization at an impasse similar to that the world had reached in the time of Christ and calls for "a reawakening of faith in the God of the majestic theophany on Mount Sinai, in the God of Elijah's vision at Horeb, in the God of the Jewish exiles in Babylonia, in the God of the Agony at Gethsemane . . ." But his basic categories are sociological.

R. H. Pfeiffer, though he has a long journey through Old Testament literary criticism,[2] devotes separate preliminary chapters to the religious, literary and historical-critical interest in the Old Testament. He puts the religious interest first. He finds that for us moderns the Old Testament is religiously significant in three ways; as inspired Scripture it continues to be norm of faith and conduct for Church and Synagogue; it is the ultimate source of their basic doctrines; it is a unique record of religious progress. The first two points, however, are merely empirical statements concerning the situation created in the past, without investigation of their validity, and the third operates only with one of the "values" provided by the Old Testament.

The year 1944 saw the appearance of a number of works directly concerned with our theme. A distinctly liberal approach marks the discussion of H. F. D. Sparks.[3] He holds that Criticism has shown that the traditional Christian attitude towards the Old Testament stands in need of drastic modification. The phrase "Word of God" as applied to it can no longer mean what it did. Historical investigation has not only demonstrated numerous errors in the Old Testament, but has shown that its writers differed little from their Gentile contemporaries. Science has demonstrated that the Old Testament ideas of cosmology and earth history are "ancient" in their character and unable to give us any enlightenment and that in the light of anthropology Old Testament custom, morality and religion are but part and parcel of a general process; the distinction between "revealed" and "natural" has, therefore, broken down. Thus, although the Old Testament may be the record of a Divine revelation, it cannot be equated with it. We may say if we will that the Old Testament not *is* but *contains* the Word of God; though we should remember as we do so that such a statement is very far from representing what the Church has for centuries maintained.

Sparks then proceeds to ask what value the Old Testament has to-day. Here he turns first to such matters as the literary excellence of the Old Testament and its importance for historians and anthropologists, but he realizes that that is only peripheral. The question is what is its Christian value both for me individually and for the Church. He points to the quandary of the cleric who at ordination is required to state that he "unfeignedly believes all the canonical Scriptures of the Old Testament", when, if he has been properly educated, he cannot possibly believe them in anything like the traditional sense. He expresses the feeling that the Church must come out into the open and declare itself. The three possibilities he sees are: (1) The Church may simply give up the Christian use of the Old

Testament; (2) It may discriminate between different parts and direct the attention of its members to some parts, rather than to others; or (3) It may retain the use of the Old Testament whole and entire, although it will certainly find itself compelled to advance reasons for doing so which are other than traditional.

Sparks rejects the radical solution and finds sentiment largely in favour of the second or moderate solution. He himself, however, espouses the third. He thinks that the bond of union between the Old Testament and the New Testament is so close that it cannot be broken and that Christian people should be taught to appreciate the entire Old Testament historically. Even the Old Testament lessons in the Anglican service must be chosen not particularly, so as to fit in with private or popular religious prejudice, but impartially, so as to illustrate the Old Testament as a whole. A rather heavy yoke of historicism!

A new slant on our subject came in that same year through H. H. Rowley, who introduced the term "relevance" to describe the relation of the Old Testament to ourselves.[4] He notes the change that has recently come over biblical studies—that of attempting to transcend the previous critical approach by seeking the abiding significance of the Bible and in particular its significance for this generation. Thereupon he undertakes to do some theological or religious undergirding by discussing such matters as revelation and inspiration. He finds revelation coming through the organ of human personality and depending for its character not merely on God but on the organ through which it comes. The writers of the Bible were real men with all the imperfections and the individuality that this implies. But God can only reveal Himself perfectly in perfect personality. That is why the Incarnation was necessary for the full revelation of God. It is not just something wholly other than the revelation of God in the Old Testament, but rather its climax and crown.

In setting forth how the failings of some writers of the Old Testament era and their false ideas and false hopes affected their writing, Rowley elaborates on Old Testament passages in which the will or purpose of God was wrongly interpreted. He rejects the accusation that this is taking away from the objective character of revelation and instituting a purely sub-

jective test for what is of God and what is not. He insists
that if God's actions or demands are ever portrayed in the Bible
in a manner inconsistent with His character as revealed in
Christ they are unworthy of Him, and the portrayal is due to
misunderstanding of Him by sincere men whose view was distorted by the eyes through which they looked upon Him. If this
elicits the suggestion that it would be better to discard the Old
Testament, Rowley replies that the latter is necessary for the
appreciation of the New Testament and that rightly understood
it is a great asset to our spiritual life. He rejects the idea of
progress in revelation so far as God is concerned; the progress
was merely in man's ability to understand and receive it. On
the other hand, the formula that the Old Testament is the
record of man's search for God is declared insufficient. Man's
search for God and God's reaching out to man are two sides of a
single process. Even man's capacity to receive Him is itself His
gift.

There are thus divine and human factors woven together in
the Old Testament. It is the record of man's growing experience
of God and progressive response to God. But Rowley feels that
such recognition of the inspiration of the Bible does not make it
final and unchallengeable authority for men. He criticizes the
Protestant Reformers for that view, and thinks the Church
should be vested with authority too. But neither can be the
ultimate authority, which is Christ Himself. "Neither Bible nor
Church can take His place, though both may lead us to Him,
for God is Spirit, and through Spirit He speaks His final Word to
us. Our desire for something lower than Spirit, something more
tangible and certain as we imagine, does not honour Christ, in
whom, and not through whom, is God to be seen."

In subsequent studies Rowley has sought to delineate the
deeper message of the Old Testament, or the Word of God in it.[5]
He sees the Old Testament not merely as preparatory to the
New, but rather the New as supplementary to the Old. Into the
making of the latter went human and divine factors that interpenetrate one another. The message of the Old Testament is
essentially religious, and that in a broad sense, affecting belief,
conduct and worship, in all of which it makes contributions of
enduring worth.

In a lecture of 1949 Rowley discussed the authority of the

Bible.[6] It is his aim here to offer evidence, "valid at the bar of reason", to support that authority. He rejects such a procedure as mere acceptance of the authority of the Bible on the authority of the Church. While he concedes that man is not only reason, and that since he is also guided by instinct and emotion there is almost certainly a non-rational factor in any man's belief in the authority of the Bible, he insists it cannot be wholly non-rational. He then seeks to adduce the arguments that will approve it to reason. He rejects equating the authority of the Bible either with inspiration or with the appeal to the inner witness of the Spirit. "Bibliolatry" is abhorrent to him— the ultimate authority is in God alone. There were other media of revelation beside the written word, and none of these is infallible; hence their authority is never absolute. Even God is limited by the spiritual maturity and sensitiveness of those He uses. It is not surprising, therefore, that in the Bible there are different levels of grandeur and loftiness. Two things are required of him who would maintain the authority of the Bible: (1) He must establish a test whereby these levels may be judged. (2) He must produce evidence that the Bible is the Word of God even if not all in the same degree.

For the test of the level of inspiration he adduces Christ, who is the supreme medium of divine revelation (essentially Luther's famous principle). So far as the Old Testament accords with the revelation in Christ, it is enduringly valid, but so far as it falls short of that it is superseded. But that does not mean that the Old Testament as such is superseded. In developing the second point, the adducing of evidence that the Bible is the Word of God, Rowley stresses the idea that the two Testaments belong together and neither is complete without the other. However, the hand of God is to be found not so much in the Bible as in the revelation of which the Bible contains the record. In that history itself, in the complex of person and event, promise and fulfilment, he discerns the guidance of God, who was active in a whole great process that culminated in the death and resurrection of Christ. The Bible itself is a unity because reflecting this unified process to which it testifies. He rejects the idea that by the same type of argument one can also prove the divine authority of Buddhism. While he finds the latter religion vindicating Paul's idea that God did not leave Himself without witness among heathen peoples (Acts 14: 17), he sees here no parallel to the complex of event and personality to which he has drawn attention in the process of divine revelation, but merely the natural spread of the influence of a teacher. It is evident, then, that Rowley's primary support for the authority of the Bible, including the Old Testament, rests on a philosophy of history.

In a recent book Rowley tries to show the dynamic unity of the Bible,[7] and this leads him to make clear that he is not thinking in terms of a purely human development that leaves God out of account, nor yet reverting to traditional dogma leaving reason out of account. He thinks it can be demonstrated, e.g., that the belief of Israel that Moses was called by God and effected the deliverance of Israel through divine aid is a more reasonable hypothesis than any other which discounts the divine element, and he shows in connection therewith what unreasonable assumptions all rival explanations of the Exodus tradition are forced to make. In speaking of the dynamic unity of the Bible Rowley does not mean that everything is on a flat level of authority. He seeks rather the continuity of religious life found in the Biblical record, mirroring as that does a long religious history. As in a personality the ideas of youth and of advancing age are not the same and yet not unrelated, so it is also with the Bible. (Cf. further, p. 280.)

In a study limited to the Prophets the Canadian scholar, R. B. Y. Scott, also pursues the relevance theme.[8] He undertakes "to state in positive terms the meaning and worth of the Hebrew prophetic writings and to indicate their profound importance, as a feature of our religious heritage having the constant freshness of a perennial stream". If the prophets do not speak of our age (and Scott—like Fullerton in 1919—is quite concerned about refuting those who seek in prophecy clairvoyant predictions of events of our own time) "they speak *to* our age because they were faced with crises and thereby can disclose the reality and nature of our crisis when speaking of their own". They are contemporaries of every generation because the truth they declare is permanently valid. What they say has the timeless quality and compelling power of authentic spiritual utterance. No explanation of them is sufficient that does not recognize that through them the Eternal God was carrying out His purpose for the redemption of mankind. Scott describes the prophets as men who had given themselves whole-heartedly to God's service, who were tremendously concerned with social conditions and public issues as marking a spiritual crisis, as having a vivid awareness of God's presence and activities in the turmoil of men's ordinary social life, as showing how their religion and ethic by its effect on the community demonstrates how a religion may become the dynamic and its ethic the directive of social transformation, as declaring the truth that God is a living God and not bound within the tradition of the past.

Scott then undertakes to show that the prophets have relevance to certain areas of life to-day. He quails a little at this assignment because he realizes that "the meaning and the moral imperative of religion for each person is for himself to recognize". But since he finds the prophets speaking largely to the *collective* mind of society and social groups, he is willing to say where he individually thinks he finds them speaking to our time.

The prophets first of all have a great deal to tell us about the nature and meaning of religion. What we learn from them on this score is not superseded (though it is illuminated) by the self-revelation of God in Jesus Christ. It is an essential element in the total Christian understanding of God and His ways. The Bible is *one* literature, and we know more about the God of Christian faith than is found in the pages of the New Testament when, like the evangelists and apostles, we read the prophetic writings with eyes opened by Jesus Christ. The relation between the Testaments, he asserts, is not simply one of succession and development, but one of interrelationship and vital continuity. The prophets, Scott then shows, make it plain that religion and ethical behaviour must form a unity. They enunciate man's social responsibility before God. They instruct us in the right evaluation of organized religious life, protecting us against its corruption and abuse and suggesting that the ends of worship are more important than the forms. They teach us that religion is not a specialized activity but a quality and attitude in all activities. Their relevance for religion in its personal aspects is to be found in what they *were*, rather than in what they said; the witness of such authentic saints carries stimulus.

17

In the second place, Scott finds the prophets having an importance for theology both because their thought is necessary to the understanding of certain major terms of New Testament theology and because the peculiar intensity of their apprehension of the ways of God demands the direct attention of the modern theologian. When we think of God in personal terms, when we speak of sin and evil, of the meaning of history, and of eschatology, we cannot ignore the thoughts of the Hebrew prophets. In connection with revelation, Scott mentions deposits "remaining from moments of it, to be added to the sum total of the knowledge of God and man".

In discussing the significance of the prophets for the work of the preacher Scott stresses their suggestiveness for messages on social justice, national responsibility, religious interpretation of historic events and on evangelism. Then he speaks of the relevance of the prophets for the cultural crisis of to-day. What Israel's prophets said long ago, as they condemned the manner of this world and pointed men to the city of God, is directly and profoundly relevant for us. The democratic struggle—the prophet's part in the spiritual ancestry of democracy—is especially singled out. They contributed the concept of a society where all had an equal right to justice and where authority was subject to a divine law of righteousness. They proclaimed the covenant society where God's way would be realized, and set before men's eyes the hope of a better day when all men would be delivered from want and fear and war.

Scott gives up the idea that what the prophets say is directly applicable:

> One cannot simply summarize and catalogue their insights and consider them disposed of when their relevance to one set of circumstances has been suggested. The dynamic of their message is not so easily exhausted, nor can its intrinsic authority be claimed for all that seems to follow from the attempt to apply it at one particular point. What really counts is a first-hand knowledge of the prophetic records, the recognition of their formative influence in our religious tradition, and their potential spiritual power over men's minds to-day. Finally we need the capacity constantly to discern afresh their relevance to the human situation of this and every age.

Since it takes an especial capacity to see this relevance it obviously cannot be made generally valid, but is a matter of faith.

A further and even more resolute bringing forward of the Old Testament came from another American quarter in that same 1944.[9] Here G. E. Wright saw not so much a relevance in the Old Testament as a challenge, placing on us a demand of decision (therein revealing an impact of modern existentialism). In accord with old Calvinistic tradition he conceives of the (Protestant) Bible as one book, and holds that there is such a thing as a "biblical religion", and that the Old Testament contributes much to it that is not duplicated in the New. He complains, furthermore, that in the last century the Protestant Church has become increasingly a New Testament Church. One reason is that the New Testament is more accessible—it takes time, study and much concentration to discover the Old Testament revelation. But even more to blame, he thinks, is the modern theology since Schleiermacher and Ritschl. They have stressed the importance of ideas. "This belief misses the really essential point about biblical revelation: that is, that God has made himself known not primarily in ideas, but in events."

Wright takes the message of the first chapter of Isaiah, giving a transposition of it into the contemporary situation of World War Two. In analysing the effect of Isaiah's message on the modern reader, Wright accuses him of evading the issue whether there is in Isaiah an actual word for us from the Lord, the Creator and ruler of the Universe. By pointing to the faults and foibles of the past we avoid those disturbing claims which the words of the prophet might have if taken seriously as spoken by God to us. But there is something within us, he asserts, that tells us Isaiah is right in his basic assertions. Where, however, is the line to be drawn between what is man's word and God's Word? Wright turns for suggestions to Jesus' use of the Old Testament—taking it as authoritative and yet feeling free to criticize it—and the similar attitude of Luther. Quoting the latter's dictum that we ourselves must decide as to whether something is God's Word and that God must confirm it to our heart, he says, "in other words conscience is between us and the Bible." He also invokes Calvin's thought that the Word must be confirmed by the internal testimony of the Holy Spirit. He infers from all this that there is an actual claim of God on us through the Old Testament. But we have to find the Word behind the words. The Word behind the words, however, is discerned only by those who are conscious of the human predicament and examine the facts of life as did the prophets, and are brought to such an attitude of prayer as Jer. 14: 7–9. But he finds it necessary to reject the view of those who, in dealing with the Old Testament, want to leave the historical situation aside entirely. The Word behind the words, he reiterates, is one that is made concrete and vivid in historical events.

In surveying the Old Testament literature Wright discovers that everything was written in states of crisis, not unlike those facing us. History, he says, is no mere story of human activity to be viewed and dissected, but the arena of the creative activity of the living, righteous, holy God. He asserts that the prophets were not interested in saying anything novel, but in confronting the people with the will of God for that particular moment of crisis. He lays down two conditions for understanding them: (1) That we be willing to stand with them at their point of vantage and experience the challenge and immediacy of God's will for that moment; (2) That we endeavour to stand in our own history and strive to find the Word of the Lord for us now. For we too are in a situation of crisis and our task is to find the Word of the Lord. There is thus a kinship between us and the Old Testament (cf. further, p. 279 f.).

Our theme has also been of particularly vital concern to several scholars approaching it from a New Testament angle. Thus M. Burrows in a recent book[10] on Biblico-theological topics sets forth his views on the problem of Scripture authority at the very outset. In general he adheres to the liberal position. He finds that the modern mind cannot accept any external compulsion in matters of belief. We cannot return to the Catholic principle of religious authority, but dogmatic assertion that the Bible is the Word of God is beset with so many difficulties that to assert it without reasonable explanation can only drive people away from the Church, even though winning fanatical approval from narrow-minded groups. He sees the solution in a properly qualified acceptance of the Bible as authority. He grants that it may seem to make the matter too involved to be worth the trouble, but answers the objection by asserting that to set up any other principle of authority, whether in philosophy, science or in immediate spiritual experience or intuition, also requires explanation and justification.

In proceeding along this line Burrows first points out that in the Bible itself authority is more a matter of what must be *done* than of what must be *believed*, and that man is judged in it according to his obedience or disobedience to the revealed will of God. God's authority resides in His superior knowledge. We accept the authority of superior knowledge everywhere in human relations. The authority of what is revealed resides in the fact of revelation itself, if only we can recognize it as such and be sure of its authenticity. But how can we do that? Burrows infers that the authority of the Bible depends upon inspiration. But he then is at pains to show that inspiration is not the divine origin of what is revealed or the process by which it is communicated. Rejecting the claims of that nature made by older theologies, he asserts that the only tenable ground of assurance for the authenticity of the revelation given in the Bible is its own inherent truth and worth. By and large, he finds, it is not the wording of the final record (which has suffered corruption and change) that is inspired; the men behind it were inspired. This leads him to examine the way in which revelation was received and here he distinguishes between "general" and "special" revelation. In the end, however, this raises the anxious question whether the inspiration given such individuals in the past is true. He does not hold that it would be fatal to Christian faith if it could be shown that all revelation came through the same means and processes as other knowledge, so that there were no such thing as direct inspiration. The only final proof is the test of experience. Since we cannot wait for a conclusive demonstration, we must commit ourselves by an act of faith without such knowledge. This is tantamount to saying that the only basis of assurance is the witness of the Spirit with the believer's own spirit.

Fully aware of all the change and diversity in the Old and New Testaments, Burrows yet perceives a unity in the Hebrew Christian tradition. The focus and principle of that unity for Christians is faith in Christ; everything is to be judged by its relation to the truth as it is in Him. Essentially, therefore, Burrows grants only a partial authority to the Old Testament in line with Luther's principle (cf. further, p. 276).

From the New Testament angle, too, A. G. Hebert has taken a particular interest in our subject. He returned to it in 1947 after dealing with it in 1941.[11] In the earlier book he already showed a fondness for mystical ideas. No one, he held, can interpret the Old Testament aright unless he takes seriously the two dogmas on which it rests: (1) that Yahweh the God of Israel is real in a sense in which none of the other gods is real; (2) That He has chosen Israel to be His people. The consequences of this would seem to be that we must all become Jews and pray only to the God of Israel. But here mysticism provides a ladder of escape. In the light of the fact of Christ's coming the Old Testament texts have taken on a fuller and richer meaning. In Christian use, for instance, the Psalms must be understood in the light of their fulfilment in Jesus the Messiah. Zion and Jersualem, the temple and the throne of David, are all to be mystically interpreted. Hebert likes to think of the Old Testament as a whole and yet not by itself but with the New Testament as its continuation. "While the Old Testament is divine it is incomplete; the several writers are incomplete when taken as individuals and separated from the whole which is Israel; and Israel as a whole is incomplete, apart from its fulfilment in the Messiah and His Ecclesia." For the Old Testament he claims inspiration though not inerrancy. "The Old Testament scriptures are imperfect because the writers can only apprehend in diverse ways various judgments of his truth; they are true because they nevertheless apprehend it."

The newer work of Hebert maintains this same position, but gives more room to the thought of a History of revelation. The Bible is the book of the divine kingdom. Through it there runs the theme of God's conflict with all that militates against His glory—an obvious echo of Calvin's emphasis on this attribute. Hebert sees the clash between the Church and secular forces going on in Israel of old as in Christendom to-day. The Old Testament is authoritative because of its relation to the divine kingdom (a) as historical record of its establishment; (b) as giving teaching about God and the way of His spiritual service which His people learned in the course of its history; (c) as declaring the end to which the divine purpose was and is moving. The book is viewed as having a function in the history of revelation, and mystical interpretation, which he would differentiate from the more arbitrary allegorical exegesis, enables us to use it as authority. Imperfections in the record are acknowledged, but these are believed to lie on the cultural level; behind and below this there is a deeper level on which its teachings are profoundly right. On the whole God has spoken in and through the record. We thus find continuing here the substance of the views of a Rothe or Hofmann.

In the same year another New Testament scholar, C. H. Dodd, writing of the biblical problem in general, was likewise compelled to think of the place of the Old Testament.[12] He differentiates between an Old Covenant and a New Covenant. The New Covenant is prior to the Church, but the Church is prior to Scripture, and of course, the same thing applies in the case of the Old Covenant: the Jewish Church is prior to Old Testament Scripture. Essentially he restates Rothe's famous definition of the Bible as "record of revelation". He holds that some of the Old Testament writings suggest that the earlier covenant was inconclusive, but he shies away from admitting that the New Covenant supplements, modifies or supersedes it; he asserts rather that it fulfils it. This means that the Old Testament is to be read in view of that for which it prepared the way, and that the New is not to be understood apart from the Old. In considering the Biblical history he finds it related at every point to the fundamental reality which lies behind all history and human experience—the living God and His Kingdom. There is furthermore a supra-historical factor entering history and directing it—revelation or the Word of God. God makes an approach to man in a way commanding his attention and elicits a response of some kind, positive or negative. In proportion as man responds the Word proves a creative factor in history. Dodd finds that the inspiration of prophets is essentially a power of insight into a situation as expressing a meaning which is God's meaning for His people. In the Old Covenant the principle of particularism works itself out to a logical conclusion; in the New Covenant Christ represents a fresh, universalistic approach of God to man. The perfect meeting of God and man toward which the whole course of the earlier history was tending is at last realized in the unity of a single personality—Jesus Christ.

This account of the views of representative professionals of biblical scholarship on both sides of the water will suffice to characterize the main lines of thought. There have been, of course, some with much more secularized standpoints, such as S. A. Cook[13] in England, or I. G. Matthews[14] in America, on whose approach we need not elaborate here. We likewise can mention only in passing such books as those of Cunliffe Jones, G. E. Phillips, J. Woods, and the volume edited by A. Richardson and W. Schweitzer.[15] Taken together they reveal impressively the degree to which the English-speaking religious world is being agitated by this topic.

A final glance at the German scene is in order. The destruction of National Socialism through the outcome of the war liberated the German Church from threatened domination by elements opposed to the Old Testament, and again allowed the free operation of all shades of opinion. In continuation of the trend existing before and during the war, there has been a pronounced effort to hold the Old Testament for Christianity as source of a living message by means of Christianizing interpretation. While the extreme devices of Vischer find no favour among leading scholars, some are, nevertheless, utilizing typology in their search for ways of expressing the unity of faith that binds us to the Old Testament saints, and a commentary series dedicated to that viewpoint is being contemplated.[16] Several significant studies from that quarter will receive attention in the next chapter.[17]

Chapter Seventeen

TOWARD A BIBLICAL THEOLOGY?

THE modern search for the meaning of the Old Testament lent a fresh importance to the discipline known as Old Testament theology.[1] For it is in this field, if anywhere, that such a meaning must be vindicated and set forth. It had frequently been noted—we fear not without some irony—that it has chiefly been a subject for posthumous publications. The German books on it by Hävernick (1848), Schultz (1869, 5th edn. 1896, E.T. by J. A. Paterson, 1892), Oehler (1873–74, 3rd edn. 1891, E.T. by G. E. Day, 1883), Kayser (1886), Riehm (1889), Dillmann (1895), and the English one of A. B. Davidson (1904), all appeared when their authors could no longer be called to account.

Before the last but one of this series of voices from the grave was heard, one of the leaders of the great critical school, B. Stade, gave a circumspect discussion of this discipline.[2] Much of what he said he repeated more briefly and sought to apply in his great book of 1905.[3]

He views Christianity as standing in historical continuity with Judaism. The appearance of Christ presupposed the existence of a set of religious and ethical ideas that had been formed in Hebrew history. Jesus connected up His own attitude with the religious faith and ethical ideals of His time and claimed to be the fulfilment of the earlier development. His message deepened the Jewish faith and ideals and remoulded them—partly even turning them into their very opposite—so that they became filled with new content; but He did not create a fresh set of religious and ethical concepts. The new thing in Christianity is the significance of Jesus Himself as perfect revelation of the Father and as abiding mediator. Jesus could set up His own authority over against that of the law, and therewith His message steps forth out of the framework of the Old Testament. New also is the life in God that He demonstrated to His fol-

lowers and the valuation placed on service to one's neighbour.
The Jewish Messianic conceptions do not exhaust the range of
His consciousness of self. But since they formed the starting-
point for it they may be viewed as the historically conditioned
form in which the new thing represented by Christianity had to
appear in order to become effective.

For Stade, "Biblical theology of the Old Testament" is the
discipline dealing with the intellectual and spiritual history
leading up to Christianity. He rejects speaking of "theology of
the Old Testament" or of "History of the Old Testament
Religion", because this leaves the New Testament out of
consideration, while "Biblical theology of the Old Testament"
preserves consciousness of the fact that theology is interested
in this subject from the angle of New Testament Christianity.
For while an interest in the preparatory history of Christianity
can be assumed for all Christians and thinking men in general,
that fact only vindicates the subject as a branch of general
study and does not yet prove it to be a necessary part of *theology*.
The justification for its inclusion in this department arises from
the needs of the Church. The latter requires that the task
envisioned above be carried out. For it has at all times, since it
rejected Marcionism, held that the revelation of God which
appeared fully in Jesus Christ was in some sense already present
in germinal form in the Old Testament. The presupposition that
the Old and New Testament revelations belong together and are
of a similar nature has never been given up, nor has the claim of
the earliest Church that the Old Testament revelation concerns
the Church and was divinely intended for it been abandoned. It
is a desideratum for the Church that this be justified theologically. At the same time it is also necessary that the uniqueness
of Christ and His revelation, which the Gnostics had emphasized
to the point of rejecting the Old Testament, be affirmed and
safeguarded, lest the higher nature of the New Testament
revelation and the new element in Christianity, as well as the
Christian insight into the nature of the objectives of salvation,
be dimmed. Both needs are met by a "Biblical theology of the
Old Testament" when it proceeds to discover the germs of
Christian thinking in the Old Testament and follows their evolution, and yet at the same time sets forth also the relative distance
separating the Old Testament revelation from that of the New.

The value of a Christian theological discipline, says Stade, is measured by the extent to which it can be used for the nurture of the new life that has gone forth from Jesus Christ. Only the revelation of the Father in and through Him can be law and doctrine for Christianity. That alone, therefore, is strictly speaking the subject of instruction in the Church. But ever since the beginning of Christianity—indeed before there was a New Testament—the Church has used the Old Testament, and no sensible person would want it to stop doing so, the more since it excellently suits the religious-educational purpose through the manifold nature of its insights and its vividness of language.

But while the fact that the Old Testament was preparatory to Christianity justifies its use in the Church, a prerequisite for such use is its Christianization; it must be understood from the angle of the New, its contents must be raised to the level of the religious and ethical ideals of the New Testament. Whatever cannot endure this process of Christianization must be left aside. For the historical understanding of the Old Testament is not the object of the Church's religious instruction, but rather its Christian understanding. Conversely, however, the historical interpretation is dominant for Biblical theology of the Old Testament as a subject of scholarly study, and the first prerequisite for a successful performance of its task is rigid adherence thereto. Thus the results of Biblico-theological study of the Old Testament would seem to be meaningless for the Church! But that is only seemingly the case. The Christian minister or teacher cannot successfully raise the Old Testament up to the Christian level and use it as means of religious instruction without damage to the Church's religious and ethical ideals, unless he is aware of the gulf that separates the two Testaments and is able to gauge its breadth properly. This is what the subject of Biblical theology of the Old Testament teaches us. By accurately portraying the development of religion under the Old Covenant it sharpens our perception of the higher religious and ethical level attained in Christianity. Whoever is not yet conscious of the fact that the contents of the Old Testament are not immediately applicable in the instruction of the Church, but only in so far as they can be interpreted on the Christian level, will become so through this study, and thus will be enabled to avoid spreading sub-Christian thinking in the Church through the medium of the Old Testament.

Stade has here put his finger on the crux of the problem. But if he thought that the individual equipped with "historical" Old Testament knowledge was able to Christianize the Old Testament by himself without some guidance he was presupposing a greater capacity than most human beings have. The question is: how can it be done? Here Stade leaves us without help, presumably considering that to be the concern of "Practical Theology". In his own book he produced what essentially was a history of the Hebrew religion. The title of Kautzsch's work, which echoes Stade's, was more properly given in its English translation *The Religion of Israel*; for it was hardly a Biblical Theology.[4] Indeed, under the impact of the history of religions the subject of that name virtually expired and Gunkel pronounced a death sentence upon it.[5]

The problem came to life again, however, in the 'twenties. Symptomatic of this was Steuernagel's plea for the usefulness of Old Testament theology as a purely historical subject, supplementary to the History of the Hebrew religion.[6] But there were deeper forces at work than that. An awareness of them prompted a new discussion of the matter by Eissfeldt.[7] He declared that it was futile to attempt to mix the historical study of the Hebrew religion with treatment of it from the angle of a subjective, living faith, as the advocates of "spiritual exegesis" and of the Dialectic theology were demanding. The historical study of this religion can never get beyond relativity and immanence, while faith, impressed with the absolute and transcendent, has not the means of comprehending the Old Testament religion as a historical entity. A theological approach artificially contracts the manifold nature of the historical phenomena, while the historical approach makes shallow the depth of the revelation which faith finds there by setting it side by side with similar religious phenomena. The two ways of looking at the subject belong to different planes and correspond to two different functions—knowledge and faith. Knowledge in the sense of historical inquiry is active; faith on the other hand knows itself seized by an eternal. Both of these approaches have to be kept separate.

The Old Testament was formed by factors of faith, and our

present faith ever and anon finds some aspect of the Old Testament religion replete with new meaning; currently the irrational and "demonic" (see p. 176) elements in it strike us most forcefully and so the historical approach, too, turns to explore them in its objective way. Faith thus stimulates knowledge and presents it with fresh themes. On the other hand knowledge, on its part, can aid and unburden faith. The life of a single generation can only find a relationship to a portion of the religion of the Old Testament. That book is too rich for it to be otherwise. Thus the prophets were unappreciated for 1800 years; then in the nineteenth century their greatness dawned on us and latterly has been very much appreciated. Who can deny that it was historical research that brought this insight? On the other hand, historical study has unburdened faith by pointing out to it the elements of the Old Testament that are below the average spiritual and moral level. These elements at the same time are not just criticized or condemned by us but are understood in the light of historical conditions.

Eissfeldt then points out how dangerous it is to make faith the criterion of history. The Old Testament gives us examples of interpretations of history governed by faith—the Deuteronomistic, with its attempt to construe history after a pattern of retribution, or that of the Chronicler who sees retribution governed by the conduct of the Hebrew kings in cultic matters. These were illusory beliefs. Historical study shows how better and deeper insights overcame these errors in the course of the Hebrew religious development.

The historical study of the Hebrew religion, Eissfeldt holds, must be carried on objectively in the interest of faith itself. It must confine itself to the Old Testament and not look over into the New. If in some situations the Old Testament religion points beyond itself, one must leave the matter open whether the New Testament and Christianity represent the fulfilment. The discipline of the History of the Old Testament Religion can thus be dealt with by men of all faiths. The theological approach, on the other hand, portrays what in the Old Testament is God's Word for the observer and for the Confession in which he stands (for one's judgment will always be conditioned by one's Confession). Such a presentation is thus limited in its usefulness to the author's own group. Little inter-confessional co-operation is possible here; only the one view or the other can finally prevail "in demonstration of Spirit and power".

Since the subject of Old Testament theology must describe the revelation faith has found and finds ever anew in the Old Testament, Eissfeldt says, it cannot take on the form of a historical presentation, for faith is concerned with the present. Revelation is above the category of time. Hence the presentation must be systematic, but not in the sense of methodically developing the material from central positions, but rather in a loci type of arrangement. Eissfeldt sees an author of such a work dealing with those matters in the Old Testament that to him are living truth. The execution will therefore be influenced by the central religious standpoint. That need not mean, however, that the Christian must seek for every Old Testament belief a fulfilment in the New Testament. There are numerous thoughts in the Old Testament that can stand by themselves and be revelation for us, the more since there often is no equivalent for them in the New Testament. In such cases the Old Testament takes on a co-equal role of authority rather than its usual subordinate one. While the History of the Hebrew religion and Old Testament theology move on different planes, the lines converge in infinity; here and now they can only form a unity in that one and the same person can treat of both.

A friendlier attitude toward the appeal for a more "theological" viewpoint in Old Testament theology was shown in W. Eichrodt's reflections on this subject.[8] But he keeps both feet planted in the historical sphere, saying that Old Testament scholarship should not be burdened with considerations of true or false—that being the prerogative of philosophy or of Dogmatic theology. Staerk had already quite a number of years before tried to place the waif Biblical theology on the doorstep of Dogmatic theology.[9] But Eichrodt saw a legitimate objective for Old Testament scholarship in trying to determine the real nature of the Old Testament religion, setting forth its structure and the inter-relationship of its component elements, and held that to be a systematic task (the term seemingly not used normatively, but rather in reference to arrangement). In the fulfilment of it the permeation of the approach by a philosophically influenced refinement of method is necessary. One must be fully conscious of the extent to which subjective factors are operative, not only in the choice of object, but in the selection the historian is forced to make in arranging the phenomena, and in the pragmatism according to which he construes. There is, too, the matter of the individual's inner predisposition to stress or favour one element or another for which he has an appreciation that some other individual does not have. On the other hand there is a rising awareness among all historians of the fact that the only possibility of bringing history to life lies in our appropriating it from some definite standpoint. Actually there is no historical science without a Philosophy of history. He finds that for the Christian Old Testament scholar the goal lies in the New Testament, and therefore it must be the task of Old Testament theology to select and arrange its material in a manner serving the end of understanding the latter. Therewith he, partly at least, confirms the objective already marked out, though not carried through, by Stade.

The impact of Comparative Religion on Old Testament science increased with the revival of Phenomenology of Religion —the study of the different types of religion and of religious ideas; a subject originally developed by Hegel. It was possible now to deal with it in the light of a far greater factual knowledge than was available in Hegel's time and in a modern realistic manner.[10]

Such study raised the question of what is distinctive or different about a given religion, and of the structure of its piety. For the case of the religion of the Old Testament the matter was taken up by F. Baumgärtel in 1932.[11] He is interested in grasping the distinctive nature of this religion as a whole. He sees it as a living relationship between man and God that is progressively purified with the march of time and relieved of those limitations which adhered to it—the process of course only finding completion in Christianity. The theme was also dealt with briefly by J. Lindblom in 1936 in a symposium devoted to the Old Testament.[12] In his opinion not every religion can be examined by the same method. For determining the nature of the Old Testament religion he recommends finding in it a certain idea of such importance that everything else can be made to depend on it, and which then will characterize the religion and differentiate it from all others. Hänel had, indeed, attempted to do this by means of the Holiness concept (p. 194). But Lindblom thinks that this idea is too widespread and too variable to suffice. He would choose the idea of God as such. He favours a systematic treatment (and thus is basically thinking of Old Testament theology). But he rules out any discussion of values or of the normative nature of the ideas from such a treatment. The Old Testament scholar should leave that to Dogmatic theology and content himself with preparing the historical materials that can be of service to the latter discipline. That one's personal religious convictions can give one a better appreciation for this or that is conceded, but that fact must remain in the background.

Lindblom finds that the proper systematization of the Old Testament ideas in a manner doing justice to reality and under organic viewpoints (in other words Old Testament theology) is the crowning task of Old Testament study. He develops in brief manner the Old Testament idea of God with due consciousness of existing similar concepts in other ancient religions. He then compares the Old Testament idea of God with the New Testament idea. Their organic connection and unity cannot be dissolved, but at the same time there are marked differences. He illustrates that from the divine love. In the New Testament God's love is turned toward the sinner; in the Old Testament the object of the divine love is Israel. This hangs together with the fact that in the Old Testament God is primarily King while in the New He is Father. But in spite of such differences many elements in the Old Testament idea of God continue to have significance for the Church. That He is the Creator protects us against dualism. That He is the God of history shields us against all forms of false mysticism. That He is transcendent, personal Will is a bulwark against pantheism. That He is holy love and holy anger prevents the abuse of the divine grace and patience. That He is leading the world to a goal preserves us from any static conception of history or any view leaving Him out of consideration in this process.

The theological task of Old Testament study was discussed by A. Weiser in the same 1936 symposium.[13] He links up with the widespread and growing consciousness that all theological disciplines must form a living unity and that true theology is only possible within the Church. One can approach the matter either from the broader angle, assigning to Old Testament study its place and objectives in the light of the whole sphere of theology, or one can start out from the Old Testament field itself and see what tasks present themselves. The second course is that chosen by him.

He sees exegesis as the basic task. It must make the Old Testament speak as it was understood (or ought to have been understood) by its contemporaries. One can only talk about an Old Testament scholarship if this historical-critical work is conscientiously done. But in which direction is the original meaning of the Old Testament to be sought? What goal does the determination of that give to exegesis? Direction and objective must flow forth from the object itself; there must be no employment of extraneous principles, such as was the case in orthodoxy when the Old Testament was looked on as a repository of proof-texts for Christian doctrines, or as prevailed in nineteenth-century liberal thought when that book was construed according to evolutionistic principles. The question is: what in any given section is the real viewpoint and spirit of the writer, his "understanding of self"? One has not yet adequately understood the Song of Deborah, for example, when one derives from it information about Hebrew tribal history and archæological matters; the real life of the thing lies in its religion and its distinctive character in this respect must be discerned. Out of the study of the whole Old Testament in such a manner there will arise an insight into what is generally characteristic of the totality. Weiser finds that two things can be singled out in describing the general understanding of existence prevailing in the Old Testament: (1) There is a dynamic view of reality running through it; (2) There is a theological way of looking at men and events—everything is regarded as from God and unto God. The Old Testament understanding of truth and reality is not a knowledge of what exists somewhere and is discerned by reason, but knowledge of reality gained in the moment of action or of some happening. It is a decision of faith in which man is confronted with ultimate reality through the act of God. It is thus that the Old Testament understands reality and it is this understanding of it that makes the preservation of that literature as Holy Scripture comprehensible. It testifies to the ages that God is present in history; it speaks of the divine reality confronting man and of human reality before God.

Old Testament study, Weiser asserts, must lead to this kind of an understanding of the Old Testament. As a theological task its concern is with man's relation to God and therein it differs from every other kind of anthropology. We are not mere spectators, facing what we see in a neutral manner, but are somehow drawn in and affected by what we read. In the dimension of divine-human relations there is no other possibility of real knowledge—in other words knowledge and faith are correlates. Since in the Old Testament the dynamic understanding of reality and the theological angle interpenetrate each other, a theological understanding of the Old Testament of the sort indicated is alone adequate to the situation and therewith also becomes the true scholarly approach.

In differentiating his position from others, Weiser discusses historicism such as that represented by Gunkel on the one hand and the idea of a systematic Biblical theology on the other. He insists that there is a subjective element operative in the so-called objective historical approach and that, since it evades the divine claim the Old Testament places on us, it really fails to be objective. For to be objective is to let the object confront us with its own understanding of being. Faith thus plays a decisive role in understanding. And he adds: only as our own existence is involved, as our own fate is in process of decision, do we understand the concerns of the Old Testament. But we are by no means to take the historical concreteness out of the ancient situations. Our task is merely to see in the situation in which we ourselves stand those relations between man and God which are the same for us as they were for the men of the Old Testament. It is not in our power, however, to achieve this for every Old Testament passage. At different times we get a better understanding of different portions of that book.

A subject of "History of the Hebrew Religion", by ruling out the question of valid truth, cannot meet the theological need. Can biblical theology do it? Weiser then asks. He believes that in this discipline a systematic treatment of Old Testament ideas is foisted on the Old Testament in accordance with Greek thought. The Old Testament knows no "doctrine" of God; the reality of God is experienced here in ever new and concrete happenings. It is contrary to the dynamic understanding of reality found in the Old Testament to systematize this subject-matter, though he concedes that there may be a certain peda-gogical value in such a marshalling of scattered facts. The Old Testament, however, puts the systematizer to shame or else is put to shame by him. Weiser's thought is that the theological task should be borne by exegesis. It is interesting to recall in passing that Barth was able to convey his original message through that channel.

In a more recent paper[14] Weiser has reaffirmed and amplified these views. He concedes that the full revelation of God does not come to us in our grappling with the Old Testament. The more deeply we look into its truths the more riddles and open questions remain. We can suffer with the men of the Old Testament and feel that like them we are *en route* to a goal still not attained. But at the same time we have an advantage over them—a source of added life and light that they do not have: the knowledge of Jesus Christ. One thing that the Old Testa-ment shows us is our sinfulness and need of redemption; the New Testament gives us the certainty of redemption through the cross.

As though to prove that scholars could publish on the subject of Old Testament theology ere they die, no less than three books of this nature appeared on the scene[15] in 1933–39.

The first was that of E. Sellin,[16] who resolutely divested the subject of all those antiquarian elements in the Old Testament that no longer have any importance for us and concentrated on the line that found its consummation in the gospel of the New Testament. This narrowing of scope makes it understandable that he felt the need of prefacing the systematic treatment with a separate account of the history of the Hebrew Religion. In his systematic part he speaks of the "teachings" of the Old Testa-ment on various topics.

L. Köhler, whose work is noteworthy for its penetrating detail, attempts to bring together the ideas of the Old Testa-ment which are, or could be, of theological importance and puts them under the heads of Theology, Anthropology and Soteri-ology.[17] The cult of Israel is treated at the end of the anthro-pology under the rather artificial construction "the self-redemption of man". He, too, thus basically follows an intellectualistic approach. For Köhler the Old Testament material is authoritative revelation wherever it fits organically into the whole Christian picture. To him the central position of the Old Testament is the assertion of God's majesty—His absolute supremacy over the world and man; he finds that viewpoint operative everywhere.

W. Eichrodt, whose attempt is on the largest scale of the three, sees a constant element in the Old Testament religion undergirding all its variations.[18] His purpose is to understand the structural unity of this Religion and interpret its deepest meaning both with consideration of its ancient environment and its connectedness with the New Testament. No extraneous scheme is thrust on the Old Testament material; the substance is developed out of the Old Testament consciousness of the God of Israel who shows Himself to be the God of the world and of the individual as well. The Covenant idea is made central—a point open to criticism. In presenting the materials the historical principle is utilized, and the book basically remains within the sphere of historicism.

A fourth major attempt to produce an Old Testament Theology—that of O. Procksch—did not appear in print until 1950, but is of earlier origin.[19] His general approach has already been set forth (p. 193 f.). He begins with a "Theology of History", taking a Christocentric view of history and of the Old Testament in the spirit of von Hofmann, and in this way tries to make the Hebrew canon relevant for the Christian. In the systematized part of the book, which follows a historical sketch of the religious development, he attempts to group the materials on each topic as far as possible around the prophetic personality chiefly associated with it.

A novel treatment of the Old Testament material in conjunction with and prefatory to New Testament concepts came from the pen of the American scholar M. Burrows.[20] The procedure necessitates selection, of course, and does not permit giving a compact and vital picture of the Old Testament religion such as can be hoped for from a book concentrating its attention on the earlier part of the canon. The attempt brings to mind the somewhat related objective of a "theology of both Testaments" suggested by G. Bertram.[21] This scholar has set forth the degree to which the Greek translation, the authoritative Old Testament for the Church of the days when our canon was formed, had been influenced by Hellenic viewpoints. He finds that the unity of the two Testaments can best be established by a Christological interpretation of the Septuagint, linking it with the Passion of Christ, after the manner of the early Christians.

One book devoted to the theology of the Old Testament has appeared in America in recent years—that of O. J. Baab.[22] He sees a fundamental unity in the Old Testament religion and finds it provided by the religious experience of the Hebrew community which continued the same through all vicissitudes of history. This religion is unique, and its main tenets have an abiding significance for us. The author deals with the more important topics in the order familiar from dogmatic theology.[23]

Turning once more from practice to theory we find another American, R. C. Dentan, discussing the history of Old Testament theology and the principles according to which it has been and should be written up.[24] He gives a preliminary definition of the subject as "that Christian theological discipline which treats of the religious ideas of the Old Testament systematically, i.e., not from the point of view of historical development, but from that of structural unity of the Old Testament religion, and which gives due regard to the historical and ideological relationship of that religion to the religion of the New Testament." Later he revises this and holds that "the scope of the subject is the normative or distinctive religion thought or assumed by the canonical books of the Old Testament, all of which have their centre on a distinctive doctrine of God"; it should include ethics and cultus, and give a picture of Old Testament piety. The first definition is more intellectualistic than the second, but it brings in the relation to the Christian order; the second could be subscribed to by a Jewish scholar. In any case Dentan remains in the sphere of the historical approach in the spirit of Eichrodt.

Soon afterward N. W. Porteous gave a discussion of the subject of Old Testament theology in a valuable British symposium.[25] He leaves it uncertain just where the line should be drawn between Old Testament theology and Dogmatic theology, but he approves of the emphasis on a historical revelation "when through the divine-human encounter, a word is spoken to which a response is made". He holds that man's response is what the Bible means by knowledge of God and that Old Testament theology is the critique of this knowledge. If this means that there must be an existential element in Old Testament theology we shall just have to bear the consequences of that. A treatment of that discipline, he declares, must keep close to life. In seeking to understand the structure of the Old Testament, not as strangers but as heirs, we shall not lose sight of the fact that Christ is its fulfilment.

During the war years the problem of a Biblical theology of the Old Testament was discussed in Germany by G. von Rad.[26] He finds the proper unifying principle in the idea of history to which that faith constantly has recourse. The Old Testament, he maintains, shows the way that God went with Israel. If one takes its teachings out of the historical frame of reference the primary peculiarity is lost sight of. A theology of the Old Testament to qualify as *heilsgeschichtlich* will have the task of setting forth the correspondence of Word of God and History in the various ways in which the former reacts on the latter. He notes that in the Old Testament the events are set in motion by a Word of God and are continuously fashioned and led to a goal by ever new Word of God. The Old Testament is thus a witness of God's continuous action in History.

Von Rad thinks that even books that do not fit in with this principle (Job, Ecclesiastes!) must be given their niche in relationship to it. He assigns an important role to the prophecy and fulfilment idea and thinks it is one of the main tasks of Old Testament theology to sketch this dialectic interplay, though he urges that it be done without any leaning on philosophies of history of modern vintage. In this connection he would even permit the use of typology to a certain degree. He also stresses the importance of the *kerygma* or the "message" aspect of the Old Testament prophetic religion. The unity of the Testaments, he claims, is provided by the concept of the Word of God; for He speaks in both.

We may note in passing that von Rad in one of his recent historical studies has tried to set forth that the Hebrew "creed" was a confession of the acts of God in past history, notably at the Exodus. The Old Testament faith is basically soteriological;

the idea of God as Creator is taken by him as completely subordinate to the belief in Him as Redeemer.[27]

Close in some respects to this scholar's viewpoint is the fresh approach undertaken by Wright. In his earlier book he had already stressed the idea that the Word behind the words of the Old Testament is one that is made concrete and vivid in historical events.[28] But that Word behind the words is discerned only by those who are willing to stand with the prophets at their point of vantage and experience the challenge and immediacy of God's will for that particular moment of crisis which concerned them, and who at the same time are ready to stand in the history of the present and seek the Word of the Lord for us now. Apparently Wright at that time imagined the message of the Old Testament as best presented in the form of biblical exegesis or exposition, as also favoured by Weiser.

But in his new book,[29] under the impact of von Rad's idea of a Hebrew confessional declaration (*heilsgeschichtliches Credo*), Wright has gone beyond this. His announced purpose is "to describe the special and characteristic nature of the biblical presentation of faith and to use the word theology for it". Whatever one may think of the idea of reviving Biblical Dogmatics (which Wright seems to have in mind), one may concede that the Old Testament writers are governed by theologies; since they are members of the same religious group these theologies will certainly have a great deal in common; ascending upwards in the scale of generalization to include the New Testament writers, one may perhaps describe an overarching element of agreement as the biblical theology in the higher sense. The question can only be: what is this *communis opinio*?

For Wright it is History, or "a God who acts" in History. The biblical presentation of faith consists of a recital of the deity's past acts. For the Old Testament these acts are the election of Israel, allegedly an inference from the Exodus deliverance, and the confirmation and clarification of it in the covenant ceremony at Sinai. He shows how this faith is made meaningful for Christians in the New Testament by typology and goes so far as to assert that it is impossible for us to discard typology without separating ourselves from biblical faith. Still, in view of the criticism incurred on that score by Vischer, he dreads typological innovations and would not go beyond what is written in the New Testament in that particular. He then turns to the confessional element in the New Testament. Following Dodd,[30] he stresses the idea that acts of God were the primary content of the Faith of the early Christians also. He finds in Paul's address at Antioch in Pisidia (Acts 13: 16 f.) a combination of the Old Testament and New Testament Creeds and presumably the sum-total then of the Biblical Faith.

In his opinion, therefore, the subject matter of Biblical theology and Dogmatic theology as well is the confessional recital of the unique events of biblical history, together with the inferences and interpretations which the Word in biblical faith by historian, prophet, psalmist or apostle and evangelist drew from them or associated with them. Wright is aware, of course, of the great variety of thought found in the Bible, but he maintains that it is never of such a nature as to constitute a totally different series of theologies because the central and especial concern with the meaning of historical events and life within history holds the whole together.

Wright, who is fond of assailing the theology of ideas of Greek derivation, here himself resorts to the Greek concept of History and the religious-phenomenological category of a "God who acts" (i.e., a voluntaristic divinity) to string together very dissimilar things in an external, unorganic manner. Some of his readers may feel that if a theology of the saving acts of God (another *Theologie der Heilstatsachen*) is in order it would be preferable to limit those acts to the ones that spell salvation for the Christian—Christ's Incarnation, Cross and Resurrection—and to have the Old Testament development construed as prophetic of the redemption in Christ, after the example of von Hofmann, Delitzsch, Orelli, Briggs and others.

A unity of the Old Testament religion, yea of the Bible and biblical religion as such, but based rather on biblical thought than on divine acts has been emphasized recently by Rowley.[31] His discussion seriously impairs the claims of those who since Kuenen and Wellhausen have been stressing the supposed anti-cultic or anti-sacrificial attitude of the prophets, and who have been finding the continuity between the New Testament and the Old in a progression from that alleged prophetic standpoint. Rowley sees the prophets merely criticizing a cult that was made a mockery by evil men. He holds that the law and the prophets are not in conflict and that the use of the Psalms was designed to make the practices of the law the organ of the spirit the prophets called for. From Old Testament sacrifice he can pass over to the New Testament sacrifice of the Cross and its celebration in the Sacraments, and therein find an underlying unity of teaching as to the supreme observances of both Old and New Testament religion.

Perhaps the most significant contributions to the theological theme to come from post-war Germany are those of F. Baumgärtel.[32] In his approach there is a resolute attempt to integrate the Old Testament heritage with that of the New (but with frank acceptance of all truth brought forward by historical research), and to focus it existentially on ourselves.

His presupposition—and he states it at the outset with commendable directness—is the Pauline Gospel of salvation: it is my being saved through Christ, my encounter with God through this Christian message, that matters. And the question for him is: do we also meet our God in the Old Testament? The affirmative to the latter question necessitates showing how this God of the Old Testament is related to the God of the New. The Christian gospel, he holds, is the yardstick wherewith the contents of the Old Testament are to be judged. But the latter are not to be taken in any other sense than that arrived at by objective historical interpretation. Baumgärtel is particularly concerned with finding some better formulation for the relationship of Old and New Testaments than that which the early Christian writings employ so prominently: the prophecy and fulfilment principle. He sees clearly that this was an ancient thought-pattern and that, however useful it may have been once, it can carry no persuasion to-day. He substitutes for it the special formulation of Eph. 3: 6, that the Christian is partaker of the promise through the gospel. Differentiating sharply between promise and prophecy he asserts that the Old Testament is promissory, not prophesying, in character. Its prophecies are not relevant for us, though they were to the contemporaries for whom they were intended. The basic thing in the Old Testament, he holds with others, is the divine assurance "I am the Lord thy God". This puts the generations of Israel under the necessity of deciding for or against God and so experiencing either the implied promise by being loyal to Him or the threat and punishment connected with defiance. The consequences of this become ever clearer in the course of Old Testament history. The Christian finds the continuity with the old order in this: that the promissory aspect of that assurance is realized in Jesus Christ.

It is apparent, then, that for the subject of Theology of the Old Testament Baumgärtel will wish to make use of the history of redemption principle (*Heilsgeschichte*), but not so much with an eye to external history as to inner development.[33] This is indeed the nub of his project as recently set forth in a fresh methodical discussion of the discipline.[34] It must be shown here, he says, that the Old Testament development is part of the self-revelation of God in Christ. For the forgiveness brought by Christ to sinful man presupposes the Old Testament judgments of God, without which that which Christ required would not have been comprehensible; and also God's promise (see above), without which Christ's appearance among this people as the One who fulfils would be incomprehensible. Repentance under the impact of the Word of God in the Old Testament order likewise is to be viewed as in organic relation with the future coming of Christ. So for the Christian the Old Testament history is from God and leading to God in Christ. Running in the form of divine promise and human response, it brings humanity to a situation where the *De profundis* cry is answered and the fulfilling and redeeming Word, Jesus Christ, is given to it by God.

The *Heilsgeschichte* of the Old Testament is a thing of the past, but for Christian faith the historical fact of Christ is at the same time one of the present, and so the things concerning Him (the events leading to His coming) also share in this characteristic. Like the witness concerning Christ, that of the *Heilsgeschichte* preceding Him awakens faith. In hearing it I realize that it concerns me both in its aspects of judgment and promise. It confronts me with the question whether I will join the true Israel in bowing before the divine majesty in confession of guilt, or remain amid the Israel that hardened its heart and go down into the judgment of God. To set this forth is a normative theological function, but unless it is undertaken one is forced to remain in the area of historicism. It is this existential approach alone, however, this present experience of the Old Testament witness, that makes the Old Testament development meaningful for me, instead of leaving it a mere historical development that may have touched the men of New Testament times but no longer need trouble me.

Heilsgeschichte as seen by us from the angle of faith in Christ, Baumgärtel claims, is not identical with the self-understanding of the Old Testament. Only the Jew can read the Old Testament in disregard of the New. Jesus Christ shattered the Jewish understanding of this sacred literature for us, so that we have to see it in a new, a Christian light. But our understanding of the Old Testament cannot be that of the early Christians either. While they no longer read their Old Testament as Jews read it, but as Christians, we are far removed from their place and situation. We cannot honestly avail ourselves, as these early Christians did, of typology to bring the Old Testament history to have direct relevance for us. We must from where we stand relate ourselves to Christ and so also to the *Heilsgeschichte* leading up to Him in a direct Christian approach. This preliminary normative manner of dealing with the Old Testament religion, however, Baumgärtel would distinguish from Dogmatic theological discussion, since the former must leave out of consideration the light that the ecclesiastical kerygma and the history of Christian thought throw upon the subject. He gives the last word on the normative position to Dogmatic theology. But how, he asks, shall the latter have the proper discernment in Old Testament matters unless the Old Testament scholar points the way and by normative statements of his own shows with what principles he operates in relating the Old Testament to his Christian standpoint?

Baumgärtel's programme thus tries to lead beyond the historicism in which all previous Old Testament theologies remain bound, and goes far toward realizing Eissfeldt's ideal of the subject and the existential approach indicated by Vischer, Bultmann and Hirsch. The laudable purpose of all these men was to give the Old Testament a present meaning; Vischer does it in terms of a revival of the understanding of the Old Testament writers by the New Testament writers—through their kind of Messianic prophecy and typology—and with the aid of a doctrine of a pre-existent Christ who was operative in the Old Testament period. Bultmann seeks the Old Testament understanding of existence on its higher levels and therein finds the Old Testament of present value for us. Hirsch takes it as the Jews of the time of Christ understood it and finds it the great antithesis to Christianity, but of permanent importance on that account. Baumgärtel's position seems closest to that of Bultmann.

We observe, then, on all sides a drift toward the normative. It is doubtful, however, whether two kinds of normative theology can be admitted—a Biblical and a Dogmatic. The task of appraising the abiding substance and worth of the historical records is hardly a halfway station on the road from a historical Biblical theology to Dogmatic theology, but is a function of the latter. If the Biblical scholar, weary of struggling with rocks and underbrush, wants to get out of the narrow ravine up which he has been toiling and gain the high plateau, where the Systematic theologian paces about, scanning broad horizons, he is free to do so. Theological history gives him ample precedent. But the Biblico-theological task itself can be greatly enriched by legitimate historical means. The photography has largely been "flat" rather than third-dimensional. To achieve the latter effect requires an improvement in our ability of seeing the reality before us, some appreciation of foreground as well as background, some power to go to the very essence of phenomena and to discern their transitional function in the vast historical process. There is room, furthermore, for two standpoints—one establishing distance and another proximity. Only the peaceful rivalry of the productions themselves can demonstrate which is the most instructive, the most useful way of dealing with the Old Testament order.

In his survey of modern theology Stephan observed that there is no happy ending to this development.[35] And this is true also of that segment of theological history we have been reviewing. The current goes on and on. But at each moment there is in the onrushing flood the desire to be merged with the river of water of life that proceeds from under the throne of God. That lends the whole course of this current an interest and significance.

NOTES

Introduction

[1] J. Orr, *The Problem of the Old Testament*, 1906. See p. 144 f.

[2] See the various "Introductions". H. H. Rowley, *The Growth of the Old Testament*, 1950 (Hutchinson's University Library, No. 45), gives an excellent outline, and on p. 174 a list of other authorities, with brief characterizations. For full insight into the whole great field of current Old Testament problems and scholarship the student should consult *The Old Testament and Modern Study, A Generation of Discovery and Research*, edited by H. H. Rowley, 1951, and *Record and Revelation*, edited H. Wheeler Robinson, 1938. Cf. also H. F. Hahn, *The Old Testament in Modern Research*, 1954.

[3] The great repository of such information is L. Diestel, *Geschichte des Alten Testaments in der Christlichen Kirche*, 1869. See further A Duff, *History of Old Testament Criticism*, 1910; E. M. Gray, *Old Testament Criticism, its Rise and Progress*, 1923.

[4] *The Old Testament in Early Christianity*. For the approach from the customary angles see R. V. G. Tasker, *The Old Testament in the New Testament*, 1947; C. H. Dodd, *According to the Scriptures*, 1953; J. Coppens, *Les harmonies des deux Testaments*, revised edn., 1949.

Chapter One
Luther and the Old Testament

[1] See T. Zahn, *Die bleibende Bedeutung des neutestamentlichen Kanons für die Kirche*, 1903, 12 f. For mediaeval matters see B. Smalley, *The Study of the Bible in the Middle Ages*, 1952.

[2] Cf. E. von Dobschütz, "Die Lehre vom vierfachen Schriftsinn", in *Harnack-Ehrung*, 1921, 1 f.

[3] K. Holl, *Gesammelte Aufsätze zur Kirchengeschichte*, vol. I, *Luther*, 6th edn., 1932, 419. This important study contains many valuable observations for the matter that here concerns us. Useful, too, is O. Scheel, *Luthers Stellung zur Heiligen Schrift*, 1902 (*Sammlung gemeinverständlicher Vorträge*, no. 29). See further, H. Bornkamm, *Luther und das Alte Testament*, 1948 (the most recent study by an authority on Luther).

[4] Holl, *loc. cit.*

[5] Holl, *op. cit.*, 420.

[6] *Ibid.*, 402.

[7] *Ibid.*, 429 f.

[8] Scheel, *op. cit.*, 43.

[9] Holl, *op. cit.*, 431.

[10] Scheel, *op. cit.*, 45.

[11] *Ibid.*, 44.

[12] *Loc. cit.*

[13] See the summary in J. Köstlin, *Luthers Theologie*, II, (1883), 257, 269 f., 273. On Semler, see p. 55 f.

[14] Scheel, *op. cit.*, 44.

[15] Compare the discussion of this in E. Troeltsch, *Vernunft und Offenbarung bei J. Gerhard und Melanchthon*, 1891, 139 f.

[16] Weimar Edition L, 643.

[17] Luther's Preface to the Old Testament, as quoted by J. Hempel, *Zeitschrift für die alttestamentliche Wissenschaft*, LIV, 1936, 298.

[18] Scheel, *op. cit.*, 43.

[19] The consequences are drawn by Hirsch (see ch. 15).

[20] W. Herrmann, *Gesammelte Schriften*, 1923, 250 f.

[21] See Scheel, *op. cit.*, 42. For the items that follow see Köstlin, *op. cit.*, 266.

[22] H. Schmidt, *Luther und das Buch der Psalmen*, 1933 (*Sammlung gemeinverständlicher Vorträge*, no. 167).

[23] *Tischreden*, ed. J. G. Walch, V, 5518.

[24] See Köstlin, *op. cit.*, 266 f. for the references to the quotations that follow.

[25] Carlstadt, *De Canonicis Scripturis* (1520), reprinted in K. A. Credner, *Zur Geschichte des Kanons*, 1847, 291 ff. He not only accepted the Jewish idea of three divisions of different degrees of authority in the Old Testament but even applied a similar principle to the New Testament, ascribing highest authority to the four gospels, second degree authority to a group comprising the Pauline epistles, 1 Peter and 1 John, but third degree authority to Hebrews, James, 2 Peter, 3 John, Jude and Revelation.

[26] A. von Harnack, *Marcion, das Evangelium vom fremden Gott*, 1924, 250 ff. (*Texte und Untersuchungen zur Geschichte der altchristlichen Literatur* vol. XLV.)

[27] The appraisal of Luther's position from a modern-conservative angle by L. Ihmels, *Die Christliche Wahrheitsgewissheit*, 2nd edn., 1908, 11 f. is well worth reading.

Chapter Two

Zwingli and Calvin and the Old Testament

[1] See P. Wernle, *Der Evangelische Glaube nach den Hauptschriften der Reformatoren*, III, *Calvin*, 1919, 268 f. His interpretative summaries are helpful.

[2] Cf. C. Sigwart, *Ulrich Zwingli. Der Charakter seiner Theologie mit besonderer Rücksicht auf Picus von Mirandula dargestellt*, 1855, 45 f. An early work of the well-known logician, and still useful.

[3] Wernle, *op. cit.*, 275.

[4] *Ibid.*, 268. M. Bucer's *Commentary on the Epistle to the Romans*

was translated by J. Owen, 1849; see 1944 reprint (Grand Rapids, Mich.), 516 f.

[5] See A. H. Hays, "The Authority of Scripture", in *From the Pyramids to Paul*, ed. by L. G. Leary, 1935, 80.

[6] Wernle, *op. cit.*, 5.

[7] Here Calvin was much influenced by Luther's *De servo arbitrio*.

[8] A. Tholuck, "Calvin als Exeget", in his *Vermischte Schriften*, II, 1839, is the fullest study. Cf. K. Fullerton, *Prophecy and Authority*, 1919, 133 f. For a special theme see L. P. Smith, "Calvin as Interpreter of Ezekiel", in *From the Pyramids to Paul*, 267 f.

[9] See Wernle, *op. cit.*, 3 f.

[10] In the final edition of *The Institutes* this is found in II, 8, 16.

[11] = II, 10 f. in the final edition.

[12] See H. W. Wolff, *Die Einheit des Bundes. Das Verhältnis von Altem und Neuem Testament bei Calvin*, 1942.

[13] Calvin's view of existence is of course extremely pessimistic.

[14] Cf. II, 11, in the final edition of *The Institutes*.

[15] Cf. M. Schulze, *Meditatio futurae vitae. Ihr Begriff und ihre herrschende Stellung im System Calvins*, 1901.

[16] M. Albertz, *Die Botschaft des Neuen Testaments*, I, pt. 1, 1947, 12.

[17] The Authorized Version in the title given the Epistle to the Hebrews asserts authorship by Paul, therein following the Alexandrian claims; it puts the Epistle after the other Pauline writings. Luther did not accept the Pauline authorship and in his Bible put Hebrews with the Catholic Epistles. That Luther's position was not unique may be seen from the fact that his contemporary, the Catholic theologian Cajetan, could deny Paul's authorship of Hebrews, hold its canonicity to be doubtful and declare that it had no authority in doctrinal matters; see Zahn, *Die bleibende Bedeutung*, 10. At Trent, however, Catholicism accepted the Pauline authorship of Hebrews.

Chapter Three

The Old Testament from the Reformation to the Middle of the Seventeenth Century

[1] This formulation, however, did not come up until early in the nineteenth century, as was shown by A. Ritschl, "Über die beiden Prinzipien des Protestantismus", *Gesammelte Aufsätze*, I, 1893, 234 f.

[2] See *Dogmatic Canons and Decrees of the Council of Trent*, New York, 1912, 7 f.; P. Schaff, *The Creeds of Christendom*, II, 1887, 79 f.

[3] Cf. the *Confessio Dosithei*, Schaff, *Creeds*, II, 401 f.

[4] Zahn, *Die bleibende Bedeutung*, 27 f.

[5] Schaff, *Creeds*, III, 233 f. A. Niemeyer, *Collectio confessionum in ecclesiis reformatis publicatarum*, 1840, 467.

[6] Niemeyer, *op. cit.*, 361 f.

[7] Zahn, *op. cit.*, 46.

[8] Schaff, *op. cit.*, 491.

[9] Schaff, *op. cit.*, 93; Die *Bekenntnisschriften der Evangelisch Lutherischen Kirche*, Berlin, 1930, 767 f.

[10] L. Ihmels, *Die Christliche Wahrheitsgewissheit*, 53 f.

[11] *Ibid.*, 54.

[12] Schaff, *op. cit.*, 600 f.

[13] Niemeyer, *op. cit.*, 730. This was directed against Capellus (p. 43).

[14] Cf. Ihmels, *op. cit.*, 55 f.

[15] G. Oehler, *Prolegomena zur Theologie des Alten Testaments*, 1845, 21.

[16] *Ibid.*, 23.

[17] H. Schöffler, *Abendland und Altes Testament*, 1937, 36 f.

[18] *Ibid.*, 73 f., 114 f.

[19] A. von Harnack, *Über den privaten Gebrauch der Heiligen Schriften in der alten Kirche*, 1912, 6 f.

[20] See A. D. White, *A History of the Warfare of Science with Theology*, 2 vols., 1910. The work takes up the sciences separately.

Chapter Four

The Reaction Against the Orthodox View of the Old Testament

[1] L. Capellus, *Arcanum punctationis revelatum*, 1624. *Critica sacra*, 1650.

[2] J. Morinus, *Exercitationes Biblicae*, 1633.

[3] R. Simon, *Histoire Critique de Vieux Testament*, 1685.

[4] J. Spencer, *De legibus Hebraeorum ritualibus*, 1685.

[5] J. Clericus, *Ars sacra*, 1697.

[6] Cf. H. P. Smith, *Essays in Biblical Interpretation*, 1921, 94 f.; J. Cocceius, *Summa doctrinae de foedere et testamento Dei*, 1648.

[7] See G. Schrenk, *Gottesreich und Bund im älteren Protestantismus*, 1923 (*Beiträge zur Förderung christlicher Theologie*, 2nd series, V).

[8] H. Grotius, *De veritate religionis Christianae*, 1627: *Adnotationes ad vetus et novum testamentum*, 1641–47. See the essay on him in A. Kuenen, *Gesammelte Abhandlungen*, tr. by K. Budde, 1894.

[9] T. Hobbes, *Leviathan, or the matter, form and authority of Government*, 1651.

[10] Spinoza, *Tractatus theologico-politicus*, 1670. For his general view of religion and its impact on his critical ideas see L. Strauss, *Die Religionskritik Spinozas als Grund seiner Bibelwissenschaft*, 1930.

[11] Cf. K. Fischer, *Geschichte der neueren Philosophie*, vol. II, (5th edn., 1909), 320, 326.

[12] His *Dictionnaire historique et critique* (1645–47) had a great influence on the 18th century mind.

[13] T. Morgan, *The Moral Philosopher*, 1737–40.

[14] W. Warburton, *Divine Legation of Moses*, 2 vols., 1737–41.

[15] Facts about the still extant manuscript in the edition of

Lessing's works edited by Petersen and Olshausen, XXII, 24. A detailed summary of this 2000 page opus was given by D. F. Strauss, *Hermann Samuel Reimarus und seine Schutzschrift*, 1862.

[16] *Beweis des Geistes und der Kraft*, 1777.

[17] See reprint in E. Schmidt, *Goezes Streitschrift gegen Lessing*, 1893.

[18] K. Fischer, *Geschichte der neueren Philosophie*, III, 648.

[19] Harnack, *Über den privaten Gebrauch der Heiligen Schriften*, 6 f.

[20] *Transzendentale Dialektik*, II, 2, para. 3.

[21] See Fischer, *Geschichte*, V, 371 f. On the incident mentioned, *ibid.*, IV, 93 f., 100.

[22] *Kants Gesammelte Schriften*, VIII, 1912, 255 f. See my *Book of the Ways of God*, 1938, 242 f.

[23] Fichte, *Versuch einer Kritik aller Offenbarung*, 1792. Cf. Fischer, *Geschichte*, VI, 221 f.

[24] See Fischer, *Geschichte*, VII, 14 f.

[25] His *Conjectures* appeared anonymously in Brussels, 1753. The work was set before the American public by Theodore Parker's translation of 1835.

[26] H. B. Witter's precedence over Astruc was forgotten until it was ferreted out by A. Lods, *Jean Astruc et la critique biblique au XVIIIe siècle*, 1924. Witter's book was *Jura Israelitarum in Palaestinam*, 1711. Cf. J. Hempel's book (chapter 12 n. 11), p. 3 f.

[27] J. A. Ernesti, *Institutio interpretis Novi Testamenti*, 1761.

[28] J. S. Semler, *Abhandlung von freier Untersuchung des Kanons*, 4 vols., 1771–75.

[29] G. T. Zachariae, *Biblische Theologie oder Untersuchung des biblischen Grundes der vornehmsten theologischen Lehren*, 5 vols., 1772–86.

[30] L. Bauer, *Theologie des Alten Testaments*, 1796.

[31] J. P. Gabler, *De justo discrimine theologiae Biblicae et dogmaticae*, 1787.

[32] J. G. Eichhorn, *Einleitung in das Alte Testament*, 5 vols., 1780–1783, 4th edn., 1823–24.

[33] W. M. L. De Wette, *Beiträge zur Einleitung in das Alte Testament*, 2 vols., 1806–7; a work really marking the beginning of the higher critical movement.

[34] See A. Ritschl, *Geschichte des Pietismus*, III, 1886, 62 f.

[35] F. Delitzsch, *Die biblisch-prophetische Theologie, ihre Fortbildung durch Chr. A. Crusius und ihre neueste Entwicklung seit der Christologie Hengstenbergs*, 1845, showed a great enthusiasm for this school's literal acceptance of biblical prophecy.

[36] On him see H. Stephan, "Hamanns Christentum und Theologie", *Zeitschrift für Theologie und Kirche*, XII, 1902, 345 f. W. Vischer frequently quotes Hamann.

[37] Cf. Fischer, *ibid.*, 666 f. Herder, *Vom Geist der ebräischen Poesie*, 1782–83 and his *Älteste Urkunde des Menschengeschlechts*, 1774, were particularly significant here.

[38] See K. Galling, "Goethe als theologischer Schriftsteller", *Evangelische Theologie*, 1949, 529 f.; H. H. Schaeder, *Goethes Erlebnis des Ostens*, 1938, 24 f. It should be mentioned that Schiller, too, took an interest in Old Testament matters in several short papers.

[39] Cf. J. Pedersen, "Die Auffassung vom Alten Testament", *Zeitschrift für die alttestamentliche Wissenschaft*, XLIX, 1931, 161 f.

Chapter Five

Schleiermacher and the Old Testament

[1] *Der Christliche Glaube nach den Grundsätzen der Evangelischen Kirche*, 2 vols., 1821 f. E.T. by H. R. Mackintosh and J. S. Stewart, *The Christian Faith*, 1928.

[2] See W. Wiesner, *Das Offenbarungsproblem in der dialektischen Theologie*, 1930, 4 f.

[3] § 3–5. In the *Reden* Schleiermacher held that the important thing was how one experiences reality; when one discerns a single living power behind all events that concern us (*individuell bestimmte Anschauung des Universums*) one has religion. Cf. W. Herrmann, *Dogmatik*, 1925, 10.

[4] § 10. He says: "Die Ursprünglichkeit der einer religiösen Gemeinschaft zu Grunde liegenden Tatsache", etc. I have worded his meaning in a free manner. It should be noted that this position implies a new beginning also for the Christian religion; the latter is not just a continuation of the Hebrew religion.

[5] § 128 f.

[6] § 12.

[7] In the light of modern studies such as have been carried on by Bousset and Reitzenstein his statement takes on fresh meaning.

[8] Bertram's studies in the Septuagint are a case in point. See Chapter 17, n. 21.

[9] He quotes Clement, *Stromata*, VI.

[10] He is thinking notably of the fourth Eclogue of Virgil.

[11] The term heathenism of course is used here in the nuance of heathenism at its best and finest, as in Plato, Epictetus, etc.

[12] § 132.

[13] This is Luther's secular view of Old Testament law.

[14] In § 14, he discusses proofs from Messianic prophecy.

[15] B. Stade, *Biblische Theologie des alten Testaments*, I, 1905, 5, considers it briefly but rejects it.

[16] Cf. W. Bousset, *Kyrios Christos. Geschichte des Christusglaubens von den Anfängen bis Irenäus*, 1913, Paul's powerful presentation of Christianity is with tools of Greek thought; no contemporary teacher of purely Semitic training could have carried through a trend of reasoning as Paul does. See H. Leisegang, *Der Apostel Paulus als Denker*, 1923, on the intellectual background presupposed. The

greatly Hellenized Septuagint, the authoritative Scripture for Gentile Christianity, must also be recalled; (cf. Bertram, "Septuaginta und Urchristentum", *Theologische Blätter*, 1925, 208 f.)

Chapter Six

The Old Testament in Nineteenth-Century Theological Thought Before Ritschl

[1] So K. I. Nitzsch, prominent exponent of the Prussian Union, in his *System der Christlichen Lehre*, 1829. Cf. K. Schwarz, *Zur Geschichte der neuesten Theologie*, 1856, 41, a writer who stood close to the time and the events.

[2] W. M. L. De Wette, *Lehrbuch der Christlichen Dogmatik*, I. *Biblische Dogmatik*, 1813.

[3] J. F. Fries, *Wissen, Glaube, Ahndung*, 1805 (re-issued by the Neo-Friesian L. Nelson, 1905). Rudolf Otto was also profoundly influenced by Fries and De Wette. See his *Kantisch-Friesische Religionsphilosophie und ihre Anwendung für die Theologie*, 1921; E. T. by E. B. Dicker, *Philosophy of Religion*, 1931.

[4] *Das Wesen des Christlichen Glaubens vom Standpunkt des Glaubens*, 1846.

[5] E. W. Hengstenberg, *Christologie des Alten Testaments*, 3 vols., 1829–35. E.T. by R. Keith, *Christology of the Old Testament*, 1836–39.

[6] See Schwarz, op. cit., 88, for the quotations given here.

[7] See Fischer, *Geschichte der neueren Philosophie*, VII, 627 f.

[8] See especially P. Tillich, *Mystik und Schuldbewusstsein in Schellings philosophischer Entwicklung*, 1912, 16 f., 131 f. (*Beiträge zur Förderung Christlicher Theologie*, XVI, 1).

[9] For analysis and discussion see Fischer *op. cit.*, VII, 794 ff.

[10] Fischer, *op. cit.*, VIII, pt. 2, 985 f.

[11] *Ibid.*, 997 f.

[12] *Ibid.*, 1171 f.

[13] See Fischer, *op. cit.*, IX, *Schopenhauer*, 488 f. Cf. also A. Schlatter, *Die Philosophische Arbeit seit Cartesius nach ihrem ethischen und religiösen Ertrag*, 2nd edn., 1910, 231 f.

[14] W. Vatke, *Die Biblische Theologie wissenschaftlich dargestellt*, I, *Die Religion des Alten Testaments*, 1835.

[15] B. Bauer, *Kritik der Geschichte der Offenbarung*, I, *Die Religion des Alten Testaments*, 1838. On his later apostasy see A. Schweitzer, *The Quest of the Historical Jesus*, 1910, 137 f.

[16] D. F. Strauss, *Leben Jesu*, 1835.

[17] His *Christentum der ersten drei Jahrhunderte*, 1853, unrolls the full panorama of his results.

[18] J. T. Beck, *Die Christliche Lehrwissenschaft*, 1838 f. On him see A. Schlatter, *J. T. Becks theologische Arbeit*, 1904 (*Beiträge zur Förderung Christlicher Theologie*, VII, 4). Beck, too, taught at Tübingen. Great, too, was the influence of A. Tholuck of Halle,

likewise a pietist, but no distinctive line of theological thought went forth from him. An interesting figure is C. A. Auberlen, whose *Die göttliche Offenbarung*, I, 1861 (not completed because of his early demise) is a model of irenic discussion.

[19] J. C. K. von Hofmann, *Weissagungen und Erfüllungen im Alten Testament und Neuen Testament*, 2 vols., 1841–44.

[20] *Schriftbeweis*, 1852–55.

[21] *Die Heilige Schrift zusammenhängend untersucht*, 13 vols., 1862–86.

[22] A. Vilmar, *Die Theologie der Tatsachen wider die Theologie der Rhetorik*, 1856. Professor at Marburg, he wielded a strong ecclesiastical and political influence and protested against the Prussian absorption of the principality and the Prussian Union enforced on the Churches.

[23] R. Rothe, *Zur Dogmatik*, 1863. Rothe was perhaps the most important Systematic-theological thinker in the period from Schleiermacher to Ritschl.

[24] *Ibid.*, 330 f.

[25] R. H. von Frank, *Die Lehre von der Christlichen Gewissheit*, 1872, § 41.

[26] G. Oehler, *Prolegomena zur Theologie des Alten Testaments*, 1845.

[27] See Introduction, n. 3.

[28] K. H. Graf, *Die geschichtlichen Bücher des Alten Testaments. Zwei geschichtliche Untersuchungen*, 1866.

[29] A. Kuenen, *De Godsdienst van Israel*, 2 vols, 1869 f.

[30] H. Ewald, *Geschichte des Volkes Israel bis auf Christus*, 5 vols., 1843–55 (2nd edn. 1851–59). E.T. by R. Martineau, *The History of Israel*, 8 vols., 1869–86.

[31] J. H. Kurtz, *Geschichte des Alten Bundes*, 2 vols., 1848 and 1855. His widely used *Lehrbuch der heiligen Geschichte*, 1843, is an abridgement of it, with extension to cover the New Testament period (E.T. by C. T. Schaeffer, *Manual of Sacred History*, 1856). Like K. Bähr, *Symbolik des Mosaischen Kultus*, 2 vols., 1837–39, he can find symbolism and typology in the Hebrew worship; in the main he applies von Hofmann's principle.

[32] *Die Lehre der Bibel von Gott oder Theologie des Alten und Neuen Bundes*, 4 vols., 1871–76. See Vol. I, *Die Lehre vom Wort Gottes*, 472 f.

[33] E. B. Pusey, *Daniel the Prophet*, 1868, p. xi f. Pusey virtually insisted that Christianity must stand or fall with the early date of Daniel.

[34] J. H. Newman, *Arians of the Fourth Century*, 1876, 153 f.

[35] Newman, *Discussions and Arguments on Various Subjects*, 1872, 246 f.

[36] Newman, *Lectures on the Doctrine of Justification*, 1874, 36 f., 145 f. I am indebted to Prof. John E. Smith for aid on Pusey and Newman.

[37] T. Parker, *A Critical and Historical Introduction to the Canonical*

Scripture of the Old Testament. Translated and enlarged from W. M. L. De Wette, 2 vols., 1843.

[38] See his *Critical History and Defense of the Old Testament*, 1845.

Chapter Seven

The Transition to the Modern Situation

[1] See especially White, *History of the Warfare of Science with Theology*, I, 232 f.

[2] *Ibid.*, II, 394 f.

[3] *Ibid.*, II, 342 f.

[4] *The Pentateuch and Joshua critically examined*, 1862 f. Cf. White, *op. cit.*, II, 350 f.; H. P. Smith, *Essays in Biblical Interpretation*, 1921, 128 f.

[5] Out of these lectures came his *The Old Testament in the Jewish Church*, 1881. On him see J. B. Pritchard, "W. Robertson Smith, Heretic", *Crozer Quarterly*, XXIV, 1947, 146 f.; T. K. Cheyne, *Founders of Old Testament Criticism*, 1893, 211 f.

[6] *Deutsche Schriften. Gesammtausgabe*, 1892, 217 f. Cf. L. Schmid, *Paul de Lagardes Kritik an Kirche, Theologie und Christentum*, 1935, 110 f.

[7] J. Wellhausen, *Geschichte Israels*, I, 1878 (in the later editions the title became *Prolegomena zur Geschichte Israels*, 1883, 1886). Wellhausen, who was Professor in the conservative Greifswald, was forced to relinquish his post and became Professor of Semitic Languages, first at Marburg then at Göttingen. He contributed greatly to the study of Islam and later also to Gospel criticism.

[8] See W. Baumgartner, "Wellhausen und der heutige Stand der alttestamentlichen Wissenschaft," *Theologische Rundschau*, 1930, 287 f.

[9] Franz Delitzsch, many of whose books were translated into English, was Professor in Leipzig. His distrust of the modern movement was expressed in his *Der tiefe Graben zwischen alter und moderner Theologie*, 1888. Cf. chapter 4, n. 35.

[10] White, II, 357 and 359. On Driver cf. Cheyne, *op. cit.*, 248 f. He was one of the foremost in scholarship, and his *Introduction to the Old Testament*, 1891, created the first really modern work of this kind in English. It was translated into German by Rothstein, 1896. Driver's contributions to Hebrew studies, to Kittel's *Biblia Hebraica* and his commentaries, are part of the heritage we all enjoy. W. Sanday was Professor in Oxford and contributed notably to New Testament scholarship. His Bampton lectures were on *Inspiration*, 1893.

[11] E. Robinson, pupil of Moses Stuart (cf. Chapter 6, n. 38) translated Gesenius' Hebrew Lexicon. Professor at Andover and later at Union Theological Seminary he won enduring scholarly fame as the father of Palestinian geography through his *Biblical*

Researches in Palestine, 3 vols., 1841–42. Cf. J. A. Bewer, "Edward Robinson as Biblical Scholar", *Journal of Biblical Literature*, LVIII, 1939, 355 f. In criticism he leaned toward Hengstenberg.

[12] C. H. Toy became Professor at Andover. His commentary on Proverbs in the *International Critical Commentary*, 1899, was noteworthy. He also wrote *Quotations in the New Testament*, 1884.

[13] C. A. Briggs had only gradually become a convert to higher criticism in spite of four years in Berlin. At his trial he argued that the Westminster Confession did not require belief in the inerrancy of Scripture, but he was suspended, nevertheless, by a vote of 298 to 116 from the Presbytery of New York. His scholarly output was considerable. For his theological position his *The Bible the Church and the Reason*, 1892, is instructive; his *Messianic Prophecy*, 1886, still operates seriously with Adamic and Noachic periods in the history of Messianic prediction. His most abiding achievements are his co-editorship of the *International Critical Commentary* (to which he contributed *The Psalms*, 2 vols., a work vitiated somewhat by his metrical theories) and his co-editorship of the great Hebrew Lexicon.

[14] F. Brown became President of Union Theological Seminary. The Hebrew Lexicon of which he was co-editor is his chief scholarly monument. At the time his defence of the young science of Assyriology in *Assyriology, its Use and Abuse*, 1885, was significant.

[15] H. P. Smith after leaving Lane Theological Seminary in consequence of his support of Dr. Briggs eventually became Professor in Meadville (later Librarian at Union Theological Seminary). He wrote some excellent books in the Old Testament field, notably a Commentary on *Samuel* in the I.C.C. series. His *Inspiration and Inerrancy*, 1893, deserves mention here; in old age he wrote his reminiscences, *The Heretic's Defence*, 1926.

[16] W. H. Green, *The Higher Criticism of the Pentateuch*, 1895; *The Unity of the Book of Genesis*, 1895. He had already taken the field against Colenso in his *The Pentateuch vindicated from the Aspersions of Bishop Colenso*, 1863. Princeton Theological Seminary long remained a seat of anti-critical attitude.

[17] W. R. Harper had a great impact on Hebrew studies in America. His Commentary on Amos and Hosea in the I.C.C. Series, 1905, was excellent. As first President of the University of Chicago he still maintained his interest in Hebrew Studies.

[18] B. W. Bacon, *The Genesis of Genesis*, 1893. Son of a noted New Haven divine, he became Professor at the Yale Divinity School and contributed notably to New Testament study.

[19] G. F. Moore, *Judges*, 1898, in the I.C.C. was an important contribution. Professor at Andover, he later transferred to Harvard. His pupil C. C. Torrey made a lasting contribution with his *Composition and Historical Value of Ezra-Nehemiah*, 1896. Professor at Yale, he became the most original biblical critic produced by America.

[20] In England A. H. Sayce, *The Higher Criticism and the Monu-*

ments, 3rd edn., 1894, was a pioneering publication along the line of archæology's "confirming" the Bible, but was not anti-critical enough to suit conservatives. Sayce, Professor at Oxford, was a man of great learning and wrote many books. The large literature of this type cannot be reviewed here. E. Schrader in Berlin did more than any contemporary to further sound use of the cuneiform sources. His *Die Keilinschriften und das Alte Testament*, 1872, was most valuable; the 3rd edn. by H. Winckler and H. Zimmern, 1901, has been one of the books most frequently cited by Old Testament scholars and though antiquated in many particulars is still useful. H. Gunkel, *Schöpfung und Chaos in Urzeit und Endzeit*, 1895, was a great eye-opener.

[21] F. Delitzsch, the son of Franz Delitzsch and Professor at Berlin, was Schrader's pupil and became the teacher of numerous Assyriologists and Old Testament scholars who delved into Assyriology. He also contributed to Hebrew lexicography and to Biblical geography. The lectures mentioned were translated as *Babel and Bible*, ed. by C. H. W. Johns, 1903.

[22] A new and revised edition was issued in 1921. There was a great outpouring of Apologetic by Old Testament scholars on this subject. E. Koenig, *Bibel und Babel*, 1902, is a good example; he re-published it in an 11th edition (re-written) as *Die moderne Babylonisirung der Bibel*, 1921.

[23] H. Winckler, who taught at Berlin, had important achievements to his credit, notably publication of the Tell el Amarna letters and his rediscovery of the capital of the Hittite Empire in Anatolia. A. Jeremias, *Das Alte Testament im Lichte des Alten Orients*, 1904, 4th edn., 1930 (E.T. *The Old Testament in the Light of the Ancient East*, 1911), became increasingly devoted to Pan-Babylonism. His *Handbuch der altorientalischen Geisteskultur*, 1913, then developed the Babylonian world-view. Both books are useful for their material. Jeremias, clergyman and *Privatdozent* at Leipzig, was a conservative theologically. In the end he was influenced by Theosophy.

[24] P. Jensen, *Das Gilgameschepos in der Weltliteratur*, I, 1906, II, 1928–29. Professor at Marburg, he contributed greatly to Assyriological studies. See H. Gunkel, "Jensens Gilgameschepos", in his *Reden und Aufsätze*, 1913.

[25] The question: what is new or original in Israel's religion? can hardly be answered yet. New texts, like those from Ras Shamra, bring increasing demonstration of Hebrew dependence.

Chapter Eight

The Old Testament in Systematic Theology since Ritschl

[1] See W. Herrmann, "Der evangelische Glaube und die Theologie Albrecht Ritschls", *Gesammelte Schriften*, 1923, I f. Ritschl was Professor at Göttingen.

[2] W. Wiesner, *Das Offenbarungsproblem in der dialektischen Theologie*, 18.

[3] A. Ritschl, *Die Christliche Lehre von der Rechtfertigung und Versöhnung*, II, 1874, 9 f.

[4] H. H. Wendt, *System der Christlichen Lehre*, 1907, belongs here; see also his *Idea and Reality of Revelation*, 1904. He was Professor at Jena and a noted New Testament scholar. A. Harnack's celebrated lectures, *Das Wesen des Christentums*, 1900, E.T. by T. B. Saunders. *What is Christianity?* reflect a similar position. J. Kaftan, *Grundriss der Dogmatik*, 1897 (8th edn., 1920), the most representative Ritschlian, veered more toward the conservative line; he was Professor in Berlin.

[5] W. Herrmann, *Der Verkehr des Christen mit Gott*, 1886, (7th edn., 1921). E.T. by J. S. Stanyon and R. W. Stewart, *The Communion of the Christian with God*, 1895. Herrmann was Professor in Marburg. His influence was world-wide, for in the face of historical criticism he provided a theology that men could preach, and his personality added weight to his message. For an appreciative study of his theology, see F. W. Schmidt, *Wilhelm Herrmann, Ein Bekenntnis zu seiner Theologie*, 1922.

[6] He has a fine passage on Hebrew monotheism in *Die Wirklichkeit Gottes*, 1914, 39 f.

[7] See *Gesammelte Aufsätze*, 19.

[8] See his posthumously-published lectures, *Dogmatik*, 1925, 34 f. E.T. by N. Micklem and K. Saunders, *Systematic Theology*, 1927.

[9] *Ibid.*, 56.

[10] M. Kaehler, *Wissenschaft der Christlichen Lehre*, 1883, (3rd edn., 1905). He was Professor at Halle-Wittenberg. Pietistic influences stemming from Tholuck and Beck here were fused with confessional Lutheran inclinations.

[11] Kaehler, *Dogmatische Zeitfragen* I, *Zur Bibelfrage*, 1907, 126, 130.

[12] *Ibid.*, 127.

[13] *Ibid.*, 140.

[14] *Ibid.*, 266 f.; cf. 410 f.

[15] The thought of Kaehler on the Biblical problem strongly influenced E. Weber, *Bibelglaube und historisch-kritische Schriftforschung*, 1913 (2nd edn., 1914), one of the most worth-while discussions from the conservative side.

[16] L. Ihmels, *Die Christliche Wahrheitsgewissheit, ihr letzter Grund und ihre Entstehung*, 1901, 2nd edn. 1908. In his valuable *Centralfragen der Dogmatik*, 2nd edn., 1912, 55 f., he shows himself primarily an adherent of Rothe's Scripture doctrine. Ihmels was Professor in Leipzig, later bishop of Saxony, and exercised a great influence as Lutheran churchman and preacher.

[17] A. Schlatter, *Das Christliche Dogma*, 1911. Primarily a New Testament scholar and an expert on the Judaism of the time of Christ, he was Professor at Tübingen. His scholarly output was

enormous. But he did not debate the N.T. issues of the day and in N.T. literary criticism was a singleton, as A. Klostermann was in the Old Testament field. His reflective-speculative approach, which makes him peculiarly difficult to read, suited the role of *Dogmatiker* better than that of exegete or historian.

[18] E. Schaeder, *Theozentrische Theologie*, 2 vols., 1909–15. He was Professor in Greifswald.

[19] Schaeder, *Das Wort Gottes. Eine systematische Untersuchung*, 1930. W. Caspari, "Das alttestamentliche Wort", *Neue Kirchliche Zeitschrift*, 1931, 752 f., is a discussion of Schaeder.

[20] E. Troeltsch, *Die Absolutheit des Christentums und die Religionsgeschichte*, 1901. See also his article *Offenbarung* in the first edition of *Die Religion in Geschichte und Gegenwart*, IV, 1913, 918 f. Troeltsch as theologian was primarily associated with Heidelberg. Transferring to Berlin he became "Kulturphilosoph". His influence was great, but his thought was viewed as destructive by churchmen. Cf. also his *Soziallehren der Christlichen Kirchen und Gruppen*, in *Gesammelte Schriften*, I, 1912, 848 f. (E.T. by O. Wyon, *Social Teaching of the Christian Churches*, 1931).

[21] I here follow his *Glaubenslehre*, 1925 (posthumous; lectures of 1911–12), p. 97 f.

[22] "Glaube und Ethos der Hebräischen Propheten", *Gesammelte Schriften*, IV, 53.

[23] *Ibid.*, 61.

[24] *Ibid.*, 820.

[25] He is thinking of the Jewish influence—Maimonides, Spinoza.

[26] Meaning Harnack, *Das Wesen des Christentums*; see note 4.

Chapter Nine
The Apologetic of Biblical Scholars

[1] Professor in Bonn and a man of tremendous industry. His own survey of his position and labours is found in *Der doppelte Wellhausenianismus im Lichte meiner Quellenforschungen*, 1927. He tried to demonstrate the reality of revelation in his *Der Offenbarungsbegriff im Alten Testament*, 2 vols., 1882. On his foray into Dogmatic theology see L. Ihmels, *Christliche Wahrheitsgewissheit*, 78 f. See also chapter 17, n. 15.

[2] W. Lotz, *Geschichte und Offenbarung im Alten Testament*, 1891, 43 f., showing also some impact from the philosophy of Lotze. The author was Professor in Erlangen and also made a worth-while contribution to Assyriology. His *Das Alte Testament und die Wissenschaft*, 1905, was one of the best books of its kind. W. Volck, *Die Bibel als Kanon*, 1885, contains excellent thought on the canonicity of the Old Testament. His *Heilige Schrift und Kritik*, 1897, is also deserving of mention. The author was Professor in Dorpat.

[3] K. Marti, *Der Einfluss der Ergebnisse der neuesten alttestamentlichen Forschungen auf Religionsgeschichte und Glaubenslehre*, 1894.

Marti became Professor in Bern and deserves to be remembered for his editorship of the *Zeitschrift für die alttestamentliche Wissenschaft* (founded by Stade) and of one of the two great German series of critical Commentaries, the *Kurzer Handcommentar zum Alten Testament*.

[4] G. Dalman, *Das Alte Testament ein Wort Gottes*, 1896. Dalman, Professor in Greifswald and long Director of the Deutsches Evangelisches Institut für Altertumswissenschaft des Heiligen Landes zu Jerusalem, and editor of its valuable *Palästinajahrbuch*, 1905–26, was widely known for his expertness in *Judaica* and his Palestine research. Books translated into English include his *Words of Jesus*, 1902; *Jesus: Jeshua*, 1939; *Sacred Sites and Ways*, 1935. He did not venture much into Biblical criticism, but the lecture here summarized reveals his attitude.

[5] R. Kittel, *Zur Theologie des Alten Testaments*, 1899. As Professor at Leipzig he played an important role. His *Biblia Hebraica*, 1906, 3rd edn., 1937, (carried through by P. Kahle, A. Alt and O. Eissfeldt) has been a great boon to all students of the Old Testament. His great opus, *Geschichte des Volkes Israel*, 3 vols., (vol. I and II, 6th edn., 1923–25), is still valuable (notably vol. III, 1927–29). An early form of his work, *Geschichte der Hebräer*, 2 vols., 1888–92, was translated as *History of the Hebrews*, 1895. His *Great Men and Movements in Israel*, 1929, tr. by C. A. Knoch and C. D. Wright, is a noble book. His *Die alttestamentliche Wissenschaft in ihren wichtigsten Ergebnissen*, 1910, 4th edn., 1921, was a useful popularization. His commentary on the Psalms (1914) is one of the best.

[6] E. Kautzsch, *Die bleibende Bedeutung des Alten Testaments*, 1902. Professor at Halle, he did yeoman service through his continued revisions of Gesenius' Hebrew grammar (the 28th edn., 1909, was translated by A. E. Cowley, 1910). The great annotated Old Testament that he edited, *Die Heilige Schrift des Alten Testaments*, 2 vols., 3rd edn., 1909; 4th edn. by A. Bertholet, 1923, has been one of the most useful tools available for the study of the Old Testament.

[7] J. Koeberle, *Die alttestamentliche Offenbarung*, 1908. While not so widely known he contributed in an able manner to the study of Old Testament theology in special monographs. On our theme see further his *Heilsgeschichtliche und religionsgeschichtliche Betrachtungsweise des Alten Testaments*, 1906.

[8] S. Oettli, conservative Swiss scholar, Professor at Greifswald and author of numerous commentaries and monographs, wrote on our subject: *Die Autorität des Alten Testaments*, 1906, (*Biblische Zeit und Streitfragen*, II, 2). F. Wilke, *Das Alte Testament und der Christliche Glaube*, 1911, likewise deserves mention. The author was Professor in Vienna.

[9] H. Gunkel, "Was bleibt vom Alten Testament?" in *Reden und Aufsätze*, (E.T. by A. K. Dallas, *What Remains of the Old Testament?* 1928.) The author, Professor in Giessen, was doubtless the most important Old Testament scholar since Wellhausen. He taught us how

to analyse and classify both Hebrew prose and poetry from the angle of the life-situations producing the varied forms of material and to discern the stylistic peculiarities. His commentaries on Genesis and on the Psalms were masterpieces.

[10] E. von Dobschütz, "The Abandonment of the Canonical Idea", *American Journal of Theology*, XIX, 1915, 416 f. Professor at Halle, he was one of the best of New Testament exegetes.

[11] G. Adam Smith, *The Higher Criticism and The Preaching of the Old Testament*, 1901. No one since Ewald has been able to make the Old Testament as inspiring as did Smith. His books on the prophets, in particular, have been invaluable to students. His *Historical Geography of the Holy Land*, 1901, and his *Historical Atlas of the Geography of the Holy Land*, 1915, were great contributions to biblical study. He was Professor in the Free Church College at Glasgow.

[12] J. E. McFadyen, *Old Testament Criticism and the Christian Church*, 1903. He was Professor in Trinity College, Glasgow; his book on *The Message of Israel*, 1931, deserves mention here.

[13] J. Orr, *The Problem of the Old Testament*, 1906. Professor in Glasgow, his field was Systematic theology, particularly Apologetics. He introduced Ritschl's theology into the English scene.

[14] C. F. Kent, *Origin and Permanent Value of the Old Testament*, 1912. Professor at the Yale Divinity School and an indefatigable worker in disseminating modern Old Testament knowledge. His most ambitious undertaking was *The Historical Bible*, 6 vols., 1908–16.

[15] K. Fullerton, *Prophecy and Authority*, 1919. Fullerton was Professor at Oberlin, Ohio. His exegetical papers in various Journals are monuments of painstaking thoroughness and critical acumen.

[16] W. Rauschenbusch, *Christianity and the Social Crisis*, 1907. His ministry among working people in New York City gave him an insight into this crisis. He became Professor in the Rochester Theological Seminary and attained a large influence.

Chapter Ten

Harnack and Delitzsch

[1] A. von Harnack, *Entstehung und Entwicklung der Kirchenverfassung und des Kirchenrechts in den zwei ersten Jahrhunderten*, 1910, 3. In speaking of a boyhood incident he recalls a quotation from the Apocrypha (Wisdom of Sol. 1:7) that influenced his whole life (*ibid.*, 4); testimony of the Holy Spirit for the Catholic Bible?

[2] A. von Harnack, *Marcion*, 253 f. See also his paper, "Die Neuheit des Evangeliums nach Marcion", *Reden und Aufsätze*, V, 1930, 128 f.

[3] F. Delitzsch, *Die grosse Täuschung*, 2 vols., 1920–21. The foreword of vol. I is dated 1914.

[4] I, 70 f.

[5] II, 18 f.

[6] II, 21, 38 f.

[7] II, 52.

[8] II, 53 f. Not all will agree with this. See W. F. Albright, "The Biblical Period", in *The Jews; their History, Culture and Religion*, ed. L. Finkelstein, 1950, 61.

[7] Josephus, *Antiquities*, XII, 318. Cf. Delitzsch, II, 62.

[10] II Macc. 12: 29–31.

[11] II, 67.

[12] I, 94.

[13] There was thus poetic justice in the fact that his Hebrew lexicon, which (as one of his American students told me) was complete to the last dot on the i, remained unpublished. His *Prolegomena eines neuen Hebräisch-aramäischen Wörterbuchs zum Alten Testament*, 1886, shows that its preparation was the work of many years.

[14] In effect this has meanwhile come to be the situation in most American theological schools, largely because Greek (which has dropped out of general education), is still insisted on, and because of all the new subjects now held more useful.

Chapter Eleven

Systematic Theology and the Old Testament after 1918

[1] See H. R. Mackintosh, *Types of Theology*, 1937, 218 f. on Kierkegaard.

[2] Barth, a Swiss clergyman, burst on the scene with his *Der Römerbrief*, 1919 (E.T. by E. C. Hoskyns, *The Epistle to the Romans*, 1933). Here again was a theologizing exegesis such as had hardly been seen since Luther's *Galaterbrief*. From the standpoint of historical exegesis it was vulnerable; cf. E. von Dobschütz, *Vom Auslegen des Neuen Testaments*, 1927, 50. But the new generation wanted something different from the husks of philology and historicism. Hence the wide acclaim it received. Barth became Professor at Basel. His subsequent theological works show the metamorphosis of a prophet into a theologian of the Church (more particularly of the Reformed Church).

[3] See Barth, *Das Wort Gottes und die Theologie*, 1924, 167 f.

[4] W. Wiesner, *Das Offenbarungsproblem in der dialektischen Theologie*, 1930, 45, a most helpful and clarifying discussion of Dialectical theology from an angle close to our present concern.

[5] Barth, *Die Lehre vom Wort Gottes. Prolegomena zur Christlichen Dogmatik*, 1927, 236. (E.T. by G. T. Thomson, *The Doctrine of the Word of God*, 1936.)

[6] Wiesner, *op. cit.*, 45.

[7] Barth, *op. cit.*, 39.

[8] *Ibid.*, 334 f.

[9] *Ibid.*, 339.

[10] *Ibid.*, 355.

[11] *Ibid.*, 361.

[12] Wiesner, *op. cit.*, 107 f.

[13] We need only mention here his *Der evangelische Glaube und das Denken der Gegenwart*, 3 vols., 1931 f.

[14] Heim, *Die Weltanschauung der Bibel*, 1920.

[15] R. Otto, *Das Heilige*, 1917 (21–22 edn., 1932). E.T. by J. W. Harvey, *The Idea of the Holy*, 1936. See also his *Religious Essays. A Supplement to The Idea of the Holy*, tr. by B. Lunn, 1931, and *The Kingdom of God and the Son of Man*, E. T. Lutterworth Press, 1938. Otto was Professor in Marburg.

[16] We mention only G. Wobbermin, *Systematische Theologie nach religionspsychologischer Methode*, 3 vols., 1913–25.

[17] Compare K. Girgensohn, *Grundriss der Dogmatik*, 1924. He was Professor at Leipzig; an early death cut short his career. His brochure *Die geschichtliche Offenbarung* in *Biblische Zeit und Streitfragen*, V, 12, 1910, is well worth reading.

[18] In *Greifswalder Reformgedanken zum theologischen Studium*, 1922, 88 f. A large literature was elicited thereby. A very full report will be found in A. Wendel, *Religionswissenschaftliche und theologische Auslegung des Alten Testaments*, 1938.

[19] See H. Gunkel, *Ausgewählte Psalmen*, 4th edn., 1917, and A. Weiser, *Die Psalmen ausgewählt, übersetzt und erklärt*, 1935.

[20] P. Tillich, "Die Idee der Offenbarung", *Zeitschrift für Theologie und Kirche*, 1927, 27 f. Tillich became Professor in Frankfurt in the philosophical field and later came to the United States, to Union Theological Seminary. His current views on revelation, as expressed in his *Systematic Theology*, I, 1950, 106 f., suggest influence on his thinking by the American emphasis on the Old Testament heritage.

[21] See his *Kirche und Kultur*, 1924, (*Sammlung gemeinverständlicher Vorträge*, 111).

[22] See his *Das Dämonische, Ein Beitrag zur Sinndeutung der Geschichte*, 1926 (same series, 119). This term goes back to Goethe, *Dichtung und Wahrheit*, IV, 20. It is used by Tillich as a symbol of the uncanny, potent, destructive capacity. Goethe saw it in the personality of a man like Napoleon.

[23] Tillich, *Kairos, Zur Geisteslage und Geistesbewegung*, 1926.

[24] Tillich, *Religiöse Verwirklichung*, 1926.

[25] F. Kattenbusch, *Die Deutsche evangelische Theologie seit Schleiermacher* (Part I, 1917); Part II, *Zeitenwende auch in der Theologie*, 1934.

Chapter Twelve

Apologetic of the 'Twenties and 'Thirties

[1] Eissfeldt, "Christentum und Altes Testament", in *Adolf von Harnack zum 70. Geburtstag*, 1921, 29 f. (Reprint from *Kartellzeitung des Eisenacher Kartells*.) Professor at Halle. Cf. n.20.

[2] E. Sellin, *Das Alte Testament und die evangelische Kirche der Gegenwart*, 1921. The author, Professor at the University of Berlin, edited the *Kommentar zum Alten Testament* series, intended as a conservative counterpart to the two great liberal series, the *Göttinger Handkommentar* edited by W. Nowack and the *Kurzer Handcommentar*, edited by K. Marti. The undertaking demonstrated that there was little difference between conservatives and liberals in higher criticism. Sellin's contributions to Old Testament scholarship were many, and he was a pioneer in organizing excavations in Palestine. See below, chapter 17, on his Old Testament Theology. His *Introduction to the Old Testament*, tr. by G. W. Montgomery, 1923, is well known.

[3] F. Baumgärtel, *Die Bedeutung des Alten Testaments für den Christen*, 1925, deserves a résumé here, but may be passed by, as his more recent views will be dealt with later.

[4] R. H. Kennett, "The Contribution of the Old Testament to the Religious Development of Mankind", in *The People and the Book*, ed. A. S. Peake, 1925, 383 f. He was Professor at Cambridge. He wrote some excellent scholarly books and was a keen critic.

[5] G. H. Box, "The Significance of the Old Testament in Relation to the New", *ibid.*, 433 f. Box was Professor in King's College, London. He wrote both in the field of Old Testament and of Judaism.

[6] G. Adam Smith, "The Hebrew Genius as Exhibited in the Old Testament" in *The Legacy of Israel*, ed. I. Abrams, A. A. Bevan, S. Singer, 1927. On Smith cf. above, chapter 9. The topic here dealt with received more detailed treatment by the American scholar (Professor in Hartford and noted for his knowledge of Islam), D. B. Macdonald, *The Hebrew Literary Genius*, 1933, and *The Hebrew Philosophical Genius; A Vindication*, 1936.

[7] F. C. Burkitt, "The Debt of Christianity to Judaism", *The Legacy of Israel*, 69 f. Professor at Cambridge, he contributed notably to the study of early Christian literature, especially the Syriac.

[8] C. G. Montefiore, *ibid*. Cf. also his essay "The Old Testament and Judaism", in *Record and Revelation*, ed. H. W. Robinson, 1938.

[9] A. S. Peake, "The Permanent Value of the Old Testament", in his *The Servant of Yahweh*, 1931. Peake had already discussed the biblical problem in his *The Bible, its Origin, its Significance and its Abiding Worth*, 1913, and *The Nature of Scripture*, 1922. He was Professor in Manchester and wrote some excellent commentaries.

[10] J. Meinhold, *Altes Testament und Evangelisches Christentum*, 1931. The author was Professor at Bonn. He wrote some excellent scholarly books; he had already clashed with ecclesiastical authorities in 1896 by his *Jesus und das Alte Testament*.

[11] J. Hempel, *Das Alte Testament und die Geschichte*, 1930, 73 f. Professor at Göttingen before the late war. Hempel was editor of the *Zeitschrift für alttestamentliche Wissenschaft* and his contributions to Old Testament scholarship are many. He analysed the religious

developments in Israel with a discernment for underlying forces and movements such as was demonstrated in other fields by a man like W. Dilthey. At the same time he is a master of criticism and at home, too, in Palestinian archæology. His *Die althebräische Literaturgeschichte*, 1930, is particularly useful.

[12] Hempel, "The Religious Value of the Old Testament", a lecture given in the U.S. and published there in *The Lutheran Church Quarterly*, 1933, 335 f.

[13] E. Brunner, "Die Bedeutung des Alten Testaments für unseren Glauben", *Zwischen den Zeiten*, 1930, 30 f. The author, second only to Barth among the Dialectic theologians, formerly Professor in Zürich, is now Professor at the International Christian University, Tokyo, Japan. It is needless to go into his general position, on which cf. Wiesner, *Das Offenbarungsproblem in der dialektischen Theologie*, 39 f., or to list here his large output in the field of Systematic theology. E.T. Lutterworth (London), Westminster (Philadelphia).

[14] In his lecture *Die Unentbehrlichkeit des Alten Testaments für die missionierende Kirche*, 1934, he stresses the importance of the Old Testament so sharply as to assert that as certainly as the Church can no longer be the Church without Jesus Christ, so little can it be the Church without the Old Testament.

[15] O. Procksch, "Die kirchliche Bedeutung des Alten Testaments", *Neue Kirchliche Zeitschrift* 1931, 295 f. Professor in Greifswald, Procksch had conservative leanings. He wrote important books in the Old Testament field. On his posthumously published Theology of the Old Testament see chapter 17, n. 19. On Girgensohn cf. chapter 11, n. 17.

[16] Procksch, "Pneumatische Exegese", *Christentum und Wissenschaft*, I, 1925, 145 f. See also his "Ziele und Grenzen der Exegese", *Neue Kirchliche Zeitschrift*, 1925, 485 f.

[17] J. Hänel, *Das Wort Gottes und das Alte Testament*, 1932. A Professor at Münster, he has contributed some worth-while work to biblical scholarship. In the wake of Otto's ideas he wrote *Die Religion der Heiligkeit*, 1931.

[18] V. Herntrich, *Völkische Religion und Altes Testament*, 1933. He contributed a book on Ezekiel in 1932. Professor in Hamburg.

[19] A. Alt, J. Begrich, G. von Rad, *Führung zum Christentum durch das Alte Testament*, 1934. Alt, Professor at Leipzig, is one of the foremost experts in historical-geographical research concerning ancient Palestine. J. Begrich had high attainments, notably in the study of Hebrew history and in pursuing Gunkel's line of research further; it is a source of regret that he was drafted into the army and killed in the Italian campaign. G. von Rad, Professor at Göttingen, has produced some important works on Pentateuchal criticism. On his views on Old Testament theology, see p. 278 f.

[20] O. Eissfeldt, *Einleitung in das Alte Testament*, 1934. One of the leading Old Testament scholars, with great achievements notably in literary criticism and in the field of Semitic Religion (i.e., the religions

represented by the inscriptions of Phœnicians and other Syrian peoples), therein continuing the labours of W. W. von Baudissin.

[21] Eissfeldt, "Geschichtliches und Übergeschichtliches", *Theologische Studien und Kritiken*, CIX, 1947, 37 f.

[22] R. Press, "Das Alte Testament als Wort Gottes", *Theologische Blätter*, 1934, 224 f. A clergyman, who has written some excellent scholarly articles.

[23] P. Volz, "Das Alte Testament und unsere Predigt", *Luthertum*, 1937, 326 f. Volz was Professor at Tübingen and wrote some important books. His Commentary on Deutero-Isaiah in Sellin's series is particularly noteworthy.

[24] G. R. Berry, "The Old Testament: A Liability or an Asset?" *Colgate Rochester Divinity School Bulletin*, 1930, 8 f. A Professor in that Baptist institution, Berry was quite radical as an Old Testament critic.

[25] J. A. Bewer, "The Christian Minister and the Old Testament", *Journal of Religion*, 1930, 16 f. He was Professor at Union Theological Seminary in New York and combined a critical attitude with deep piety. His *Literature of the Old Testament*, 1922, is the leading *Literaturgeschichte* on this subject in English, and has been widely used for a generation. His *Annotations on the Prophets* in the *Harper's Annotated Bible Series* promise to be very useful for years to come.

[26] "The Authority of the Old Testament", *ibid.*, 1936, 1 f.

[27] W. F. Lofthouse, "The Old Testament and Christianity", in *Record and Revelation*, edited by H. W. Robinson, 1938, 458 f. Formerly Principal of Handsworth College, Birmingham, he has written scholarly papers and contributed a volume to the Clarendon Bible.

[28] H. W. Robinson, "The Philosophy of Revelation", *ibid.*, 303 f. This gives his thought *in nuce*. See also his *Inspiration and Revelation in the Old Testament*, 1946; *Redemption and Revelation*, 1942. He was Principal of Regent's Park College, Oxford. His output was large and not confined to the Old Testament field.

[29] E. G. Kraeling, *The Book of the Ways of God*, 1938, (1939 in the American edition). The author was active both as clergyman and teacher; in the latter capacity he taught Old Testament at Union Theological Seminary and for some years also Semitic Languages at Columbia University. He recently published the oldest find of Aramaic papyri from the Jewish colony at Elephantine, *The Brooklyn Museum Aramaic Papyri*, 1953.

Chapter Thirteen

The Revival of the New Testament Approach

[1] A spokesman of dissatisfaction with biblical exegesis as carried on by Old Testament scholars was the clergyman C. Cramer. His book, *Amos, Versuch einer theologischen Interpretation*, 1930, assails

the emphasis placed on the personalities of the prophets and would understand them and their message entirely from the doctrine of the divine election of Israel. But that, too, is historicism and gives the Old Testament no immediate significance for us. Subsequently he followed Vischer's line. See also his "Hegel oder Herder oder——", *Theologische Blätter*, 1932, 140 f. H. Hellbardt, "Die Auslegung des Alten Testaments als theologische Disziplin", *ibid.*, 1937, 129 f., holds Christ contained in the Old Testament as in consubstantiation. See Eichrodt's criticism of this in "Zur Frage der theologischen Exegese des Alten Testaments", *ibid.*, 1931, 73 f.

[2] W. Vischer, "Das Alte Testament und die Verkündigung", *Theologische Blätter*, 1931, 1 f. See his earlier "Das Alte Testament als Wort Gottes", *Zwischen den Zeiten*, 1927, 379 f. *Die Bedeutung des Alten Testaments für das Christliche Leben*, 2nd edn., 1927.

[3] Vischer, *Das Christuszeugnis des Alten Testaments*. I, *Das Gesetz*, 1934 (E.T. by A. B. Crabtree, *The Witness of the Old Testament to Christ*, 1949). II, *Die Propheten*, 1942. Vol. III is still due.

[4] Separate themes from the Pentateuch were treated in his *Jahweh der Gott Kains*, 1929; "Der Gott Abrahams, Isaaks und Jakobs", *Zwischen den Zeiten*, 1930.

[5] A separate theme from "the Prophets" was treated in "Der Gottesknecht", *Jahrbuch der Theologischen Schule zu Bethel*, 1930.

[6] Separate subjects from "the Writings" were *Esther*, 1937 (in *Theologische Existenz Heute*, no. 48) and *Hiob, ein Zeuge Jesu Christi*, 5th edn., 1942.

[7] R. Abramowski, "Vom Streit um das Alte Testament", *Theologische Rundschau*, 1947, 65 f.

[8] For a critique see G. von Rad, "Das Christuszeugnis des Alten Testaments", *Theologische Blätter*, 1935, 249 f.; also the valuable remarks of Baumgärtel, p. 91 f. of the work mentioned below, note 32 to chapter 17.

Chapter Fourteen

The Old Testament and the Existential Question

[1] Cf. W. Wiesner, *Der Offenbarungsbegriff in der dialektischen Theologie*, 76 f.

[2] E. Grisebach, *Erkenntnis und Glaube*, 1923.

[3] M. Heidegger, *Sein und Zeit*, I, 1927.

[4] F. Gogarten, *Glaube und Wirklichkeit*, 1928. Gogarten was Professor in Breslau.

[5] Gogarten, "Einheit von Evangelium und Volkstum", *Deutsche Theologie*, 1933.

[6] Gogarten, "Ist Volksgesetz Gottesgesetz?" *ibid.*, 1934.

[7] R. Bultmann, "Die Bedeutung des Alten Testaments für den Christlichen Glauben", *Glauben und Verstehen. Gesammelte Aufsätze*, 1933. The author was one of the most radical New Testament

critics; his *Geschichte der Synoptischen Tradition*, 1921, was particularly important. Professor at Marburg, he has recently become a storm centre of discussion through his "Das Problem der Entmythologisirung der Neutestamentlichen Verkündigung", in his *Offenbarung und Heilsgeschehen*, 1941; reprinted in *Kerygma und Mythos; Diskussionen und Stimmen zum Problem der Entmythogisirung*, ed. H. W. Bartsch, 2nd edn., 2 vols., 1951–52. A good survey in A. N. Wilder, "Mythology and the New Testament", *Journal of Biblical Literature*, LXIX, 1950, 113 f.

⁸ Bultmann, "Ursprung und Sinn der Typologie als hermeneutische Methode", *Theologische Literaturzeitung*, 1950, 205 f.

Chapter Fifteen

The Old Testament as Antithesis to Christianity

¹ E. Hirsch, *Das Alte Testament und die Predigt des Evangeliums*, 1936. The author was Professor in Göttingen prior to the late war. He has published a great deal—most recently a *Geschichte der neueren evangelischen Theologie*, 4 vols., 1949–52.

² See his *Christliche Freiheit und Politische Bindung*, 1935, 76 f.

³ I have changed his terminology in the interest of lucidity in English presentation; he speaks of *lex simplex* and *lex in lege*.

⁴ See his *Luthers Deutsche Bibel*, 1928.

⁵ His *Kierkegaardstudien*, 2 vols., 1933, show his interest in this thinker.

⁶ *Das vierte Evangelium*, 1936, 320 f.

⁷ See above, p. 176.

⁸ *Das Alte Testament*, 71 f.

⁹ He gives the reference to Kierkegaard as *Papirer* 1/1 A 151 (1854).

¹⁰ *Pap.* 11/1 A 184 (1854).

¹¹ For a criticism from this angle see G. von Rad, "Gesetz und Evangelium im alten Testament", *Theologische Blätter*, 1937, 41 f.; J. Hempel, *Zeitschrift für die alttestamentliche Wissenschaft*, LIV, 1936, 298 f.

Chapter Sixteen

Recent Discussions

¹ W. F. Albright, *From the Stone Age to Christianity*, 1940. The author, Professor at John Hopkins University in Baltimore, is the most versatile Orientalist of our time and has played a great role as a pioneer of truly scientific Palestinian archæology. (See his Pelican Book, *The Archæology of Palestine*, 1949.) He edits the *Bulletin of the American Schools of Oriental Research*.

² R. H. Pfeiffer, *Introduction to the Old Testament*, 1940, the most detailed modern work of its kind and bibliographically the most

informative. The author, who teaches at Harvard, is a keen Old Testament critic and has achievements in Assyriology to his credit as well.

[3] H. F. D. Sparks, *The Old Testament in the Christian Church*, 1944. The author is a Professor at Oxford University.

[4] H. H. Rowley, *The Relevance of the Bible*, 1942. The author is a Professor at Manchester University and one of the most learned and productive of Old Testament scholars. He is a prime mover in international co-operation and understanding on the part of men engaged in Old Testament study, and edits the valuable Book List put out annually by the *Society for Old Testament Study*.

[5] See further his *The Rediscovery of the Old Testament*, 1946; *The Relevance of Apocalyptic*, 1944.

[6] *The Authority of the Bible*, 1949 (Joseph Smith Lecture); *The Unity of the Bible*, 1953.

[7] *The Unity of the Bible*, 1953.

[8] R. B. Y. Scott, *The Relevance of the Prophets*, 1944. The author is Professor at McGill University, Montreal.

[9] G. E. Wright, *The Challenge of Israel's Faith*, 1944. See further, chapter 17. The author, noted for his work in Palestinian archæology and geography, is Professor at the McCormick Theological Seminary in Chicago. He edits the *Biblical Archæologist*, a publication of the American Schools of Oriental Research that does much to disseminate knowledge about recent discoveries. Of other pertinent studies by Wright we may mention here his *The Old Testament Against its Environment*, 1950; his lecture *The Old Testament; Impediment or Bulwark of the Christian Faith*, 1945; also his article, "Interpreting the Old Testament", *Theology Today*, III, 1946, 176 f.

[10] M. Burrows, *Outline of Biblical Theology*, 1946 (see further, chapter 17). The author is Professor at Yale; his role in obtaining permission to publish the Dead Sea scrolls and in editing them so promptly deserves particular mention.

[11] A. G. Hebert, *The Authority of the Old Testament*, 1947; *The Throne of David, A Study of the Fulfilment of the Old Testament in Christ and his Church*, 1941. The author was Professor of New Testament at Kelham (Newark).

[12] C. H. Dodd, *The Bible Today*, 1946. The author was Professor at Cambridge and is a New Testament scholar of high rank, with many publications to his credit. He had already written a book on the Biblical problem, *The Authority of the Bible*, 1928, 3rd edn., 1952.

[13] S. A. Cook, *The Rebirth of Christianity*, 1942; see earlier his *The "Truth" of the Bible*, 1938. Professor at Cambridge, he was a master scholar of the school devoted to historical and comparative religious study. His *The Old Testament; A Reinterpretation*, 1936, presents the modern critical view afresh.

[14] I. G. Matthews, *The Religious Pilgrimage of Israel*, 1947. The author was Professor at Crozer Theological Seminary, and has a humanistic approach.

[15] H. Cunliffe Jones, *The Authority of the Biblical Revelation*, 1946. W. J. Phythian Adams, *The People and the Presence*, 1942. G. E. Phillips, *The Old Testament in the World Church*, 1942. C. R. North, *The Old Testament Interpretation of History*, 1946. J. Woods, *The Old Testament in the Church*, 1949. W. A. C. Elmslie, *How Came our Faith*, 1948. W. A. Smart, *Still the Bible Speaks*, 1948. *Biblical Authority To-day*, ed. A. Richardson and W. Schweitzer, 1951.

[16] G. von Rad, "Typologische Auslegung des Alten Testaments"; W. Zimmerli, "Verheissung und Erfüllung", in a discussion of principles for a projected new Commentary series, *Evangelische Theologie*, XII, 1952–53, nos. 1/2. See the critique of both contributions by Baumgärtel in the work to be cited, chapter 17 n. 32, p. 106 f. On typology see J. Daniélou, *Sacramentum futuri; Études sur les origines de la typologie biblique*, 1950.

[17] Two noteworthy studies from the German quarter are K. Elliger, *Die Bedeutung der Geschichte Israels für die Kirche Jesu Christi*, 1948, and H. W. Hertzberg, *Werdende Kirche im Alten Testament*, 1950.

Chapter Seventeen

Toward a Biblical Theology?

[1] On the origin of this discipline see above, p. 56.

[2] B. Stade, "Über die Aufgaben der biblischen Theologie des Alten Testaments", *Zeitschrift für Theologie und Kirche*, III, 1893, 30 f. Reprinted in his *Akademische Abhandlungen*, 2nd edn., 1907, 77 f. Stade was Professor in Giessen, founder of the leading Old Testament journal, the *Zeitschrift für die alttestamentliche Wissenschaft*. See on him Gunkel, "Bernhard Stade", in his *Reden und Aufsätze*.

[3] B. Stade, *Biblische Theologie des Alten Testaments*, I, 1905; Vol. II, *Die Jüdische Religion von der Zeit Esras bis zum Zeitalter Christi*, 1911, was done by A. Bertholet.

[4] E. Kautzsch, *Biblische Theologie des Alten Testaments*, 1911 (As *The Religion of Israel* it appeared in the Extra Volume of Hastings, *Dictionary of the Bible*, 1904, 612 f.). B. Duhm's noteworthy *Theologie der Propheten*, 1875, also used "Theology" in this manner.

[5] *Die Religion in Geschichte und Gegenwart*, 2nd edn., I, 1089 f. art. *Biblische Theologie und Biblische Religionsgeschichte*).

[6] C. Steuernagel, "Alttestamentliche Theologie und alttestamentliche Religionsgeschichte", *Vom Alten Testament; Festschrift Karl Marti*, ed. K. Budde, 1925, 266 f. He was Professor in Breslau.

[7] O. Eissfeldt, "Israelitisch-jüdische Religionsgeschichte und alttestamentliche Theologie", *Zeitschrift für die alttestamentliche Wissenschaft*, XLIV, 1926, 1 f.

[8] W. Eichrodt, "Hat die alttestamentliche Theologie noch selbständige Bedeutung in der alttestamentlichen Wissenschaft?" *ibid.*, XLVII, 1929, 83 f.

[9] W. Staerk, "Religionsgeschichte und Religionsphilosophie in ihrer Bedeutung für die biblische Theologie des Alten Testaments", *Zeitschrift für Theologie und Kirche*, N.F., IV, 1923, 289 f.

[10] G. van der Leeuw, *Phänomenologie der Religion*, 1935.

[11] F. Baumgärtel, *Die Eigenart der alttestamentlichen Frömmigkeit*, 1932.

[12] J. Lindblom, "Zur Frage der Eigenart der alttestamentlichen Religion", in *Werden und Wesen des Alten Testaments*, ed. P. Volz, F. Stummer, J. Hempel, 1936, 128 f.

[13] A. Weiser, "Die Theologische Aufgabe der alttestamentlichen Wissenschaft", *ibid.*, 207 f.

[14] Weiser, "Vom Verständnis des Alten Testaments", *Zeitschrift für die alttestamentliche Wissenschaft*, LXI, 1945-48, 17 f.

[15] Mention should be made of E. Koenig, *Theologie des Alten Testaments*, 1922, a work of conservative character with too much space expended on rebuttal of loose statements or extreme views of other scholars. He also wrote a *Geschichte der alttestamentlichen Religion*, 1912. On him see chapter 9, n. 1.

[16] E. Sellin, *Theologie des Alten Testaments*, 2 vols., 1933. On him see chapter 12, n. 2.

[17] L. Köhler, *Theologie des Alten Testaments*, 1936 (3rd edn., 1953). E.T. in preparation, Lutterworth Press, 1955. Professor in Zürich. His new Hebrew Dictionary (with Aramaic supplement by W. Baumgartner), providing both English and German renderings, will prove a useful tool for students and scholars.

[18] W. Eichrodt, *Theologie des Alten Testaments*, 3 vols., 1933-38. The author is Professor in Basel. He has written numerous papers bearing on the theological theme, beginning with *Ist die altisraelitische Nationalreligion Offenbarungsreligion?* 1925. See now his *Man in the Old Testament*, tr. by K. and R. Gregor Smith, 1951.

[19] O. Procksch, *Theologie des Alten Testaments*, 1950. On him cf. chapter 12, n. 15. His paper "Geschichte als Glaubensinhalt", *Neue Kirchliche Zeitschrift*, 1925, 485 f. also merits attention.

[20] M. Burrows, *An Outline of Biblical Theology*, 1946. See above, p. 260 f.

[21] G. Bertram, "Die Aufgabe einer Theologie beider Testamente", *Kirche im Angriff*, XII, 1936, 416 f. He is Professor in Jena.

[22] O. J. Baab, *Theology of the Old Testament*, 1949. The author is Professor at the Garrett Biblical Institute, Evanston, Ill., U.S.A. Cf. also his article "Old Testament Theology: its Possibility and Methodology", in *The Study of the Bible Today and Tomorrow* ed. by H. R. Willoughby, 1947, 401 f.

[23] Mention should be made here of N. H. Snaith, *The Distinctive Ideas of the Old Testament*, 1950. H. W. Robinson's discussion, "The Characteristic Doctrines", in *Record and Revelation*, 321 f., should likewise not be overlooked. His other essay in that volume was outlined above, p. 216.

[24] R. C. Dentan, *Preface to Old Testament Theology*, 1950. He is

Professor at the Berkeley Divinity School in New Haven, Conn., U.S.A.

[25] N. W. Porteous, "Old Testament Theology", in *The Old Testament and Modern Study*, ed. H. H. Rowley, 1951, 311 f. He is Professor at the University of Edinburgh.

[26] G. von Rad, "Grundprobleme einer biblischen Theologie des alten Testaments", *Theologische Literaturzeitung*, 1943, 226 f. In connection with the idea of history emphasized by von Rad, cf. M. Noth, *Geschichte und Gotteswort im Alten Testament*, 1950 (E.T. in Bulletin of the John Rylands Library, March, 1950). The author is one of the leading Old Testament scholars of our time. The paper shows from the historical side how difficult is the theological task.

[27] von Rad, "Das Problem des alttestamentlichen Schöpfungsglaubens", *Werden und Wesen des Alten Testaments*, 138 f. The study referred to is *Das formgeschichtliche Problem des Hexateuchs*, 1938.

[28] G. E. Wright, *The Challenge of Israel's Faith* (see chapter 16, n. 9).

[29] Wright, *God who Acts; Biblical Theology as Recital*, 1952.

[30] C. H. Dodd, *The Apostolic Preaching and its Developments*, 1936.

[31] H. H. Rowley, "The Unity of the Old Testament", *Bulletin of the John Rylands Library*, XXIX, 1946, No. 2; *The Unity of the Bible*, 1953 (cf. above chapter 16, n. 4).

[32] F. Baumgärtel, *Verheissung. Zur Frage des evangelischen Verständnisses des Alten Testaments*, 1952. Also his related paper "Das alttestamentliche Geschehen als heilsgeschichtliches Geschehen", in *Geschichte und Altes Testament, Albrecht Alt zum 70 Geburtstag*, 1953, 13 f. For his antithesis to von Rad see his "Der Dissensus im Verständnis des Alten Testaments", *Evangelische Theologie*, 1954, 298 f. This scholar is Professor at Erlangen and wrote a valuable study on Job. Cf. also n. 11 above.

[33] We may note in passing that the Systematic theological discussion of H. Richard Niebuhr, *The Meaning of Revelation*, 1941, also stresses "internal history", "where value does not mean strength as in external history, but quality, and time is not quantitative but organic and social, so that what is past is not gone but abides in us as our memory and what is future is not non-existent but already present in us as our potentiality".

[34] F. Baumgärtel, "Erwägungen zur Darstellung der Theologie des Alten Testaments", *Theologische Literaturzeitung*, 1951, 258 f.

[35] H. Stephan, *Geschichte der evangelischen Theologie seit dem Deutschen Idealismus*, 1938, 328.

INDEX

SUBJECTS

311

Subjects cont.

Subjects cont.

Subjects cont.

Subjects cont.

NAMES*

* Except those of Antiquity, which are in the Index of Subjects.

Names cont.

Names cont.

SCRIPTURE PASSAGES

Scripture passages cont.

The British Folklorists

A HISTORY

THE BRITISH
FOLKLORISTS

A HISTORY

by

RICHARD M. DORSON

THE UNIVERSITY OF CHICAGO PRESS

Library of Congress Catalog Card Number: 68–16689

The University of Chicago Press, Chicago 60637

Routledge & Kegan Paul Ltd., London E.C.4

© 1968 Richard M. Dorson. All rights reserved

Published 1968

Printed in the United States of America

For Dan and Ruth Boorstin

Preface

T HIS BOOK BEGAN A LONG TIME AGO, in the summer of 1948, when on a casual visit to my sister who lived in London I stumbled across the library of The Folk-Lore Society. The library was housed in University College of the University of London. A bomb dropped on the main library building during the war had forced a temporary rearrangement of the books. The folklore collection was then located on overflowing shelves hidden behind the medical library. All summer I spent in that dusty haven, making acquaintance with the Great Team. In 1949–50, 1951, 1963, and 1964–65 I returned, pursuing the trail of the British folklorists in the British Museum reading room and in the Cambridge University library and attending meetings of the Society with so illustrious a heritage.

During the years since that first summer, the power and eloquence of these giants of folklore were never long out of my mind, even when I was deeply immersed in my own American folklore. More and more I came to feel that familiarity with the brilliant history of folklore science in England was as indispensable for the American, and indeed for the European, Asian, or African student of folklore, as for the British. The birth and growth of the idea of folklore and the magnetism in that idea for many powerful minds in diverse callings formed a story as marvellous as any folktale. Here I have tried to tell that story.

Among my benefactors I am grateful to the John Simon Guggenheim Memorial Foundation for twice enabling me to make extended sojourns in England, and to its directors, Henry Allen Moe and Gordon N. Ray, for their sympathetic interest. The International Studies Advisory Committee of Indiana University under the chairmanship of Edward H. Buehrig has aided me with grants for travel expenses and clerical assistance. To Katharine Briggs, President of The Folk-Lore Society, I am indebted for suggestions and encouragement and to Christina Hole, Hon. Editor of *Folklore*, for permission to reproduce portraits of some of the leading figures of the Society. During my year in Cambridge, Edward M. Wilson, professor of Spanish in Emmanuel College and former Hon. Secretary

[v]

of The Folk-Lore Society, showed me many kindnesses. Mrs. H. A. Lake Barnett, Hon. Treasurer of the Society, graciously allowed me to see Sir George Laurence Gomme's scrapbook of clippings of the 1891 International Folklore Congress. Sheri Harvey and Lydia Fish have rendered invaluable assistance in checking references and in assuming other tedious chores.

R. M. D.

Contents

Illustrations

I *The Antiquaries*

SELDOM IN THE HISTORY of learning has a new subject announced its arrival so explicitly and with such self-assurance as did folklore. Writing to a respected English weekly, the *Athenaeum,* on August 22, 1846, the antiquary William John Thoms (1803–1885) declared, 'What we in England designate as Popular Antiquities . . . would be most aptly described by a good Saxon compound, Folk-Lore. . . .' Within a year Thoms could proudly announce that his term had achieved household currency. In the following decades it would enter many languages and become in Britain and the United States a much mooted and bruited label, covering a vast span of notions, from the scientific study of primitive belief to the vocalizing of pop groups heard today. But its coiner intended 'folk-lore' to designate a serious cultural inquiry, and his successors explored the subject with an intellectual vigour and brilliance that excited all England in the late Victorian decades. The classicist and medievalist, anthropologist and psychologist, historian and archaeologist, literary scholar and philologist, as well as the parson, the doctor, and the schoolmaster, found stimulus and reward in the methods of folklore. In 1878, as if to confirm its permanence, a dedicated group of private scholars calling themselves folklorists founded a Folk-Lore Society and in 1891 organized an international Folk-Lore Congress. Their compatriots abroad, who governed colonies, planted missions, and travelled the globe, diligently amassed folk traditions and customs, the better to understand subject peoples and alien cultures.

How the theory and pursuit of folklore evolved in England and were transported throughout the British Isles, the British Empire, and the world at large is the story of this book. And our first question must be, where does the story properly begin?

This complex and intricate chapter of intellectual history does not commence with the letter of Thoms, which confirmed the merit of an exploration well under way. To whom was Thoms indebted?

[1]

The inquiry he furthered did not, as some might suspect, owe its impetus to the Renaissance interest in classical mythology, although handbooks in mythology were abundant; nor did it derive from the Romantic affection for folksong, although an enduring interest in ballad studies had commenced in 1765 with Bishop Percy's *Reliques of Ancient English Poetry*.

The key phrase in Thoms's proposal is 'popular antiquities,' a term too cumbersome for his taste but well understood by his countrymen. The quest for antiquities of all kinds had intrigued Englishmen throughout the seventeenth and eighteenth centuries. They wrote books on Greek, Roman, and Norman antiquities; on the antiquities of numerous English towns and counties which they often coupled with 'natural history,' 'scenery,' and 'curiosities'; on the antiquities of abbeys and cathedrals, of Oxford University and the Inns of Court. In earliest usage the term 'antiquities' signified the physical, visible remains of the historic past in England. The emergence of national sentiment in Elizabethan times was accompanied by the New Learning, practised by bibliophiles and foot-loose scholars, liberating the study of the past from the theological tracts of the monks. A strong interest in Roman ruins and relics characterized this learning, as a virile nation aspiring to greatness viewed the remnants of an ancient empire scattered about its island home. The Roman fort, the Saxon church, the Celtic burial mound proved alluring to a new genus of historical antiquary, whose researches took the form of walking tours during which he surveyed the local trophies—urn, coin, barrow, monument—and added his notes and sketches on these artifacts to his collection of manuscripts and monkish chronicles.

Exemplar and father of these researches was William Camden (1551–1623), whose *Britannia*, an historical survey of British topography and antiquities, was destined to become an institution and a landmark. First issued in a small Latin edition in 1586, it was translated into English and greatly extended by subsequent editors, notably Edmund Gibson (1695) and Richard Gough (1789). In his preface Camden plainly states the historical basis of antiquarian studies, saying that his friend, the geographer Abraham Ortelius, 'did very earnestly sollicit me to acquaint the World with *Britain*, that ancient Island; that is, to restore Britain to its Antiquities, and its Antiquities to Britain.' This he had endeavoured to do, notwithstanding 'Some there are who cry down the study of Antiquity with much contempt, as too curious a search after what is past. . . .'[1] The lasting success of the *Britannia* refuted this objection, and

[1] *Camden's Britannia*, published by Edmund Gibson (London, 1695), 'Mr Camden's

[2]

ensured the acceptance of antiquities as a proper field of inquiry, especially in the form of county history, following the divisions of the *Britannia*. Camden's predecessor, John Leland (*ca.* 1503–52), who planned the work Camden achieved, styled himself *Antiquarius* and was appointed King's Antiquary in 1533. By the eighteenth century 'antiquary' had become a title respected and esteemed.

The concept of antiquities, even in its earliest formulation, was not restricted to written and material records of the past; it also covered oral traditions. When Camden in 1607 published a small book of commonplace notes, *Remaines of a Greater Worke, concerning Britaine*, he included with descriptions of old costumes and coins a list of proverbs harking back to early times. For the *Remaines* and the *Britannia* Camden employed the walking tour as a technique for mining local history and tradition. On his tours he observed topography and interviewed residents. A section of the *Britannia* devoted to 'Manners and Customs of the Ancient Irish' reveals his success at gathering folk memories. Consider the superstitions he gathered about horses. Irishmen of old would not clean the feet of horses or gather grass for them on a Saturday, but would do so on holy days. The owner of a horse must eat an even number of eggs, or he will endanger his animal. A jockey should not eat eggs, but in the event of doing so must then wash his hands. To ensure the health of his horses, the owner should refuse the loan of fire to his neighbours. Whoever praised a horse or other animal must say 'God save him!' or spit on the creature; if an illness still resulted, the owner should seek out the admirer and whisper the Lord's Prayer in his right ear. If someone with bewitching eyes looked at a horse and caused it sickness, the owner requested an old woman to utter prayers. (The fear of the evil eye persists in Ireland and in Mediterranean countries.) To cure worms in horses' hooves, the horseman brought to his house on two Mondays and a Thursday a witch who breathed on the afflicted part, 'cherished' it, and repeated a secret charm. When a horse died, his master hung the legs inside his house and revered the hooves.[1]

Camden related these and similar practices, demonstrating the value of the horse to the early Irish, as an aspect of British antiquities. His partiality to the oral testimony of local inhabitants, and his shrewd historical analysis of such testimony, is seen in the following tradition he recorded in Kent.

[1] *Britannia*, col. 1047.

Preface.' An excellent essay on 'William Camden and the *Britannia*' by Stuart Piggott is in the *Proceedings of the British Academy*, XXXVII (1951), 199–217.

'Tis a current report among the Inhabitants that Julius Caesar encampt here in his second expedition against the Britains, and that thence it was call'd *Julham*, as if one should say Julius's *station or house*; and if I mistake not, they have truth on their side. For Caesar himself tells us, that after he had march'd by night 12 miles from the shore, he first encounter'd the Britains upon a River, and after he had beat them into the woods, that he encamp'd there; where the Britons having cut down a great number of trees, were posted in a place wonderfully fortify'd both by nature and art.

Now this place is exactly twelve miles from the sea-coast, nor is there e're a river between; so that of necessity his first march must have been hither; where he kept his men encamp'd for ten days, till he had refitted his fleet shatter'd very much by a tempest, and got it to shore. Below this town is a green *barrow*, said to be the burying place of one *Jul Laber* many ages since; who some will tell you was a *Giant*, others a *Witch*. For my own part, imagining all along that there might be something of real Antiquity couch'd under that name, I am almost perswaded that *Laberius Durus* the Tribune, slain by the Britains in their march from the Camp we spoke of, was buried here; and that from him the *Barrow* was called *Jul-laber*.[1]

Here is an ingenious reconstruction of a Roman antiquity, employing a physical site and a community legend to forge a link with mighty Caesar. Camden sloughs off the covering of folk belief to find underneath a genuine core of ancient history. The moral for later antiquaries is plainly marked: the factual story behind the Roman ruin may still survive, dipped in legend, on the lips of the natives, and offer clues to the historian.

The *Britannia* and the *Remaines* stirred noble patrons and inquiring gentry to collect and preserve antiquities. Three years after the death of Camden there was born in Wiltshire a worthy successor to his interests, gossipy, gregarious John Aubrey (1626–97), who emphasized the oral and marvellous element in antiquarian studies. Aubrey typified the seventeenth-century antiquary, probing deep into his home county; a debt-ridden country squire, educated at Oxford and the Middle Temple, his curiosity extended to all manner of local traditional subjects, and throughout his life he accumulated notes and compiled bulky manuscripts from his reading, conversations, and walking trips. 'I was much inclined by my Genius

[1] *Britannia*, 'Kent,' p. 197.

from childhood, to the love of antiquities,' he wrote, 'and my Fate dropt me in a countrey most suitable for such enquiries.'[1] In Aubrey the concept of antiquities found not only an ardent and devoted champion, but also a broad interpreter. He linked antiquities to 'natural history' and 'preternatural' events, and looked toward living people as repositories of tradition. His most famous work, the *Brief Lives*, quarried by biographers and historians of Stuart times, is stuffed with personal anecdotes. Twice-told legends are strewn throughout other works: his vast compilation, 'Monumenta Britannica or a Miscellanie of British Antiquities'; the Natural History and Antiquities he assembled for both his native Wiltshire and adjacent Surrey (the latter alternatively titled 'A Perambulation of the County of Surrey'); the compendium of customs and notions surviving from classical and biblical times he called 'Remaines of Gentilisme and Judaisme'; and the one book published during his lifetime, the *Miscellanies* (1696), a record of supernatural experiences and conceptions current in his day which could pass for the notebook of a modern folklore collector.

The central historical fact in Aubrey's own life was the civil war between the forces of the King and of the Parliament. He had to withdraw temporarily from Oxford in 1642 when military forces occupied the city. In 1651, two years after the beheading of Charles I, Aubrey witnessed the execution of a Puritan minister, Christopher Love, for high treason. 'Shortly after his suffring the skye began to thicken and at last was envellopt in blacke dismall Cloud, and all that night and till next noon such Thunder, lightning, and Tempest as if the Machine of the world has been dissolving.'[2] The Restoration of Charles II in May, 1660, brought about the imprisonment of Aubrey's friend James Harrington, the political philosopher, whose durance produced a mad idea that his perspiration turned to flies and bees. So Aubrey gratified his appetite for the wondrous and remarkable in the midst of revolution and upheaval. With the sure instinct of the tradition-hunter, he recognized the rupture in society caused by new inventions and new political forms, and the damaging effect of these innovations on the old peasant culture.

Before Printing, Old-wives Tales were ingeniose, and since Printing came in fashion, till a little before the Civill-warres,

---

[1] Anthony Powell, *John Aubrey and his Friends* (London: Mercury Books, 1963), p. 274. Quoted by Powell from Aubrey's 'Description of the North Division of Wiltshire.'
[2] *Ibid.*, pp. 70–1. Quoted by Powell, from Anthony Wood's Manuscripts, Bodleian Library.

the ordinary sort of People were not taught to reade. Now-a-
dayes Bookes are common, and most of the poor people understand letters; and the many good Bookes, and variety of
Turnes of Affaires, have putt all the old Fables out of doors:
and the divine art of Printing and Gunpowder have frighted
away Robin-goodfellow and the Fayries.[1]

At so early a date this is an extraordinarily acute insight into
the ways of oral folklore. Aubrey furthermore pointed out a sharp
historical division, in the middle decades of the seventeenth century, between the old, tradition-soaked culture and the new
mechanical civilization. He saw this rupture affecting not only tales
and fables but also ancient customs and festivals dating from
Roman times, which had endured, and indeed blended with, Roman
Catholic and Anglican rituals. From his own childhood in Wiltshire
and his strolls in other counties, Aubrey remembered local usages
now vanished with the smoke and turmoil of internal strife, for 'the
Civill Warres comeing on have putt out all these Rites, or customs
quite out of fashion.'[2] No longer did gentlemen keep in their dwellings merry harpers who sang and composed ballads, nor tilt in
tournaments; no longer did country folk dance and sing in the
churches at Christmas-time, or place a penny for St. Peter in a
corpse's mouth, or sit on the parish porch at midnight of Midsummer's Eve to see apparitions of those to die in the coming year;
no more did shepherds wear their old Roman garb of long, white,
woollen cloaks. Gone was the bizarre custom of sin-eating.

In the County of Hereford was an old Custome at Funeralls
to hire poor people, who were to take upon them all the Sinnes
of the party deceased. One of these (I remember) lived in a
Cottage on Rosse-high way: He was a long, leane, ugly lament-
able poor raskal. The manner was that when the Corps was
brought out of the house and layd on a Biere: a Loafe of bread
was brought out, and delivered to the sinne-eater over the
Corps, as also a Mazar-bowle of maple (Gossips bowle) full of
beer, which he was to drinke up, and sixpence in money, in consideration whereof he tooke upon him (ipso facto) all the
Sinnes of the Defunct, and freed him (or her) from Walking
after they were dead. This custome alludes (me thinkes) something to the Scape goat in the old Lawe.[3]

---

[1] Oliver L. Dick (ed.), *Aubrey's Brief Lives* (2nd ed.; London: Secker and Warburg,
1950), p. xxxiii. Quoted by Dick in his Introduction, 'The Life and Times of John
Aubrey,' from Aubrey's 'Remaines of Gentilisme and Judaisme.'
[2] *Ibid.*, p. xxxvi. Quoted by Dick from Aubrey's 'The Natural History of Wiltshire.'
[3] *Ibid.*, p. lxvii. Quoted by Dick, from 'Remaines of Gentilisme and Judaisme.'

Nineteenth-century folklorists like Edwin Sidney Hartland sought zealously in Herefordshire for traces of sin-eating, which they considered, like Aubrey, a pagan survival of once widely adopted funerary rites, perhaps originally involving sacrifice. Since these country ceremonies were disappearing, Aubrey's antiquarian spirit was moved to record them for the sake of comprehending the past. 'Old Customs and old wives fables are grosse things, but yet ought not to be buried in Oblivion; there may be some trueth and usefulnesse be picked out of them, besides 'tis a pleasure to consider the Errours that enveloped former ages: as also the present.'[1] Here is probably the earliest statement in English of the value in recording folk traditions. Again he says, 'I know that some will nauseate these old Fables: but I doe profes to regard them as the most considerable pieces of Antiquity I collect.'[2]

All his writings display Aubrey's fondness for the lively anecdote and the ominous legend. The celebrated *Lives* strings together little stories; thus Aubrey speaks of the 'Tradicion of the Countrey people in Dorset' that Cardinal Morton was a shoemaker's son.[3] In his 'Natural History and Antiquities of the County of Surrey' he ponders the series of injuries that befell all who chopped down an oak tree in 1657, and this reminds him of the fate affecting the Earl of Winchelsea in Kent, whose wife and son died soon after the Earl felled a grove of oaks. In his county perambulations and commentaries on monumental antiquities Aubrey inserts such items incidentally, but he devotes two books entirely to these curiosities. In the *Miscellanies* he gathers together specimens of 'day and local' fatalities occurring at predestined times and places, omens, dreams, apparitions, prophecies, marvels, magic, knockings, blows invisible, visions in a glass, glances of love and envy, converse with angels and spirits, transportation in the air, second-sighted persons. Some of his occult information he gleaned from earlier writers; he cites two of the most famous witch-books, Joseph Glanvill's *Saducismus Triumphatus* (1681) and Richard Baxter's *The Certainty of the Worlds of Spirits* (1691); he reprints a collection of day-fatalities issued in 1678 by a John Gibbon; and he was in close touch with Sir William Dugdale, author of *The Antiquities of Warwickshire* (1656), a model county history following in the wake of Camden. Dugdale told Aubrey of an apparition he himself had seen, which prophesied events later borne out, and of a second-sighted Highlander who had

[1] *Ibid.*, p. lxv. Quoted by Dick, from 'Remaines of Gentilisme and Judaisme.'
[2] Powell, *op. cit.*, p. 66. Quoted by Powell from the Aubrey Manuscripts, Bodleian Library.
[3] Dick, *op. cit.*, pp. lx–lxi. Quoted by Dick from a letter by Aubrey to Anthony Wood.

foretold the death of Charles I. Sir William had written down these accounts in his own book of miscellanies, which Aubrey had seen in the museum at Oxford.[1] But many cases Aubrey obtained at first hand, from his own immediate world. Thus he learned about day-fatalities.

> I had a Maternal Uncle, that died the Third of *March* last 1678, which was the Anniversary day of his Birth; and (which is a Truth exceeding strange) many years ago he foretold the day of his Death to be that of his Birth; and he also averred the same but about the Week before his departure.[2]

At harvest-time in a field of Warminster parish in Wiltshire, one of the parishioners took up two sheaves of wheat, crying '*Now for* Richard, *Now for* Henry,' till at last he let fall the sheaf representing Richard and cried, '*Now for King* Henry, Richard *is slain.*' This acting took place the very day and hour of the fight at Bosworth Field between King Richard III and Henry VII in 1485 which placed Henry on the throne to found the Tudor line. 'When I was a School-boy, I have heard this confidently delivered by Tradition, by some Old Men of our Country.'[3] Again, Aubrey heard directly from a painter living at Stowel in Somersetshire how he was cured of a wen as big as a pullet's egg by rubbing his cheek against a dead woman's hand after saying the Lord's Prayer and begging a blessing. The painter avowed this not only to Aubrey but also to his clergyman companion, Andrew Paschal.[4] The circumstantial detail and personal source of Aubrey's wonders are again well illustrated in the following ghost relation.

> Mr. *Caisho Burroughs* was one of the most beautiful Men in *England,* and very Valiant, but very proud and blood-thirsty: There was then in *London* a very Beautiful *Italian* Lady, who fell so extreamly in Love with him, that she did let him enjoy her, which she had never let any Man do before: Wherefore, said she, I shall request this favour of you, never to tell any one of it. The Gentlewoman died: and afterwards in a Tavern in *London* he spake of it: and there going to make water, the Ghost of the Gentlewoman did appear to him. He was afterwards troubled with the Apparition of her, even sometimes in company when he was drinking; but he only percieved [*sic*] it: Before she did appear he did find a chilness upon his Spirits; she did appear to him in the Morning before he was killed in a

---

[1] *Miscellanies*, collected by J. Aubrey, Esq. (London: printed for Edward Castle, 1696), pp. 66–7.   [2] *Ibid.*, p. 6.   [3] *Ibid.*, p. 88.   [4] *Ibid.*, p. 98.

Duel. This account I have from an intimate Friend of mine, who was an acquaintance of his.[1]

All these miscellanies—Aubrey had no better term at his disposal—follow a certain thread. They present personal encounters and experiences with 'preternatural' forces. Spectral signs, sounds, and sights foretell death or reveal the presence of the walking dead. Spirits and angels, ghosts and fairies appear to mortals or speak with them. The kernels of these little narratives belong entirely to the traditions of English supernaturalism; the same themes attracted Andrew Lang two centuries later, when he sought to blend the study of folklore with psychical research. In form the episodes are casual and conversational, lacking the taut structure of fictional folktales. Today they are known among folklorists as memorats, a designation suggested by the Swedish scholar Carl von Sydow. Aubrey searched them out with a sure instinct, and an editor of his work in 1881 referred to the *Miscellanies* as one of the indispensable books on the folklore shelf.

The editor, James Britten, a compiler of English country words and plant-names, was entrusted by The Folk-Lore Society with the publication of Aubrey's other folklore book, which had lain in manuscript in the British Museum since 1688. This was the 'Remaines of Gentilisme and Judaisme,' an omnium-gatherum of all kinds of local customs, observances, practices, and usages. Aubrey jotted down descriptions of these entertaining habits and cited classical and biblical authorities to indicate their ancient provenance, hence his title. His entries ranged over Christmas and New Year's holidaymaking, charms to tie the tongues of foes, the casting and drawing of lots, revels and wakes, shepherds and garlands, funeral and nuptial rites and other such matter, piled together in scrapbook fashion. Frequently he was able to identify a pagan rite or magical formula in some idle pastime of village youths. Thus 'Cocklebread.'

> Young wenches have a wanton sport, wch they call moulding of Cocklebread; viz. they gett upon a Table-board, and then gather-up their knees & their coates with their hands as high as they can, and then they wabble to and fro with their Buttocks as if the [y] were kneading of Dowgh with their A——, and say these words, viz.:
>
> My Dame is sick & gonne to bed,
> And I'le go mowld my cockle-bread.

[1] *Ibid.*, pp. 60–1.

[9]

Aubrey at first imagined this a mere wanton game, but a reference in Burchardus led him to recognize the sport as no make-believe but a relic of love magic, for the dough was indeed thus 'moulded,' then baked into bread and given to a favoured male, who would adore the maid thenceforth.[1]

Although not published for nearly two centuries, the *Remaines* enjoyed a considerable reputation among antiquaries, and was quarried for two major folklore volumes, the 1813 edition prepared by Sir Henry Ellis of John Brand's *Observations on Popular Antiquities*, and the *Anecdotes and Traditions* assembled in 1839 by William John Thoms, who enriched the extracts with his own notes. When The Folk-Lore Society printed the entire manuscript in 1881, with extracts of folklore from Aubrey's other writings in an appendix, the folklorists of the golden age were acknowledging a direct debt to their predecessor. Aubrey directed the concept of antiquities as formulated by Leland and Camden toward local tradition and called attention to the disappearance of popular customs in the vortex of social and political revolution.

The *Miscellanies* and the manuscript 'Remaines' increased the great Brand-Ellis compilation of popular antiquities, whose two stout volumes formed a much vaster *Remaines*, culled from myriad sources. Brand was the giant antiquary-folklorist of the late eighteenth century, as Aubrey was of the late seventeenth. His magnum opus, destined to become the cornerstone of British folk-lore science, was, like most of the work in that science, a collaborative and cumulative effort. If Ellis edited Brand, Brand had already edited and absorbed Bourne.

Henry Bourne, a clergyman with antiquarian interests (1694–1733), was born a year before Aubrey's death. He was the son of a tailor in Newcastle-upon-Tyne and, with the help of friends who released him from his apprenticeship to a glazier, attended Christ's College at Cambridge University. After graduating in 1720 he assumed the curateship of All Hallows Church in Newcastle, a living he held for the remainder of his short life. To posterity he left a history of Newcastle, published three years after his death, and a singular tract combining his roles of clergyman and antiquary. It was titled *Antiquitates Vulgares; or, the Antiquities of the Common People. Giving an Account of several of their Opinions and Cere-*

---

[1] John Aubrey, *Remaines of Gentilisme and Judaisme*, edited and annotated by James Britten (London: Publications of the Folk-Lore Society, IV, 1881), p. 43 and note, p. 225, where Britten says that Aubrey has correctly solved the enigmatic reference to 'Cockell-Bread' in George Peele's *The Old Wives Tale* (1595).

monies. With proper Reflections upon each of them; shewing which may be retain'd, and which ought to be laid aside. By Henry Bourne, M.A., Curate of the Parochial Chapel of *All-Saints* in *Newcastle* upon Tyne. Newcastle, printed by J. White for the Author, 1725.

As the title page indicated, this was indeed a cautionary and hortatory work, kindled with Reformation ire and zeal, berating papist and heathen ideas insinuated into Christian rituals. The annual round of calendar customs, from the celebration of the New Year to the feast of Christmas, had degenerated into a year-long orgy. Holy days once reverent and Christlike had turned into bouts of libertinism and revelry. Bourne's chapter headings reduced the general complaint to specific charges: 'Of the Christmas Carol, an ancient Custom: The common Observation of it very unbecoming.' The text then descends to particulars:

> Was this performed with What Reverence and Decency, which are due to a Song of this Nature, in Honour of the Nativity, and Glory to our Lord, it would be very commendable; but to sing it, as is generally done, in the midst of *Rioting and Chambering, and Wantoness*, is no Honour, but Disgrace; no Glory, but an Affront to that Holy Season, a Scandal to Religion, and a Sin against Christ.[1]

So, too, the chapter 'Of New-Year's-Day's Ceremonies' cites 'Mumming, a Custom which ought to be laid aside.' Mumming has led to 'Uncleanness and Debauchery,' in direct opposition to the Word of God, as given in Deuteronomy xxii, where the Lord abjures man and woman not to wear each other's clothes. And so on throughout the year. Shrovetide, although properly purged of public confessions by the Church of England, is now given over to 'Rioting, and Gaming and Drunkenness.' St. Valentine's Day, while cleansed of its olden superstition, brings amorous exchanges, leading to scandal and ruin. Some observances Bourne concedes to be harmless. Palm Sunday has been stripped of the idolatrous superstitions it received from the papists, and if the young people enjoy carrying palm branches in their hands as an emblem of the season, so be it—but would it not be more fitting for them to carry 'the Palm of good Workes'?

The Newcastle curate was passionately seeking reform of religious abuses, not attempting to expand the stock of antiquities. His sources, copiously cited, are the Latin writings of the early church fathers and English bishops; the books of Scripture, particularly the Old Testament; sound classical authorities like Socrates

[1] Henry Bourne, *Antiquitates Vulgares* (Newcastle: J. White, 1725), p. 141.

[11]

and Plutarch, Virgil and Cicero; a sprinkling of English chroniclers, poets, and philosophers, from the Venerable Bede and Gregory of Tours to Shakespeare and Locke. Right and rational conduct is the theme, and vulgar superstitions, nursed by monkish Romanism and heathen lusts, are the foe. To outward appearances, Bourne had composed another reformist tract, a preachment against idolatry and sin, based on scriptural exegesis. But he drew upon novel sources, his own observations of the festal orgies and the papist rites he so deplored.

Henry Bourne was a shrewd observer. He wrote about the populace kindling fires on Midsummer's Eve, seeing spirits exorcized in haunted houses, carousing at wakes, worshipping at wells and fountains. He knew 'Of country conversation in a Winter's Evening,' centring on ghosts and spirits. He saw how the interwoven strands of folk tradition formed a separate culture from the rational, sober, and pious ways of learned men. These patterns of behaviour he called 'the antiquities of the common people,' regarding them as a base counterpart to the physical antiquities left by Roman generals and Saxon kings. Bourne's explanation for such 'antiquitates vulgares' was made in simple theological terms; these were heathen errors renewed and enlarged by the medieval church. The light of reason and the truth of God would soon blow them away.

Bourne took pleasure in linking pagan and papist as perpetrators of a vulgar antiquity. In the chapter 'Of visiting Wells and Fountains,' he wrote:

> There need be no Question, but as this Custom is practically Heathenish, so it is also originally: For the Heathens were wont to worship Streams and Fountains, and to suppose that the Nymphs, whom they imagin'd the Goddesses of the Waters, presided over them. As the Papists have borrowed many of their silly and superstitious Ceremonies from the Religion of the Heathens, so this in particular, a sottish, stupid, and abominable Custom, they could borrow no where else. *For we had no such Custom*, neither at any Time *the Churches of GOD.*[1]

Bourne scorned the Devil with his cloven hoof, seducing the ignorant and seeking to draw men from God with silly omens of salt-spilling, hares crossing one's path, crickets chirping. Ghosts and spirits emanated from the 'Fears and Fancies, and weak Brains of Men' on which the papists played. The spectres and apparitions

[1] Henry Bourne, *Antiquitates Vulgares* (Newcastle: J. White, 1725), p. 69.

seen at tombs and temples in antiquity, and reported by St. Athanasius and other church fathers, were not walking and talking spirits—these were Romish inventions—but most likely good angels appearing in the likeness of the saints. Only so much would Bourne concede to the supernatural.

For half a century Bourne's tract lay unnoticed, while the temper of England changed. The papist threat receded before entrenched and liberal Anglicanism. Nourished by trade and industry, the merchant and yeoman classes emerged as a new public. Latin, the language of scholars, yielded to English as the general tongue (thus the Gibson edition of the *Britannia*, 1695). The self-discovery of England proceeded through the tour over improved roads (Roger Gale to Oxford and Stonehenge, 1705; Daniel Defoe to manufacturing centres, 1724). Spurred by the classical bent of the early eighteenth century, the tours invested Roman remains with added interest, as a link between two great peoples. Between 1710 and 1730 a score of books were written on British and Romano-British antiquities, and in 1718 the Society of Antiquaries was founded on solid and permanent footing.

In 1777 the *Antiquitates Vulgares* saw print again in a curious form, and with scant praise allowed to its author, whose name on the title page appeared in a secondary position. John Brand (1744–1806) took the credit, and he called the book *Observations on Popular Antiquities*. Brand's contribution lay in commentaries following each of Bourne's chapters which swelled the work by one-fourth. 'Popular Antiquities' designated the mental heirlooms of the past found in the superstitious fancies of the populace, but no longer a target of reform so much as a proper subject for antiquarian study.

Brand became a Fellow of the Society of Antiquaries in the year his book was published, and served as resident secretary in London from 1784 until his death. His career resembles Bourne's, for Brand also grew up in Newcastle-upon-Tyne, entered the church, and wrote a history of Newcastle. Bound apprentice to his uncle, a cordwainer, he was enabled by friends to attend Lincoln College in Oxford University, and became a curate at Cramlington in 1774. Ten years later his patron, the Duke of Northumberland, presented him with a London rectory. The first edition of the *Observations* was also published at Newcastle, like the work of Bourne it incorporated. In Brand, however, the antiquary quite eclipsed the cleric, and he focused his energies on running down every printed reference he could find to any kind of popular antiquity.

Attracted by the matter of Bourne's book, he faced the problem of how best to proceed. Obviously with some distaste, he decided to print each chapter in its entirety as a springboard for his own additions and emendations.

> Mr Bourne complains in his Preface of the *invidious* Behaviour of some of his Townsmen:—It is beneath a Man, *conscious of inward Worth*, to *complain* of that which he ought always to *despise*.—Posterity seems to have done him very ample Justice for their Insults:—A Copy of the *Antiquitates Vulgares* has of late fetched seven or eight Shillings in London. —Many perhaps will think the Purchasers mistook an Accident for Merit, and confounded the Idea of *Scarceness* with that of *intrinsic Value*.—I received this Information from one of the Society of Antiquaries, who understands the Subject too well himself to be mistaken in his Opinion of the Merit of those who have written upon it. On the weight of that Opinion alone I have been induced to preserve every Line that our Author has left us in that Work.[1]

This decision suited Brand's temperament, for he was primarily an accumulator of clippings and jotter of notes, and Bourne's topics gave him a frame in which to disgorge some of his ever-mounting mass of materials. His ungracious attitude toward Bourne commenced in the Preface and continued throughout the chapter postscripts. 'Mr Bourne, my Predecessor in this Walk, has not, from whatever Cause, done Justice to the Subject he undertook to treat of,' he announced, adding more gently:

> New Lights have arisen since his Time. The English Antique has become a general and fashionable Study; and the Discoveries of the very respectable Society of Antiquaries have rendered the Recesses of Papal and Heathen Antiquities easier of access.[2]

In addition Brand promised some discoveries of his own of customs yet retained in the north, which would surprise the learned residents of southern England.

Bourne's view on the reason for the continuance of superstitious customs was accepted by Brand, who declared in his preface, 'Christian, or rather Papal Rome, borrowed her Rites, Notions, and Ceremonies, in the most luxurious Abundance from ancient and Heathen Rome. . . .' The common people in their naïve credulity still believe that only a 'Popish priest' could lay a spirit. With clear apprehension of his subject, Brand drew a distinction between men

[1] John Brand, *Observations on Popular Antiquities: including the whole of Mr. Bourne's Antiquitates Vulgares* (Newcastle-upon-Tyne, 1777), pp. 18–19 n.
[2] *Ibid.*, p. vi.

of learning and *the People*, between the *written Word*, which had been wiped clean by public authority of the old superstitions, and *oral Tradition*, which kept them alive. The italics are Brand's, and his use of these phrases shows his grasp of the central concepts of folklore methods.[1]

On the ticklish question of scriptural support for the validity of spirits, apparitions, and dreams, a question which Bourne had considered closely, Brand took the modern position of cultural relativism. 'The sacred Writings, given for very different Purposes, and to Nations whose Genius and Manners by no means resembled our own, cannot in my Opinion, with any Propriety, be applied to *this Subject*.'[2] They should be treated like miracles, which no reasonable man claims can be currently performed. And elsewhere he cautions against the fashion in Bourne's day for clergymen to interlard every statement with a 'spice of Divinity.' If clergymen do not spend too much time in lighter studies, then 'none but narrow-minded Bigots will think the Investigation of antient Manners an improper *Amusement* for them.'[3]

Brand's 'Observations' often reinforced Bourne's thesis of Roman-popish origins. If Bourne wonders why so much luxury and intemperance prevail at Shrovetide, he should have realized that the season's drunkenness is a vestige of the Romish carnival. In Northumberland the vulgar consider the leaves of the purple-flowered lady's thistle to be splashed with the milk of the Virgin Mary, hence its name, shortened from Our Lady. On this folk etymology Brand dryly comments, 'An ingenious little Invention of Popery, and which, no doubt, has been of Service to the Cause of Superstition.' Dreams are strongly heeded by the vulgar because, Brand conjectures, the heathens and Romanists assigned guardian genii to each part of the body, and to special trades and occupations, and through dreams these invisible guardians inform their wards of imminent dangers. From his boyhood Brand remembered an ingenious method of making an artificial sun dance on Easter Sunday, by setting a vessel of water in the open air to catch the sun's reflection, and now he recognizes this artifice as 'a *Relique* of *Popish Legerdemain*.' Yet in a lighter moment he gibes at awe of priests by the vulgar; Bourne is jealous, because Protestant clergy are not credited with the black arts![4]

One pagan-Romish rite described by Brand foreshadows the elaborate theory of harvest ritualism James G. Frazer would construct in *The Golden Bough*.

[1] *Ibid.*, p. iv.   [2] *Ibid.*, p. 410.   [3] *Ibid.*, p. 73.
[4] *Ibid.*, pp. 233, 409, 293–5, 247 n., 113.

[15]

Vacina, . . . among the Antients, was the Name of the Goddess to whom the Rustics sacrificed at the Conclusion of
Harvest.

Moresin [author of a manuscript on Roman calendar customs
in Brand's possession] tells us, that *Popery*, in Imitation of this,
brings home her Chaplets of Corn, which she suspends on
Poles; that Offerings are made on the Altars of her tutelar
Gods, while Thanks are returned for the collected Stores, and
Prayers are put up for future Rest and Ease. Images too of
Straw, or Stubble, he tells us, are wont to be carried about on
this Occasion; and in England he himself saw the Country
People bringing home in a Cart (I suppose from the Field) a
Figure made of *Corn*, round which Men and Women promiscu-
ously singing, followed a Piper or a Drum.—A Vestage [*sic*] of
this Custom is still preserved in some Places in the North: Not
Half a Century ago they used every where to dress up some-
thing, similar to the Figure above described, at the End of
Harvest, which was called a *Kern Baby*. I had this Informa-
tion from an old Woman at a Village in Northumberland.—The
Reader may perhaps smile, but I am not ashamed of my
Evidence. In a Case of this Nature *old Women* are respectable
Authorities.[1]

Here is suggested a technique and a target for the English folk-
lore movement: inquiry of elderly villagers into seasonal customs
supposedly reflecting primitive fertility rituals.

Brand did not limit popular antiquities to the memories of rustics. He introduced the term 'mercantile antiquity' to apply to
customs connected with the trades. Even schoolboys might inherit
antiquities. Eton boys who stopped passers-by and stage coaches
on Salt Hill near Windsor, gave them salt, and extorted money
from them, could be aping ritual jinks of old St. Nicholas' Day.
Unable to insert all of his choice morsels in the chapter Observations, Brand added thirty entries in an appendix, covering such
matters as cock-fighting and tobacco, witches and gypsies, the vulgar sayings 'Deuce take you' and 'Under the rose,' Pancake Tuesday
and Royal-Oak Day, Will-with-the-Wisp and the Wandering Jew,
the ring-finger and the truelove knot.

Captivated by his discoveries, Brand continued to clip and file
and copy from volumes of local history and travels as they appeared
and from the rare works he kept adding to his magnificent anti-

---

[1] John Brand, *Observations on Popular Antiquities: including the whole of Mr.
Bourne's Antiquitates Vulgares* (Newcastle-upon-Tyne, 1777), pp. 306–7.

quarian library. By 1795 he was writing a preface for a new edition, but materials accumulated faster than he could digest them, and the publication of the score of volumes in Sir John Sinclair's *Statistical Account of Scotland* (1791–99), with its detailed reports on provincial customs, finally engulfed him. Two years after the death of the redoubtable antiquary, his revised manuscript was sold along with his personal library; a preliminary notice in the *Gentleman's Magazine* for November, 1807, announced the auction.

BRAND'S POPULAR ANTIQUITIES

Mr Stewart, in January, 1808, will submit, by Auction, the well-known and valuable Work, intituled POPULAR ANTIQUITIES; enlarged on a very extended Plan, being the Labour of Thirty Years, and compressed in Five Volumes; the last Edition, interleaved with Writing Paper, in Two Volumes, and the Three Volumes Thick Quarto, in MS. wrote entirely of new Matter, in the neat and elegant hand of Mr Brand. . . .

This announcement was also carried as the final item of the *Bibliotheca Brandiana*, Part II, No. 4064 (Part I had listed 8,611 items and 243 manuscripts), with the enticement that the manuscript was left 'in such a complete state, that the purchaser will have little or nothing to do but to go to press the moment he is in possession of this most invaluable treasure.'

As Sir Henry Ellis would learn, this claim of readiness was somewhat exaggerated. But fourteen co-publishers, who entrusted the manuscript to him, thought it worth a purchase price of £600. As Keeper of Manuscripts of the British Museum, and Secretary of the Society of Antiquaries, Ellis was a logical executor to prepare the giant tome for publication. He found with the manuscript Brand's sketch for a new arrangement, which he followed. While he was engaged on this task, a London edition, reset but without alteration in content, appeared in 1810, but it was shortly eclipsed by the sumptuous, weighty, truly monumental two quarto volumes issued in 1813, announced as *Observations on Popular Antiquaries: chiefly illustrating the origin of our Vulgar Customs, Ceremonies and Superstitions*. By John Brand; arranged and revised, with additions, by Henry Ellis. This mighty work laid the foundations for a science of folklore, and became a landmark in the history of English thought.

In the new format, the original sections of Bourne's treatise are dispersed, to sink into the mass of quotations, tailnotes, footnotes, thoughts, and afterthoughts which comprise the huge, undigested scrapbook. Set in three sizes of type, the *Popular Antiquities* gives

[17]

the impression of notes upon notes upon notes, with ever increasing eyestrain. The two bulky volumes are divided between the feasts and fasts of the calendar year and the habits and fancies flourishing in everyday usage. Ellis thus explains the division:

> In the first volume, it will be seen, the days of more particular note in the Calendar are taken in chronological order; the Customs at Country Wakes, Sheep-shearings, and other rural practices, form a sort of Supplement; and these are again followed by such usages and ceremonies as are not assignable to any particular period of the year.
>
> In the second volume, the Customs and Ceremonies of Common Life are introduced, followed by the numerous train of Popular Notions, Sports, and Errors.[1]

As his contribution, Ellis indicates the collation of quoted passages with their sources, 'a service which has added very much to the correctness of the Work,' the preparing of the Index, and the adding of some further notes, in brackets. In effect he saw the manuscript through press, a considerable task, but the achievement, with its flaws, belongs primarily to Brand and his herculean efforts over three decades.

The 1813 edition of the *Observations on Popular Antiquities* came forth at the right time for the right public, the intellectually curious, non-academic Victorians, absorbed in their England and the by-ways of its culture, hobbyists with a purpose, amateur antiquaries blessed with leisure and private libraries. For them, as well as for professional men of letters and learning, Brand-Ellis became a vade mecum, an automatic reference and authority on antique custom and odd superstition. Further, the *Popular Antiquities* whetted the taste for bygones; it was a work for the owner to enlarge with newspaper clippings and literary references, just as Brand himself had elaborated upon his own first edition. Interleaved copies of Brand-Ellis, with copious marginalia and inserts, are to be seen in the British Museum, The Folklore Society library, and in private hands, and one can conjecture the relish with which they were expanded. Indeed, such an enriched copy of the 1777 edition, annotated by his bibliophile friend Francis Douce, was used by Brand. By his range and wealth of illustrative examples, Brand had defined an unknown and unsuspected area of civilization, the traditional culture of the common people, rooted in a pagan antiquity, and so of interest to

---

[1] John Brand, *Observations on Popular Antiquities: chiefly illustrating the origin of our vulgar customs, ceremonies, and superstitions.* Arranged and revised, with additions, by Henry Ellis (2 vols.; London, 1813), I, v–vi. Hereafter this edition will be referred to as Brand-Ellis.

the educated gentry. He declared that 'nothing can be foreign to our enquiry, much less beneath our notice, that concerns the smallest of the Vulgar: of those little ones who occupy the lowest Place in the Political Arrangement of human Beings.'[1]

An idea of the growth of the 1813 edition over the 1777 edition can be gained by comparing their treatment of the same topic. The earlier edition devotes seven pages to 'May Day,' three by Bourne and four by Brand. Together they cite nine printed sources and one personal source in the text and notes. In the 1813 publication, 'May Day Customs' covers fourteen quarto pages, while 'May Poles' receives a separate eleven-page section. For 'May Day Customs' Brand now cites forty-nine literary and two oral sources, divided between his main narrative and the ever-proliferating notes. Ellis adds one reference from Aubrey's manuscript, the 'Remaines of Gentilisme.' This galaxy of sources embraces poetical accounts of May Day merrymaking by Chaucer, Shakespeare, Milton, and Gray; town, county, and national histories; travel books; works on witchcraft, dialects, and domestic manners; four Latin treatises; a newspaper story and a magazine article; an account of *The Laws of the Market* (1677) and a play, *Whimsies: or a true Cast of Characters* (1631). No smooth essay emerges from these half a hundred references. The welter of commentaries deals with May Day festivities as practised from Cornwall to Scotland by kings and chimney sweeps, milkmaids and Londoners; with laws governing, and verses celebrating, the festal day; with pertinent superstitions, such as May being an unlucky month for marriage; and with guesses at the origin of May Day, such as the view that the May games once offered honour and homage to a goddess of fertility. For the reader who wished to know what had been observed and written about May Day in the British Isles, Brand-Ellis provides the complete lexicon, unsifted but exhaustive. It seemed indeed that the single-minded antiquary and his editor had scoured all the printed and manuscript resources of the island.

In the tranquil mood of the nineteenth century, with the wars of church and state safely behind and the battle of reason over superstition clearly won, Victorian gentry could smile at vulgar antiquities as the heritage of the unlettered and the unknowing. On witchcraft and fairy lore and other supernaturalism, Brand wrote as a rationalist and cynic for fellow rationalists, unconcerned as yet with psychological or physiological explanations. Gleefully he exposed the miraculous cures for the King's Evil, the scrofulous rash which only the king's touch could remove; even Samuel Johnson

---

[1] *Ibid.*, I, ix.

as a youth had submitted to the royal hand. Brand quoted an old man who confessed having gone to court simply to receive the gold touch-piece, for which he was quite willing to announce a cure. 'We now,' wrote Brand triumphantly, 'without the smallest danger of incurring the suspicion of Disloyalty, can safely pronounce that the royal touch for the King's Evil, is to be referred to the head of Physical Charms, evincing that no order of Men escaped the antient contagion of Superstition.'[1]

Untroubled by any commitment to take seriously these vulgar notions, even on royal authority, readers could browse and forage for curiosa through the pages of the *Popular Antiquities*. They would find, for example, antique practices of marriage and courtship, such as the convention that a man might sell his wife if he delivered her with a halter about her neck ('It is painful to observe, that instances of this occur frequently in our Newspapers'). In the north of England young men contended with each other on the altar for the bride's garter, on occasion even throwing her down in their zeal. ('I have sometimes thought this a Fragment of the antient Ceremony of loosening the Virgin Zone, or Girdle, a Custom that needs no explanation.') An assured love charm for a suitor to employ on a reluctant maid is reported: thread a needle with one of her hairs and run it through the fatty flesh of a dead man, say the brawn of the arms or the calf of the leg, whereon she will dash madly after her erstwhile pursuer. From Aubrey's *Miscellanies*, Brand culled a personal observation that befell the Wiltshire antiquary in 1694 on the day of St. John the Baptist. Walking in the pasture behind Montague House, Aubrey had noticed a score of 'well habited' young women, kneeling on the grass and apparently busy weeding. A youth informed him that they were looking under the root of a plantain for a coal, which must be found that day and hour; they would put it under their heads that night, and dream of their future husbands.[2]

And so on, for myriad topics of olden lore covering seven hundred thick quarto pages. The pleasure of rummaging for vulgar antiquities in the great treasure chest of Brand-Ellis overcame the distaste of readers for its obvious faults of structure and composition, which critics immediately perceived. A lengthy review essay in the *Quarterly Review* for July, 1814, sharply pointed out these defects.

The interminable length and confusion of the notes, nine-

[1] Brand-Ellis, II, 599–600.
[2] *Ibid.*, 37, 56–7, 605; I, 267.

tenths of which ought to have been incorporated in the text, and the immethodical manner in which Mr Brand has treated his subject, are equally objectionable. . . . He takes no general view of his subject, and his desultory collections are made with so little care, and the notes and the texts are so frequently at variance with each other, that the reader is left without any other help than his own sagacity may afford him, to arrive at any conclusion whatever.[1]

The anonymous critic considered unnecessary Brand's apology for the ' "seeming unimportance of the subject". There are few departments of literature which have a better claim upon our attention.'[2] If Brand's work fell short, his field of inquiry was now firmly recognized.

It is in its cumulative, overwhelming effect that the *Popular Antiquities* made its impact. Brand was able to show, by the sheer mass of his materials and the diversity of his sources, how deeply these customs and ceremonies and superstitious usages permeated English life. Whoever had taken note of English ways and manners —poet, traveller, antiquary, satirist, essayist, literary editor, playwright, dialect compiler, county chronicler, the writer on necromancy, the ballad-maker—all seemingly had captured some popular antiquity, which lay undetected in their pages until scooped out and placed with its kin by the indefatigable Brand.

Some manuscripts, prints, tracts, and treatises consulted by Brand were rare and unknown. One of his most frequently quoted sources was a manuscript which he described in his Preface of 1777.

> A learned Performance by a Doctor Moresin in the Time of James I and dedicated to that Monarch, is also luckily in my Possession. It is written in Latin, and entitled 'The Origin and Increase of Depravity in Religion'; containing a very masterly Parallel between the Rites, Notions, &c. of *Heathen* and those of *Papal* Rome.[3]

In the printed catalogue of Brand's library, the manuscript is listed under items 4432 and 4490, *Moresinum Depravatae Religionis Orgo et Incrementum* (Edinburgh, 1593, 1594). Brand cited it continually to support his thesis of the heathen-popish origins of popular antiquities. In the 1777 preface he also mentioned owning

one of those antient Romish Calendars of singular Curiosity,

---

[1] *Quarterly Review*, XI (July, 1814), 279, 285.
[2] *Ibid.*, p. 259.   [3] Brand, *op. cit.*, p. viii.

which contains under the immoveable Feasts and Fasts, . . . a variety of brief Observations, contributing not a little to the elucidation of many of our popular Customs, and proving them to have been sent over from Rome. . . .

Another special favourite of Brand was the *Ritual of Divine Offices* by Durand, who lived at the end of the twelfth century, 'a Work inimical to every Idea of rational Worship, but to the Enquirer into the Origin of our popular Ceremonies, an invaluable Magazine of the most interesting Intelligence.'[1] In the 1777 edition, Moresin and Durand are the two most quoted authorities.

His friend Douce, the learned and generous book-collector, loaned Brand many a prize. 'A curious little Book, the property of Francis Douce, Esquire, lies before me,' he notes. 'It is entitled "Divers Crab-tree Lectures that Shrews read to their Husbands, &c." 12 mo. Lond. 1639.' Elsewhere Brand alludes to such items owned by Douce as a 'curious Print' titled 'An exact Representation of the humorous Procession of the Richmond Wedding of Abram Kendrick and Mary Westurn'; 'an antient illuminated missal'; 'a curious Dutch Mezzotinto'; 'the curious Collection of Prints, illustrating antient Customs, in the Library of Francis Douce, Esq.' He used Douce's translation of a thirteenth-century Anglo-Norman carol.[2]

The *Bibliotheca Brandiana*, listing for sale Brand's personal library, reveals any number of tantalizing titles among its 10,000 entries. Here is Arnold's *Chronicle of the Customs of London*, almost an incunabulum, 1521; *A Treatise on the Second Sight, Dreams, and Apparitions*, 1763; *Curious Tracts on Astrology and Magick* (undated); *An Essay on the Study of Antiquities*, Oxford, 1782, and a host of other works on antiquities; *Compleat History of Magic, Sorcery, and Witchcraft*, 1716; *A New Dictionary of the Terms, ancient and Modern, of the canting Crew in its several Tribes of Gipsies, Beggars, Thieves, Cheats, &c.*; a manuscript of Cornish dialect; *Enquiry into the Causes of Prodigies and Miracles*, 1727; collections of ballads, jests, proverbs, witch trials, prophecies; *Narrative of Evil Spirits in the House of Master Jan Smagge, Farmer in Canvy Islands, Essex*, 1709; *Tracts (very curious), viz., A great Wonder in Heaven, shewing the late Apparitions and Prodigious Noyse of War and Battels, seene on Edge-Hill, neere Keinton, in Northamptonshire*, 1642.[3] And so on.

---

[1] Quoted, Brand, *op. cit.*, p. viii, p. vii.
[2] Brand-Ellis, *op. cit.*, II, 110 n., 111 n.; I, 300 *b*, 371; II, 62 *c*, 16 n.
[3] Taken from *Bibliotheca Brandiana*. A Catalogue of the Unique, Scarce, Rare, Curious and numerous Collection of Works on the Antiquity, Topography and decayed Intelligence of Great Britain and Ireland, from the first invention of Printing

One encounters, on the other hand, among Brand's suppliers a number of familiar and honoured titles, classics of one kind or another in the English tongue. Tucked in his notes are Robert Burton's *The Anatomy of Melancholy* (1621), John Selden's *Table-Talk* (1689), Reginald Scot's *The Discouerie of Witchcraft* (1584), Thomas Browne's *Pseudodoxia Epidemica* (1646), better known by the title of its running heads, 'Enquiries into Vulgar and Common Errors,' Gilbert White's *Natural History and Antiquities of Selborne* (1789), Samuel Johnson's *A Journey to the Western Islands of Scotland* (1775), Richard Hakluyt's *Divers Voyages touching the Discouerie of America* (1582), and Laurence Sterne's *A Sentimental Journey* (1768). Of literary classics, the roster seems virtually complete, and one of Brand's accomplishments was to demonstrate the debts of poets, dramatists, and prose-writers to the bubbling springs of popular tradition. These debts are more readily understood when one considers that the rise of Elizabethan literature, breaking with priestly Latin and courtly French, depended on yeoman speech and was written in large part by yeoman authors bred in the life of the countryside, with its fairs and festivals and games and old-wives' tales; the cities served as market fairs for country people, and London developed as a cluster of market towns. So the pages of Brand-Ellis are dotted with allusions to playwrights Ben Jonson, Massinger, Congreve, Dekker, Beaumont and Fletcher, Heywood, and their obscure fellows gathered in Robert Dodsley's *A Select Collection of Old Plays*. For instance, from Thomas Heywood's '*Philocothoniste, or the Drunkard, opened, dissected and anatomized*' (1035), Brand extracted the following popular idioms applied to a drunk:

> He is foxt, hee is flawed, he is flustered, hee is suttle, cup-shot, cut in the leg or backe, hee hath seene the French King, he hath swallowed an Haire or a Taverne-Token, hee hath whipt the Cat, he hath been at the Scriveners and learn'd to make Indentures, hee hath bit his Grannam, or is bit by a Barne-Weesell, with an hundred such-like Adages and Sentences.[1]

Shakespeare was often cited, along with editors Isaac Reed, George Steevens, and Francis Douce, who explained the Bard's localisms.

In erecting his substantial section on 'Fairy Mythology,' Brand

[1] Brand-Ellis, *op. cit.*, II, 233 n.

down to the present Time . . . being the entire Library of the late Rev. John Brand (First Part sold May 6, 1807, and the thirty-six days following).

referred to Milton's 'L'Allegro,' James Collins' 'Ode on the Popular Superstitions of the Highlands of Scotland,' William Browne's *Britannia's Pastorals*, Allan Ramsay's *Poems*, Chaucer's *The Canterbury Tales* ('The Wife of Bath'), a 'political ballad' by Bishop Corbet, 'The Fairies Farewell,' James Gay's 'Fable of the Mother, Nurse and Fairy,' and Martin Lluellin's poems. He found fairy lore in Percy's 'Antient Ballads' and in an 'old Ballad of Robin Goodfellow.' From Shakespeare he gathered relevant passages in *The Tempest*, *Romeo and Juliet*, and *King Lear*. These poetical descriptions of the fairy people Brand blended with his customary melange of sources: the many volumes of the *Statistical Account of Scotland*, yielding folkways from one parish after another; histories, descriptions, and journeys to Kent, Cumberland, Staffordshire, Orkney, the Isle of Man, 'Part of Scotland,' the Western Islands, the south of Ireland; and odd and out-of-the-way imprints beloved of the antiquary. Assembled side by side, these extracts, quotations, and summaries bore witness to the existence of a powerful fairy tradition; later students would analyse this heap of materials to point out inner relationships and principles.[1]

Among other kinds of sources, Brand recognized the value of dictionaries, glossaries, and proverb compilations in throwing light on popular antiquities. Vernacular speech preserved fossils of old pastimes and fancies. So Brand resorted regularly to the *Collection of English Proverbs* by John Ray (Cambridge, 1670, and succeeding editions), who had absorbed the list in Camden's *Remaines*. Brand confirmed Ray's statement that 'to stang' scholars at Christmastime was an expression used in Cambridge colleges to mean the practice of making students who missed chapel ride a colt-staff. One illustration from Ray can show the interdependence of proverbial phrase and a popular, if controversial antiquity.

Kentish *long-tails*

Those are mistaken who found this Proverb on a miracle of *Austin* the Monk; who preached in an *English* village, and being himself and his associates beat and abused by the *Pagans* there, who opprobriously tied *Fish-tails* to their back-sides; in revenge thereof such appendants grew to the hind-parts of all that generation. For the scene of this lying wonder was not laid in any part of *Kent*, but pretended many miles off, nigh *Cerne* in *Dorsetshire*. I conceive it first of outlandish extraction, and cast by foreigners as a note of disgrace on all *English* men, though it chanceth to stick only on the *Kentish* at this day.

[1] Brand-Ellis, *op. cit.*, II, pp. 327–50.

What the original or occasion of it at first was is hard to say; whether from wearing a pouch or bag to carry their baggage in behind their backs; whilst probably the proud *Monsieurs* had their Lacquies for that purpose; or whether from the mention'd story of *Austin*. I am sure there are some at this day in forreign parts, who can hardly be perswaded but that *English men* have tails.

Why this nickname (cut off from the rest of *England*) continues still entail'd on *Kent*, the reason may be (as the Doctour conjectures) because that County lies nearest to *France*, and the *French* are beheld as the first founders of this aspersion.[1]

In this traditional saying is imbedded a saint's legend, which Ray rationalizes into an etymology based on an early mode of transport and peppers with doses of anti-Romanism and outraged nationalism.

A word-book which appeared after Brand's death and on which Ellis drew substantially was *An Etymological Dictionary: illustrating the words in their different significations, by examples from ancient and modern writers; shewing their affinity to those of other languages, and especially the northern; explaining many terms, which, though now obsolete in England, were formerly common to both countries; and elucidating National Rites, Customs, and Institutions, in their analogy to those of other nations: to which is prefixed, A dissertation on the origin of the Scottish language* by John Jamieson, D.D. Two volumes (quarto), Edinburgh, 1808. Jamieson, a member of the Society of Antiquaries of Scotland, relied for his literary references on antiquarian studies and firmly linked them to his own inquiries, saying in his Preface, 'The use of such a work . . . must facilitate the progress of those . . . investigating the records of antiquity.'[2] Ancient customs whose meaning has become obscured may be explained through words or phrases referring to them in the common speech. Jamieson recalled that Dr. Johnson once advised Boswell to compile a dictionary of Scotticisms, on the manner of Ray's glossary of north country words.

A third meritorious work joining dialect, proverbs, and beliefs and useful for Brand-Ellis was bookseller Francis Grose's *A Provincial Glossary, with a collection of Local Proverbs, and Popular Superstitions* (1787, enlarged 2nd edition, 1790). The section on 'Superstitions' resembles Aubrey's *Miscellanies* in its choice of

---

[1] John Ray, *A Collection of English Proverbs* (Cambridge, 1670), pp. 233–4. Ray acknowledged his debt to Thomas Fuller, *The History of the Worthies of England* (London, 1662).

[2] John Jamieson, *An Etymological Dictionary* (Edinburgh, 1808), I, iii.

topics: A Witch, A Sorcerer or Magician, Fairies, The Second-Sight, Omens portending Death, Charms and Ceremonies for Knowing Future Events, and Things Lucky and Unlucky. For these vulgar notions Grose combed the 'most celebrated authors' on the subject, from King James I to Reginald Scot and Aubrey. But he also reveals a lively sense of oral tradition, lauding Shakespeare's realistic use of horror-laden nursery tales, and he himself uses verbal sources for his own examples, a number of which he had

> collected from the mouths of village historians, as they were related to a closing circle of attentive hearers, assembled in a winter's evening, round the capacious chimney of an old hall or manor-house; for, formerly, in countries remote from the metropolis, or which had no immediate intercourse with it, before newspapers and stage-coaches had imported scepticism, and made every ploughman and thresher a politician and free-thinker, ghosts, fairies, and witches, with bloody murders, committed by tinkers, formed a principal part of rural conversation, in all large assemblies, and particularly those in Christmas holidays, during the burning of the yule-block.[1]

Like Aubrey, Grose recognized the withering of popular fancy induced by literacy and rationalism and the greater need for antiquaries to preserve fading relics.

Grose belongs with a number of eighteenth-century antiquaries and travellers in the decades between Aubrey and Brand who worked in fields bordering on and dipping into popular antiquities. Until Brand extracted and brought together these materials, their common essence went unperceived. In the history of the folklore concept, it is Brand's *Observations on Popular Antiquities* which brought into focus the relevant labours of such stalwart antiquaries as John Stow and Joseph Strutt, Francis Grose and Thomas Pennant, who properly should be introduced in this discussion of Brand's sources.

A Falstaffian figure, rotund and jovial, gifted as an artist, lexicographer and bookman, Francis Grose (1731?–1791) perhaps best represents the complete antiquary of the eighteenth century. He was founder and editor of *The Antiquarian Repertory: a Miscellany, intended to preserve and illustrate several valuable Remains of Old Times. Adorned with elegant sculptures* (Vol. I, 1775, and thereafter at irregular intervals). Brand read sympathetically its several issues dedicated to the serious pursuit of 'Antiquarian Learning,' every man being at heart an antiquarian, as Grose contended in his Intro-

[1] Francis Grose, *A Provincial Glossary* (London, 1790), pp. vii–viii.

duction. Occasionally its contents crossed the line from physical to popular antiquities in such matters as an 'extraordinary Relation' of a ghost, a 'ridiculous charm' for ague, the customs of church ale and bride ale, a legend of buying and selling the Devil, the awarding 'Of the Bacon of Dunmow Priory' by hallowed custom to happy spouses, and north Wiltshire folkways culled from Aubrey's manuscript.

Grose produced a shelf of notable works on popular language and antiquities. His *A Classical Dictionary of the Vulgar Tongue* (1785) became a minor classic. He wrote on English *Military Antiquities Respecting a History of the English Army* (2 vols., 1786–8), and toured the British Isles for his handsomely illustrated folio and quarto tomes, *The Antiquities of England and Wales* (6 vols., 1773–87); *The Antiquities of Scotland* (2 vols., 1789–91); and *The Antiquities of Ireland* (2 vols., 1791–5), begun the year of his death and completed by Edward Ledwick. While his interests were directed primarily to remains as 'sepulchral monuments' and 'ancient castles and monasteries,' he followed Camden and Aubrey in the employment of the walking tour and the guided conversation to uncover old words, sayings, and superstitions. The following entry from the *Classical Dictionary* shows the link between traditional saying and legend relished by Grose.

Jack of Legs, a tall long-legged man; also a giant, said to be buried in Weston Church, near Baldock, in Hertfordshire, where there are two stones fourteen feet distant, said to be the head and feet stones of his grave. This giant, says Salmon, as fame goes, lived in a wood here, and was a great robber, but a generous one, for he plundered the rich to feed the poor; he frequently took bread for this purpose from the Baldock bakers, who catching him at an advantage, put out his eyes, and afterwards hanged him on a knoll in Baldock field. At his death he made one request, which was, that he might have his bow and arrow put into his hand, and on shooting it off, where the arrow fell, they would bury him: which being granted, the arrow fell into Weston churchyard. About seventy years ago, a very large thigh bone was taken out of the church chest, where it had lain many years for a shew, and was sold by the clerk to Sir John Tredeskin, who, it is said, put it up among the rarities of Oxford.

Elements of Robin Hood, in the generous outlawry and the manner of the hero's selecting his burial ground, are clearly present. The dictionary was filled with folklore plums: games, customs, proverbs, expressions picked up during Grose's nocturnal prowls into raffish public houses. 'Hobson's Choice' is there, meaning 'That or none: from old Hobson, a famous carrier of Cambridge, who used to let horses to the students; but never permitted them to chuse,' always deciding on the suitable mount himself. 'Boh' entered the vulgar tongue in memory of a Danish general who so terrified his enemy Foh 'that he caused him to bewray himself.' Consequently one smelling a stink would exclaim 'Foh!' Boh also contributed to the slur, 'He cannot say Boh to a goose,' meaning he is a cowardly fellow. A story told of Ben Jonson has the playwright in humble dress meeting a nobleman, who sneered, 'You Ben Jonson! why you look as if you could not say "Boh" to a goose!' 'Boh!' said Ben.

Grose himself became a subject of legend, for his ready wit and swollen figure. A butcher in the Dublin meat market is supposed to have said to him, 'Well, sir, though you don't want anything at present, only say you buy your meat of me; and by G—— you'll make my fortune.' Robert Burns composed verses about Grose after meeting the antiquary in Scotland:

> If in your bounds ye chance to light
> Upon a fine, fat, fodgel wight
> O' stature short, but genius bright,
>   That's he, mark weel—
> And wow! he has an unco slight
>   O' cauk and keel.
>
> It's tauld he was a sodger bred,
> And ane wad rather fa'n than fled:
> But now he's quat the spurtle-blade,
>   And dog-skin wallet,
> And taen the —— *Antiquarian trade*,
>   I think they call it.[1]

Topographical antiquaries industriously combing the shires turned up many nuggets appreciated by Brand. Representative is Robert Plot, Keeper of the Ashmolean Museum and professor of 'Chymistry' at Oxford University. His folio editions of *The Natural History of Oxford-shire* (1677, 2nd edition 1705) and of *The Natural History of Stafford-shire* (1686) touch on matters preternatural. In the first work he offers 'a *Relation*, as strange as 'tis true,' of knock-

[1] Terms are from Francis Grose, *A Classical Dictionary of the Vulgar Tongue* (London, 1785), p. 92. The third edition, revised by Pierce Egan (London, 1823), contains a 'Biographical Sketch of Francis Grose, Esq.' (pp. xxix–xl). The verses by Burns are quoted on p. xxiii.

ings on doors, tables, or shelves that announced impending deaths to the family of Captain Basil Wood of Brise-Norton. In his Staffordshire annals, Plot records other family death omens: the Cumberfords of Cumberford Hall always heard knocks before a fatality, no matter how far distant the doomed kinsman might be; the Burdet family were forewarned by a drumming noise from the chimneys for six or eight weeks running; and down in Devon the Oxenhams knew of a death to come when a white-breasted bird fluttered about their beds.[1]

Plot also relates a remarkable dream that came to the father of Sir Henry Wotton, Provost of Eaton. The elder Wotton dreamed that the University treasury was robbed by five townsmen and poor scholars; on awakening he wrote from Kent to his son, then a student at Queen's College Oxford; the letter arrived the day after the robbery, 'when the University and the City were both in a perplext Inquest of the Thieves,' and led to their apprehension.[2]

Fairy rings engage Plot's attention, as they did the country people. Vacillating between natural and unnatural explanations, he speculates on whether they were caused by lightning, or marked out by witches for their rendezvous, or served as the dancing places of 'those little pygmy Spirits they call Elves or Fairys.'[3] On one point he feels certain, that only those places worn bare like a pathway might be assigned to fallen spirits.

The professor of Chymistry listened to ale-house stories of human interest, such as the adventure at the black mere of Morridge, familiar to all inhabitants of Leek. The mere was reputedly bottomless and ill-omened, cattle would not drink of it, nor birds fly over it (allegations Plot finds to be false). On a black evening one of the ale-house crowd for a wager repaired to the mere, to find there a ruffian about to drown a poor woman he had got with child; the man of Leek frightened away the blackguard and brought back the near-naked damsel to his cronies as proof of his courage and the marvellous providence of the Lord.[4]

England was more than an aggregate of counties, she was also London, and London boasted her own loyal antiquary, John Stow (1525?–1605), whose name regularly occurs in Brand's notes. Having heard of various gentlemen engaged in publishing the 'perambulations' of their shires, Stow felt impelled to do the same for

---

[1] Robert Plot, *The Natural History of Oxford-shire, Being an Essay towards the Natural History of England* (2nd ed., Oxford, 1705), pp. 208, 329–30.
[2] Robert Plot, *The Natural History of Stafford-shire* (Oxford, 1686), p. 214.
[3] Plot, *Oxford-shire*, pp. 9, 14. [4] Plot, *Stafford-shire*, pp. 290–1.

his city. In 'The Epistle Dedicatoire' he wrote, '. . . I have attempted the discovery of *London*, my native soile and countrie. . . .' He called his book *A Survay of London. Contayning the Originall, Antiquity, Increase, Moderne Estate, and Description of that Citie*, written in the yeare 1598, by Iohn Stow, Citizen of London. A second edition of 1603, grown from 483 to 580 pages, carried the further announcement: 'Since by the same Author increased, with divers rare notes of Antiquity.' An edition of 1633 remained the same size, but as London grew so did the book, and when it next saw print, in 1720, the modest 8vo format had exploded to two mammoth folios, guided by John Strype, who had digested old John Stow much as Brand had swallowed Bourne. Brand used both the Strype and Stow editions, but leaned on Stow for 'Sportes and pastimes of old time used in this citie,' exemplified by a fishmonger's procession with more than a thousand horses, Christmas pageantry governed by the Lord of Misrule, a 'stage play that lasted eight daies'; leaping, dancing, shooting, and wrestling; baiting of bears and bulls; and May games featuring the execution of Robin Hood and his men before the king.

The folklore of London, first recognized by Brand, has continued to receive attention. Henry Mayhew's encyclopedic study, *London Labour and the London Poor* (1851–62) has been shown to harbour abundant folk traditions.[1] The most ardent champion of folklore science in the 1870's and after, George Laurence Gomme, was knighted for his books on the history and institutions of London, and his two interests often overlapped.

Another giant who crops up continually in Brand's references is Joseph Strutt (1749–1802), called 'the father of English antiquaries.' Strutt said of himself, 'My love for my national antiquities is greater than I can express.'[2] He devoted his life to their pursuit, beginning in 1773 at the age of twenty-four with *The Regal and Ecclesiastical Antiquities of England*. In the next three years he published in three volumes, *Horda-Angel-Cynnan: The Manners and Customs, Arms and Habits of the Inhabitants of England*. Other works of Strutt on which Brand relied were *The Chronicle of England: from the Arrival of Caesar to the End of the Saxon Heptarchy* (1777), and *A Complete View of the Dress and Habits of the People of England, from the Establishment of the Saxons in Britain to the Present Time, illustrated by engravings taken from the most authentic*

[1] Donald McKelvie, 'Aspects of Oral Tradition and Belief in an Industrial Region,' *Folk Life*, I (1963), 79. 'He [Mayhew] was a folklorist by default perhaps, but none the less a folklorist.'
[2] William Strutt, *A Memoir of the Life of Joseph Strutt, 1749–1802* (London, 1896), p. 23. Printed for private circulation.

remains of Antiquity (2 volumes, 1796–99). But his most famous work, whose ungainly Saxon title dropped away in favour of the subtitle 'Sports and Pastimes' after the early editions, was *Glig-Gamena Angel-Deod, or the Sports and Pastimes of the People of England: including the Rural and Domestic Recreations, May-Games, Mummeries, Pageants; Processions, and Pompous Spectacles, from the earliest period to the present time: illustrated by Engravings selected from Ancient Paintings; in which are represented most of the popular diversions* (1801). Brand follows Strutt's section in *The Chronicle of England* in the 'English aera,' commencing at the close of the thirteenth century, when Norman and Saxon customs had completely blended. Once he speaks of 'Strutt's Additions to Camden,' and the 1813 Brand-Ellis alludes to 'Mr Strutt's Notes, . . . communicated by Francis Douce,' more evidence of the links between the great antiquaries.[1]

Strutt's diversified undertakings were united through their common antiquarian outlook and method. In his survey of English costume, he devotes a chapter to the habits of minstrels and players, fools and jesters, mummers and maskers, and returns to this subject in his chef d'œuvre on English sports and pastimes. This last work gave him the idea of writing a fictional narrative illustrating the usage of the fifteenth century, which he nearly completed during the last year of his life; it remained for Sir Walter Scott to put the finishing touches on *Queenhoo-Hall* in 1808, and initiate his own series of romances filled with the antiquarian spirit.

Of his life work, Strutt wrote:

> The study of antiquities is, in itself, both amusing and useful. It not only leads to extensive discoveries in ancient records, but in great measure proves the truth and authenticity of those venerable remains; it brings to light many important matters which (without the study) would yet be buried in oblivion, and explains and illustrates such dark passages as would otherwise be quite unknown.[2]

Since the antiquarianism of Joseph Strutt was of the library, a digging among rare manuscripts and missals, Brand additionally required the fresh eye of the observer viewing older ceremonies extant among the people. In the emerging literature of tours and travels he found ample rewards, both in accounts by Englishmen 'perambulating' the countryside, such as Benjamin Heath Malkin's *The Scenery, Antiquities and Biography of South Wales, from*

---

[1] Brand, *op. cit.*, p. 43 n.; Brand-Ellis, *op. cit.*, II, 273a.
[2] William Strutt, *op. cit.*, p. 22.

Materials collected during Two Excursions in the Year 1803 (1804), or by European visitors closely examining English manners and behaviour, as Henri Misson's *Memoirs and Observations in his Travels over England* (1719, translated by John Ozell from the French edition of 1698). But by all odds the author-traveller from whom Brand borrowed most conspicuously was his contemporary Thomas Pennant (1726–98).

Pennant's *A Tour in Scotland, MDCCLXIX* came out the same year it was composed, 1769, with a second volume following three years later. It speedily attained celebrity, thanks to its intimate delineations of sequestered Scottish clans, as remote from Londoners in the eighteenth century as Africans of the Congo seem to Europeans in the twentieth. Four editions of the two hefty volumes had appeared by 1775. (It was as a series of letters to Pennant that the author of an even more renowned work, Gilbert White, presented *The Natural History and Antiquities of Selborne* in 1789, by contrast an exploration of the writer's native heath.) Brand quotes not only the *Tour in Scotland* but also relies heavily on a manuscript describing Pennant's journey in Wales.

Amidst his detailed observations on agriculture, industry, architecture, antiquities, and amusements, Pennant pauses to comment contemptuously on the barbarous ideas of the Highlanders.

Superstitions

The country is perfectly highland; and in spite of the intercourse this and the neighbouring parts have of late years had with the rest of the world, it still retains some of its antient customs and superstitions: they decline daily, but least their memory should be lost, I shall mention several that are still practised, or but very lately disused in the tract I had passed over. Such a record will have this advantage, when the follies are quite extinct, in teaching the unshackled and enlightened mind the difference between the pure ceremonies of religion, and the wild and anile flights of superstition.

Spectres

The belief in spectres still exists; of which I had a remarkable proof while I was in the county of *Breadalbane*. A poor visionary, who had been working in his cabbage garden, imagined that he was raised suddenly into the air, and conveyed over a wall into an adjacent corn-field; that he found himself surrounded by a crowd of men and women, many of whom he knew to have been dead some years, and who appeared to him skimming over the tops of the unbended corn, and mingling together like bees going to hive: that they spoke an unknown language, and with a hollow sound: that they very roughly pushed him to and fro; but on his uttering the name of God, all vanished but a female sprite, who seizing him by the shoulder, obliged him to promise an assignation, at that very hour, that day sevenight: that he then found that his hair was all tied in double knots, and that he had almost lost the use of his speech: that he kept his word with the spectre, whom he soon saw come floating thro' the air towards him: that he spoke to her, but she told him at that time she was in too much haste to attend to him, but bid him go away, and no harm should befall him; and so the affair rested when I left the country.[1]

This spectral flight has its counterparts, and Pennant notes that Aubrey in his *Miscellanies* gives 'two ridiculous relations of almost similar facts' reported in Devonshire and Murray. Elsewhere the traveller describes the Bel-tein May Day offering of a caudle of eggs, butter, oatmeal, and milk proffered by the Highlanders to the guardians of their flocks and herds. He remarks on the powers of second-sight ascribed to Molly Mac-leane, of the Isle of Rum in the Hebrides; of prophecy with a well-scraped blade bone of mutton; of Kenneah Oaur of Sutherland who predicted the forced migrations of his people. He wonders at the ceremony of late-wake at Highland funerals, a two-day frolic of dancing, crying, and bag-pipe-playing. All such curiosities were communicated to Pennant 'by a gentlemen resident on the spot where they were performed.'[2]

Brand's dependence on the random reports of travellers ended, for Scotland at any rate, with the publication in twenty-one volumes of the work that finally engulfed him, Sir John Sinclair's *The Statistical Account of Scotland, Drawn up from the communications of the ministers of the different parishes* (1791–9). The topics covered by this systematic inquiry, as indicated in a list submitted by the editor to the co-operating clergy, include many facts and figures about the size, location, agriculture, minerals, schools, and houses of the parish, but sections are also provided for antiquities and the manners and customs of the people.

The travellers even at best furnish but casual and surface glimpses of customs and traditions they encountered in transit, and for which, in the minds of such enlightened passers-by as Pennant, they might feel only scorn. Brand himself, occupied with his

---

[1] Thomas Pennant, *A Tour in Scotland, MDCCLXIX*, 2 vols. (4th ed.; Dublin, 1775), I, 95–6. [2] *Ibid.*, I, 96 n., 97 n.

literary extracting, never indulged in direct collecting of popular antiquities, save in a few rare cases where his servant—the primary bridge between the gentry and the folk—supplied him with some tibits. 'My servant, B. Jelkes, who is from Warwickshire, informs me that there is a custom in that county,' he began on two occasions, and went on to mention the customs of good wives preparing seed cake at Allhallows' Eve, and of the poor 'going a corning'— begging corn of the farmers—on St. Thomas' Day. A few other scraps personally communicated to him came from His Grace the Duke of Northumberland, concerning a Christmas carol on the Scottish border; from a 'credible person' born in a Suffolk village, who told of a rural Christmas custom of hunting owls and squirrels; and from a Devonshire clergyman, speaking about the 'Blind Days' of March, the first three of the month, when no farmer would sow seed. And in his discussion of cockfighting and beliefs about cocks, Brand recalled that a collier in the northern pits allegedly let a gamecock down a pit suspected of foul air; and once while ministering to a sick miner, Brand had heard the cock crow and seen it suspended in a bag over the miner's head.[1]

These are the few scattered instances where the compiler of the *Popular Antiquities* himself drew from the wells of tradition. The next step forward in transmuting the concept of popular antiquities into the science of folklore would be the direct soliciting of eyewitness accounts and personal reports of rural ceremonies and usages.

Beside the Brand-Ellis edition of the *Observations on Popular Antiquities*, the curious Victorian might well place on his shelves or parlour table another formidable reference work, the *Every-Day Book* and *Table-Book* of William Hone (1780–1842). Bookseller, journalist, publisher, author, editor, reformer, Hone has won a minor but secure reputation as a fiery and caustic pamphleteer of the Regency period, sentenced to prison in 1817 for his bold attacks and biting caricatures of the Tory Establishment. A champion of liberty and equality against power and privilege, his early career as political journalist and social critic is linked to the *Every-Day Book* by his feeling for the working class. As a pamphleteer he followed the tradition of Tom Paine in addressing his satires and squibs, enlivened with the cartoons of George Cruikshank, to the ordinary reader. The polemical street literature he wrote and sold from his little bookshop on the Strand led him to the popular oral literature he sought to record in his serials. As suited his temper and instincts,

---

[1] Brand-Ellis, *op. cit.*, I, 309 *u*, 350 *b*, 377 note, 379 *m*, 462 note, 428 *s*.

Hone took a hard-headed, sceptical attitude toward the idolatries fastened by medieval monks upon country folk, an attitude at variance with the nostalgic gaze of the romantic poets; and he also disagreed with Wordsworth and Coleridge on political grounds. In turn Coleridge denounced Hone as a 'liberticide.'[1]

Hone conceived of the *Every-Day Book; or Everlasting Calendar of Popular Amusements, Sports, Pastimes, Ceremonies, Manners, Customs, and Events* as a weekly miscellany containing appropriate reading matter for the days and seasons. Saints' legends, holiday observances, and biographical notices furnished ready-made filler for particular dates, and the editor interspersed descriptions of landscape, curious narratives, and, increasingly, the contributions of correspondents on the subjects in his title. The initial interest was slight, and Hone was arrested for bankruptcy and consigned to the King's Bench. There he continued to edit the *Every-Day Book*, which ran from January, 1825, to December, 1827. Hone then initiated the *Table-Book* on the same plan, but omitting daily dates, and this lasted through 1827. The parts of the *Every-Day Book* and the *Table-Book* were each bound in two fat volumes of eight hundred and fifty pages, and a combined three-volume edition appeared in 1830. The *Year Book* followed in 1831–2, by which time Hone had made his mark, receiving £400 for the task from his publisher, William Tegg. Tegg continued to reissue the three works until 1874. Their popularity was considerably abetted by the lively drawings of Cruikshank. Sir Walter Scott, Robert Southey, and Charles Lamb all praised these compendiums, Lamb even writing verses to 'ingenuous Hone.'

Other publications by Hone that display his interest in antiquities are *Sixty Curious and Authentic Narratives and Anecdotes Respecting Extraordinary Characters* (1819, reprinted in Boston, 1825), a book of horrors and credulities, and a folio edition of Strutt's *The Sports and Pastimes of the People of England* (1830). Hone knew well the production of his precursors, and an early issue of *The Every-Day Book*, for June 24, 1826, firmly stresses his indebtedness to Brand.

A large paper copy of Brand's 'Popular Antiquities,' with MS. notes upon it by a gentleman of great reputation as an antiquary, and who has publicly distinguished himself by

---

[1] Herschel M. Sikes, 'William Hone: Regency Patriot, Parodist, and Pamphleteer,' *Newberry Library Bulletin*, V, No. 8 (July, 1961), 281–94. A biography has been written by Frederick W. Hackwood, *William Hone, His Life and Times* (London and Leipzig: T. Fisher Unwin, 1920).

[35]

erudite dissertations on certain usages of ancient times, was some time ago most obligingly forwarded by that gentleman to the editor of the *Every-Day Book*, with permission to use the valuable manuscript additions. Hitherto it happened, from peculiar circumstances, that the advantage has not been available, but this and future sheets will be enriched from that source.

Hone had known Brand and remembered him as 'a tall, robust, Johnsonian sort of man,' without Johnson's stoop.

The *Every-Day Book* and its sequels regularly refer to Brand, to revise, corroborate, or amplify a point; the *Table-Book* commences with encomiums of Francis Douce and prints substantial passages on 'Old Customs and Manners' from Aubrey's manuscripts in the Ashmolean Museum at Oxford; Hone refers familiarly to Francis Grose and his *Antiquarian Repertory*; and he had read out-of-the-way collections such as Anne Grant's *Essays on the Superstitions of the Highlanders of Scotland* (1811) and William G. Stewart's *The Popular Superstitions and Festive Amusements of the Highlanders of Scotland* (1823). He devotes one article to such renowned antiquaries as Pennant, Grose, Jacob Bryant, George Steevens, Richard Farmer, Samuel Paterson, Isaac Reed, and John Nichols. But while Hone was clearly building upon the past in his investigations of popular customs, he sought energetically to break new ground. His innovation was the development of a corps of contributor-correspondents, who would be stimulated by the descriptions of popular customs reprinted from antiquarian sources in the *Every-Day Book* to send in like ceremonies they had personally witnessed. Instead of the connoisseur of old customs simply interleaving his copy of the *Popular Antiquities*, he could now publish his fresh observation in a forthcoming issue of Hone's weekly, and perhaps induce someone else in turn to write up his local variation of the event or usage. Hone made this aim explicit:

Mr. Reddock's paper on this subject [Hogmany], at page 13, has elicited the following letter from a literary gentleman, concerning a dramatic representation in England similar to that which Mr. Reddock instances at Falkirk, and other parts of North Britain. Such communications are particularly acceptable; because they show to what extent usages prevail, and wherein they differ in different parts of the country. It will be gratifying to every one who peruses this work, and highly so to the editor, if he is obliged by letters from readers acquainted with customs in their own vicinity, similar to those that they are informed of in other counties, and particularly if they will take the trouble to describe them in every particular. By this means, the *Every-Day Book* will become what it is designed to be made,—*a storehouse of past and present manners and customs*. Any customs of any place or season that have not already appeared in the work, are earnestly solicited from those who have the means of furnishing the information.[1]

To insure as far as possible the accuracy of the reports dispatched to him, Hone required, 'as absolutely indispensable,' that all writers submit their name and address to the editor. He will not print anonymous communications, nor reprint extracts from 'an old book' or 'an excellent authority' unless authors and titles are named. When a correspondent challenged the editor on an alleged error, Hone defended himself, but expressed his gratitude for the intent, adding, 'I aim to be accurate, and can truly say that it costs me more time to establish the facts I adduce, than to write and arrange the materials after I have convinced myself of their authority.' Thus did Hone through his columns and on his wrappers train his readers in scholarly habits.[2]

He kept returning to his main theme, quoting a correspondent who declared that the 'character and manners of a people may be often correctly ascertained by an attentive examination of their familiar customs and sayings.' Such investigations enlarge the knowledge of human nature, illustrate national history, mark the fluctuation of language, and explain the usages of antiquity. Hence, through communications about these daily occurrences, the *Every-Day Book* can become in the best sense 'an assemblage of anecdotes, fragments, remarks and vestiges, collected and recollected. . . .' To encourage and stimulate firsthand reports, Hone issued specific requests on his wrappers. He urged readers in all parts of England to collect every carol they heard in the Christmas season of 1825 and convey them to him, along with associated manners and customs practised in the neighbourhood, to augment his printed collection of over ninety carols. Another time he invited his readers to submit all possible facts and anecdotes concerning Bow bells and all who are born within the sound of Bow bells. A solicitation of harvest customs brought a rich response in varieties of harvest songs and feasts, forms of 'crying the neck,' and health-drinking catches. Once Hone queried about the 'remarkable usage' of swearing on the horns

---

[1] William Hone, *The Every-Day Book and Table Book; or, Everlasting Calendar of Popular Amusements, Sports, Pastimes, Ceremonies, Manners, Customs and Events*. 3 vols. (London: Thomas Tegg, 1838), II, col. 73, 'Hogmany' (January 16). The first two volumes are the *Every-Day Book* and the third is the *Table Book*.
[2] *Ibid.*, II, col. 662, 'Strand Maypole' (May 13).

at Highgate, and asked what lay behind the question, 'Have you been sworn at Highgate?' Almost tearfully he pleaded for information about the farcical election of the mayor of Garrat, through 'the loan of handbills, advertisements, scraps, or any thing any way connected with the subject'; readers had not responded to his previous entreaties, perhaps feeling that such matters were beneath their notice.[1]

The columns of these miscellanies evince Hone's success in spurring his readers to observe and describe customs and usages in their vicinity. As he had wished, they entered into the spirit of a common enterprise both amusing and instructive and scouted the countryside for unreported institutions of rural life. Here a correspondent announces a new discovery:

> Sir,—Although your unique and curious work, the *Every-Day Book*, abounds with very interesting accounts of festivals, fairs, wassails, wakes, and other particulars concerning our country manners, and will be prized by future generations as a rare and valuable collection of the pastimes and customs of their forefathers, still much of the same nature remains to be related; and as I am anxious that the *Country Statute*, or *Mop*, (according to the version of the country people generally,) should be snatched from oblivion, I send you a description of this custom, which, I hope, will be deemed worthy a place in the *Table-Book*. . . .
>
> Some months ago I solicited the assistance of a friend, a respectable farmer, residing at Wootton, in Warwickshire, who not only very readily promised to give me every information on the subject, but proposed that I should pass a week at his farm at the time these Statutes were holding.[2]

There followed in detail an account of the Mop, an annual meeting of landowners and rustics, like a fair, to arrange service for the coming year and haggle over wages; after the hiring, the countrymen paired off with the lasses and rushed to the public houses. This lengthy paper indicates the degree of interest in amateur ethnography kindled by Hone, whose readers were actually seeking out and questioning farmers and farmwives in their neighbourhood. Contributions flowed in from residents in the counties, and from

[1] *Op. cit.*, II, col. 1275, 'Extraordinary News' (September 30); I, col. 1604, 'Christmas Carols' (December 24); II, cols. 1154–82, [Harvest Customs] (September); II, cols. 79–87, 'Swearing on the Horns at Highgate' (January 16); II, cols. 865–6, 'For the Every-Day Book' (June 23).
[2] *Ibid.*, III, Part 1, col. 171–2, 'Statutes and Mops' (Vol. III, the *Table Book*, does not give entries by days and is divided into two parts).

persons of varied backgrounds; a former surgeon on a Greenland whaler wrote in to report a May Day celebration he witnessed aboard ship in 1824. Hone regretted the paucity of Irish contributions, and partially compensates by reprinting excerpts from the *Researches in the South of Ireland* (1824) of T. Crofton Croker, soon to make his name as a collector of Irish tales.

Hone's interests extended beyond the mere recording of popular customs and beliefs to recognition of social change and speculation about the origins of ritual. 'The *Every-Day Book* has presented a more striking view of the changes of manners and customs than any book which has gone before it,' Hone announced in his columns. He prints, for example, a notice on the transition in April fool jokes, due to changing apparel; and he reprints from the Sunday *Advertiser* of July 19, 1807, the history of a festal fireworks, known as 'The Bleeding Image,' which had evolved from the 1518 execution of a soldier in Paris into a harmless merriment. The arrest of superstition was a chief factor in promoting useful change.

On the question of origins, Hone engaged in bold conjecture. Some of his and his correspondents' interpretations echo the Brand-Bourne thesis, and speak of 'accommodation of the Romish church to the pagan usages.' The vulgar belief in the ability of the hot-cross bun to protect the house from fire when suspended from the ceiling on Good Friday is 'a relic of the old superstition' surviving the Reformation and the most notorious symbol of Roman Catholicism left in England. Allied is the notion current in the west of England that the crossed stripes on the back of the ass are symbolic of the ride of Christ. For laying bare these Romish remains, one reader offered congratulations.

> You, Mr Editor, have exposed with a masterly hand the superstitions and monkery of the olden time, for which you have my best thanks, in common, I believe, with those of nine out of every ten in the nation; but should a Mr Hone arise two hundred years hence, I think he would have something to say upon these *our* times.[1]

Hone the rationalist, disgusted with superstitious credulities, ran afoul of Hone the ethnologist, intrigued by popular antiquities, and his pages reveal his dilemma as he exhorts his countrymen to note down the old ceremonies and then on occasion ruthlessly exposes them as frauds. From his knowledge of political journalism, he could recognize the origins of certain wonders as purely partisan concoctions. They were cast in the mould of spectral and preter-

---

[1] *Ibid.*, II, col. 1577, 'St. Clement' (November 23).

natural occurrences sold as broadsheets and in pamphlets and chap-books to the credulous populace, but their intent was to malign the party they ostensibly supported. With the decline of partisan zeal, the writers and vendors of these pieces found their business dwind-ling, and continued to impose upon the vulgar for personal gain. So reasoned Hone, in reprinting a rare quarto tract, 'A TRUE ACCOUNT *of divers most strange and prodigious* APPARITIONS *seen in the Air* at Poins-town, in the county of Tipperary, in Ireland: March the Second, 1678–9. Attested by Sixteen Persons that were Eye-Witnesses.' Although allegedly published in Dublin, Hone declared it was forged in London, and probably never reached Poinstown, and even if it did, few there would be able to read it, and of those none would care enough to issue a contradiction. In similar fashion, a hawker in Somersetshire will bruit a wonderful account of an ap-parition in Hertfordshire, and when he reaches that county, astonish the populace with an account of the same wonder in Somerset.[1]

In the same spirit, the editor of the *Every-Day Book* printed an instance of deception practised on Yorkshire folk who believed that on St. Mark's Eve, according to the Old Calendar, spirits of those who are to die in the coming year will approach the church door at midnight. Some of the bolder peasantry would attempt to view the spot, and taking advantage of their dread, Joe Brown imperson-ated the Barguest, frightened the villagers out of their wits, and robbed their homes.[2]

Yet historical origins for village observances did exist, and when he came upon such explanations, Hone printed them gladly. A correspondent wrote that at Alnwick, in Northumberland, in February, 1824, thirteen persons desirous of obtaining the freedom of Alnwick waded through the local pond and planted a holly tree at the door of the house once belonging to King John. According to the tradition, King John nearly drowned in that pond, and saved his life only by clinging to a holly tree; thereupon he dictated the conditions governing the freedom of Alnwick. And so with the Ludlow rope pulling, in which an eye-witness on February 7, 1826, averred that nearly two thousand persons were involved; tradition assigned the origin to a siege of Ludlow by Henry VI, which led to the rise of two factions in the town, one wishing to give admit-tance to the king, the other supporting the pretensions of the Duke of York.[3] Better substantiated than either of these is the following

[1] Hone, *op. cit.*, II, cols. 278–82, 'Strange Narrative' (March 2).
[2] *Ibid.*, II, cols. 548–51, 'Joe Brown—The Church Watch' (April 24).
[3] *Ibid.*, II, cols. 249–50, 'The Freeman's Well at Alnwick' (February 22; the so-called Freeman's Well is actually a pond); II, cols. 256–7, 'A Shrovetide Custom' (February 25).

[40]

account sent to the *Every-Day Book* of a relatively young custom, begun in 1694.

Newark Custom, founded on a dream

A curious traditional story of a very extraordinary deliverance of alderman Hercules Clay, and his family, by a dream, is at your service.

I am, &c.

Benjamin Johnson

On March 11, every year, at Newark-upon-Trent, penny loaves are given away to every one who chooses to appear at the town-hall, and apply for them, in commemoration of the deliverance of Hercules Clay, during the siege of Newark by the parliamentary forces. This Hercules Clay, by will dated 11th of December, 1694, gave to the mayor and aldermen one hundred pounds, to be placed at interest by the vicar's consent for his benefit, to preach a sermon on the 11th day of March, annually, and another hundred pounds to be secured and applied in like manner for the poor of the town of Newark, which is distributed as abovementioned. The occasion of this bequest was singular. During the bombardment of the town of Newark, by the parliament army under Oliver Cromwell, Clay (then a tradesman residing in Newark market-place) dreamed three nights successively, that his house was set fire to by the besiegers. Impressed by the repetition of this warning, as he considered it, he quitted his house, and in the course of a few hours after the prediction was fulfilled.[1]

A fire bomb landed on his house. And thereafter, on the 11th of March, the minister preached a sermon on the power of dreams. Folk belief, custom, and history all happily blend in this well-documented example of how a local observance gets its start.

As evidence mounted, even the most rabid anti-papist could see that no simple theory of monkish accretions to pagan idolatries explained the genesis of rural ceremonies. Some indeed appeared to have originated in circumstances of local history impinging on national events and personages, and these were a source of honest village pride. Or perhaps a simple comical incident had given rise to an annual usage, as in the custom of 'beating the lapstone' at Nettleton, near Burton, the day after Christmas. On this occasion, the shoemakers beat the lapstone of all water-drinkers, in memory of a neighbour, Thomas Stickler, who had not tasted malt liquor

---

[1] *Ibid.*, II, cols. 367–8, 'Newark Custom, Founded on a Dream' (March 11).

for twenty years and then became tipsy from a mere half pint of ale drunk at his shoemaker's one Christmas. Tottering back to his house, he was met by his good dame, who inquired, 'John, where have you been?—why, you are in liquor?' 'No, I am not,' John hiccuped. 'I've only *fell over the lapstone*, and that has *beaten my leg*, so as I can't walk quite right.'[1]

Again, conflicting views of the origin of a given ceremony undermine any pat monistic theory. What means the business of 'Riding the Black Lad' in Ashton-under-Lyne on Easter Monday, when a straw man is dragged through the streets, forced to beg liquor for its thirsty attendants, shot at, and burned? Some hold that the figure represents Sir Ralph Assheton, vice-chancellor under Henry VI, who rode through his lands on Easter Monday in black armour and extracted penalties from those tenants who had not cleared their corn of gool (marygold). On one of his visits he was shot and killed. Far from prosecuting the murderer, the tenants took up a collection to kill Sir Ralph each year in effigy. An appealing reconstruction, especially to social critics. But the defenders of nobility counter with the thesis that the dummy stood for a border hero, Thomas Ashton, who carried off the royal standard from the Scottish king's tent in a border battle, for which feat Edward III knighted him; Sir Thomas then donated a sum to perpetuate this ride in his own honour.[2]

In addition to country fêtes, the *Every-Day Book* and its sequels captured many other varieties of popular lore. London street cries, charms against witches, remarkable epitaphs, powers of second-sight, spectral sights (even one beheld by the editor), children's games, death 'fetches,' and indeed the whole gamut of popular antiquities enter Hone's pages. A new strain that occasionally emerges is the humorous lore of exaggeration and eccentricity. Halfway through his serial, Hone introduced a series of sketches about local characters who had grown into mock heroes of village legend. One such was The Reverend Mr. Alcock, or Burnsal, near Skipton in Yorkshire: 'Every inhabitant of Craven has heard tales of this eccentric person, and numberless are the anecdotes told of him.'[3] A scapegrace from Penryn was memorialized in the following epitaph:

Here lies William Smith: and what is somewhat rarish,
He was born, bred, and hang'd in this here parish.[4]

[1] Hone, *op. cit.*, III, Part 1, col. 85, 'Customs, Beating the Lapstone.'
[2] *Ibid.*, II, cols. 467–70, 'Riding the Black Lad' (March 27).
[3] *Ibid.*, III, Part 1, cols. 634–5, 'Clerical Errors.'
[4] *Ibid.*, III, Part 2, col. 153, 'Remarkable Epitaphs.'

Once in a while the tall tale crops up, as in the straight-faced yarn of the Fenland man who periodically left his miasmatic valley to seek an upland wife and so replenish his finances from her dowry, knowing that no outsider could survive long in the Fens.[1] Then there are the notorious liars who pleaded guilty in court but were released, the juries distrusting their word. Akin is an anecdote related as having transpired in the lovely village of Temple Sowerby in Westmorland (although it is an international tale type, No. 1920, 'Contest in Lying'): The villagers on May Day indulged in a story-telling contest to see who could produce the greatest lie. First prize was a grindstone, second a sharp hone for a razor, and for mediocre liars there were consolation prizes of dull whetstones, with the people serving as judges and later repairing to the inn. Once the Bishop of Carlisle passed by the village green in his carriage, and on learning of the reason for the assemblage, lectured the townsfolk on their iniquity, concluding, 'For my part I never told a lie in my life.' The judges promptly awarded him the hone.[2]

The *Year-Book* of 1832 ended Hone's activity as an editorial compiler of popular customs and usages, although his format would be repeated, notably by Moses A. Richardson in *The Local Historian's Table Book* (8 vols., 1841–6), and by the Scottish publisher Robert Chambers in *The Book of Days* (2 vols., 1863–4). With Brand and Hone to consult, no alert Englishman thenceforth would be unaware of the popular antiquities lodged in a thousand printed sources and visible in hundreds of country towns. The stage was set for talented Victorians to explore this newly charted area of English studies.

[1] *Ibid.*, II, cols. 923–4, 'Laying Out of Wives' (July 6).
[2] *Ibid.*, II, cols. 599–600, 'May Day Story-Telling' (May 1).

II   The Antiquary-Folklorists

IN THE DECADE 1834 to 1844 newly formed scholarly societies in London brought together in satisfying communion antiquaries and bookmen of like interests. During these years the Camden, Parker, Percy, Shakespeare, Aelfric, Caxton, and Sydenham societies were founded, with the active members devoting their energies to the scholarly editing and publishing of valuable literary, historical, and religious manuscripts, documents, tracts, and studies. These flourishing societies, headed by an earl or lord and maintained by private scholars of the middle class, suggest the congenial atmosphere for intellectual pursuits which prevailed outside the universities in nineteenth-century England. The blessings of empire and trade, peace and prosperity, stability and reform, in proper balance, made possible this efflorescence of humanistic learning.

Eventually the folklore movement would have its own Folk-Lore Society. In its infancy, it drew strength from the antiquarian clubs, particularly the Percy and Camden, whose activities bordered on the sphere of popular antiquities. Six antiquaries contributed creatively to the emerging study of folklore, and one would give it its name.

[1   THOMAS CROFTON CROKER]

In 1825 a volume entitled *Fairy Legends and Traditions of the South of Ireland* appeared on London bookstalls under the imprint of John Murray but lacking the name of an author. He was soon discovered to be a clerk in the Admiralty named Thomas Crofton Croker (1798–1854), and his book met with such success that the publisher sent him scurrying back to Ireland to collect materials for a sequel. Croker came down with a fever during his hasty field trip, and Murray had to wait until 1828 to issue the second and third series. The brothers Grimm translated the first volume into German within the year, a French edition came out within three years, and the work was re-issued throughout the century. Wilhelm Grimm wrote a highly cordial letter to 'the man whose valuable collection of Irish Tales and Legends occupied us for several months last summer,' and attached an 'Essay on the Fairies' with a request for its translation into English. Sir Walter Scott opened an enthusiastic correspondence with Croker, noting some fairylore items, and soon made his acquaintance in London.[1]

The immediate recognition accorded *Fairy Legends* was well deserved, and the volumes still stand as an original contribution to the development of folklore studies. They represent the first intentional field collection to be made in Great Britain, in that sense paralleling the Grimms' *Household Tales*. Their contents differed, embracing not *Märchen* or fictional fairy tales, but traditional stories about demonic beings rife among the Irish peasantry. It was Jacob Grimm of the *Deutsche Mythologie*, not of the *Kinder- und Hausmärchen*, who was fascinated by the Irish legends. Croker wrote up skeletal motifs and incidents into full-dress sketches, interlarded with descriptions of scenery and background and specimens of humorous colloquial dialogue, much in the manner of the Anglo-Irish character literature of the time. Although the archness of the humour and the fluency of the narratives give an overly literary effect, the basic authenticity of most tales seems evident. Thus in a note to one tale Croker wrote, 'The figure of "a salmon with a cravat round its neck, and a pair of new top-boots", is perhaps rather too absurd, but it has been judged best to give the legend as received. . . .'[2] And in his preface to the second series he reprinted newspaper accounts of 1820 and 1827 about murders attributed to fairies, to reinforce the truth of his stories, and weaken the charge that they no longer were accepted.

A quondam friend Thomas Keightley (see next section) asserted that several tales were falsified, and a number of the genuine ones supplied by himself and other unnamed contributors.[3] In response

[1] T. F. Dillon Croker, 'Memoir of the Late Thomas Crofton Croker, Esq.,' *Gentleman's Magazine*, n.s. XLII (October, 1854), 397–401. This memoir, by the author's son, is reprinted in the 1859 edition of *Fairy Legends* edited by Thomas Wright, and contains valuable data on the history of the work. John Hennig has provided useful information on 'The Brothers Grimm and T. C. Croker' in *Modern Language Review*, XLI (1946), 44–54. Hennig has also written on French editions of Croker's *Fairy Legends* in 'Contes Irlandais,' *Modern Language Review*, XLII (1947), 237–42; XLIII (1948), 92–3.
[2] *Fairy Legends and Traditions of the South of Ireland* (London: John Murray, 1825), p. 7 n.
[3] Thomas Keightley, *Tales and Popular Fictions* (London: Whittaker and Co., 1834), p. 180. 'My share was a fair proportion of the tales, and a very large proportion of the Notes in the first and second volumes.' Keightley named seven tales specifically as his, and reprinted four of them as an appendix to his *The Fairy Mythology*. Other

to their protests Croker reduced his later edition of 1834 from fifty to forty tales, presumably all of his own collecting. In fairness to Croker it must be said that he had the original idea of securing fairy traditions, and stimulated Keightley to collect, or rather to recollect. In the notes appended to each tale, which please the modern folklorist more than the embellished texts, Croker (or the unnamed Keightley) indicate the oral sources in a general way, sometimes even affirming that a tale had been set down verbatim, mention local variants, and discuss similar stories collected by Thiele in Denmark and the Grimms in Germany. Storytelling situations customarily introduce the narratives, and frequently convey a strong sense of verisimilitude.

The kitchen of some country houses in Ireland presents in no ways a bad modern translation of the ancient feudal hall. Traces of clanship still linger round its hearth in the numerous dependants on 'the master's' bounty. Nurses, foster-brothers, and other hangers on, are there as matter of right, while the strolling piper, full of mirth and music, the benighted traveller, even the passing beggar, are received with a hearty welcome, and each contributes planxty, song, or superstitious tale, towards the evening's amusement.

An assembly, such as has been described, had collected round the kitchen fire of Ballyrahenhouse, at the foot of the Galtee mountains, when, as is ever the case, one tale of wonder called forth another; and with the advance of the evening each succeeding story was received with deep and deeper attention. The history of Cough na Looba's dance with the black friar at Rahill, and the fearful tradition of *Coum an 'ir morriv* (the dead man's hollow), were listened to in breathless silence. A pause followed the last relation, and all eyes rested on the narrator, an old nurse who occupied the post of honour, that next the fireside. She was seated in that peculiar position which the Irish name '*Currigguib*,' a position generally assumed by a veteran and determined story-teller. Her haunches resting upon the ground, and her feet bundled under the body; her arms folded across and supported by her knees, and the out-stretched chin of her hooded head pressing on the upper arm; which compact arrangement nearly reduced the whole figure into a perfect triangle.[1]

[1] *Fairy Legends and Traditions of the South of Ireland* (London: John Murray, 1834), pp. 274–5.

contributors to Croker's book are named in Séamus O' Casaide, 'Crofton Croker's Irish Fairy Legends,' *Béaloideas*, X (1940), 289–91.

An advantage in Croker's method, as compared with the severe field notes of the modern scientific collector, can be seen in this passage, where the setting for the marvellous adventure achieves a three-dimensional vividness. In spite of the literary veneer, *Fairy Legends* presents an orderly arrangement of homogeneous traditions. The legends chiefly involve beings from the spirit world who loom so large in the Irish folk imagination: the cluricaune (variant of leprechaun), the mischievous fairy shoemaker who carried a magic shilling and knew the whereabouts of treasure; the dullahan, whom Scott had encountered as a gloomy headless spectre on a visit to Ireland; the phooka, a prankish horse who conducted benighted travellers on fearful rides—creatures still traditional.[1]

A host of common folklore motifs, familiar in *Sagen* and popular belief, enter the tales. Treasure is lost when the diggers break silence; rent money given the poor tenant by a friendly fairy turns to gingerbread in the hands of the stony-hearted agent; a monk sleeps a hundred years, and the imprints of his knees in solid rock still startle tourists. In his commentaries Croker recognizes, even with the relatively limited collections then available, the widespread currency of such ideas. In the legendary return to earth of the chieftain O'Donoghue he perceives the heroic formula of the popular champion who periodically returns to his people; he spotted at once the continental parallels to the treasure dreamer who goes to London Bridge and is told by a stranger of a treasure buried back in Ireland—a legend later employed by Gomme to illustrate his thesis of prehistoric survivals in folklore; and the vision of the spectral coach with its headless steeds and driver he likens to the aerial wild huntsman that Jacob Grimm has discussed. Croker ventured little into theory, save for a few paragraphs, speculating on origins, that explain the legends of underwater cities and spectral hunters naturalistically; they arise from tricks played on the eyes and ears, which interpret misty mirages and hounds baying in the wind in terms of fairylore. So had the great myths originated. Of primitive rituals and barbaric survivals Croker has nothing to say.

Friendship and exchange of information with the Grimms and Scott were a fruitful byproduct of *Fairy Legends*. Because the Grimms translated Croker's first volume, adding a knowledgeable introduction, he dedicated his third volume to them, translated

[1] Visiting Ireland in November, 1951, I heard some of Croker's tales in current variants. See R. M. Dorson, 'Collecting in County Kerry,' *Journal of American Folklore*, LXVI (1953), 29–31, 33–4, for the pooka, the luharacan, and the London Bridge treasure legend.

their treatise, and printed a long dedicatory letter to 'Dr. Wilhelm Grimm.' He wrote, 'You will perceive that a considerable portion consists in a close translation of your introductory essay to the *Irische Elfenmärchen*. . . . The corrections and additional notes which you have favoured me with are inserted in their proper places. . . .'[1] The third volume of 1828, which was not reprinted, has special interest for the folklore student, both for the Grimms' lengthy essay, and for its scope, which extends to all of Britain. Ireland plays little part, as Croker devotes his portion of the book to 'The Mabinogion and Fairy Legends of Wales,' using materials from correspondents. He also sought for English fairy legends, but had little luck apart from one account of a fairy sighted within three miles of London. The Grimms in turn spend a scant dozen pages discussing 'The Elves in Ireland,' against forty on 'The Elves in Scotland,' followed by a hundred 'On the Nature of the Elves' in which they organize systematically their information on elfin behaviour. For their Scotch data, in which they take pride, they rely largely on W. Grant Stewart's *The Popular Superstitions and Festive Amusements of the Highlanders of Scotland* (Edinburgh, 1823), a work valuable for its oral traditions and apparently, as they gleefully remark, unfamiliar to the compiler of the Irish fairy legends. The brothers also resort to Scott's essay on fairy mythology and his notes to the *Lady of the Lake*.[2] But they beg to differ with Scott's method, in their separation of beliefs belonging to different ages and their demonstration of the effect of Christianity on the fairy faith. Their method enables them to study mythology historically.[3]

Scott too reacted with delight to the first number of *Fairy Legends*, writing Croker a letter from Abbotsford on April 27, 1825, which Croker immediately printed in the second edition of the first series. In his letter Scott commented on the close resemblance of Irish fictions to the Scottish, save for the cluricaune and the banshee. But witches, water bulls, and little people were to be seen in Scotland, and Sir Walter reported in droll style a shepherd's sight of a fairy court. Croker dedicated the second volume to Scott and printed a long document from him in the third volume. 'A rummager of our records,' wrote the Waverley romancer, 'sent me

---

[1] *Fairy Legends and Traditions of the South of Ireland*. Part III (London: John Murray, 1828), pp. iii, v.
[2] 'We have also availed ourselves of the Essay on Fairies, in the second volume of Walter Scott's Ministrelsy of the Scottish Border, 4th Edit Edinb. 1810, II, p. 109–183, and the Introduction, I, 99–103, of his notes to the Lady of the Lake. . . .' *Ibid.*, p. 13).
[3] *Ibid.*, p. 54.

the other day a most singular trial of an old woman, who was tried, condemned, and burned alive for holding too close a connexion with Elf-land.'[1] The account of the trial supported the point made by the Grimms on the overlapping of witch and fairy superstitions.

Scott and Croker met at a breakfast party given by the novelist's son-in-law, J. G. Lockhart, in Pall Mall on October 20, 1826, and each left an account of the other. The baronet of Abbotsford noted in his diary: 'Crofton Croker, author of the Irish Fairy Tales—little as a dwarf, keen-eyed as a hawk, and of easy, prepossessing manners.'[2] In a letter to his sister Croker recorded his own overflowing emotions.

When I was introduced to the 'Great Unknown' I really had not the power of speaking; it was a strange feeling of embarrassment, which I do not remember having felt before in so strong a manner, and of course to his 'I am glad to see you, Mr Croker, you and I are not unknown to each other,' I could say nothing. He contrived to say something neat to every one in the kindest manner, a well-turned compliment, without, however, the slightest appearance of flattery, something at which every one felt gratified. . . . He mentioned my Fairy Legends, and hoped he should soon have the very great enjoyment of reading the Second Volume. 'You are our—I speak of the Celtic Nations (said Sir Walter)—great authority now on Fairy Superstition, and have made Fairy Land your Kingdom; most sincerely do I hope it may prove a golden inheritance to you. To me (continued Sir Walter) it is the land of promise of much future entertainment. I have been reading the German translation of your Tales and the Grimms' very elaborate Introduction'. . . . But really I blush, or ought to blush, at writing all this flattery: yet I must confess it was most sweet from such a man.[3]

Acclaimed by such eminent authorities on tale and legend, Croker's work stayed in print for years, and was reissued after his death in a new edition prepared by his friend and 'fellow-labourer' Thomas Wright, who called it one of the best collections of fairy legends in the language.[4]

[1] *Ibid.*, p. xvi.
[2] J. G. Lockhart, *Memoirs of the Life of Sir Water Scott, Bart.*, III (Edinburgh and London, 1837), p. 360.
[3] 'Sir Walter Scott and Mr Crofton Croker,' *Gentleman's Magazine*, n.s. XLII (November, 1854), pp. 452–3.
[4] *Fairy Legends and Traditions of the South of Ireland*. A new and complete edition, edited by T. Wright, with a memoir of the author, by his son, T. F. Dillon Croker (London: William Tegg [n.d.]). This useful edition, itself reprinted, contains 'The

Fairy Legends significantly advanced the cause of popular antiquities in the British Isles by demonstrating the continued existence
of supposedly dead and bygone superstitions. Croker stumbled on
the idea of field work more or less accidentally. His first walking
trips when a boy through southern Ireland in 1812 and 1815
brought him in contact with the peasants and started him collecting songs and tales. The poet Tom Moore expressed thanks to
Croker in 1818 for communicating to him many curious fragments
of ancient Irish poetry and some interesting traditions current in
the country. In 1821, after he had settled in London, Croker revisited the counties of Cork, Waterford and Limerick, and gathered
further data, published in 1824, as *Researches in the South of
Ireland, illustrative of the scenery, architectural remains, and the
manners and superstitions of the peasantry*, a handsome quarto
volume belying the modest preface that the contents consisted of
sketchy field notes strung together. The antiquarian point of view
and its impulse toward folklore shows very clearly in *Researches*,
where inquiries into both material and oral remains of the past fit
easily side by side. One insight into Croker's difficulties with the
natives is amusingly illustrated by this dialogue:

> 'Pray is this the nearest road to——?'
> 'Is it to —— you are going? fait' and that's not the nearest
> road—being 'tis no road at all.'
> 'Then had I better go yon way?'
> 'Och! indeed and I wouldn't advise you going that way at
> all. 'Tis few people goes that way, for there's a big black dog
> there, and he'll ate you up entirely.'
> 'Which way then can I go?'
> '*Fait!* and the best way you'd go is just to be staying
> where you are.'[1]

This sounds exactly like Yankee talk. Croker managed to gain
the confidence of the 'lower orders,' in ways which unfortunately
he has not described, and his chapter on 'Fairies and Supernatural
Agency' shows a firm grasp of the material he published at length
the following year. Here the writing and comment are completely
straightforward, without the adornment of *Fairy Legends*, and

[1] *Researches in the South of Ireland* (London: John Murray, 1824), p. 27.

Editor's Preface' (iii–vi), 'Memoir of the Author' (vii–xxii), with three letters from
Scott, 'The Author's Preface to the First Volume, Second Edition' (xxiii–xxvii), and
'The Author's Preface to the Second Volume' (xxviii–xxxi), in the edition I have
used, which is undated. An edition with different pagination has the date Feb. 1st,
1862, after Wright's Preface.

provide a meaty exposition of the fairy mythology. Croker speaks with authority on 'the most common of fairy fictions,' namely the tale of the abducted woman who beholds the fairies by rubbing their magic ointment on her eye, and (in 1824) adumbrates the laws of fairy behaviour which Hartland decades later traced so cleverly. Croker appreciates the peculiarly Irish character of fairy kidnappings, and remarks on the absence of second-sight, so prevalent in the Scottish Highlands, among the Irish peasantry. The chapters on 'Keens and Death Ceremonies' and 'Manners and Customs' probe further into folk tradition with commendable realism; the belief that the left hand of a corpse dipped in a milk pail makes the milk it holds creamier, suits the atmosphere of grim poverty.

Croker wrote and edited further works related to folk materials, although none came close in importance to *Fairy Legends*. *The Legends of the Lakes: or, Sayings and Doings at Killarney* (1829) came not from his own field work but from that of a schoolfellow and retired soldier, R. Adolphus Lynch of Killarney, who tried collecting after reading *Fairy Legends*. Croker bought his materials, and arranged them to fit in with descriptions of the local scenery; a boatman rowing the author-traveller to some celebrated spot, or the driver of the surrey, relates a *Sage* connected with the locality. The artificial gaiety of the narrative and the secondhand nature of its contents impair its value.

Another folklore volume grew out of the chapter on keens in *Researches* and was published by the Percy Society in 1844 as *The Keen of the South of Ireland: as illustrative of Irish political and domestic history, manners, music, and superstitions*. Croker himself translated the Gaelic originals he had collected and uncovered a rich vein of Irish folk tradition in these wild death laments, often incorporating macabre murders and curses. He also edited collections of Irish historical and popular songs and led the active life of a versatile antiquary and man of letters. He wrote a pantomime based on one of his fairy legends and two novelettes, edited journals, memoirs, and plays, assisted in the founding of the Camden and Percy societies and the British Archaeological Association, was elected a Fellow of the Society of Antiquaries, collected a private museum of Irish ethnographical specimens—all while holding a government clerkship, so that he apologized in his work on the keens for not having time to re-read his hasty translations! Widely read as well as prolific, he kept up with folklore and antiquarian scholarship, and the catalogue of his library shows such works as Roby's *Popular Traditions of England*, Dalyell's *The Darker*

Superstitions of Scotland, and Stewart's *Popular Superstitions of the Highlanders* (no doubt acquired after the Grimms' comment on its omission!) that attest his familiarity with the scanty folk collections of his time.[1] It was his special contribution to expand the shelf of British oral folklore.

[2 THOMAS KEIGHTLEY]

Perhaps the most important result of Croker's collecting lay in the books he stimulated an Irish friend to write. The friend, Thomas Keightley (1789–1872), has expressed his debt in this way:

> One of my earliest literary friends in London was T. Crofton Croker, who was then engaged in collecting materials for the Fairy Legends of the South of Ireland. He of course applied to his friends for aid and information; and I, having most leisure, and, I may add, most knowledge, was able to give him the greatest amount of assistance. My inquiries on the subject led to the writing of the present work, which was succeeded by the Mythology of Ancient Greece and Italy, and the Tales and Popular Fictions; so that, in effect, if Mr Croker had not planned the Fairy Legends, these works, be their value what it may, would in all probability never have been written.[2]

The Fairy Mythology, which grew out of Keightley's collaboration with Croker, and the *Tales and Popular Fictions* published six years later (1834) stand out as the two most mature English studies on comparative folklore in the first half of the century. A strangely brash and rather pathetic figure, Keightley annoys us with his trumpetings of his own merit and then softens us with his candid confession to a life of London hackwork. Poor health caused him to renounce his career at the Irish bar and come to London in 1824, where he prepared a historical manual for school use with such success that he was encouraged to turn out histories of Greece, Rome, India, and England, editions of Milton and Shakespeare, and similar schoolroom materials adopted, he tells us, at Eton, Harrow, Rugby, and 'most of the other great public schools.'[3] Keightley possessed two talents for this work which served him

[1] *Catalogue of the greater part of the Library of the late Thomas Crofton Croker* ... printed 11 December 1854.
[2] *The Fairy Mythology, Illustrative of the Romance and Superstition of Various Countries*, a new edition, revised and greatly enlarged (London, 1850), p. vii.
[3] *The Mythology of Ancient Greece and Italy*, 2nd ed. (London: Whittaker and Co., 1838), p. iv.

well in his folklore writing, the ability to compress a long narrative into an easy, fluent synopsis, and a feeling for 'the people.' He preferred to write of Greece and Rome rather than the Orient because Oriental history 'is the history of Khalifs, Shahs and Sultans—not of the people.'[1]

Recalling fairy legends for Croker from his youth in Leinster, where a cowherd had filled him with 'shanahas,' Keightley felt the fascination of this new subject. Palgrave's articles in the *Quarterly Review*[2] gave him literary handholds, and his own active mind pursued the trail thus opened. He called this trail 'Popular Mythology,' and expressed surprise that Scott alone had pointed to it, in his essay on 'Fairy Superstition.' 'But since the Essay was written, much has appeared, and he has himself called upon his friend Mr. Douce to compile a work "upon the origin of popular fiction, and the transmission of similar tales from age to age and from country to country"—a proof that, in his opinion, something remained to be done.'[3] Douce not having answered the call, Keightley had taken it on himself, with apologies to Sir Walter for his different approach. From a variety of literary works and collections—and Keightley claimed to have read in twenty odd languages and dialects—he culled the peasant stories of sprites seen in homes, farms, and fields throughout the British Isles and the countries of Europe, for his successful compilation of fairy mythology. The frame that Keightley reared in 1828 was filled amply in an expanded edition in 1850, making use of Grimms' *Deutsche Mythologie* and other works that had appeared in the meantime. In his 1850 preface he remarked that, as he had begun his literary labours with the fairy studies, so now he closed them with the same subject; yet he lived to write a third preface to the 1860 edition, in which he refers to 'the neglect of what Mr. Thoms has very happily designated "Folk-lore," ' in his single use of the term.[4]

For an early book of folklore *The Fairy Mythology* sets high standards. Keightley showed an awareness of the sanctity of oral tradition not previously evident among the English folklorists, including himself, for he shamefacedly confessed to decorating

[1] Quoted in Samuel Warren, *A Popular and Practical Introduction to Law Studies*, 3rd ed. (London, 1863), I, 236.

[2] Sir Francis Palgrave, *Quarterly Review*, XXI (1819), 91–112, and XXII (1820), 348–80. These articles, 'Antiquities of Nursery Literature' and 'Popular Mythology of the Middle Ages,' are frequently cited by early folklorists; see the tribute of William J. Thoms in *Legends and Lays of Germany* (London, 1834), p. v.

[3] *The Fairy Mythology* (London: William Harrison Ainsworth, 1828), I, viii.

[4] *The Fairy Mythology, Illustrative of the Romance and Superstition of Various Countries*, a new edition, revised and greatly enlarged (London, 1860), p. 298.

[53]

tales for Croker's book, and even to transplanting a German legend to Ireland—which, *mirabile dictu*, he later discovered actually existed there. He discriminates between the composed songs and 'genuine legends' in Cromek-Cunningham's *Remains of Nithsdale and Galloway Song*, questions whether a Normandy collector has not transferred tales from adjacent Brittany, rejects London-bred Milton as a fairylore source because he knew only 'book superstitions,' and in his comments on collectors and informants demands as high standards as any modern purist.[1] In these respects *The Fairy Mythology* proves a decided advance over Croker's *Fairy Legends*, whose literary touches nevertheless fooled the Grimms, hampered by a foreign idiom. Keightley relates and translates the tales simply and acknowledges his sources faithfully. The range of these sources shows clever detective work. For the British section, for example, where the gleanings seemed so barren, he brings a rich harvest, drawn from early chroniclers like Gervase of Tilbury, travellers such as Waldron, the poets from Chaucer to Spenser, and folklore amateurs in the Brand tradition. He appreciates the worth of Mrs. Bray's pixie stories, and speaks highly of Hugh Miller—although, oddly, he culls from his geological classic, *The Old Red Sandstone*, and ignores his *Scenes and Legends*. In foreign literatures Keightley seems surprisingly at ease, and one reads his estimations of Straparola and Basile with wonder that he should so early have recognized their value as the first collectors of wonder tales.

Keightley, not content with the ferreting out of fairylore, arranged his samples according to a systematic scheme of racial geography. He sought to prove that fairy belief descended from primitive Gotho-Germanic religions and thence spread to the weaker Celtic-Cymric peoples; that is, the Norwegian *nis* and German *kobold* antedated the Irish fairy and Scottish brownie. Early Irish literature includes no fairies, yet modern Irish lore contains elf-creatures like those in old Teutonic belief, ergo an invasion has occurred. Here Keightley's thinking echoes that of the Grimms—whose works on *Marchen*, *Sagen*, and mythology liberally sprinkle his notes.[2] Even in the dark age of folklore, when virtually nothing was known of traditions outside Europe, Keightley probed at the boundaries, opening with the Persian *peries* and

[1] *The Fairy Mythology, Illustrative of the Romance and Superstition of Various Countries*, a new edition, revised and greatly enlarged (London, 1860), pp. 364, 350, 472 n., 348.

[2] He concludes his later editions with the acknowledgement: 'The labours of MM. Grimm in this department of philosophy can never be too highly praised.' *Ibid.*, p. 511.

closing with the Jewish *shedeem* and African *yumboes* (told him by a woman who had heard of them from a native Jaloff servant). He never overpressed his analogues, and his statement on folklore's perpetual puzzle, how to explain the similarity of widespread tales, anticipates Andrew Lang and still makes good sense today:

> As I advanced in my researches, I was every day more and more struck with the great similarity that pervades the legends of different countries. This is by many accounted for by sup- posing nations, of common origin, to have brought these legends from a common country; thus bestowing on the simplest incident an unknown antiquity. To me this looks like applying a lever to raise a feather . . . we should not leave out of view the sameness that runs through the acts and thoughts of men, which wearies us in history, in fiction, and in common life. For my own part, were a collection of Mexican, Esquimaux, or New Zealand tales to appear, I should be no more surprised to find them corresponding with European ones than I should be at seeing a Chinese magpie (if such thing be) constructing its nest after the same fashion as an English one. . . . The truth I apprehend to be this: some tales and legends are transmitted; others are, to speak geologically, independent formations. When, in a tale of some length, a number of circumstances are the same, and follow in the same order, I would term it trans- mitted. . . . Other circumstances may be referred to what we may call the poverty of human invention; such are the swords of sharpness, and the shoes of swiftness, everywhere to be met with. . . . There is a third class, which I find more difficult to dispose of. Mr Morier heard Whittington and his Cat in Persia; Magalotti told it in Italy, of one Ansaldo degli Ormanni; and two churches in Denmark were raised by the possessors of similar lucky cats. Who now can take it upon him to assign the birth-place of this legend? And is it not possible that the European and Asiatic versions of so simple a fiction may be independent?[1]

The idea that men's minds work similarly when composing brief *Sagen* was restated by Keightley in his reasonable introduction to *Mythology of Ancient Greece and Italy*. The classic myths often correspond to legends of later days. A pagan Greek explains the colour of the hyacinth as the bleeding of Ajax; a Christian sees in the cross printed on the shoulders of an ass a relic of the Lord's

---

[1] *The Fairy Mythology*, 1828, I, ix–xi. In later editions the index noted 'Similar Legends.'

ride. 'Each wished to give some account of an unusual appearance.'[1] So men everywhere devise simple legends to account for the appearance of nature, according to their own cultural data.

Complex tales are another matter, and in his *Tales and Popular Fictions; Their Resemblance, and Transmission from Country to Country*,[2] Keightley points out some unusual correspondences his reading in romances, sagas, epics, and folktales had detected. In support of the theory laid down in *The Fairy Mythology*, he divides the volume into stories which he believes had crossed from the Middle East to western Europe, a second group which strikingly resemble each other but have grown independently, and a third class that give him pause. For his first division, he proffers complex tales with striking motifs, such as wooden horses that fly and singing birds that recover lost children, which had spread westward across Europe as single units.[3] Centuries before Galland translated the *Arabian Nights*, the marvellous fictions of Persia and India had stolen into the Mediterranean along the trade routes from Syria and Egypt to Venice and thence west even to Ireland. When the Grimms stoutly maintain that their isolated Keuterberg village could not have imported tales, Keightley declares that their version crept into town from a traveller who had read or heard of the *Thousand and One Nights*. When they point to strictly German features, such as the cry of 'Hilloa' peculiar to the cowherds of Keuterberg, he contends this points not to the story's birthplace but to its stopping place.[4]

When a champion fights a mortal battle with a father he has never seen, as did Sohrab in Persia, Cuchullin in Ireland, and Theseus in Greece, Keightley remarks the striking resemblance, but draws back from any claim for diffusion. He fails to hint at the Chadwicks' brilliant heroic age concept that explains these parallelisms as the result of comparable conditions of society, but he distinguishes perceptively between the complex organism of a wonder tale and the episodic motif that freely circulates through folk literature.

At a third grouping Keightley shakes his head in puzzlement, and leaves it on middle ground between unified plots and inde-

---

[1] *The Mythology of Ancient Greece and Italy, intended chiefly for the use of students at the universities and the higher classes in schools* (London, 1831), p. 5. A second edition, 'considerably enlarged and improved,' appeared in 1838.

[2] The only edition was published in London in 1834 by Whittaker and Co.

[3] Motif D1626. 1, *Artificial flying horse*, in Stith Thompson's motif-index; and Type 707, *The Three Golden Sons* (Grimm No. 96, 'The Three Little Birds'), in the Aarne-Thompson type-index.

[4] *Tales and Popular Fictions*, p. 115 n. He writes shrewdly: 'It is curious to observe how by these means tales are localised.'

pendent analogues. The fortunes that lucky cats bring their masters and the ways in which weak but crafty men outwit giants and ogres seem too close for independent invention but too loose for cohesive texts; Keightley is on the verge of the modern recognition of motif groups. In his nine chapters Keightley browses through literature and legend with eminent good sense, relishing to the full the folklorist's joy in locating identical and close-seeming fictions, but not pressing too far his discoveries.

In the preface to his work, Keightley announces that he had completed his inquiries into popular traditions and superstitions and exhausted the public's attention. The remainder of his literary life went into other labours, and these two early books, with a few scattered articles, stand as his contribution to folklore. Though his books are risky pioneer inquiries, they justify his own self-praise. Without *The Fairy Mythology* Hartland could never have produced *The Science of Fairy Tales*; Clouston's analyses of diffusion in his *Popular Tales and Fictions* enlarge the insights provided in the *Tales and Popular Fictions*. As Croker first gathered tales in the field, so Keightley first compared them in the library.

[3 FRANCIS DOUCE]

Reminiscing about his first literary contacts, William Thoms recalled how fifty years earlier, when he was contemplating his *Early Prose Romances*, he met 'that ripe scholar, Francis Douce [1757–1834], who received me with a warmth and cordiality . . . [that] never abated.' Thoms glows with gratitude to his friend, mentor, and consultant. 'He encouraged me in every way: lent me books—aye, and MSS.; answered all my inquiries, poured out his stores of learning, encouraged my visits. . . .'[1]

The debt thus fervently proclaimed by the father of folklore was felt by many of his fellow antiquaries. Brand and Ellis both drew upon Douce's erudition for the *Popular Antiquities*, and his name appears in numerous notes on their later editions. Hone regularly invoked 'My Douce, whose attainments include more erudition concerning the origin and progress of English customs than any other antiquarian possesses.'[2] With his customary self-gratulation, Keightley quoted Douce's words of praise for his *Tales and Popular Fictions*.[3] When first presenting his *Fairy*

[1] *Notes and Queries*, ed. William Thoms, 5th Ser., VI (1876), 1.
[2] *Every-Day Book*, I, col. 111.
[3] Thomas Keightley, *The Fairy Mythology* (London, 1860), p. vi. Keightley quotes Douce as saying 'it was many, many years indeed, since he had read a book which yielded him so much delight.'

Mythology to the public, he remarked how Sir Walter Scott had called on 'his friend Mr Douce' to do just this sort of book,[1] and elsewhere Scott's biographer tells us of the border novelist's reliance on Douce in matters traditional.[2] Douce's generosity in assisting writers and scholars became near-legend. Southey, in search of the sources of the *Morte d'Arthur*, asked his publishers to forward a letter to Douce, as 'He has great information upon these subjects, and is liberal in communicating it.'[3] Thomas Wright refers to Douce's views on the *Gesta Romanorum* as one refers to a standard authority.[4] Through the antiquarian folk writings of the time Douce's name runs like a thread, in notes, prefaces, and acknowledgements of literary favours; he cleared the obstacles and opened up pathways for his colleagues following the course of folk-tale wanderings. 'Mr Douce first directed my attention to this passage,' Keightley notes briefly in reference to the appearance in the fifteenth century of the flying-horse story, which helped clinch his argument that this was a Persian tale moved to Europe.[5] In *Notes and Queries*, editor Thoms lets fly an inquiry into the mythic giant, Woglog, 'of whom my venerable friend, the late Mr. Douce, was wont to discourse, and whose history he was anxious to learn.'[6]

Douce himself published very little. He served the cause of antiquarian studies as a skilled and indefatigable collector, an encyclopedic consultant, and a central junction for his many anti-quary friends. The *Catalogue of the Printed Books and Manuscripts Bequeathed by Francis Douce, Esq. to the Bodleian Library* (Oxford, 1840) contains among its varied treasures most of the folklore titles then published—Aubrey, Reginald Scot, Glanville, Stewart, Brand, with special collections of jestbooks, *fabulae*, *facetiae*, and editions of Fortunatus—and we can see the very titles that Thoms drew upon in his *A Collection of Early Prose Romances*. Douce's friend, Thomas Dibdin, the leading bibliophilist of his times, has left us a charming picture of the trophies that adorned the collector's home:

His maple-wooded bookcases rejoice the eye by the peculiar harmony of the tint with the rich furniture which they enclose.

[1] Keightley, *The Fairy Mythology* (London, William Harrison Ainsworth, 1828), I, viii. Thoms, quoting the same passage, adds, 'To this call, it is much to be regretted, that Mr Douce has not replied' (*Lays and Legends of Germany* [London, 1834], p. v).
[2] J. G. Lockhart, *Memoirs of the Life of Sir Walter Scott, Bart.* (Edinburgh, 1845), p. 102.
[3] *Selections from the Letters of Robert Southey*, ed. John Wood Warter (London, 1856), III, 49.
[4] Wright, *Essays on Subjects connected with the Literature*, II, 63.
[5] Thomas Keightley, *Tales and Popular Fictions* (London, 1834), p. 69.
[6] *Notes and Queries*, ed. Thoms, 3rd Ser., X (1866), 68.

Here a bit of old, bright stained glass, exhibiting the true long-lost *ruby tint*; there, an inkstand, adorned in high cameo-relief, by the skill of *John of Bologna*; a little regiment, pyramidically piled, of the rarest China cups, out of which seven successive Emperors of China quaffed the essence of bohea. Persian boxes, Raffaell-ware, diptychs, and chess-men— the latter used by Charles V. and Francis I., on their dining together, *tête-à-tête*, not long after the battle of Pavia. Korans, missals, precious manuscripts; Marc Antonios, Albert Durers, Roman coins—the very staff with which Regiomontanus used to walk on his housetop by moonlight, after making certain calculations in his calendar!! Magic lore, and choice madrigals sung by Queen Elizabeth's private band; brave prick-songs! and the parchment roll which Handel wielded in beating time on the first representation of his Messiah. But his belles-lettres, facetiae, old poetry, and rare prints form a combination which hath no compeer!—and, septuagenarian as he is, I wish him a good score of years to shot his guns, and to fire them off with effect.[1]

Here are exhibited the manifold interests of the London antiquary, whose zeal for acquiring and examining the curios of the past would produce as one by-product the study of folklore. As we might expect, Douce possessed the eccentric traits of the genus antiquarius. 'He would neither bend nor bow to any man breathing,' wrote Dibdin. When Joseph Ritson, the ballad editor, called on Douce one day for lunch, he noticed some *animalcula* in the cheese and protested in horror—not on grounds of revulsion, but of personal affront, for Ritson had written a heartfelt book, *An Essay on Abstinence from Animal Food.* On Ritson asking 'if he meant to insult him,' Douce rose in the air and stated '*the door was before him,*' and never allowed Ritson through it again.[2] The streak of vain sensitivity in Douce's make-up led him to abandon writing when his one major work met with some criticism.

That work, the *Illustrations of Shakespeare, and of Ancient Manners,* abounds in folklore notes, the more significant since they precede the expanded 1813 edition of Brand.[3] The plays of Shakespeare on which Douce wrote textual comments, after the fashion of Steevens and Ritson, served him chiefly as a spring-

[1] Thomas Dibdin, *Reminiscences of a Literary Life* (London, 1836), II, 638 n.
[2] *Ibid.*, pp. 770–1 n.
[3] The full title adds 'with Dissertations on the Clowns and Fools of Shakespeare; on the collection of popular tales entitled *Gesta Romanorum*; and on the English morris dance,' 2 vols. (London, 1807).

board for antiquarian discussion. 'One design of these volumes has been to augment the knowledge of our popular customs and antiquities, in which respect alone the writings of Shakespeare have suggested better hints, and furnished ampler materials than those of any one besides.'[1] So, in his notes on *The Tempest*, he deals with the sailors' omen of St. Elmo's fire, the Elizabethan awe of the enchanted Bermuda islands, the man in the moon, fairy mythology, and travellers' tales of fabulous beasts. His sheaf of references to such folk beliefs reveals the range of the dedicated bookman. On St. Elmo's fire he cites Pliny, Seneca, Erasmus, etymological dictionaries, and books of travel; for the man in the moon, he refers to Chaucer and Dante, the Jews, the 'Cingalese,' and the Chinese.[2]

A suggestive theme in several notes directs attention to the Roman background of much European folk tradition. Since Jacob Grimm would soon command overwhelming support for his thesis of Germanic origins, Douce's Romanic emphasis deserves its due. In a lengthy note on Hecate, the witch in *Macbeth*, he develops the point that Diana-Hecate and other Roman deities passed into popular fairylore and witchlore in the Middle Ages.[3] Another Roman lineage provides Douce with an original folklore disquisition when he follows the phrase in *Henry V*, '*figo* for thy friendship,' through the network of phallic symbols, gestures of disdain, and amulets against the evil eye depicting the gesture (the thumb thrust through two fingers). One plate shows a Spanish amulet displaying both the phallic hand and the Madonna and child, thus combining the potency of Roman and Christian cultures.[4]

Two 'dissertations' of folklore interest follow the Shakespeare notes. In the first, 'On the Gesta Romanorum,' a learned biblio-graphical argument leads to a summary of stories in the 'English gesta,' some with comparative notes that constitute an early listing of folktale variants in written literature. Commenting on the faithful dog who saves an infant from a serpent but is then mistakenly slain by his master, Douce points to an Eastern appearance in the *Fables of Pilpay*, and a Western appearance in the Welsh legend of Gelert.[5] One can appreciate why Scott, after reading this essay, called on its author to make the study of story migration which Keightley finally undertook.

The second treatise speculated 'On the Ancient English Morris Dance.' Strutt erred in disavowing its connection with Morisco

---

[1] Douce, *Illustrations of Shakespeare*, I, ix.   [2] *Ibid.*, pp. 3–5, 15–17.
[3] *Ibid.*, pp. 383–94.   [4] *Ibid.*, pp. 492–501.
[5] Stith Thompson, *Motif-Index of Folk Literature*, B331.2, 'Llewellyn and his dog.'

(Moorish) dances; he overstated its linkage with the May games of Robin Hood.[1] Douce here shows the breadth of a catholic folklorist, for none of his colleagues brought folk dance within their purview.

Soured at carping criticisms of his one major effort, Douce retired to his library and bestowed its rich resources on friends pursuing the intricate trails of wandering fictions.

[4 THOMAS WRIGHT]

In a discursive essay 'On Dr Grimm's German Mythology,' written as a review article and republished in book form in 1846, an antiquary wrote these appreciative words:

> There is no subject of inquiry relating to the history of a people more interesting than its popular mythology and superstitions. In these we trace the early formation of nations, their identity or analogy, their changes, as well as the inner texture of the national character, more deeply than in any other circumstances, even in language itself. It has been brought before us in all its generality by the *Mythologie* of Dr. Jacob Grimm, one of the most admirable books that Germany has ever sent us.[2]

Thomas Wright (1810–77) could speak with some authority, for he knew familiarly the medieval literature in which were imbedded relics of pagan folk belief, and he himself shared the Grimms' interest in popular traditions. In his complimentary essay he grasped precisely Jacob Grimm's key concept, the carry-over and partial blending of Germanic with Christian supernaturalism among the peasantry, and provided his own examples from unpublished Anglo-Saxon documents. These early Christian writings condemned heathen idolaters, like the man who, 'deceived by the illusion of hobgoblins, believes and confesses that he goes or rides in the company of her whom the foolish peasantry call Herodias or Diana, and with immense multitude, and that he obeys her commands.'[3] By considering these folk practices which the monks condemned, and abstracting others which they absorbed, like the pranks of the Devil, one could reconstruct the pagan mythology.

---

[1] The current interpretation subordinates Moors and Robin Hood to origins in fertility ritual; see Gertrude Kurath on 'Morris' and 'Morisca' in the *Standard Dictionary of Folklore, Mythology, and Legend* (New York, 1950), II, 750, 747.

[2] Thomas Wright, *Essays on Subjects connected with the Literature, Popular Superstitions, and History of England in the Middle Ages* (London: John Russell Smith, 1846), I, 237.   [3] *Ibid.*, p. 243.

This method of Jacob Grimm, which Wright and his fellow antiquaries so greatly admired, steered into allied channels much of Wright's own work.

Wright perfectly typifies the early Victorian antiquary-scholar, with his prodigious output, his sweeping range of interests in the records of the past from literature to artifacts, and his vigorous espousal of learned societies. One hundred and twenty-nine titles in the British Museum catalogue carry his name; he served as secretary of both the Camden and Percy societies for many years, editing numerous volumes in their behalf, and founded several abortive enterprises, such as a Historical Society of Science and the *Archaeologist and Journal of Antiquarian Science*. On these two projects he worked jointly with a friend from Cambridge days, James Orchard Halliwell (later Halliwell-Phillips), destined to become a reputed Shakespearean scholar, but also with a flair for folklore. These antiquarian and literary societies brought potential folklorists in touch with each other; we find Wright, Halliwell, Croker, and Thoms serving as council members for the Percy Society in 1845, while the founding group of the British Archaeological Association, in 1843, included Wright, Croker, Thomas Pettigrew, who the next year published a volume on medical superstitions, and Charles Roach Smith, a diligent archaeologist who conducted a column on antiquities in the *Gentleman's Magazine*.[1] In Croker especially Wright found a brotherly spirit, and he edited posthumous issues of Croker's *Fairy Legends* and Killarney legends. His introduction to the fairy volume praised its accuracy and value for historical and ethnological study.[2] In his *History of Ireland* (1854), Wright expressed his debt to Croker's '*remarkably interesting* private museum of Irish antiquities.'

Wright's own folklore writings carry the marks of his antiquarian brand of scholarship. They cover a variety of topics— Robin Hood ballads and legends of Purgatory, witchcraft narratives and saints' miracles—with a broad, rather than deep, erudition. The extended review and the piecemeal essay form his customary expression, and the fully developed treatment of a branch of folklore, like Keightley's *Fairy Mythology*, never emerges. His two volumes of *Narratives of Sorcery and Magic from the most authentic sources* merely paraphrase the grim and frightful documents on which they rely, and their contribution lies in the editorial assem-

[1] Charles Roach Smith, *Retrospections: Social and Archaeological*, 3 vols. (London, 1883, 1886, 1891), speaks of both Wright and Croker in some detail. See especially I, 76–85, 251–7.
[2] T. Crofton Croker, *Fairy Legends and Traditions of the South of Ireland*, ed. T. Wright (London, 1862), p. iv.

bling of English witchcraft episodes from late medieval and Reformation times.

Wright's most considerable contribution to folklore lies in his collected *Essays on Subjects connected with the Literature, Popular Superstitions, and History of England in the Middle Ages.* Half of the twenty essays deal with folk traditions, usually rooted in the twelfth and thirteenth centuries but enduring to modern times. Medieval letters branched into popular lore with the twelfth-century chronicles of 'The Cambrian Giraldus, Gervase of Tilbury, William of Newbury, and several others, [who] give us so much curious information on the popular mythology of their time. . . .'[1] The fairy *Sagen* in the chronicles and saints' legends extended both ways in time; they could be pushed back to the elf-creatures of Anglo-Saxon belief, *à la* Grimm, and traced forward to the oral tales of the living peasantry, and Wright reflected along both lines. Much of his writing pivots about this central idea, the persistence of Teutonic-Saxon demonology through successive cultural overlays—the historical approach to folklore that Gomme would later work out in detailed time sequences. Writing, like Douce and Halliwell, 'Of the National Fairy Mythology of England,' Wright charts a whole chronology of demon lore. The Anglo-Saxon monsters of Beowulf re-emerge in the devils of the medieval monks; French verse, Greek and Italian tales, astrology and witchcraft all contribute in later centuries to the spirit world of today's peasant. Wright reiterates this theme in 'Friar Rush and the Frolicsome Elves,' which follows the thread of the elfin character through its shifting forms, in the fire-dragons of Beowulf, the elves of the saints' legends, and the fairies of the romances. Elsewhere he sees in English folk wizards of the high Middle Ages, like Eustace the monk and Fulke Fitz Warine the outlaw, generic figures of popular lore; Robin Hood merely served as a new peg for traditional ballad exploits previously attached to similar characters.[2] Because the oral tales that always exist can be viewed only at certain points in time when they have accidentally lodged in manuscripts, to be coloured by scribes, their continuity escapes notice. Here Wright displays a firm grasp of folk material in recognizing the literary corruption of oral tradition. Peasant tales about goblins and boggarts he prefers to the monkish chronicles and metrical romances, with their Christian and courtly additions, as mirrors of ancient belief. And he illustrates with a Welsh devil tale he himself had

[1] Wright, *op. cit.*, II, 12.
[2] *Ibid.*, in the essays on 'The Story of Eustace the Monk,' 'The History of Fulke Fitz Warine,' and 'On the Popular Cycle of the Robin Hood Ballads.'

heard—of how Morgan Jones fooled Satan by presenting his fowling piece to the Fiend as a pipe and pulling the trigger—a genuine folktale still current.[1]

Wright probes with the comparative as well as the historical method. Beginning modestly, he picks up a collection of modern Greek superstitions (written in Latin), notes the likeness of *naragidae* with fairies and *callicantzara* to changelings, and concludes by comparing Greek and Yorkshire tempest-dragons.[2] And a volume on French traditions leads him to correlate Bayeux and English superstitions.[3] That these parallels in the lore of two countries might be pushed to broad conclusions Wright finally realized in his most important folklore essay, 'On the History and Transmission of Popular Stories.' Lacking field collections from which to speculate, he perceives nevertheless the eastern provenance of many tales that drift westward on the lips of Saracen jongleurs, or through medieval translations and monkish collections of moral anecdotes. To the *Gesta Romanorum* he pays special due, for funnelling classic and Oriental fictions into Renaissance Europe. Wright drives home his point with comparative variants which show the loss of cultural meaning when an Indian story moves west. A countryman takes a lamb to market; six sharpers lined up at intervals ask him how much he is asking for his dog; eventually he becomes convinced that it is a dog and sells it at a low price. Transferred to the Western world, the hoax loses its original point —that Hindus regard the dog as unclean.[4]

Wright understands the oral as well as the literary movement of folktales. He concludes his essay with three examples of the same trickster narrative from twelfth-century Germany, sixteenth-century France, and contemporary Ireland (Samuel Lover's story of 'Great Fairly and Little Fairly'). Literary borrowing seems unlikely here, so the tale 'must have been preserved in all these countries traditionally. The fables and legends now current among the peasantry are the fictions of the middle ages.' Wright has discerned a genuine folktale, 'The Clever Boy.'[5] Elsewhere he recognizes the oral quality of manuscript Latin stories,[6] and

---

[1] Wright, *op. cit.*, pp. 34–7. (This is Type 1157, 'The Gun as Tobacco Pipe'; see my *Bloodstoppers and Bearwalkers* [Cambridge, 1952], pp. 143–4, 200 n., for a Finnish-American example.)
[2] *Ibid.*, I, 283–304.   [3] *Ibid.*, p. 126.
[4] *Cf.* Stith Thompson, *Motif-Index of Folk Literature* (6 vols.; Bloomington, 1955–1958), J2300, 'Gullible Fools,' e.g., J2317, 'Well man made to believe that he is sick.'
[5] This is Type 1542 in the Aarne-Thompson type-index. (A version in the French-Canadian tradition was told me by Willard Truckey in Marquette, Michigan, in 1946.)
[6] *A Selection of Latin Stories, from manuscripts of the thirteenth and fourteenth centuries,*

unerringly inserts into a social history of the Middle Ages the folk-tale we now know as 'The Obstinate Wife.'[1]

Sometimes Wright's scholarship gets blurred by his anti-Catholic rage—an emotion characteristic of the early antiquarians—and he assails the clergy for deluding the peasants with miracles and saints' legends: saints are invested with the attributes of pagan folk heroes to awe the populace.[2] Wright's preface to his monograph on *St. Patrick's Purgatory* becomes at times a diatribe against papal Rome for corrupting the 'pure religion of the gospel' with vulgar beliefs.[3] Likewise, in the foreword to *Narratives of Sorcery and Magic*, he accuses the Roman church of nursing barbarous folk ideas, that it might charge its enemies with devil worship.[4] In his wrath Wright demoted the churchman to a position beneath the heathen. 'Thus, while the unconverted Saxon revered the barrow, because he believed that it was from time to time revisited by the spirit of its tenant, the English monk, with a grosser superstition, worshipped the bones, the last mouldering witnesses of his mortality.'[5] The irate antiquary failed to consider that Protestantism also generated folklore in divine providence and devilish witchcraft. In the next generation, Clodd, the freethinker, would rend The Folk-Lore Society with a similar analysis of superstition hidden in Christian ritual.

Wright's solid editorial labours bequeathed to folklore a number of medieval writings strewn with legends and popular tales. He edited the histories both of Giraldus Cambrensis and Walter Map, twelfth-century chroniclers with a flair for the marvellous;[6] *A Selection of Latin Stories*, in whose introduction he restated his views on Eastern origins and the popular basis of medieval tales; the popular legend of St. Brandan, in which he saw some similarity with Sinbad;[7] a manuscript copy of *The Seven Sages*, a medieval

[1] Thomas Wright, *A History of Domestic Manners and Sentiments in England During the Middle Ages* (London, 1832), pp. 287–8. The tale is Type 1365.
[2] See Thomas Wright, 'On Saints' Lives and Miracles,' *Essays on Archaeological Subjects* (London, 1861), I, 227–67.
[3] Thomas Wright, *St. Patrick's Purgatory; an essay on the legends of Purgatory, Hell, and Paradise, current during the Middle Ages* (London, 1844), pp. v–vii.
[4] Thomas Wright, *Narratives of Sorcery and Magic, from the most Authentic Sources*, 2nd ed. (London, 1851), I, vi–vii. [5] Wright, 'On Saints' Lives and Miracles,' p. 237.
[6] *The Historical Works of Giraldus Cambrensis*, rev. and ed. Thomas Wright (London, 1883); *Gualteri Mapes De Nugis Curialium*, ed. Thomas Wright (Camden Society, 1850).
[7] *St. Brandan: A Medieval Legend of the Sea, in English Verse and Prose*, ed. Thomas Wright, Percy Society, No. 48 (London, 1844).

ed. Thomas Wright, Percy Society, No. 28 (London, 1842), pp. viii–ix: '. . . many of these tales appear to have been taken down from oral recitation, and they seem to have been transmitted by a similar medium to later ages.'

Arabian Nights stemming from India;[1] and, among more fugitive pieces, two fourteenth-century poems, 'The Tale of the Basyn' and 'The Frere and the Boy,' which were in effect versified legends. Wright's preface to these poems typifies his approach to folklore:

> Our earlier ballads and stories illustrative of the popular superstitions and mythology are however scarce, and, when we meet with them, are worthy of preservation. I am sure, therefore, that no excuse will be necessary for printing, in preference to many other curious poems, two of the most generally popular of our tales of magic and enchantment in the earliest forms that we at present know.

Wright traces their literary history as black-letter and broadside ballads, penny chapbooks, and peasant *Märchen* in Grimm, and notes how monk became Quaker and friar becomes Jew in different cultural contexts. In his volume on Christian legends of the upper and lower worlds, *St. Patrick's Purgatory*, Wright performs an editorial service in bringing together summaries of the legendary visions of Purgatory scattered through medieval literature. He reiterates his theses, that saints' legends of the Church owe much to the fairy legends of the peasantry, and that popular oral lore, largely subterranean, underlies the seemingly isolated literary production with folk motifs—in this case, of course, Dante's *Divine Comedy*. Thomas Wright understood the folklore content of the thinly Christianized chronicles, poems, and hagiography of the Middle Ages, and his remarks thereon can still be read with profit.

[5 JAMES ORCHARD HALLIWELL-PHILLIPPS]

A mercurial and tempestuous personality, James Orchard Halliwell (1820–89; he became Halliwell-Phillipps in 1872) was in his early career an enthusiastic devotee of 'antiquarian literature.' He collaborated closely with Thomas Wright, ten years his senior, whom he met at Cambridge University, and became his benefactor during Wright's difficult later years. The many sides of Halliwell's life and activities call for detailed treatment. A prodigy, who published his first book, a study of a mathematician, at eighteen, he was elected at that age a Fellow of both the Society of Antiquaries and the Royal Society. Off to a whirlwind start as rare book and

[1] *The Seven Sages, in English Verse* (from MS, University of Cambridge), ed. Thomas Wright, Percy Society, No. 53 (London, 1845); *Introduction to the Seven Sages*, ed. Thomas Wright, Percy Society, No. 64 (London, 1846).
[2] *The Tale of the Basyn and The Frere and the Boy, Two early tales of magic*, ed. Thomas Wright (London, 1836).

manuscript collector, organizer and participant in antiquarian societies, prolific editor and scholar, at twenty-four Halliwell fell into disgrace, charged with the theft of manuscripts from Trinity College, Cambridge. His marriage in 1842 to the daughter of Sir Thomas Phillipps led to bitter estrangement from his father-in-law, an astringent character, himself the match of Halliwell. Phillipps objected to the precarious financial position of the young scholar, who was obliged to keep selling his collections to meet his debts.[1] Not until his wife's inheritance upon the death of her father in 1867 was Halliwell's position eased.

Although Halliwell lived well into the heyday of the anthropological folklore school, from the 1840's on he became increasingly occupied with Shakespearean research, and his folkloristic period belongs to the years before mid-century. He edited numerous reprints for the Camden, Percy, and Shakespeare societies, and issued with Wright in 1841-2 ten numbers of *The Archaeologist and Journal of Antiquarian Science*. Ranging over many forms of popular literature, he often touched on folklore subjects.

His major folklore publications fell under the head of traditional rhymes. *The Nursery Rhymes of England, collected principally from oral tradition,* which he first published in 1842 for the Percy Society, found a responsive audience quite outside scholarly circles, reaching a fifth edition by 1853. Indeed, there was little meat for antiquaries; Halliwell was content to print most of the familiar verses without comment, with only a few short notes to heighten interest in certain rhymes. Halliwell recognized in the last pair of some nonsense lines given him by a Professor de Morgan in Dorsetshire a quotation from a fifteenth-century manuscript (reprinted by Halliwell and Wright in their *Reliquiae Antiquae*):

> In fir tar is,
> In oak none is,
> In mud eel is,
> In clay none is.
> Goat eat ivy,
> Mare eat oats.[2]

In our time the last two lines have stimulated a popular song.

The political implications of some nursery jingles intrigued Halliwell. In one he perceived an obsolete sense of the word 'tory,'

[1] The breakdown of relations between Phillipps and Halliwell is traced by A. N. L. Munby in *The Family Affairs of Sir Thomas Phillipps* (Cambridge: at the University Press, 1952), pp. 37-53.

[2] James Orchard Halliwell, *The Nursery Rhymes of England*, 4th edition (London: John Russell Smith, 1846), LXXXIX, p. 47.

which had once signified a bog-trotting rascal; and he referred for particulars to Crofton Croker's *Researches in the South of Ireland.*

> Ho! Master Teague, what is your story?
> I went to the wood and kill'd a *tory*;
> I went to the wood and kill'd another;
> Was it the same, or was it his brother?
> I hunted him in, and I hunted him out,
> Three times through the bog, about and about;
> When out of a bush I saw his head,
> So I fired my gun, and I shot him dead.[1]

These matters of origin and interpretation occupied Halliwell far more in a sequel volume of 1849, *Popular Rhymes and Nursery Tales*, which joined Aubrey's *Miscellanies* and Brand's *Popular Antiquities*—quoted regularly in its pages—as an indispensable title for the new breed of folklorist. Ray, Grose, Hone, Douce, and Thoms also enter his notes.

Much more than a collection, the *Popular Rhymes* offered historical and comparative analysis of its verses and tales. It amplified the scope of the earlier rhyme-book with a section of nineteen folktales, obtained both from oral sources and from chapbooks. The chapter rubrics were now much tighter and more definitive: Nursery Antiquities, Fireside Nursery Stories, Game-Rhymes, Alphabet-Rhymes, Riddle-Rhymes, Nature-Songs, Proverb-Rhymes, Places and Families, Superstition-Rhymes, Custom-Rhymes, and Nursery-Songs. Halliwell conceded his debt to Robert Chambers' 'elegant work,' *The Popular Rhymes of Scotland* (1826), but also stressed the differences in content. Together the two 'vernacular anthologies' contained nearly all that was worth preserving of 'the natural literature of Great Britain.'

In the *Popular Rhymes* Halliwell called attention to 'Nursery Antiquities,' the somewhat paradoxical title of his opening chapter. With persuasive evidence, he urged the venerable age of many trivialities found on children's lips. This 'nursery traditional literature' formed a part of 'vernacular rural literature,' and needed no apology on aesthetic grounds; Sir Walter Scott himself had expressed his preference for these inherited rhymes and tales over the 'prosaic good-boy stories' now dished out for the moral edification of English youth.

To establish the antiquity of household jingles and legends, Halliwell had recourse to sixteenth- and seventeenth-century manuscripts he knew so well. By citing Aubrey's 'Remaines of

---

[1] *The Nursery Rhymes of England,* 5th ed. (London, 1853), XIV, p. 7.

[68]

Gentilisme' he was able to show that a bit of doggerel had circulated for two hundred years, having once been part of a game called 'leap-candle,' in which girls danced over a candle on the floor chanting:

> The tailor of Biciter,
> He has but one eye,
> He cannot cut a pair of green galagaskins,[1]
> If he were to die.[2]

In Aubrey's *Miscellanies* of 1696 Halliwell found a precedent for this rhyming proverb of ominous import:

> When Easter falls in our Lady's-lap,
> Then let England beware a rap.[3]

And again Aubrey gave him the clue, along with Gough's edition of Camden's *Britannia*, to the legend connected with the plant called Danes'-blood or Danewort. The plant derived its names from the battle between the Danes and the Anglo-Saxons at Sherston in 1016, when the blood of the Danes stained the battlefield and coloured the plant. A fabled warrior known as Rattlebone distinguished himself that day, and was memorialized in rhyme. Eight centuries after, schoolboys seeing his statue chanted:

> Fight on, Rattlebone,
> And thou shalt have Sherstone;
> If Sherstone will not do,
> Then Easton Grey and Pinkney too.

Supposedly this promise was made to Rattlebone by his king.[4]

These examples illustrate Halliwell's technique of uncovering the adult historical and political implications behind a child's innocuous rhyme. Like Chambers, he was attracted by the rhymed verses which summarized a legend, preserved a ballad, spiced a game, enclosed a charm, or expressed a proverb or riddle. A little couplet or quatrain recited in the home might thus open out into an antique and meaningful tradition. Since fairies always spoke in rhyme, as Halliwell notes, a simple jingle often led into fairy mythology:

> Oh, lend a hammer and a nail,
> Which we want to mend our pail.

---

[1] *Galagaskins:* wide, loose trousers.
[2] Halliwell, *Popular Rhymes and Nursery Tales* (London: John Russell Smith, 1849), p. 16. See also *Nursery Rhymes* (4th ed., 1846), CCCCIV, p. 186.
[3] *Popular Rhymes and Nursery Tales*, p. 184.
[4] *Popular Rhymes and Nursery Tales*, 'Sherston Magna,' pp. 198–9.

A Devonshire pixy made this request of a Worcestershire ploughman, according to Halliwell's source, Jabez Allies. The incident thus fell within the large class of stories about fairies offered presents.[1]

To trace the ancestry of his rhymes, Halliwell resorted to archaic words and historical allusions within the verses, or to references to popular jingles made by poets of old. A 'very curious ballad' entitled 'Namby Pamby,' written about 1720 and in the possession of Crofton Croker, helped confirm the age of such favourite game-rhymes as 'London Bridge is broken down' and a string of others. Shakespeare, Herrick, John Heywood yielded fragments of nursery literature. Many a popular enigma or jest of the moment had enjoyed its round of popularity in previous times, Halliwell was quick to point out, ridiculing the claim that they were new inventions or American imports:

> To revert to the lengthened transmission of jokes, I may mention my discovery of the following in MS. Addit. 5008, in the British Museum, a journal of the time of Queen Elizabeth. The anecdote, by some means, went the round of the provincial press in 1843, as of modern composition. 'On a very rainy day, a man, entering his house, was accosted by his wife in the following manner: "Now, my dear, while you are wet, go and fetch me a bucket of water." He obeyed, brought the water and threw it all over her, saying at the same time, "Now, my dear, while you are wet, go and fetch another!" ' [2]

The long section in the *Popular Rhymes* on 'Fireside Nursery Stories' was the first to present the English folktale as a distinct form of antiquarian literature. Halliwell garnered a third of his sheaf of eighteen tales from word-of-mouth, and for the rest chose chapbook narratives apparently close to oral variants. In the latter class fell 'Jack and the Giants,' 'Tom Hickathrift,' and 'Puss in Boots,' and by printing them he hoped to elicit living instances of 'the traditional tale as related by the English peasantry.' Lacking a complete text, he took unjustifiable liberties, surrounding with his own words the rhymes which, he saw at once, obviously fitted into the tale of 'The Frog King and Iron Henry,' collected by the

---

[1] *Popular Rhymes and Nursery Tales*, p. 190. The work of Jabez Allies, *On the Ancient British, Roman, and Saxon Antiquities of Worcestershire* (London, 1840), has nothing on folklore, but the greatly expanded edition of 1852 adds *and Folk-lore* after *Antiquities*. The rhyme is given on p. 419. Halliwell obviously saw it in the pamphlet Allies published in 1846, *Folk-lore, on the Ignis Fatuus, or Will-o'-the-Wisp, and the Fairies*, reprinted with additions in the second edition (London and Worcester, 1852), pp. 409–70.

[2] *Popular Rhymes and Nursery Tales*, p. 154.

1. FRANCIS GROSE

2. WILLIAM HONE

Grimms and Chambers, and commented on by Scott, who believed the enchanted frog originally to have been a crocodile. But the few oral tales he did gather in full—'Lazy Jack' from Yorkshire, 'The Story of Mr. Vinegar,' and 'The Princess of Canterbury' from the West—hinted at further riches.

Besides the collections of rhymed lore, Halliwell edited dictionaries of dialect words and reprints of jestbooks, ballads, and fairy beliefs, all with a bearing on folklore. In *Illustrations of the Fairy Mythology of A Midsummer Night's Dream*, which he published for the Shakespeare Society in 1845, he assembled thirty-nine extracts from diverse literary sources dealing with the fairy creed prior to and during Shakespeare's time. This project joined two of his central interests, folklore and Shakespeare, and marks a transition from the first to the second. In the *Popular Rhymes* he conjectured that 'Shakespeare, who has alluded so much and so intricately to the vernacular rural literature of his day, has more notices of nursery-rhymes and tales than research has hitherto elicited,' although he could only identify one, the indelicate verse in *King Lear* beginning 'Pillicock sat on Pillicock hill.'[1] His aim in the *Illustrations* was to uncover the themes of the Elizabethan fairy tradition on which Shakespeare drew and to which he coupled his own inventive fancy.

The resulting compendium placed on record valuable source materials, chosen from metrical romances, chapbooks, poems, songs, plays, manuscripts, tracts, and pamphlets. They ran the gamut from the poetic compositions of Michael Drayton and Robert Herrick to literal accounts of fairy beings observed in Cornwall, Wiltshire, the Isle of Man, and Ireland. For these direct reports of fairy behaviour the editor relied on Aubrey's manuscript histories of Wiltshire and Surrey, George Waldron's *The History and Description of the Isle of Man* (1726), one of Brand's favourite hunting grounds, and Joseph Ritson's *Fairy Tales* (1831), a venture comparable to Halliwell's, but without the specific Shakespearean focus. A rare pamphlet in the British Museum provided Halliwell with 'a very interesting document in the history of Fairy Mythology.' Its title told the story: *Strange and Wonderful News from the county of Wicklow in Ireland, or, a Full and True Relation of what happened to one Dr Moore (late Schoolmaster in London). How he was taken invisibly from his friends, what happened to him in his absence, and how and by what means he was found, and brought back to the same Place. (With Allowance).* London, printed for T. K., 1678. The editor did not draw into a conclusive essay the inferences

[1] *Ibid.*, p. 14.

present in his introductory notes. He pointed out that Shakespeare could have drawn the Puck–Robin Goodfellow character from folk tradition, but for romancing between a mortal and a fairy, evidence of tradition was practically non-existent, save for one scarce tract of 1613. It remained for Thoms, two years later, to write an essay on Shakespeare's debt to folklore.

An impressive production of this period relevant to folklore was *A Dictionary of Archaic and Provincial Words*, published by Halliwell in two thick volumes in 1847. It grew from his interest in Shakespeare's language, and he used for a model the *Glossary* prepared by Robert Nares in 1822 from notes to the variorum edition of Shakespeare.[1] Besides being itself a treasury of folk speech and provincialisms, the *Dictionary* contained a host of entries among its 51,027 words glossing traditional games, customs, foods, and beliefs. Under 'Fairy' he listed such expressions reminiscent of an older faith as *fairy-butter, fairy-circles, fairy-rings, fairy-darts, fairy-loaves, fairy-pipes, fairy-money*, applied to kinds of natural phenomena and local antiquities. Folk games came to light in archaisms like *barley-beak, cob-nut, kit-cat*. An intriguing note explained the sport of *Hunting-the-Wren*:

> The custom still prevalent in Ireland, the Isle of Man, and some other places, on St. Stephen's day, of hunting the wren, is one of very considerable antiquity. Its origin is only accounted for by tradition. Aubrey, having mentioned the last battle fought in the North of Ireland between the Protestants and the Papists, says:— 'Near the same place a party of the Protestants had been surprised sleeping by the Popish Irish, were it not for several wrens that just wakened them by dancing, and pecking on the drums as the enemy were approaching. For this reason the wild Irish mortally hate these birds to this day, calling them the devil's servants, and killing them whenever they catch them; they teach their children to thrust them full of thorns; you'll see sometimes on holidays a whole parish running like madmen from hedge to hedge wren-hunting. In the Isle of Man, on St. Stephen's Day, the children of the village procure a wren, attach it with a string to a branch of holly, decorate the branch with pieces of riband that they beg

---

[1] Robert Nares, *A Glossary; or, Collection of Words, Phrases, Names, and Allusions to Customs, Proverbs, etc. which have been thought to require illustration, in the works of English authors* (London, 1822). A new edition in two volumes was prepared by Halliwell and Thomas Wright in 1859.

from the various houses, singing the following ridiculous lines:—

> We'll hunt the wren, says Robin to Bobbin;
> We'll hunt the wren, says Richard to Robin;
> We'll hunt the wren, says Jack o' th' land;
> We'll hunt the wren, says every one.

Eight other verses followed. So a local expression led—with the help of the faithful Aubrey—into a historical legend, a holiday pastime, and a child's verse, neatly interwoven and sprinkled with anti-papist sentiment.

Halliwell depended on Aubrey in other instances, for the suggestive *cockel-bread*; *Cobloaf*, a crusty, uneven loaf stolen at Christmas; *Toms-of-bedlam*, mad vagabonds who roamed the country before the civil wars; and *ivy*. *Ivy* invoked a custom once observed in Oxfordshire permitting the maidservant to ask the manservant to dress the house with ivy, and if refused, to steal his breeches and nail them up on the yard gate.

Another service Halliwell rendered to popular literature was in reprinting early jestbooks, some unfortunately in absurdly small editions of twenty-six copies. He edited in this manner *The Jokes of the Cambridge Coffee Houses in the Seventeenth Century* (1841); *The Will of Wit . . . reprinted from the rare edition of 1599* (1860); and *Conceits, Clinches, Flashes, and Whimzies, a Jest-Book of the Seventeenth Century, hitherto unknown to Bibliographers, reprinted from the unique copy of 1639* (1860). Halliwell failed to trace the pedigrees of the humorous anecdotes whose lease on life he renewed, and, save for a few references to Thoms' *Anecdotes and Traditions*, suggested no variants. He did recognize one Cambridge jest as an ancient Greek story, told of a pedant by Hierocles. 'A poor scholar having almost been drowned in his first attempt at swimming, vowed that he would never enter the water again until he was a complete master of the art.'[1] Another seventeenth-century chestnut lives on today:

> A vagrant boy lying abroad in the street one winter's night, began crying 'Fire! Fire!' The people looked out of their windows, and asked 'Where! where!' 'I would I knew myself,' quoth the boy. 'for I would then go and warm myself.'[2]

---

[1] *The Jokes of the Cambridge Coffee-Houses in the Seventeenth Century*, edited by James Orchard Halliwell (Cambridge and London, 1841), p. 9, 'A Good Swimmer.'
[2] *Ibid.*, p. 19, 'A Patent Sto e.' A twentieth-century variant collected in northern Michigan, an elaborate version told on Cornish miners, can be found in my 'Dialect Stories of the Upper Peninsula,' *Journal of American Folklore*, LXI (1948), 127.

Later in the century, William Alexander Clouston would show the wide dispersion of slight comic fictions.

In the realm of ballad literature too, Halliwell reprinted antiquarian pieces. In a forty-page tract, *Ballads and Poems respecting Hugh of Lincoln. A boy alleged to have been murdered by the Jews in the year MCCLV* (1849), he juxtaposed nine recountings of the grisly episode fixed in ballad and legend. In the canon of English and Scottish popular ballads created by Francis James Child this is number 155. Halliwell also edited *Early Naval Ballads of England* (1841) and, with Thomas Wright, *Ancient Ballads and Broadsides published in England in the Sixteenth Century, chiefly in the earlier years of the reign of Queen Elizabeth* (1867). Although printed broadside ballads, these topical pieces sometimes drifted into oral remembrance, and their themes of monstrous births and walking ghosts reflected supernatural ideas of the seventeenth century.

The full record of Halliwelliana contains numerous items falling in the borderland between popular and oral literature.[1] Halliwell understood the oral basis of folklore, and when he had the chance, as on his walking trips through Cornwall and Wales, he listened for local legends. His ramble through Cornwall in 1861 was urged by a desire to see the antiquities described by William Borlase in his *Observations on the Antiquities Historical and Monumental, of the County of Cornwall* (1754), but in addition he wished to view this 'chosen Land of the Giants, as is asserted in our folk-lore,' in order to 'trace what now remain of the traditions respecting them.'[2] In the course of his tour he did set down some local traditions, about the cruelty of the Spanish invaders of 1595 and the power of pixies who dazzled travellers with sudden mists. But his best old wives' tales came from earlier antiquaries, like Borlase himself, telling of the Scillonian who believed he had raised a hurricane by digging up the Giants' Graves.[3] In writing up an excursion to northern Wales, Halliwell relied for legends far more on printed extracts than village conversation.[4] His master area lay not in the field but in the library, especially in the fugitive publications of the sixteenth and seventeenth centuries drenched in Tudor and Stuart folk notions.

[1] *Halliwelliana: a Bibliography of the Publications of James Orchard Halliwell-Phillipps* was published by Justin Winsor (Harvard Library Bibliographical Contributions, No. 10, Cambridge, Mass., 1881).
[2] J. O. Halliwell, *Rambles in Western Cornwall by the Footsteps of the Giants* (London: John Russell Smith, 1861), p. vii.
[3] *Ibid.*, pp. 157–9, 204, 226–32.
[4] J. O. Halliwell, *Notes of Family Excursions in North Wales* (London: printed for the author, 1860). When he does report a 'local tradition' of large stones let drop from her apron by a giant's wife, it is in paraphrase and without source (pp. 120–1).

[6 WILLIAM JOHN THOMS]

To describe the contents of a volume he had assembled in 1834, William John Thoms (1803–85) found it necessary to employ a variety of phrases. He called the book *Lays and Legends of Germany*, and presented it as first of a series for various nations, 'illustrative of their Traditions.' On the title page he quoted Sir John Malcolm: 'He who desires to be well acquainted with a people will not reject their Popular Stories or Local Superstitions.' In his introduction he referred to 'Old Wives Legends,' 'Fire-side Stories,' 'National Tales,' and 'Legendary Lore' as meriting philosophical reflection. Twelve years later, Thoms devised a short, crisp, suggestive, and all-inclusive term to replace these and other slippery synonyms doing duty to define the materials in which he was deeply engrossed: folk-lore.

A civil servant like his father, who had been a clerk in the Treasury, Thoms held successive posts that supported him without unduly encroaching on his freedom. He served as clerk in the secretary's office at Chelsea Hospital until 1845, then as clerk in the printed-paper office of the House of Lords until 1863, when he was given the congenial post of deputy librarian of the House, resigning because of advanced years in 1882. All the while he participated actively in the antiquarian societies, being elected a fellow of the Society of Antiquaries in 1838, and appointed secretary of the Camden Society the same year, a position he filled until 1872; he was also a council member of the Percy Society, and prepared reprint editions for both the Percy and the Camden.

In his pursuit of literary antiquities, Thoms was first and foremost an editor, of original editions, miscellanies, and departments in periodicals. His initial publication, *A Collection of Early Prose Romances* (3 vols., 1828), bring together, with the aid of Douce's library, 'scattered specimens of popular fiction' paralleling the metrical romances which Ellis, Joseph Ritson, and others had made known. These medieval narratives of such characters as 'Doctor Faustus,' 'Robert the Devyl,' 'Friar Rush,' and 'Friar Bacon' were often enough, as Thoms recognizes, founded on traditions and handed down without dependence on verse form. Eventually printed in popular chapbooks of the seventeenth and eighteenth centuries, they bulge with folklore elements of magical and miraculous, heroic and picaresque deeds and adventures, and clearly bear an affinity with wandering oral fictions. Thoms points out analogues to the legends of Vergil in the *Arabian Nights* and the French *fabliaux*, to Friar Rush in such comparable sprites as Robin

[75]

Goodfellow, Puck, the Scottish Red Cap, the Saxon Hudken, and the Norwegian Nisse, and he sees their resemblance to two of the *Household Tales* of the Grimms. His comments on 'Friar Bacon' emphasize the popular and folk character of its hero.

The history of Fryar Bacon as related in these pages, was probably written towards the close of the sixteenth century, and is we may suppose a collection of the various traditions respecting him which were current among all classes of the community when the narrative was compiled. Many of the incidents contained in it are widely diffused in other shapes, and the name of our hero has doubtless often been connected with them merely from their being mutual subjects of popular fable: but the Brazen Head and the wonderful Perspective Glass, which he is reported to have made, seem deserving of particular notice, though any credit which may be given to him for his exertions in constructing such a head, 'by the which hee would have walled England round with brass,' he will I fear have to share with so many who are said to have possessed similar skill in the construction of magical images that it will be considerably diminished.[1]

Reprinted and enlarged in 1858, as *Early English Prose Romances*, the set became a standard library item, and a writer in *Notes and Queries* referred to the 'familiar books which occupy a handy place not upon my shelves only or the shelves of antiquaries.'[2]

Turning from medieval romances to popular fictions generally, Thoms conceived a plan for a series to be titled *Lays and Legends of Various Nations*. The only volumes issued, all in 1834 and his rarest works, were for Germany, France, Spain, and Tartary. They were slight compilations of less than a hundred pages, save for Germany, which ran to three times the size of the others. In the introduction to the volume for Germany he sketched the intellectual background of the series. The examination of popular tales and legends in a philosophical spirit was a study of recent growth. Sir Walter Scott, in an oft-quoted passage from his notes to *The Lady of the Lake* (1810), had stated that a 'work of great interest might be compiled upon the origin of popular fiction and the transmission of similar tales from age to age, and from country to country; the mythology of one period would then appear to pass into the romance of the next century, and that into the nursery tale of the subsequent

---

[1] *A Collection of Early Prose Romances*, edited by William J. Thoms (3 vols.; London: William Pickering, 1828), I, 'The History of Friar Bacon,' p. iv.
[2] *Notes and Queries*, 2nd series, VII (June 11, 1859), 470.

ages.' Thoms regretted that his friend Douce, who was so well qualified, had not responded to Sir Walter's request, but it had stimulated Sir Francis Palgrave to write articles on 'The Antiquities of Nursery Literature' and 'Popular Superstitions of the Middle Ages' in the *Quarterly Review*, and had led to the graceful and ingenious volumes by Thomas Keightley, *Fairy Mythology* and *Tales and Popular Fictions*. Although Thoms might gently disagree with some of its conclusions, this latter work, issued in 1834, seemed indeed to fulfil Scott's desire. In the same breath should be mentioned Croker's estimable *Fairy Legends from the South of Ireland*, which had so gratified 'the antiquarian enquirer into the wide field of romantic fiction.' With the translation and notes to the 'German Popular Stories' of the Grimms (Thoms must be referring to the translation made by Edgar Taylor in that year) the select list of English works on legendary lore was complete.

Thoms now proposed to extend that list with his selections of national tales. He recognized the paucity of popular traditions available, and the reasons why, remarking how the French had neglected their fairylore, and sighing over opportunities lost by the narrow-minded type of antiquary.

How incurious are the majority of us, except on the subject which we deem the one all worthy of our attention. How many an antiquary, who has travelled miles to see a druidical monument, has cried 'Pish'—at the legend with which his peasant guide would illustrate it, when reflection would have told him, that under the garb of fiction the truth of history is frequently concealed. Cambray's Monumens Celtique is full of allusions to traditions, the particulars of which are for the most part studiously suppressed.[1]

Britain too was sadly neglected. How regrettable that none of the zealous inquirers into popular mythology—Palgrave or Keightley or Croker—had yet dedicated himself to the 'preservation of the Legends of our "*Father Land*".'[2] To this task Thoms now addressed himself, beseeching the readers of the *Lays and Legends of Germany* to send him, care of the publisher, George Cowie in the Strand, 'any inedited English Lays or Legends they might possess.' In the sister volume for Spain he referred to a Yorkshire story suggesting Shakespeare's *The Taming of the Shrew* ' . . . which we expect to be able to lay before our readers, among the curious stores which we

[1] *Lays and Legends of France* (London: George Cowie, 1834), p. vi n.
[2] *Lays and Legends of Germany* (London: George Cowie, 1834), p. viii.

have in reserve for them in the Lays and Legends of England.'[1] The book on which he had his heart set never appeared, and long after he published in the *Folk-Lore Record* (1879) four medieval legends sent him by Thomas Wright for inclusion in the unfinished work, which had lain for forty-five years among Thoms' papers.[2] Nor did the volumes announced in his notes for Greece, Denmark, Bohemia, and Ireland materialize.

The failure of the series was due not to any fault in the idea, which before the end of the century was executed successfully by German and French editors, but to its timing and method. In 1834 Thoms had little to choose from but literary and secondary writings based on folk themes, and appeals to book readers to send fresh materials to the publisher was not the way to build a network of regular correspondents; Thoms profited by the lesson. At that early date he could not cull from European field collections, save for Germany, and even so he complained at Edgar Taylor's translation of the *Kinder- und Hausmärchen* as too free, omitting homely expressions and repetitions, while the Grimms' *Deutsche Sagen* was not (and to this day still is not) translated into English, and lacked comparative notes. For France, Thoms resorted to the heroic poems and Norman *fabliaux* of the Middle Ages, for Spain to Southey's rendering of *Chronicle of the Cid*, for Tartary to Adolfus Bergmann's excursions in Tartary, loaned him by Sir Francis Palgrave. Thoms clearly favoured folk over literary versions, and sharply distinguished between the 'composed "Contes Tartares" of Thomas Simon Guevllette' and the 'genuine traditions' of Bergmann.

This abortive series should be remembered for its imaginative vision. Its editor perceived both the national and the comparative aspects of oral literature. He contrasted the vivacious and sportive character of the French tales with the horror-laden and witch-ridden atmosphere of the German legends; at the same time he remarked on the numerous resemblances, too close for coincidence, between fictions of East and West.[3]

Undeterred by the setback of this enterprise, Thoms continued his antiquarian researches. In *The Book of the Court* (1838), he considered the functions and prerogatives of the royal household. At times this aristocratic subject dipped into antiquities of the

---

[1] *Lays and Legends of Spain* (London: George Cowie, 1834), p. 54 n.

[2] 'Four Transcripts by the late Thomas Wright, F.S.A.,' communicated by William J., Thoms, F.S.A., *Folk-Lore Record*, II (1879), 165–79. Thoms proposed these be printed 'as a memorial of one who has in his numerous publications done so much to illustrate the folk-lore and early literature of England.' One tale, 'The Miller at the Professor's Examination,' is a variant of Type 924A.

[3] *Lays and Legends of Tartary* (London: George Cowie, 1834), p. 72 n.

people, as in the Court practice of distributing alms and bounty on Maundy Thursday preceding Good Friday. 'Maundy' presumably derived from the *maunds* or baskets containing the gifts, *maunds* coming from Latin 'mandatum' through Old French.

The following year Thoms brought out for the Camden Society *Anecdotes and Traditions, illustrative of Early English History and Literature.* He restricted his source to unpublished manuscripts in the British Museum, principally Aubrey's 'Remaines of Gentilisme and Judaisme.' Now he was on the trail of two distinct forms of folk material, the brief, personal tale and the country superstition. To defend his interest in these seeming trifles, he quotes the poet Robert Southey on anecdotes, in particular one about Cromwell in his youth quarrelling and punching Prince Charles in the nose, a story preserved by the Reverend Mark Noble as a tradition of Hinchinbrook. Southey observes, in his usual common-sense manner:

> Such anecdotes, relating to such a man, even though they may be of doubtful authenticity, are not unworthy of preservation. The fabulous history of every country is part of its history, and ought not to be omitted by later and more enlightened historians; because it has been believed at one time, and while it was believed it influenced the imagination, and thereby, in some degree, the opinions and character of the people. *Biographical Fables*, on the other hand, are worthy of notice, because they show in what manner the celebrity of the personage, in whose honour or dishonour they have been invented, has acted upon his countrymen.[1]

This admirable statement, though anathema to the scientific historian drawing his cleaver between fact and fable, was a joy to Thoms. One illustration can show how Thoms extracted historical information from the period anecdote. From the jest collection of Roger L'Estrange he printed a story about Queen Elizabeth, who was greeted by one in the crowd with 'God blesse your *Royall* Majestie!' and then with 'God blesse your *Noble* Grace!' 'Why, how now,' cried the Queen, 'am I tenne groates worse than I was e'en now?' Thoms explained that ten groats was the difference in value between the old ryal or royal and the noble, which were then reckoned at ten shillings and six shillings, eight pence, respectively.

---

[1] *Anecdotes and Traditions, illustrative of Early English History and Literature, derived from ms. sources* (London: printed for The Camden Society, 1839), pp. vi–vii. The story can be found in Mark Noble, *Memoirs of the Protectoral-House of Cromwell* (2nd ed.; Birmingham: printed by Pearson and Rollason, 1787), I, 94.

Thus for the pun, but the chief point of interest, Thoms added, was to see the transition from the title 'your Grace' to 'your Majesty' as the correct form of address for the English sovereign, during the later Tudor and early Stuart reigns.[1]

In his section on rural superstitions, drawn from Aubrey and from John Collet's diary of local customs, Thoms followed the path of earlier antiquaries. To an account of dressing wells with flowers, taken from Aubrey, he appended his favourite authorities, Jacob Grimm's *Deutsche Mythologie*, Brand-Ellis, and Hone, and supported their position that this was another case of Christianity adopting heathen rites.[2] Thoms felt that his materials offered fresh proofs to Grimm in his reconstruction of national mythology, and this service alone should justify publication of these humble anecdotes and traditions.

Once again Thoms made his obeisance to Jacob Grimm, in preparing *The History of Reynard the Fox, from the edition printed by Caxton in 1481. With notes, and an introductory sketch of the literary history of the romance*, by William J. Thoms, published for the Percy Society in 1844. The editor softened passages that seemed too coarse. In his introduction Thoms lauded Grimm's study of the medieval beast-fable, *Reinhart Fuchs* (1834), and endorsed the thesis that popular tales of speaking animals could not be satirical, whereas the literary fable elaborating on these tales was indeed a satire aimed at the laxness of court and clergy. Francis Douce told Thoms that he read *Reynard the Fox* to Mrs. Douce every Christmas, whereupon Thoms inquired if he skipped passages.

The year 1846 was to prove momentous. Two more books came out, editions of chapbook stories like those in the *English Prose Romances*, rewritten for children, under the titles *Gammer Gurton's Famous Histories* and *Gammer Gurton's Pleasant Stories*. Newly revised and amended, by Amb[rose] Mer[ton].[3] But these were not memorable, save for the pseudonym. It appeared again, under a letter printed in the *Athenaeum* for August 22, 1846, a letter which bore as a caption a word never before seen in print: 'FOLK-LORE.'

The *Athenaeum* was a leading weekly review of literature, science, and the arts, and a likely sounding board for Thoms' purposes. This was nothing less than using its readership to cast a net for the

---

[1] *Anecdotes and Traditions*, p. 66.
[2] *Ibid.*, pp. 92–3 n.
[3] The full titles are *Gammer Gurton's Famous Histories of Sir Guy of Warwick, Sir Bevis of Hampton, Tom Hickathrift, Friar Bacon, Robin Hood, and the King and the Cobbler*; and *Gammer Gurton's Pleasant Stories of Patient Grissel, The Princess Rosetta, & Robin Goodfellow, and Ballads of the Beggar's Daughter, The Babes in the Wood, and Fair Rosamond* (Westminster, 1846).

traditions he now termed 'folk-lore.' Thoms-Merton had selected his medium carefully. 'Your pages have so often given evidence,' he began, 'of the interest which you take in what we in England designate as Popular Antiquities, or Popular Literature. . . .' He then drew a breath and in a parenthetical aside unveiled his brain child: '(though by-the-bye it is more a Lore than a Literature, and would be most aptly described by a good Saxon compound, Folk-Lore,—*The Lore of the People*).' Back to the original plea: '. . . that I am not without hopes of enlisting your aid in garnering the few ears which are remaining, scattered over that field from which our forefathers might have gathered a goodly crop.'[1]

In a paragraph-long opening sentence he had named the field and charted its course. Thoms' letter has achieved a certain belated recognition,[2] but it can only be understood in the context of its intellectual origins. The document does not stand alone, but caps a movement with its own antiquity. Thoms knew intimately the work of his predecessors, and stated his ambition of accomplishing ten times more effectively through the pages of the *Athenaeum* what Hone had attempted in the *Every-Day Book*. For his theoretical goals Thoms referred to the second edition of Jacob Grimm's *Deutsche Mythologie* (1844), which he called one of the most remarkable books of the century. He hoped that some future Grimm would arise in England to reconstruct the ancient heathen mythology of Britain in the same brilliant fashion that Grimm had done from the thousand scattered fragments of superstitious belief still to be found. For instance, the *Deutsche Mythologie* treated the prophetic role of the cuckoo in popular mythology, and mentioned the notion that the cuckoo never sings until he has thrice eaten his fill of cherries. Recently 'Ambrose Merton' learned of a Yorkshire nursery rhyme illustrating this idea:

> Cuckoo, Cherry-tree,
> Come down and tell me
> How many years I have to live.

Each child then shook the tree, and the number of cherries that fell betokened the years of his life ahead. Brand-Ellis and Hone had failed to describe the custom connected with the rhyme, but the full performance, as Grimm had often demonstrated, might well offer the key to an ancient heathen rite.

In his letter the following week, in the now established depart-

---

[1] *Athenaeum*, August 22, 1846 (No. 982), 'Folk-Lore,' pp. 862–3.
[2] It was, for instance, reprinted by Duncan Emrich in his article ' "Folk-Lore": William John Thoms,' *California Folklore Quarterly*, V (1946), 355–74.

ment of 'Folk-Lore,' Thoms invoked Grimm to illustrate the philological method of tracing the mythological roots of folklore. The question was, what signified 'Old Scratch' as a euphemism for the Devil? Brand suggests it means the Devil can appear only in the shape of an old man; but Grimm follows the name through High German monuments to a sprite known as the Schrat, who is described in an old German poem (included by the Grimms in their 'Essay on the Irish Legends,' translated in the third volume of Croker's *Fairy Legends of the South of Ireland*). So, as in the case of the innocent cuckoo rhyme, a sliver of pagan mythology is uncovered.

Even if Brand erred on this point, Thoms tenders homage to 'that huge mass of imperfectly digested materials which may be said to constitute the text book of the students of our English "Folk-Lore," Brand's "Popular Antiquities"....'[1] Already he had quoted from Keightley's *The Fairy Mythology* and from Shakespeare to assert the vitality of the fairy belief in English popular lore. So in his first two letters Merton-Thoms made plain his special debts: to Brand and Hone, Croker and Keightley, and the incomparable Grimms.

For the special studies of these antiquaries and mythologists Thoms had now devised an appropriate label which would, he hoped, catch the attention of the intellectually curious. Four times in his initial letter did he employ the term, and made sure that his readers knew the neologism was his: '... remember I claim the honour of introducing the epithet Folk-Lore ... into the literature of this country.' But he aspired to be more than a name-coiner; he wished to father a new field of learning.

The instrument to cultivate this field would be the regular department devoted to folklore and open to contributors. When Thoms first presented his plan, Charles Wentworth Dilke, editor of the *Athenaeum*, accepted it sympathetically—on condition that the genial antiquary do the screening and pruning—a condition that must have delighted, if it did not actually originate with, Thoms. A cautious postscript appended to 'Ambrose Merton's' letter, presumably by Dilke, reveals his deliberations before agreeing to open columns to 'valuable salvage for the future historian of old customs and feelings.' He fears a deluge of trivia, and warns readers to keep their communications short, and rarely indeed to exceed two columns. The success of the venture would depend upon whether 'our antiquarian correspondents be earnest and well-informed.' All

---

[1] *Athenaeum*, August 29, 1846 (No. 983), 'The Epithet "Old Scratch",' p. 887.

contributions would be carefully sifted, 'both as regards value, authenticity, and novelty.'

Even before their baptism, the materials of folklore had appeared in the pages of the *Athenaeum*, and the same folio page on which Thoms' letter commenced was given over, in happy juxtaposition, to a book review quoting meaty passages on Manx omens, fairy doctors, and inaugural rites of the kings and judges of old. A perspicuous editor, especially one catering in good part to the membership of antiquarian societies, could see about him the tides running in support of Thoms' proposals.

Thoms took his editorial supervision seriously, as we see in a comment he made in his column for September 19, 1846.

> We have retrenched those portions of R. P.'s communication which treated of generalities only. That there is a vast body of 'traditionary lore' floating among our peasantry, cannot be doubted. Our object in opening our columns to communications on the subject of Folk-Lore was, not to establish that fact, but to collect the legendary fragments themselves. The 'many stories' told to R. P. are what we are desirous of preserving— not the fact that they were so told.

Actual texts, not vague allusions, were desired, and Thoms had his problem getting this thought home. He continues his instructions—just as Hone did—in his columns for October 17, where he informs correspondents writing about local feasts to specify the day of consecration of the parish church, and the saint to whom it was dedicated; and in transmitting old words and popular phrases, which are 'proper subjects for Folk-Lore communications,' to give full title and page references to their source. To suggest specific topics of 'Popular Mythology and Observances' which readers might seek, in his second letter Thoms listed rural feasts, fairy legends, Devonshire pixies, the Essex spectral coach drawn by headless horses, the foolish men of Coggeshall, the Cornish magistrate Tregeagle, the Yorkshire barguest. First to respond was his antiquary friend from the Camden Society, John Bruce, in the issue for September 5, discussing 'Medical Superstitions—the Ash-tree.' Bruce wrote about the folk remedy for curing a child with rickets by passing him through a split ash which was then swathed and plastered over with loam; if the tree healed, the child would recover. Bruce speculates whether this and cognate 'passing through' cures indicate a ceremony of regeneration. He hopes that continental as well as British antiquaries will enter into 'mutual communication' on such matters, and he also desires that 'Mr. Merton' will give the

[83]

substance of Grimm's collections that bear on this or any other subject.

As might be expected, Thoms lost no time in replying to what seems like a planted query, and the following week cites the *Deutsche Mythologie* at length, finding a reference to Benjamin Thorpe's *Ancient Laws and Institutes of England* (1840) forbidding 'tree worshipings and stone worshipings and that devil's craft whereby children are drawn through the earth.' Now the department was well launched, with the whole apparatus of folklore investigation outlined: direct field observation, accurate reporting, communication of specific data, and then the comparative commentary by 'Merton,' if this were beyond the resources of the writer, tracing the custom or notion to its heathen lair with the aid of Grimm and the English antiquaries.

Some goodly prizes did swim into the net cast by Ambrose Merton. His query on Tregeagle brought a quick response, by September 5, with an extended discourse on the legends of Tregeagle, the Cornish magistrate endowed with diabolical powers; the signature H. belonged to Robert Hunt, whose copious collection of Cornish traditions was published in 1865. A Worcestershire antiquary, Jabez Allies, sent to Thoms a forty-six-page pamphlet he had written, *Ignis Fatuus, or Will-o'-the-Wisp, and the Fairies*, containing local reports of elfin beings. Thoms printed an extract in the department for September 17. One passage especially caught his eye, for it offered an English counterpart to the legend of the wild hunt, which Jacob Grimm had analysed at length in the *Deutsche Mythologie*.

The Seven Whistlers

Whether these were fairies, or wizards, or Fates, I cannot pretend to say; but I have been informed by Mr. John Presdee, late of Alfrick, and now of Worcester, that the country people, used to talk a good deal about the Seven Whistlers, when he was a boy, and that he frequently heard his late grandfather, John Presdee, who lived at Cuckold's Knoll, in Suckley, say that he oftentimes, at night, when he happened to be upon the hill by his house, heard six out of the Seven Whistlers pass over his head: but that no more than six of them were ever heard by him, or by any one else, to whistle at one time; and should the seven whistle together, the world would be at an end. This is a very remarkable legend;—and it is strange that such a fancy should have been credited down to nearly this our time. It probably took its rise either from the

[84]

occasional peculiar whistling of the wind, or from flights of wild fowl, such as plovers, widgeons, or teal, which do sometimes fly at night, and make a rather singular whistling noise.

As was by now his regular technique, refined through his 'Lays and Legends' series and the *Anecdotes and Traditions*, Thoms appended a scholarly comment to explain the significance of the tradition in Teutonic mythology. Characteristically he alluded to a German *Märchen* and *Sage* to illustrate by analogy its pagan ideas.

This remarkable legend, as Mr. Allies very properly designates it, is clearly connected with two curious points in Popular Mythology:—one, that which represents the departed soul as flying away in the shape of a bird—an instance of which the reader will remember in the pathetic story of 'The Juniper Tree,' in the translation of the 'Kinder- und Haus-Märchen,' where the spirit of Margery's little brother, whom his stepmother had so cruelly put to death, flies from the Juniper Tree in the likeness of a bird. The second point of connexion is with that extensive class of legends relating to what is known in this country as the Wild Host,—of which the Wild Huntsman, in 'Der Freyschütz,' is perhaps the most familiar type. In one of the German legends quoted by Grimm, from Otmar's 'Collection,' mention is made of a spirit called Tutosel, or *Toot-Owl*, said to have been a nun; who, after her death, was, for some crime, condemned to associate with the Wild Hunstman,—and who is ofttimes heard in the air, where she joins her tooting, or whistling '*uhu*,' to his well-known and dreaded cry.[1]

The relation with Allies bore fruit, and when Allies reissued his 1840 work on the antiquities of his county, the new edition of 1852 included the term 'folklore' in its title, *On the Ancient British, Roman and Saxon Antiquities and Folk-Lore of Worcestershire*. The twelfth chapter reprinted the pamphlet on the 'Ignis Fatuus.'

Other meaty contributions reached the *Athenaeum*, dealing with 'Legends of the Small People of Devonshire and Cornwall' (October 10, 1846, signed again by H.), and 'The Pixies of Devonshire' (October 24, signed by R. J. K.), paraphrasing reports of the locals about encounters with strange, small beings. But Thoms' hopes of enlisting a steady corps of semi-professional correspondents failed to materialize, and by the end of 1847 he was filling his department with a series of his own on 'The Folk-Lore of Shakespeare.'[2] In the

[1] *Athenaeum*, September 17, 1846 (No. 986), p. 955.
[2] The series ran in nine consecutive instalments, beginning September 4, with a

[85]

opening article, signed by 'William Thoms,' the author reveals the identity of Ambrose Merton and expresses innocent satisfaction at the 'universal adoption' of his coinage 'folk-lore,' which in less than twelve months had almost achieved the status of a household word. The first book to adopt the word into its title, Thomas Sternberg's *The Dialect and Folk-Lore of Northamptonshire*, appeared in 1851.

In his Shakespeare articles, Thoms singled out the fairy mythology present in *A Midsummer Night's Dream* as a springboard for quotations for Shakespeare and other poets, synopses of legends, and philological speculations about origins. His purpose was to demonstrate the core of folklore truth at the heart of the Bard's poetic drama; Shakespeare was a faithful folklorist, immersed in the elfin legendry of his countrymen, and indeed its most gifted expositor. Thoms rode too hard this appealing thesis, which had already attracted Douce and Halliwell. As usual, he found in the Grimms some of his most striking references. Triumphantly he linked Queen Mab to the night-hag, through a legend in the *Deutsche Sagen* of the Alp who misbehaves like Mab. But Teutonic and Celtic streams flow happily together; the name Mab derives from Mabh, chief of the Irish fairies. On such thin evidence Thoms endeavours to 'throw a light over the writings of the Poet of the People from the side of our popular literature, customs, and superstitions.'[1]

If the *Athenaeum* launched folk-lore, it did not long remain its sponsor. In 1848 only one issue carried folklore, and although the column resumed briefly in August, 1849, by now Thoms had conceived a new venture, *Notes & Queries*, which began on November 3 under his sole editorship. This 'little paper you once proposed, in which we could all ask and answer one another's questions' (as Thoms later recalled the Reverend Samuel Maitland saying to him),[2] served a variety of antiquarian interests, with folklore playing a large role. In the first number Thoms devoted an article to saints' legends, which should be 'more frequently consulted for illustrations of our folk-lore and popular observances,' and he gives an example of how the pawnbroker's symbol of three golden balls originated in the legend of St. Nicholas. By February 2, 1850, Thoms felt secure enough to print an editorial note on '*Folk Lore*,' saying correspondents had been begging him to open his columns to articles and notes 'on our fast-fading *Folk Lore*,' as had the

[1] *Athenaeum*, November 6, 1847 (No. 1045), p. 1150.
[2] *Notes and Queries*, VI (July 15, 1876), 41.

tenth appearing on December 11. It was reprinted as one 'notelet' in Thoms' *Three Notelets on Shakespeare* (London: John Russell Smith, 1865).

3. THOMAS WRIGHT

4. WILLIAM JOHN THOMS

Athenaeum, and accordingly he would assure 'our own numerous readers that any contributions illustrative of *The Folk Lore of England,* the Manners, Customs, Observances, Superstitions, Ballads, Proverbs, &c., of the Olden Time, will always find welcome admission to our pages.' He promised to enrich such communications with extracts from the works of continental antiquaries. This announcement, which sounds suspiciously like Ambrose Merton writing to William Thoms, inaugurated a department that endured all through Thoms' editorship, until he retired on September 28, 1872, and thereafter remained a standard feature. The folklore columns of *Notes & Queries* are rich pickings for the folklorist, who can browse through the 3,000 entries under 'Folk Lore' for the twenty-two years Thoms guided the paper. He himself, during the first four years, wrote on such matters as metrical charms, a Saxon weather proverb in Wiltshire, the Irish nonsense tale of Sir Gammer Vans, the German trickster Eulenspiegel, the mysterious giant Woglog, and likenesses between English and Flemish carols.

For the middle period of the English folklore movement, Thoms steadily maintained interest and continuity in folklore topics through *Notes & Queries,* while new ideas were germinating which would raise folklore from an antiquarian to a scientific pursuit. Meanwhile he rendered still further contributions. In 1849 he prepared an English edition of *The Primeval Antiquities of Denmark,* by J. J. A. Worsaae (translated, and applied to the illustration of similar remains in England, by William J. Thoms). Here was an opportunity to make available for the English public a key work on the antiquities of a people whose history was linked with that of England, to undertake comparative analysis, and occasionally to relate physical to popular antiquities. Thus he pointed out that the burial custom of placing 'death shoes' beside the corpse was based on the old belief, revealed in a Yorkshire dirge in Aubrey's 'Remaines,' that the souls of the dead had to 'pass through a great lande full of thornes and furzen.'[1] More books followed. The new edition of *Early English Prose Romances* came out in 1858, *Choice Notes from 'Notes and Queries': Folk-Lore* in 1859, and the *Three Notelets on Shakespeare,* part of which had appeared in the *Athenaeum* as 'The Folk Lore of Shakespeare,' in 1865. Then in 1873 Thoms, who had been vigorously pursuing the theme in *Notes & Queries,* published a study of *Human Longevity, Its Facts and Its Fictions,* including an inquiry into some of the more remarkable instances, and suggestions for testing reputed cases, illustrated by examples. His findings disclosed that the majority of cases reported

[1] *The Primeval Antiquities of Denmark* (London: John Henry Parker, 1849), p. xxi.

on centenarians could not be substantiated, and were to be attributed to hearsay, bragging, or folklore. Finally, in 1876, he undertook a new edition of John Stow's *A Survey of London, Written in the Year 1658*. The folklorist expanded on the labours of his predecessor with notes on Christmas celebrations taken from Brand-Ellis, the city fool from Douce, medieval secret societies from Keightley, and punishments for witchcraft from Grimm.

Of these titles, *Choice Notes* proved especially valuable for the folklorist, and made its way to the charmed shelf that held Aubrey's *Miscellanies*, Brand's *Popular Antiquities*, Hone's *Every-Day Book*, and Halliwell's *Popular Rhymes and Nursery Tales*. Thoms (whose name did not appear on the title-page) culled his choice samples from the twelve volumes of the first series, which ran from 1849 to 1855. In a way it fulfilled his dream of preparing a book on English legendary lore. This handy compendium reflects Thoms' approach to folklore, a synthesis of Brand and Hone: local instances of popular antiquities are supplied and politely contemplated by gentlemen correspondents. Placed side by side as they came to hand, they furnished curious if miscellaneous information on country charms and cures, legends of castles and pools, appearances of spectres and pixies, reports of the evil eye and the devil's marks, and the whole panoply of custom and superstition. Popular antiquities thrive still, and *Choice Notes* displays them as living folklore. If at present these scraps appear 'little better than the drivellings of antiquated crones,' they will provide some future Grimm with the materials to erect 'a complete system of the ancient mythology of these islands.'[1] Thoms did not worry about repeating himself.

A typical note gives information on the 'Legend of John of Horsill':

> Tradition states he held the manors of Ribbesford and Highlington, near Bewdley (Worcestershire), about the twelfth century. Several legends, approaching very near to facts, are extant in this neighbourhood concerning him; one of the best authenticated is as follows:
>
> Hunting one day near the Severn, he started a fine buck, which took the direction of the river; fearing to lose it, he discharged an arrow, which, piercing it through, continued its flight, and struck a salmon, which had (as is customary with such fish in shallow streams) leaped from the surface of the water, with so much force as to transfix it. This being thought

---

[1] *Choice Notes from 'Notes and Queries': Folk Lore* (London: Bell and Daldy, 1859), pp. v–vi.

a very extraordinary shot (as indeed it was), a stone carving
representing it was fixed over the west door of Ribbesford
Church, then in course of erection. A description of this carving
is, I believe, in Nash's *History of Worcestershire*, but without
any mention of the legend. The carving merely shows a rude
human figure with a bow, and a salmon transfixed with an
arrow before it. A few facts concerning this 'John of Horsill'
would be hailed with much pleasure by your well wisher.

Kidderminster   H. Corville Warde[1]

Intriguing as is this account, the folklorist of a later date regrets
that the correspondent, in the fashion of his time, paraphrases the
tradition instead of giving the exact words of a named raconteur.
The legend is offered in fragmented form, without attempt at
further research, even to verifying the one reference cited; these
correspondents are not attempting scholarly monographs. They are
attracted by the strong local associations, in this case with a
medieval lord of the manor, the river of the district, and the village
church. The marvellous oral tradition had been tangibly enshrined
in stone, a correlation between the popular and the physical
antiquity doubling the appeal of each.

As his final and crowning achievement, Thoms signing himself
'An Old Folk-Lorist,' participated in the correspondence with
George Laurence Gomme in *Notes & Queries* in 1876 which resulted
in the formation of The Folk-Lore Society two years later.[2] He
urged that 'not a day should be lost in organizing such a society,'
and after it came into being he served as its director from 1878 until
his death in 1885. His Preface to its first volume, the *Folk-Lore
Record*, modestly reviewed his own part in establishing the value of
folklore as a study worthy of its own society.[3] By 1878 the word
and the concept of folklore had spread far around the world and
moved a long way from the notion of popular antiquities. Brilliant
theorizers would now hold the stage, and the memory of Thoms,
assiduous antiquary, editor, organizer, would slowly fade. Yet his
creative act named and defined the field. Nietzsche has appraised
this kind of genius.

Originalität. Was ist Originalität? Etwas sehen, das noch
keinen Namen trägt, noch nicht genannt werden kann, ob es
gleich vor aller Augen liegt. Wie die Menschen gewöhnlich sind,
macht ihnen der Name ein Ding überhaupt sichtbar. Die
Originalen sind zumeist auch die Namengeber gewesen.[4]

---

[1] *Ibid.*, p. 134.   [2] *Notes and Queries*, 5th Series, VI (July 1, 1876), 12.
[3] *Folk-Lore Record*, I (1878), xiii–xvi.   [4] *Die Fröhliche Wissenschaft* (1882), par. 261.

Originality. What is Originality? To see something that as yet
bears no name, cannot yet be named, although it lies immediately before all eyes. Men being the way they are, the name
first makes a thing really visible to them. The people endowed
with originality have chiefly been the name-givers.

III The Literary Folklorists

IN THE EARLY DECADES of the nineteenth century the antiquarian spirit escaped the book-lined walls of the British
Museum and the austere parlours of archaeological societies and
spread across meadows and green valleys. The historical romancers
adopted antiquities and bathed the medieval past in a shimmering
haze, through which moved armoured knights and ladies fair,
shielded from elves, demons, and assorted goblins by magicians
and soothsayers. Nature-poets rediscovered old ballads and
savoured old wives' tales, finding in them models for their own
creations, which they attached to a Roman camp site, Saxon burial
mound, Norman cathedral, towering crag, or desolate moor. As a
friend of Sir Walter Scott testified, 'He was but half satisfied with
the most beautiful scenery when he could not connect it with some
local legend.'[1]

Wordsworth and Coleridge, Southey and Scott are names one
thinks of when considering the lyrical romanticism of early nineteenth-century poets and their consuming interest in country folk.
The mood was of course international, spreading from Germany
where the collections of the brothers Grimm served to support the
theories of the poet Johann Gottfried von Herder, who in the late
eighteenth century first suggested that separate racial strains might
be traced in folklore. In Norway, Finland, Hungary, Serbia, and
elsewhere, scholars found special national qualities in the history,
literature, language, and folklore of their terrain. Now the folk are
transformed from a superstitious, backward peasantry to a pastoral
people attuned to nature and glowing with a natural morality.

For the science of folklore this romantic interlude between the
tenets of rationalism and the methods of positivism brought
dangers. It interrupted the sober search for the raw materials of
folklore, and diverted attention to the evocation of atmosphere

[1] Henry A. Beers, *A History of English Romanticism in the Nineteenth Century*
(London, 1902), p. 12.

and the tenderer emotions. From the point of view of the literary craftsman there was no problem; he turned to the humble people of the village and their own poetry and legends for the inspiration of his muse. But from the point of view of the folklorist the results were unfortunate: the presentation of folk traditions was blurred and diluted with literary mannerisms. The end product may have been literature but was not folklore.

The successive editions of the first and most famous collection of folktales, the *Kinder- und Hausmärchen*, display the risks attendant on the literary approach to folklore. Jacob and Wilhelm Grimm prepared in 1812 the first book of orally told traditional tales, in striking contrast to the literary revision of such tales which had engaged writers from Ovid to Boccaccio; but as their work caught fire and prompted new publication, instead of refining their empirical techniques for accurate recording of the spoken texts, they increasingly took liberties with the narratives, inserting phrases and developing character portrayals, with the intent of clarifying the story line and bringing forth the inner expression of the peasant soul.[1] From this convention but a short step was needed to the doctrine that a collector could completely rewrite the oral fiction in his own style.

Among English men of letters, Robert Southey (1774–1843) best exemplifies the professional writer with a taste for antiquities and folklore. Born in Bristol and brought up in Bath, he hankered for the lore of the countryside but depended on his eclectic reading and contacts with antiquaries for acquaintance with popular mythology. He visited Scott at Ashetiel in the autumn of 1805; in 1813 Scott magnanimously relinquished the poet laureateship to Southey. While admiring Scott as 'a man of great talent and genius,' he criticized the Border Ballads for mixing modern with antique words—'polished steel and rusty iron!'—an indication of Southey's own sense of faithfulness to tradition.[2] He speaks of dining with T. Crofton Croker, and writes his publishers, Longmans and Company, inclosing a letter for Mr. Douce with queries on the *Morte d'Arthur*, since he is so well informed and helpful upon these subjects.[3] In a letter to a correspondent he shows familiarity with the writings of Aubrey and states his own suspended judgment of the reality of spirits.

[1] This development is well traced by Alfred and Mary Elizabeth David, 'A Literary Approach to the Brothers Grimm,' *Journal of the Folklore Institute*, I (1964), 180–96.
[2] Charles Cuthbert Southey, *The Life and Correspondence of Robert Southey*, 6 vols. (London, 1849–50), II, 211–12.
[3] *Selections from the Letters of Robert Southey*, edited by his son-in-law, John Wood Warter, 4 vols. (London, 1856), III, 49.

To C. W. Williams Wynn, Bristol, Jan. 15, 1799

Captain Bell's vision is in Aubrey's 'Miscellanies' also. It looks like a lie. I am not a disbeliever in these things, but that story is not among the credible ones. It is a curious subject, the truth of supernatural warnings and appearances. I mean some day to state the *pro* and *con* in the M. Magazine, and invite controversy, for it has never been fairly and reasonably examined. I lean to belief myself. . . . Pray buy me the ghost book . . . if you should meet with a ghost, a witch, or a devil, pray send them to me.[1]

And to Wynn he also writes of 'getting scent of a tremendous story about King Arthur, to be found in Gervase of Tilbury, concerning his *family of apparitions*.'[2]

In his *Common-Place Book*, Southey jotted down and excerpted passages from his readings on an immense variety of subjects, ranging over Remarkable Facts in Natural History, Characteristic English Anecdotes, Voyages and Travels, Orientalia, and American Tribes. These extracts reveal clearly enough his bent toward outlandish customs. Here is an entry on 'Water-spouts, Curious Superstition,' detailing a practice of French sailors to cut the air athwart a waterspout with a black-handled knife, while pronouncing holy words from the Gospel of St. John—'a foul superstition, which may be accompanied with some implicit compact with the Devil. . . .' An account of 'The Magician Siribio and the Prophetic Bird' tells of the ruined city Sibiris, allegedly built by the magician Sibirio, on a mountain overlooking the Nile; on the mountain top the magician placed a bird, which in time of plenty turned its head toward the river, and in time of scarcity toward the desert. It would also turn toward an approaching enemy, clapping its wings and crying loudly to warn the citizens. And from Cotton Mather comes an 'Indian Superstition of sacrificing [a dog] to the Devil,' to prevent English dogs barking at them. From Richard [or Robert, pseud.] Burton's *The Surprising Miracles of Nature and Art* (1683), Southey culled the wonder of the groaning boards, a phenomenon observed in London in 1682. Elm planks were said to groan when touched with a red hot iron; one was presented to the king. A Cumbrian belief caught his attention: a person suffering from the whooping, or king, cough must request a prescription from a woman whose married name is the same as her maiden name, or from a parson on horseback with these words,

---

[1] *Ibid.*, I, 64. [2] *Ibid.*, p. 308.

'Honest friend of a pyebald horse, tell me what's good for the king cough?'[1]

Southey made effective use of such nuggets in his verse and prose compositions. A clutch of ballads he wrote in 1796 is wedded to folk themes. 'The Witch' links together some well-known motifs: the black cat as familiar, broomstick-riding, charms against a witch —a pebble with a hole in it hung over the manger or a horseshoe nailed to the threshold. As a schoolboy Southey heard as a factual account the story he wrote as 'Mary the Maid of the Inn.' The events were said to have occurred in the north of England, but he was astute enough to recognize a similar incident related in Plot's *History of Staffordshire*. From a poem of 1635 by Thomas Heywood, with notes on a Finnish legend, he was moved to compose the ballad of 'Donica,' the tale of a maiden in whose dead body the devil walked for two years, until a magician removed a hidden charm, whereupon the body fell lifeless. And from Heywood he obtained a Rhine legend of an incubus for the ballad 'Rudiger.'[2] Among his prose writings, Southey's best known folkloric creation is the nursery tale of 'The Three Bears,' included in 1837 in the fourth volume of his stream of personal miscellanies, *The Doctor*. When Joseph Jacobs reprinted 'The Three Bears' in *English Fairy Tales* (1890), he believed it Southey's own invention and a unique example of the literary parentage of a folktale. But in *More English Fairy Tales* (1894), Jacobs unearthed an oral variant with a fox instead of an old woman as the interloper in the bears' home— Goldilocks came later—which he believed to be an older form than Southey's, and current opinion is that Southey, as he claimed, was reproducing a popular tale.[3]

Attracted by oral and traditional legends, Southey perceived their migratory character. In the 'Madociana' he included a story of Alexander the Great, who used a diving bell to observe the fishes, and commented on how widely it was known, in medieval Spanish, German, and Welsh romances, and even among the Malays, who could not have obtained it from Europe, as Alexander was not the hero of their tale. (But here the poet laureate fails to allow for the process of substitution.) 'The number of good stories of all kinds which are common to the Orientals and Europeans, are more likely to have been brought home by peaceable travellers, than by the

---

[1] *Southey's Common-Place Book*, edited by his son-in-law, John Wood Warter, 4 vols. (London, 1849–51), I, 380–1; II, 467; IV, 374, 531.
[2] *The Poetical Works of Robert Southey* (Paris: A. and W. Galignani, 1829), pp. 628–30, 635–6, 637–9.
[3] Katharine M. Briggs has written 'The Three Bears,' *IV International Congress for Folk-Narrative Research in Athens*, ed. G. A. Megas (Athens, 1965), pp. 53–7.

Crusaders.' And he suspects that Jewish pedlars acted as the great go-betweens.[1] This is shrewd speculation on the transmission of folktales.

Southey directly contributed to the folklore movement by suggesting a work he himself might have attempted under favouring circumstances, but which he generously encouraged and supported. In one of his letters to the novelist Anna Eliza Bray (1790–1883), he remarks, 'Such gleanings of tradition are very delightful to me. How often have I had cause to wish that I had, while it was possible, preserved all that the elders of my own family could have told me of *their* elders, and of the little circle in which they lived— of their own times and the times before them!'[2] And he mourns that, except for an aunt in Taunton, he has for many years been the oldest of his race. In Mrs. Bray, however, he found an alter ego; her novels dealt with leading families of Devonshire and Cornwall, and her second husband, the Reverend Edward A. Bray, as vicar of Tavistock and an eager antiquary, was in close touch with Devon people and places. In a letter Southey wrote her in 1831, which she later printed in the preface of the book it proposed, he outlined his idea for a new kind of topographic history.

> I should like to see from you what English literature yet wants—a good specimen of local history, not the antiquities, nor the natural history, nor both together (as in White's delightful book about Selborne), nor the statistics, but everything about a parish that can be made interesting—all of its history, traditions and manners that can be saved from oblivion. . . .[3]

The following year he pursued the subject, writing: 'Gather up all the traditions you can, and even the nursery songs: no one can tell of what value they may prove to an antiquary.' He and his son had been reading with absorption a curious Danish collection of local stories wise and silly, and in them he saw matter a-plenty 'for fancy and for reflection, to point a moral, or work up into a poem,' and in addition to elucidate the history of a bygone time.[4] Southey here must be alluding to a work by Paul Henri Mallet, originally published in French in 1755 and translated into English

---

[1] Southey, *Life and Correspondence*, II, 318–19.
[2] Southey, *Selections*, IV, 436.
[3] Alluded to in the opening pages of the 1836 edition, and printed in full in the preface to the 1879 edition.
[4] Quoted by Mrs. Bray, *A Description of the Part of Devonshire Bordering on the Tamar and the Tavy*, 3 vols. (London: John Murray, 1836), II, 275, as a Preface to a sheaf of witch, spectre, and devil tales.

in 1770 by Thomas Percy, of 'Reliques' fame, as *Northern Antiquities: or A Description of the Manners, Customs, Religion and Laws of the Ancient Danes.* A reprint was issued in Edinburgh in 1809. This antiquarian treatise first stirred Europeans to the romance of Norse mythology.[1] Southey hoped England would yield comparable treasures. To the well-established formula of 'Natural History and Antiquities' of the shire Southey would now add as a major component the village and family traditions which had hitherto received only passing attention.

Mrs. Bray responded at once to the suggestion and by 1836 had completed a three-volume work entitled *A Description of the Part of Devonshire Bordering on the Tamar and the Tavy; its Natural History, Manners, Customs, Superstitions, Scenery, Antiquities, Biography of Eminent Persons, etc. in a Series of Letters to Robert Southey, Esq.* Another lot, issued in 1838, carried the title *Traditions, Legends, Superstitions, and Sketches of Devonshire on the Borders of the Tamar and the Tavy* as a start. The best-known title was to be *The Borders of the Tamar and the Tavy*, from Mrs. Bray's two-volume abridgment of 1879.

Since Gilbert White had cast the *Natural History and Antiquities of Selborne* into a series of letters to Thomas Pennant, Mrs. Bray had a ready precedent for the format of her Devonshire gleanings. She mailed each chapter in the form of a letter to Southey, who wrote back appreciatively, offering comments on special points. To close the circle, he reviewed pleasurably and discursively in the *Quarterly Review*, to which he contributed regularly, the book addressed to himself.[2] On receiving the published volumes, early in 1836, he wrote Mrs. Bray within forty-eight hours, congratulating her for 'bringing together in it many things well worthy of preservation, which must otherwise have been forgotten, because there would have been none to collect them, and you have collected them just in time.'[3] The old story! Yet, in a manner familiar to all folklore collectors, Mrs. Bray wished she had started a little sooner, before the death at a great age of Mrs. Mary Adams of Tavistock, 'the depository of every legend or story connected with this neighbourhood,' handed down the generations for centuries.[4]

One of Southey's commentaries was so rich in lore that Mrs. Bray published it as a note to her own account of Drake legends.

You have indeed collected a rich harvest of traditions concerning Sir Francis Drake. I had heard of his shooting the

[1] Henry A. Beers, *A History of English Romanticism in the Eighteenth Century* (London, 1899), p. 190. [2] *Quarterly Review*, LIX (1737), 275–312.
[3] Southey, *Selections*, IV, 436. [4] Bray, *op. cit.*, I, 263 n.

gulf; and of his pushing the boy overboard who knew that they were under London bridge. My story of the stone is yours of the marriage: with this variation, that instead of a ball coming up through the earth, a huge round stone fell through the air upon the train of the intended bride's gown, as she was on the way to church; upon which she turned back, saying, she knew it came from her husband. My story adds that the stone is still used as a weight upon the harrow of the farm; and if it be removed from the estate in which it fell, always returns thither. Yours is much the grander fiction. My story says, moreover, that it was not long before Sir Francis returned, and in the dress of a beggar asked alms of his wife at her own door; but in the midst of his feigned tale, a smile escaped him, and he was recognized, and of course joyfully embraced. This is borrowed from Guy, Earl of Warwick, and is found also in other romances. The miracle of leading the water is common in the lives of the saints, and especially of the Irish saints, who generally led it up hill to make the miracle the greater.[1]

The poet laureate speculated that Spaniards first told such stories about Drake, believing that he trafficked with the Devil, and communicated them to English fellow-Catholics, who found the black arts comely when practised by their hero. Lope de Vega had indeed heard from Spanish soldiers in the Armada who had been prisoners in England that Drake's countrymen praised him for dealing with the Devil.

Mrs. Bray's reports of the pixies in Devon also struck a responsive chord in her correspondent. 'I knew them of old by Coleridge's poem about them, which was written before he and I met in 1794,' he wrote back, 'but your stories were new to me, and have amused my fireside greatly.'[2] He added regretfully that the pixies were not apparent in his harsher countryside, although boggles and barguests had been sighted, usually in animal form. The growth of large towns and the coming of factories to the country destroy these superstitions, Southey observed, pondering the legends of the Devon moors.

The Borders of the Tamar and the Tavy did not so much initiate a new kind of domestic history as divert into a new channel literary treatments of legendry. Mrs. Bray's volumes of 1836 have a double ancestry, on the one side the topographical antiquities, on the other the romantic embroideries of local traditions by poets and

---

[1] *Ibid.*, II, 174–5 n.   [2] Southey, *Selections*, IV, 280–1.

fiction writers. In this vein fall Allan Cunningham's *Traditional Tales of the English and Scottish Peasantry* (1822), John Roby's *The Traditions of Lancashire* (1829), Samuel Lover's *Legends and Stories of Ireland* (1831), and Andrew Pickens' *Traditionary Stories of Old Families, and Legendary Illustrations of Family History* (1833). The prefaces as well as titles give lip service to oral sources. Cunningham, a minor Scottish poet and romancer (see Chapter IV, section 2), declares in a perceptive Foreword to his *Traditional Tales* that 'the old narrative fire-side mode of story-telling . . . has not been departed from,' and thanks the 'humble and wandering novelists' who supplied him with his themes. But the reader finds little resemblance to any tale ever voiced by man or woman. Here are verbose, long-drawn-out narratives strewn with repetitive descriptions of mournful heaths and sombre crags, alternating with stilted conversations spoken by withered hags and weatherbeaten mariners. Yet imbedded in their prolix depths are solid kernels of folk belief: visions and prophecies, witches and jonahs of the sea, fairies, and spectral sights.

A representative and influential work in this genre was *The Traditions of Lancashire*, written in 1829 by a successful banker, John Roby (1793–1850). The first series of two handsomely illustrated volumes was sold in royal octavo with proofs and etchings for four pounds, four shillings, and in demy octavo for two pounds, two shillings, making it a prize acquisition for a gentleman's library, and yet a second edition was called for within a year, and a second series, uniform with the first, was published in 1831. Doubting that a banker could write in such vein, readers speculated as to the true author, suggesting Crofton Croker, who did in fact contribute one tradition, on 'The Bar-Gaist.' After the first series appeared, Sir Francis Palgrave congratulated Roby for having made a valuable addition both to English literature and English topography, 'for these popular traditions form . . . an important feature in topographical history,' and urged him to continue.[1] Sir Walter Scott referred to Roby's story of Mab's Cross in his introduction of 1832 to *The Betrothed, or Tales of the Crusaders*, and in his work on *Demonology and Witchcraft* alluded to Roby's account of the witch Demdike.[2] A more popular and somewhat condensed edition in three volumes was issued in 1841, and reprinted two years later, under the title *Popular Traditions of Lancashire*, intended for

---

[1] *The Legendary and Poetical Remains of John Roby, with a sketch of his literary life and character*, by his Widow (London, 1854), pp. 28–9.

[2] John Roby, *Popular Traditions of Lancashire*, 3 vols. (3rd edition; London: Henry G. Bohn, 1843), Preface; I, 100; II, 217 n.

the general reading public. In the Preface the author expressed his hope of 'supplying a void in English literature which has long been a matter of surprise to the scholars of other nations,' and so was launching this series on 'The Popular Traditions of England' with 'Series the First, Lancashire.' Then in his Introduction he expanded on the value such a 'collection of English traditions' would have 'for illustrating English history, manners, and customs now obsolete' or as 'legends, having truth for their basis.'[1] The proposed series never materialized, but Roby's work continued to find readers, reaching a sixth edition in 1906. In 1911 a volume of *Lancashire Legends, selected from Roby's 'Traditions of Lancashire,'* was edited by Mary Dowdall and E. T. Campagne, with drastic curtailment of its windier passages. *Traditions of Lancashire* reached print yet again in 1928 and 1930.

In his prefatory remarks and scattered observations, Roby wrote with seeming authority on traditions. Disclaiming expert knowledge and even any pretension to the name of 'antiquary,' he rested his case squarely on his access to spoken traditions.

In the northern counties, and more particularly in Lancashire . . . it may readily be imagined that a number of interesting legends, anecdotes, and scraps of family history, are floating about, hitherto preserved chiefly in the shape of oral tradition. The antiquary, in most instances, rejects the information that does not present itself in the form of an authentic and well-attested fact; and legendary lore, in particular, he throws aside, as worthless and unprofitable. The author of the 'Traditions of Lancashire,' in leaving the dry and heraldic pedigrees which unfortunately constitute the great bulk of those works that bear the name of county histories, enters on the more entertaining, though sometimes apocryphal narratives, which exemplify and embellish the records of our forefathers.

A native of Lancashire, and residing there during the greater part of his life, he has been enabled to collect a mass of local traditions, now fast dying from the memories of the inhabitants. It is his object to perpetuate these interesting relics of the past, and to present them in a form that may be generally acceptable, divested of the dust and dross in which the originals are but too often disfigured, so as to appear worthless and uninviting.[2]

Brave and promising words, but the implications of the final

---

[1] *Ibid.*, I, 20. [2] John Roby, *Traditions of Lancashire*, 2 vols. (London, 1829), I, v–vi.

sentence would undo them, for as it turned out Roby lacked any respect for the texts of oral tradition, even in paraphrase. Roby seems not to have known the work of the antiquaries in London converging on the concept of folklore, and his citations even to standbys like Brand and Reginald Scot are meagre. His emphatic employment of the term 'tradition' and the compound 'oral tradition' is surprisingly prophetic of modern usage. In his home town of Rochdale he gave a course of four lectures, illustrated with sketches he drew as he talked, on 'Tradition, as connected with, and illustrating history, antiquities, and Romance'; and he wrote that history and learning build on tradition, providing current examples of historical investigation—an Amazonian society, a one-legged people—that verified tradition. But he was alone in his reliance on the term. In a note to a ballad he placed within a story, he commented that the music to the words was *'traditionary,* if we may be allowed the expression.'[1]

Roby was cognizant of similarities between British traditions and those of modern Scandinavia, classical Greece, and ancient India. He saw a correspondence between the worship of Juno and the frolic of English country girls racing for an undergarment in a village competition; he remarked on the appearance of the 'most cockney of all cockney tales,' that of Dick Whittington and his cat, in Persia.[2] But these are fleeting references.

In his conception of the nature and quality of oral tradition, Roby actually showed little understanding and positive disdain. With the romanticists he regarded folk products as disfigured and imperfect specimens in the mouths of the peasants, whose wild beauty and full figure must be restored by a creative mind. His widow revealed his literary method as involving two stages, first, the collecting of the materials, and second, through his imaginative powers, abetted by his relish of the supernatural, the 'weaving them into tales of romantic interests,' with a copy of Thomas D. Fosbroke's *Encyclopaedia of Antiquities* (1825) at his elbow to check period costume and furnishings.[3] It is clear that Roby's contact with oral legends irritated and frustrated him. In attempting to pin down a boggart seen in the vicinity of Clegg Hall, two miles northeast of Rochdale, who was 'the subject of many an absurd and marvellous story among the country chroniclers,' Roby found the accounts so desultory, various, vague, and unintelligible, as to defy his efforts to weave them into one continuous narrative.[4]

---

[1] Roby, *Remains*, p. 40; Roby, *Popular Traditions*, pp. 3 ff., 209.
[2] Roby, *Popular Traditions*, pp. 15, 19.   [3] Roby, *Remains*, p. 22.
[4] John Roby, *Traditions of Lancashire, Second Series*, 2 vols. (London, 1831), II, 3.

As we now know, oral legends take the form of fragmentary incidents rather than symmetrical wholes. All Roby could discover was the memory of a villainous murder in the thirteenth or fourteenth century, perpetrated by a wicked uncle who threw two orphan nephews into the moat, that he might seize their inheritance; thereafter an angry and troubled spirit haunted Clegg Hall. So much for the tradition, but upon it Roby constructed a fifty-page romance: counterfeiters used the haunted chamber to mask their operations, until one fell in love with Alice, the daughter of the mansion.

Later folklorists continued to refer to Roby's traditions, until published field collections from Lancashire in the 1870's rendered them obsolete. Occasional slivers of undiluted lore found in the notes or passing remarks in these leaden romances deal with the Gabriel Ratchets, as the ominous Wild Huntsmen were called in Lancashire; the wonder-working Hand of Father Arrowsmith, preserved in a silk bag at Garswood and still resorted to by diseased persons seeking the cures the divine promised when executed for his faith at Lancaster by William III (Roby says he actually was found guilty of rape); the seer Edward Kelly, reputed to have a compact with the Devil; the huge woad stone quoited to Monstone Edge by Robin Hood from his bed six miles away; and the witch unmasked when the bewitched cow, driven from the shippen by a pair of breeches thrown over its horns, made straight for her mill-dam.[1] Roby uncovered these traditions and then buried them in cumbersome fictions.

Samuel Lover (1797–1868) resembles Roby as a literary adapter of oral tales, but differs considerably in style. His is the cloyingly comic Anglo-Irish sketch, in contrast to the gloomy Gothic romance. Born in Dublin and educated at Dublin University, Lover moved to London in 1835 and made his livelihood as a professional Irish jack-of-all-letters—novelist, poet, painter, composer, playwright. His *Legends and Stories of Ireland* appeared in 1831 and inspired a rival volume bearing his name, *Popular Stories and Legends of the Peasantry of Ireland,* to which he merely contributed six illustrations, as he indignantly announced in his *Legends and Stories of Ireland, Second Series* (1834). Nor did the deceitful work contain 'a single legend in its pages,' he added bitterly. From this outburst one would expect to find a clear concept of legend in his own writings.

In his first preface he declares that his sources are the 'village

[1] Roby, *Popular Traditions* (1843), II, 234; Roby, *Traditions of Lancashire, Second Series* (1831), II, 186; Roby, *Popular Traditions* (1843), I, 267 n., 96–8; II, 225–6.

crone and mountain guide,' whose tales he recited to friends round his fireside in the manner of their tellers. He had gone deep into the 'western wilds of Ireland' to gather these native 'Rigmaroles.' Being induced to publish them, he apologizes to his readers because 'some of them are essentially *oral* in their character,' and may suffer in being reduced to writing, but he is intent on preserving the manner of the Irish peasantry. Throughout his pieces there are allusions to individual narrators.

> From this lady I heard some characteristic stories and prevalent superstitions of the country. Many of these she had obtained from an old boatman, one of the crew that manned Mr. ——'s boat; and often, as he sat at the helm, he delivered his 'round, unvarnish'd tale'. . . .[1]

This acknowledgment is all the more persuasive because it indicates a primary oral source fed by an earlier oral source. At times Lover sounds like a skilled collector, when he speaks of honouring the narrator's beliefs, or when he portrays a raconteur like Paddy the Sport, 'a tall, loose-made, middle-aged man . . . fond of wearing an oil-skinned hat and a red waistcoat,' and much given to tobacco and whiskey. Paddy was known for spinning marvellous yarns, of the fairy tale and ghost-story variety, and for his clever repartee filled with long bows. When his master asked him why he was so hoarse, Paddy replied: 'Indeed, Sir, it's a cowld I got, and indeed myself doesn't know how I cotch cowld, barrin' that I slep' in a field last night, and forgot to shut the gate afther me.' When trying to steal peas, he sees the fairies; a spirit shakes him in bed, and a young lord dies soon after; he tells of a clever fox who throws a pursuing ranger's brogues in the fire and so escapes. His distinction between fairies and spirits sounds knowledgeable:

> . . . the fairies doesn't love to be seen, and seldom at all you get a sight iv them; and that's the differ I was speakin' iv to you betune fairies and sper'ts. Now, the sper'ts is always seen, in some shape or other; and maybe it id be a bird, or a shafe o' corn, or a big stone, or a hape o' dung, or the like o' that, and never know 'twas a sper't at all, antil you wor made sinsible av it, some how or other; maybe it id be that you wor comin' home from a friend's house late at night, and you might fall down, and couldn't keep a leg undher you, and not know why, barrin' it was a sper't misled you—and maybe it's in a ditch you'd find yourself asleep in the mornin' when you woke.[2]

---

[1] Samuel Lover, *Legends and Stories of Ireland* (2nd edition; Dublin: W. F. Wakeman, 1832), p. 18. [2] *Ibid.*, pp. 213–14. The story of 'Paddy the Sport' is on pp. 197–226.

This is probably a good deal more Lover than Paddy. Current studies have shown that the borderline between fairies, spirits, and ghosts in folk belief is tenuous and continually crossed. Such morsels of folklore as do come to the surface are surrounded by arch dialogue, whimsical euphemisms, and coy characterizations. The Devil is 'his sable majesty.' Comic Paddy, the stage Hibernian, eccentric and lovable, camouflages the peasant storyteller and becomes the antic spirit of elfin fun.[1]

In some instances, instead of elaborating freely upon a graveyard superstition or a saint's legend, Lover follows a well-structured folktale. 'Paddy the Piper' is a localized story of Type 120 ('Getting Rid of the Man-Eating Calf') with Paddy fleeing from the Hessians and Orangemen, when he discovers a corpse hanged by the rebels in the cow-house. He steals his boots and runs off; at the fair he meets Shamus, who has come to sell his cow, thinking it ate up the boots; Paddy finds that breeches made from the cow's hide compel the wearer to jig to his pipes. Curiously this folktale is told as a true incident befalling a soldier at the battle of Culloden. 'The Legend of the Little Weaver of Duleek Gate. A Tale of Chivalry' is again a local form of Type 1640, best known in the Grimms' version of 'The Brave Tailor' who killed seven flies with one swat and posted a placard around his neck saying 'Seven at One Blow,' leading his enemies to think he had destroyed seven giants. But Lover is not consistent in his employment of *Märchen* and legends, and the promises of his prefaces to present oral recitations are not borne out by his written fictions. Southey may have influenced him, and Lover dedicated his story 'The Curse of Kishogue' to the poet laureate for its resemblance to Southey's 'The Curse of Kehama,' founded on Hindu mythology.

In the light of the fictionalized folklore sketches written by Roby and Lover, the factual treatment of Devonshire legends and traditions by Mrs. Bray assumes the greater value in the history of the folklore concept. As a practising novelist, she might well have produced imaginary or embroidered sketches, and she did bring out in 1854 a children's book called *A Peep at the Pixies, or Legends of the West*, fancifully rewriting some of the elfin stories she had gathered in Dartmoor and North Cornwall. But in *The Borders of the Tamar and the Tavy* she set down in paraphrase the local beliefs and oral narratives she heard in southern England, and so, as Southey had hoped, softened the impersonal topographical

---

[1] Bayle Bernard, in *The Life of Samuel Lover*, 2 vols. (London, 1874), considers Lover's stories a 'model method' of dealing with Irish fairy lore, for the native elf is a true Irishman (I, 205).

history into a meandering domestic chronicle, with much attention to folk observances.

The modern reader may well be repelled by the florid feminine style of Mrs. Bray and the interminable descriptions of the landscape one must traverse before encountering flesh and blood figures. One senses that Mrs. Bray's sympathies were with Southey when she wrote him, 'You are a poet, and have, therefore, no doubt a very friendly feeling towards those little pleasant elves that have supplied you with many a wild and fanciful dream of fairy land.'[1] A legend of pixies tending the grave of an old lady who guarded their tulips would, she feels, make a good subject for a poem. Still she provides an adequate account of the pixies, whom the Devon peasants regarded as the souls of unbaptized infants, and her garnerings were cited in subsequent studies, such as Keightley's amplified edition of *The Fairy Mythology*. Fairy legends later to become well publicized are in her pages: of the pixy who never performed any further household and barnyard chores after receiving a new suit, for fear he would spoil it; of the midwife given a magic ointment enabling her to see the fairies, and deliver their baby, but who was stricken blind when she used it to detect a pixy thief. Witches were also accessible in Dartmoor:

> Our guide, indeed, was not very sceptical; for he said that an ill-minded old woman, who is still alive and lives near him, had *bewitched himself*, so that for seventeen weeks he never slept an hour, nor ate more than a biscuit or two; that he never felt hungry nor sleepy; that always at twelve o'clock at night, precisely, such pains as of pricking of pins, would so torment him in his side, that he was obliged to be taken out of bed, and that he would sit up till six o'clock in the morning, when these tortures regularly left him![2]

This continuing belief of Devon peasants in witchcraft and the Devil's agency explained their attributing to Sir Francis Drake the powers of a necromancer, and in the legends surrounding Drake, 'the old warrior' as he was called, Mrs. Bray made her richest haul. His wizardry enabled him to create fire ships out of wooden blocks to destroy the Spanish Armada; to bring a flowing stream into Plymouth; to move an enormous stone with the help of the Devil; and while overseas to fire a cannon ball through the globe into the church in Plymouth to prevent his wife's remarriage.[3]

Heathen charms were another prize, although the old folk would

[1] Bray, *A Description*, I, 169.   [2] *Ibid.*, p. 261.   [3] *Ibid.*, II, 168–74.

not tell them to Mrs. Bray, for fear their efficacy would be destroyed if they appeared in print, and she had to obtain them through an intermediary, Mary Colling. As Mrs. Bray correctly noted, these secret verses were passed from man to woman and woman to man. One would heal a scald or burn. Another was a 'barbarous string of rhymes to stop an effusion of blood':

> Jesus was born in Bethlehem,
> Baptized in river Jordan, when
> The water was wild in the wood,
> The person was just and good,
> God spake, and the water stood
> And so shall now thy blood—
> In the name of the Father, son, &c.[1]

Bloodstopping charms and powers have since been widely reported throughout Britain and the United States. Also familiar today is the rhyme of the cuckoo, which Mrs. Bray heard in Devonshire. She commented that in druidical times the British priesthood had hailed the cuckoo's note as the harbinger of May Eve sacrifices. Devonians still regarded the bird as ill-omened; to hear him for the first time from one's left was bad luck.

> In the month of April,
> He opens his bill;
> In the month of May,
> He singeth all day;
> In the month of June,
> He alters his tune;
> In the month of July
> Away he doth fly.[2]

Various other folk matters receive attention. The spirit of a suicide walks over its grave at midnight; harvesters 'holla the nack' to appease the spirit of the harvest; diseased persons creep through a tolmen to be cured; the locals charm an adder by drawing a circle around it with an ash rod; a parson quiets a storm by speaking in Latin to a spirit in the Red Sea; a peasant salts his 'feyther' in a chest for the winter. Mrs. Bray omitted place-name legends which, 'being wholly fictitious, have, of course, no admission in these letters'—a curious gap in her perception of folk tradition.[3] Her commentaries are few, except to restate views on pagan and druidical origins, and her reference works sparse: Brand, of course; Edward Davies, *The Mythology and Rites of the British Druids*

[1] *Ibid.*, I, 334.   [2] *Ibid.*, p. 326.   [3] *Ibid.*, p. 273.

(1809); and, echoing Roby, the 'excellent and laborious' *Encyclopaedia of Antiquities* of the Reverend Thomas D. Fosbroke.

In sum, the quantity of folklore lodged among the letters is not large, but found a rightful place in the parish annals of Dartmoor. Mrs. Bray saw the Devonian peasants as a separate people! '. . . in no part of England has the march of intellect marched at a slower pace than on the moor. Many of its inhabitants cannot read; they speak the broadest Devonshire.'[1] Resisting the tendency to embalm them in romantic fiction, the vicar's wife listened to their talk and prepared the way for systematic fieldworkers.

[1] Bray, *A Description*, I, p. 337.

IV   The First Scottish Folklorists

[1   WALTER SCOTT]

O N   BOTH SIDES OF THE BORDER, Sir Walter Scott (1771–1832) was the first major figure to cultivate the literary uses of folklore with sympathy and comprehension. Himself an adopted son of the Border, his genius extended north and south and helped link the activities of English and Scottish folklorists. He cherished equally his loves for antiquities, oral lore, and romantic fiction, and if his greatest energies and former fame were attached to the historical romance, he served well the cause of antiquarian folklore. His towering influence sparked interest in Scottish traditions in the opening decades of the nineteenth century.

Scott displayed his several interlaced interests and passions in his first substantial work, the three-volume *Minstrelsy of the Scottish Border, Consisting of Historical and Romantic Ballads, Collected in the Southern Counties of Scotland; with a Few of Modern Date, Founded upon Local Tradition* (1802–3), which he amplified with notes and 'occasional dissertations' on 'popular superstitions, and legendary history.' These additions, Scott hoped, would 'contribute somewhat to the history of my native country.'[1] His ambivalent literary and scholarly attitudes toward ballads and legends are evident in the *Minstrelsy,* and again in *The Border Antiquities of England and Scotland; Comprising Specimens of Architecture and Sculpture, and Other Vestiges of Former Ages, Accompanied by Descriptions. Together with Illustrations of Remarkable Incidents in Border History and Tradition, and Original Poetry* (1814–17). In these twin quarto volumes physical and popular antiquities, Border lore, and literary invention happily mingle. Even in his spate of Waverley novels, begun in 1814, Sir Walter felt concern for the full and proper acknowledgment of his traditional sources.[2] As

---

[1] *Minstrelsy of the Scottish Border,* 3 vols. (Kelso: James Ballantyne, 1802), I, cix.

[2] Coleman O. Parsons has written an impressively documented study, *Witchcraft and*

one critic remarked, 'Scott was himself so genuinely an antiquary that he must have resolved that all these old legends should live on unadorned, in addition to their being handed down as parts of his novels. . . .' Accordingly, the author bolstered his novels with meaty prefaces and copious notes concerning primary sources, for which 'he ransacked old chronicles and musty records, consulted with peasants, gamekeepers, wayfaring pilgrims, and bedridden sibyls.'[1]

Indeed the Waverley novels sired books of tradition. Aware of the links between the romances and local legendry, a youthful admirer, Robert Chambers, gathered together in 1822—and in an expanded edition of 1825—*Illustrations of the Author of Waverley, being Notices and Anecdotes of Real Characters, Scenes, and Incidents, Supposed to be Described in his Works*. Scott's own informative glosses to his stories were published as a unit in 1833, the year after his death, in three volumes titled *Introductions and Notes and Illustrations to the Novels, Tales, and Romances, of the Author of Waverley*, a publication of special value for the student of folklore in literature. The two productions were nicely complementary, as in their sections on David Ritchie, the deformed hermit regarded as a malignant fairy, who suggested to Scott his romance of *The Black Dwarf*. Scott thanked Chambers and Chambers thanked Scott for revealing anecdotes about 'Bowed Davie.'[2] Add to these titles the *Letters on Demonology and Witchcraft* of 1830, and an imposing mass of folkloristic commentary by the author of Waverley is assembled.

Scott was indeed part antiquary, and knew familiarly his predecessors in the garden of antiquities. He completed the manuscript of Joseph Strutt's *Queenhoo-Hall* in the winter of 1807–8 for the publisher John Murray, a romance endeavouring to illustrate manners, speech, and customs during the reign of Henry VI. Dipping deep into the sources for his notes to the ballads and romances, he cites Gervase of Tilbury and Gough's *Camden* on early precedents of current wonders; refers to the third edition of Reginald Scot's *Discovery of Witchcraft* (1665) for its parade of 'absurd and superstitious ideas concerning witches'[3]; takes from Aubrey's *Miscel-*

[1] M. H. H. Macarney, 'Sir Walter Scott's Use of the Preface,' *Longman's Magazine*, LXVI (August, 1905), 370–1.
[2] *Introductions and Notes and Illustrations to the Novels, Tales, and Romances of the Author of Waverley*, I (Edinburgh: printed for Robert Cadell, Edinburgh, and Whittaker & Co., London, 1833), pp. 349–50; Robert Chambers, *Illustrations of the Author of Waverley* (3rd ed.; London and Edinburgh: W. & R. Chambers, 1884), p. 76.
[3] Scott, *Introductions*, I, 208.

Demonology in Scott's Fiction, with chapters on the Supernatural in Scottish Literature (Edinburgh and London: Oliver & Boyd, 1964).

lanies the family spectre of Tullochgorn, hairy May Moulach;[1] alludes to Brand and Hone, Pennant and Roby and Croker. He exchanged letters and books with Jacob Grimm in 1814 and 1815, expressing pleasure that two ballads from his *Minstrelsy* had been translated for a journal edited by Jacob, and voicing a desire to see the newly published *Kindermärchen*, which Jacob later sent him. He informs Grimm that he reads German with facility, and has often enjoyed the *Volksmährchen* of Musäus. In fact, Scott eventually accumulated a library of some three hundred books in German on antiquities and folklore. The correspondence terminated when Scott plunged his energies into the Waverley novels, but for a stretch he matched the erudition of Jacob, and shared with the brothers their folkloric passion.[2] In his appreciation of the Grimms, Scott was of course squarely in the lineage of Wright, Thoms, Croker, and other British antiquaries.

In one detailed letter to Jacob Grimm, Scott spoke knowledgeably of Douce as 'by far our most diligent investigator of the history of popular fiction,' but gently downgraded him as a collector of minute information rather than a broad theorizer.[3] Sir Walter wrote directly to Douce in 1804, thanking him for literary favours given the Scotsman on a recent visit to London, and again in 1808 on receipt of Douce's *Illustrations of Shakespeare*. Its note on 'Fools of Shakespeare' stirred his recollection of *all-licensed* fools, half-knaves, and half-numskulls, maintained in the great houses of Scotland half a century earlier, and still remembered for their *bon mots* and quips.[4]

More than any of his contemporaries, Sir Walter balanced his relish for library antiquities with his zest for the field. His imagination was kindled by tales he heard in his youth in the Highlands, then largely inaccessible. Listening to old warriors relating their adventures in the Jacobite uprising of the '45, he was struck by the 'ancient traditions and high spirit of a people, who, living in a civilized age and country, retained so strong a tincture of manners belonging to an early period of society. . . .'[5] This kind of a subculture offers the ideal field area for the folklorist, but Scott was continually torn between his ethnographical and literary bents, and he recognized that they frequently led from the same starting

[1] Scott, *Minstrelsy*, I, lxxxvi.
[2] Edward V. K. Brill, 'The Correspondence between Jacob Grimm and Walter Scott,' *Hessische Blätter für Volkskunde*, LIV (1963), 489–509.
[3] *Ibid.*, p. 496.
[4] *Letters of Sir Walter Scott; Addressed to the Rev. R. Polwhele; D. Gilbert, Esq.; Francis Douce, Esq. etc. etc.* (London: J. B. Nichols and Son, 1832), pp. 17–18, 91–3.
[5] Scott, *Introductions*, I, 10.

point in different directions. He explained this disharmony in his introduction to *Guy Mannering*:

> ... the manner in which the novels were composed cannot be better illustrated than by reciting the simple narrative on which Guy Mannering was originally founded; but to which, in the progress of the work, the production ceased to bear any, even the most distant resemblance. The tale was originally told me by an old servant of my father's, an excellent old Highlander, without a fault, unless a preference to mountain dew over less potent liquors be accounted one. He believed as firmly in the story, as in any part of his creed.[1]

And then for a dozen pages he recounts the narration of old John McKinley about a benighted traveller who turns out to be an astrologer, and predicts evil for the new baby of the house when he comes of age. Having reached twenty-one, the youth travels to the astrologer, wrestles with the demon, wins, and marries the sage's daughter. Yet these themes of prophecy, trial, love, and marriage failed to provide the stuff of romance. Other legends Sir Walter found even more intractable. He planned an abortive romance, to 'turn upon a fine legend of superstition' current in his part of the Border around Abbotsford, the feats of the magician-poet-prophet Thomas of Hersildoune, popularly known as Thomas the Rhymer, who would return from the land of faery to protect his people during some future convulsion of society. A stranger, who is Thomas, leads a horse-dealer to a hillside cavern where knights are sleeping and tells him to choose between drawing a sword or blowing a horn which hang in the cavern; if he chooses correctly, the knights will rise; but the horse-dealer blows the horn, and falls dead. Scott knew this as a well-travelled tale, attached to Highland glens and Northumberland coal mines, and recorded in Reginald Scot's *The Discoverie of Witchcraft*; later, E. S. Hartland would allude to continental versions in his analysis of the myth of the Returning Hero. 'Although admitting of much poetical ornament,' Scott observed, 'it is clear that this legend would have formed but an unhappy foundation for a prose story, and must have degenerated into a mere fairy tale.'[2] In this distinction, between the structure of the folktale and the composition of an historical romance, lay Scott's problem, and as a literary craftsman he necessarily sacrificed the integrity of the first for the artistry of the second.

If he took liberties in his fiction, Scott stayed close to genuine

---

[1] Scott, *Introductions*, I, p. 131.   [2] *Ibid.*, p. 42.

folk traditions in his introductions and notes, and his fecund mind ranged over numerous beliefs and marvels imbedded in Border lore. Inevitably he discussed the fairy mythology, remarking that the 'elfin people' were popularly believed to haunt the craggy sources of the river Forth; he synopsized the celebrated tract, *The Secret Commonwealth of Elves, Fauns, and Fairies* (1691) by Robert Kirk, in which the minister and Gaelic scholar of Aberfoyle parish in Perthshire recounted his abduction by the fairies.[1] Scrupulously Scott pointed out a mistaken attribution in early editions of *The Heart of Midlothian* for the legend about the fairy boy of Leith, who flew overseas every Thursday before midnight to meet the fairies, and on his return could reveal to any questioner that person's fortune. This wonder came not from Richard Baxter's *The Certainty of Worlds of Spirits* (1691), but Richard Barton's [*sic*] *Pandaemonium, or, The Devil's Cloyster* (1684).[2] The Waverley novelist knew that vulgar opinion believed running streams could bar magic forces, and cited in evidence Robert Burns' tale *Tam o' Shanter.* Commenting on his own ballad *Lord Soulis*, Scott explained that *redcap* was the name for a spirit which haunted every old castle in southern Scotland, and he went on to mention the necromancer Michael Scot, who assigned evil spirits the endless task of twisting ropes of sand, still observable in unfinished strands ridged along the seashore.[3] Other mysterious creatures he noticed were the mermaid, the monstrous sea-snake, the malignant Brown Man of the Muirs, and the water-kelpie. For this last sprite the Reverend Dr. John Jamieson, then working on *An Etymological Dictionary of the Scottish Language* (two volumes, 1808), wrote a dialect poem, 'Water-Kelpie,' which Scott printed in the *Minstrelsy* and elucidated with this commentary:

> A very common tale in Scotland is here alluded to by the poet. On the banks of a rapid stream the water spirit was heard repeatedly to exclaim, in a dismal tone, 'The hour is come, but not the man'; when a person coming up, contrary to all remonstrances, endeavoured to ford the stream, and perished in the attempt. The original story is to be found in Gervase of Tilbury.—In the parish of Castleton, the same story is told, with this variation, that the bye-standers prevented, by force, the predestined individual from entering the river, and shut him up in the church, where he was next

[1] *Ibid.*, p. 341; II, 58, 109–10.
[2] *Ibid.*, I, 456. But Scott still erred; the author's name was Bovet not Barton.
[3] Scott, *Minstrelsy*, II, 372, 334–5.

morning found suffocated, with his face lying immersed in the baptismal font.[1]

Up in Cromarty, Hugh Miller would also relate the episode. The same incident is linked with many rivers in Norway, and indeed is known throughout Europe.[2]

Clan feuds and Border strife had seared their way deep into Scottish folk memory, and exercised a special attraction for the romancer. He knew of Border children born with broadaxe marks on their necks and blood drops spattered on their arms.[3] Rob Roy, the hero of one novel, had perpetrated his Robin Hood exploits within forty miles of Glasgow on the lawless side of the Border early in the eighteenth century, and stories of his exploits continued to divide the MacGregor and Campbell clans.[4] In the grim, righteous Covenanters, who in 1557 organized their band of nobles as a 'Congregation of the Lord' to safeguard their Calvinistic Protestantism and Scottish nationalism, and fought in the 1670's and '80's against the imposition of episcopacy on their church, Scott found heroic martyrs of legend, and his story for *Old Mortality*. A ready-made devil was John Graham of Claverhouse, viscount of Dundee, killed at the battle of Killiecrankie in 1689. Persecuted Covenanting sects like the Camerons regarded Satan and his fiends as their omnipresent foe, harassing them with disasters great and small, from a sudden flood to the casting of a horseshoe; Claverhouse they believed to be a minion of Satan. A charm from the Devil enabled him to resist leaden bullets, and only a silver button fired by his own servant finally killed him. Scott acknowledges that he followed popular tradition in giving Claverhouse a black instead of a sorrel charger, as befitted the character of its donor, the Evil One himself, who had performed a Caesarean operation on the dam. 'This horse was so fleet, and its rider so expert,' he observed, 'that they are said to have outstripped and *coted*, or turned, a hare upon the Bran-Law, near the head of Moffat Water, where the descent is so precipitous, that no merely earthly horse could keep its feet, or merely mortal rider could keep the saddle.' Tradition alleged that a cup of wine given Clavers by his butler turned to clotted blood, and that cold water boiled at the touch of his foot.[5]

[1] Scott, *Minstrelsy*, III (2nd ed., Edinburgh, 1803), 365–6; T. F. Henderson edition (Edinburgh and London, New York, 1902), IV, 345–6.
[2] Reidar Th. Christiansen (ed.), *Folktales of Norway* (Chicago and London, 1964), p. 67, gives a text and refers to a study by Robert Wildhaber in *Rheinisches Jahrbuch für Volkskunde*, IX (1958), 65–88.
[3] Scott, *Introductions*, III, 116.
[4] *Ibid.*, I, 220.   [5] *Ibid.*, pp. 458, 392–3; Scott, *Minstrelsy*, pp. 193–5.

Robert the Bruce appears in Sir Walter's notes as a hero of legend. Before the Bruce's triumph over the British in the battle of Bannockburn in 1314, he prayed to a casket supposedly holding the luminous silver arm of St. Fillan. But the king's chaplain, a man of little faith, had removed the arm for safekeeping. Of a sudden the casket opened and shut, and onlookers saw that the saint had returned his arm to its receptacle, in assurance of victory.[1]

Spectre-haunted castles attracted Scott, both as a likely subject for sombre ballad and romance and as a prominent feature of Scottish lore. He dwells on the castle of Hermitage, sunk into the ground by the load of its iniquities. The door of the dungeon where Lord Soulis conferred with evil spirits was opened only once in seven years by a demon to whom he gave the keys on leaving the castle; into this chamber no peasant dared look, or even to thrust a willow stick through the door chinks, for when he pulled it out it would be completely peeled. So too did the ruins of Cadyow Castle, along the banks of the river Esk, near Auchindinny, hold their share of guilt. Here Lord Bothwellhaugh cruelly cast out his wife to obtain her barony; her ghost, clad in white, carrying her child, hovered around the ruins. When the stones were moved to a new site four miles distant, the spectre moved its quarters too, and continued to terrify the domestics. The common people believed that all formidable, ancient castles were constructed by the Picts, who propitiated the spirit of the soil by bathing the foundation stone in the sacrificial blood of a human victim. Likewise did the Gaels immure alive some poor mortal as a foundation sacrifice. St. Columba was supposed to have thus buried St. Oran, to appease the spirits who levelled each night the structure reared during the day.[2]

Sir Walter was not oblivious of the humorous lore which only slowly gained the attention of folklorists. The practice along the Border of giving nicknames to propertyless persons sharing the same name led to comic inventions and jests. Scott remembered in the little village of Lustruther that four natives all bore the name of Andrew or Dandie Oliver, and were distinguished by the nicknames Dandie Eassil-gate, Dandie Wassil-gate, Dandie Thumbie, and Dandie Dumbie. The first two took their sobriquets from their residences east and west in town, the third from a malformation of the thumb, and the fourth from his taciturnity. In a comparable village, a beggar woman passing through and receiving no alms is supposed to have asked if there were any Christians in Annandale.

[1] Scott, *Minstrelsy*, III (2nd ed., Edinburgh, 1803), p. 391.
[2] *Ibid.*, II, 334; III, 398; II, 371.

To which a resident replied, 'Na, na, there are nae Christians here; we are a' Johnstones and Jardines.' This conversation follows the thread of an international tale type (1833e), in which an illiterate woman misunderstands the simple questions of a missionary. In another note, on 'Scottish domestics,' he relates an obviously travelled anecdote of a master and his quick-tongued servant. Commanded to leave his position immediately for a gross offence, the domestic replied, 'In troth, and that will I not. If your honour disna ken when ye hae a gude servant, I ken when I hae a gude master, and go away I will not.' After a similar breach, the master said, 'John, you and I shall never sleep under the same roof again.' Whereon John answered, 'Whare the deil can your honour be ganging?'[1]

Household ceremonies that play a part in the novels are further explained in the notes. The groaning malt and the *ken-no*, as the special ale and rich cheese were called which women of the family offered at the birth to the unsuspecting males, perhaps harked back to secret rites of the *Bona Dea*. The lykewake, or custom of watching the dead body, was based in the superstition that the disembodied spirit of the deceased hovered around the corpse in the interval between death and burial, and if properly invoked, could cause the dead body to speak and reveal any foul play involved. But these charms, dependent on leaving the door open, were attended with mortal risks.

The following story, which is frequently related by the peasants of Scotland, will illustrate the imaginary danger of leaving the door ajar. In former times, a man and his wife lived in a solitary cottage, on one of the extensive border fells. One day, the husband died suddenly; and his wife, who was equally afraid of staying alone by the corpse, or leaving the dead body by itself, repeatedly went to the door, and looked anxiously over the lonely moor, for the sight of some person approaching. In her confusion and alarm, she accidentally left the door ajar, when the corpse suddenly started up, and sat in, the bed, frowning and grinning at her frightfully. She sat alone, crying bitterly, unable to avoid the fascination of the dead man's eye, and too much terrified to break the sudden silence, till a Catholic priest, passing over the wild, entered the cottage. He first set the door quite open, then put his little finger in his mouth, and said the paternoster backwards, when the horrid look of the corpse relaxed, it fell back on the bed, and behaved itself as a dead man ought to do.[2]

[1] Scott, *Introductions*, I, 167; Type 1833e, *ibid.*, p. 386.
[2] Scott, *Minstrelsy*, III, 252.

Many other folk matters engrossed Sir Walter, spells of gypsies and witches, second sight and prophetic dreams, and the gushing of blood from a corpse at a murderer's touch.

In his various notes and prefaces, Scott had commented on many topics of supernatural and local tradition, and finally he felt impelled to organize his materials and thoughts into a single work. The *Letters on Demonology and Witchcraft*, published in 1830, two years before his death, brings to fruition and synthesis his lifelong interest in these subjects, and is the first full-scale treatise in English on what before long would be called folklore. The *Letters* (addressed to Scott's son-in-law, J. G. Lockhart) promptly took a place beside Brand's *Popular Antiquities* as an immediate authority and reference in matters supernatural and archaic.

Unlike the *Popular Antiquities*, the *Letters* were fluently written and adroitly organized. The florid manner of the Waverley novels has given way to a closely reasoned prose, but the old narrative skill remains, employed to vivify the cases of spectral sights and witchcraft trials paraded before the reader.

The ten *Letters*, though untitled, were abstracted in a table of contents. Their main subjects may be listed as follows: I, Imaginary Apparitions; II, Scripture and the Question of Witches and Demons; III, Heathen Sources of Demonology; IV, the Fairy Mythology; V, Fairy and Witch Beliefs; VI, Christianity and Demonology in the Sixteenth and Seventeenth Centuries; VII, Witchcraft in Europe; VIII, Witchcraft in England; IX, Witchcraft in Scotland; X, Ghost Stories.

While the subject matter often overlaps with and dips into the *Popular Antiquities*, Scott was less concerned than Brand with calendrical custom, and more with supernatural belief. Theological polemics also coloured his outlook, but the anti-papism of Bourne and Brand gives way to a broader animus against all divisions of Christianity, the Calvinist as well as the Catholic, who identify witchcraft with heresy to strengthen their own 'evil power.' Scott writes as a rationalist and latitudinarian Christian, weighing the evidence for and against apparitions, witches, and ghosts in the light of reason and with the guidance of the Church, but at too early a date to benefit from empirical science, ethnology, and the Higher Criticism. His threads of argument bring into order the mass of legendary traditions recorded in the British Isles from Aubrey through Hone.

Scott is addressing himself to three main questions: the reality of ghosts and apparitions; the genesis and character of fairies, witches, and demons, according to the reports of their observers;

and the historical relationship of witchcraft to the Church and civil law.

In his first and last *Letters*, Scott explains away a number of ghost and spectre tales on rational grounds. The evidence of human eyes and ears is known to be fallible; the army of marching companies seen in 1686 on the banks of the Clyde by two-thirds of the assembled multitude was due to inflamed imaginations and mass suggestibility. Rustics have mistaken ordinary noises for the sound of the Wild Hunt rushing overhead. Perhaps a ghost is invented, as in the case of the Highlander who testified in court in 1749 that the ghost of an English sergeant had revealed to him the details of his murder; under cross-examination the Highlander stated that the English ghost spoke to him in Gaelic. Scott conjectures that the Highland plaintiff invented the ghost, a figure plausible to his countrymen, in order to avoid turning informer.

The novelist himself gives instances of his own exposure to spectres when he slept in ghost-haunted castles, but while his youthful—as contrasted to his more mature—sensibilities evoked sensations, spirits failed to materialize. Tersely he concludes, 'It is the same with all those that are called accredited ghost stories usually told at the fireside. They want evidence.'[1] Yet he appreciates the sincerity of believers, and relates a powerful ghost story personally told him by William Clerk, chief clerk to the Jury Court, Edinburgh, of a captain who shot a sailor, and was thereafter haunted by his ghost to the point where he plunged overboard. On the side of his own personal belief, he acknowledges that 'The abstract possibility of apparitions must be admitted by every one who believes in a Deity, and his superintending omnipotence.'[2] Scott was verging on the yet unmapped field of psychical research, which would later intrigue his fellow Scot, Andrew Lang. He discusses dreams, sleepwalking, visions, hallucinations. One of his narratives deals with a gay blade who went out on the town night after night and kept seeing green goblins on his return. His physician prescribed a complete rest in the country; the patient recovered, and enjoyed his new life so much that he decided to move permanently, and had his furniture shipped down from the city. As soon as the furniture arrived, he began seeing the goblins again. The traditional character of these phenomena interest Scott less than the question they raise of wilful or involuntary deception.

With visible fairies and witches, Scott does consider traditional elements. He examines the sources of popular demonology among

---

[1] Scott, *Letters on Demonology and Witchcraft, addressed to J. G. Lockhart* (London: John Murray, 1830), p. 359.   [2] *Ibid.*, p. 47.

the ancient heathens, as reflected in classic mythology and reinforced by pagans of modern times. Scott had read in Cotton
Mather's *Magnalia*, and singles out the Massachusetts Puritan's
vivid examples of Indian—and the white man's—credence in
shamanistic magic. In the vein of Brand, but with his own personal
knowledge as supplement, he sets forth examples of pagan customs
for appeasing devils still practised in Scotland. In the Beltane
ceremony (already noticed by Pennant), cakes were ritually baked
on the first of May and dedicated to the demons associated with
birds and beasts of prey, that they might spare the flocks and
herds. Coming to recent British sources, Scott shows wide acquaintance with the literature on the fairies, on which he had already
written in the *Minstrelsy*. He cites standard older works like
Joseph Glanvill's *Saducismus Triumphatus* (1700) and the field
collection of his friend Crofton Croker. In the legend of Thomas
the Rhymer he recognizes 'the first, and most distinguished instance, of a man alleged to have obtained supernatural knowledge
by means of the fairies.'[1] He mentions other versions of this
tradition of the Sleeping Army, one in Reginald Scot, and one
personally known to him from Sheriffmoor. The relation between
the human magicmaker and the otherworld fairy especially intrigues
Scott. Often an accused and convicted witch confessed to obtaining
her powers of sorcery from the fairies, as Scott learned from reading
Robert Pitcairn's records of *Criminal Trials in Scotland*. Alice
Pearson, who was tried in 1588 for practising occult arts, testified
that a green man had once come to her. This association of fairy
and witch foreshadows the point that would be made by Katharine
Briggs in *The Anatomy of Puck* (1959), on the blending and merging
of spectral and malevolent beings. A connection between a ghost
and fairyland appeared in a curious experience Scott reports from
a seaport town in North Berwick. A weaver beheld the figure of
his first wife, who asked him to rescue her from Elfland. The
baffled weaver turned for advice to his clergyman, who pondered
how to counsel his parishioner; finally he admonished, 'Think of
her as a saint in heaven and not as a prisoner in Elfland.'

In his *Letters* on witchcraft in Europe and the British Isles, Scott
states that much stronger and clearer evidence is available for this
than for other kinds of supernatural belief because of legal accusa-
tions against witches presented to judges. His comments explaining
the witch mania are shrewd. He points out that, in view of other
articles of faith in the sixteenth century, such as the detection of
murderers by divining rods, treating the sword instead of the

[1] *Ibid.*, p. 140.

wound, the curing of warts by sympathetic magic—credited by Francis Bacon—necromancy ascribed to wicked women does not seem far-fetched. This core of belief was, however, manipulated in a truly diabolical fashion for ecclesiastical, political, and personal ends. Heresy was linked with witchcraft, so that the established Church would label a group of gathered Protestants a Sabbath of hags and fiends—but the Calvinists made the same charges against their foes. Wealthy persons too became targets, so that their inquisitors could despoil them. Perhaps a childish lie would start an inexorable train of tragic accusation; Scott thinks this happened in the witch-crazed village of Mohra in Sweden, where a tardy boy, lying late abed, claimed that witches had carried him to the devil's block-house at Blockula. The nefarious Mathew Hopkins, the self-reputed witch-finder, found profit in calling at English towns in 1645 and 1646 and spying out and torturing hapless victims till they confessed. Even the sceptical Sir Thomas Browne, who rejected so many 'Vulgar Errours' of the seventeenth century, once gave evidence against a witch. When mischief followed close upon a threat, as could happen coincidentally and did happen in cases related by Scott, lawyers cited these facts as grim evidence, under the charge *damnum minatum et malum secutum*. With the rise of rationalism and scepticism in the eighteenth century, witchcraft passed out of the courts and back to hearth-fire gossip. The novelist recalls in his own time how an old woman raising chickens wished ill on a grain farmer unable to carry her grain to market; on the way a wheel of his cart came off and his grain was damaged. In an earlier day she would have paid with her life.

The *Letters* tell a story of the battle between reason and unreason. Packed with illustrative narratives, they offered a rich resource for antiquarian folklorists in the ensuing decades.

[2 ALLAN CUNNINGHAM]

When *Marmion* reached the bookstalls in 1810, a young admirer travelled seventy miles on foot from Dalswintor to Edinburgh to meet its author. He missed him, and Allan Cunningham did not greet his hero until Scott came to London in 1820 to receive a baronetcy. The author of Waverley sat for a marble bust by the sculptor Francis Chantrey, whom Cunningham had served as secretary for ten years, after leaving Scotland for London. In 1821 Scott returned to London for the coronation of George IV. Cunningham saw him again, and recorded their conversation on ballads and tales.

5. ROBERT CHAMBERS

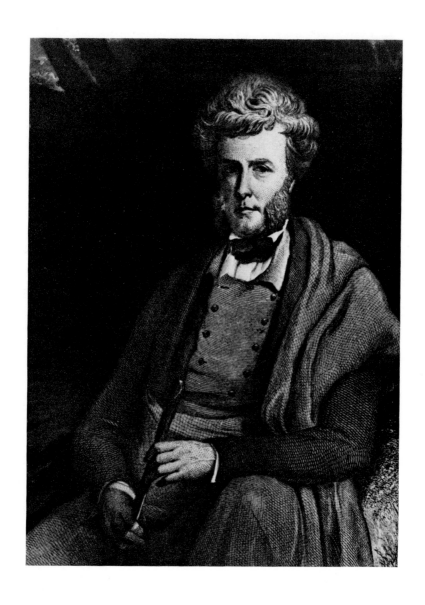

6. HUGH MILLER

C.—I have gathered many such things myself, Sir Walter, and as I still propose to make a collection of all Scottish songs of poetic merit, I shall work up many of my stray verses and curious anecdotes in the notes.

S.—I am glad that you are about such a thing. Any help which I can give you, you may command. Ask me any questions, no matter how many, I shall answer them if I can. Don't be timid in your selection. Our ancestors fought boldly, spoke boldly, and sang boldly too. I can help you to an old characteristic ditty not yet in print:—

> There dwelt a man into the wast,
>   And Ogin he was cruel,
> For on his bridal night ar e'en
>   He gat up and grat for gruel.
>
> They brought to him a gude sheep's head,
>   A bason, and a towel;
> Gar take thee whim-whams far frae me,
>   I winna want my gruel.

C.—I never heard that verse before. The hero seems related to the bridegroom of Nithsdale:—

> The bridegroom grat as the sun gade down;
> The bridegroom grat as the sun gade down;
> To ony man I'll gie a hunder marks sae free,
> This night that will bed wi' a bride for me.

S.—A cowardly loon enough. I know of many crumbs and fragments of verse which will be useful to your work. The Border was once peopled with poets, for every one that could fight could make ballads, some of them of great power and pathos. Some such people as the minstrels were living less than a century ago.

C.—I knew a man, the last of a race of district tale-tellers, who used to boast of the golden days of his youth, and say, that the world, with all its knowledge, was grown sixpence a-day worse for him.

S.—How was that? How did he make his living? By telling tales, or singing ballads?

C.—By both. He had a devout tale for the old, and a merry song for the young. He was a sort of beggar.

S.—Out upon thee, Allan. Dost thou call that begging?
Why, man, we make our bread by story-telling, and honest
bread it is.[1]

The common folklore interests of the two Scottish men of letters,
one already famous, the other now forgotten, are apparent in this
recollection, set down in Cunningham's high-flown style. Clearly
the younger man felt the powerful fascination of Border traditions,
and looked to Scott for direction, with the predictable consequence
that his own writing career meandered in the marchland between
literary composition and folklore collecting. Scott became his
mentor, and obtained cadetships for his sons.

Cunningham was born in Keir, in Dumfriesshire, and apprenticed
to his brother, a stonemason. At the age of twenty-five, in 1809, he
met the engraver Robert H. Cromek, and showed him a sheaf of
his poems which he described as old songs. The following year
Cromek published them under his own name as *Remains of Nithsdale and Galloway Song, with Historical and Traditional Notices
relative to the Manners and Customs of the Peasantry*. In an im-
broglio much like the feud between Croker and Keightley over the
Fairy Traditions of the South of Ireland, Cunningham alleged that
every piece in the book save for two scraps was written by him,
while Cromek claimed that Cunningham had represented the ballads
to him as traditional not original. In an edition issued seventy
years later, the publisher, Alexander Gardner of Paisley, acknowledged Cunningham's authorship, saying in a prefatory note,
' . . . the volume is interesting as the production of a representative
Scotsman, whose songs are at least founded on ballad and traditionary lore, and whose expositions of the manners and customs
of the peasantry of his native district, embodied in the work are
replete with information which every antiquarian must prize.'[2]
The appendixes treating folklore subjects offer fresh information,
and point to the road Cunningham might have taken had he guide-
posts to follow. They deal with such matters as 'Scottish Games,'
'History of Witchcraft, sketched from the popular tales of the
peasantry of Nithsdale and Galloway,' 'Character of the Scottish
Lowland Fairies, from the Popular Belief of Nithsdale and Galloway,' and an 'Account of Billie Blin',' a notorious Scottish brownie.

In these essays Cunningham records traditions of nefarious
witches and fairies attached to known local characters. The gyre

---

[1] Rev. David Hogg, *Life of Allan Cunningham, with Selections from his Works and
Correspondence* (Dumfries: John Anderson & Son, 1875), pp. 203–4.
[2] *Remains of Nithsdale and Galloway Song* (Paisley: Alexander Gardner, 1880),
publisher's note.

Carline turns waves into mud, and a bewitched cow is burned. There is talk of the 'ill or uncannie een' (evil eye) and the counter-charm from a rowan tree; elf-shooting; the curing of a breath-blasted child; a changeling; the resistance by a husband to the fairies' seduction of his wife; a brownie's aid to a lady in childbirth. Writing on the Scottish brownies, Cunningham (alias Cromek) remarked that some features had already been given the public by Mr. Scott in his *Minstrelsy* of the Scottish Border, but that this discussion was the more complete. He further criticized Scott's ballad of 'Cospatrick' in the *Minstrelsy* as patchwork, and false to fairy-tale consistency in omitting the brownie Billie Blin' and having inanimate objects like bed, blanket, and sheets speak out in place of Billie.[1] In such ways Cunningham showed the instinct of the simon-pure folklorist. He singled out informants, noting 'This curious legend is one among a considerable number which were copied from the recital of a peasant-woman of Galloway, upwards of ninety years of age.'[2] Cunningham voices the perennial lament that modern life will doom the old traditional lore,

There is an old Scotch adage—

> Whare the scythe cuts and the sock rives
> Hae done wi' *fairies* an' *bee-bykes!*

The land once ripped by the ploughshare, or the sward once passed over by the scythe proclaimed the banishment of the Fairies from holding residence there ever after. The quick progress of Lowland agriculture will completely overthrow their empire; none now are seen, save solitary and dejected fugitives, ruminating among the ruins of their fallen kingdom![3]

How the fertile soil of folk belief nourishes the growth of tales and ballads was readily understood by the poet-antiquary. In printing a fragment of 'Lady Margerie'—

> But when brother Henry's cruel brand
> Had done the bloody deed,
> The silver-buttons flew off his coat,
> And his nose began to bleed.—

he explains the meaning of the last two lines as a 'preternatural sign' denoting a murderer among the 'vulgar' in Scotland.[4]

[1] *Remains of Nithsdale and Galloway Song*, now first published by R. H. Cromek (London: printed for T. Cadell and W. Davies, 1810), pp. 338 n., 206–7.
[2] *Ibid.*, p. 205.
[3] *Ibid.*, pp. 309–10, in Appendix F, 'Character of the Scottish Lowland Fairies, from the Popular Belief of Nithsdale and Galloway.'   [4] *Ibid.*, p. 224.

In 1813 Cunningham brought out under his own name *Songs: chiefly in the Rural Language of Scotland,* in the poetic tradition of Robert Burns and his friend James Hogg, the 'Ettrick Shepherd.' These poems employed folk speech but were subjective lyrics rather than—as in Scott's *Border Minstrelsy*—imitations of folk ballads.

The climax of Cunningham's efforts with folk materials, before he turned to other writing projects, came in his *Traditional Tales of the English and Scottish Peasantry,* issued in two volumes in 1822. A perceptive Preface showed clearly enough the author's intimacy with oral narratives, but the promise of his title was not realized in the contents. An entry in Scott's diary for November 14, 1826, appraised the work of his disciple in friendly but candid terms.

> We breakfasted at honest Allan Cunningham's—honest Allan—a leal and true Scotsman of the old cast. A man of genius, besides, who only requires the tact of knowing when and where to stop, to attain the universal praise which ought to follow it. I look upon the alteration of 'It's hame and it's hame,' and 'A wet sheet and a flowing sea,' as among the best songs going. His prose has often admirable passages, but he is obscure and overlays his meaning, which will not do nowadays, when he who runs must read.[1]

A modern reader may well feel that Sir Walter was charitable indeed, and that the windy, wordy, artificial style of the 'leal' Scott contrasts oddly with the tang of peasant speech. These verbose narrations do exhibit a sea witch who curses ships, the ghost of a shipwrecked lady murdered for her gold by a fisherman, a cup-bearer to the fairies, spectral troops that presage death. But traditional tales they are not, and they might more accurately have been titled 'Literary Tales Faintly Suggested by Oral Traditions of the Scottish Peasantry.' In 1822 the distinction between invention and tradition was not very meaningful to Cunningham, nor to most of his contemporaries.

[3 ROBERT CHAMBERS]

In March, 1824, a Scottish youth of twenty-two published the first part of a serial work entitled *Traditions of Edinburgh,* still a unique collection of urban folklore. Young Robert Chambers

---

[1] John G. Lockhart, *Memoirs of the Life of Sir Walter Scott, Bart.,* 7 vols. (Edinburgh, 1837–38), VI, 385.

(1802–71) dedicated his second volume, 'respectfully and grate-fully,' to Sir Walter Scott, Bart., who furnished him with materials after reading the first volume. Scott had indeed once contemplated such an enterprise himself. So a friendship developed which Chambers had avidly sought. When still in his teens, he had sent the Waverley novelist a transcript of songs from *Lady of the Lake*, in a peculiar calligraphy designed as a means of attracting the attention of persons superior to himself. The technique worked.

When George IV some months afterwards came to Edin-burgh, good Sir Walter remembered me, and procured for me the business of writing the address of the Royal Society of Edinburgh to his Majesty, for which I was handsomely paid. Several other learned bodies followed the example, for Sir Walter Scott was the arbiter of everything during that frantic time, and thus I was substantially benefited by his means.

According to what Mr. Constable [Scott's publisher] told me, the great man liked me, in part because he understood I was from Tweedside. On seeing the earlier numbers of the *Traditions*, he expressed astonishment as to 'where the boy got all the information.' But I did not see or hear from him till the first volume had been completed. He then called upon me one day, along with Mr. Lockhart. I was overwhelmed with the honour, for Sir Walter Scott was almost an object of worship to me. I literally could not utter a word . . . A very few days after this visit, Sir Walter sent me, along with a kind letter, a packet of manuscript, consisting of sixteen folio pages, in his usual close handwriting, and containing all the reminiscences he could at the time summon up of old persons and things in Edinburgh. Such a treasure to me! And such a gift from the greatest literary man of the age to the humblest![1]

Even more generosity followed, for Scott contributed to Chambers' next work, *The Popular Rhymes of Scotland* (1826), allowing his young friend to walk home with him from Parliament House and listen to Sir Walter's stores of information on subjects of their mutual interests. In his third folklore work, *Scottish Jests and Anecdotes* (1832), Chambers included a section on 'Mots of Sir Walter Scott,' naming one of his idol's chief informants, 'Mrs. Murray Keith, a venerable Scotch lady, from whom Sir Walter Scott derived many of the traditionary stories and anecdotes wrought up in his admirable fictions. . . .' When the novelist denied

---

[1] William Chambers, *Memoir of William and Robert Chambers* (13th ed.; Edinburgh and London: W. & R. Chambers, 1884), pp. 205–7.

using—or misusing—her tales, she exclaimed, 'What, d'ye think I dinna ken my ain groats among other folk's kail?'[1]

Still other writings on tradition linked the two in this early period of Chambers' authorship. In 1817 Chambers wrote a piece on the Black Dwarf in the *Scots Magazine*, which Scott reprinted in the preface to his novel *The Black Dwarf*; William Chambers, Robert's brother, published in 1820 *The Life and Anecdotes of the Black Dwarf, or David Ritchie*, gathering together the tales attributing to 'Bowed Davie' the destruction of sheep and cattle by fairy power. In 1823 Robert Chambers brought out the *Illustrations of the Author of Waverley: being Notices and Anecdotes of Real Characters, Scenes, and Incidents Supposed to be Described in his Works.*

By the age of thirty, Chambers had published three collections based on oral traditions, each exploring a little-examined portion of the folk inheritance. Yet the next three decades of his crowded life as an Edinburgh publisher, editor, and author took Chambers away from folklore, and he never returned to it until the crowning work of his life, which hastened his death, *The Book of Days* (2 vols., 1862–4). Still, this output in itself represents a substantial and creative contribution to the folklore movement.

An antiquary should by rights be elderly, but Chambers developed his antiquarian interests as a stripling. In his first score of years, however, he had lived a lifetime of struggle and poverty. Born in Peebles in 1802, the son of a once prosperous drapery merchant who went bankrupt, Robert moved to Edinburgh in his eleventh year to continue his schooling, living with his elder brother William in an unheated, unlighted room. After school he roamed the Old Town absorbing its legends for the book he would issue before long. For lack of entrance fee he was forced to surrender his hope of a university education. At one point he clerked in Pilrig at four shillings a week, walking the ten miles each way to and from his home on a foot lamed from birth. At sixteen he set up as a bookseller, with stock from his father's library and his schoolbooks, in Leith Walk in Edinburgh, and from then on maintained himself.[2] Meanwhile William had set up a creaky little printing press, and on this he cranked out Robert's *Traditions of Edinburgh* in parts, the sale of one part financing the printing of a sequel.[3] Scott visited the shop to meet the author.

[1] *Scottish Jests and Anecdotes. To which are added, a selection of choice English and Irish jests* (Edinburgh: William Tait, 1832), p. 32.

[2] A. Turnbull, *William and Robert Chambers 1800–1883* (Edinburgh and London: W. & R. Chambers, Ltd., n.d.), a twenty-four-page commemorative pamphlet.

[3] Coleman O. Parsons, *Serial Publication of Traditions of Edinburgh* (London: The

In time the brothers became eminent public figures of Edinburgh, and partners in a well-known publishing firm. In March, 1965, the present writer called at the firm's office on Thistle Street, purchased a copy of the *Traditions of Edinburgh*, still in print, and had it autographed by the firm's director, the great-great-grandson of Robert Chambers.

Chambers considered himself an antiquary, and in his writings continually employed the term 'antiquities,' which he related to 'oral intelligence' in preference to bookish sources. So in *Traditions of Edinburgh* he paints this picture of a district especially congenial to his subject:

> The West Bow is a place abounding more in antiquities than any other part of the city, and, what could not fail to render these antiquities interesting to the public, is the circumstance that they are all accompanied in their preservation by anecdotes of a curious and amusing description. . . . From its peculiarly venerable aspect,—the dark profundities and *culs de sac* that descend from behind it,—its numerous decayed houses with aerial dove-cot-looking gables projecting over the street . . . it seems a place full of grandmothers' tales and quite calculated to maintain a wizard or a ghost in its community. Both of these it has accordingly done within the last century and a half, in the person of the notorious Weir, who first served them in the one capacity, and lastly in the other.[1]

Robert quickly adapted his relish for country traditions to his new urban environment. At Mackay's Classical Academy he met Edinburgh boys who filled his ears with marvellous stories of 'reputed wizards, noted eccentric characters, and remarkable criminals,'[2] such as the Major Weir referred to above, who was executed in 1670 for a series of atrocities. For a hundred years thereafter, no person would live in the demon-infested dwellings, and when a family finally moved in, they experienced the sensation of going downstairs when they were ascending and of going upstairs when they were descending. What schoolboys talked about in fevered tones, elderly residents could amplify from well-stocked memory. A friend gave young Chambers a letter to the venerable Charles Kirkpatrick Sharpe, who knew the scandals of Charles II

[1] Robert Chambers, *Traditions of Edinburgh*, 2 vols. (Edinburgh, printed for W. & C. Tait, 1825), I, 116–17.   [2] Chambers, *Memoir*, p. 128.

Bibliographical Society, 1933), untangles the knots in the several overlapping editions of the *Traditions*. Six serial numbers were issued from March, 1824, to September, 1825.

as if it were yesteryear. Robert talked with others who remembered the Scottish capital during the early reign of George III. One old gentleman could recall fifty titled personages who as late as 1769 dwelt in the Old Town, before it faded into a cluster of tall tenements and dingy closes. This 'ancient native,' who once knew everyone in town and could scarcely place a single face half a century later, complained that he beheld more streets now than persons then.

From such human reservoirs of civic events and personalities Robert pieced together the Edinburgh traditions. They were issued as small brochures, an appropriate form of street literature, aimed to attract volunteered additions, until publisher William gathered them together. Sensibly Robert divided his findings under the rubrics of 'Old Houses' and 'Characters,' the two chief magnets of urban legends. Many old homes possessed their macabre or bizarre tradition. Here Lady Eglintoune died at the age of ninety-one, in 1780, dining with her pet rats and washing her face in sow's milk. The handsome Patersone house yonder was financed from a stake won by shoemaker John Patersone playing golf with the Duke of York against two English noblemen to determine whether the game was of Scotch or English origin. (The third edition of the *Traditions* in 1826 gives a variant account from the first of 1824.) Argyle Square in the Old Town received its name from an incident dating back ninety years. The Duke of Argyle, on learning of the death abroad of George I, quickly apprised his favourite tailor, who at once bought up all the black cloth in town, secured a monopoly on the sale of mourning cloth, and reaped a small fortune, with which he built some of the houses in Argyle Square, naming them for his patron. Another 'well-authenticated' tradition of similar vintage affirmed that the magistrates once offered a resident of Canonmills all the ground between Gabriel's Road and the Gallowlee, in perpetual fee, at the annual rent of a crown bowl of punch, but he rejected it, for the worthless land produced only heath and whins. A century later it yielded rents of ten thousand pounds a year. In one old ducal home lived the idiot son of the second Duke of York, who was said to have killed and roasted a little kitchen boy on the day the Union of Scotland and England was effected (May 1, 1707); the common people said it was a judgment upon the Duke for supporting the Union. In the fire-gutted alley of Beth's Wynd, the evil-looking cellars of certain crazy old houses were believed by old wives of the wynd to have been shut at the time of the plague, which would burst forth anew if they were ever opened.[1]

[1] Chambers, *Traditions*, II, 219–20.

Some houses became legendary because of eccentric characters who lived in and even still haunted them, while other characters attained notoriety independent of a particular edifice. The *Traditions* captured a medley of such personages, from the highborn to the lowliest. At one end of the spectrum were the slightly mad Duchess Catherine, who invited finely dressed ladies to walk and made them sit around her on a dunghill; and despondent Lord Lovat, who lay abed for two years after his wife left him and started up only when he heard Prince Charlie had landed: 'Lassie, bring me my brogues—I'll rise noo!' Once being aroused with important tidings, the aged lord was discovered still in bed, between two buxom, naked Highland lasses, whereon he explained that his thinning blood required the application of animal warmth. At the other end of the social scale were equally mad individuals. 'Daft Jamie' Duff, well remembered by Edinburgh citizens for his antic ways, and written into *Guy Mannering* by Scott, would run around the race-course at Leith bare-legged and switching his sides, under the impression that he was both rider and horse; he carried all gifts of food home to his mother, even putting soup in his pocket, and throwing vittles and garbage on her lap; he loved to attend funerals. 'Daft Jamie' died in 1788, and his escapades lingered in memory well after his death.[1] Characters like these could well explain the interest in tales of numskulls and fools which led the Scottish folklorist William Alexander Clouston to write *The Book of Noodles* in 1888.

There were many other figures of fun and infamy whom Chambers transferred from talk to print: Archibald MacCoul, the rhyming tobacconist; Willie-and-the-Bottle, who could stand on his head on top of a bottle; Claudero the satirist and blackmailer; 'Drunken Charlie' Stewart who had been wounded at Culloden in the '45, and ever after when drunk would attack whomever he met in the King's livery, usually being locked up in consequence. More memorable than these was 'Bowed Joseph,' a proletarian hero who commanded the meal-mobs and directed their riots, for instance ordering them to burn the furnishings of a cruel landlord. A domestic tyrant too, he made his wife walk behind him. Once in jail he blithely walked out past the guards whistling unconcernedly. Denied admission into a city parade, he reacted characteristically:

When the foolish craft of shoemakers used, in former times, to parade the High Street, West Bow, and Grassmarket, with inverted tin kettles on their heads, and schoolboys' rulers in

---

[1] *Ibid.*, I, 292 ff.; II, 9, 11, 64, 69.

their hands, *Bowed Joseph*, who, though a leader and commander on every other public occasion, was not admitted into this procession, on account of his being only a cobbler, dressed himself in his best clothes, with a royal crown painted and gilt, and a wooden truncheon and marched pompously through the city, till he came to the Netherbow, where he planted himself in the middle of the street, to await the approach of the procession, which he, as a citizen of Edinburgh, proposed to welcome into the town. When the royal shoemaker came to the Netherbow Port, Joseph stood forth, removed the truncheon from his haunch, flourished it in the air, and, pointing it to the ground, with much dignity of manner, addressed his pastework Majesty in these words—'Oh, great King Crispianus! what are we in thy sight, but a parcel of puir slaister-kytes —creeshy coblers—sons of bitches?' And we have been told that this ceremony was performed in a style of admirable burlesque.[1]

Bowed Joseph died about 1780 in a fall from a stagecoach when drunk. Drinking accidents and incidents blended with anecdotes of colourfully named drinking clubs, taverns, oyster cellars, and such gathering places for the convivial and morose, where traditions of the city were perpetuated and initiated.

The *Traditions of Edinburgh* introduced a concept only now beginning to attract serious attention, the concept of urban folklore. From its inception on the continent and in Great Britain, the subject of antiquities and superstitions had been associated with the peasantry and the countryside, with landscape and the elements. Chambers recognized the vitality of communal legends in the throbbing metropolis, and of their constant renewal through the interplay of character and incident. Throughout the *Traditions*, he named informants and stayed close to oral report.

In the related work he published soon after, Chambers again displayed an original insight into the formation of oral tradition. *The Popular Rhymes of Scotland, with Illustrations, Collected from Tradition* first came out in 1826. A third and amplified edition, whose Preface was dated 1841, carried the imprint of William and Robert Chambers, now active publishers in their own right; a quarto edition of 1842 bore the title *Popular Rhymes, Fireside Stories, and Amusements, of Scotland*. The first Preface directly stated the antiquarian impulse behind the collection.

In the peculiar eyes of antiquaries, I trust the Work will find favour upon a distinct account. There can be no doubt,

---

[1] Chambers, *Traditions*, II, 148–9.

that many of the 'ratt rimes,' preserved in this, and to be preserved in the succeeding series, though they may now appear vulgar and nugatory, contain materials of obsolete manners of which the present generation would gladly know more, and are the relics of a body of Scottish poetry long antecedent to any which has yet met the attention of collectors.[1]

And the compiler solicited 'Rhymes and Traditionary Anecdotes' from readers.

Again in the 1842 Preface he wrote, 'The purpose of this work is to supply a presumed desideratum in popular antiquities.' Nevertheless, these rhymes and their attached legends had not won the concentrated attention of Brand and his fellows; what manner of lore were they? They were not nursery rhymes, as the title might suggest, but a borderline and ill-defined form between verse and prose, in which a snatch of verse often summed up an anecdote or tradition known to the listeners. Chambers considered these rhymed verses a segment of the popular poetry uncollected by ballad antiquaries like Bishop Percy and Walter Scott, and a complement to the fireside folksongs that regaled Scottish families before the rise of the printed book. He called them 'relics of the old natural literature of my native country.'[2] Some referred to events and stories, some described the peculiar features of a locality and its inhabitants, some were predictions, usually associated with the famous poet-prophet Thomas the Rhymer. They might be sung or recited to soothe the babe in the cradle, to enliven the wits on the village green, or to transmit the wisdom of the cottage. Intensely local in reference and allusion, they yet closely resembled, as Chambers pointed out, rhymes in England and Germany, and no doubt in other Teutonic countries, a proof of their common origin in a distant mythological past—according to the gospel of Jacob Grimm.

An example of a local legend encapsuled in a rhyme was the jingle chanted by villagers of Whittinghame, in East Lothian:

> Oh weel's me noo, Ive gotten a name;
> They ca' me short-hoggers o' Whittinghame![3]

[1] Robert Chambers, *Popular Rhymes of Scotland, with illustrations, collected from tradition* (Edinburgh: William Hunter, and Charles Smith & Co., and London, James Duncan, 1826), Preface, v–vi.
[2] Robert Chambers, *Popular Rhymes, Fireside Stories, and Amusements, of Scotland* (Edinburgh: published by William and Robert Chambers, 1842), Preface.
[3] Chambers, *Popular Rhymes* (1826 ed.), p. 9. All references are to this edition.

By itself the verse is meaningless to an outsider, but to the good people of Whittinghame it carried a complex story. An unwed mother murdered her unwanted child by a large tree outside the village, where ever after, on dark nights, its ghost would run distractedly between the tree and the churchyard, bewailing its lack of a name and its consequent sentence to earthly haunts. One night a drunkard reeling home sighted the spirit and convivially remarked, 'How's a' wi' ye this morning, Short-Hoggers?' Whereon the delighted ghost ran away crying out the verse above and, rejoicing in his newly awarded name, was seen no more. The name 'Short-Hoggers' suggests that the spirit wore short stockings without feet, probably as a result of his many years of fruitless walking. Chambers received this information from an 'informant' (his word, now an accepted term) who in turn had heard the legend and rhyme from an old woman of Whittinghame who had actually seen the ghost.

In this and in other legends, Chambers' novel approach led into well-established patterns of folk tradition. Thus he compiled a section on 'brownies,' the Scottish elf, on the basis of such little rhymes as

Ha! Ha! Ha!
Brownie has't a'![1]

alluding to the brownies' self-declared delight in sipping stolen milk. Chambers went on to relate the episode of a brownie rounding up the sheep into the fold with such alacrity that he also, unwittingly, collected a number of hares, who caused him to exclaim, 'Confound thae wee gray anes! they cost me mair trouble than a' the lave o' them.' This tall tale is found in the Welsh manuscript of *The Red Book of Hergest* in the fourteenth century, and in western North America today.[2]

A good portion of Chambers' entries take the form of place-name etymologies, local sayings, and 'popular reproaches.' The villagers of Guthrie explained the origin of its name from an ancient occurrence. A shipwrecked Scottish king asked a poor fisherwoman, 'Will ye gut ane to me, gudewife?' She answered, 'I'll gut three. Thereupon he responded:

'Then Gut Three
Your Name Sall Be!'[3]

---

[1] Chambers, *Popular Rhymes*, p. 271.
[2] *Ibid.*, p. 274 n. Warren E. Roberts has discussed 'The Sheep Herder and the Rabbits' in *Journal of the Folklore Institute*, III (1966), 43–9.
[3] Chambers, *Popular Rhymes*, pp. 182–3.

What Chambers labels 'Popular Reproaches,' folklorists today usually call 'blason populaire,' and recognize as a distinct species of tradition, the jeering slogan or proverbial taunt hurled in malicious fun by one country, region, or town against another. Chambers succinctly defines the form.

There is a nationality in districts as well as in countries: nay, the people living on different sides of a streamlet, or of the same hill, sometimes entertain prejudices against each other, not less virulent than those of the inhabitants of the different sides of the British Channel or the Pyrenees. This has given rise, in Scotland, to an infinite number of phrases, expressive of vituperation, obloquy, or contempt, which are applied to the inhabitants of various places by those whose lot it is to reside in the immediate vicinity. Some of these are versified, and have the appearance of remnants of old songs; others are merely couplets or single lines, generally referring to some circumstances in the history of the subject, which originally called forth the ridicule of the neighbours, and continues to do so traditionally.[1]

And he adds that in England too almost all the counties enjoy such standing jokes against each other. Thus the natives of Wiltshire were called 'Moon-rakers,' after a group of them sought to rake in to shore the moon's reflection in a pool—a famous noodle tale told on the wise men of Gotham and their kinsmen in distant places. The Scots seemed to exceed in neighbourly ridicule. 'Lousie Lauther' was the rude designation applied by outlying villagers to Lauder in Berwickshire. When asked the reason, one derider replied in the following vein:

Deed, I think there's nae muckle need o' proving the matter, for yere ain skins should ken better than I can tell ye; but there's just ae thing I'll swear to, and that is, that nae farer gane than yesterday, as I was commin' owre to the town, I met a Lauder chest o' drawers takin' the road for Edinburgh, o' its ain accord, as hard as it could hotch![2]

A village in East Lothian had to suffer the barbed taunt, 'Stick us a' in Aberlady!' after an unhappy husband there had complained to his fellow-townsmen that he believed he was being cuckolded. 'Deed, billy,' replied an unsympathetic crony, 'gin that be yere story, ye might *stick us a' in Aberlady!*' The saying became pro-

[1] *Ibid.*, pp. 123–4.
[2] *Ibid.*, pp. 123, 136–7.

verbial, and an Englishman who was gulled into crying it out in the street of the town was savagely stoned.[1]

Sayings and snickers of this sort could be loosely classified as jokes, and by a natural sequence Chambers published in 1832 *Scottish Jests and Anecdotes. To which are added, a choice selection of English and Irish jests.* In his Preface he states that they were collected from all imaginable sources, 'but mostly from the mouths of the people themselves.' Here again Chambers was breaking trail, for this was no Joe Miller collection of old chestnuts, but a record of witticisms and humorous stories enhanced with local, regional, and national sauces. One cycle dealt with incidents of speaking out impromptu in kirk, another with jokes of the Jacobites, a third with the superiority of the Scotch peasant, while others clustered around celebrated Scotsmen like David Hume, Hugh Blair, and Walter Scott. The short comic traditional story lacks any clear-cut English term; joke is too loose; the combination of jest and anecdote in Chambers' title is happy, suggesting the humorous element and the historical anchorage. This form of oral narrative is still the stepchild of the professional folklorist.

Chambers speculated about the Scotch sense of humour, as compared with the English, and found it less refined in classic wit and more given to fantastic imagery, but noteworthy for its sarcasm, repartee, the dry satire that punctures affectation, and the broad household jollity arising from grotesque ideas. Speaking of the Jacobites, he commented that, in lieu of arms or letters, they possessed an armoury of jests with which to annoy the enemy, as the stock in trade of a depressed faction. These bold generalities indicate the theoretical bent of Chambers' mind; but he lacked analytical tools with which to harness his intuitions.

A few specimens may illustrate the naïveté of Scottish country characters as depicted in anecdotal humour. On the outbreak of war the government imposed a tax on candles, thereby raising the price. A Scottish goodwife in Greenock asked her chandler, Simon Macbeth, the reason for the price rise. 'It's a' owin' to the war,' replied Simon. 'The war!' echoed the astonished matron. 'Gracious me, are they gaun to fight by cannel light?'[2]

A bailie of Lochmaben, in Dumfriesshire, one of the least favoured of Scotch burghs, received a letter from a Parliamentary candidate soliciting his support. When he opened the letter, the servant delivering it observed, 'Sir, you hold the letter by the wrong end.' 'Hoot mon,' answered the bailie testily, 'gie yoursell

---

[1] Chambers, *Popular Rhymes*, pp. 138–9.
[2] *Ibid.*, p. 16.

[132]

nae trouble about that; d'ye think I wad be fit to be a bailie o'
Lochmaben, gin I couldna read a letter at ony end?'[1]

Along with the comedy of rustic ignorance is found, perhaps
surprisingly among the dour Scots, the Munchausen humour of the
marvellous. The town clerk of Stirling, Mr. Finlayson, was noted
in the late seventeenth century for his hyperbole. Once visiting the
Earl of Monteith in his castle at Talla, he was asked by the earl if
he had ever seen the sailing cherry tree, and on answering no, was
told that it was 'a tree that has grown out at a goose's mouth, from
a stone the bird had swallowed, and which she bears about with
her in her voyages round the loch. Now, Finlayson,' continued the
earl, 'can you, with all your powers of memory and fancy, match
my story of the Cherry Tree?' 'Perhaps I can,' said Finlayson
quietly. 'When Oliver Cromwell was at Airth, one of his cannon
sent a ball to Stirling, and lodged it in the mouth of a trumpet
which one of the men in the castle was sounding in defiance.' 'Was
the trumpeter killed?' 'No, my lord; he blew the ball back, and
killed the artillery-man who had fired it.'[2]

Some of the humour seems too grim for laughter. An anecdote
of the '45 rebellion is told on a party of volunteers in the royal
service who were captured by the Highland army at the battle of
Falkirk and herded into a barn in the village of St. Ninians, where
they languished all evening without food or water. Finally a Glasgow militiaman asked the Celtic sergeant guarding them if they
could not get victuals or drink, reminding him that the fortunes of
war might reverse the tables another time. 'What the muckle
deevil,' roared the Highlander, 'do you want wi' ta vittal and
drink? you hang ta morn whether or no!'[3]

In each of these stories, local places and persons are named, and
the anecdotes, as distinct from jokes, are set in historical scenes and
situations. They might well be international in form or theme; the
dialogue between Finlayson and the Earl of Monteith falls into the
pattern of the lying contest (Type 1820). But they derive from
Scottish folk memory.

As bookseller, bookmaker, and bookwriter, Robert Chambers
wore interchangeable hats, and he produced a spectacular number
of volumes. Their central theme was the Scottish tradition, unfolded in history, biography, scenery, lore, and antiquities. Among
his relevant titles in these early years should be mentioned, in the
realm of popular poetry, *The Scottish Ballads* (1829) and *The
Scottish Songs* (2 vols., 1829); of landscape and antiquities, *The*

---

[1] *Ibid.*, p. 84.
[2] *Ibid.*, pp. 105–6.   [3] *Ibid.*, p. 22.

Picture of Scotland (2 vols., 1827), *A Picture of Stirling* (1830), *Minor Antiquities of Edinburgh* (1833), and *The Land of Burns* (1840, with John Wilson). As a leal Scotsman, he edited *Robert Forbes'· Jacobite Memoirs of the Rebellion of 1745* (1834), an event productive of so much Scottish folk tradition, and *The Poetical Works of Robert Burns* (1838), and he undertook the four-volume *A Biographical Dictionary of Eminent Scotsmen* (1835). Swamped with these and other labours far afield, Chambers veered from his first love of Scottish traditionary lore until late in life his most ambitious enterprise brought into focus all the resources he had acquired and accumulated in this vein. This was *The Book of Days. A Miscellany of Popular Antiquities in connection with the Calendar including Anecdote, Biography, & History, Curiosities of Literature and Oddities of Human Life and Character* (2 vols., 1863–4).

The Book of Days brings to a close, and a suitable climax, the collection of popular antiquities as an approach to folklore. Even before its appearance, the modern technique of folklore collecting had been triumphantly initiated by John Francis Campbell of Islay, the Scotch Gaelic folklorist, in his *Popular Tales of the West Highlands* (4 vols., 1860–2). Yet *The Book of Days* is full of rich rewards. It combines the Aubrey-Brand-Hone concept of miscellaneous popular antiquities, clearly enough credited in the title and the internal references, and equally accepts Thoms' term and view of folklore as living, migratory oral tradition. In his statement of purpose, Chambers outlined half-a-dozen general categories intended to make his volumes 'a repertory of old fireside ideas in general, as well as a means of improving the fireside wisdom of the present day.' His rubrics covered the Church calendar of popular festivals and saints' days, with their Christian antiquities; seasonal phenomena; 'Folk-Lore of the United Kingdom—namely, Popular Notions and Observances connected with Times and Seasons'; notable events, biographies, and historical anecdotes connected with the days of the year; articles on popular archaeology; and curious fugitive pieces. The format was thus pretty much that of Hone, with folklore specifically added.

The intellectual trail that Chambers followed could not be more distinctly marked. He acclaims all the major antiquaries. Here in an entry on New Year's gifts are invocations of Brand-Ellis and Fosbroke; a notice on 'Unlucky Days' refers to Aubrey's *Miscellanies*; there is a piece on Jacob Grimm early in the first volume. Other items deal with John Stow, with 'Dr. Borlase, the Cornish Antiquary,' author of *The Natural History of Cornwall* (1758), and with 'Dr. [William] Stukeley, the Antiquary, and his Speculations';

7. JOHN GRAHAM DALYELL

8. ROBERT BROWN JR.

'Humphrey Wanley, the Antiquary', son of the author of *Wonders of the Little World* (1678), a curious miscellany in its day; 'An Antiquary of the Olden Type,' Browne Willis. Douce is cited on St. Valentine's Day; Plot and his *Natural History of Staffordshire* on 'Oddities of Family History'; Grose on a legend of live burial; Bourne and Strutt on the church bell that tolls for the departed; Reginald Scot on rhyming rats to death. *The Book of Days* was not the reflection of an individual mind, but of the Victorian community sharing the same preconceptions and resources. 'A correspondent sends us the following account of a custom in South Lancashire,' writes Chambers, ' . . . of which he can find no notice in Brand, or Strutt, or Hone, or in *Notes and Queries*, and which has therefore the recommendation of novelty, though old. . . .'[1] In like manner Chambers himself, speculating about spectral dogs, whom he arranges ingeniously in three categories, first observes that neither Brand in his *Popular Antiquities* nor Scott in his *Witchcraft and Demonology* had taken notice of this special class of apparitions. A century later a folktale collection would carry the title *Dog Ghosts and Other Texas Negro Folk Tales*.[2]

Coupled with the allusions to, and thumbnail sketches of, the hallowed antiquaries of earlier generations, who cultivated popular antiquities, are novel folkloric matters. With some pride Chambers introduced for the first time the subject of the 'folk-lore of playing cards,' claiming that the widespread divinatory practices connected with cards in Britain and throughout the Commonwealth, even if they involved no more than screening lucky from unlucky cards, belonged in the province of folklore. Fortunetellers of course practised divination with cards. Astutely Chambers remarked, ' . . . the fortunetellers are the moralists, as well as the consolers of the lower classes. They supply a want that society either cannot or will not do.' Elsewhere he discourses on the 'folk-lore of nail-cutting,' giving a rhyme for the days and a superstition from Sir Thomas Browne.[3]

Beyond his use and ready acceptance of Thoms' neologism, Chambers grasped surely the constituent elements in folklore, such as legend, tradition, and superstition, and these terms continually recur in *The Book of Days*. In one pithy note on '*Tradition and*

[1] Robert Chambers, *The Book of Days, A Miscellany of Popular Antiquities in connection with the Calendar including Anecdote, Biography, & History, Curiosities of Literature and Oddities of Human Life and Character*, 2 vols. (London & Edinburgh: W. & R. Chambers, ca. 1869), I, 31, 41–2, 49, 478–9, 212–13, 329–30; II, 26, 341–2; I, 255–7, 306–8, 804–8, 548–9; II, 103–4; I, 546.
[2] *Ibid.*, II, 433–6. *Dog Ghosts* was collected by J. Mason Brewer (Austin, Texas, 1958). [3] Chambers, *The Book of Days*, I, 281–4, 526.

Truth' he gives his shrewd opinion on a problem that has never ceased to tantalize folklorists, the veracity of oral historical tradition:

The value of popular tradition as evidence in antiquarian inquiries cannot be disputed, though in every instance it should be received with the greatest caution. A few instances of traditions, existing from a very remote period and verified in our own days, are worthy of notice.[1]

As an example, he then told of Norie's Law, a funeral mound in Fifeshire, which actually led to a tomb of a warrior with silver armour.

Family legends and traditional ghosts attracted Chambers as a vigorous sprout of English folklore. Thus he related the story behind the Tichborne Dole, first appearing in the *Winchester Observer* and frequently set forth in books on English local customs up to the present day. Told on one of the oldest families in Hampshire, the legend has a sadistic lord promising his bedridden lady a dole of bread to the poor from the proceeds of as much land as she could crawl over while a brand burned—hence the designation 'Tichborne Dole' for this annual almsgiving. Before her death Lady Mabella predicted that, if the dole were discontinued, the family tree would produce seven sons followed by seven daughters—a curious prediction, since the seventh son is regarded in folk belief as endowed with special powers.[2]

These family legends, while they circulated among the villagers, originated with, and persisted among, the aristocracy. So the return from the dead of Sir Tristram Beresford, ancestor of the Waterford family and Protestant supporter during the Revolution, was talked about in the parlours of his descendants and their friends among the British upper classes. His widow met his spirit in the woods, and he led her by the hand.

For evermore that lady wore
A covering on her wrist.[3]

So Scott wrote, in his ballad version of the episode. The black ribbon concealing the spot on her wrist touched by the ghost was matched in a similar experience recounted by Anne M. Grant in her *Essays on the Superstitions of the Highlanders in Scotland* (1811), with the widow permanently exhibiting a blue mark on her wrist.

[1] Chambers, *The Book of Days*, I, pp. 337-8.
[2] *Ibid.*, pp. 166-8.   [3] *Ibid.*, pp. 785-6.

Chambers referred to other parallels in religious and spiritual writings by Richard Baxter and Henry More.

The editor of *The Book of Days* fully recognized the migratory nature of these seemingly local traditions of the ancestral mansion. He pointed to the peregrinations of a romantic story attached to Littlecote Hall in Wiltshire, and handed down in the family of Lord Chief-Justice Popham from the time of Queen Elizabeth. Aubrey had first placed it on record; Scott had received a version from Lord Webb Seymour, inserting it as a ballad in his romance of *Rokeby* and giving the outline in his notes; but the same tradition was localized in Edinburgh and was also told by Sir Nathaniel Wraxall.[1] Authentic or not, the legends of manorial customs reflected the historic facts and behaviour of a now vanished society, Chambers was quick to remark, in introducing a perquisite exercised by the Lord of Chetwode Manor in Bucks. For killing a large boar the Lord was given the right to collect a toll from travellers crossing the river Rhyne—and gleefully Chambers noted that Thomas Blount had overlooked this right in his *Jocular Customs of Ancient Tenures* (1679), one of Brand's favourite hunting grounds.[2]

These indications of folklore acumen could easily be multiplied. In treating of omens of death among ancient families, and offering two examples from Scott, Chambers regretted the inadequacy of the information, which so often failed to relate the omen to the family.[3] He cast a broad net, and comprehended modern as well as ancient lore. 'No modern ghost-story has been more talked of in England, than one in which the seers were two military officers named Sherbroke and Wynyard.'[4] Yet for all its pleasures, *The Book of Days* necessarily remained what it was intended to be, a miscellany of popular antiquities; it could not rise above its formula. The clever perceptions of talented Robert Chambers never reached the level of philosophic synthesis.

[4 HUGH MILLER]

On the death of Hugh Miller, by his own hand, the day before Christmas, 1856, the Scottish and English newspapers carried striking tributes to the stonemason who became a celebrated geologist, editor, and public figure.[5] These obituaries surveyed his various talents, in literature, science, journalism, and theology, but none described him as a folklorist—a term still young. The fame of

---

[1] *Ibid.*, II, 554–6.   [2] *Ibid.*, pp. 517–19.   [3] *Ibid.*, pp. 731–2.   [4] *Ibid.*, p. 448.
[5] See the 'Memorials of the Death and Character of Hugh Miller,' in Hugh Miller, *The Testimony of the Rocks* (Boston, 1857), pp. 7–30.

Hugh Miller has gradually receded. His attempt to wed geological and scriptural truth, while it won him the friendship of Louis Agassiz in America, placed him on untenable scientific grounds; the Free Church movement he espoused is forgotten; and his heavily descriptive prose, contrived and prolix, though not without charm, cannot hold modern readers. Yet Hugh Miller deserves the close attention and firm respect of one audience today, for he contributed two very remarkable books to the first shelf of British folklore.

In *Scenes and Legends of the North of Scotland* (1835; new, expanded edition, 1850), published in his thirty-third year, Miller presented a wide range of traditional tales from his home of Cromarty, an isolated peninsular seaport on the Highland border, windswept and gale-lashed by the North Sea. His autobiography, *My Schools and Schoolmasters* (1854), contains much incidental information on the varied sources of folklore to which he was exposed. These two books reveal what the whole literature of folklore rarely divulges, the place that folk tradition occupies in the life of a town, and in the life of a man.

Miller did not set out deliberately to record tales, in the manner of the modern field collector, but he possessed the folklore instinct and eagerly drank in the 'traditionary history' that surrounded him at every turn. To his Uncle James, a harnessmaker who absorbed all the antiquarian lore of castle and crag and sepulchre on his country journeys, he listened with unending delight. Visiting his cousin George in the Highlands, young Hugh sat in on evening storyfests about bitter and ancient Gaelic legends of giant Fions fighting great boars with poisonous bristles. Yarns of the sea had always washed over the Cromarty youth. As a boy he repeatedly heard mate Jack Grant relate the narrow escape of Hugh's father, a sea captain, in a storm that broke his ship on the Findhorn bar; a woman and child had drowned in an inside cabin, and Jack had earlier seen their wraiths walking on deck with the captain. Later, when Hugh voyaged along the Scottish coast, he spent evenings in the forecastle listening to sailors' narratives strongly tinctured with the supernatural. Coming across a band of gypsies, Miller was amazed at their power to lie, from the oldest to the youngest, who 'lisped in fiction.' He never forgot the old woman's marvellous lie of curing a young nobleman whose eye hung halfway down his cheek; she slit a hole at the back of his neck, seized the end of a sinew, and pulled the orb snugly into place—then tied a knot in the ligament to keep it there.[1]

[1] Hugh Miller, *My Schools and Schoolmasters* (Edinburgh, 1907), pp. 34–5, 104–5, 357–8, 386–7.

The oral history which to this day folklorists have unfortunately slighted, Miller absorbed avidly. He never forgot the older generation's recollections of stirring events now coated with legend: of the battle of Culloden in the '45', of royalist horrors inflicted on the Highland rebels, of the buccaneer adventures of his own great-grandfather, John Feddes.

And I have felt a strange interest in these glimpses of a past so unlike the present, when thus presented to the mind as personal reminiscences, or as well-attested traditions, removed from the original witnesses by but a single stage. All for instance, which I have yet read of witch-burnings has failed to impress me so strongly as the recollections of an old lady who in 1722 was carried in her nurse's arms . . . to witness a witch-execution in the neighbourhood of Dornoch—the last which took place in Scotland. The lady well remembered the awe-struck yet excited crowd, the lighting of the fire, and the miserable appearance of the poor fatuous creature whom it was kindled to consume, and who seemed to be so little aware of her situation, that she held out her thin shrivelled hands to warm them at the blaze.[1]

Here the Cromarty stonemason described the word-of-mouth history which in olden times and still today, on the lips of Indians or Europeans or Africans, invariably acquires folk elements. So he relates how the folk adjudged innocent a Highlander swinging on the gibbet when a white pigeon half encircled the corpse; and how an old woman's dog, separated from the battlefield of Culloden by a lofty hill, howled eerily in its direction, 'looking as if he saw a spirit.'[2]

Besides savouring folk history, Miller appreciated its kin, personal history, where an eloquent bard enlarged on his own strange and wonderful experiences. In a garrulous stonemason named Jock Mo-ghoal, he found a most masterful saga man.

As recorded in his narratives, his life was one long epic poem, filled with strange and startling adventures, and furnished with an extraordinary machinery of the wild and supernatural; and though all knew that Jock made imagination supply, in his histories, the place of memory, not even Ulysses or Aeneas . . . could have attracted more notice at the courts of Alcinous or

[1] *Ibid.*, p. 125.
[2] *Ibid.*, pp. 125–6, 128; for reminiscences of Culloden see also Miller's *Essays, Historical and Biographical, Political and Social, Literary and Scientific*, ed. Peter Bayne (Boston, 1865), 'The Centenary of the "Forty-Five",' pp. 101–2.

Dido, than Jock in the barrack. The workmen, on the mornings after his greater narratives, used to look one another full in the face, and ask, with a smile rather incipient than fully manifest, whether 'Jock wasna perfectly wonderfu' last nicht?'[1]

In one of his sagas, Jock told how he spied a girl friend in Edinburgh across the street—his future wife—and in walking over to greet her was struck by a chariot. His sweetheart took him, in great pain, to an old hag who offered to defer the agony; Jock acquiesced, made his way home safely in spite of robbers, mists, and snowstorms, and four weeks later, as the hag had stated, he heard the rattle of a chariot, felt a smashing blow on his breastbone, and staggered to bed for six weeks. Perceptively Miller comments that such fabulous autobiographers can always be found in the 'less artificial' states of society.

On reading *My Schools and Schoolmasters*, Robert Chambers was moved to write its author, in a letter of March 1, 1854, 'Your autobiography has set me a-thinking of my own youthful days, which were like yours in point of hardship and humiliation, though different in many important circumstances.' And Chambers spotted the folklore, repeating in *The Book of Days* Miller's account of his cousin George's dream of the sleeper whose soul escapes through his mouth in the form of a fly. An old resident of Ross-shire implicitly believed in this phenomenon, and had on several occasions seen the indistinct little form leaving the open mouths of dying Highlanders. The publisher was reminded of the same legend attached to Gontran the Good, king of Burgundy, in the sixth century. In the twentieth century it has also been reported in Japan and North America.[2]

With so wide a range of oral sources at his command, and the impulse to absorb them, the Cromarty author was in a position to write an unusual volume of folklore. On the other hand, no disciplined approach to the field as yet existed to guide him, and he knew only the techniques of Sir Walter Scott, Allan Cunningham, and Robert Chambers. Nevertheless, the *Scenes and Legends of the North of Scotland* exceeds all expectation for a pioneer collection of local narratives and merits a recognition it has never received, as a superb record of folk traditions seen in their full context of village society and history. Miller knew the bleak Scottish town, not yet robbed by the great industrial cities of its cultural individuality,.

---

[1] Miller, *My Schools*, pp. 208–9.

[2] William Chambers, *Memoir of William and Robert Chambers* (Edinburgh and London, 1884), p. 129; Robert Chambers, *The Book of Days* (London and Edinburgh, 1869), I, 276–7; Keigo Seki (ed.), *Folktales of Japan* (Chicago, 1963), pp. 157–60.

with an intimacy no visiting collecter could ever attain.[1] Unspoiled by preconceptions of modern folklore science, he set down whatever he heard and saw in the way of traditions.

Detailed contemporary letters from the early 1830's afford us considerable insight into the purposes and circumstances governing the publication of the *Scenes and Legends*. This work was intended by Miller to launch a promising literary and intellectual career; previously he had printed only a volume of poems at his own expense, whose faults he soon perceived, and a pamphlet on the herring fisheries. Young Miller had high aspirations, and enjoyed local celebrity in Cromarty for his learning, but he sought a larger audience. Knowing his birth town best of all subjects, through his long-established family roots and antiquarian interests, he conceived the idea of writing a 'traditional history' such as Gilbert White's *Natural History and Antiquities of Selborne* (London: 1789). What White had done to illuminate the atmosphere of every English town, Miller would do for Scottish parishes, through the representative model of Cromarty.[2] This larger ambition explains the inconsistencies in the book, which records grim folk belief and rude dialect in company with artificial literary passages describing emotions and landscape. Miller wished to take his place in English literature, by virtue of a book on folklore.

He found the usual difficulties in securing a publisher. For three years from 1833 to 1835, his letters reveal his efforts and frustration. In one priggish statement he declares his unwillingness to publish a subscription, but in the end, after Edinburgh publishers had rejected his manuscript with some praise and criticism of its too lengthy moralizing, he concluded a subscription arrangement with Adam Black, future Lord Provost of Edinburgh.[3] Miller had continued to polish his *Scenes* all the while, writing that 'If ever my Traditions get abroad they will be all the better for having stayed so long at home.'[4] The book made its way slowly, even with favouring reviews and Miller's imploring letters to literary friends and patrons.[5] Curiously, when Miller's reputation ultimately justified a reissue in 1850 (and thereafter the work went through successive editions), it appeared in enlarged form, despite the

---

[1] According to W. M. Mackenzie, *Hugh Miller, A Critical Study* (London, 1905), p. 2, the population of Cromarty at this time numbered about 1,500.
[2] See his letter to Sir Thomas Dick Lauder (to whom he inscribed the *Scenes*) of March, 1833, in Peter Bayne, *The Life and Letters of Hugh Miller*, 2 vols. (Boston, 1871), II, 43–5.
[3] *Ibid.*, I, 300–2; II, 50.   [4] *Ibid.*, I, 374.
[5] See his letters to Allan Cunningham and Sir George Mackenzie, *ibid.*, II, 45–9. The reception of the book is described in *My Schools*, pp. 512–13.

criticisms of the first publishers' readers. The author added sketches he had contributed to *Chambers Journal*, after the publication of the *Scenes*, and others he had written before 1835 but not included in the first printing.[1]

Neither Miller nor his public understood very precisely what he had written. The line between oral tradition and creative fiction had not yet been clearly drawn; Miller admits to merging memory and imagination, and discloses his bias in one especially revealing aside. 'This part of the country contains a rich and as yet unexplored mine of tradition; but some of the stories are of too wild and fantastic a character for furnishing a suitable basis for a prose tale; and the great bulk of them, though they might prove interesting when wrought up together, are too simple and too naked of both detail and description to stand alone.'[2] He is always thinking of tradition in terms of literary possibilities and goes on to say that he has imaginatively endowed legends with landscape and dialogue and movement. Some fictional efforts did come from his pen, but shortly after the publication of the *Scenes* he turned to journalistic and scientific writings.

The Cromarty mason must have been something of a character himself. 'He was tall and athletic,' recalls one traveller to Cromarty, 'and had a large head, made to look huge by a rusty profusion of not very carefully remembered hair.' The visitor described the red sandstone whiskers, the keen grey eyes, freckled face, and slouching walk, borne down as it were by his own massive intelligence and brooding ambitions.[3] Hugh Miller achieved the fame he so earnestly wished in his own lifetime, but posterity may remember him best for this literary excursion of his youth.

In regarding folklore as the raw stuff of literature, Miller drew inspiration and technique from his illustrious countryman, Sir Walter Scott, whose name runs through the *Schools and Schoolmasters* like a Greek deity. When he moved to Edinburgh to edit *The Witness*, awestruck Hugh lingered in Castle Street for a glimpse of the great man, without success. He refers familiarly to Scott's *Letters on Demonology and Witchcraft* and quotes Scott's folklore tales and notes to illuminate Cromarty legends. The water-kelpie whom Sir Walter described in *Guy Mannering*—the stream's spirit cries, 'The hour's come but not the man,' whereon a rider rushes up to the bank and perishes in attempting to cross—reminded Miller of a striking variant in his own Ross-shire. When the courier rode up to

---

[1] Lydia Miller (Mrs. Hugh Miller), in the Preface to her husband's *Tales and Sketches* (6th ed.; Edinburgh, 1872), p. xiii, and Miller's note to the second edition of *Scenes and Legends*.   [2] *Life and Letters*, I, 420.   [3] J. R. Robertson, in *ibid.*, p. 383.

the stream, following the kelpie's cry, a group of Highlanders cutting corn seized him and thrust him into a nearby chapel, to save him from his fate. When the hour of death had passed, they unlocked the door and found the man lying dead, his face buried in a small stone font whose few pints of water had suffocated him when he fell down in a fit.[1] Again Scott sharpens Miller's insight, in connection with the grey-bearded goblin that haunted Craighouse Castle. A herdboy told Hugh, 'Oh, they're saying it's the spirit of the man that was killed on the foundation-stone, just after it was laid, and then built intil the wa' by the masons, that he might *keep* the castle by coming back again; and *they're saying* that a' the verra auld houses in the kintra had murderit men built intil them in that way, and that they have a' o' them their bogle.' Miller immediately recognized the antique tradition of building sacrifice, and quoted Scott on its modern transference to pirates, who customarily buried a Negro or a Spaniard with their loot to guard it.[2]

Thus inspired by Sir Walter and driven by his own urge for recognition, the humbly born writer explored every aspect of Cromarty life for its sheaves of lore and gathered them in his *Scenes and Legends*. Some sketches Miller elaborated from the bare motifs, as he admitted, with imaginary dialogue and scenic backdrop, but others he set down plainly, in their grim, tart, or comic oral style. Historical and humorous tradition he treated more scrupulously than supernatural incidents, which tended to stimulate his fancy.

The coastal sea and the bay of Cromarty figure prominently in the mass of tales. Fishermen, sailors, and smugglers crowd the pages, for the men of Cromarty divided their time between farm and fishery. We hear a wealth of marine belief: of whistling for winds and soothing the waves; of the Witch of Tarbat, who transported a ship inland and drowned her own husband and son in a hurricane; and of the conviction that relatives of the drowned always persecute the wreck's survivor.[3] When the herrings suddenly deserted Crom-

[1] *My Schools*, pp. 202–3. See Motif M341.2.3, 'Prophecy: death by drowning.' Accounts of the water-kelpie are given in John G. Dalyell, *The Darker Superstitions of Scotland* (Glasgow, 1835), pp. 543–4; Walter Gregor, *Notes on the Folk-Lore of the North-East of Scotland* (London, 1881), pp. 66–7; John G. Campbell, *Superstitions of the Highlands and Islands of Scotland* (Glasgow, 1900), p. 215; Alasdair A. MacGregor, *The Peat-Fire Flame: Folk-Tales and Traditions of the Highlands and Islands* (Edinburgh and London, 1937), pp. 68–71, 116–19.

[2] *My Schools*, pp. 232–3. See Motifs S261, 'Foundation sacrifice,' and N571, 'Devil (demon) as guardian of treasure,' in Stith Thompson, *Motif-Index of Folk Literature*, 6 vols. (Bloomington, Indiana, 1955–8).

[3] *Scenes and Legends of the North of Scotland; or, The Traditional History of Cromarty* (8th ed.; Edinburgh, 1869), pp. 58–9, 282–9, 62. For sea lore see Motifs G283, 'Witches have control over weather,' D2142.0.1, 'Magician (witch) controls winds,' and D2151.3, 'Magic control of waves'; Eve B. Simpson, *Folk Lore in Lowland*

arty, folk explanations arose to explain the disaster: fighting men had spilled angry blood in the sea, or a minister had cursed taunting fishermen packing their catch on a Sunday. Tradition claimed that in one lucky season surplus fish were used to fertilize the fields—a reason given in Cornwall for the disappearance of the hake.[1] A quarantine fleet that lay off Cromarty to isolate the cholera in the eighteenth century gave rise to rumours that mysteriously surfaced again in 1831, when another fleet dropped anchor. The fish were said to be poisoned, from eating victims thrown overboard; a graverobber found not the money he sought but the dread fever; one ingenious soul saved his townsmen by trapping the plague, formed into a yellow cloud, in a linen bag burying the bag under a churchyard stone.[2] Fragmentary reports clustered around the mermaid, who Cromarty folk were wont to spy along the shore, braiding her long yellow tresses and defying a hardy man to best her. To one who could, she granted three wishes, and John Reid thus compelled her to guarantee him his beloved. Only under compulsion would the mermaid use her power for good, and the sight of her might presage evil; shortly after she was seen washing bloody clothes in the loch, the church roof collapsed and killed many inside.[3]

Throughout the dour chapters of Cromarty life, the kirk stands sharply athwart the town, an edifice of Calvinistic granite hewn by staunch Presbyterian Covenanters. To folklore it contributed the religious stories about Donald Roy, the Presbyterian elder, and Miller's own great-great-grandfather, stories passed down through the family line as wondrous truth. Donald became converted when,

[1] *Scenes and Legends*, pp. 256–7. Simpson gives folk reasons for the desertion of the herrings, pp. 141–2. For the disappearance of hake from the Cornish fishing towns see Robert Hunt, *Popular Romances of the West of England* (2nd series; London, 1865), pp. 152–3; R. M. Dorson, *Bloodstoppers and Bearwalkers* (Cambridge, Mass., 1952), pp. 110–11.

[2] *Scenes and Legends*, p. 244. An Englishman frightened an Indian in colonial New England by declaring that a hole in the ground, used for storing powder, contained the plague; an Indian chief later asked the Englishman to release it against his enemies (*America Begins*, ed. R. M. Dorson [New York: 1950], p. 302, quoting Thomas Morton's *New English Canaan*, 1632).

[3] *Scenes and Legends*, chap. 20, pp. 290–304. Motif B81 is 'Mermaid.' Legends of Cornish mermaids are given by Robert Hunt, *Popular Romances of the West of England* (1st series; London, 1865), Nos. 56–62. In 'The Old Man of Cury' (pp. 159–63), a captive mermaid gives her captor three wishes in payment for her release. See also Campbell, 'The Mermaid,' in *Superstitions*, pp. 201–2; MacGregor, 'Mermaid Traditions,' in *The Peat-Fire Flame*, pp. 105–6.

Scotland (London, 1908), 'Fishermen's Superstitions,' pp. 118–44. G. L. Kittredge, *Witchcraft in Old and New England* (Cambridge, Mass., 1929), chap. 8, 'Wind and Weather,' pp. 159–60, gives examples of witches who traffic in winds; R. M. Dorson, *Jonathan Draws the Long Bow* (Cambridge, Mass., 1946), pp. 245–7, abstracts Maine sea superstitions from the writings of George S. Wasson.

returning from the playing fields instead of the church on successive Sundays, he found his cattle dead. He developed the power of second-sight and could foretell catastrophe and good fortune. Praying once in a Catholic lady's home, he caused twelve images to topple in the chapel and brought about his hostess' conversion.[1]

With clever perception, Miller bracketed the visionary Presbyterian with a Highland seer whose uncanny prophecies still agitated the talk of later generations. The so-called heathenism of the one and the Christian faith of the other incorporated the same class of 'neutral superstitions,' which carry over from the false to the true religion. Unlike temperamentally as were the Highland clansman and the Covenanting elder, they shared an ancient and universal belief in dream, vision, and miracle. So Miller boldly introduced Kenneth Ore, the seventeenth-century seer from Ross-shire. Kenneth first learned of his divinatory gift when gazing at a smooth stone that warned him of a plot against his life. Ever after he foresaw troubled events; he foretold that a raven would drink blood three days running on a hill in Sutherlandshire, that a cow would calve on Top of Fairburn Tower, and that dramshops would arise at the end of every furrow.[2] Miller is sceptic enough to declare that only fulfilled prophecies are remembered.

Moving now into the murky area of popular credulity in unnatural beings, the folk historian of Cromarty speaks on evil spirits, ghostly apparitions, and green fairies. Wherever he scratched the surfaces of Scottish border life, wells of supernatural belief opened up. Pondering in the burying grounds of St. Regulus and Kirk-Michael, or recalling the ghost tales of an 'elderly relative' with whom he journeyed through neighbouring parishes, Miller evoked a score of spectral narratives. The very apartment in which he wrote had seen and heard wraiths and distress cries that presaged death.[3] The Devil appeared in divers guises in the north of

---

[1] *Scenes and Legends*, pp. 145–50. Accomplishments of Protestant ministers in popular fancy often closely parallel Catholic saints' legends; see C. Grant Loomis, *White Magic* (Cambridge, Mass., 1948), chap. 5, 'Divine Foresight and Knowledge,' and chap. 6, 'Power Over Matter.'

[2] *Scenes and Legends*, pp. 163–5. Kenneth Ore is presented at full length in Alexander Mackenzie, *The Prophecies of the Brahan Seer*, with introductory chapter by Andrew Lang (Stirling, Scotland, 1899). Lang points out that the Brahan seer, unlike his fellow Highlanders, used a divining stone. Mackenzie quotes Hugh Miller on Ore, pp. 7–8. (I also have a copy of a tenth edition, dated 1942.)

[3] *Scenes and Legends*, p. 358. Scottish death omens and wraiths are discussed by James Napier, *Folk Lore: or, Superstitious Beliefs in the West of Scotland within this Century* (Paisley, 1879), pp. 56–9; also by Gregor, *Notes on the Folk-Lore of the North-east of Scotland*, pp. 203–5; and see the section, 'Apparitions, Wraiths, the Second Sight,' in *Scottish Fairy and Folk Tales*, ed. Sir George Douglas (London, n.d.), pp. 193–215.

Scotland, as a black dog emitting flame when Donald Roy thought evil, or an ugly beast who vanished in a lightning flash, or a lively stranger who paused at the edge of a clergyman's light. In two instances the Evil One claimed a human soul for services rendered, and a servant who used the Devil's name caught sight of his lost mistress chained in a cavern and guarded by two large dogs.[1] A variety of revenants pester the living. One returns to fulfil a death compact, another to rebuke a farmer courting near the grave of his late wife (he died within a fortnight), a third to redeem her sin in stealing the pack of a murdered pedlar. The ghost of a second murdered pedlar walks until his natural life span is up—which leads Miller to wonder if this is not Arminian rather than Calvinist tradition! A protective mother returns from the grave to cover her freezing babes. Not all ghosts are purposeful, Miller recognizes, and in one elaborate episode involving the mysterious death of a miller, he stresses the lack of motivation of the spectre that afterward haunted the miller's companion.[2]

Where ghostly revenants are known around the world, other beings display a purely Celtic background. Green goblins and sylphs commit evil in vague traditions. The genius of smallpox takes the form of a wandering green lady; another green lady bathes a goblin child in the blood of a household's youngest inmate; yet a third implores a deaf farmer reading a Bible to tell him if there is any hope for such as she.[3] Unlike such goblins, the fairies are diminutive, three feet in height, wearing gray suits with red caps, and seem better known in popular memory. Only shortly before Miller's lifetime, specified individuals had beheld the fairies at the Burn of Eathie, and many had reported activity in the meal mill of Eathie at night, when the miller had gone home. One ne'er-do-well who attempted to stay the night at the mill was seen no more (some

[1] *Scenes and Legends*, pp. 146, 166, 168, 169–76. See Motifs G303.3, 'Forms in which the devil appears,' and G303.9.5, 'The devil as an abductor.' Dalyell (*Darker Superstitions*), has material on evoking Satan, Satan's forms, and Satanic pacts, pp. 528, 547, 553–5, 577–80; Gregor (*Notes*), speaks of 'Devil compacts,' pp. 74–5, and Campbell (*Superstitions*), of 'The Devil,' pp. 292–312.

[2] *Scenes and Legends*, pp. 359–70, 376. See such motifs as E411, 'Dead cannot rest because of sin'; E413, 'Murdered person cannot rest in grave'; E415, 'Dead cannot rest until work is finished'; E323.2, 'Dead mother returns to aid persecuted children.' Scottish ghostlore can be found in Gregor, *Notes*, chap. 13, 'Ghosts,' pp. 68–70; MacGregor, *The Peat-Fire Flame*, 'Ghost Tales and Haunted Places,' pp. 282–311. Louis C. Jones stresses the neutrality of many modern ghosts in 'The Ghosts of New York: an Analytical Study,' *Journal of American Folklore*, LVII (1944), 246.

[3] *Scenes and Legends*, pp. 70–3. The classification of these evil demons is not easily made, the more so since green is the characteristic fairy colour (Campbell, *Superstitions*, p. 155), and since the diminutive fairies and Satanic metamorphoses are often popularly confused (Dalyell, *Darker Superstitions*, p. 534). Motif V361 is suggested here: 'Christian child killed to furnish blood for Jewish rite.'

say he came back after seven years), but a bold young farmer
accomplished the feat, and saved himself in the manner of Ulysses
in the cave of Polyphemus. He told an inquisitive old fairy that his
name was 'Mysel' an' Mysel' ' and then hit him in the face with a
roasted duck. The blinded creature screamed to his companions
that 'Mysel' an' Mysel' ' had done the injury.[1]

Some of these witch, goblin, ghost, and fairy legends cling to
definite landmarks in and about Cromarty, and geographical sites
offered Miller the chief thread of his desultory and rambling volume.
He wanders along the shore or across the bluffs and woods and
meadows, and pauses at the spot where a celebrated event allegedly
occurred. This technique was advantageous because many Cromarty traditions are local legends and, besides, the writer's taste led
him to associate scenery and tales. 'There is a natural connexion,'
he writes, 'between wild scenes and wild legends,' and he misses no
opportunity to support the contention. His opening pages discuss
etymological legends about the Sutor Mountains, said to be named
either for giant shoemakers (soutar—shoemaker) who used the
promontories as work stools, or by an ardent maiden who pointed
out to her reproachful lover the embracing peaks that resembled
'tongueless suitors.'[2] Sludach Spring gushes irregularly ever since
a tacksman flung mud in it, even though he later atoned by wiping
the spring with a clean linen towel.[3] A high precipice known as the
Caithness-man's Leap memorializes a tremendous and fortuitous
descent by a thief, shot by the enraged farmer.[4] Behind the
magical properties of Fiddler's Well lies a strange account. A con-
sumptive young man whose best friend has just died of consumption is told by a field bee to dig at the spot where the well now

[1] Scenes and Legends, pp. 466–70. This is Motif K602, 'Noman.' W. A. Clouston gives
variants from Northumberland and Finland in The Book of Noodles (London, 1888),
p. 194 n. Campbell offers abundant material on 'The Fairies' and 'Tales Illustrative
of Fairy Superstition,' in the first two chapters of Superstitions of the Highlands and
Islands of Scotland, pp. 1–155; see also MacGregor's first chapter (in The Peat-Fire
Flame), 'Faeries: Their Propensities and Activities,' pp. 1–28; Simpson (Folk Lore in
Lowland Scotland), 'Fairies,' pp. 82–117; Douglas (Scottish Fairy and Folk Tales),
'Fairy Tales,' pp. 103–39.
[2] Scenes and Legends, pp. 13–15. Place-name legends are, of course, common in
folklore; the juxtaposition here between an old myth and a modern pun has special
interest. Some New England examples are given in R. M. Dorson, Jonathan Draws
the Long Bow (Cambridge, Mass., 1946), pp. 188–98.
[3] Scenes and Legends, pp. 5–7. See Motifs H1193, 'Causing dry spring to flow again
task,' and H1292.1, 'Why has spring gone dry.' MacGregor (The Peat-Fire Flame,
p. 145) tells of an abused well that moved its locale.
[4] Scenes and Legends, pp. 264–6. Peabody's Leap, on the Vermont side of Lake
Champlain, similarly commemorates a tremendous jump made by pioneer Timothy
Peabody in escaping from Indians (Charles M. Skinner, American Myths and Legends
[Philadelphia and London, 1903], I, 52–4).

flows, and drink its water in the morning, to be cured. Others also have benefited from the water.[1] A widely honoured European tradition, the sleeping host who will arise when a visitor blows the bugle or smites the mace within his mountain fastness, becomes attached to the Dropping Cave. There dauntless Willie Millar blew the bugle, but the charm failed to work, and he found himself tumbling on the sod before the cave.[2]

Such *Natursagen* early attracted the attention of continental folklorists, but the historical legends which Miller gathered with equal zest still remain virgin territory. He set down stark and vivid memories of the '45, the fateful year (1745) when the Stuart Pretender (Charles Edward) and his Highland allies marched on the throne, pillaging the border and lowland towns on their way, until they met their Armageddon the next year on the battlefield of Culloden. Often these remembrances dwell on humorous incidents tied to the Highland marauders. One lone follower of the Pretender rushed out to greet them, crying 'You're welcome.' 'Welcome or not, give me your shoes,' replied the invader. Amazon Nannie Miller, when the Cromarty men had fled, dealt summarily with two Highland warriors who sought to 'spulzie' (rob) her; instead, they fled precipitately before her wrath, after she had ducked one in the meal barrel. Anyway, it was said that the ill-gotten gains of looters in the '45 would never benefit their possessors. One poor fisherman, seeing his boat broken by the king's men in their pursuit of the Pretender, sighed out, 'Gain King, gain Pretender, waes me, I'm the loser gain wha like.' Hugh's grandfather had seen one disappointed Jacobite who swore he would never cut or comb his hair until Charles Edward was crowned, and walked around like a huge mobile cabbage, 'for his hair stuck out nearly a foot on each side of his head, and was matted into a kind of felt.'[3] The American and French revolutions also generated local traditions. A ballad grew around the tragic killing by Donald Munro of his two sons, who had enlisted in the English army for the purpose of seeing their father in America. Omens and prodigies were seen on the outbreak of war with France, armies fighting in the air and the sky deluged with

[1] *Scenes and Legends*, pp. 339–41. Well legends of Celtic Scotland, often involving curative properties, appear in MacGregor, *The Peat-Fire Flame*, chap. 12, 'Well Lore,' pp. 144–56.
[2] *Scenes and Legends*, pp. 332–6. This is Motif E502, 'The Sleeping Army.' E. S. Hartland has a full discussion of this migratory legend in *The Science of Fairy Tales* (London, 1891), pp. 207 ff.
[3] *Scenes and Legends*, pp. 320–5. MacGregor (*The Peat-Fire Flame*) testifies that this cycle of traditions survives to the present; see his chap. 23, 'Folk-Tales of the '15 and the '45,' pp. 312–28.

blood. The horrors of epidemic and starvation as well as of wars lingered in folk memory.[1]

Probably the richest vein of lore that Miller tapped lay in the local characters, whose idiosyncrasies he described with sympathetic fidelity. These are pertinacious, obdurate, and fanatic personalities whose eccentric behaviour had passed into the unwritten history of Cromarty. Chiefly they possess an unswerving single-mindedness. Donald Miller steadfastly rebuilt the bulwarks separating his farm from the stormy sea and finally conquered it by constructing a fourth bulwark. Threatened with the loss of his farm if he voted against his laird's choice for minister, and locked in his room by his good wife to make sure that he did not, Roderick Ross crawled out the narrow window and sped to church to give his self-dooming vote. Sandy Wood carried his determination beyond the grave. His garden mysteriously shrunk each year, till he discovered his neighbour stealthily shifting the boundary stones that separated their lands; then the rogue accused Sandy of the deed, before the townspeople. To insure getting the ear of the Lord first on Judgment Day, Sandy had himself buried hard by the moor of Navity, where God was expected to interview the risen. A visiting Englishman, hearing the tale, heaped dirt on Sandy's grave, to keep him from securing this unfair headstart; happily, the villagers, who had come to appreciate Sandy's side, shovelled off the dirt. Other portraits deal with the genteel, impoverished painter Morrison, who once painted two sisters without realizing one had taken the other's place; with the fierce dominie, such a terror to his pupils that a lady, seeing him in church years after she had sat in his class, fainted dead away; with the shiftless lad who failed as a ploughman and cabinet-maker but who achieved national fame as an inventor of nautical instruments. Some odd sticks Miller captures with a single telling anecdote, like the simple curate, father of twenty, who admired the bonny lass on his knee and wished she were his daughter—which indeed she was. Little Jenny grew up to be Hugh Miller's great-great-grandmother.[2]

Still other kinds of folk matter are scattered throughout the *Scenes and Legends.* Of the local sayings that acquired a proverbial currency, three became attached to the lone pro-American Whig in

---

[1] *Scenes and Legends*, pp. 475–6, 485, 246–9, 308–17. The ballad story suggests Motif N731.2, 'Father-son combat' (Sohrab and Rustum). Seventeenth-century omens of war are reprinted in *America Begins*, ed. R. M. Dorson, pp. 399–400, 150, 151.

[2] *Scenes and Legends*, pp. 30–6, 349–54, 215–20, 415–16, 424–31, 144. On a visit to Cromarty in August, 1967, I heard the story of Sandy Wood. Local characters have not as yet been studied or much collected by folklorists.

town, John Holm. 'All in vain, like John Holm's plan of the fort,' referred to a cat's obliterating with its tail the replica of Fort George carefully traced by John in the hearthstone ashes. Local customs are represented in the incongruous practice of cockfighting under the supervision of the parish schoolmaster, and in Scottish versions of Halloween rites. Haunted homes and castles, prophetic dreams, and curious traditions that defy classification—the presence of a cock averts a meteor's fall; a web of linen made from stolen lint soars into the air and drops in a lake—these intersperse the meaty volume.[1]

One puts down the book to marvel at the density and breadth of oral narration within the borders of a single community. Yet the major fictional forms of storytelling—complex *Märchen*, humorous exaggeration, romantic *novelle*—are lacking. This is a country of legend, of the believed tale, and fictions that wander into town are sharply localized. The most meaningful distinction among the multiple narratives, and one hinted at by Miller, lies in layers of belief. Tales nearest in time, like those about the '45 or Donald Roy the elder, are received most implicitly, while the ones dating from remote, perhaps pre-Christian days, when giants and evil goblins formed part of a comprehensive mythology, seem shadowy and are only half-credited.[2] In this conception Miller anticipates Gomme, who believed that folklore could be used to reconstruct past historical periods. But he also foreshadows Lang, who held that mankind everywhere thinks alike in the savage state that precedes civilization. Miller notes the resemblance between old Scottish and New Zealand native battle-axes and of the giant legends whereby Tonga Islanders and the early inhabitants of Cromarty explain the appearance of mountains.

Though making little attempt to segregate his materials into rigid categories, the future geologist did speculate on their natural divisions. Lacking any terminology for labeling stories, he divided them into 'three great classes,' those founded on real local events, those which are pure invention, and those which blend fact and

---

[1] *Scenes and Legends*, pp. 376–7, 420–3, 63–6, 73–4, 61. In *My Schools and Schoolmasters* Miller gives a delicious example of proverbial coinage, relegated to a footnote (p. 298). Some lads gave an eagle, shot by Hugh's Uncle James, to a half-witted old woman called 'Dribble Drone,' saying it was a great goose. She cooked and ate it, and was heard to remark, 'Unco sweet, but oh! teuch, teuch!' The saying was later applied to any tough fish or meat.

[2] References to the different time layers behind folklore can be found in *Scenes and Legends*, pp. 58, 70, 161; to the uniformity of human invention, pp. 15–16. Mackenzie (*Hugh Miller*) has a perceptive chapter on 'History and Folklore,' pointing out Lang's polygenetic theory as stated by Miller (pp. 69–70).

imagination.[1] Clearly he placed many tales into the first rather than the third group because of his own credulity in both supernatural and unusual natural events. Like Andrew Lang, he possessed his own modicum of belief, and saw a spectral arm the night his father drowned.[2] Again, he accepted as true many extraordinary occurrences simply because they departed from precedent.

Invention generally loves a beaten track—it has its rules and its formulas, beyond which it rarely ventures to expatiate; but the course of real events is narrowed by no such contracting barrier; the range of possibility is by far too extensive to be fully occupied by the anticipative powers of imagination; and hence it is that true stories are often stranger than fictions, and that their very strangeness, and their dissimilarity from all the models of literary plot and fable, guarantee in some measure their character as authentic.[3]

The recurrence of folktales around the world has borne out Miller's shrewd insight that plots and motifs are easier to borrow than to create. But with greater access to collections of legends, he might have recognized a 'beaten track' in some Cromarty happenings. The very episode that prompted the above induction, a fugitive's mighty leap over a cliff, finds its close counterpart across the Atlantic (see n. 4, p. 147). Still, the stonemason realized the peregrinations behind certain traditions and observed that the same rumours attached to a quarantine fleet stationed in the bay in the seventeenth century had become attached to another such fleet nearly a hundred years later.

His mind plays briefly with classes of tellers as well as tales, and he recognizes 'that the different sorts of stories were not lodged indiscriminately in every sort of mind'—the people who cherished the narratives of one particular class frequently rejecting those of another. But he ends up lamely, saying that women, being more poetical, are attracted to the more imaginative legends. One factor in impressing him with the truth of stories lay in the minute detail provided by rural narrators, whom he likens to the Dutch painters.[4] These hints at inspection of oral style he unfortunately fails to pursue.

[1] *Scenes and Legends*, pp. 3–4. Miller stoutly affirms the inimitability of the common people's style in telling true narratives, as distinct from fictitious ones.
[2] *My Schools*, p. 24. See also the omen of the sandstone slab, pp. 236–7, which Hugh dropped over a wall for an augury in a mood of depression. Instead of smashing, it lit on its edge in soft greensward, whereupon Hugh believed he was meant to recover.
[3] *Scenes and Legends*, pp. 263–4.
[4] *Ibid.*, pp. 4, 7.

For the most part Miller recorded and presented his folklore un-analytically, aware that he was dealing with 'traditionary history,' but never consciously attempting to found or further a new study. Perhaps this lack of technical training gives his work its greatest value, for he never separated lore from life, as does the modern collector, but set his narratives amidst the bleak and relentless rigours of existence in a Highland coastal town.

[5 COLLECTORS OF SUPERSTITIONS: GRANT, STEWART, DALYELL]

While Scott and Chambers, Cunningham and Miller were interesting themselves and their readers in Scottish lore, three dissimilar works appeared on the subject of superstitions in Scotland. Each used 'superstition' in its title in a broad sense, much as Thoms would shortly use 'folk-lore.'

In 1811 Anne MacVicar Grant (1755–1838) brought out two volumes of *Essays on the Superstitions of the Highlanders of Scotland.* The authoress was more intriguing than her book. Born in Glasgow, she was taken to the American colonies at the age of three in 1758. Her father, Duncan MacVicar, was serving there as a lieutenant in a Highland regiment. He stayed on after the close of the French and Italian Wars in 1765, speculating in land in New York state; his daughter grew up in Albany, learning to speak with Dutchmen and Indians. MacVicar returned to Glasgow in 1768, still holding his thousands of acres in the hope of a killing, but all were confiscated during the American Revolution. In 1773 he accepted the post of barrack master at Fort Augustus in the northern parish of Abertaff, and a new life began for Anne in the Highlands. She moved to the neighbouring parish of Laggan in 1779 after her marriage to the Reverend James Grant, and bore him twelve children, only one of whom outlived her. On the death of her husband in 1801 she turned to writing for remuneration, and published poems, letters, and memoirs capitalizing on her American and Highland experiences. In 1810 she took up residence in Edinburgh, supervising the education and morals of young ladies, and mingling in literary society. Her fame rivalled that of *Ossian*'s MacPherson, and her visitors included Scott, Southey, James Hogg, and Wordsworth.[1]

[1] Roderick Barron, 'A Highland Lady of Letters: Mrs. Grant of Laggan,' *Transactions of the Gaelic Society of Inverness*, XLII (1965), 68–90, is informative and discerning.

In view of her talents and opportunities, the *Essays* make disappointing reading. They are filled with moralistic sentiments, scenic raptures, and long-winded reflections. Anne Grant was clearly struck by the fantastic ways and convictions of the Highlanders but, unlike Mrs. Bray benefiting from Southey's counsel, lacked any guide to channel her materials. Scattered through her pages are wordy accounts of castle spectres, apparitions, fairies, prophecies, and second-sight. The thread, if one exists, lies in the conflict and resolution between the Presbyterian values of the kirk, embodied in her husband, and the supernatural creed of the Highlanders. The minister's wife walked and visited throughout the district, coming to know the families in nearly every cottage; some of the old men and women had lived through the '45. She was therefore able to insert in her essays a number of incidents personally told her of unnatural visitations and afflictions, or 'air-drawn terrors.'

Sympathetic, Mrs. Grant perceived some benefits in the devoutly credited superstitions. Highlanders regarded the rite of baptism and invocation of the Deity as means of disarming fairies and other sprites dangerous to newborn babes. Parental vanity and envy were checked through the prohibition against onlookers praising the babe, which would thereby be exposed to evil eyes and evil spirits. A nurse or dairymaid would instantly say, 'God save the bairn or the beast,' if a child or cow were inadvertently admired. When Queen Mary visited the North, staying at Inverness, a lady of Ross-shire of the Monro family gathered her twelve sons, dressed in Lincoln green and mounted on sable horses, and her twelve daughters, all in white on white steeds, to present to Her Majesty. Overwhelmed, the queen gave up her chair to the mother, saying, in the words of those who talked to Mrs. Grant, 'Madam, ye sud tak this chaire, ye best deserve it.' But the royal admiration brought an early death to the children.[1]

Even the most intelligent, well educated, and staunchly Presbyterian Highlander could succumb to a superstition. Mrs. Grant tells of a native in the vale of Glenorchy who warred against superstitions, but credited the second-sight. As evidence he recounted an incident befalling a Presbyterian pastor who one evening saw two small lights rise over a churchyard, cross a river to a hamlet opposite, and return with a larger light, whereupon all three sank into the earth. On inquiring the next morning, the clergyman learned that two young children of a blacksmith, now an old man

---

[1] Grant, *Essays on the Superstitions of the Highlanders of Scotland*, 2 vols. (London: printed for Longman, Hurst, Rees, Orme, and Brown, 1811), I, 163–73.

living across the river, were buried behind the church. Within the hour he received a message to come to the bedside of the smith, who died the next day.[1]

One ghostly encounter set down by Mrs. Grant was noticed by Hone and studied by Andrew Lang. Its special interest lay in the tangible mark left on the living by the dead.

A gentleman died in Strathspey, three score years since, and left a widow with a large family. He, though the head of an ancient house, left not much behind him; and his widow found it necessary to pay the most sedulous attention to all the small profits of a farm, &c. for the benefit of her family: She possessed among other things a mill, part of the grist of which she allowed to the miller, and took the rest to herself, as a kind of rent. She often walked down from her house to see whether her due was regularly put in the place allotted for it. One evening she staid longer than usual, and returned to her house as it grew dusk; her way lay through a little wood, and she had to cross a brook, over a temporary bridge made of fallen trees. As she was approaching with some doubt and hesitation towards it, she saw on the other side, her husband very well drest, in tartan, with a handsome silver mounted dirk, and pistols, such as he used to wear on occasions of display.

He came to her, took her hand, and led her over the bridge with the utmost attention, then walking up the wood, he said to her; 'Oh Marjory, Marjory, by what fatality have you been tempted to come thus rashly alone, when the sun is gone to sleep.' It is in this manner that they express, what we should call sunset.

The spectre disappeared, and Marjory arrived at home in great terror, fainted immediately, and on her recovery from her swoon, thought of nothing but preparing for her departure.

She lived however for a week, and was visited by many of her friends. Had they been sceptical enough to doubt her assertion, she carried about with her, a testimony to enforce her belief. Her wrist, where the ghost had laid hold of her hand, was blue, and had the appearance of being mortified. This is quite consistent with the system; for it appears that Marjory was punished for her impiety in daring the powers of darkness, without using the precaution appointed in such cases.[2]

[1] Grant, *Essays on the Superstitions of the Highlanders of Scotland*, 2 vols. (London, 1811), I, 256–61.
[2] *Ibid.*, pp. 216–18.

In some of her comments Mrs. Grant tentatively suggests classes of spectres. Mountain ghosts seem 'moral, rational, and prudent,' as in the foregoing account, in which the spectral husband judiciously warns his wife against being out late at night. A second group of spirits possesses a more capricious and enigmatic character. Shadowy card-players were beheld one night in the great room of the castle by a youth on guard, who died in delirium three days later.[1]

This rough attempt at classifying supernatural beings was carried out more systematically by William Grant Stewart in *The Popular Superstitions and Festive Amusements of the Highlanders of Scotland* (1823; new edition, 1851), the book on which the Grimms relied heavily in the essay prefacing their translation of Croker's Irish fairy legends. The jocose style, the oral basis, and the choice of subject all coincided with Croker's better known work. While cognizant of the writings on Scottish superstitions by Burns, Scott, Mrs. Grant, and others, Stewart felt the need for an organized account of the habits and 'similitudes' of Highland ghosts, fairies, and witches. 'By visiting the most celebrated professors of traditional lore in the district,' Stewart said of himself, 'he speedily acquired not only a fundamental knowledge of the reigning principles of superstition, but likewise an inexhaustible store of tales and traditions.'[2] He confessed he had been obliged to abridge these 'primitive relations,' but maintained he had borrowed the language directly from the mouths of the Highland narrators and translated it in a manner intelligible, he hoped, for *peasant readers*!

The Table of Contents impressed readers like the Grimms with its formal chapter divisions, slicing up supernatural beings according to their properties, powers, and traits, adverse and favourable. Actually the promised treaties proved to be a series of pegs on which to hang a number of striking personal narratives, given presumably in the words of their speakers. For so early a tract, preceding Croker and Keightley and Scott's *Letters on Demonology and Witchcraft*, it broke new ground, bringing into focus the separate features of the ghost, fairy, and witch, with brief glances at the brownie, spunky and water-kelpie. Stewart's emphasis is on contrast, where Scott, and later Jeremiah Curtin, would point out overlapping aspects.

Along with the arch commentary, Stewart provided valuable

---

[1] *Ibid.*, pp. 226–30.
[2] Stewart, *The Popular Superstitions and Festive Amusements of the Highlanders of Scotland* (Edinburgh: printed for Archibald Constable and Company, 1823), p. xiii.

firsthand spirit stories. The Highland ghost was, like his flesh and blood counterpart, devoted to his master. When one clansman died without returning an axe (iron possessing magical efficacy) and a whisky barrel he had borrowed, the ghost haunted a friend until he absorbed the message and took back the articles. Stewart disclosed spectral secrets: embrace a ghost and lift it off the ground if you wish to make it speak; cure murrain in cattle with juice extracted from a corpse's head excavated in a churchyard, always making due apologies to its ghost. The sheaf of fairy reports was especially rich and revealing. Two fiddlers, decoyed by Thomas the Rhymer to play for the fairies in Inverness, emerged a hundred years later after what seemed to them a one-night stand. A midwife seized by the fairies assisted in a fairy accouchement at Cairngorm. A seal-hunter, led underwater by a supposed sealskin merchant who was actually one of the fairy tribe of seals, was implored to heal the wound he had inflicted that morning on a suffering fairy seal. The wizard Michael Scott learned his necromancy from a wise woman to whom he gave the middle part of a white snake he had killed. Witch tales too offered excitement. Witches in the form of cats sank the ship of the sailor-hero John Garve Macgillichallun of Razay. Witches were themselves sunk in their riddles (i.e. sieves) when a bystander uttered the words 'Go in the name of the Best.'

These intimate revelations anticipated the findings about fairy, ghost, and witch behaviour written late in the century by Hartland and Lang. The supernatural lapse of time in fairyland, the abduction of midwives and seduction of mortals by the fairies, the shipwrecking powers of the witch, the helpful qualities of ghost and fairy, are all illustrated in Stewart's *Highlanders*. He might more aptly have titled his book 'Traditions' rather than 'Superstitions,' although he did set forth a few elaborate formulas. For protection against fairy spells, gather the herb 'Mohan' from a mountain cliff untrod by man, feed it to a cow, and of the milk make a cheese, which will ever after safeguard its eater. Against witchcraft the recipe was even more painstaking.

> . . . notice is privately communicated to all those householders who reside within the nearest two running streams, to extinguish their lights and fires on some appointed morning . . . a spinning-wheel, or some other convenient instrument, calculated to produce fire by friction, is set to work with the most furious earnestness by the unfortunate sufferer, and all who wish well to his cause. Relieving each other by turns, they drive on with such persevering diligence, that at length the

spindle of the wheel, ignited by excessive friction, emits '*Forlorn Fire*' in abundance, which, by the application of tow, or some other combustible material, is widely extended over the whole neighbourhood. Communicating the fire to the tow, the tow communicates it to a candle, the candle to a fir-torch, the torch to a cartful of peats, which the master of the ceremonies, with pious ejaculations for the success of the experiment, distributes to messengers, who will proceed with portions of it to the different houses within the two running streams, to kindle the different fires. By the influence of this operation, the machinations and spells of witchcraft 'are rendered null and void,' and in the language of Scots law, 'of no avail, force, strength, or effect, with all that has followed, or may follow thereupon.'[1]

Should even this potent remedy fail, recourse could be had to a stone of wondrous protective properties cherished in the Willox family.

In a concluding section Stewart describes 'Highland Festive Amusements' he had witnessed: Hallowe'en, Christmas, New-Year's Eve, Fasten's Eve, Belton Eve, christenings, weddings, wakes, funerals. Ghosts and fairies mingle with the guests at these affairs, their presence evoking the charms and divination spells rife on these occasions. So a hopeful swain would steal out to the peat-stack on Hallowe'en, sow a handful of hemp-seed and chant:

> Hemp-seed I saw thee,
> Hemp-seed I saw thee,
> And he who is my true love
> Come after me and pu' thee.

Then looking over his shoulder, he would see the apparition of the desired one pulling the hemp. If hemp-seed were not on hand, the quester could ride the floor-besom in the manner of a witch three times round the peat-stack, and on the last circuit the apparition would appear.[2]

While Anne Grant and Stewart were finding supernatural beliefs among the Highland cottagers, Sir John Graham Dalyell (1775–1851) was amassing them from the manuscripts and printed books in the Advocates' Library at Edinburgh. His collection was published under the title *The Darker Superstitions of Scotland illustrated from History and Practice* (1834). Dalyell was a consulting advocate, inventor of a self-regulating calendar, author of a score of

[1] *The Popular Superstitions and Festive Amusements of the Highlanders of Scotland*, pp. 215–16.
[2] *Ibid.*, p. 282.

books on subjects varying from sea disasters to Scottish history to the humbler forms of animated nature. His memorialist honoured him as a 'thorough linguist, mathematician, mechanist, antiquary, genealogist, musician, historian, and zoologist.'[1] In *The Darker Superstitions* he arranged an inventory of charms, predictions, incantations, taboos, magical formulas, healing remedies, elixirs, and enchantments from parish records, witch trials, classical writings, books of travellers and antiquaries, and theological treatises.

The eighteen chapters presented overlapping but suggestive rubrics: Of an Evil Eye, Invocations and Maledictions; Occult Infection and Cure of Maladies; Miscellaneous Remedies, or Antidotes to Disease; Amulets; Analogies to Propitiating Sacrifice; Propitiatory Charms; Faculties ascribed to Sorcerers; Superstitions relative to Marriage; Doctrine of Sympathy; Ingredients and Instruments of Superstition and Sorcery; Mystical Plants; Mystical Animals; Mystical Mankind; Prognostication, Divination; Imaginary Beings; Spectral Illusions; The Tongues; Tests, Trial, Conviction, and Punishment of Sorcery. An eleven-page index and scrupulous documentation of the far-flung sources made the *Darker Superstitions* the most scholarly encyclopaedia of British folk beliefs in its time; indeed, it had no rivals. Drawbacks were its Calvinist condemnation of the black arts, its heaped-up clutter of extracts, and a lugubrious style. 'Mankind have peopled the boundless regions traversed by the celestial orbs,' wrote Dalyell in his chapter on *Imaginary Beings*, 'with beings resembling themselves, yet invested with a superior nature, an invisible, etherial, definite figure, which, losing its tenuity, may sink to the earth, and become susceptible to mortal view.'[2]

Among the myriad sources sifted by Dalyell, some of the familiar names recur. In his discourse on the evil eye he cites Reginald Scot's *Discoverie of Witchcraft* (1584), Gough's edition of Camden's *Britannia*, Aubrey's *Miscellanies*, an oft-quoted reference (1696), Robert Kirk's *Secret Commonwealth* of 1691, in Robert Jamieson's edition (1815). He excerpts Pennant on an amulet to ease the pain of childbirth, Croker on the Shetland water horse, Brand-Ellis on hunting the wren in Ireland and horseshoes nailed over London doors for luck, and Thomas Browne's *Pseudodoxia Epidemica* on the denial of sulphurous flames in hell.[3] Dalyell made considerable use of the handsome collection of manuscripts and tracts on Scottish

[1] 'Memoir of Sir John Graham Dalyell, Knight and Baronet,' in *The Powers of the Creator Displayed in the Creation*, III (London: John Van Voorst, 1858), xlii.
[2] John Graham Dalyell, *The Darker Superstitions of Scotland, Illustrated from History and Practice* (Edinburgh: Waugh and Innes, 1834), p. 525.
[3] *Ibid.*, pp. 131, 544, 423, 148, 436.

church history accumulated a century earlier and deposited in the Advocates' Library in Edinburgh by Robert Woodrow (Wodrow), minister of Eastwood. In its published form, in four large quarto volumes (1842–43), Wodrow's *Analecta: or Materials for a History of Remarkable Providences; Mostly Relating to Scotch Ministers and Christians*, would delight Andrew Lang with its copious testimonials of faith in divine wonders. In manuscript form the *Analecta* served Dalyell equally well. From it he culled second-sighted visions, of the defeat at the battle of Bothwell Bridge, and of gentlemen bathed in blood who died soon after; an account of a lady accused by her minister of having fellowship with the Devil; a report of a church bell that would not toll after its heathenish parish deposed its minister; the prophetic dream of a 'popish lady' that a coach would overturn in the river.[1]

To Dalyell's credit, he went beyond the mere cataloguing of superstitions and sought to uncover a controlling idea, such as the 'doctrine of sympathy,' which gave a rational air to wild beliefs. This principle accounted for cures effected by a healer who touched the girdle of an afflicted person when that person lay in pain at some distance; for counter-spells against a witch performed by burning the object or animal bewitched, and so burning the witch; and for the inflicting of injury and death to a hated one by piercing waxen images of the human model. In these latter cases, surmised Dalyell, an inflamed imagination disturbed the mind and body of the human target. To make his point he related the 'familiar anecdote' ascribed to Dr. Pitcairn who, meeting an acquaintance in Edinburgh, capriciously told him his hours were numbered. The man went to bed and never rose again. Further to Dalyell's credit, he did not rest content with image-tormenting sorceries culled from sixteenth- and seventeenth-century trials of Scotch witches, but, anticipating the doctrine of survivals formulated by the anthropologist E. B. Tylor, pointed to image destruction among the Hindoos, on the continent, in ancient Rome. In conclusion, Dalyell moralized on the universal human tendency of evildoers to exploit their weaker brethren.[2]

By mid-century a considerable mass of legends, beliefs, and supernatural lore rife among the peasantry in Scotland and England had been excavated and placed on public view. But as yet no body of theory had tested these materials, which rested precariously in a no man's land between the provinces of the poet and the antiquary.

[1] *Ibid.*, pp. 473, 476, 579, 269, 479.
[2] *Ibid.*, ch. 13, 'Doctrine of Sympathy,' pp. 317–71.

V   The Mythological Folklorists

I N ENGLAND AND SCOTLAND the folklore-minded antiquaries
and romancers had by the middle of the nineteenth century won
the preliminary round in their battle for recognition. The field had
been fairly defined and circumscribed, thanks to its crisp new name.
In the pages of *Notes and Queries*, Thoms was accumulating fresh
items of tradition and steadily reminding the intellectually curious
of the existence of lower-class culture. Yet, while admitting the
charm and intrigue of the subject, the casual onlooker might well
question the deeper purpose and philosophic basis of folklore. The
urge to discredit Romish festivals by demonstrating their pagan
origins and vulgar survivals had lost its appeal to a comfortable
Anglican Establishment, and smacked too much of outworn
theological polemics. Jacob Grimm's hypothesis of common Aryan
origins for Indo-European languages and mythologies, with its persuasive philological proofs, provided the intellectual backbone for the
English collectors and romancers; but this was a Teutonic theory
based on Germanic materials, and in any event the Grimms' major
source material, the *Märchen*, was barely visible in merry old
England. The pursuers of folklore wavered uncertainly between
literary embroidering and antiquarian exposition of their hard-won
treasures.

At this juncture two novel systems of thought emerged upon the
intellectual scene to exploit the raw data of folklore. The protagonists of these systems engaged in a duel which occupied the last
three decades of the century, and attracted the attention of the
English nation and the outside world. First to develop, in the 1850's,
was the science of comparative mythology, revivified by philological researches applied to India rather than to Europe. Meanwhile another trail led from Darwin's *On the Origin of Species* (1859)
and the theory of biological evolution to the science of anthropology
and the theory of cultural evolution, a theory which by the 1870's
infected a stellar group of anthropological folklorists. There is a good

deal of overlap and riposte between the two contending schools of folklore, but from Max Müller's seminal essay of 1856 to Andrew Lang's opening salvo in an article in 1873, the new mythological interpretation of folklore ruled uncontested.

Born in Germany in 1823 in the town of Dessau, Friedrich Max Müller came to England in 1846, attained a professorship at Oxford, and until his death in 1900 lived and wrote and participated in the midst of English intellectual life. At the University of Leipzig, which he attended from 1838 to 1841, he shifted from conventional classical studies to the enticing new field of Sanskrit, and felt as if he were peering into the dawn of civilization. Later studies took him to Berlin in 1844 to hear Franz Bopp, a founder of comparative philology, and to Paris in 1845, to collate Sanskrit manuscripts under the direction of Eugene Burnouf. In Paris he starved himself and slept only one night out of three in order to devote every possible moment to his researches.[1] In 1846 he crossed the channel to London to seek the support of the East India Company in his goal of translating the Sacred Books of India from Sanskrit into English. At the age of twenty-six he had found his life's work and love, the Vedic studies which would unveil the language, thought, mythology, and folklore of the Aryan peoples. In the next decades he won a vast audience with limpid essays on such forbidding subjects as the science of language and the religion of India, and became so famous that in 1875 several European governments joined to lure him back to the Continent from Oxford; he was persuaded to stay by a special decree at Convocation and a prayerful eulogy from the dean of Christ Church College. The college broke precedent with an offer of a chair free from all teaching duties.[2]

Translating and pondering over the Vedas with the eyes of a comparative philologist, Müller perceived family resemblances in the metaphorical names of the ancient gods of India and Greece which led him to evolve a striking theory. This he presented in 1856 in a lengthy essay titled 'Comparative Mythology,' an essay that reoriented all previous thinking about the origin of myths.[3] Handbooks and manuals of mythology had flourished ever since the Renaissance re-established the classics; Thomas Keightley had

---

[1] Max Müller, *My Autobiography, A Fragment* (New York, 1909), chaps. 5 and 6, gives rich details on Müller's early years in France and England.

[2] Georgiana Max Müller, *The Life and Letters of the Right Honourable Friedrich Max Müller*, 2 vols. (New York, London, and Bombay, 1902), II, 7, and Appendix C, 'Speech of Dean Liddell,' 475–9.

[3] Müller, *Oxford Essays* (Oxford, 1856), pp. 1–87, reprinted in *Chips from a German Workshop*, 4 vols. (London, 1867–75), II, 1–143.

written one study, *The Mythology of Ancient Greece and Italy* (1831), but even Keightley with his folklore instinct produced only a conventional treatment of the Homeric gods and heroes as pretty nature allegories. Müller now offered a key to the understanding of Aryan traditions, whether myths of the gods, legends of heroes, or tales of adventurers, through the method of comparative philology and the new revelation of Vedic Sanskrit.

Both Müller and Lang puzzled over an anomaly no scholar had explained, the barbarous elements in Greek myths. How could so civilized a people repeat such degrading stories about their gods? The mystery can be cleared up, Müller reasoned, by tracing the names of the Greek deities to their Sanskrit equivalents, and then reading in the Veda, the oldest literary monument of the Aryan peoples, to perceive the true nature of the gods. All the Indo-European peoples belonged to a common Aryan stock; after the migration of the European groups from their Indic homeland, the parent language, and the mythology it related, splintered into various offshoots. A time came when the original meanings of the names of the Vedic gods were forgotten, and survived only in mythical phrases and proverbs of uncertain sense. Stories then developed to explain these phrases. From this 'disease of language' myths were born.

Müller postulated a 'mythopoeic' age when truly noble conceptions of the Aryan gods first arose. This age occurred, not at the beginning of civilization, but at a stage early enough so that language could not convey abstract notions. Two processes developed to carry the burden of communication: polyonomy, where one word carried many meanings, and homonymy, where one idea became attached to different words. Dyâus, the supreme god, might be understood as sky, sun, air, dawn, light, brightness. Conversely, a number of different words might signify the sun, with its complex of associations. These phenomena of mythopoeic thought and speech thickened the confusion resulting from the 'disease of language.'

Metaphors thus operated in two ways. The same verb root, for instance 'to shine,' could form the name of the sun or a term for the brightness of thought. Then again, nouns so formed could be transferred poetically to other objects; the rays of the sun become fingers, clouds are called mountains, the rain clouds are referred to as cows with heavy udders, the lightning receives the appellation arrow or serpent. These metaphorical words are 'appellatives,' and form the substance of myths.[1] Müller always stressed that solar

[1] Müller, *Lectures on the Science of Language, delivered at the Royal Institution of Great*

[162]

interpretation must be based on strict phonetic rules. The 'ponderous squibs' that reduced the nursery song of sixpence, or Napoleon, or a gentleman named Mr. Bright, or Max Müller himself, to solar myths, all went wide of the mark in ridiculing the excesses of comparative mythologists who failed to *identify* similar gods and heroes with etymological proofs.[1]

Clearly, mythopoeic man constructed his pantheon around the sun, the dawn, and the sky. How could it be otherwise? Müller asked.

> What we call the Morning, the ancient Aryans called the Sun or the Dawn. . . . What we call Noon, and Evening, and Night, what we call Spring and Winter, what we call Year, and Time, and Life, and Eternity—all this the ancient Aryans called *Sun*. And yet wise people wonder and say, How curious that the ancient Aryans should have had so many solar myths. Why, every time we say 'Good morning,' we commit a solar myth. Every poet who sings about 'the May driving the Winter from the field again' commits a solar myth. Every 'Christmas number' of our newspapers—ringing out the old year and ringing in the new—is brimful of solar myths. Be not afraid of solar myths. . . .[2]

[1] Müller, *Natural Religion: The Gifford Lectures Delivered before the University of Glasgow in 1888* (London, 1889), p. 487. For these squibs see 'The Oxford Solar Myth' by the Reverend R. F. Littledale, in Max Müller, *Comparative Mythology, An Essay*, ed. Abram Smythe Palmer (London and New York, 1909), pp. xxxi–xlvii, reprinted from *Kottabos*, a magazine of Trinity College, Dublin, No. 5 (1870), which proves Max Müller to be a solar myth; anon., 'John Gilpin as a Solar Hero,' *Fraser's Magazine*, n.s., XXIII (March, 1881), 353–71; E. B. Tylor, *Primitive Culture*, 3rd ed. (London, 1891), I, 319–20 (the Song of Sixpence, Cortès, and Julius Caesar are 'solarized').

[2] Müller, *India: What Can it Teach Us? A Course of Lectures delivered before the University of Cambridge* (New York, 1883), p. 216. Cf. these similar statements: 'I look upon the sunrise and sunset, on the daily return of day and night, on the battle between light and darkness, on the whole solar drama in all its details that is acted every day, every month, every year, in heaven and in earth, as the principal subject of early mythology' (*Lectures on the Science of Language, Second Series*, p. 537). '. . . there was but one name by which they [mythopoeic men] could express love—there was but one similitude for the roseate bloom that betrays the dawn of love—it was the blush of the day, the rising of the sun. "The sun has risen," they said, where we say, "I love"; "The sun has set," they said, where we say, "I have loved"' (*Chips from a German Workshop* [New York, 1872], II, 128, from 'Comparative Mythology' [1856]). 'Was not the Sunrise to him [mythopoeic man] the first wonder, the first beginning of all reflection, all thought, all philosophy? Was it not to him the first revelation, the first beginning of all trust, of all religion?' (*Selected Essays on Language, Mythology, and Religion* [London, 1881], I, 599–600). ' "Is everything the Dawn? Is everything the Sun?" This question I had asked myself many times before

Britain in February, March, April, and May, 1863, 2nd Ser. (New York, 1869), p. 371, in the lecture on 'Metaphor.'

The major triumph of comparative mythology lay in the equation Dyâus=Zeus, which associated the supreme gods of the Greeks and Vedic pantheons. If they were identical, their families of lesser gods and goddesses must equally be kin. Dyâus is the Vedic sky-god, and now the ugly mystery of the Greek myth of Cronus and Zeus is cleared up. Cronus castrated his father, Uranus, at the behest of his mother, Gaea, who was both Uranus' wife and daughter. Cronus then married his own sister and swallowed his children as fast as they were born. But Zeus escaped when his mother substituted for him a stone swaddled like a baby. Then Zeus compelled Cronus to disgorge his brothers and sisters. Scarcely a fitting tale to introduce the beauties of Greek mythology to the younger generation! But now we see plainly that the marriage of Uranus and Gaea represents the union of heaven and earth. The paternal cannibalism of Cronus originally signified the heavens devouring, and later releasing, the clouds, and the act of Zeus depicts the final separation of heaven and earth, and the commencement of man's history.[1]

In making their equations, Müller and other comparative philologists of his day filled their pages with a series of acrostic puzzles that inevitably arrived, after conjecture, surmise, and supposition, at a predestined goal. For Müller it was the sun, for Kuhn the storm clouds, for Schwartz the wind, for Preller the sky. With increasing acerbity Müller told Lang and all non-Sanskritists to stay out of these arguments,[2] but on occasion he did provide English readers with homely examples of the 'forgetfulness of language,' which he dubbed 'modern mythology.' The arms of Oxford, displaying an ox crossing a ford, represented such a popular etymology. Look how 'cocoa' has absorbed 'cacao,' how 'God' is associated with 'good,' how 'lark,' as sport, suggests the bird. We speak of 'swallowing' one's pride, and perhaps an early swallower was named Cronus. One dramatic illustration that Müller offered to clinch his point dealt with the modern myth of the barnacle goose, reported by sailors and travellers who had seen birds hatched from shellfish. Working back in time through his sources, Müller eventually arrived at a twelfth-century Irish version from Giraldus

[1] Müller, 'Jupiter, the Supreme Aryan God,' *Lectures on the Science of Language, Second Series*, pp. 432–80; 'The Lesson of Jupiter,' *Nineteenth Century*, XVIII (Oct., 1885), 626–50.

[2] E.g., *Natural Religion*, p. 449: '. . . no one who is not an expert, has anything to say here.' In 1897 Müller wrote Lang personally, 'Still less could I understand why you should have attacked me, or rather my masters, without learning Sanscrit. . . .' (*Life and Letters*, II, 381).

it was addressed to me by others . . . but I am bound to say that my own researches lead me again and again to the dawn and the sun as the chief burden of the myths of the Aryan race' (*Lectures on the Science of Language, Second Series*, p. 520).

Cambrensis. Then he gives the key. Irish birds would be called Hiberniculae, a name eventually shortened to Berniculae, which easily becomes Bernacula, and is confused with 'barnacles.' In this way linguistic confusion creates the myth of birds being born from barnacles. Similarly, speculates Müller, the legend of Dick Whittington and his cat could have arisen from misapprehension of the French 'achat,' trade, to which Whittington actually owed his wealth, but which in English was rendered 'a cat.'[1] Unravel this kind of verbal confusion, and the puzzling elements in Greek myths appear as legends springing up around divine names which, before the Aryan separation, signified the sun and the dawn.

From the appearance of his 1856 essay on 'Comparative Mythology' until the end of his life Müller expanded, championed, and defended his theory. *Lectures on the Science of Language, Second Series* (1864) included five chapters relating to solar mythology. Three years later Müller brought together in the second volume of his *Chips from a German Workshop* his occasional 'Essays on Mythology, Traditions, and Customs,' dating from (and including) his epochal monograph. This volume particularly intrigues the intellectual historian by recording Müller's reactions, in the form of review-essays, to classical folklore works emerging in the 1860's: the tale-collections of Callaway, Dasent, and Campbell, and the seminal researches of Tylor. A lecture 'On the Philosophy of Mythology' formed part of the *Introduction to the Science of Religion* (1873).[2] In his *Lectures on the Origin and Growth of Religion, as Illustrated by the Religions of India* (1878), Müller turned critic, and to the question 'Is Fetishism a Primitive Form of Religion?' replied with a strong negative; at the same time he discussed the problem of securing from savages reliable evidence on their beliefs. Here Müller strikes at the anthropological evolutionists. The chapters on 'The Lessons of the Veda' and 'Vedic Deities' in *India: What Can It Teach Us* (1883) tentatively apply the solar theory to savages.

He considerably extended his critique of rival methods in his Gifford Lectures for 1888 on *Natural Religion* (1889), in analysing the three schools of mythology contending in England. In *Physical Religion* (1891), Müller devoted particular attention to Agni, the Vedic god of fire, and demonstrated his religious and mythological components in two chapters, 'The Mythological Development of Agni' and 'Religion, Myth, and Custom.' Again in *Anthropological*

---

[1] Müller, *Natural Religion*, p. 441; 'Solar Myths,' pp. 904–5; *Lectures on the Science of Languages, Second Series*, pp. 556–68, in Lecture XII, 'Modern Mythology.'

[2] This lecture was reprinted in Müller's *Selected Essays on Language, Mythology, and Religion*, I (London, 1881), along with other folkloristic essays previously published in *Chips*, II, and a lecture of 1870, 'On the Migration of Fables.'

Religion (1892), the four-time Gifford lecturer touched on such favourite themes as the unreliability of anthropological evidence, and the contradictory reports about savage ideas and ways. Because mythology formed a vital link in his chain of being, along with thought, language, and religion, Müller rarely omitted the solar theory from his general discussions of cultural and religious origins. In these books Müller never mentioned Lang by name, although he referred continually to 'ethno-psychological' mythologists who studied the tales of savages without learning their languages. Lang remarked on this omission in his review of a new edition of the *Chips* (1894), a review which finally drew blood and led Müller to produce two thick volumes on *Contributions to the Science of Mythology* (1897).[1] Here he massed the arguments of his lifelong researches for a personal clash with Lang, repeated everything he had previously written, and repeated his repetitions throughout the twin volumes.

In 1873 Lang launched his first attack on Müller's solar mythology with an article in the *Fortnightly Review* on 'Mythology and Fairy Tales.' For the next three decades he peppered Müller with a barrage of criticisms centred on his alleged neglect of ethnological data, and exploiting the internal differences among the celestial mythologists. Müller never conceded an inch. He stuck fast to his etymologies, and berated Lang for discussing Sanskrit matters on which he was ignorant. However, he dissociated himself from any conclusions not based on the identifications of Greek and Sanskrit proper names, and considered his follower Cox unwary for submitting proofs based solely on analogies.[2] While Lang never learned Sanskrit, his opponent increasingly considered ethnological materials. Further, Müller strongly counterattacked the ethnological position, and criticized the ambiguities and convenient vagueness of such terms as totemism, animism, fetishism, and savages.[3] He disparaged the data obtained from savages by missionaries and travellers as credulous, biased, and coloured by

[1] Müller does not identify the review in his several repetitions of Lang's comment in *Contributions to the Science of Mythology*, 2 vols. (London, New York, and Bombay, 1897), I, 11, 32, 184. He does mention Lang, and only with praise, in articles in the *Nineteenth Century* on 'The Savage,' XVII (Jan., 1885), 117, and 'Solar Myths,' XVIII (Dec., 1885), 905.

[2] See, e.g., Müller's concluding remarks in his review of Cox's *A Manual of Mythology*, in *Chips from a German Workshop*, II, 154–9, where he points out the possibility of ancient myths being transferred to historical heroes; and his expression of misgivings about 'The Analogical School,' in *Natural Religion*, p. 486.

[3] Müller, 'The Savage,' *Nineteenth Century*, XVII (Jan., 1885), 109–32; *Contributions to the Science of Mythology*, I, 7, 185 *et seq.*; *Anthropological Religion*, Appendix III, 'On Totems and Their Various Origin,' pp. 403–10; *Lectures on the Origin and Growth of Religion as Illustrated by the Religions of India* (London, 1878), pp. 52–127.

public opinion and priestly authority, and demanded that observers master the native languages.[1] (English anthropologists today criticize their American colleagues for not learning languages.) Are all savages alike? he asked, and answered that further study of savage myths and customs would reveal more contradictions than ever the philologists brewed, 'with this important difference, that scholars can judge of etymologies by themselves, while many a Baron Munchhausen escapes entirely from our cross-examination.'[2] Think what a hodgepodge of creeds and customs a curious Finn would find in England, especially if he had to rely on interpreters! Unless the motive is the same in each case, the customs extracted from different cultures are not true analogies.

So Müller anticipated the lethal shafts modern anthropology would direct at comparative ethnologists such as Frazer. For totemism he reserved his choicest barbs. Totems conveniently appeared wherever the ethnologists found some belief or rite involving an animal. Should Müller's friend, Abeken, whose name means small ape, and who displays an ape in his coat of arms, be assigned the ape as his totem? 'It is true I never saw him eating an ape, but I feel certain this was not from any regard for his supposed ancestor or totem, but was with him a mere matter of taste.'[3] What do animism and totemism explain, in any event? To say that the myth of Daphne can be understood because Samoans and Sarawakians believed women could change into trees is to explain *ignotum per ignotius*; why would they believe such a thing?[4] Müller thus threw back at Lang his charge that philology failed to account for the nasty and senseless stories about Greek gods.

Far from abandoning his philological 'fortress,' Müller sallied forth to annex folklore territory. The ethno-psychological school shared his objectives, and he would gladly work with them, provided they observed proper scholarly caution and learned languages.[5] Müller stoutly asserted his friendship for ethnology. He spoke warmly of Tylor, whose *Researches into the Early History of Mankind* he reviewed sympathetically, but with the admonition that the comparison of customs should keep within the bounds of comparative languages.[6] Indeed, he quoted 'My friend, Mr.

[1] Müller, *Anthropological Religion*, Appendix V, 'On the Untrustworthiness of Anthropological Evidence,' pp. 413–35.
[2] Müller, *Contributions to the Science of Mythology*, I, 280.
[3] *Ibid.*, II, 600.   [4] Müller, *Natural Religion*, p. 441.
[5] Müller reiterates the necessity to learn languages, and not simply engage in the 'pleasant reading' of folklore, in *Contributions to the Science of Mythology*, I, 5, 23–4, 28, 128, 232, 286; II, 462, 830–1.
[6] Müller, *Chips from a German Workshop*, II, 'On Manners and Customs,' pp. 248–283, esp. p. 260.

Tylor,' in support of solar mythology, and for evidence on the unreliability of travellers' reports.¹ Müller himself had strenuously
pleaded for the establishment of an archives on 'Ethnological
Records of the English Colonies,' recognizing the great opportunity
afforded by the dominions, colonies, and missionary societies of the
British Empire, but the project was allowed to languish.² He had
once compiled a Mohawk grammar, and would certainly learn
savage tongues if time permitted.³ Since life was finite, he must
rely on scholarly missionaries who had themselves translated the
tales of primitive peoples; and so he consulted closely with Patte-
son, Codrington, and Gill on Melanesian and Polynesian dialects,
with Bleek and Hahn on African folklore,⁴ and on American Indian
dialects with Horatio Hale, future president of the American Folk-
lore Society, to whom he wrote in 1883, 'I am glad to hear of your
projects. I feel sure that there is no time to be lost in securing the
floating fragments of the great shipwreck of the American languages. When you have stirred up a national interest in it for the
North of America, you should try to form a Committee for the
South. The Emperor of Brazil would be sure to help, provided the
work is done by *real scholars*.'⁵ Müller knew the work of the Reverend
J. S. Whitmee, who hoped to collect 'choice myths and songs' that
would make possible a comparative study of Polynesian mytho-
logy.⁶ And he supplied a Preface for the book of traditions brought
back from the island of Mangaia by the Reverend W. Wyatt Gill,
in which he pointed eagerly to this record of mythopoeic men who
believe in gods and offer them human sacrifices.⁷ In 1891 the
Oxford don served as president of the Ethnological Section of the
British Association.⁸

The modern reader of Max Müller's mythological theory may find
himself astonished at the sophistication of the Sanskrit scholar in
matters ethnological. With admirable insight he dissected the
stereotyped notion of a 'savage,' to show how the qualities imputed
to him applied just as readily to the civilized man. 'When we read

¹ Müller, *Contributions to the Science of Mythology*, I, 143; *Lectures on the Origin and Growth of Religion*, p. 91.
² Müller, *Natural Religion*, p. 505.
³ *Ibid.*, p. 515; *Life and Letters*, II, 129; *Anthropological Religion*, pp. 169–71, where Müller gives the fullest details of his contact with an educated Mohawk.
⁴ Müller, 'The Savage,' p. 117; *Natural Religion*, pp. 515–17; 'Mythology among the Hottentots,' *Nineteenth Century* (Jan., 1882), pp. 33–8.
⁵ Müller, *Life and Letters*, II, 145–6.
⁶ Müller, *Lectures on the Origin and Growth of Religion*, pp. 74–5.
⁷ William Wyatt Gill, *Myths and Songs from the South Pacific* (London, 1876). In his Preface (pp. v–xviii) Müller explicitly rejects any single explanation for mythology, whether fetishism or the disease of language.
⁸ Müller, *Contributions to the Science of Mythology*, I, 11.

some of the more recent works on anthropology, the primordial savage seems to be not unlike one of those hideous india-rubber dolls that can be squeezed into every possible shape, and made to utter every possible noise. . . .'[1] Contemporary 'savages' have lived as long as civilized races and are nothing like primitive man. Actually the Andaman Islanders enjoyed a felicitous existence that a European labourer would gladly embrace.[2]

Then, after playfully juxtaposing the contradictory reports about savages, which reveal only the ignorance of the beholders, Müller does an unexpected turnabout. In an article entitled 'Solar Myths,' he relies exclusively on 'scholarlike' ethnologists to support his thesis. Almost in the words of Lang, he speaks about 'the surprising coincidence in the folklore, the superstitions and customs of the most remote races,' and proceeds to explore this mystery. He finds that among the non-Aryan peoples also, the trail always leads back through the disease of language to a solar myth. Legends of the Polynesian Maui become intelligible when we recognize that his name signifies the sun, or fire, or the day; the Hottentot deity Tsui-goab, now understood as Broken-Knee, originally meant the red dawn or the rising sun; Michabo, the Great Hare of the Algonkins, can be traced back to the god of light. So, thanks to the ethnological school of comparative mythology, the preoccupation of early man everywhere with the life-giving sun, about which he spun his legends and riddles and myths, becomes manifest.[3]

In his books too Müller compares crude New Zealand origin tales with Greek myths, and juxtaposes the Polynesian Maui with gods of the Veda, in the manner of Lang, but in the interests of solarism.[4] The *Kalevala* fascinated him as much as the Scot, and he corresponded with Krohn about Finnish folklore.[5] Like the most confirmed ethno-folklorist, he culled myths from the Eskimos, the Hottentots, and the Estonians, to illustrate the male and female personifications of sun, moon, and stars already known from his Aryan examples.[6] He produces superstitious customs of Scottish, Irish, and German peasants, which acquire a mythological hue.[7] And he makes a vigorous plea for the methods of comparative

---

[1] Müller, 'The Savage,' p. 111.
[2] Müller, *Anthropological Religion*, 'The Andaman Islanders,' pp. 173–80.
[3] Müller, 'Solar Myths,' pp. 900–22, esp. pp. 902, 906, 919.
[4] Müller, *Natural Religion*, p. 516; *India: What Can It Teach Us?*, pp. 169–75.
[5] Müller, *Anthropological Religion*, Appendix VIII, 'The Kalevala,' pp. 440–6.
[6] Müller, *Selected Essays on Language, Mythology and Religion*, chap. X, 'On the Philosophy of Mythology,' I, 609–15. Note, e.g., 'Among Finns and Lapps, among Zulus and Maoris, among Khonds and Karens, we sometimes find the most startling analogies. . . .'
[7] Müller, *Physical Religion*, Lecture XII, 'Religion, Myth, and Custom,' pp. 286–93.

folklore in studying mythology, before Lang had ever published a full-scale attack on his system.[1] Reading these comments, one recognizes that Lang was often pillorying a straw man—as Müller protested.[2]

In comparing non-Aryan with Aryan myths, Müller remained ever faithful to philological principles and the solar viewpoint. If myths had degenerated into heroic legends, and these into nursery tales, the reflection of the sun still shone, even in Red Riding Hood and Cinderella, and perhaps could be retraced etymologically.[3] He praised the eth $\frac{o}{o}$ logical work of Lewis Morgan and John Wesley Powell in the United States, based entirely on linguistics, and pointed triumphantly to the etymology for Gitse-Manito whose root, 'to warm,' clearly led back to the sun.[4] Müller's own inquiries into Mordvinian myths, relying on collections made by linguistic scholars, revealed the same solar origins he had traced for Vedic gods. When Letts spoke of the golden boat that sinks into the sea, or the apple that falls from the tree, they referred unwittingly to the setting sun.[5]

At the end of the long debate, it was Lang who gave ground. *Modern Mythology* finds him curiously on the defensive, qualifying his position on totemism, and admitting the differences between himself and Frazer on totemic survivals. Instead of referring to Samoan 'totems,' Lang will henceforth speak of Samoan 'sacred animals,' as more exact, since to prove sacred beasts are totems required definite evidence.[6] In revising his *Myth, Ritual, and Religion* in 1899, Lang made such extensive concessions that Hartland, who reviewed the new edition in *Folk-Lore*, the organ of the

[1] Müller, in *Chips from a German Workshop*, V (New York, 1881), p. 89. 'How much the student of Aryan mythology and ethnology may gain for his own progress by allowing himself a wider survey over the traditions and customs of the whole human race, is best known to those who have studied the works of Klemm, Waitz, Bastian, Sir John Lubbock, Mr. Tylor, and Dr. Callaway' (in 'On the Philosophy of Mythology,' 1871).

[2] Lang's comments in *Modern Mythology*, p. xx, alleging prejudice on Müller's part against ethnological collections, are manifestly unfair. The unbiased reader will, I believe, agree with the statements of Müller that he was not an adversary but more nearly a collaborator with Lang (*Contributions to the Science of Mythology*, I, 11; *Life and Letters*, II, 381, where Müller writes Lang, '. . . I am perfectly certain that some good may be got from the study of savages for the elucidation of Aryan myths. I never could find out why I should be thought to be opposed to Agriology, because I was an aryologist. *L'un n'empeche pas l'autre*' (8 July 1897). Note that Müller, as well as Lang, was a charter member of The Folk-Lore Society in 1878.

[3] Müller, 'Solar Myths,' p. 916.

[4] Müller, *Natural Religion*, pp. 508–10, and 511 n.

[5] Müller, *Contributions to the Science of Mythology*, I, 235 et seq.; II, 433–5.

[6] Lang, *Modern Mythology*, pp. 85, 142–3. Lang writes that he begged Müller not to read the book, and vowed not to criticize his ideas again ('Max Müller,' *Contemporary Review*, LXXVIII [1900], 785).

anthropological school, averred Lang had delivered himself into his opponents' hands.[1] Speculating on religious origins, Lang came to accept, on the basis of anthropological evidence, the same conception of 'high gods' and pure spiritual ideas among primitive peoples that Müller supported intuitively and philosophically. Lang challenged Tylor on the animistic origins of religious belief, and ceased to present the upward ascent of man as a clear-cut evolutionary climb.[2] In his new edition he added the sentence, 'The lowest savagery scarcely ever, if ever, wholly loses sight of a heavenly father,' after the statement, 'The most brilliant civilization of the world never expelled the old savage from its myth and ritual.' Again, he appends two new sentences to his chapter on 'Mexican Divine Myths' to soften the original conclusion that even the Spanish Inquisition advanced over barbarous Mexican ritual. The new ending holds that wild polytheistic myths grow around gods unknown to low savage races, who recognize a 'moral primal Being.'[3] In asserting the godliness of early man, Lang elevates the savage mentality, and so injures his thesis that survivals or borrowings from savages explain the irrational elements in myths and fairy tales.

Influential as was the solar theory of Max Müller among the Victorians, a rival myth-interpretation of slightly varied emphasis also attracted considerable attention. This was the lightning school of celestial mythologists, championed by the German Sanskritist Adalbert Kuhn in his work *Die Herabkunft des Feuers und des Göttertranks* (*On the Descent of Fire and the Drink of the Gods*, 1859). Where Müller himself imported and translated his system into England, Kuhn remained in Germany and was made known to the English public through a book by Walter Keating Kelly, *Curiosities of Indo-European Tradition and Folk Lore* (1863). Kelly expressed at the outset his intention to present the 'remarkable discoveries' of the successors to Jacob Grimm, who deserved the same recognition Jacob had justly received abroad. Among these post-Grimm scholars, Dr. Kuhn ranked as one of the foremost of the philological mythologists, and Kelly did not hesitate to say that his *Descent of Fire* marked a new epoch in the science of mythology.

Wherever possible Kelly illustrated Kuhn's principles from British and Irish folklore, and regretted 'how much we are behind the Germans, not only as to our own insight into the meaning of

[1] *Folk-Lore*, X (1899), 346–8. Hartland was then engaged in a dispute with Lang over the nature of Australian aboriginal religious ideas.
[2] See Lang's Preface to the new edition of *Myth, Ritual, and Religion*, 2 vols. (London, New York, Bombay, and Calcutta, 1913), I, xvi.
[3] Lang, *Myth, Ritual, and Religion* (1913 ed.), II, 298, 105. Cf. 1887 ed., II, 280, 81.

[171]

such relics of the past, but also as to our industry in collecting them.'[1] The *Curiosities* undoubtedly helped stimulate fieldwork, and is frequently cited in the county collections. Kelly paid tribute to Thoms for commenting, in his Preface to *Choice Notes*, that the study of folklore would rise from a pleasant pastime to a science. Henceforth, Kelly concluded, every careful collector of every scrap of folklore, novel or well-marked, will be serving the ethnologist and philosophic historian. This synthesis of Sanskrit myth-reading with local English folklore gave Kelly's one mythological work an immediacy lacking in the multifarious writings of Müller.

What the sun was to Müller, lightning was to Kuhn. He begins, like Müller, with the equation Dyâus=Zeus as the supreme Indo-European god of heaven, and develops further analogies between Vedic and Greek deities. The gandarves of ancient India he links up with the Grecian centaurs as cloud demons who enjoyed imbibing a heavenly drink, called soma in India and ambrosia in Greece. Soma attracted many Indo-European myths and legends, dealing with the descent of fire (i.e. lightning), the soul of man, and the drink of the gods. The wine butt of the centaurs corresponded to the soma vessel of the gandarves, and the same word signified both butt and cloud. Euripides speaks of the fountains of ambrosia, the drink of immortality, lying at the edge of the ocean, where heaven and earth meet, and the clouds rise and fall. And a starry nymph of the rainy constellation, the Hyades, who sired the centaurs, was named Ambrosia.

To Kuhn and Kelly, Prometheus appears as a fire-maker through the lightning rather than the fire-bringer. This role is apparent in the myth relating how he split the head of Zeus, from which Athene sprang forth all armed, an act symbolizing the birth of the lightning goddess from the cloud. The Vedic Mâtarisvan, a fire-kindling god, corresponds to Prometheus.

In the *Curiosities* solar gods and symbols are usually subordinated to the lightning. Kuhn took notice of such figures as Savitar, a sun-god with a beaming chariot drawn by golden-coloured mares called Haritas, in whom Max Müller recognized the original of the Greek Charities. The Cyclops, the giants with one eye round as a wheel in their foreheads, were a whole people of suns. But the sun was overshadowed by the lightning. The giants and ogres of nursery tales had descended from a numerous tribe of demons known to the southern Aryans as Râkshasas, huge, misshapen giants, formed like clouds, with hair and beard the colour of the red lightning. When-

[1] Walter K. Kelly, *Curiosities of Indo-European Tradition and Folk Lore* (London: Chapman and Hall, 1863), p. ix.

ever the great god Indra hurled his thunderbolt, it returned to his hand. Hence up to the present day in Germany, as Mannhardt states, and in Hertfordshire and Essex, as Kelly has personally observed, country people throw the windows wide open during a thunderstorm, to allow the lightning egress.

Actually sun and lightning were related ideas, for the sun was regarded not only as the heavenly fire but also as the immediate source of the lightning. When black clouds concealed the sun, the early Aryans believed that its light had been extinguished and needed rekindling. The complex of symbols meshing fire, sun, lightning, and the solar wheel—a symbol first expounded by Jacob Grimm—was clearly evinced in the festal ceremonies of the Celtic needfire, the Scottish Beltane, and St. John's fires. For illustration Kuhn described a German village ceremony on St. John's Day, climaxed with a group of townspeople pushing a fiery wheel to the top of a hill and then rolling it down into the stream below. Comparably, in the Vedic legend of Indra's fight with the midsummer demons, the sun stands on top of the cloud mountain. Analogies also appear in the popular Norse tale from Dasent of the wonder-working mill which filled the sea with salt. The mill owner, Frodi, is the sun god Freyr; the stone of his quern is the disk of the sun, and its handle is the fire-kindler. A European legend of a robber in a castle who seizes maidens, and is transformed by one into a granite block, receives this analysis. 'The legend is transparent in all its details. It is a meteoric drama, with its action and scenery transplanted from sky to earth. The robber and ravisher is the storm-god who issues from his cloud-castle, and chases the white-cloud maidens; but his force is spent, his cloud-castle collapses, and he is banned by the power of nature's magic.'[1]

The familiar *Märchen* of the lucky boy and his magic objects emerges in a tidy exegesis of sun plus lightning. In the tale the lad journeys with a buck goat that spits gold, a hen that lays golden eggs, and a table that covers itself with the choicest food. When a rascally innkeeper steals these treasures, a magic stick jumps out of the boy's bag and pummels the innkeeper until he returns them, whereupon the stock leaps into the boy's hand.

The table in this story is the all-nourishing cloud. The buck-goat is another emblem of the clouds, and the gold it spits is the golden light of the sun that streams through the fleecy coverings of the sky. The hen's golden egg is the sun itself. The demon of darkness has stolen these things; the cloud

[1] *Ibid.*, p. 93.

gives no rain, but hangs dusky in the sky, veiling the light of the sun. Then the lightning spear of the ancient storm-god Odin leaps out from the bag that concealed it (the cloud again), the robber falls, the rain patters down, the sun shines once more.[1]

In tracing local stories and country beliefs to thunder gods and lightning myths, Kelly fascinated English readers. Where Scott puzzled over the legend of Thomas the Rhymer finding a sleeping army in a cavern on the Scottish border, Kelly confidently pronounced the Sleeping Hero and the warriors to represent Odin and his host. Peas, cats' eyes, sieves, fern-seed, wish-rods all contain mythic elements which account for their use in household magic.

Max Müller sought to reconcile the differences between his solar theory and Kuhn's 'metereological' theories by identifying a common Sanskrit root for sun, lightning, and fire.[2] It was these variations of celestial symbolism among the Sanskritists that Lang would remorselessly ridicule.

The solar theory was carried to lengths far exceeding the etymological boundaries of Max Müller by his most aggressive disciple, George William Cox. An Oxford graduate, clergyman, self-styled baronet (his claim was posthumously denied), and a popular writer on Greek history and mythology, Cox developed what his master called the 'analogical' school of comparative mythology. He presented this viewpoint first in conventional retellings of classical myths, *Tales from Greek Mythology* (1861), and *Tales of the Gods and Heroes* (1862),[3] then in a deceptive *Manual of Mythology* (1867), which by a series of leading questions and loaded answers converted innocent school children to solarism, until finally he engulfed the adult reading public with two large volumes on *The Mythology of the Aryan Nations* (1870), and *An Introduction to the Science of Comparative Mythology and Folklore* (1881). Throughout these writings Cox quotes, cites, and invokes the name of Max Müller on nearly every page, and reduces all Aryan myths, legends, and fairy tales to the contest between sun and night. Müller's 'Essay on Comparative Mythology' first charmed him into a field previously 'repulsive.' Building on that solid foundation, he had completely reconstructed the original mythology of India and

[1] Walter K. Kelly, *Curiosities of Indo-European Tradition and Folk Lore* (London: Chapman and Hall, 1863), p. 211.
[2] Müller, *Physical Religion* (New York, 1891), p. 186.
[3] These are combined in No. 721 of Everyman's Library, *Tales of Ancient Greece* (London and New York, 1915, frequently reprinted), whose introduction has no doubt misled countless younger readers into interpreting all Greek myths as activities of the sun.

Greece, through one new insight: the resemblance of all Aryan narratives to each other. Max Müller had demonstrated by etymological proofs the identity of certain Homeric and Vedic gods, and their common origin, through 'failure of memory' (which Cox preferred to 'disease of language'), in phrases about the sun. Now Sir George will interpret the meaning of myths and legends which defined philological assault, through the comparison of their narrative elements.[1] By this method, the striking fact becomes apparent that every Greek hero performed the same feats, be he Achilles, Odysseus, Heracles, Theseus, Bellerophon, Appollon, Meleagros, or even Paris. Where his master regarded Paris as the night, Cox sees in him aspects of both night and day; Paris begins his career as a power of darkness, but ends as a solar deity.[2] Continually Cox calls attention to the similarities in the legends of heroes, to their spears and arrows and invincible darts which represent the rays of the sun, to their wonderful steeds and magic swords. All their adventures follow the same pattern of a long westward journey filled with labours and struggles, and this is the course of the daily sun. 'The story of the sun starting in weakness and ending in victory, waging a long warfare against darkness, clouds, and storms, and scattering them all in the end, is the story of all patient self-sacrifice, of all Christian devotion.'[3] The Achilleus is a splendid solar epic, portraying the contest between sun and night, and reaching its climax when Achilles tramples on the blood of his enemies as the glorious sun tramples out the dark clouds.[4]

Sir George of course had no patience with euhemerism. He blasted the article asserting the historicity of heroes in the eighth edition of the *Encyclopaedia Britannica* and denied all factual basis for the saga of Grettir or the cycle of King Arthur, or any other solar hero. Four-fifths of the folklore of northern Europe he swept into his solar net. Legends of death are blood-stained sunsets; stupid demons and ogres are the dark powers who must be conquered by light-born heroes; the episodes of heroes hidden in caves reflect the waxing and waning year.[5] Sigurd, William Tell, Roland, the biblical David, all tell the same tale (and in his last mythological

---

[1] Cox, *The Mythology of the Aryan Nations*, 2 vols. (London, 1870; reprinted 1882), I, v–vii.
[2] *Ibid.*, I, 21 n., 65 n.; II, 75–6.
[3] *Ibid.*, I, 168; *cf.* pp. 49, 153, 291, 308; and *A Manual of Mythology, in the Form of Question and Answer*, 1st American ed., from the 2nd London ed. (New York, 1868), pp. 39, 70, 78, 81, 104, 109, 117, 119, 211, for references to parallels between solar heroes; indeed, Cox never introduces a hero without indicating these parallels.
[4] Cox, *The Mythology of the Aryan Nations*, I, 267.
[5] *Ibid.*, I, 170 n., 308, 322–5, 409, 135 n.

study Cox annexed Beowulf and Hamlet).[1] The fairy tales too conform to the elemental pattern. All the humble heroes who find riches and conquer dragons, whether Boots or the frog prince or Cinderella, are solar deities; Hansel and Gretel are dawn children, and the ubiquitous gold that rewards the valiant hero is the golden light of the sun.[2] Under Cox's solar touch black becomes white, for the name of the horse 'Black' can signify light and whiteness, as befits the steed of a solar hero.[3] Small wonder that Max Müller confessed dizziness at viewing this solar empire he had innocently opened up.[4]

Certain insights in Cox's work show a growing sophistication toward folklore. His extension of Müller's etymological equations into the area of structural comparisons was actually moving onto the sounder ground of type and motif analysis. The great heroes of epic and legend do betray astonishing resemblances, which have evoked the historical thesis of the Chadwicks that comparable periods of cultural history produce an 'Heroic Age,' and the ritual-origins theory popularized by Lord Raglan, who substitutes the dying and reborn god for the waning and waxing sun. Cox recognized common elements in myths, legends, and *Märchen*, and understood more perceptively than Müller that a cluster of incidents hangs together to form a folktale complex. He pointed out that Müller had confused a fable in the Hitopadesa with the Master Thief, and commented, 'The possible affinity of thievish stratagems in all countries can scarcely account for a series of extraordinary incidents and astounding tricks following each other in the same order, although utterly different in their outward garb and colouring.'[5] He himself then confused the Master Thief with the legend of Rhampsinitus.[6] To protect his pan-Aryan theory, Cox had to deny the possibility that solar legends spread by borrowing, and obtusely contended that the greater the resemblance, the less the chance for diffusion! He conceived of borrowing in purely literary terms, and argued that a borrowed tale must perfectly match its original. Similar but not identical narratives indicate a common

[1] Cox, *An Introduction to the Science of Comparative Mythology and Folklore* (London, 1881), pp. 309, 307.
[2] Cox, *The Mythology of the Aryan Nations*, I, 159 n., 132 n. Frequently the fairy-tale hero wears a 'garment of humiliation' representative of the toiling, unrequited sun.
[3] *Ibid.*, I, 247 n.
[4] Müller, *Natural Religion*, p. 495.
[5] Cox, *The Mythology of the Aryan Nations*, I, 113.
[6] 'The Master Thief' is Type 1525 in Antti Aarne and Stith Thompson, *The Types of the Folktale* (Helsinki, 1961); 'Rhampsinitus' is Type 950. Cox used this supposed tale for evidence against borrowing; see his 'The Migration of Popular Stories,' *Fraser's* Magazine, n.s., XXII (July, 1880), 96–111.

source in Vedic India.[1] Mythology and folklore converge in Cox's solarism, and he claimed as their only distinction the possibility of subjecting a myth to philological analysis.[2]

In his well-known introduction to the Hunt edition of Grimm's *Household Tales*, Lang dealt at length with the theories of Sir George, and in some perplexity. Although so clearly a disciple of Müller, yet Cox revealed to Lang some independence of mind and even the makings of an anthropological folklorist.[3] (See pp. 209–10.) Accordingly Cox never became the *bête noire* to Lang that Müller was, and Lang judged that Cox suffered not so much from his own wrong thinking as from improper guidance.[4]

Robert Brown, Junior, F.S.A., of Barton-on-Humber (1844–1912) laboured manfully during the 1870's and '80's to establish the influence of the ancient Semitic cultures on Hellenic religious mythology. Invitingly he wrote, 'he who is wearied with the familiar aroma of the Aryan field of research may stimulate and refresh his jaded senses with new perfumes wafted from the shores of the Euphrates and the Nile.'[5] As Max Müller sought to draw the Greek pantheon into the folds of Vedic conceptions, so Robert Brown, the Assyriologist and Egyptologist, attempted to clasp Hellas within the orbit of Near Eastern cults and myths. Comparative mythology had launched a powerful pincers movement on classical Greece, from India and from Egypt, which bid fair to rob Athens of most claims to originality. If Müller demanded that mythologists study Sanskrit, and Lang insisted they read ethnology, Brown declared they must acquaint themselves with the latest research on Chaldea, Assyria, Phoenicia, Arabia, Persia, and Egypt. Semitic Asia had contributed at least as many divinities to the Greek pantheon as had Aryan India![6] The extent of these contributions Brown measured in studies of *Poseidôn* (1872), *The Great Dionysiak Myth* (2 vols., 1877–78), *The Unicorn* (1881), and *The Myth of Kirkê* (1883), and summarized his position, in the face of Lang's taunts, in *Semitic Influence in Hellenic Mythology* (1898).[7]

[1] Cox, *The Mythology of the Aryan Nations*, I, 145.
[2] Cox, *An Introduction to the Science of Comparative Mythology and Folklore*, p. 7 n.
[3] Lang, 'Household Tales: Their Origin, Diffusion, and Relation to the Higher Myths,' Introduction to *Grimm's Household Tales*, with the author's notes, trans. and ed. Margaret Hunt, 2 vols. (London, 1910), I, xxiv–xxv, xxxv, xl.
[4] See Lang's note, *ibid.*, p. xxiv.
[5] Robert Brown, *The Great Dionysiak Myth*, 2 vols. (London, 1877–78), I, 162.
[6] *Ibid.*, I, vi; II, 334.
[7] Other relevant publications are *The Religion of Zoroaster* (1879), *The Religion and Mythology of the Aryans of Northern Europe* (1880), *Language, and Theories of its Origin* (1881), *The Law of Kosmic Order* (1882), *Eridanus: River and Constellation* (1883), *Researches into the Origin of the Primitive Constellations of the Greeks, Phoeni-*

Although this last work originated as a rebuttal to *Modern Mythology*, Brown by no means slavishly followed Müller and Cox. His Semitic bias naturally led him into differences with the Vedic scholar, whose school he criticized for excessive pan-Aryanism.[1] Cox rather than Müller dominates Brown's footnotes, and the 'Aryo-Semitic' mythologist steadily refers to the interpretations in *The Mythology of the Aryan Nations*, with due respect to its author (who returned the compliment), but with cavils at his neglect of Semitic gods.[2] Brown's thesis compelled him to grant some historical basis to legends, in spite of all the harsh words then accorded euhemerism, for he necessarily supported his arguments with geographical and historical facts of commerce, travel, and migration throughout the Aegean area. Cox and Müller laughed away all history behind myth, secure in the one historical point that Aryan peoples emigrated from India and carried their language and myths with them; but Brown had to demonstrate that physical contact, not an ancient linguistic inheritance, gave Greek deities a Semitic gloss. Art and archaeology documented his position and clothed the bare bones of philology.[3] Therefore, he called into evidence the Egyptian character of a splendid belt worn by Heracles, or the Phoenician skill at packaging reflected in the 'curious knot' Circe taught Odysseus how to tie.[4] To show his eclecticism, Brown scoffed at some excesses of the 'Natural Phenomena Theory.'[5] How could Polyphemos be the eye of the sun, blinded by the solar hero Odysseus, for would the sun blind himself? How could Skeiron, the wind, be first slain and then devoured by a tortoise?[6]

[1] Brown, *The Great Dionysiak Myth*, I, 4; 'Reply to Prof. Max Müller on "The Etymology of Dionysos," ' *Academy* (19 Aug., 1882), cited in Brown, *The Myth of Kirkê: including the visit of Odysseus to the Shades. An Homerik Study* (London, 1883), p. 83 n.

[2] E.g., Brown, *The Great Dionysiak Myth*, II, 139–40, [Theseus and the Minotaur]; I, 420–26 [statue of Demeter]; 'Posidônic Theory of Rev. G. W. Cox,' *Poseidôn: A Link Between Semite, Hamite, and Aryan* (London, 1872), pp. 5–9. In his Preface to a new edition of *The Mythology of the Aryan Nations* (1882), Cox pays especial tribute to the researches of Robert Brown. In *The Unicorn: A Mythological Investigation* (London, 1881), p. 73, Brown cites the acceptance by Cox of his view of Bakchos-Melqarth.

[3] Brown, *The Great Dionysiak Myth*, II, 140, 213; *Semitic Influence in Hellenic Mythology, with special reference to the recent mythological works of the Rt. Hon. Prof. F. Max Müller and Mr. Andrew Lang* (London, Edinburgh, Oxford, 1898), p. 202.

[4] Brown, *The Myth of Kirkê*, pp. 163–92.

[5] Brown, *The Great Dionysiak Myth*, I, 229, '. . . one key will never open all locks'; *Poseidon*, pp. 79–80.

[6] Brown, *Poseidôn*, pp. 39–40; *The Great Dionysiak Myth*, I, 229.

cians and Babylonians (1899, 1900), *Mr. Gladstone As I Knew Him, And Other Essays* (1902), esp. 'Studies in Pausanias,' pp. 93–235.

Most of Brown's explications, however, conform to rigid solar orthodoxy. The trip of Odysseus to the underworld represents the span of a day and a night, during which the sun descends beyond the horizon, and all the mythical figures the solar hero meets in the depths are also solar characters: Tityos stretched on the ground attacked by two vultures is the sun besieged by the powers of darkness; Tantalos reaching for water that always recedes is the suffering sun, and so is Sisyphos, trying vainly to push a solar stone over the brow of the hill that is heaven, and so of course is Heracles, drawing his bow in the midst of the dead. Thus the dead sun suffers every night.[1] Throughout the massive data on Dionysos the solar character of the complex divinity predominates. One myth associated with his name has a lion chase a leopard into a cave; the leopard emerges from another entrance, re-enters the cave and devours the lion, who has been caught fast, from behind. Here the lion is the flaming sun, and the cave and the leopard are both the dark night; night mounts into heaven behind the hidden sun and gnaws him to death—although he will be reborn at the east portal next morning.[2] No narrow solar mythologist, Brown displayed lunar and stellar sympathies, and analysed the unicorn as 'the wild white, fierce, chaste Moon,' and Circe as the moon-goddess beloved by the solar Heracles. Medusa is the 'Serpentine-full-moon, the victim of the solar Perseus,' and her petrifying stare signifies the moon-glare of a soundless night.[3]

On every occasion Brown reasserted the Semitic provenience of gods and myths found in Greece. After following the trail of Dionysos through the poets and dramatists and cults, in gems and vases and epithets, Brown placed the origin of the vast complex in Chaldea. 'Here, then, is Dumuzi-Tammuz on Assyrian and Kaldean ground, side by side, and in truth identical with Dian-nisi-Dionysos, the judge-of-men, the ruling, judging, sinking, life-giving, all-sustaining Sun, diurnal and nocturnal. . . .'[4] As the myth travelled westward across the Aegean, Hellenic culture softened some of its wilder orgiastic features, although traces remained in the Eleusinian mysteries. The sea-god Poseidôn too originated in Chaldea, and entered Greece through Phoenicia and Libya; he resembles the biblical Noah and the Chaldean Oannês, a creature that rose out of

---

[1] Brown, *The Myth of Kirkê*, pp. 157–62.
[2] Brown, *The Great Dionysiak Myth*, II, 9–11; also *The Unicorn*, 'The Contest between the Lion and the Leopard,' pp. 73–8. In *The Myth of Kirkê*, Brown resolves two variants of the death of Odysseus as the same solar myth, by making a ray-fish the young sun that drops on the bald head of Odysseus, the old sun (p. 23).
[3] Brown, *The Unicorn*, p. 1; *The Myth of Kirkê*, pp. 47, 53.
[4] Brown, *The Great Dionysiak Myth*, II, 332.

the sea and instructed men in the arts and letters.[1] An Egyptian papyrus of the Twelfth Dynasty first presents in mythical form the great solar voyage across heaven, as the tale of an archaic sea captain who visited the land of shadows.[2] From such data, Brown felt justified in capping the debate between Lang and Müller with the formation of the new Aryo-Semitic school of comparative mythology.[3]

Lacking the sparkle of Lang and the limpid style of Müller, Brown appears at a disadvantage when he comes fuming into the controversy. His antiquarian volumes are filled with rejoinders to dead authorities, classical quotations, genealogical tables of deities, philological equations, and the accumulation of recondite evidence more or less germane to the inquiry. In *Semitic Influence in Hellenic Mythology*, Brown tried to match Lang at his own game of taunt and gibe, not without some trepidation in tackling an opponent who might have given pause to Heracles himself. Brown and Müller both complained that Lang's numerous journalistic outlets, daily, weekly, and monthly, gave him opportunity to throw up an artificial cloud of scorn over solar mythology.[4] Now the Egyptologist bitterly accused Lang of misrepresenting himself, Müller, and Cox: he pointed to the world-wide evidence for solar myths (which Lang never denied), and attacked the theory of totemism and survivals on the grounds that Hellenic constellation-names and legends derive not from savages but from the advanced civilization of the Phoenicians.[5] If philologists disagree, one can still be right; and they do agree on the general outlines of the natural phenomena theory. Brown's intense pique emerges on nearly every page, and produces a curious appendix, entitled 'Professor Aguchekikos On Totemism,' intended as a *jeu d'esprit* paraphrasing the anti-solar arguments of Lang himself. The satire purports to be a review written in A.D. 4886 of a learned study on *Anglican Totemism* in the Victorian epoch, which infers the prevalence of totemism from the animal names of clans, such as the Bulls and the Bears, who once struggled in a 'stock exchange,' and from such archaic expressions as calling a man 'a snake in the grass.'[6]

Isolated in Barton-on-Humber, Robert Brown suffered from a feeling of being ignored or brushed aside by Lang and the intellec-

---

[1] Brown, *Poseidôn*, pp. 2, 110–16.
[2] Brown, *The Myth of Kirkê*, pp. 167, 101.
[3] Brown, *Semitic Influence in Hellenic Mythology*, p. ix.
[4] *Ibid.*, pp. 23–4; *cf.* Müller, *Contributions to the Science of Comparative Mythology*, I, vii.
[5] Brown, *Semitic Influence in Hellenic Mythology*, pp. 29–31, 54–66.
[6] *Ibid.*, pp. 205–15.

tual establishment. He refers to a debate with Lang in *The Academy* over solar matters in which, 'according to general opinion the brilliant journalist came off but second best.'[1] Lang actually did devote waspish attention to Brown. In one chapter in *Custom and Myth* on 'Star Myths,' he belittled Brown's thesis that the Akkadians, and peoples of comparable culture, named the zodiacal signs after myths and festivals connected with the months.[2] Lang attacked this thesis in another chapter, 'Moly and Mandragora.'[3] (See p. 211.) In the 1898 edition of *Custom and Myth*, Lang wrote a special Preface, 'Apollo, the Mouse, and Mr. Robert Brown, Junior, F.S.A., M.R.S.A.,' a title based on another chapter in *Custom and Myth*, 'Apollo and the Mouse,' which Brown had criticized in his *Semitic Influence in Hellenic Mythology* (1898). There Brown cited evidence from Frazer's *The Golden Bough* to disprove Lang's suggestion that the worship of Apollo was connected with a mouse totem. Frazer's examples showed that mice were worshipped not as totemic deities but simply as vermin to be placated and induced to depart. Apollo remains a sun god. This point Lang conceded, although contending that it was merely one of alternative hypotheses, and he then turned to consider Brown's 'many grudges' against him. Brown alleged that Lang had 'treated his opinions with utmost contempt' in a slighting reference to *The Great Dionysiak Myth* in the article on 'Mythology' in the *Encyclopaedia Britannica*, and in a derisive attack in the *Saturday Review*. Lang made a distinction between contempt and disagreement, and chastised Brown for descending to personal polemics.[4]

A word must be given to the massive two-volume work on *Zoological Mythology, or The Legends of Animals*, by Angelo De Gubernatis, which appeared in 1872. The Italian professor of Sanskrit published this work in English as a tribute, no doubt, to the reputation of Max Müller and the lively interest in England in comparative mythology. Ruefully the author remarked, 'It has fallen to me to study the least elevated department of mythology,'[5] the

---

[1] *Ibid.*, pp. 30–1, 54–66.
[2] Lang, *Custom and Myth* (London, 1893), p. 137.
[3] Lang, 'Moly and Mandragora,' in *Custom and Myth*, pp. 143–55.
[4] This polemical preface appears only in the 1898 edition, pp. i–xix, and was withdrawn in later reprintings of *Custom and Myth*.
[5] Gubernatis, *Zoological Mythology, or The Legends of Animals*, 2 vols. (New York and London, 1872), II, 425. Gubernatis also compiled a mythological herbarium, *La Mythologie des Plantes, ou Les Légendes du Règne Végétal*, 2 vols. (Paris, 1878), in dictionary form; the first volume treats mythical heroes and phenomena with plant associations (the sun is like a tree), the second considers plants as they appear in myths. Gubernatis diverges from Müller on 'Bernacles,' which he traces to a bird-producing tree in India (I, 65–70).

appearance of gods in animal forms, assumed when they broke a taboo, or served a term of punishment. A vast body of popular lore now described the actions of Aryan gods in animal disguises, where formerly they had appeared as celestial phenomena. Beginning with myths about the sacred bull and cows of the Rigvedas, who represent the sun-god Indras and the clouds, Gubernatis moved to Slavonic and other European parallel tales, and then systematically considered further beasts recurring in *Märchen*, in the usual solar terms. The soul of the ass is the sun; the whale is the night; the peacock is the starry sky; the crab is the moon; birds of prey are lightning and thunderbolts; the serpent-devil is the power of darkness.[1] In Jack and the Beanstalk, Jack's mother is the blind cow, that is, the darkened aurora; she scatters beans, and the bean of abundance, which is the moon, grows up to the sky; this Jack climbs to the wealth of the morning light.[2] Gubernatis necessarily brought many folktales within his net, and recognized some kinships; for instance, he discerned the tale-type of the man or animal trapped by putting his hands or paws in the cleft of a tree trunk,[3] and he uncovered the legend of the peasant who overheard the talking bulls on Christmas eve prophesy his own death.[4]

The mythological disputants of the period continually refer to this zoological compendium. Brown praised Gubernatis for recognizing the solar character of the hog,[5] and Lang scoffed at him for interpreting the cat as the moon and the mouse as the shadows of night. How, when the moon-cat is away, can there be any light to make playful mice-shadows?[6] Even the sympathetic reviewer in *The Scotsman* complained that this overdose of celestial interpretations was blunting his confidence in comparative mythology.[7]

The cause of solar mythology persisted into the twentieth century, with Müller's drooping banner being raised again by the Reverend Abram Smythe Palmer, doctor of divinity, sometime

[1] Gubernatis, *Zoological Mythology*, I, 370; II, 337, 322, 356, 181, 390.
[2] *Ibid.*, I, 244. Cf. this interpretation with that of the modern psychoanalytical school, which considers 'beans' and 'stalk' as symbols for the testicles and penis, and sees the tale as a masturbation fantasy (William H. Desmonde, 'Jack and the Beanstalk,' *American Imago*, VIII [Sept., 1951], 287–8).
[3] *Ibid.*, II, 113. This is Type 38, 'Claw in Split Tree.'
[4] *Ibid.*, I, 258 n. Motif B251.1.2.2., 'Cows speak to one another on Christmas' is well-known, but the death prophecy is not. I heard the full tale from a Mississippi-born Negro.
[5] Brown, *The Myth of Kirkê*, pp. 54–5.
[6] Lang, *Custom and Myth*, p. 117.
[7] Unsigned review, *The Scotsman*, 26 Dec. 1872. The lengthy review omits to mention the phallic as well as solar interpretations rendered by Gubernatis (see, e.g., *Zoological Mythology*, II, 9–10), with far more boldness than by squeamish Robert Brown (*The Myth of Kirkê*, p. 23 n.; *The Great Dionysiak Myth*, I, 7 n.).

lecturer at the University of Dublin, and author-editor of a dozen books on lexical and biblical subjects. Palmer applied the solar thesis to religious and classical myths and extended the disease-of-language process to English words, coining the term 'folk-etymology.'

These twin interests often intersected. In *Leaves from a Word-Hunter's Note-Book* (1876), Palmer devoted a chapter to the words West and North and their mythological associations with the region of darkness, the land of departed souls. For the key symbol of sunrise he of course quoted Müller's essay of 1856, and for the sunset he credited the researches of Müller, Cox, and De Gubernatis as having proved beyond question its poetic representation in the descent of Orpheus, Odysseus, and other heroes to the infernal underworld.[1]

In 1882 Palmer brought out a thick compendium with a title Müller could have phrased: *Folk-Etymology, A Dictionary of Verbal Corruptions or Words Perverted in Form or Meaning by False Derivation or Mistaken Analogy.* Among the assembled instances were several choice specimens of verbal confusion leading directly into mythic ideas—even in 'England.'

So far back as the time of Procopius England was popularly regarded by the people on the opposite shore of the continent as the land of souls or departed spirits. It is still believed in Brittany that a weird boat laden with souls is ferried across the English channel every night. . . . It has been conjectured that this superstition arose from a misunderstanding of *England,* formerly *Engeland,* as *engle-land,* 'The Angel land,' engel being an angel in German, A. Saxon, &c. . . . In German folk-lore Engel-land in German literally means both the land of the Angels and of the English. In the former sense Engelland is a later semi-Christian transfiguration of the former Teutonic Home of the angel-like Light Elves—good fays who were said to be more beautiful than the sun.[2]

The folk etymology of *Gabriel Hounds* also opened up a web of beliefs. As used in the northern counties the term signified a yelping sound heard in the air, undoubtedly the cry of a flock of wild geese, but construed as an omen of calamity. In Leeds the word was *gabble-retchet,* and brought to the mind's eye the souls of unbaptized children flitting about their parents' dwelling. In Devonshire it was

---

[1] *Leaves from a Word-Hunter's Note-Book* (London: Trubner & Co., 1876), pp. 278, 293.
[2] *Folk-Etymology* (London: George Bell and Sons, 1882), p. 111.

THE MYTHOLOGICAL FOLKLORISTS

wish-hounds, in Cornwall *dandy-dogs*, in Wales *Hell-hounds* (Cwm Anwm). The old English form was *Gabrielle rache*, the *rache* or *ratche* being a hound in Anglo-Saxon, while *Gabriel* was corrupted from *gabaren*, a corpse; hence 'corpse-hounds.' In another context, Gabriel was the angel of death among the Hebrews, and the Talmud described him as the spirit of thunder, facts leading to his aerial elevation in the folk mind. And Palmer quotes a verse from Words-worth and a comment from the antiquary Dr. Plot on the popular belief in Gabriel's hounds coursing overhead.

These folk etymologies continued to intrigue Palmer, who ampli-fied his choicest specimens in a little volume of essays, *The Folk and Their Word-Lore* (1904). Here he illustrated 'modern mythology' with the Scotch word *rat-rhyme, rot-rhyme, rott-rime*, originally sug-gesting rote memory, from Old French *rote*. But the sound of the word conjured up the idea of a rhyme to charm away rats. Palmer cited Chambers' *Book of Days*, in turn quoting Reginald Scot, on this point, as well as Ben Jonson and Shakespeare, who had alluded to an Irish practice of rhyming rats to death. 'So folk-lore is evolved out of folk-etymology.'[1]

An even more striking instance of this process was offered in 'The Hand of Glory.' Burglars seeing a corpse on a scaffold would cut off one of the dead man's hands and carry it with them to cast slumber over the inmates of any house they robbed. Such was the belief as registered in the *Ingoldsby Legends*, in Scott's *The Anti-quary*, in Brand's *Popular Antiquities*. The English phrase was a translation of the French 'main de gloire,' which was a corruption from *mandragora*, the plant endowed with magical properties enabling it to shine at night.[2]

In the realm of folk-etymology Palmer was on strong ground, but he did not sense the incompatibility of this process with the solar symbolism he devoutly espoused.

> The mythologising faculty everywhere regarded the rising sun going forth to his daily conflict and victory as a warrior-god, whose spear and arrows were the bright rays which he scattered around him; while the dark water, over which he mounted triumphant, and the clouds of night which he put to flight, were the vanquished monsters which he destroyed, either the devouring serpent of the deep or the flying dragons of the air.

[1] *The Folk and Their Word-Lore* (London: George Routledge and Sons, Ltd., 1904), pp. 123–4.
[2] *Ibid.*, pp. 124–5.

So he wrote in *Babylonian Influence on the Bible and Popular Beliefs* (1897).[1] He returned to the Babylonian evidence and to his etymologies in *Some Curios from a Word-Collector's Cabinet* (1907), with the Hebrew term *Shamash*, the public crier of the synagogue. In the language of ancient Babylonia this was the name for any servant, and also a proper name for the sun god as servant or attendant of the moon god. Thus the servant sun god rose and set each day as he was bidden. Buddhists too hailed the sun as the travelling servant of the Lord.

Besides sun =servant =Shamash, Palmer also correlated sun and Son, quoting Müller and Lang on the sun as progenitor and father, or his own creator, and Crooke's *Folklore of Northern India* on the 'common idea in folk-lore that women may be made mothers by the prolific action of the sun.'[2]

With all his solar devotion, it was only fitting that Palmer brought out a special edition of Müller's *Comparative Mythology, An Essay*, in 1909. While reprinting a parody by R. F. Littledale, 'The Oxford Solar Myth,' he himself completely indorsed Müller's 'epoch-making' treatise with a barrage of references from ethnology and poetry for his own long 'Introductory Preface on Solar Mythology.' Cox's excesses he regretted. In his Preface, Palmer placed poetic invocations of dawns and sunset side by side with sun hero extracts from savage myths.

A crowning solar work, *The Samson-Saga and Its Place in Comparative Religion*, appeared late on the scene, in 1913. Palmer showed sound instinct in regarding the figure of Samson in the Book of Judges as a legendary character containing 'many elements of popular tradition well known to the student of folk-lore. . . .'[3] Then he went on to assert that the story of Samson was an ancient solar legend once current in Babylonia and localized with additions in Canaan. Samson was to the Hebrews what Herakles was among the Greeks, the descendant of the sun hero Gilgamesh.

If Samson the radiant strong man is the sun, Delilah, who shears his locks (rays), enfeebles him, and leads him to an end of humiliation and blindness, is the night. The whole saga is a drama of sunset. The famous riddle told by Samson suggests primitive riddles linked, as Müller has shown, with mythological presentments of sun, moon, and atmosphere. That the sun could have his course impeded or fettered in mythic fancy is seen in Polynesian legends

[1] (London: David Nutt, 1897), p. 19.
[2] *Some Curios from a Word-Collector's Cabinet* (London: George Routledge and Sons, n.d. [1907]), p. 90.
[3] *The Samson-Saga and Its Place in Comparative Religion* (London: Sir Isaac Pitman & Sons, Ltd., 1913), p. v.

[185]

and German peasant stories of the sun-catcher who binds the sun fast with cords.

Did the clerical lexicographer feel any qualms at solar interpretation so late in the day? No; he placed himself squarely with the 'new school of folk-lore,' and quoted Lang's *Custom and Myth* to support the argument that similar environments produced similar mythopoeic responses. Frazer was his authority for the view that myth and history were not mutually exclusive opposites. In one respect Palmer did deviate from Müller, in using 'folk-lore' and 'mythology' compatibly, and with no sense of conflict between rival theories. But no one was listening to the Reverend A. Smythe Palmer when *The Samson-Saga* appeared, for solar mythology had then sunk into a back eddy, far removed from the mainstream of folklore theory.

VI   The Savage Folklorists

IN THE HISTORY of the idea of folklore in England, the first
scholar whose fame still lives is Sir Edward Burnet Tylor, the
father of anthropology and godfather of the anthropological school
of folklorists. The conventional view sees before Tylor a darkness
conveniently cloaking forgotten antiquaries and mythologists and,
after him, a modern group, bold in theory and rigorous in technique, springing up in response to his seminal works. Andrew Lang,
the most illustrious member of this group, is paired with Tylor in
a thousand references, and it was to Tylor that he dedicated *Custom
and Myth*, his first book on folklore. Lang with his shafts of ridicule
brought Max Müller and the celestial mythologists down to earth
and erected over their bones the new structure of folklore science
based on anthropology. In *Researches into the Early History of
Mankind* (1865), Tylor distinguished between folklore and mythology, whose materials played so vital a part in his inquiry. Folklore
represented the contemporary superstitions and nursery tales of
civilized peoples. Mythology preserved the explanations in story
form which all peoples, from the primitive to the highly developed,
fashioned to account for their supernatural origins. Folklore belonged only to the last and highest stage of cultural progression and
embodied survivals from the earlier stages. Mythology appeared at
all stages, but in varying degrees of simplicity and sophistication
according to the advancement of the race. In *Primitive Culture*
(1871) Tylor formulated the doctrine of survivals and the theory of
animism, two celebrated concepts, the first wholly and the second
substantially dependent on folklore materials.

Tylor's Theory of Mythology

Turning first to Tylor's theory of mythology, we recognize at
once how prominent a place he accorded mythmaking in his
treatises; but wonder of wonders, he follows almost slavishly the
solar analyses of Max Müller.

In myths Tylor beheld the philosophic expression of savages, recording their views of the world and its supernatural creators and rulers at the dawn of history. Failing to comprehend the proper character of myths, innumerable commentators weighted them down with the 'rubbish' of allegorical and euhemeristic glosses, finding either sophisticated morality fables or altered transcripts of history. In so doing they have almost totally ignored or misunderstood the actual history contained in myths, which reflect the primitive condition and mental outlook of early man. The happy recovery of myth secrets, wrote Tylor, was 'due to modern students who have with vast labour and skill searched the ancient language, poetry, and folk-lore of our own race, from the cottage tales collected by the brothers Grimm to the Rig-Veda edited by Max Müller.'[1]

In *Researches*, Tylor considered with obvious relish two vexing problems posed by myths: What degree of historical truth, if any, do they contain? Were similar myths the result of diffusion or independent invention? To these questions he addressed himself with such sanity and clarity, and so expansive a command of the literature of myth, that many of his commentaries are still unsurpassed. Rejecting any monistic thesis, he placed mythical narratives on a spectrum running from the historically valid to the purely inventive, and allowing for intermediate types, such as 'myths of observation,' fattened upon a single observed fact. The discovery of fossil bones often set in motion elaborate histories of gods and giants and monsters. A narrator able to point out landmarks mentioned in the story, and to ascribe personal names and local places to the alleged event, could coat a myth with seeming facts, Tylor astutely observed. Turning from historical to geographical aspects of myths, he offered illustrations 'of the more general analogies running through the Folk-lore of the world. . . .'[2] And he roamed over the five continents sampling widespread myths: of the tortoise-creator, revered in both the Old and the New World; of the man swallowed by the great fish in legends of the Chippewa Indians, Polynesians, the ancient Hindus, Christians who have been told of Jonah and the whale, and German peasants who hear of Little Red Riding Hood gobbled up by the wolf. In marginal cases Tylor will let his reader decide whether a myth has one or many points of origin, but he stood fast by his main proposition, the universality of the mythmaking faculty among all races and peoples.

[1] *Researches into the Early History of Mankind and the Development of Civilization* (London: John Murray, 1865), p. 256.
[2] *Ibid.*, p. 325.

In *Primitive Culture*, Tylor fitted the myths of mankind into his evolutionary system. After dismissing the several erroneous readings of myth, he presented the ethnological, the true one, which dovetailed with the comparativist school of Müller, treating myths of literate peoples. At the earliest level, savages constructed nature myths that revealed their simple animistic perception of nature. At a higher level, man shaped philosophic and historic myths to provide answers for the mysteries of the universe. In unravelling these myths, Tylor endorsed the two chief principles of solar mythology: by personifying nature primeval man first created nature myths; and through epithet and metaphor—Müller's 'disease of language' —he bred fresh mythic fancies. The key used by Müller to open classical myth could also unlock the minds of savages. If savages thought the clouds driven across the sky seemed like cows being led to pasture or fancied the sun to resemble a glittering chariot, they must have treated the resemblances as realities and given names and adventures to the celestial charioteer and herdsman. Surely the Polynesian Maui was a solar hero worthy to set alongside Heracles and Achilles. Throughout *Researches, Primitive Culture*, and his textbook *Anthropology, An Introduction to the Study of Man and Civilization* (1881), Tylor praised and echoed the heavenly symbolism of Müller, Adalbert Kuhn, and George Cox. Max Müller is indeed one of his favourite authorities, cited for his lectures on the science of language and Vedic religion as well as for his comparative mythology.

The solar drama beloved by Müller was equally cherished by Tylor.

Day is daily swallowed up by Night, to be set free again at dawn, and from time to time suffers a like but shorter durance in the maw of the Eclipse and the Storm-cloud; Summer is overcome and prisoned by dark Winter, to be again set free. It is a plausible opinion that such scenes from the great nature-drama of the conflict of light and darkness are, generally speaking, the simple facts, which in many lands and ages have been told in mythic shape, as legends of a Hero or Maiden devoured by a Monster, and hacked out again or disgorged.[1]

Legends and nursery tales of mortals being swallowed alive enact mythically this daily and seasonal plot. No nature myth is more widely dispersed than the 'theme of night and day, where with mythic truth the devoured victims were afterwards disgorged or

[1] *Primitive Culture: Researches into the Development of Mythology, Philosophy, Religion, Art and Custom.* 2 vols. (London: John Murray, 1871), I, 302.

[189]

set free.'[1] And Tylor regrets that Red Riding Hood in the English version is unfaithful to the German version, where the hunter rips up the sleeping wolf and the little maiden in red stained cloak steps out safe and sound. Paraphrasing Müller, Tylor asserts that people who say 'The sun is swallowed up by night' are expressing metaphorically an action that barbaric man once construed literally. Legendary journeys to the underworld are poetic adaptations of the sun's daily descent into darkness. The myth of the sunset has dyed the dogmas of classical sages and modern divines, who follow the savage poets in equating the West and the night with the regions of the dead.[2]

One latter-day mythologist saw no discrepancy in lumping together Müller and Tylor in the course of his solar explications. Abram Smythe Palmer regularly paired the rival theorists in his quotations and notes. In a chapter of *Leaves from a Word-Hunter's Notebook* (1876), he cited Müller on the mythic importance of the sunrise, and then turned to Tylor for the mythic importance of the sunset, quoting an apposite passage from *Primitive Culture*. Palmer thanked the 'same learned anthropologist' for a number of illustrations of the 'world-wide superstition,' which he proceeded to set forth, mixing examples culled from Tylor with others taken from Kuhn, Cox, and Walter K. Kelly. Several pages later he reaffirmed the solar character of the legends of Orpheus, Odysseus, and other heroes who visited the infernal regions and brought back the golden treasures of the dawn, saying, 'The researches of Max Müller, Cox and De Gubernatis have placed this beyond question, and the most widely-dispersed savage legends, Mr. Tylor assures us, from Polynesia and America, give new confirmation to the theory.'[3] In *The Samson-Saga*, Palmer relied on Tylor's amassed examples of sun-catcher myths to reinforce the evidence supplied by Müller and others.

Tylor's espousal of Müller's celestial mythology caused the admirers of the father of anthropology considerable embarrassment in later years. His biographer, Robert Ranulph Marett, Tylor's own pupil and successor and with Tylor and Lang a member of Balliol College, did his best to skirt the damaging tributes to solarism by singling out for emphasis his master's slight demurrers.[4] With his

---

[1] *Anthropology. An Introduction to the Study of Man and Civilization*. With Introduction by A. C. Haddon, The Thinker's Library, No. 14, 2 vols. (London: Watts & Co., 1930), I, 126.
[2] *Primitive Culture*, II, 44.
[3] Abram Smythe Palmer, *Leaves from a Word-Hunter's Note-Book* (London: Trübner & Co., 1876), pp. 287, 293.
[4] R. R. Marett, *Tylor* (London: Chapman and Hall, 1936), pp. 82–3. Marett cites

customary balance, Tylor did reject the excesses of the solar theory, showing how easily the nursery 'Song of Sixpence' or the heroes Cortes and Caesar could be solarized. He chided a 'learned but rash mythologist' who read into the nursery rhyme, 'The cow jumped over the moon,' the remnant of an old nature myth, the cow having replaced a cloud.[1] Instead of this guesswork Tylor demanded evidence. In the third edition of *Researches*, issued in 1878, Tylor did withdraw in part from his solar allegiance, in deference to the tumult raised in the meanwhile by Lang.[2] But the pages of exposition interpreting Maui as a sun god remained firmly in the text.

The reader of Lang, seeing his constant invocations of Tylor, would never guess the true nature of Tylor's mythological thought. For instance, in Lang's celebrated 'Introduction' to *Grimm's Household Tales* in the Margaret Hunt translation, he allows Tylor one mild statement suggesting 'there is a quaint touch of sun-myth in a tale [of the Wolf and the Seven Kids] which took its present shape since the invention of clocks,' but two paragraphs later he underscores a strong denunciation by Tylor of foolhardy mythologists who find myths of sun and sky and dawn wherever they look. This selective use of quotations gives the quite false impression that Tylor and Lang shared the same viewpoint.[3]

In summary, Tylor differs gently from Müller in assigning myth formation by animistic analogies to the 'lower races' and through the flowering of verbal metaphor to the 'higher races.' But both processes fully accept the primacy of the sun, along with the moon and the stars, in kindling man's mythopoeic imagination. In effect, Tylor broadened the territory of solar mythology to include savages.

Tylor's Interest in Folklore

As primitive peoples composed myths, so peasants preserved folklore, the tattered remnants of savage myths and animistic beliefs. In his Introduction to *Researches*, outlining his plan to investigate the early mental condition of man, Tylor continually

[1] *Anthropology*, I, 127.
[2] In the third edition of *Primitive Culture*, Tylor adds a note correcting his statement that the pied fantail of New Zealand sings only at sunset. 'Thus the argument connecting the sunset-song with the story as a sunset-myth falls away' (I, 336-7).
[3] *Grimm's Household Tales*, translated from the German and edited by Margaret Hunt (London: G. Bell and Sons, 1910), I, xviii-xix.

Researches, 3rd ed. (1878), p. 153 n.: 'The author, after ten years' more experience, would now rather say more cautiously, not that Quetzalcoatl is the Sun personified, but that his story contains episodes seemingly drawn from sun-myth.' Marett refers in a note (p. 82) to Lang's 'The Great Gladstone Myth' in *In the Wrong Paradise and Other Stories* (1886) along with Tylor's solar squib on Julius Caesar (*Primitive Culture*, I, 319).

invokes the materials of folklore. One of the problems he proposed to tackle was how to account for the origin of similar customs, arts, and legends found among widely distributed peoples. He will depend on indirect evidence supplied by 'Antiquities, Language, and Mythology.' Historical connections between Europe, Egypt, and Africa can be demonstrated through nursery tales, such as 'The Ungrateful Serpent Returned to Captivity' (now classified as Type 155), found both in the *Arabian Nights* and in Wilhelm Bleek's collection of Hottentot folktales, *Reynard the Fox in South Africa* (1864). If the beast fable was formerly considered a mere 'cock-and-bull story,' George Webbe Dasent, translator of *Popular Tales from the Norse* (1859), has given it a new prestige by pointing out resemblances between Norse and African stories that must have shared a similar past. Tylor also talks about dreams and ghosts, which he will study in seeking to reconstruct the history of man's belief in the soul. Indeed, the reader beginning *Researches* might well anticipate a monograph on folklore.

Nor would he be far misled. Folklore appears conspicuously in four of the succeeding chapters, 'Images and Names,' 'Some Remarkable Customs,' 'Historical Traditions and Myths of Observation,' and 'Geographical Distribution of Myths.' Examining childlike ideas imbedded in ethnological reports of savages, Tylor often has recourse to myths and legends, magic and taboo. What the doll is to the child, the image or idol was to primitive man. In the works of nature the child-man sees the marks made by his gods. So in the giant cavity in the rock at Ceylon the Brahman saw a footprint planted by the god Siva; the Buddhist ascribed it to Gautama Buddha and the Moslem to Adam after his expulsion from Paradise, while Christians were divided between claims made for St. Thomas and the Queen of Ethiopia. As with tangible images, so with intangible names; they must be handled with care and awe and concealed when necessary, for power over the name, by childlike confusion of words and things, conferred power over the person. Image and name magic might coincide, and Tylor quotes the *Daemonologie* of King James I, as excerpted in Brand, to the effect that 'the devil teaches how to make pictures of wax or clay, that by roasting thereof, the persons that they bear the name of may be continually melted or dried away by continual sickness.'[1] Again in his discussion of remarkable customs, Tylor seizes on folkloristic practices widely scattered among savage peoples and with echoes in the upper strata of civilization. One such practice was the sorcery of the shaman, who by sleight of hand extracted bits of wood, stone,

[1] *Researches*, p. 125.

and hair from the diseased. Another was the institution of the couvade, in which the father suffers the pain of childbirth through empathy with his wife or, in unusual cases, with his unborn son.

In other chapters, too, Tylor levies upon oral traditions. His essay on 'Growth and Decline of Culture' commences with an appraisal of traditional history and its effects as a record of early inventions and discoveries, say in mining, glassmaking, or netting. Mythic inventors became entwined with or replaced historical ones, hence the ethnologist examining an historical tradition must carefully weigh the internal against the external evidence. Quetzalcoatl, allegedly the bringer of civilization to the Mexican people, turns out to be, according to the key of Max Müller, the brightest of solar deities.

In *Primitive Culture* Tylor codifies his observations on the behaviour of folklore within a new concept, 'Survival in Culture,' to which he devotes two powerful chapters. The happy term 'survivals' would spur folklore collectors and theorists into an alluring chase, and soon displace the pejorative 'superstitions' in the terminology of the anthropological folklorist. According to the doctrine of survivals, the irrational beliefs and practices of the European peasantry, so at variance with the enlightened views of the educated classes, preserve the fragments of an ancient, lower culture, the culture of primitive man. Consequently these survivals not only illuminate the past history of the race but also confirm the broad theory of development, as opposed to the theory of degeneration, which Tylor vigorously counters. While the main march of mankind is upward, from savagery through barbarism to ascending levels of civilization, relics of savagery, such as witchcraft, still survive among civilized peoples, and occasionally burst into revivals, as in the fad of spiritualism, a revival of primitive sorcery.

In assembling his ethnographic examples of a given cultural theme or trait, Tylor regularly leads his reader from specimens reported among the lowest races by travellers and missionaries, through intermediate illustrations, culled from classical writers or Sanskrit chroniclers or Chinese historians, along to the final analogues in nineteenth-century folklore collections. The continuity he thus outlines from savage to peasant opens the exciting possibility of working backward in time from peasant to savage. Tylor frames the comparison at the outset of his inquiries:

> Look at the modern European peasant using his hatchet and his hoe, see his food boiling or roasting over the log-fire, observe the exact place which beer holds in his calculation of happiness,

hear his tale of the ghost in the nearest haunted house, and of the farmer's niece who was bewitched with knots in her inside till she fell into fits and died. If we choose out in this way things which have altered little in a long course of centuries, we may draw a picture where there shall be scarce a hand's breadth of difference between an English ploughman and a negro of Central Africa.[1]

This was the equation which inspired a generation of folklorists to examine peasant folk culture with loving care and to plot its likenesses with tribal behaviour. Such phrases as 'city savages' and 'street Arabs' carried the notion of survival even into urban society, although Tylor felt their suggestion of degradation misleading. No doubt he would have approved forward-looking labels for primitives, perhaps 'nature's gentlemen' or 'desert aristocrats.' No opprobrium was attached to those habits and ideas discarded by the front marchers of civilization lingering on in back corners as survivals of remote antiquity. Rather, they were honoured relics to be eagerly noted, whether the Somerset hand-loom, the Midsummer bonfire, the All Souls' supper for the spirits of the dead, or the ordeal of the Key and the Bible.

The doctrine of survivals was related to the concept of animism, to which Tylor devotes seven pithy chapters, advancing his thesis of the development of religious ideas from the initial notion of a disembodied spirit or soul upward to the belief in higher spiritual beings. Animistic survivals especially delight him. Thus in the practice of selling soul-mass cakes he beholds a survival of funeral sacrifices. In the custom of ghost-laying he sees a vestige of soul interment, although the once serious savage rite was now, as so often, reduced to jest. (On this matter Tylor cites Grose as quoted in Brand.) The primitive idea of separable spirits lurks still in the familiar English traditions surrounding St. John's Eve, the night on which apparitions leave the bodies of those doomed to die in the coming year and accompany the clergyman to the church door.[2] Even tree worship persists in the villages.

> The peasant folklore of Europe still knows of willows that bleed and weep and speak when hewn, of the fairy maiden that sits within the fir-tree, of that old tree in Rugaard forest that must not be felled, for an elf dwells within, of that old tree on the Heinzenberg near Zell, which uttered its complaint when the woodman cut it down, for in it was Our Lady, whose chapel now stands upon the spot.[3]

[1] *Primitive Culture*, I, 6. [2] *Ibid.*, II, 38, 140. [3] *Ibid.*, p. 201.

In the realm of folklore and mythology, with which so much of his theory of culture is concerned, Tylor was not scrapping outworn theses and exposing errors of method; he was building upon the pyramided labours of all his predecessors, and he knew them well. The philological mythology of Jacob Grimm, the compilations of the antiquaries and nineteenth-century collectors, both in Britain and on the Continent, the celestial mythology of Müller and Kuhn, served him equally. Brand and Pennant, Halliwell and Hunt, Walter Scott and Campbell of Islay furnished him with instance upon instance of survivals in the peasant folklore of the British Isles. Nor did he lack for European illustrations. For Germany, besides the Grimms, he liked *Der deutsche Volksaberglaube der Gegenwart* of Adolf Wuttke, particularly valuable in presenting folk beliefs directly rather than as a part of tales. For Norway he relied on George Webbe Dasent's *Popular Tales from the Norse*, admiring its use of the comparative method of folktale analysis. For Slavic traditions he utilized Ignaz Johann Hanusch's *Die Wissenschaft des Slawonische Mythos*, gleaning such morsels as this eyewitness' view of a dying man: 'Ha! with the shriek the spirit flutters from the mouth, flies up to the tree, from tree to tree, hither and thither till the dead is burned.'[1]

For the folklore-minded readers whom Tylor instantly inspired—and whom he can still inspire—his achievement was twofold. His extensive scouring and sampling of folklore and myths from all over the world demonstrated the similarities and interrelationships in the traditions of primitive and civilized peoples. And he brought to intellectual synthesis the labours of the English antiquary-folklorists of the preceding three centuries. Folklore could now take its place with the new empirical sciences. All the ethnographic facts Tylor patiently assembled into his intricate model pointed to a law of progression governing the evolution of the human race. Although in his second edition of *Primitive Culture* Tylor felt it necessary to add a prefatory note explaining his seeming neglect of Darwin and Spencer, saying that his system was organized from a different viewpoint, he was clearly responsive to their philosophy. The uniform, upward moving stages of culture form his plot; inexorable but beneficent laws of institutional survival determine which parts of the culture should wither away and which should bloom at a given stage. In the evolution of mythic structures, the observer could trace man's thought rising from the simple personification of nature to speculative world-histories. In the folklore of peasants, the observer could witness on the edge of his own enlightened culture the

[1] *Ibid.*, p. 25.

[195]

relics of barbaric rites. And to observe the primary stage of myth, and the living enactment of primitive sorcery, he need only turn to the savages still enduring in his own day. By piecing together these beginnings and ends, the ethnologist and folklorist could win a noble triumph indeed, the reconstruction of the early history of man.

Tylor's Influence on Anthropological Folklorists

Seven years after the first publication of *Primitive Culture* a Folk-Lore Society was formed whose energetic founders were deeply committed to the thesis of unilinear cultural evolution. Andrew Lang proclaimed a 'method of folk-lore' based on Tylor's analogy between savage myth and peasant custom. Sidney Hartland sought for the substratum of savage ritual and belief contained in nursery tale and classical legend. Edward Clodd wrote two books on survivals of name magic, a Tylorian proposition. Alfred Nutt linked ancient Celtic myth with modern Gaelic folktale. George Laurence Gomme titled one of his books *Ethnology in Folklore*. Through their writings the name of Tylor echoes like that of a household god. Clodd has told in his *Memories* (1916) how *Primitive Culture* powerfully influenced his decision to reject the Bible as Revelation and to accept the evolution of spiritual thought in man. Tylor himself was a founding member of the Society, served on its council, and was elected vice-president. He contributed an introduction to the Society's memoir of 1888, the collection of *Aino Folk-Tales* by Basil Hall Chamberlain, and commented happily on the primitive Ainos' implicit acceptance of their family tales, which served them as explanatory myths, venerated like physical theorems in modern society. 'Those who maintain the serious value of folk-lore, as embodying early but quite real stages of philosophy among mankind, will be grateful for this collection. . . .'[1]

Yet the ethnological folklorists who so admired Tylor and so avidly embraced the doctrine of survivals unanimously ridiculed Müller and the camp followers of solar mythology. The explanation is that they drew selectively from the gospel of Tylor according to the exegesis of Lang. Save for two preliminary works by Gomme, all the major publications of the anthropological school were published after Lang's *Custom and Myth* (1884) set forth the principles of the new folklore science. Lang's opening broadside at Müller was fired in a magazine article of 1873, seven years before Gomme's first folklore monograph. The personal relationship between Tylor and

[1] Introduction to Basil Hall Chamberlain, *Aino Folk-Tales* (London: Publications of the Folk-Lore Society, XXII, 1888), p. viii.

Lang at Oxford helped to identify the ideas of Lang with those of his mentor. But on their interpretation of mythology they were poles apart. Where Tylor had been content to place ethnology and comparative mythology side by side, or stage by stage, in friendly relationship, Lang demolished the hypothesis of disease-of-language among the Aryans and filled the vacuum with a continuous chain of savage survivals. The irrational elements in classical myths were due not to metaphoric misunderstanding but to lingering barbarisms.

The Tylor venerated by the ethnological folklorists was the Tylor who found survivals in one folklore category after another: children's games, nursery tales, proverbs, riddles, blessings, taboos, witchcraft. They seized on his persuasive examples of an idle pastime, a popular saying, or a conjurer's trick traceable to a once meaningful and perhaps shocking savage rite. Thus the innocent child's sport and rhyme of 'Petit Bonhomme' concealed a vicious ritual over a thousand years old; where now children toss about an object, once savages hurled a live baby back and forth until it died, believing that its death conferred power on the final holder. The innocuous phrase 'to haul over the coals' referred perhaps to the ordeal of passing through the fire; and in his own time Tylor could report a news story of an Irishwoman in New York standing her child on burning coals to see if it was a changeling. In the friendly custom of drinking one's health could be seen a vestige of libations offered the gods and the dead. Fear of saving a drowning man—an incident in Scott's novel *The Pirate*—stemmed from the old belief that a water spirit was claiming the body. Riddles and number rhymes and playground games threw light on the childlike beginnings of languages and numeral systems.[1]

This thesis of survival was the part of Tylor's work annexed by Lang and transmitted to his fellow folklorists.

Supporters of Tylor

Savages kept coming into closer view. The idea of prehistory as a separate and special part of the human record which could be investigated through archaeology and ethnology was advanced in 1865 by John Lubbock (later Lord Avebury) in the best-selling *Pre-Historic Times, as illustrated by Ancient Remains, and the Manners and Customs of Modern Savages.* Lubbock was much less the folklorist than Tylor, but he complemented the ethnologist with his archaeological reconstructions and devoted considerable attention to visible savages—Maoris and Fijians and Ojibwa Indians. He concentrated on the most primitive or 'non-metallic' savages, and

[1] *Primitive Culture*, I, 70, 76–7, 97–9, 215, 219, 240.

through direct scrutiny of their habits sought to fill in his picture of Stone Age man known only from artifacts. This method of examining surviving remnants of nearly extinct species was familiar to scientists, Lubbock pointed out:

Many mammalia which are extinct in Europe have representatives still living in other countries. Our fossil pachyderms, for instance, would be almost unintelligible but for the species which still inhabit some parts of Asia and Africa; the secondary marsupials are illustrated by their existing representatives in Australia and South America; and in the same manner if we wish clearly to understand the antiquities of Europe, we must compare them with the rude implements and weapons still, or until lately, used by savage races in other parts of the world. In fact, the Van Diemener and South American are to the antiquary what the opossum and the sloth are to the geologist. [1]

Lubbock further explored his subject with another popular book, first published in 1870, *The Origin of Civilisation and the Primitive Condition of Man: Mental and Social Condition of Savages*. Again while covering much of Tylor's ground, he comments only briefly on oral literature, although inescapably touching on matters of concern to the folklorist, such as sorcery and ghost belief. He very nearly articulates the doctrine of survivals, which Tylor would present the following year, when he speaks of 'traces of water-worship' evident in the offerings left at holy wells in Scotland, which he had himself seen, and in the belief in the kelpie, a water spirit appearing as a man, woman, horse, or bull. Cooking utensils attracted Lubbock more than traditional superstitions, but his writings helped bring savages into the limelight, and no writer on savages could avoid mention of superstition. Lubbock jocosely related an anecdote of an Englishwoman ferried across Saratoga Lake by a Mohawk Indian, to whom she kept blattering, in spite of the Mohawk conviction that disaster would befall any person who talked on those waters. Laughed at by the lady for his fears, the Mohawk replied simply, 'The Great Spirit is merciful, and knows that a white woman cannot hold her tongue.' [2]

A frankly popular work by James Anson Farrer, a writer on varied subjects from military customs to literary forgeries, helped broaden the concept of savage folklore. This was *Primitive Manners*

---

[1] John Lubbock, *Pre-Historic Times, as illustrated by Ancient Remains, and the Manners and Customs of Modern Savages* (London and Edinburgh, 1865), p. 336.
[2] Lubbock, *The Origin of Civilisation and the Primitive Condition of Man* (London: Longmans, Green, and Co., 1870), p. 23.

9. MAX MÜLLER

10. ANDREW LANG

and Customs, published in 1879, a digest of ideas made familiar by Tylor, Lubbock, and Spencer. From Tylor he drew the emphasis on savages, from Lubbock the notion of 'prehistoric antiquity,' from Spencer the vision of social evolution. The book brought together in compact form instances of 'savage'—a word he used continuously and in seven of his nine chapter titles—moral philosophy, political notions, wedding customs. It began with an exposition of 'Some Savage Myths and Beliefs' and concluded with essays on 'The Fairy-Lore of Savages' and 'Comparative Folk-Lore.' Among related topics Farrer discussed savage forms of prayer and their survival in modern folklore:

> As savages have been known to apologize to a slain elephant or bear, assuring it that its death was accidental, so it is said that in parts of Germany a woodcutter will still (or would recently) beg the pardon of a fine healthy tree before cutting it down. In our own midland counties there is a feeling to this day against binding up elder-wood with other faggots; and in Suffolk it is believed misfortune will ensue if ever it is burnt. In Germany formerly an elder-tree might not be cut down entirely; and Grimm was himself an eye-witness of a peasant praying with bare head and folded hands before venturing to cut its branches.[1]

And so on. The English custom of apple-howling or wassailing, and the German practice of presenting fruit trees with money on New Year's Day, both illustrated the continuing belief in the propitiation of tree spirits. Farrer's interest lay in proving modern superstitions to be the remains of ancient barbarism rather than ancient mythology, originating in the savage state of mind that had produced the myths. This state of mind was still visible in European usages and folktales. A farmer in the North Riding attributed the loss of a cow to his own remissness in failing to inform it of his wife's death. European peasants still burned cut hair, a practice comparable to customs among the Fijians and Zulus, who seek thus to eliminate injurious demons.

Farrer saw three possible explanations for similar rituals appearing in widely removed places: community of origin, transmission from people to people, or independent development pursuant to the laws of mental growth governing all races. Farrer strongly voted for the third. To drive home his point, he printed side by side abstracts of savage and European folktales which presented close

[1] James Anson Farrer, *Primitive Manners and Customs* (London: Chatto and Windus, 1879), p. 76.

analogies. Today a folklorist would regard these as obvious variants of the same tale-type, introduced by Europeans into South Africa and among the North American Indians; but before the day of tale-indexes, the case for uniform mental processes convinced a good many. Farrer's book especially appealed to Andrew Lang, who quoted it regularly, as did other folklorists. Lang applauded Farrer's conclusion, that the science of comparative folklore would corroborate the findings of archaeology in demonstrating the progress of man from savagery to culture. Farrer nicely balanced the folklore of the savage and of modern man. If horseshoes no longer hung over the threshold of London houses in the West End, as Aubrey reported in his *Miscellanies* in the seventeenth century, they still appeared over the threshold of country cottages. French omnibus and railway companies have discovered that passengers abruptly dwindle on Fridays; German soldiers lying dead on the Franco-Prussian battlefield were found to carry word charms as shields against swords or bullets.

To support his point that popular superstitions were still abundant in the nineteenth century, Farrer listed ten key works published more or less recently. The first seven, all from Britain, were: 1) All the volumes of *Notes and Queries*, Index, Folk-Lore; 2) Harland and Wilkinson, *Lancashire Folk-Lore*, 1867; 3) Henderson's *Notes on the Folk-Lore of the Northern Counties of England and the Borders*, 1866; 4) Kelly's *Curiosities of Indo-European Tradition and Folk-lore*, 1863; 5) Stewart's *Popular Superstitions of the Highlanders of Scotland*, 1851; 6) Sternberg's *Dialect and Folk-Lore of Northamptonshire*, 1851; and 7) Thorpe's *Northern Mythology*, 1851.[1] This was a noteworthy list of collections for a field as yet lacking professional workers, and each title commanded attention as an original pioneering effort.

Farrer left the subject of folklore after the one book in order to pass on to his next assignment, but the area of inquiry to which he called attention increasingly fascinated the folklorists.

Another volume often cited by late-nineteenth-century ethno-folklorists was a detailed and turgid treatise by Charles Francis Keary, *Outlines of Primitive Belief among the Indo-European Races*, appearing in 1882. Keary had already associated himself with the concept of prehistory in a volume written four years earlier, *The Dawn of History: An Introduction to Pre-historic Study*. In *Outlines* he used the historical rather than the comparative-mythological

---

[1] James Anson Farrer, *Primitive Manners and Customs* (London, 1879), p. 280 n. The last three titles were Birlinger, *Volksthümliches aus Schwaben*, 1861; Koehler, *Volksbrauch im Voigtlande*, 1867; and Bosquet, *La Normandie Romanesque*, 1845.

method to explore the region of prehistoric belief on the ground that the stratum of primitive beliefs preceded the formation of myths in time, and should be considered first. Excluding savages from his inquiry, he hit directly at the Aryan mythologists on their home ground, by examining the uncivilized notions of the early Aryans and the German heathens. In so doing he reduced the distinction between the savages of Tylor and the Aryans of Müller; the primitive heathens in India and Europe too possessed the savage mentality.

These investigations of the savage mind by Tylor, Lubbock, Farrer, and Keary prepared the way for a fully developed anthropological theory of folklore. The formation of The Folk-Lore Society in 1878, with 'savage' folklorists as key organizers, marked the triumph of ethnology over comparative mythology. What had once been a dilettante quest for antiquities of an irrelevant past had now become a serious quest to recapture the mind of early man. The temporary obsession with the classical heritage of ancient India and its Grecian offspring receded before the allure of still older mysteries to be unveiled in the dim mists of the primeval past.

VII   The Great Team of Folklorists

ENTHUSIASTIC SUPPORTERS of the anthropological approach to folklore began corresponding in 1876 about a folklore organization, and within two years they had organized The Folk-Lore Society in London. Now the field of folklore was baptized, defined, solidified, and equipped with a cause. Its cause was to establish a science devoted to reconstructing the world view of pre-historic savages from the contemporary lore of peasants. The whirl-pool of activity and the ferment of excitement that lasted from 1878 to the first World War drew many talented scholars and collectors into the Society, but the phenomenal achievements of six giants gave the movement its thrust. Between them, Andrew Lang, George Laurence Gomme, Alfred Nutt, Edwin Sidney Hartland, Edward Clodd, and William Alexander Clouston produced a whole library of folklore writings, from multivolumed treatises to pithy articles, prefaces, lectures, addresses, reviews, and notes. Co-operating closely with each other, they formed a 'great team' whose collective efforts wrote a brilliant chapter in the history of modern thought.

These anthropological folklorists built on the labours of their pre-decessors, and to some extent they matched the roles played by the earlier group of antiquary folklorists. Gomme succeeds Thoms as the crusader for folklore, and Thoms almost literally hands the mantle over to his successor, who devoted his private life to further-ing a science of folklore. Alfred Nutt the publisher, whose books carried the imprint of his father, David Nutt, and who was a Celtic scholar of distinction in his own right, fills a comparable function to that played by Francis Douce, the generous bibliophile. The house of Nutt, known for its educational and foreign lists, sponsored numerous titles on folklore, frequently at a loss which Alfred had to recoup on more popular titles. Hartland recast the subject matter of Keightley's *The Fairy Mythology* into his *The Science of Fairy Tales*, the first of his masterful explorations of savage tales and customs. Clouston in turn expanded on Keightley's *Tales and Popu-*

lar Fictions in his two-volume study, *Popular Tales and Fictions,* spinning a web of interrelated stories from the Himalayas to the Highlands. Intellectually, Clodd the outspoken freethinker is the descendant of the rationalist Wright, extending the folklore attack on Romanism to cover all Christian dogma. Lang's miraculous output finds precedent in the versatile productivity of Halliwell.

The intimate connections of the earlier group are also duplicated. As the firm friendships of Thoms and Douce, Halliwell and Wright, Croker and Keightley (until they quarrelled) were fostered by the several antiquarian societies to which they belonged, so did the new Folk-Lore Society provide a regular meeting ground for the anthropological folklorists who dominated the Society in its first twenty years. Successively, five of the six served presidential terms, covering the period 1888–1902.[1] (Clouston, who lived in Glasgow, was necessarily less active in the Society.) For a number of years Gomme was director of the Society, Clodd its treasurer, Nutt its publisher, and Lang and Hartland members of its executive council. Nutt published the organ, initiated in 1878 as the *Folk-Lore Record,* altered to the *Folk-Lore Journal* in 1883 and to *Folk-Lore,* its enduring title, in 1888. He also published the Society's monograph series, as well as the short-lived *Archaeological Review,* which was incorporated with *Folk-Lore* in 1890, and he engineered the successful pamphlet series 'Popular Studies in Mythology, Romance and Folklore,' to which he and Hartland contributed five of the first six numbers.

Acknowledgments and mutual references in their greater and lesser works further underscore the group's close partnerships. Thus Gomme in *Folk-Lore as an Historical Science* tendered 'Mr. Lang most grateful thanks, for he took an immense deal of trouble and gave me the advantage of his searching criticism.' In turn, Hartland in *The Science of Fairy Tales* stated his 'obligations to Mr. G. L. Gomme, F.S.A., who has so readily acceded to my request that he would read the proof-sheets, and whose suggestions have been of the greatest value.' As one of a hundred instances, in a paper on 'The Science of Folk-Lore' developing his own thought Gomme referred in consecutive paragraphs to statements by Lang, Nutt, and Hartland in their running dialogue on the definition and classification of folklore.[2] In this way they commended and corrected each other in the public conversation so fruitful for the Victorians.

---

[1] Lang served as president in 1888 and 1889 and was the first non-titled president; Gomme served from 1890 through 1894, Clodd in 1895 and 1896, Nutt in 1897, 1898, and 1899, and Hartland in 1900 and 1901.
[2] *Folk-Lore Journal,* III (1885), 4–5.

In one of his monthly columns in *Longman's Magazine*, Lang apologized for an error in the previous issue saying, 'Before the article was published, but when it was too late to alter it, Mr. Alfred Nutt kindly drew my attention to a very elaborate, mystical, and "Druidical" chant of the same kind....'[1] In the same column he reprinted a rare English *Märchen* from Suffolk unearthed by Clodd in the *Ipswich Journal*. Describing his intellectual friendships in his chatty *Memories*, Clodd included sketches of Lang and Gomme. He spoke of his 'jolly talks' with Gomme on survivals of early inheritance customs, and of the 'kindly acts' of Lang who volunteered to read the proofs of his friend's book when he detested reading his own. Clodd affectionately dedicated his *Magic in Names* to Hartland in 1920, when only they survived of the initial group. Clouston dedicated *Flowers from a Persian Garden* in an open letter of friendship and gratitude to Hartland, and *Literary Coincidences*, which contained two folklore essays, to Nutt; it was Hartland who wrote Clouston's obituary in *Folk-Lore*. At the International Folk-Lore Congress held in London in 1891 under the sponsorship of The Folk-Lore Society, a high point in English folklore, Lang served as president, Hartland as chairman of the folktale section, and Gomme and Nutt presented papers. Nutt then acted as co-editor and publisher for the Proceedings of the congress.

All during these years the group corresponded intimately with each other on Society and scholarly business, their letters in themselves comprising a vast output.[2]

The stature of these evening folklorists greatly enhanced the subject to which they lent their energies. None were permanently connected with universities, each wrote his books as an avocation, and yet their drive and enthusiasm enabled them to outproduce most academic scholars. Lang left his fellowship at Merton College, Oxford, to make his living in London as a free-lance literary journalist and become one of the most celebrated men of letters of his day. Clodd entered the banking business in London, and from that staid base gained a wide notoriety for his championing of evolutionism in its extreme form of free thought; he wrote a best-seller, *The Childhood of the World*, as a primer of evolution for children. The name of Alfred Nutt was highly respected in publishing circles. Edwin Sidney Hartland was a solicitor by profession and served a term as mayor of Gloucester. George Laurence Gomme was knighted in

---

[1] 'At the Sign of the Ship,' *Longman's Magazine*, XIII (February, 1889), 439.
[2] The extensive Clodd correspondence preserved in the Brotherton Collection of the University of Leeds Library includes numerous letters exchanged with Gomme, Lang, and Hartland.

1911 for his service as Clerk of the London County Council and for his five books on the early history and institutions of London. Clouston worked as newspaper editor and feature writer, while compiling books on such varied topics as Dr. Johnson's aphorisms and hieroglyphic Bibles. As Robert Ranulph Marett, the rector of Exeter College, Oxford, wrote in *Folk-Lore*, '. . . one and all were in a good sense men of the world, accustomed to judge and to act in the light of hard facts; so that their unbounded enthusiasm, the almost boyish abandon with which they devoted the hours saved from the daily round to the speculative reconstruction of human history in its widest aspects, was tempered by a stern resolve to be neither sentimental nor slipshod. . . .'[1]

United as they were in a common cause to construct a solid discipline of folklore and to demolish the false claims of comparative mythology, the giants nevertheless jousted vigorously with each other. Once the enemy had fled, they probed each other's pet theories, to ensure that all remained in a state of scientific grace. Clodd drew blood from Lang in lancing Lang's thesis of psychic folklore. Nutt brought heavy artillery to bear on Gomme's cherished theory of racial strains in folklore, and Lang provided a coup de grâce. Hartland marshalled impressive evidence to discredit Lang's espousal of high gods among the Australian aborigines. Gomme ticked off Lang for debasing the coin of folklore by writing fairy stories for children. But against the claims of the diffusionists, Groome or Jacobs or the American Newell, they closed ranks in spirited defence of cultural evolutionism. In concluding his severe critique of Gomme's racial theory, Nutt could still say, 'Differ as we may . . . Mr. Gomme and I can continue to work harmoniously in the same society. We feel no impulse to start rival bodies or to excommunicate each other, and are content to leave it to time and the progress of research to decide which, if either, of us be in the right.'[2]

Broadly and deeply devoted to folklore science, the great team spread their influence at home and abroad. While not themselves fieldworkers, they actively encouraged county residents in England and colonial administrators overseas to collect data. They spoke too for all the British Isles. Lang the Borderer displayed a filial interest in Anglo-Scots traditions. Nutt the Celticist collaborated with the Gaelic folklorists of Ireland and Scotland. Hartland, living adjacent to Wales, assisted in Welsh folklore inquiries. The world was their province, and Britain their beloved capital.

[1] In his obituary of Hartland in *Folk-Lore*, XXXVIII (1927), 83-4.
[2] *Folk-Lore*, X (1899), 149.

[1 ANDREW LANG]

Now, with regard to all these strange usages, what is the method of folklore? The method is, when an apparently irrational and anomalous custom is found in any country, to look for a country where . . . the practice is . . . in harmony with the manners and ideas of the people among whom it prevails . . . . the peculiarity of the method of folklore is that it will venture to compare . . . the myths of the most widely severed races.[1]

So Andrew Lang (1844–1912) expounded 'The Method of Folklore' in 1884 in his book of essays *Custom and Myth*, aimed against the comparative mythologists who would limit their comparisons to Aryan-speaking peoples. Lang could have made his reputation as a folklorist alone, but he made many other and larger reputations.

A battery of experts at St. Andrews University has lectured on his manifold interests, from the classics, religion, Scottish history, poetry, biography, and anthropology to golf and fishing.[2] No lecture was devoted to folklore, perhaps his fondest sport. His fecundity and wit were the despair of his contemporaries, who writhed at his thrusts in morning leaders, weekly and monthly reviews and columns, and incessant addresses, prefaces, and essays interlarded among a stream of scholarly and literary books. His bibliography of books and pamphlets runs to nearly five hundred titles.[3]

A son of the Border, born in Selkirk, Scotland, educated at St. Andrews and Glasgow University, awarded a fellowship to Balliol College, Oxford, in 1864, Lang commenced his career conventionally as a student of the classics, until his mind stirred to the new anthropology. His first books dealt with the Homeric question, but he was soon considering the nature of savage mythmaking as part of the subject matter of classical mythology. Like Max Müller, he puzzled over the brutal and irrational features of Greek myths, but the explanation through Vedic Sanskrit gave him no satisfaction. In May, 1873, he fired the opening salvo in a withering attack on Müller's system that lasted until the latter's death in 1900; the article, 'Mythology and Fairy Tales,' in the *Fortnightly Review*, rejected philology for ethnology as the handmaiden of folklore. The following

---

[1] *Custom and Myth* (London, 1901), pp. 21, 23.
[2] *Concerning Andrew Lang*. Being the Andrew Lang Lectures delivered before the University of St. Andrews 1927–37 (Oxford, 1949). The Andrew Lang Lecture of 25 April 1951 by Herbert J. Rose, *Andrew Lang, His Place in Anthropology*, was separately issued (Edinburgh, 1951).
[3] Roger Lancelyn Green has appended 'A Short-Title Bibliography of the Works of Andrew Lang' to his *Andrew Lang, A Critical Biography* (Leicester, 1946).

years found him reviewing a variety of new books on folk literature and supernaturalism in *The Academy,* and he printed letters 'On Founding a Folklore Society' in *The Academy* for December 1 and 15, 1877. Within a year he contributed an article on 'The Folk-Lore of France' to the first volume of the new journal, the *Folk-Lore Record,* delineating the uniquely Gallic elements in French oral literature, and he wrote a preface to the second volume in 1879 restating his theory. By this time he was well launched into the folklore side of his multiple writing activities.

Lang's Anthropological Theory of Folklore

In the history of the English folklore movement, the influence of E. B. Tylor on Andrew Lang is a crucial relationship. Lang met the anthropologist in 1872 at Balliol College, to which they both belonged. Although he read in classics, Lang had already felt the allure of savages and totemism induced by the 'epoch-making' work of John Ferguson McLennan, *Primitive Marriage* (1865). The intellectual excitement in primitive man aroused by Tylor and Lubbock speedily communicated itself to him. Writing in 1907, in a tribute to Tylor, he recalled the ferment of the decade he inherited as a student.

It is to be noted that, in 1860–1870, a fresh scientific interest in matters anthropological was 'in the air.' Probably it took its rise, not so much in Darwin's famous theory of evolution, as in the long-ignored or ridiculed discoveries of the relics of Palaeolithic man by M. Boucher de Perthes. Mr. Henry Christy, a friend of Mr. Tylor, and Sir John Evans, helped greatly to establish the authenticity of the discoveries of M. Boucher de Perthes, and while they were mainly exercised with the development of man's weapons, implements, and arts, Mr. Tylor, with Lord Avebury, studied his mental development as revealed in his customs, institutions, and beliefs. Mr. McLennan and Sir Henry Maine were contemporaneously laying the foundation of the study of earlier and later jurisprudence.[1]

Lang went on to recapture the delight he had experienced on reading *Primitive Culture,* written so attractively that an intelligent child could peruse the chapter on 'Survival in Culture' and 'become a folk-lorist unawares.' He acknowledged a divergence between the views of his master and of himself on the perplexing enigma of the countless coincidences in the oral and material culture of races. Lang favoured coincident and multiple invention, while Tylor

[1] 'Edward Burnet Tylor,' in *Anthropological Essays presented to E. B. Tylor in Honour of his 75th Birthday Oct. 2, 1907* (Oxford, 1907), pp. 3–4.

leaned more to the borrowing of myths and *Märchen* between peoples. They differed too on spiritualism, Tylor dismissing it as a 'monstrous farrago,' while Lang thought the element of animism—though not of automatism—to be a survival. And they disagreed in their attitudes on Max Müller, into whose 'adjacent garden' Tylor never threw a stone. Yet, recognizing their triadic bond, Lang uses the phrase of Müller to describe anthropology as 'Mr. Tylor's Science.' In the end this new science triumphed over the solar theory, with aid on the Continent from Wilhelm Mannhardt, 'who paid more attention to European folk-lore with its survivals of early ritual than did Mr. Tylor.' Lang made confession of his 'giant ignorance' of Mannhardt when working out the method of comparative folklore.[1]

During the 1870's and '80's Lang was busy erecting an anthropological theory of folklore and demolishing the claims of solar mythology. His premises flowed directly from the conclusions of Tylor and were elaborated in 'The Method of Folklore,' the opening essay of his group of papers published in 1884 under the title *Custom and Myth* and frequently reprinted. The folklorist could compare relics or survivals obtained from conscientious collectors with the existing customs and traditions of savages, as recorded by travellers and missionaries, and perceive a continuity. Everywhere the same beliefs, and survivals of beliefs, manifested themselves; primitive man ascribed spirits to the trees, the animals, and the elements; he worshipped the animal protector of his clan, he credited the shaman with powers of transformation. These concepts of animism, totemism, and fetishism continually appear in myths and fairy tales, which hark back to the stage of culture when men did not sharply distinguish between the human and the natural world. Hence the study of survivals can assist in reconstructing the earliest stages of human life and culture, much as the fossil bones of a prehistoric creature could conjure up an extinct species. The technique lay in comparing the more advanced Aryan traditions with non-Aryan myths and legends of lesser peoples over the world. So there is nothing surprising in the myth of Cronus swallowing his children, for obviously it dates from an era of cannibalism. We learn about Greek gods from red Indian totems.

Armed with this method, Lang turned its cutting-edge into Müller's delicate hypotheses. Again and again he pointed to the disagreements among the experts on the Greek-Vedic equations, the cornerstone of Müller's edifice. Then he asked embarrassing ques-

---

[1] 'Edward Burnet Tylor,' in *Anthropological Essays* etc., pp. 7, 9, 13, 10. Edward Clodd, *Memories* (London, 1916), quoting Lang, p. 209.

tions. Since all primitive men have myths, why did not myths originate before the Mythopoeic Age? Why would mythopoeic man
remember phrases and forget their meanings? Why does Müller
devise the cumbersome processes of polyonymy and homonymy to
explain a very simple phenomenon, namely that savages regarded
the elements as persons? Lang pointed out possibilities for error
within the etymological method. Old legends regularly gravitate
to new and more modern heroes, whose names will merely mislead
the inquirer. Red Indians and other savages often adopt the names
of elements for their personal names, and these too would produce
false scents. Folk-etymologies explaining supposed origins of names
exist, of course, but mainly in connection with place-names. In any
case, how can comparative mythology explain the myths of non-
Aryan races, lower in culture than the Vedic Aryans, unacquainted
with Sanskrit, yet possessing legends similar to those found in
India and Greece? The answer Lang provided, on the foundations
laid by Tylor, came from ethnology and its view of the ladderlike
ascent of all men, regardless of their race or language.

In his lengthy Introduction to the Margaret Hunt edition of
Grimm's Household Tales, Lang considered in detail the solar theories
of both Müller and Cox. He used the opportunity afforded by the
presence of the German *Märchen* to press home his counter-theory
in an essay entitled 'Household Tales: Their Origin, Diffusion, and
Relation to the Higher Myths.' The deviations of the self-styled
baronet Cox from the orthodox position of his master Müller baffled
Lang and turned the edge of his wit, for on some points Cox veered
so abruptly from Müller that he landed squarely in the arms of Lang.
When Sir George posited an animistic state of savagery conducive
to mythmaking, and conceived that animistic ideas grew from
savage thought, not from confused language, Lang naturally applauded. The foe of solarism approved the way Cox refused to trace
myths merely through names, as Müller demanded, and he supported Cox's view that *Märchen* can be both the remains and the
sources of myth.

A mystified Lang could not see how Sir George, quoting Müller
chapter and verse, drew inferences congenial to the anthropological
view. Cox should have gone to the evidence about savage customs
and ideas, not to the philologists, Lang said, and then his correct
inferences might have led to correct conclusions. Unfortunately,
those conclusions echoed Müller's in reading the sun and the clouds
and the dew into every myth and tale, and Lang mocked the two
solarists impartially when he came to analyse their reconstructions.
He laughed polyonymy and the forgetfulness-of-words into the

ground, as he attempted by these processes to explain the Jason myth, and then he showed how simply the anthropologists could decipher the primitive elements of the story. Had Cox been born a bit later he might have been saved, Lang suggests, mindful that *The Mythology of the Aryan Nations* was published in 1870, a year before *Primitive Culture,* and so written at a time when 'philologists were inclined to believe that their analysis of language was the true, perhaps the only key, to knowledge of what men had been in the pre-historic past. It is now generally recognized . . . that the sciences of Anthropology and Archaeology also throw much light on the human past. . . .'[1] As Cox cited Müller, so Lang cited Tylor, but selectively and somewhat unfairly, since solarists as well as ethnologists could quote Tylor. In fact, Müller did invoke the father of anthropology as an expert witness that uncritical missionaries and travellers ignorant of native languages could not be relied upon in the study of savage mythology and religion. Lang retorted that Tylor applied tests of reliability, such as a pattern of consensus or recurrence, to determine valid data, and that upon such data he had written a number of chapters in *Primitive Culture.* Also, Lang recalled Tylor's caution against rash inferences which, on the strength of fancied resemblances, deduced myths of the sun and sky and dawn in every household tale. And he excerpts Tylor's parody of 'The Song of Sixpence.' So did the disputants quote the scriptural authority to their own purpose.

In the final portion of his essay, Lang marshalled his arguments for the value of studying savage folktales, singling out African collections to compare with Aryan. In scouring the bibliography, he came up with Bushmen, Swahili, Basuto, Zulu, Hottentot, and Madagascar specimens, and he also indicated the scanty but still usable resources from the South Pacific and North America. He then proceeded to illustrate, in tabular form, correspondences between savage and European tales in such matters as heroes who are helped by animals, who marry animals, who are transformed into animals, who are captured by cannibals, and who descend to Hades. Above the theme of the savage tale he placed the related savage idea, such as belief in kinship with animals. Hence this idea is found as a survival in European household stories, which no longer reflect the institutions of primitive culture and mentality. At a still higher level are found the myths of early civilizations.

Turning from Müller and Cox to debate with Robert Brown, Lang further refined his 'savage' approach. Lang flicked Brown

[1] Lang, Introduction to *Grimm's Household Tales,* trans. and ed. Margaret Hunt (London, 1910), I, xxiv, note.

with the same whip he used on all his adversaries, including his friends, but on this victim he drew the most blood. Brown refers furiously to an anonymous review of *The Myth of Kirkê*, obviously by Lang, in the *Saturday Review*, where the Scot had ridiculed the solar theory, saying that Robinson Crusoe, like Odysseus, lived in a cave and so must be the sun.[1] In *Custom and Myth*, Lang called the views elaborated by Brown in *The Law of Kosmic Order*, that the Akkadians named the stars after celestial myths, 'far-fetched and unconvincing.' Even granting that the Greeks obtained their star-names from Chaldea, did the Eskimos and Melanesians name stars in debt to Akkadian fancies? More likely, the Akkadians must have inherited from a savage past beliefs which they used in naming the constellations.[2]

The Akkadian theory, sighs Lang, is becoming as overdone as the Aryan. In the chapter 'Moly and Mandragora' in *Custom and Myth*, Lang challenges Brown's analysis of the magic herb moly, given to Odysseus to ward off the siren Circe. Brown construed moly as originally a star, known to the ancient Akkadians, which guarded a solar hero; Lang thought it simply a magical herb of the kind everywhere credited by savages. He quotes Brown in *The Academy* for January 3, 1885, as contending that 'if Odysseus and Kirkê were sun and moon here is a good starting-point for the theory that the moly was stellar.' Then he inserts the lance. 'This reminds one of the preacher who demonstrated the existence of the Trinity thus: "For is there not, my brethren, one sun, and one moon,—and one multitude of stars?" '[3] In his Preface to a new edition of *Custom and Myth* in 1898, Lang replied to Brown's work earlier that year, *Semitic Influence in Hellenic Mythology*, with a point-by-point rejoinder, 'Apollo, the Mouse, and Mr. Robert Brown, Junior, F.S.A., M.R.S.A.' (See p. 181.) There Lang declared that a 'gentleman of Mr. Brown's calibre' should not 'intermingle his criticisms on my mythological work with personal remarks' and that he 'needed a lesson.'

Lang never denied the presence of solar myths, and lunar and star myths as well, and offered copious examples in his *Myth, Ritual and Religion*, published in two volumes in 1887. Here he pursued the development of primitive mythology and worship set forth by Tylor in the final half of *Primitive Culture*. Heavenly myths took form not from any 'disease of language' but from the animistic stage of culture, in which early man personalized the elements and

---

[1] Robert Brown, *Semitic Influence in Hellenic Mythology* (London, 1898), pp. 30–1.
[2] Lang, *Custom and Myth* (London, New York, and Bombay, 1898), p. 137.
[3] *Ibid.*, p. 155 n.

accepted metamorphosis. Thus the mythical Zeus has 'all the powers of the medicine-man and all the passions of the barbarian.'[1] Relentlessly Lang bombarded the solar mythologists with examples from Australia, Africa, North and South America, and the South Pacific islands of savage traditions resembling those of civilized peoples. The believed tales of barbarians survive in the myths and *Märchen* of a later day, and account for their odd features. 'It is almost as necessary for a young god or hero to slay monsters as for a young lady to be presented at court; and we may hesitate to explain all these legends of an useful feat of courage as nature-myths.'[2] Where Müller and his followers invariably interpret the hero vanquishing the dragon as the sun conquering the night, Lang sees an ancient storytelling formula, based on the actual hunting of a wild beast.

Andrew Lang flourished on controversy, and his anthropological method of folklore was honed during his sharp debate with the mythologists. As late as 1897 he was writing *Modern Mythology, A Reply to Max Müller*, a minutely detailed answer to the weighty two-volume attack he finally goaded the Sanskrit scholar into making earlier that year in *Contributions to a Science of Mythology*. In the end Lang had vastly enlarged the concept of folklore from Tylor's restricted sense of European peasant traditions to the oral inheritance of all races. If Tylor drew the analogy between the peasant and the savage, it remained for Lang to insist that the folklorist collect and study the customs and tales of primitive peoples. In late Victorian England, a perfect situation existed within the framework of Empire to pursue this end.

Lang as a Psycho-Folklorist

As the anthropological school of folklore gained ascendancy over the mythological, Lang's interest gravitated to other frictional areas, in particular that of psychic lore. In an arresting essay, 'The Comparative Study of Ghost Stories,' in the *Nineteenth Century* for April, 1885, he proposed that the psycho-folklorist of the present reinforce his contemporary data with the illustrations unwittingly set down in the past. Only so could one get a long-range view on ghostlore and appreciate its timeless rather than temporal features. As with the fairy tales, it was the universality, the correspondence, the recurrence that pleased and puzzled him, and which he called 'the *mythical* tendencies of ghost stories.'[3]

Lang's writings on spiritualistic lore are as usual scattered

---

[1] Lang, *Myth, Ritual and Religion* (London, 1913), II, 193–4. [2] *Ibid.*, p. 196.
[3] See also his remarks in *Longman's Magazine*, XXIII (February, 1894), 437–40.

through essays, prefaces, addresses, columns, and books. The rising curve of his interest in psychic matters can be seen in the department 'At the Sign of the Ship' which he conducted in *Longman's Magazine* from 1885 to 1905, commenting on the manifold topics that appealed to him, from poetry to golf, in effect maintaining his private journal for public inspection. Of two hundred and forty-one 'Ships,' one hundred and thirty-six contained folklore entries, and the figure might have been higher except that 'folklore bores many just people so terribly.' The Ships are filled to their holds with dreams, hallucinations, apparitions, conjure tricks, coincidences, crystal-gazing, *déjà vu*, poltergeists, dowsing, spirit rapping, telepathy—the whole gamut of modern mysteries. By treating these topics 'scientifically'—that is, with the principles of scientific research—he hoped to distinguish the folklore tale from the factual phenomenon, the magician's trick from the real event, the faulty from the true perception. He claimed the scientist's prerogative of pushing back the area of the unknown; conceivably there was 'something' in these mysteries other than hoax or delusion, and his own temperament induced in him a partial belief. The Scot saw ghosts, had strange dreams, talked with Scottish neighbours about their second-sighted visions and with London friends who saw scenes in crystal balls.

One mystery that particularly intrigued him was the so-called Fire Walk, in which native performers walked barefooted over red-hot stones without injury. In his column he printed descriptions from correspondents in Trinidad, India, and Japan, and cited others from Tahiti and the Fiji Islands taken from *Folk-Lore*. His summary article on 'Passing Through the Fire' in the *Contemporary Review* for August, 1896, and the chapter on 'The Fire-Walk' in *Magic and Religion* (1901) end inconclusively with his failure to discover the trick, if trick it was. 'Maybe we could all walk through the fire if we tried!' he guessed.

Eventually his papers on psychic lore grew into two books. In *Cock Lane and Common-Sense* (1894), he boldly asserted that no age had a pre-emption on the marvellous, that rationalism bred its ghosts and revivalism its miracles. One of his favourite source-books for Scottish providences was Robert Wodrow's *Analecta*. Through the ages the same ghostly tales are told; why these particular ones? The first job of the folklorist was to isolate the key plots, and this he could do by colligating ancient and medieval wonders with modern counterparts found among civilized and savage peoples.[1] In *The Book of Dreams and Ghosts* (1897), he traced

---

[1] *Cock Lane and Common-Sense* (London, 1894), pp. 136–7.

the legend of the Ghostly Compact for over seven centuries, isolating story after story in which the revenant sears a scar into the hand of its living partner (as in the Highland account related by Anne Grant). Lang sought to identify a genuine pattern of psychic experience, and in his endless analyses of cases ran one species to earth, so he thought, in the authentic type of haunted-house story, nothing more than 'pretty frequent, inexplicable noises, with occasional aimless apparitions.' The findings of the Society for Psychical Research (of which body he became president in 1911) tallied with his own historical inquiries, giving him the double check he desired.

The enthusiasts for psychical research founded their society in 1882 and, like the folklorists, were attempting to develop a new science. In the Ships and elsewhere, Lang refers with keen interest to such exploratory works as Frederic W. H. Myers, Frank Podmore, and Edmund Gurney's *Phantasms of the Living* (1886), Podmore's *Apparitions and Thought-Transference* (1894), and Myers' *Human Personality and its Survival of Bodily Death* (1903). Increasingly he recommended a synthesis of the two fields in approaching topics of mutual concern. In an extended Introduction to Robert Kirk's *The Secret Commonwealth of Elves, Fauns, and Fairies* (1893), Lang pressed home his desire for a scientific approach to the supernatural.

Kirk, the minister of Aberfoyle, who set down his celebrated account of faerydom in 1594, appealed to his fellow Scot as an early 'student in folk-lore and in psychical research—topics that run into each other.'[1] Kirk was investigating the laws of fairy behaviour on a rational basis. In his own view, Lang disagreed with the theory advanced by David MacRitchie in *The Testimony of Tradition* (1890) that belief in fairies stemmed from folk memories of a vanished race, preferring to link it with ideas about Hades. To this lingering belief in a shadowy underground race Lang added reinforcing data collected by the Society for Psychical Research on 'double-men' or *Doppelgängers*, poltergeists, and the visions of the second-sighted. One poltergeist of 1649, 'The Just Devil of Woodstock,' he culled from Scott who had picked it up from Hone; in this way Lang meshed folklore with psychic evidence.

As a son of the Border, Lang naturally speculated about second-sight from the perspective of psycho-folklore. In *The Making of Religion* (1898), he offered many savage examples of seers which

---

[1] *The Secret Commonwealth of Elves, Fauns, and Fairies.* A Study in Folk-Lore & Psychical Research. The Text by Robert Kirk, M.A., Minister of Aberfoyle, A.D. 1691. The Comment by Andrew Lang, M.A., A.D. 1893 (London, 1893), p. xv.

11. ALFRED NUTT

12. EDWARD CLODD

tended to confirm modern reports of the Society for Psychical Research. Again in his remarks on 'The Brahan Seer and Second Sight,' introducing Alexander Mackenzie's *The Prophecies of the Brahan Seer* (1899), he called for more recording of the use of divining stones in the Highlands, in the 'interests of Folk Lore, or Psychology, or both.' The Brahan seer was Kenneth Mackenzie, a seventeenth-century predictor of the Isle of Lewis, whose prophecies had entered tradition. Lang was willing to believe in seers, if their predictions could be properly checked. He gave instances from his own knowledge which he had been able to verify. A literary lady told him of a vision of a stranger who thrust a knife into the left side of her friend. Lang offered to bet one hundred pounds against the possibility of the vision being fulfilled. Several months later the lady met the man of the vision at the entrance to her friend's house; he was a surgeon who had just operated, unsuccessfully, on her friend's left side. In the Ships, too, Lang commented on crystal-gazing, expressing pleasure at finding ancient examples of scrying in Hartland's *The Legend of Perseus* and contemporary examples among the Red Indians and Maoris, to corroborate the testimony of his own acquaintances.

But in such matters he displayed too subjective an interest for his hard-headed colleagues. 'Now I am in disgrace with the Folk-Lore Society,' he writes plaintively, 'for maintaining that this world-wide practice arises from the simple fact that some people *do* see hallucinatory pictures in glass balls, in carafes of water, in ink, and, generally, in any clear depth.'[1] Lang here refers to a sharp clash with Edward Clodd, who jibed at him in his presidential address of 1895 to the Folk-Lore Society, alleging that crystal visions came from a disordered liver and pointing to the number of spirit mediums who had been exposed.[2] Never one to sidestep a controversy, Lang rebutted the same year in the pages of *Folk-Lore* with his 'Protest of a Psycho-Folklorist.'

> What I cannot understand is this: as long as a savage, mediaeval, or classical belief (as in Fire-Walking) rests only on tradition it interests the folklorist. As soon as contemporary evidence of honourable men avers that the belief reposes on a fact, Folklore drops the subject. . . . I don't care what the cause is, from sleight of hand to the action of demons. . . . If Mr. Clodd explains all by a disordered liver, then a disordered liver is the origin of a picturesque piece of folklore.[3]

[1] *Longman's Magazine*, XXVII (November, 1895), 104–5.
[2] *Folk-Lore*, VI (March, 1895), 78–81.   [3] *Ibid.*, VI (September, 1895), 247, 239, 238.

Clodd replied to the protest by vigorously attacking the pseudo-scientific methods of psychical research for its a priori assumptions and for the fallibility of sense perceptions at best. He offered rational explanations for Fire Walking and repeated his charge that modern spiritualism was nothing but savage animism in new dress —that is, a survival, as Tylor had said.[1] In a later, briefer skirmish, Clodd went so far as to place Lang 'in the movement which arrests the explanation of the occult on scientific lines.' This was in his review in *Folk-Lore* in 1905 of Northcote W. Thomas' *Crystal-Gazing: Its History and Practice,* for which Lang provided a sympathetic introduction.[2] Clodd considered that Lang still accepted mysteries in a scientific age.

Like Walter Scott before him, Lang sought to deal soberly with the supernaturalism of modern life, substituting for the self-evident light of reason the empirical tests of science as formulated by the Society for Psychical Research. His original evolutionary thesis tended to fade before the realization that ghost stories seemed more congenial to Englishmen than to savages, and he considered each case on its own terms, endeavouring to separate the fraudulent from the genuine psychic event. But his fellow-folklorists thought their leader had been led up the garden path by seductive sirens posing as spiritualistic mediums.

Tales and Ballads

In some of his writings, Lang was content to consider the major folklore genres as categories in themselves, apart from polemical theory. The folktale had appealed to him from his childhood, and in the Ships he took advantage of his strategic editorial post to stimulate collectors, in the manner of Hone and Thoms. Correspondents sent him variants of tales and customs he had printed, and he in turn printed and commented on their variants in later numbers, so that certain themes recur over the months and even the years. In the early Ships, he dwelt on English and continental *Märchen,* and he encouraged schoolmasters and clergymen at home and missionaries and travellers abroad to supply examples. Lang's imagination was aroused by the chance of unearthing the rare oral tradition, vitiated by two centuries of cheaply printed chapbooks. His examples brought to light several good specimens of native folktales, including one prize from Devonshire, where the simple hero who answers three questions successfully bears the name of

---

[1] *Folk-Lore*, VI (September, 1895), pp. 248–58.
[2] *Ibid.*, XVI (December, 1905), 479–80. See also *ibid.*, XVII (June, 1906), 231–3; *ibid.*, XVII (September, 1906), 373–4.

Robin Hood. These stories turned his thoughts 'to study national character in traditional tales,' and he mused over the spare rationalism of English *Märchen*.

Note how Suffolk fancy economises in miracle: Cap o' Rushes has fine clothes of her own, and needs no friendly beast, no fairy godmother, to provide them for her. We have no king here, but 'a very rich gentleman,' and no 'fairy prince with happy eyes and lighter-footed than the fox,' but merely 'the master's son.' . . . The English, too, is very plain and pleasant; it is a work-a-day, unassuming English story, with the romance reduced to the lowest possible power.[1]

Here is a different Lang from the indefatigable demonstrator of the universal traits in popular tales; it is the nationalist folk interpreter of his sparkling early essay on 'The Folk-Lore of France' in the *Folk-Lore Record* for 1878. There he speaks of the scanty content of French folksongs, and the satiric humour and worldly wisdom in French *Märchen*. On the whole, French folklore is less imaginative and harsher than the traditions in sister nations. 'One misses the pleasant spontaneity and good nature of the Norse legends, the intensity of the Scotch ballad, the poetry of Celtic stories.'[2] He asks searching questions about the pagan and ecclesiastical elements in the heritage of the French peasant. Yet he pursues them no further, and the whole intriguing question of national folklore ends there.

This foray into national traditions runs strangely counter to his 'damnable iteration' of the universal traits in folktales. In the 'discourse' he provided in 1887 to William Adlington's translation of *The Most Pleasant and Delectable Tale of the Marriage of Cupid and Psyche*, he stresses that every essential idea and incident in the story, no matter how bizarre they now appear, once must have seemed commonplace enough. Hence there was little point in trying to demonstrate one historic point of origin among one particular people for ideas of metamorphosis and enchantment. Lang's most extensive discussion of folktales was his lengthy Introduction to *Perrault's Popular Tales* (1888), which he intended in part as an essay on 'the study of Popular Tales in general.' There were only eight *contes* in Perrault's slender volume, but most were destined for immortality: Beauty and the Beast, Little Red Riding Hood,

---

[1] *Longman's Magazine*, XIII (February, 1889), 445. The tales Lang collected in *Longman's* were reprinted in *Folk-Lore*, I (1890), 289–312, under the title 'English and Scotch Fairy Tales.'
[2] *Folk-Lore Record*, I (1878), 117.

Bluebeard, Puss in Boots, Cinderella, Hop o' My Thumb. Perrault, who served his brother, the Receiver-General of Paris, from 1654 to 1664, and assisted Colbert in the planning of royal buildings, placed the *Histoires ou Contes du Temps passé* in the mouth of his young son. 'It is to this union of old age and childhood, then, of peasant memories, and memories of Versailles, to this kindly handling of venerable legends, that Perrault's *Contes* owe their perennial charm,' judged Lang.[1] Here he is at his most judicious, not overpressing survivals, giving full value to borrowing, and he quotes Lönnrot on a story-swapping session between Finnish, Russian, and Swedish fishers. He concludes with cautions against the Aryan theory of the Grimms and the Indianist theory of Benfey and Cosquin, but substitutes no dogma of his own. Independent invention, migration in both ancient and modern times, the combining of separate incidents in similar ways, and literary influences all play their part in the 'sphinx of popular tales.'[2]

When the evidence for borrowing in an historic period was clear, he reverted to Tylor's position that dissemination does not upset the evolutionary theory, for the 'receiving folk' must be receptive to the ideas of the 'transmitting folk.' He developed this point in his presidential address to the International Folk-Tale Congress of 1891.[3] Confronted two years later with the first comparative study of a folktale, *Cinderella*, by Marian Roalfe Cox, to which he supplied a preface, he was disappointed to find so few ancient and savage variants among the three hundred and forty-five. 'Perhaps the examination of *Cinderella* statistics will lead to nothing very remarkable,' he observes wryly in a Ship for June, 1893. Yet in October, 1896, he restates the basic article of his creed. 'All peoples notoriously tell the same myths, fairy tales, fables, and improper stories, repeat the same proverbs, are amused by the same riddles or devinettes, and practise the same, or closely analogous, religious rites and mysteries.'[4]

His later introductions to collections of tales are brief repetitions of the creed. He was happy to introduce Mrs. Langloh Parker's *Australian Legendary Tales* (1896) and *More Australian Legendary Tales* (1898), for here was the savage mind at close view. The latter year he also ushered before the public an edition of *The Arabian Nights Entertainments*. Once more he commented on savage sur-

[1] *Perrault's Popular Tales*. Edited from the Original Edition, with Introduction, &c. by Andrew Lang (Oxford, 1888), p. xxxii.
[2] *Ibid.*, p. cxv.
[3] *The International Folk-Lore Congress, 1891, Papers and Transactions*, ed. Joseph Jacobs and Alfred Nutt (London, 1892), 1–12.
[4] *Longman's Magazine*, XXVIII (October, 1896), 632.

vivals in folktales in a Preface to Elphinstone Dayrell's *Folk Stories from Southern Nigeria* (1910). In a final statement, his 1911 article on 'Tale' for the eleventh edition of the *Encyclopaedia Britannica*, he accepted oral dissemination along with cultural uniformity as a factor explaining the diffusion of folktales.

Alone of his co-workers Lang also flirted with the ballad and its teasing problems. As early as 1875 he entered the controversy with his article on 'Ballads' in the *Encyclopaedia Britannica*, in which he took a communalist position. In *Longman's* he printed a Suffolk fragment about a mysterious 'Duke of Bedford,' hoping to get more information, and Scotch texts of 'Jon Come Kisse Me Now' and 'Oh gin I were where Gaudie rins.'[1] The work of Francis Child evoked his admiration and led him to say that the English had sadly neglected their own folksongs. In one Ship he refers to a correspondence with Child, who conceded merit for Lang's argument on the antiquity of the ballad of the 'Queen's Marie.'[2] He wrote Child's obituary in *Folk-Lore* and reviewed with praise the Sargent-Kittredge one-volume selection from Child.[3] He assembled *Border Ballads* in 1888 and *A Collection of Ballads* in 1897, observing 'Perhaps the editor may be allowed to say that he does not merely plough with Professor Child's heifer, but has made a study of ballads from his boyhood.'[4] In one excursion into folksong materials in Europe, he wrote an introduction for Domenico Comparetti's *Traditional Poetry of the Finns* (1899). As an Homeric scholar he was interested in the composition of the *Kalevala* and the popular poetry of savages and their similarities and differences.

Over the years Lang modified his original position on communal origins. In his articles on balladry for Chambers' *Cyclopaedia of English Literature* (1901) and in 'Notes on Ballad Origins' (1903) in *Folk-Lore*, he accepted individual contributions and re-creation as components of the 'popular fancy,' which he still maintained to be the source of folksongs. Scottish blood prevailed over the scientific temper when he edited *Sir Walter Scott and the Border Minstrelsy* (1910) and defended Sir Walter's loose editorial methods.

That puckish spirit of controversy which marks so much of Lang's scholarly writing and which, fortunately for him, found an audience which could stomach tedious debates, dominates his folklore work. His reviews, essays, and books were primarily running

---

[1] *Ibid.*, XVII (December, 1890), 217–18; *ibid.*, XXVII (November, 1895), 107–8; *ibid.*, XXIII (February, 1894), 436–7.
[2] *Ibid.*, XXVII (November, 1895), 108.
[3] The obituary appeared in *Folk-Lore*, VII (1896), 416–17, and the review in *ibid.*, XVI (1905), 238–40.
[4] *A Collection of Ballads* (London, 1910), p. xxii.

duels, demolishing the enemy's hypothesis and defending his own, and when arguments languished, his scholarship drooped. Seminal ideas are scattered through the Ships, which for want of foils he never followed up. In one column he criticizes a literary history for neglecting the connections between folklore and literature. 'The relations between the popular genius, in *Volkslieder* and *Märchen*, on one side, and accomplished literary art, epic, lyric, dramatic, on the other, deserve careful and adequate study,' he observes, adding that a very interesting book might be written on the evolution of literature from this point of view. 'There is a come and go, a va-et-vient, or running debtor and creditor account between the popular and the artistic genius,' he muses, and thinks of Perrault and Theocritus, Scott, and Coleridge. Yet this book, which he was supremely qualified to write, never emerged from his three-page essay, and he returned to his dreams and phantasms.[1] In other Ships he glances at the folklore of the stage and folk anecdotes of professors, and he makes shrewd observations on heroic legend in explaining why Joan of Arc failed to magnetize legends because '. . . the Maid had a great dislike for nonsense and a sharp tongue. . . . A person, however extraordinary, who habitually adopts this line does not encourage the growth of Folk Lore, and there is much more about Wallace than about Joan of Arc.'[2] Lang's fertile mind roved widely over topics being investigated by folklorists today, but the intellectual currents of his time channelled his protean talents into psycho-folklore and the hunt for survivals.

[2   GEORGE   LAURENCE   GOMME]

'I should like it to be settled once for all that folk-lore is a science,' declared George Laurence Gomme (1853–1916) in the keynote statement to his life work.[3] The 'organization man' of the great team, he served as honourable secretary, director, and from 1890 through 1894, president of The Folk-Lore Society. His zeal for the science of folklore was coupled with a scholarly devotion to the history and government of London—an outgrowth of his position as statistical officer and Clerk of the London County Council, the central municipal governing body in England. Especially did he relish the prehistory of English village institutions. These often entwined interests gave a special character to Gomme's research,

[1] *Longman's Magazine*, XXVI (October, 1895), 649–52.
[2] *Ibid.*, XXIV (June, 1894), 214.
[3] *Folk-Lore Journal*, III (1885), 1.

which looked backward to early British man rather than to early black, yellow, or red man.

In 1880 Gomme published his first book on folklore, *Primitive Folk-Moots; or Open-Air Assemblies in Britain*, which he dedicated to William John Thoms. Here he introduced his method of utilizing current folktales, customs, and usages as data for reconstructing an institutional antiquity of prehistoric Britain. Folktales might indeed preserve mythological conceptions, as so many commentators had stressed, but for Gomme their prime secrets lay in the primitive political institutions they mirrored.

But the most archaic traces of popular opinion as to the open-air meetings of assemblies are to be found in some of our traditional folk-tales. The folk-tale is itself a survival from primitive times, and in some cases it has brought away with its fairy narrative remnants of archaic social existence.[1]

He broadened his investigations in 1883 with *Folk-Lore Relics of Early Village Life* and in 1890 with *The Village Community, with Special Reference to the Origin and Form of its Survivals in Britain*. Amplifying these particular studies into a general method, he produced *Ethnology in Folk-Lore* (1892) and his most ambitious work, *Folk-Lore as an Historical Science* (1908). As an indication of how his studies overlapped, in this last work he devotes much attention to a treasure legend tied to London Bridge, in support of his thesis that folk traditions contain important historical information; the legend revealed the strategic site of London in Roman times.

In another series of books, Gomme dug into the past of his beloved London. Tylor himself had remarked in passing on the splendid opportunities open to the antiquary in exploring the capital city, where one could find 'relics side by side of the London mammoth and the London savage.'[2] Gomme's titles on this subject included *The London County Council* (1888), *London in the Reign of Victoria, 1837–97* (1898), *The Governance of London* (1907), *The Making of London* (1912) and *London* (1914). Only in their central city of Londinium had the Romans left an ethnic impress on tradition, for they were too far advanced and too physically aloof in their walled cities from the agricultural Aryans to disturb their sacred tribal organization. Related publications were *The Literature of Local Institutions* (1886) and *Lectures on the Principles of Local Government* (1897), the last being lectures delivered at the London School of Economics.

[1] *Primitive Folk-Moots* (London, 1880), p. 201.
[2] E. B. Tylor, *Primitive Culture* (London, 1871), I, 53.

On the recommendation of the Council of The Folk-Lore Society, Gomme prepared a trim *Handbook of Folklore* (1890), designed to serve amateur collectors in the countryside. Hartland contributed the section on the folktale. After some discussion as to its scope, Gomme prevailed in his view that the entries should be confined to the materials of English tradition. (In the revision and considerable expansion undertaken by Charlotte Burne in 1914, the entries were adapted to overseas collectors among primitive peoples.) The *Handbook* stands up well today in the ordering of its categories and the clarity of its leading questions, designed to aid the novice and stimulate the country parson or schoolteacher to inquire among the locals for items of tradition. As the first collector's manual in English it marks a milestone, codifying the folk materials assembled since Brand. The questionnaire form rendered visible the main lines of tradition already established and encouraged further additions.

In addition to his own monographs, Gomme was extremely active with editorial and bibliographical projects. Between 1886 and 1905 he served as general editor for The Gentleman's Magazine Library, a classified selection from the file of the richly stocked *Gentleman's Magazine*, covering the period from 1731 to 1868. Of the twenty-nine volumes edited, sixteen dealt with the topography of English counties, and six others with *Archaeology* and *Architectural Antiquities* and *Romano-British Remains*. Of direct concern for the folklorist were the volumes dealing with *Manners and Customs* (1883), *Dialect, Proverbs and Word-Lore* (1884), *Popular Superstitions* (1884), and *English Traditional Lore* (1885). For much of the eighteenth and nineteenth centuries the *Gentleman's Magazine* notably served the antiquarian interests of cultivated gentry. In sorting out and reprinting their notes, essays, and correspondence, Gomme stimulated an aspect of the folklore movement that complemented fieldwork: the location and reprinting of the folklore buried in manuscripts and local printed sources. In another series of five titles, *Chap-books and Folk-Lore Tracts*, which he co-edited with H. B. Wheatley for the Villon Society in 1885, Gomme edited two volumes himself, *The History of Thomas Hickathrift* and *Mother Bunch's Closet*. Chapbooks often constituted the only extant evidence of well-known folktales and legends for the period before field-collecting. Gomme's Introduction describing the exploits of Hickathrift, the legendary strong man from Northumberland, is a model paper on the interweaving of oral and subliterary traditions.

Of all the great team, Gomme was the most persistent and determined champion of the scientific credentials of folklore. The Folk-Lore Society provided the agency to establish rigorous standards, and the more influential the Society became, the further toward maturity would the science advance. In his first annual report as honourable secretary of The Folk-Lore Society in 1879, he charted the field and defined its goals. In his sweeping view, faithful to the new doctrine of Tylor and Lang, folklore embraced all the culture of the people excluded from the official religion and history.

It represents itself in civilized history by strange and uncouth customs; superstitious associations with animals, birds, flowers, trees, and topographical objects, and with the events of human life; the belief in witchcraft, fairies, and spirits; the traditional ballads and proverbial sayings incident to particular localities; the retention of popular names for hills, streams, caverns, springs, tumuli; fountains, fields, trees, &c., and all such out-of-the-way lore. In savage life all these things are extant, not as survivals but as actual portions of the prevalent state of society. The Folk-Lore survivals of civilization and the Folk-Status of savage tribes both, therefore, belong to the primitive history of mankind; and in collecting and printing these relics of one epoch, from two such widely different sources, the Folk-Lore Society will produce that necessary comparison and illustration which is of so much service to the anthropologist.[1]

He concluded with a strenuous call to the Society to engage in *collecting materials*, a task that must precede the 'equally important work' of placing these collections 'rightly in the scientific divisions of human history.'

In spite of his vast debt to Tylor, Gomme was fully conscious of the services rendered by earlier antiquaries, and he paid them tribute in a piece on 'Folk-Lore and the Folk-Lore Society' in 1880 in the first number of *The Antiquary*. 'In Folk-Lore . . . we have a most valuable relic of olden times,' he began. 'We owe its title, if not its introduction, to the deep insight of a now veteran antiquary—Mr. Thoms.' But even before Thoms, Sir Francis Palgrave had 'discovered the archaeology hid in our popular superstitions and customs, and his article in the *Quarterly Review* remains a sort of general text to this day.' Sir Walter Scott came in for his meed of praise for having 'dipped very deeply into all these things—using them, as we all know, to the best advantage in his incomparable novels, and bringing them into historical

---

[1] *Folk-Lore Record*, II (1879), 4.

prominence in his "Letters on Demonology and Witchcraft" and in the introduction to his *Minstrelsy of the Scottish Border*.' Thanks to these innovators, a firm interest in the study of popular customs and superstitions now existed; Brand's *Popular Antiquities* had been republished; new specialized studies and labours were under way. 'And thus the work of collection began and is still going on, and should continue until every scrap of Folk-Lore is recorded in print.' Now raised to the 'platform of the sciences,' folklore offers to the student of comparative jurisprudence and of primitive politics clues he could obtain nowhere else. Indeed, the first question the folklorist should ask himself after he completes his field mission is, 'What does my collection illustrate in the life of primitive man, and how, therefore, can it best be fitted in with what is already known?' For an example, marriage customs among primitive peoples formerly carried much more weight than in their present form in modern survivals, involving inter-community and inter-tribal relations, and thus should not be classified among domestic affairs.[1]

This is Gomme the exhorter, encourager, organizer, and promoter of folklore researches. There was another Gomme, the propounder of a theory which would employ the materials of folklore to reconstruct the institutional life of pre-Aryan Britain. The shift in Gomme's thought from his initial orthodox Tylorian survivalism to his final position is seen in his last statement on 'Folklore' in 1913 for James Hastings' *Encyclopaedia of Religion and Ethics*. There he declared that savage custom, rite, and belief should not be classed as folklore, although they often are because they invite close comparison with the materials of folklore, but such classifying confuses the respective divisions of anthropology and folklore. A distinction between traditional and psychological folklore, which had unfortunately been lumped together, should be made. Traditional folklore belongs to groups of people who do not share in the towering civilization that looms over them but who look back to an earlier day. Psychological folklore pertains to persons or generations of persons of stunted mental capacity unable to comprehend the phenomena of nature or the results of civilization. Under this heading are found only beliefs, not customs or rites, and they relate only to the present.[2]

While Lang in his presidential address to the 1891 folklore congress had declared he could not distinguish between anthropology

---

[1] *The Antiquary*, I (1880), 13–15.
[2] 'Folklore,' in *Encyclopaedia of Religion and Ethics*, ed. James Hastings (Edinburgh, 1908–15), VI, 57–9.

and folklore, Gomme insisted on a clear division of labour and objectives. 'Mr. Gomme at first stood almost alone in his protest that the lore of the uncultivated classes of a civilised state must not be treated in the same way as the lore of the absolutely uncultured savage,' Nutt stated at the time. Gomme wished to restrict the term folklore to the former group, and 'to define it as the "scientific study of the survivals of archaic beliefs, customs, and traditions in modern times." '[1]

In effect, Gomme found his savages in Britain. Where Tylor and Lang debated about totemism among the Australian aborigines or the Red Indians or tribal Africans, Gomme looked for the primitive past on his own island. The distinction between Aryan civilization and savage culture so sharply drawn by the anthropological folklorists, and which he had initially accepted, gave way to a view of historic layers of ethnic cultures, divisible into pre-Aryan and Aryan, with Celtic, Roman, and Saxon subdivisions. Each invader has left his ethnic stamp on the conquered race below him in the evolutionary scale. By the analysis of survivals and the use of the comparative method the folklorist could reconstruct the historical sequence of these ethnic periods. He could illuminate the prehistory of savage Britain. Take totemism. Bringing together a mass of evidence in an 1889 article in the *Archaeological Review* on 'Totemism in Britain,' Gomme documented his thesis that early man in Britain worshipped totemic deities. He piled up one example after another of survival and relic illustrating totem belief and totem clan systems. Certain districts only preserved taboos against killing particular animals or birds, or even looking at or naming them, and the distribution pattern suggested physical areas once peopled by believers in totem ancestors. As one of hundreds of examples, Gomme cited a prejudice against white cows in Scotland, reported by Dalyell in his *The Darker Superstitions of Scotland*; Dalyell had speculated that the sentiment derived from a religious taboo once held against consuming the product of a sacred animal, and Gomme praised him for so shrewd a deduction made at a time (1834) when scientific principles and theories of folklore origins had not yet been advanced.

While the totem organization survived as a name system, it faded out by the time nomadic tribes became sedentary, and never entered the peasant life of the nation. Gomme's prize specimen, culled from an Irish collector, directly connected a family patronymic with an animal totem. 'In very ancient times some of the clan

[1] Alfred Nutt, 'Recent Archaeological Research, No. II, Folk-Lore,' *Archaeological Review*, III (1889), 74.

Coneely, one of the early septs of the county, were changed by "art magical" into seals; since then no Coneely can kill a seal without afterwards having bad luck. Seals are called Coneelys, and on this account many of the name changed it to Connolly.'[1]

The following year in *The Village Community*, Gomme hammered away at the prevalent view that Aryan peoples and civilization had created peasant village institutions. Looking to modern savage cultures, he pointed out features of Basuto, Dyak, and Fiji village social organization also surviving in Britain. Again, a year later, the International Folk-Lore Congress of 1891 afforded him opportunity to advance his thesis in a paper on 'The Non-Aryan Origin of Agricultural Institutions.'

> My proposition is that the history of the village community in Britain is the history of the economical condition of the non-Aryan aborigines; that the history of the tribal community is the history of the Aryan conquerors, who appear as overlords; and that the Romans, except as another wave of Aryan conquerors at an advanced stage of civilisation, had very little to do with shaping the village institutions of Britain.[2]

Where Lang and Hartland wished to peer back into the philosophy and cosmology of primitive man on some dark continent, particularly as expressed through myth, Gomme looked for the institutional forms of political and social life developed by the early inhabitants of the British Isles. He proposed still to employ the comparative method, and chose India as a chief testing ground, for here primitive economics and traditional religion interacted in daily village life and could throw light on the prehistoric state of village organization in Britain. In village India the ethnological folklorist could see peasant life whole; he no longer could do so in England, not only because primitive institutions had disintegrated but because the English state had obscured the true nature of peasant economic life by burying it under a network of manorial laws. The prehistory of village agriculture was not to be found in the history of English manorial custom, written from the point of view of the landowning class, but from the traditions of the peasantry themselves. In England an observer could still detect primitive economic habits, but only in conjunction with survivals of religious rite.

[1] 'Totemism in Britain,' *Archaeological Review*, III (1889), 219. The full article covers pages 217–42, 350–75.
[2] *The International Folk-Lore Congress, 1891, Papers and Transactions*, ed. Joseph Jacobs and Alfred Nutt (London, 1892), p. 356.

These peasant traditions survived from an earlier race van-
quished by the Aryan invader. In *Ethnology in Folklore* (1892),
Gomme emphasizes this belief to point up the contrast between his
position and the survivalism of Lang and Frazer. Savage customs
were not introduced into Scotland, Warwickshire, and Greece by
Scotchmen, Englishmen, and Greeks, but by pre-Aryans on a level
of culture with that of savage Africans. 'Has anyone attempted to
realise the effects of a permanent residence of a civilised people
amidst a lower civilisation, the members of which are cruel, crafty,
and unscrupulous?' he asked, and pointed to the stories by Feni-
more Cooper about the white man and his relations with the Red
Indians.[1] In England the racial distinction may no longer be
seen so starkly, but Gomme believed that the labourers in the
Cambridgeshire fens were little better than savages (and here he
anticipated the uncovering of remarkable oral traditions among
the Fenmen in the 1960's, indicative of a distinct subculture),
while Mrs. Bray has brought to view the 'Devonshire savage' in
her book of letters to Southey. The Arabian custom of well-worship
plainly survived in a decaying state as a non-Aryan cult in the
British Isles; changes could be analysed as a result of symbolism,
substitution, and amalgamation. As race succeeds race the beliefs
pass on; the peasants of the north counties still say that Peg o'Nell
of Ribble River claims a life every seven years, and so they share
with the savages of old the conviction that drowning persons
should not be rescued.

Gomme's theory came under attack from his successor to the
presidency, Alfred Nutt, who gave an address in 1898 on 'The Discrimination of Racial Elements in the Folklore of the British
Isles.[2] In effect, Nutt denied the possibility of such discrimination
in prehistoric times. In his closely reasoned argument, he contended
that a common literature and language in the Celtic-speaking,
Brythonic-speaking (Wales and Cornwall), and English-speaking
areas had obscured racial elements in folklore. The difficulties
presented in separating the Aryan races increased tenfold when
one sought to isolate pre-Aryan folk philosophy and folk literature
after a lapse of twenty-five hundred years. Folklore research along
racial lines should be confined to the historic record, and therefore
to Aryan groups, such as the Gael in Scotland and Ireland, who
had lived apart for three centuries.

Such tenets struck at Gomme's most cherished hypotheses, and
he marshalled his resources in rebuttal. In doing so, he drew upon

[1] *Ethnology in Folklore* (London, 1892), p. 41.
[2] Printed in *Folk-Lore*, IX (March, 1898), 30–52.

[227]

a memoir read to the British Association in 1896, which he now redrafted for a paper he read to The Folk-Lore Society on November 15, 1898: 'Ethnological Data in Folklore: A Criticism of the President's Address in January, 1898.' (It was reprinted in *Folk-Lore* the following year.)[1] Gomme stated his position forcefully. First, he would look to folk custom, ritual, and belief rather than to folk literature for ethnological survivals. Second, he would not confine himself to the historic record but would employ folklore independently to cast light on prehistory. Third, he would set forth a method for comparative folklore research along scientific lines.

This method was ingenious. Gomme postulated that a modern peasant custom could not simply be equated with a modern savage custom; both must be traced back to ancient savagery and considered in the full-fleshed social organization to which they once belonged. Surviving examples of beliefs and customs should be compared on the basis of their constituent elements, which would be divided into 'radicals' and 'divergences.' Recurring radical elements marked the line of decay. Applying this process of comparison and classification to surviving customs involving fire, Gomme perceived a system of fire-worship once associated with a prehistoric *tribal* civilization. In surviving practices he was able to recognize the ritual of carrying a sacred flame from the tribal fire to the household fire. The tribe can be identified as Aryan. Dissimilar customs therefore must belong to a pre-Aryan people.

The next step called for Gomme to locate on a map of Britain all the places where a particular custom was known, connecting these points with a straight line. If the physical map is then withdrawn, there remains the 'geographical test-figure.' A number of test figures may be constructed in turn and compared. Thus for customs of water-worship, which Gomme had reason to believe were non-Aryan, a very different test figure resulted from that produced by a survey of Aryan fire-customs.

By this method Gomme intended to trace folklore survivals from a fragmented present to a racially differentiated, clear-cut past. In certain ways he anticipated current folklore techniques such as motif-analysis and folk-atlas mapping. But his system rested on vulnerable hypotheses which were soon pricked by his close associates.

[1] *Folk-Lore*, X (June, 1899), 129–43. Gomme's paper read to the British Association in 1896 was printed in *Report of the British Association for the Advancement of Science* (London, 1896), 'On the Method of Determining the Value of Folklore as Ethnological Data,' pp. 626–56.

Nutt delivered 'A Reply to the Foregoing Criticism' at the same Society meeting, and it was printed immediately following Gomme's exposition.[1] The publisher reiterated the primacy of folk literature as a test of racial elements. Did not all the Greeks claim Homer as their bard long after their institutions and rituals had altered or withered? As for folk customs, Gomme has failed to allow for regional variations among the same racial stock in his concept of divergences. In plotting his maps he begins with the surviving customs to demonstrate historical settlements, but more properly he should have begun with historical evidence of population movements.

The climactic work of Gomme, his *Folk-Lore as an Historical Science*, instead of convincing his critics, led to further jabs. In a six-page review in *Folk-Lore*, Lang raised a series of pernickety questions. How can a fact revealed by tradition be proved correct except by historical methods? What does Gomme mean by the vague word 'tribal,' which he appears to use in opposition to 'agricultural'? How can he distinguish between English and Greek and ancient Egyptian racial folklore strains when they share so many elements in common with savages in Australia and Africa?[2] In his review in *Man*, Hartland challenged Gomme's theory of totemic origins being connected with primitive agricultural institutions and criticized his statement concerning '. . . the industrialism of early woman, from which originated the domestication of animals, the cultivation of fruits and cereals, and the appropriation of such trees and shrubs as were necessary to primitive economics. . . .'[3] Hartland pointed out that domestic animals and cultivated plants did not bulk large in savage totems, and that the notion of collective group worship contradicted the accepted theory of individual origins of totems.

Not his enemies but his friends levelled Gomme's proud edifice.[4]

[3   ALFRED   NUTT]

The folklorist truly deserving the name . . . must bring with him principles based upon world-wide inquiries; he must ever

[1] *Ibid.*, X (June, 1899), 143–9.   [2] *Ibid.*, XIX (1908), 241–6.
[3] Quoted in Hartland's review in *Man*, VIII (1908), No. 68, pp. 125–8.
[4] Criticisms of Gomme's survival theory in *The Village Community* are made by F. W. Maitland in 'The Survival of Archaic Communities,' *Law Quarterly Review*, IX (London, 1893), 36–50, esp. pp. 49–50. The editor, Sir Frederick Pollock, then appended a note suggesting *imitation* and *parallelism* as alternative explanations to *survival* of apparently archaic institutions.

be prepared to test the evidence yielded, say, by Berkshire or Devon, in the light of material gathered it may be in Greenland or Polynesia, vouched for by the oldest known records of humanity, or by the latest Antipodean newspaper.[1]

So in his third and final address as president of The Folk-Lore Society did Alfred Nutt (1856–1912) outline the rigorous and awesome demands to be faced by the aspiring student of folklore. In his own published writings he concentrated on Gaelic Ireland and Scotland in meaty essays, prefaces, notes, and papers, frequently in collaboration with others. In 1881 he printed in the *Folk-Lore Journal* a treatise on 'The Aryan Expulsion and Return Formula in the Folk and Hero Tales of the Celts.' Here Nutt was applying to Celtic traditions a pattern of heroic legend devised in the 1870's by the Austrian J. G. von Hahn. Nutt found correspondences that were not very close, and he concluded that Celtic hero stories were independent rather than borrowed, thus supporting the principle of universal cultural similarities so dear to Lang and the anthropological folklorists.

During the '80's, Nutt continued to write weighty papers on interrelated themes and in 1888 he brought them together under the title *Studies on the Legend of the Holy Grail, with Especial Reference to the Hypothesis of its Celtic Origin*. This formed Publication XXIII of The Folk-Lore Society. The author bemoaned the fact that no British Grimm had done for Celtic mythology what Jacob had done for Teutonic. Patiently he amassed evidence to demonstrate that the Grail romances had not sired a debased and shrunken folklore found today on peasant lips but had themselves derived from a worthy and poetic folk tradition. In the *Märchen* and legends collected by Campbell and Grimm, telling of a hero robbed of magic gifts who regains them or of a sleeping hero surrounded by his warriors in a magic castle, Nutt perceived incidents related to the Grail story. The magic castle vanishes at dawn, since sleep is brother to death and night brother to the otherworld. So does the current folktale embody the older myth. But the folktale continues, coexisting with and enduring long after the romance has been buried in manuscript. The two independent offshoots betray a startling 'kinship of moral ideas,' clearly the result of the fixed laws that govern the 'spontaneous, flower-like character' of folk tradition.

The few partisans of the theory that folk-tradition is only a later and weakened echo of the higher culture of the race are

[1] *Folk-Lore*, X (1899), 71.

13. GEORGE LAURENCE GOMME

14. ALICE BERTHA GOMME

invited to study the present case. A Celtic tale, after supplying an important element to the Christianised Grail legend, has gone on its way entirely unaffected by the new shape which that legend assumed, and yet it has worked out a moral conception of fundamental likeness to one set forth in the legend. It would be difficult to find a more perfect instance of the spontaneous, evolutional character of tradition contended for by what, in default of a better name, must be called the anthropological school of folk-lorists.[1]

The moral basis of romance and folktale is equally evident. In the one case, wealth, learning, power, or salvation is the reward; in the other, the fairy-tale ending brings happiness and affection. Nutt was always uneasy about his admitted preference for Celtic over Germanic examples of romance-like folktales, but claimed that 'the romances are historically associated with Celtic tradition.'

Every year brought a noteworthy contribution. In 1889 in the *Archaeological Review* Nutt wrote valuable appraisals of 'Celtic Myth and Saga—A Survey of Recent Literature' and 'Recent Archaeological Research—No. II, Folk-Lore,' assessing the state of folklore studies in the 1880's. In 1890 he provided one hundred pages of comparative notes to the Scottish collection assembled and translated by the Reverend D. MacInnes, *Waifs and Strays of Celtic Tradition. Argyllshire Series.—No. II. Folk and Hero Tales.* The same year he contributed to Douglas Hyde's *Beside the Fire; A Collection of Gaelic Folk Stories.* In 1891 he presented a comprehensive discussion on 'Problems of Heroic Legend' at the International Folk-Lore Congress held in London.[2] In 1893 he printed in *Folk-Lore* 'The Lai of Eliduc and the *Märchen* of Little Snow-White,' offering a case study of his special thesis. The Scottish Gaelic tale of Gold-tree and Silver-tree, newly collected in the Highlands, belonged to the same story type which in the tenth century had produced the *lai* of Eliduc; hence the medieval romance emanated from a mythic narrative shared by the Aryan peoples.[3] In 1895 he considered the belief system of the Irish peasant in his Preface to *Tales of the Fairies and of the Ghost World, Collected from Oral Tradition in South-west Munster* by Jeremiah Curtin, an American folklorist of Irish parentage.

[1] *Studies in the Legend of the Holy Grail* (London, 1888), pp. 257–8.
[2] Printed in *The International Folk-Lore Congress, 1891, Papers and Transactions*, ed. Joseph Jacobs and Alfred Nutt (London, 1892), pp. 113–34.
[3] 'The Lai of Eliduc and the Märchen of Little Snow-White,' *Folk-Lore*, III (1892), 26–48.

In his major folklore publication Nutt collaborated with the well-known Celtic scholar Kuno Meyer in a two-volume edition of a medieval Celtic manuscript which Meyer translated and edited and Alfred published. This was *The Voyage of Bran* (1895–7), bearing the subtitle 'With an Essay upon the Irish vision of the happy otherworld and the Celtic doctrine of rebirth' by Alfred Nutt. The essay on 'The Happy Otherworld in the Mythico-Romantic Literature of the Irish,' occupied over two hundred pages in the first volume; all of volume two was devoted to 'The Celtic Doctrine of Re-birth.' Applying the survival theory of Tylor and Lang, Nutt made extensive use of nineteenth-century fairylore to elucidate the beliefs found in ancient Irish literature.

In his first of three presidential addresses to The Folk-Lore Society, in 1897, Nutt further developed his favourite theme. His topic, 'The Fairy Mythology of English Literature: Its Origin and Nature,' dealt with a matter explored earlier in the century by Halliwell (whose *Illustrations of Fairy Mythology* he cited as a main source), Thoms, and Douce, but with the altered premises of the anthropological school plus his own Celtic bias. In the 'wonderful half-century: 1580–1630,' the fairy realm depicted by Shakespeare and reproduced by a host of contemporary and later poets —Drayton, Ben Jonson, Herrick, Milton—faithfully represented an ancient fairy creed. 'What I shall essay to prove is that in reality sixteenth-century folk-belief and mediaeval fairy-romance derive their origin from one and the same set of beliefs and rites. . . .'[1] Nutt developed his argument with the aid of living folklore. The same term, *aes sidhe*, designating the ancient pantheon known as the Tuatha de Danaan, is heard in current Irish traditions and is found in Irish manuscripts preserving tales from nine hundred to eleven hundred years old. In England the Roman conquest snapped the continuity of fairylore, but the Celtic evidence clearly illustrates the kinship of impish Puck and courtly Oberon in heroic sagas and agricultural myths. The Irish fairies guard the flocks and herds and protect the vegetation. To the possible objection that Shakespeare's fairies are Teutonic rather than Celtic, Nutt replies that in pre-Christian antiquity Teuton and Celt were as one, just as modern German and Irish peasants share common beliefs. In descriptions of the Dionysian rituals can be seen a primitive, sacrificial cult of the soil common to all Europe. 'Have we not in rites such as these the source of tales found everywhere in the peasant fairy lore of Europe and represented with special vividness in Celtic folklore?'[2]

[1] *Folk-Lore*, VIII (1897), 32. The whole address covers pp. 29–53.   [2] *Ibid.*, p. 48.

Since Shakespeare's time, the elemental, capricious powers reflected in the fairies have been degraded by latter-day writers into 'simpering puppets.' So Nutt joined his veneration for Celtic lore with due esteem for the Bard.

This line of thought led Nutt in his address of 1898 to challenge the ideas of Gomme by stressing Aryan against pre-Aryan races and folk literature against folk custom as the most rewarding work areas for the folklorist.

In 1899 Nutt addressed the Society on 'Britain and Folklore' and spoke in an eloquent vein of sophisticated nationalism. The British Isles were favoured by a variety of circumstances for the complex study of folklore. They possessed the primitive stratum of 'archaic literature' in a far better state of preservation than it was found in Germany, France, Scandinavia, or Russia. Their imperialist position brought the savage races of the world under the same rule as the peasant at home. Nutt referred to an address by his successor as president, Sidney Hartland, to the Gloucester Philosophical Society emphasizing the practical value of folklore to the legislator. The publisher went on to draw a parallel between modern Britain and ancient Rome, whose tribunes recognized the customary laws of the less advanced peoples whom they governed.[1]

Beginning in 1899, Nutt published and contributed to a delightful series of pamphlets designed for the intellectually curious public, *Popular Studies in Mythology, Romance and Folk-Lore*. These booklets, which usually ran from forty to eighty pages, presented the high points of their complex topics in straightforward, nontechnical prose, and supplied a selected bibliography for further readings. Nutt wrote the first, on *Celtic and Mediaeval Romance* (1899), and followed this with No. 3, *Ossian and the Ossianic Literature Connected with His Name* (1899), No. 6, *The Fairy Mythology of Shakespeare* (1900), and No. 8, *Cuchulainn, the Irish Achilles* (1900).

In 1910, the year of Nutt's death, there appeared in *Folk-Lore*, along with his obituary, a succinct final statement, 'How Far is the Lore of the Folk Racial?' He reviewed continental scholarship from the Renaissance on as it shifted from an overly national to an overly universal basis, and restated his own credo that the artistic folklore visible in Britain offered the best chance of examining racial stores. For if the political chieftain of old had compromised his institutions with the conqueror, the bard fought to retain his poetic inheritance.[2]

---

[1] The address was printed in *Folk-Lore*, X (March, 1899), pp. 71–86.
[2] 'How Far is the Lore of the Folk Racial?' *Folk-Lore*, XXI (1910), 379–84.

The sum of this solid and substantial folklore scholarship is a unified achievement, applying the doctrine of survivals to illuminate medieval Celtic literature through modern Gaelic folklore. Nutt saw in his own speciality of Celtic studies the opportunity to test on an uncluttered ground the perennial question of folklore origins, early or late, savage or post-Christian. In his survey article of 1889, 'Celtic Myth and Saga,' he referred ominously to exponents of the 'revelationist' position who beheld in Norse mythology, Haitian voodoo, Arthurian romance, and European folktales the fragments of classical and Christian legends. To clarify the issue Nutt turned to analogies:

> On the sea shore we may pick up fossils from which we can reconstruct the history, reaching back into a past incalculably remote, of lands and seas with their distinctive floras and faunas; we may also pick up worn and rounded bits of what we with difficulty recognise as fragments of ginger beer bottles flung away perhaps only six months before. According to which of these two analogies are we to classify the items of folk-lore? Mr. Leland has recently told us that the gipsies all over Europe and in many parts of Africa have a superstitious regard for the Maria Theresa thaler; are other widespread superstitions of equally recent date?

He then drove home his claim.

> In answering these questions the importance of Celtic tradition cannot be over-estimated. No other Aryan civilisation has developed itself so independently of the two great influences, Hellenic and Hebraic, which have moulded the modern world; nowhere else is the course of development less perplexed by cross currents; nowhere else can the great issues be kept more steadily in view.[1]

For the Celticist, the enemy lay not with the heavenly mythologists but with the revelationists who would eliminate his pagan Aryans as the artistic troubadours of folk literature. Surprisingly, Nutt considered the anthropological folklorist and comparative mythologist as basically united in their studies of myths, legends, ritual and legal customs, and traditions. From their controversy of the past twenty years, the investigators of Aryan and non-Aryan races had learned to make common cause in the 'orthodox' doctrine which has now won acceptance. It is this doctrine that the

[1] 'Celtic Myth and Saga—A Survey of Recent Literature,' *Archaeological Review*, II (September, 1888–February, 1889), 136.

so-called revelationists, like former Prime Minister Gladstone, are now challenging with their theory—very occasionally demonstrable—of folklore as degenerate superstition coming in the wake of revealed Christianity.[1]

So wrote Nutt, who as a close observer of and participant in these disputations was able to set down a first-hand record of this transitional chapter in the history of folklore. He retraces the nineteenth-century growth of interest in Aryan philology and mythology which by the 1850's had established as cultural norms of a single race the mythologies of ancient India, Greece, and Scandinavia, embodied in the Vedas, the Homeric epics, and the Eddas. Alongside them are to be measured the beliefs of folklore. Kelly's *Curiosities of Indo-European Folk-Lore and Tradition* is cited as a representative popular treatment using this method. Then came the researches of Wilhelm Mannhardt in Germany, beginning with his *Germanische Mythen* in 1858, which only slowly compelled scholars to recognize that many rustic rites and conceptions could not be referred to the official mythologies. In England, Tylor and Lang were elaborating the system based on the unity of myth and rite among all races.

Indeed, the history of our study of late is very largely that of Mr. Lang's researches, of the influence they have exercised, of the comment and opposition they have called forth. When the Folk-Lore Society elected him to its presidential chair last year, every genuine folk-lorist recognised the election as at once an act of justice and a manifesto; the present generation of students had put their master in his rightful place. Mr. Lang was the first to bring the facts of savage mythology to bear upon that theory which resolved the god and hero tales of the various Aryan tribes into a series of nature-myths. . . . But along with . . . Mannhardt's sympathy for the neglected and rustic sides of mythology, with Professor Tylor's divinatory grasp of the psychological attitude of uncultured man, Mr. Lang displayed that interest in, and that feeling for the growth and nature of cult and institution which is one of the most marked features of the modern historical spirit. He thus

---

[1] 'Its partisans hold with Professor Bugge that the Norse mythology is in the main a retelling of classic fable and Christian legend; with Dr. Gaster that Folk-tales are mostly later than Christianity; with W. Forster that the Arthurian romances have nothing Celtic about them, but are simple exercises of the individual fancy upon well-worn romantic themes largely derived from the East; and . . . with Mr. Newell that Voodoo rites are not African in their origin but are a simple echo of European witch superstitions imported into Hayti in the seventeenth century' (*ibid.*, p. 136).

attracted the support of many students of the classical mythologies who had found the Aryan nature-myth system too
doctrinaire in its methods and too capricious in its results, and
had turned to the ritual side of religion, as affording a surer
basis for investigation.[1]

What was the orthodoxy which Lang ministered as high priest?
Nutt restated the dogmas succinctly: The belief and fancy of the
relatively uncultured European peasant and the absolutely uncultured savage are substantially the same, and observations made
in the one case may be used to supplement and control observations
made in the other. Nutt speaks of the 'archaeological' and 'ethnological' folklorist who complement each other's work in happy
combination, and he looks for the same precision and 'reign of law'
in folklore as in the geology of Lyell and the archaeology of the
modern excavator. 'In the January number of this *Review*, Mr.
Arthur Evans supplies an admirable example of this method in his
discussion of the date and meaning of Stonehenge; he seeks a clue
to the mystery among practices still prevalent in India and in the
Caucasus.'[2] So will the student of the fragmented creed of the
European peasantry seek clarification from the full forms of ritual
and myth among Redskin and Negro.

Thus in midstream Nutt reviewed the past, assessed the present,
and forecast the future of folklore studies. The evolutionists can
point happily to the original work done by Frazer on totemism
among savages, by Karl Pearson on matriarchalism among the
ancient Germans, and by Gomme on the origin of local English
institutions of the pre-Roman period. In their inquiries lay proof
that 'the facts of folk-lore, when interpreted in the light of the
evolution theory, may affect problems with which at first sight they
have nothing in common.'[3] On the negative side, Nutt realizes that
many of the earlier collections were made under the inspiration of
outmoded theories, and hence the enormous data of folklore need
to be reco-ordinated. Moving toward a common front, active members of the new Folk-Lore Society had engaged in a spirited discussion of the 'science of folk-lore' in Volume II of the *Folk-Lore
Journal* in 1879, and in committee had laboured to bring forth a
'Handbook to the Science of Folk-Lore' with especial attention
to tales and customs. This handbook would enable future collectors
to assemble their materials in a form most adaptable to the uses

[1] 'Recent Archaeological Research—No. II, Folk-Lore,' *Archaeological Review*, III
(April, 1889), 78.
[2] *Ibid.*, pp. 75-6.
[3] *Ibid.*, p. 85.

of the evolutionists. In this way the proper direction of the science seemed assured.

The calm confidence of Nutt and his colleagues in their principles and programme was always a shade disturbed by the 'borrowing theory,' most successfully applied to folktales. Nutt gave this diffusionist thesis a grudging nod.

> It assumes that the myths, legends, ritual and legal customs, and traditions which form the subject-matter of the studies both of comparative mythology and of folk-lore, are to be regarded not as the fossil remains by which the sequence of strata in the mental and social evolution of mankind can be determined, but as the distorted and degraded fragments of religious and social systems with which we are familiar at first hand. It postulates that the phenomena under consideration existed in an original and perfect shape in some definite centre, whence they were diffused, suffering change in the process. . . . In the study of folk-tales, the borrowing-theory has never lacked adherents since the publication of Benfey's *Pantschatantra*, the overwhelming erudition of which gave the theory standing and authority.[1]

The scholar-publisher then accorded recognition to Theodor Benfey's French disciple, Emmanuel Cosquin, editor of the *Contes populaires de Lorraine*, and to William Alexander Clouston, whose painstaking but carefully circumscribed treatises in 'comparative storyology' had given credit to the borrowing theory, concealing its vagueness and looseness. This searching appraisal showed how intensely Nutt had thought through his intellectual position.

In the following years Nutt pursued evolutionism with his own Celtic-Gaelic slant. The one question he continually raised throughout his prefaces, notes, and monographs was the relationship between the living folklore of the Gaelic-speaking peasant and the ancient Irish romances. His predestined answer boldly upheld the continuity of the fairy belief for a thousand years. In 'the pre-Christian kings of the euhemerising annalists, the wizard champions of the bardic reciters, the ruined angels of the Christian moralist,' he perceived the 'good people' known in the current tales of Irish peat-cutters.[2] Unlike the rest of Europe, reft by the Reformation, in Ireland the older and newer creeds blend harmoniously. Traces

---

[1] *Ibid.*, pp. 79–80.
[2] Preface to Jeremiah Curtin, *Tales of the Fairies and of the Ghost World* (London, 1895), p. vii.

of the great agricultural festivals of the past (Aryan, not pre-Aryan as Gomme would have it), at which fairy deities were ritually honoured, are found in modern tales. Where the folklorist usually had only the ancient record or the modern folklore with which to work, in Ireland he possessed both links in the chain extending from past to present. Concrete examples confirmed this view; Jeremiah Curtin's tale of John Shea and the treasure preserved the machinery of archaic Gaelic romance and even the pristine name of the 'mythic marvel-land,' Lochlin, but the narration is ascribed to a man who died in 1847. So too the powers of a pagan wizard-lord are easily transferred to St. Martin. 'What a lesson for those to whom the saint's presence suggests a late and purely Christian origin for the whole story!'[1] Nutt is delighted to get in his dig at the revelationists. One tale, of fairy dwellers in a cromlech mound, seems to support the hypothesis of David MacRitchie that the fairies are actually race memories of an underground pigmy people; but Nutt counters with the thought that these mounds are sanctified graves, and he wonders whether the fairy belief has not sprung out of ancestor-worship and, after a brilliant poetical interlude, is now reverting to its first phase.

The fairy belief is obviously as tenacious as the ghost belief is tenuous, Nutt conjectures, in appraising the two classes of stories in Curtin's collection. The ghost seems a late intruder, rarely evident in early Gaelic legend. Reluctant to concede a post-Christian development without a countersuggestion, Nutt speculated as to whether the idea of ghosts could not actually have derived from an 'older, ruder race' than the Aryan Celts. To avoid the revelationists he would even accept Gomme's pre-Aryanism!

All the complex questions arising from the more than thousand-year stretch of Irish literature and fairylore should be referred to a central condition. This is the opposition and harmonizing of the Gaelic agricultural ritualism and romantic mythology with an alien, Christian ritualism and romance. Witchcraft might well be a by-product of the collision between the two faiths. The fairy belief has continued underneath the Christian overlay, and preserves elements of pre-Christian worship. Thus the mortal of modern legend borne to fairyland for a fleeting period that turns out to be a lengthy span may once have been an actual participant in an agricultural revel. Carried away by the ecstasy of the rite, he could indeed have lost all sense of time and space. The factor that Nutt discounted was literary invention. If the bards no longer romanced

[1] Preface to Jeremiah Curtin, *Tales of the Fairies and of the Ghost World* (London, 1895), p. vii.

about Finn and Cuchulainn, the peasants continue yet to tell their unadorned tales.[1]

In his general discussions on problems of folklore, Nutt asserted the distinctive quality of Gaelic expression. Writing on heroic legend and the question of the historic basis of tradition, he singled out the father and son combat as a mythical pan-Aryan tale coming to finest flower in the Celtic version of Cuchulainn and Connla and the Persian version of Sohrab and Rustum.[2]

Paying tribute in her obituary to Nutt in *Folk-Lore*, Jessie Weston commended his valiant fight for the principle that medieval romance might be elucidated through modern folklore, and that folk tradition, not literary composition, formed the backbone of the old romances. Foreign critics had scorned Mr. Nutt's efforts. Then in 1910 John Lawson attempted to span classical mythology and contemporary tradition in *Modern Greek Folklore and Ancient Greek Religion*, bridging an even wider span and honouring the principle for which the folklorist-publisher fought so valiantly.[3]

[4 EDWIN SIDNEY HARTLAND]

'The time may come when the conquests of folk-lore shall be reckoned among the most remarkable and in their results the most important achievements of inductive reasoning,' wrote Edwin Sidney Hartland (1848–1927) in the *Folk-Lore Journal* in 1885.[4] He had begun his donations of thoughtful, wide-ranging articles and reviews the year before, and for forty years he remained a steadfast and impressive contributor.

The Gloucester solicitor's interests first centred on folk narratives. In 1890 he brought out a compact edition of *English Fairy and other Folk Tales*, judiciously selected from the available sources, which were all too rarely first-hand oral texts. But he captured the oral tradition in its secondary forms in chapbooks, county collections, and periodicals. In 1891 he produced a masterly treatise, *The Science of Fairy Tales, An Enquiry into the Fairy Mythology*, applying the doctrine of survivals to the tales and ideas of savages and peasants. Its opening chapter on 'The Art of Story-Telling'

---

[1] 'The Celtic Doctrine of Re-birth,' in *The Voyage of Bran* (London, 1897), II, 226; *The Fairy Mythology of Shakespeare* (London, 1900), p. 29.
[2] 'Problems of Heroic Legend,' *The International Folk-Lore Congress, 1891, Papers and Transactions* (London, 1892), p. 128.
[3] Jessie L. Weston, 'Alfred Nutt: an Appreciation,' *Folk-Lore*, XXI (1910), 512–14. In the same volume, pp. 335–7, Edward Clodd wrote 'In Memoriam: Alfred Nutt.'
[4] In a symposium on 'The Science of Folk-Lore,' *Folk-Lore Journal*, III (1885), 120.

remains a model statement on the settings and oral carriers of folk-
tales. In 1892 he edited the first volume, dealing with his home
county, Gloucestershire, in the series of *County Folk-Lore, Printed
Extracts*, issued by The Folk-Lore Society, and provided a Preface,
'Suggestions for the Systematic Collection of the Folk-Lore of
Gloucestershire.' For the next few years Hartland was engaged on
a mammoth enterprise, pursuing the ramifications of a single narrative theme as it wound in and out of savage rites, classical myths,
and European *Märchen* through the evolving course of civilization.
The first volume of *The Legend of Perseus: A Study of Tradition in
Story, Custom and Belief*, with a subtitle 'The Supernatural Birth,'
came out in 1894 under the imprint of David Nutt. Volume II,
subtitled 'The Life Token,' appeared in 1895, and Volume III,
subtitled 'Andromeda. Medusa,' in 1896. In its day *The Legend of
Perseus* enjoyed a reputation almost commensurate with *The
Golden Bough*. It is still the most extensive application of the
anthropological method of folklore to a single traditional story.

This monumental effort should not eclipse other related activities
dispersed along several fronts. These were the years when Hartland's reviewing for *Folk-Lore* was at flood tide; beginning in 1890
he wrote cluster reviews of dozens of folktale books in *Folk-Lore*. In
that journal alone he published twenty-one reviews in 1897 and
seventeen in 1898. In 1898 and 1899 he engaged spiritedly with
Lang over the origins of Australian gods. In 1899 and 1900 he prepared two booklets for the series Nutt published on *Popular Studies
in Mythology, Romance and Folk-Lore*, the two of chief interest to
folklorists being *Folk-Lore: What is It and What is the Good of It?*
(No. 2) and *Mythology and Folktales: their Relation and Interpretation* (No. 7), introducing to a lay audience the system of the
evolutionary school. In 1900 and 1901 he delivered to The Folk-
Lore Society presidential addresses revolving around totemism
among savages and the social organization of South African tribes.
Within this decade he also offered presidential papers to Section H
(Anthropology) of the British Association, in 1906, and to Section I
(Religions of the Lower Cultures) of the Third International Congress for the History of Religions, in 1908. In 1909 he wrote a
Preface for Marie Trevelyan's *Folklore and Folk Stories of Wales*
as well as materially assisting her with the work.

A gradual shift in Hartland's preoccupations from folk narrative
to primitive institutions is seen in his next major work, published
in 1909 in two volumes, again by Nutt, *Primitive Paternity: the
Myth of Supernatural Birth in relation to the History of the Family*.
The same year he wrote an introduction to Captain Hugh O'Sulli-

van's *Collection of Dinka Laws and Customs*, and in 1912 he performed the same service for Ella Leather's bulky *The Folk-Lore of Herefordshire*. In 1914 appeared his collection of essays *Ritual and Belief: Studies in the History of Religion*. By 1921 he had moved completely into Tylorian anthropology with *Primitive Society: the Beginnings of the Family and the Reckoning of Descent*. In 1923 he edited, for the Cymmrodorion Society, Walter Map's *De Nugis Curialium*, a twelfth-century travel book filled with folklore. His final work was *Primitive Law* (1924). These selected titles indicate Hartland's main concerns with the folktale, Welsh folklore, and the survivals of primitive institutions and religious ideas among modern savages.

The dedication and sweep of Hartland's approach to folklore are seen in many ringing pronouncements. In the running debate in the *Folk-Lore Journal* on 'The Science of Folk-Lore,' he speaks for a broad concept, saying, 'I decline to be limited to *survivals*, or to *archaic* beliefs and customs.'[1] He prefers the term 'uncivilised' to archaic and deems the whole world of primitive man, not simply Britain or the Aryan race, to be the province of the folklorist. Alone on the Council of The Folk-Lore Society, he voted against a restrictive definition of folklore in the *Handbook*. The thought of early man, as it struggled from an untrained imagination toward a disciplined reason, was what intrigued students of folklore who should therefore seek, in the recent words of Henri Gaidoz in *Mélusine*, to 'reconstituer la genese des croyances et des usages.' Human nature was everywhere constant and man's ideas substantially the same. The science of folklore sought to recover their original modes and the laws of their divergence, and so to demonstrate the constitution of the mind. But the processes of folklore continue still. 'I contend that Tradition is always being created anew, and that traditions of modern origin wherever found are as much within our province as ancient ones.'[2] And Hartland cites historical personages like Mary, Queen of Scots and Oliver Cromwell who in their time attract the uncultivated mind and magnetize floating tales. Instances of recent superstitions forming among people of all degrees of civilization throw light on how older, now meaningless practices were generated.

In his address as chairman of the Folk-Tale section of the International Folk-Lore Congress of 1891, Hartland emphasizes the high value of folktales in the quest of the folklorist to illuminate primitive beliefs and practices and the very structure and develop-

[1] In a symposium on 'The Science of Folk-Lore,' *Folk-Lore Journal*, III (1885), 117.
[2] *Ibid.*, p. 120.

ment of the human mind. For in tales chiefly do the 'speculative portions of a savage creed take shape.'[1] Already Hartland was worried by the 'disseminationist' theory which Franz Boas was inculcating among his Columbia University anthropology students, and took pains to remove its fangs with the counter-theory of 'cultural receptivity.' If tales passed from people to people by borrowing, obviously the internal content of tales could not then be produced to prove the uniform mental development of mankind—a thorn that had pricked Tylor and Lang. So Hartland contends that if 'a wandering story, thus finding an appropriate soil and climate, settle down and flourish, it follows that the ideas it expresses correspond to those current among the "folk" of its new home.'[2] In short, the culture of the transmitting folk and of the receiving folk must be identical. A Maori myth would not lodge among the English peasantry. By this reasoning Hartland hoped to safeguard his thesis that modern tales could be examined for evidence of primitive thought and custom. As for the distinction between tales told for pleasure and for truth, this does not count too heavily against the doctrine of survivals, for the ideas and manners conveyed in *Märchen* must be intelligible to their listeners, and have been taken for facts in the not too remote past.

One of Hartland's overriding concerns was to reduce the artificial walls between *Märchen* and sagas and superstitions and rites and trace them back to the seedbed of savage philosophy. The superstitious belief is encrusted under a poetic myth or local saga and tied to a definite locality as a real event; eventually the saga breaks loose from its moorings and floats off as a timeless *Märchen.* In explaining *Folklore: What is It and What is the Good of It?* he singles out a wart cure commonly known to nineteenth-century Britishers and follows its course backward in time to the ceremonies of savages employing primitive magic.

> The portion of Anthropology with which folklore deals is the mental and spiritual side of humanity. It is now well established that the most civilised races have all fought their way slowly upwards from a condition of savagery. Now, savages can neither read nor write; yet they manage to collect and store up a considerable amount of knowledge of a certain kind, and to hand on from one generation to another a definite social organisation and certain invariable rules of procedure in all the events of life. The knowledge, organisation, and

---

[1] *The International Folk-Lore Congress, 1891, Papers and Transactions* (London, 1892), p. 16. The whole address covers pp. 15–39. [2] *Ibid.*, p. 19.

rules thus gathered and formulated are preserved in the memory, and communicated by word of mouth and by actions of various kinds. To this mode of preservation and communication, as well as to the things thus preserved and communicated, the name of Tradition is given; and Folklore is the science of Tradition.[1]

The laws governing tradition, although shifting and uncertain, could be isolated and articulated, and in *The Science of Fairy Tales*, Hartland sets them forth. Worship of a heathen god never totally suppressed by Christianity can be detected in the ubiquitous legend of the sleeping hero entombed with his warriors who will return to succour his people in time of need; and the sleeping hero passes into the *Märchen* hero unaware of the passage of time in the fairyland or otherworld he has entered. King Arthur and Jack the Giant Killer are descendants of the same protective deity. So too in the world-wide *Märchen* of the swan maiden who is changed from a bird to a beautiful woman, Hartland perceives direct trace of the totemic worship of a goddess.

In *The Legend of Perseus*, he lays before the world the results of an exhaustive application of folklore science to one mythic tale. First he slices the classical versions of the myth, as refined by Ovid and Strabo, Pausanias and Lucian, into component 'trains of incident': the Supernatural Birth, the Life Token, the Witch and her Evil Eye. Each mushrooms into its own separate volume, as Hartland relentlessly assembles examples from tradition, the source of the literary forms. In their literary dressing of the primitive saga, the poets had politely discarded such coarse elements as the external soul of the ogre, or the delousing of the sleeping hero by his maiden lover. Once launched on his hunt, Hartland finds in collections of *Märchen*, legends, customs, and superstitions a chain of beliefs held from 'the shores of the Arctic Ocean to the islands of the Southern Seas.'[2] Thus in hunting down the idea of the life-token, the object whose destruction also destroys its owner wherever he may be, Hartland has recourse to legends of sacred wells and trees, accounts of funeral and marriage practices, beliefs such as the couvade containing notions of intimate blood-ties, and practices of sympathetic magic and leechcraft in which an external object transferred to itself the human disease or affliction. This protracted investigation lights up the myth.

. . . our inquiry . . . has also furnished us with the reason why the life-token was left behind when the hero started on

[1] *Folklore: What is It and What is the Good of It?* (London, 1899), pp. 6–7.
[2] *The Legend of Perseus*, 3 vols. (London, 1894–6), II, 445.

his adventures, why his brothers followed him, and why in many cases the slaughtered dragon found an avenger. The hero and his brothers were one body. The Medusa-witch, in striking him, struck them; and their plain duty was revenge. So likewise when the hero slew the dragon, the surviving kin of the dragon, whether mother or brother, must in return compass the hero's death.[1]

This is a different world from that conjured up by the solar mythologists, who saw in Perseus a sun hero, in the baleful Medusa a moon goddess, and in the dragon a deity of night. Hartland felt that his painstaking efforts had established the prehistoric age of a *Märchen* known in folklore and literature, and demonstrated the fact that older, ruder forms survived along with the higher literary versions appearing in the upward march of civilization. Further, he was able to 'circumscribe the native region of the tale' in the area of Europe, southwest Asia, and northern Africa.[2] This conclusion points forward to the goals of the twentieth-century comparativists of the Finnish school, who by close analysis of variants hope to locate the starting point of a complex tale. Hartland's primary aim was something quite different, to show the pervasiveness of the Perseus story and its elements among many peoples at different levels of civilization over a long stretch of time, as evidence of the uniformity of mental processes.

In *The Academy* an anonymous reviewer—perhaps Lang—of *The Supernatural Birth* compared Frazer's cautious inference at the termination of *The Golden Bough* with Hartland's forthright announcement.

Mr. Frazer invites us in the closing sentence of his book to listen to the bells of Rome ringing the Angelus as we linger at eventide in the once sacred grove of Nemi, where the incarnate tree-god was slain; but only 'he who hath ears to hear' will interpret the vague hint. Mr. Hartland, more boldly, makes the birth of Perseus from the fecundation of Danaë by Zeus in the form of a shower of gold, the text of discourse on legends of supernatural conceptions all the world over.[3]

Unlike Frazer, Hartland was first and foremost a champion of the folklore method sharpened by ethnology. He saw a host of

---

[1] *The Legend of Perseus*, 3 vols. (London, 1894–6), II, 444.
[2] *Ibid.*, III (London, 1896), 187.
[3] *The Academy*, No. 1176 (November 17, 1894), 397.

practical values in folklore science: means for promoting Empire administration, missionary work, class harmony, insights into the past, and appreciation of English and Hebrew literature. Folklore had 'vast possibilities that will revolutionise our conceptions of human history,' illustrating the common human nature of savage Tasmanian and cultivated Englishman.[1]

Nevertheless, Hartland clung ever more firmly to the evolutionist view that stressed the differences between primitive and civilized man. If they shared a common humanity, they were an æon apart in the development of their ideas and institutions. The solicitor read with disbelief Lang's *The Making of Religion*, controverting the orthodox anthropological concepts of Tylor on the growth of gods from ghosts. When in his incendiary presidential address Clodd had carried Tylor's theory to a conclusion involving Christian dogma, the banker believed that Hartland, Nutt, and Lang were all defending with him this advanced and delicate position. Now suddenly Lang had defected, no doubt under the spell of his spiritualist and occult fancies. Hartland corresponded with Clodd about the matter and gathered his legalistic arguments for a frontal assault, 'The "High Gods" of Australia,' that appeared in *Folk-Lore* in the last issue of 1898, in the year of publication of *The Making of Religion*. Although taken by surprise, Lang rallied in time to print 'Australian Gods: A Reply' in the first number for 1899, answering the multiple criticisms with close detail and his usual wit; Hartland's 'A Rejoinder' followed immediately in the same number.[2] Much of the debate was circumstantial and technical, turning on the interpretation and acceptability of reports by ethnologists and myth-collectors and possible missionary influences, but the issue was clear. Lang found support among the primitive aborigines of Australia for his surmise that early man possessed the conception of a moral Being, an All-Father, God. Hartland riddled the evidence, pointed to the obscene rites and gross legends connected with Daramulum and other deities, and berated Lang for offering analogies with the Ten Commandments and biblical passages that could not properly be applied to savage thought. The discussion was largely anthropological, as both parties recognized, but it contained two points of special concern for the folklorist. Hartland challenged the use of modern spiritualism to confirm the visions of savages, saying 'As students of folklore we must be content to leave the inquiry to scientific psychologists.'[3] Then

---

[1] *Folklore: What is It and What is the Good of It?*, p. 44.
[2] *Folk-Lore*, IX (December, 1898), 290–329; *ibid.*, X (March, 1899), 1–57.
[3] 'The "High Gods" of Australia,' *Folk-Lore*, IX (December, 1898), 291.

he requested some means of distinguishing between the noble religious ideas Lang perceived and the ugly, vicious myths Spencer and Gillen found among the Australian savages. 'Perhaps Mr. Lang will tell us that this legend of Daramulum's death is a part of the folklore, of the mythology, and not of the religious belief of the Murring tribes.'[1]

Hartland wrote this with obvious sarcasm, but Lang claimed in rebuttal that ideas of the high god could and did co-exist with grotesque tales about the god. Which is more probable, that a god-ideal originally held could not be lived up to, or that a medicine man would be elevated to a god? Lang preferred to believe that gods preceded ghosts and high myths came before low myths. *Märchen* about the Christian God were known to circulate among peasants. His arguments had their force, but these are strange words to come from the champion of savage survivals in folktales, and Hartland made him wriggle uncomfortably in his altered stance. In his review in *Folk-Lore* in 1899 of Lang's revised edition of *Myth, Ritual, and Religion,* the solicitor of Gloucester caustically noted the changes Lang had entered since the first edition, now giving savages credit for entertaining the idea of a moral Creator. These changes, Hartland alleged, had virtually handed the victory to the critics of evolutionism and the survivals doctrine.

In his presidential addresses to The Folk-Lore Society in 1900 and 1901 Hartland concentrated on contemporary savage institutions and considered the intricate questions surrounding totemism among the tribes of Australia and South Africa. These addresses enunciated both his imperialist view of folklore research within the British Empire and his increasing emphasis on folklore as anthropology. As the science of folklore grew from a dilettantish infancy, its practitioners inevitably shifted their 'base of operations from European tradition to savage tradition.'[2] Only through a careful study of savage life and custom as a whole was it possible to understand the folklore of Europe. Today the folklorist

> perceives that between the tradition of the Irish peasant and the tradition of the Maori no generic difference exists, but both are equally folklore, and in grasping the importance of folklore as thus conceived for any investigation into the past of the human race, the study of folklore has become frankly anthropological. It is no longer possible, even if it were desired, to draw a line between the science of folklore and that side of

[1] 'The "High Gods" of Australia,' *Folk-Lore,* IX (December, 1898), p. 296.
[2] *Ibid.,* XI (1900), 78.

15. EDWIN SIDNEY HARTLAND

16. MOSES GASTER

anthropology which deals with the earlier intellectual, spiritual, and institutional development of mankind. They are one and the same.[1]

This was exactly opposite the position Gomme had reached.

For his illustrative examples Hartland examined the social systems of South African tribes residing on British territory, retracing the path of totemic belief from mother-right to patriarchy to tribal cult to ancestor-worship. Always he referred to mythic narratives as a documentary source, thus employing 'the folklore of South Africa' to help answer questions about the origins of religious belief.[2] Hartland was thus applying the concept of folklore to the province claimed exclusively six decades later by cultural and social anthropologists, who have dropped 'folklore' from their terminology.

Nowhere are Hartland's powers of clear analysis and legal reasoning more evident than in his abundant reviews. In *Folk-Lore* alone he wrote nearly two hundred reviews with unfaltering grace and judgment. Who would know the literature of the folklore movement can do no better than begin with his reviews, which include titles in French, German, Dutch, Italian, and Latin. He also contributed to the journal the obituaries of William Alexander Clouston, the Reverend Walter Gregor, ex-Prime Minister William E. Gladstone, Sir John Rhys, Paul Sébillot, and Charlotte Burne.

In the course of his writing career, Hartland became more and more the ethnologist. His *Primitive Paternity* links the traditions of folklore to the problems of kinship relations and social organization which have become central to the interests of social anthropologists. Hartland built upon *The Legend of Perseus*, incorporating a good deal of his earlier abstracts of legends and beliefs dealing with marvellous conceptions, rebirths, and reincarnations. But now his trail led back to the family institutions of primitive man, who could not perceive the connection between sexual intercourse and procreation. Hence the family structure of civilized nations, based on the idea of two parents, the father and the mother, recedes in savage times into the institution of father-right and the still earlier mother-right, with only one parent as the acknowledged guardian of the child. From the evidence gathered since his earlier study by explorers, missionaries, and anthropologists, Hartland added still extant examples of family relationships among primitive peoples who failed to understand the results of procreation. Now the data of tale, belief, custom, and practice meshed neatly to confirm

[1] *Ibid.*, pp. 56–7.   [2] *Ibid.*, XII (1901), 15–40.

Hartland's insight concerning primitive ideas about paternity originally glimpsed sixteen years earlier. All the proofs converge: vestiges of the idea among the higher races; widespread and inter-related beliefs, customs, and institutions among the lower races pointing to the possession by all primitive men of the same general body of traditional philosophy concerning birth and fatherhood. The conclusion is clear, supported by folklore and ethnology: early man was ignorant of the nature of reproduction and resorted to magical and mythical explanations.

Since the demise of Hartland, social anthropology and folklore studies have followed ever diverging courses, forgetful of the happy union between the two he had promoted so successfully.

[5 EDWARD CLODD]

In 'A Fragment of Autobiography' Edward Clodd (1840–1930) wrote:

I was born at Margate on the first of July 1840. The brig of which my father was captain traded between that port and the North. My parents lived in Queen Street, Margate, till my early childhood, when they removed to Aldeburgh, of which town both were natives. I come of sailor and farmer stock. The ancestors on my father's side lived, some at Parham and some at Framlingham; my maternal grandfather was a Green-land whaler.[1]

Clodd's parents hoped to see their son become a minister of the gospel, but instead he grew into one of the doughtiest freethinkers of his age.

As a youth with little education Edward went to London and secured a clerkship for six months without pay at Cornhill in 1855. He became clerk in the London Joint Stock Bank in 1862, and was appointed secretary in 1872, remaining a respected figure in the banking business until his retirement in 1915. During these years Clodd took advantage of the London libraries and lecture societies to broaden his knowledge, and he stirred to the new currents of evolutionism and rationalism exciting intellectuals in the '60's and '70's. His own mental evolution took a course directly away from the austere Baptism of his parents toward a theism based on cultural relativism, and ending in a bold agnosticism. He criticized all those who bowed to the supernatural, from Church prelates to

[1] Edward Clodd, *Memories* (London, 1916), p. 1.

[248]

spiritualists, as slaves of primitive beliefs, and to document his charges gave copious examples from the anthropological folklore he knew so well.

Clodd's genial personality, breadth of interests, and social affability placed him at the centre of a talented circle, whom he frequently entertained at his Aldeburgh home on the east coast. To his seaside cottage came George Gissing, Leslie Stephen, Thomas Hardy, William Butler Yeats, J. M. Barrie, George Washington Cable, H. G. Wells, and Walter Savage Landor, historians F. York Powell, J. B. Bury, and George M. Trevelyan, jurist Sir Frederick Pollock, the diplomat Sir Alfred Lyall, and archaeologist Sir W. M. Flinders Petrie. He knew dons, scientists, editors, travellers, and a goodly share of folklorists. His house guests included George Laurence and Alice Gomme, Hartland, Lang (whom he frequently saw at the Savile Club in London), F. Hindes Groome, Frazer, Sir John Rhys.[1]

In his snatch of autobiography Clodd recalled the excitement of Darwinianism and the Higher Criticism in the 1860's, shared by many of these friends. Darwin himself was reluctant to extend evolutionism to man's mental and spiritual development, fearing further prejudice to his theory, so it was Thomas Henry Huxley's *Evidence as to Man's Place in Nature* (1863) and Tylor's *Primitive Culture* (1871) that made the leap, and opened Clodd's eyes to the Bible text, 'Ye shall know the truth and the truth shall make you free.' In a sense Clodd harks back to Bourne, who criticized popular antiquities as Romish and pagan survivals, but Clodd would lay all Christendom open to the same charge of sheltering heathen ideas.

The literary banker, as he was known in London, first attracted wide attention in 1875 with a primer of evolutionary thought, *The Childhood of Religions, embracing a simple Account of the Birth and Growth of Myths and Legends*, a book often reprinted in the United States as well as England and translated into many languages, European and heathen. Fortunately for the book's success, it was written while the author was still a theist and could still separate primitive from revealed religions. The same year saw the publication of his address to the Sunday Lecture Society on 'The Birth and Growth of Myth, and its Survival in Folk-Lore, Legend, and Dogma.' This lecture grew into a book on folklore, *Myths and Dreams* (1885), applying a strictly Tylorian measurement to the stuff of dreams, with none of the psychic leanings of Lang, and no hint of Freudian revelations to come. Prehistoric man, like the child, confused dreams with reality. In his animistic outlook he

---

[1] Joseph McCabe, *Edward Clodd, A Memoir* (London, 1932), pp. 99–100.

[249]

endowed animals with speech and objects with life and then wove tales around his imagined encounters with talking wolves and angry rocks and spectres of the night; so too he recounted the story of his dreamed experiences that further blurred the distinction between live beings and apparitions. The belief in a separable soul or heart is found still in the folktale of Punchkin and can be traced back to a barbarian's dream.[1]

In village traditions of his native Suffolk, Clodd found evidence to support his broad theories. A well preserved West Suffolk tale of the Rumpelstiltskin type inspired his article for the *Folk-Lore Journal* in 1889 on 'The Philosophy of Rumpelstiltskin,' pointing out the tale's core in the savage belief in the power attached to a name. In 1889 he introduced the volume for Suffolk in the Folk-Lore Society's series, *County Folklore, Printed Extracts*, whose clippings and extracts of Suffolk lore were assembled by Lady Eveline Camilla Gurdon. Clodd happily noted many evidences of survivals, saying 'we have but to scratch the rustic to find the barbarian underneath.'

One theme especially fascinated the banker, the savage's identification of a name with the object named, and his awe and fear of the name. Clodd had devoted a chapter in *Myths and Dreams* to this notion, and following his lucky Suffolk find he elaborated on the subject in a book-length treatise, *Tom Tit Tot, an Essay on Savage Philosophy in Folk-Tale* (1898). Beginning with the Rumpelstiltskin cycle of tales, Clodd pursued the myriad appearances of name spells throughout primitive magic and taboo.

In the 1890's Clodd assumed a prominent role as a spokesman for the domain of folklore. In 1895 he was elected to the presidency of The Folk-Lore Society, and on September 16 of that year he addressed the Anthropological Section of the British Association, meeting at Ipswich, on 'General Conclusions in Regard to Folklore.' It was, he observed, the first time folklore had enjoyed any distinctive representation at the British Association for the Advancement of Science. Folklore and anthropology were twin sciences, dividing respectively the studies of the psychical and physical sides of man.

> . . . comparative anatomy has settled our place in the long succession of life; anthropology, in its branches of ethnology and prehistoric archaeology, has defined the differences between the races of mankind. . . . What remains of abiding prac-

[1] 'The Philosophy of Punchkin,' *Folk-Lore Journal*, II (1884), 302. The whole article covers pp. 289–303.

tical importance lies chiefly within the province of folklore to deal with. For you can exclude it from no department where the thought of man comes into play.[1]

Coming late to maturity, folklore has profited from the senior sciences, Clodd continued. After discarding its antiquarian phase, when collectors sought out the strange and unique with no sense that they were handling living records of the past, folklore endeavoured to trace the origin and migration of myths and tales, but this too was a blind alley, delighting with its instances and coincidences of similar legends and anecdotes found in far removed places. (And Clodd used the opportunity to give examples.) But now folklore has moved from the secondary to the primary quest, seeking to explain 'the presence and persistence of barbaric elements in customs, rituals, and beliefs forming integral parts of the theologies of civilised peoples.'

In his presidential address of 1895 to The Folk-Lore Society, Clodd amplified these remarks on the realm of the folklorist.[2] Beginning in low key, he reported friends asking him why middle-aged persons, apparently in their second childhood, met once a month to tell each other creepy stories. To them he replied that folklore was no objectless pursuit for dilettantes but a noble enterprise taking the entire thought of man as its province and covering all the 'dim and dateless past,' with no part 'common or unclean.' Folklore can supply the key to man's interpretation of himself and his surroundings. It is the psychical side of anthropology, beginning with primitive man's 'zoomorphizing' of his world, a world in which human beings and beasts, the animate and the inanimate, blend and flow one into the other. Here the folklorist finds his *materia prima*. This primal stuff enters the cycles of folktales, the systems of black and white magic, the bodies of myth, festival, ceremonial custom, barbaric philosophy, and finally the great religions with their imposing rites.

No reader of Tylor could object to this presentation, although the conclusion carried a stick of dynamite. The following year, in his second address, Clodd lighted the fuse.[3] He began again with a tribute to Alfred Nutt, but where in 1895 he thanked the publisher-scholar for helping finance the publications of the Society, in 1896 he praised Nutt for elucidating Christianity's debt to classic

---

[1] Clodd's paper to the British Association is printed in a clipping pasted on the back page of a volume deposited in the library of The Folk-Lore Society, London, titled 'Edward Clodd, Presidential Addresses to Folk Lore Society 1895–96. With Criticisms.'

[2] *Folk-Lore*, VI (1895), 54–81.   [3] *Ibid.*, VI (1896), 35–60.

paganism. Thus the Celtic idea of Elysium could be seen recurring in the full span of Aryan mythology—Christian, classic, and Oriental. Here was a specific illustration of the 'weighty support' folklore could provide to the theory of unity and continuity which included man in the universal order. Unhampered by narrow attachment to any particular creed, the folklorist searched for the related ideas incarnated in all. 'Without bias, without assumptions of relative truth or falsity, he searches into origins, traces variations, compares and classifies, and relates the several families to one ordinal group.'[1] With this scientific principle as a banner, Clodd proceeded to examine just such clusters of folk-religious concepts. A mass of examples, accumulated by Frazer in *The Golden Bough* and easily expanded from both Catholic and Protestant rituals, confirmed the savage basis of the sacramental act, namely that by eating an organism the eater acquired its physical and mental qualities. From Sidney Hartland's *The Legend of Perseus* the speaker elicited a string of scattered traditions of virgin births and supernatural fecundation. One could turn to the daily papers and find savage folklore still current. The gist of these remarks, summarized Clodd, marching toward his climax, is that popular belief has changed very little and only superficially since primeval days; the old animism still informs the higher creeds. Hence the rite of baptism cannot be understood without reference to barbaric lustrations and water-worship generally. The acceptance of divine interference in petty human affairs (so characteristic of Puritanism) recalls the barbaric worship of gods who behave like spiteful men. Exorcism as practiced by the Catholic priest echoes the demon-chasing incantations of the shaman.

Here was the doctrine of survivals carried to its ultimate conclusion. Folklore's 'high mission,' Clodd ended, 'is to contribute to the freedom of the spirit, to deliver those who, being children of superstition, are therefore the prisoners of fear.'[2]

Not all of Clodd's audience were ready for deliverance. On January 29, 1896, a letter was posted to him from two members of the Council of the Society, J. P. Emslie and T. W. E. Higgins, commencing 'Might we beg of you, in the interests of the Folk-Lore Society, not to allow your last presidential address to be printed in "Folk-Lore"?' The second sentence explained why. 'There were certain passages in it which caused both of us, as Christians, great pain.' The complainants were sure that other Christian members of the Society would feel the same way and resign. On February 3 they wrote again, thanking Clodd for attempting, although too

[1] *Folk-Lore*, VI (1896), 41.   [2] *Ibid.*, p. 59.

late, to stay the printer's hand, refusing to answer the points he had made in refutation, and confining themselves simply to the question, 'Would the publication of your address be beneficial or otherwise to the Society?' This they proposed to discuss at the next Council meeting. Meanwhile Clodd had already been advised of their attitude by a friend, another council member, T. Fairman Ordish, who in a letter of January 27 revealed that Emslie had asked him to join in the protest. Ordish stalled Emslie by suggesting he communicate his views in writing to the Publications Committee. To Clodd, Ordish expressed his admiration.

For myself, I think the destruction of error must precede the synthesis of truth, and I shall be extremely sorry if we have to limit the effect of your epoch-making address. I imagine that hereafter it may stand as a landmark in the intellectual emancipation of our time, with Tyndall's Belfast address and one or two of Huxley's more pregnant pronouncements.

Hartland too had written Clodd on January 29, from Gloucester. His letter indicates the problem faced by the founding fathers of The Folk-Lore Society, who must now harmonize their zeal for the scientific pursuit of truth with the practical needs of cajoling members with only a dilettante interest in matters folkish.

My dear Clodd:
I saw Higgins' letter, and I think Mr. Elford Higgins in the character of martyr of revealed truth is an edifying spectacle. Except your far too generous references to myself (for which I had no opportunity after the meeting to thank you) and except a personal reference to Jesus Christ (which old associations and sentiment would probably have withheld from my life)—Of course this does not involve the least shade of reflection on you for using it. It is merely personal feeling for which I have been unable to rid myself—[*inserted comment*] I do not recollect a single word you uttered which I should not be proud to have said. These things must have been said, and said from the chair, sooner or later.
At the same time we must recognize that there are many members whose guineas are valuable and who are apt to take offence because they have no valid basis of argument to combat them; and we must consider how best to obviate their objections. I should not be disposed to suppress the address. I should resist it. Nor should I allow any thing more than what

was absolutely necessary to show that the utterance was not meant to bind objecting members personally. For my part and without knowing your reasons more fully I do not see what harm a temperately worded disclaimer could do. It would probably satisfy the clerically-minded members, and would to us be an exhibition of their inability to seriously oppugn your conclusions. I have suggested to Gomme that the address and report of the council, and in fact the whole minutes of the meeting, should be postponed to the June no. of the Journal. They would come then in the natural chronological order, and the postponement would give time for feelings to cool down, for this year's subscriptions to be paid, and for a careful consideration of the course to be taken.

And more in the same vein. Those who have gone into the questions thoroughly would certainly support Clodd's position, but many members 'only skim the surface of things.' Hartland appreciates and echoes Clodd's desire to do 'what is best for the Society's interests.'

So the address was printed. On reading it William E. Gladstone, the former Prime Minister and himself a writer on mythology who saw in myths the degraded remnants of revelation, sent in his resignation, in a letter dated May 11, 1896, from Hawarden Castle, Chester.

I have read the address delivered by Mr. Clodd as President of the Folk Lore Society, and printed on behalf and at the expense of the Society in its record of transactions for the current quarter.

As an original member (so I believe) of the Society, I have understood its purpose to be the collection and due presentation of the facts of Folk Lore, and have regarded it as an institution of great value.

The address of the President (not the first as I observe which he has delivered) appears to me in no way to be within the purposes of the Society, and I am not willing that such addresses should be printed at the charge and on behalf of the subscribers.

I think it is best to abstain from stating grounds, though I should readily give them if it could serve any useful purpose.

I have read the apology offered in F. L., which justifies the publication, and leads to the belief that such publications may be repeated.

It cannot be expected that the Society should renounce such

proceedings in order to meet the views of a subscriber: but, finding that I have misunderstood the scope and aim of the Society, I request you to be good enough to remove my name from the list of subscribers, and to cancel the authority under which my contribution is drawn. The subscription is a public act, and I may possibly think it right to make public the circumstances of my withdrawal.

I remain sir
Your obedient servant
W. E. Gladstone[1]

F. A. Milne Esq.

But other responses were encouraging. Sir Alfred C. Lyall, one of Clodd's closest friends, expressed his interest in the address, which brought back to him the pleasure he had experienced in collecting folklore in India. Lyall did feel some scepticism at overriding 'good serviceable theories' of folklore, as Frazer had done in *The Golden Bough*, and he thought that Clodd had pushed evolution too far in giving prehistoric roots to Christian symbolism. 'I fancy that you treat as evolution certain practices which have no more than an accidental likeness to primitive belief.'

There was no doubt in the mind of another of Clodd's close friends and fellow-agnostic, Grant Allen, who read the paper in proof, and wrote his sentiments in an undated letter.

> Just read Address. What a capital paper! So clear, so learned, so bold, so cogent! But no wonder it roused discussion and searching of mind, for it almost commits the Society to an anti-Christian attitude. . . . Fred Whelen tells me there is danger of large secessions from the Society on account of your heterodox pronouncement; if so, and if you want new members, I shall be proud if you will enroll me among you.
>
> It struck me in reading the address that my book, now in Kidd's hands, supplies to some extent just such faithful dealing with the application of folk-lore and ethnology to the Christian religion as your paper desiderates.

The book Allen referred to was his *The Evolution of the Idea of God* (1897).

If Council members of the Society demurred from engaging their president in debate, wounded parties on the outside held no such scruples. The Catholic Truth Society issued a twenty-four page

---

[1] These letters are attached to the volume from Clodd's personal library referred to in n. 1, p. 251.

pamphlet in London, price one penny, titled *Folk-Lore Ex Cathedra: being an examination of Mr. Edward Clodd's presidential address to the Folk-Lore Society, 1896.* Its opening sentence suggested a certain displeasure. 'The inspiring doctrine of man's essential bestiality has no more enthusiastic and devoted apostle than Mr. Edward Clodd.' Construing the address as a 'formal assault upon the position of Christianity, all along the line,' the anonymous author proceeded to challenge Clodd's evidence of comparative rites, wholly dependent upon Frazer, but making no mention of the one people from whom Christianity evolved, the Jews. No 'intelligent student of antiquity, Catholic or non-Catholic,' would deny origins of Christian ceremonies in pagan customs, but this is a far different matter from asserting that 'the feast of our Lady's Purification is simply the natural development of a licentious Pagan Orgy.' No infidel has ever dared deny the fact of the crucifixion, in spite of all the prehistoric tradition about symbolic crosses and the worship of trees and serpents. If the crucifixion is no myth, no barbaric idea, no fragment of folklore, neither are vague traditions about virginal births and the eating of gods. Still, concludes the pamphlet, ' . . . there is no conclusion so preposterous that it might not be demonstrated by the slipshod, unscientific methods of investigation followed by Mr. Edward Clodd, and his imitators.'[1]

Lang too was drawn into the general controversy. Meeting Clodd at the Savile Club one day, he addressed him as 'Brer Jackal.' When Clodd looked askance, Lang explained that the mystery would be cleared up in the Catholic *Month.* A perusal of the issue for September, 1898, disclosed a fierce review of Lang's *The Making of Religion,* referring to the 'Clodds, the Allens, the Langs,' and other popularizers of evolution as jackals in the lion's wake—the lion being Tylor.[2]

Following the storm of his presidency, Clodd plunged more deeply than ever into his evolutionist and anti-theist polemics. Mention should be made of his Introduction to an edition of *Fairy Tales from Hans Andersen,* brought out by Wells, Gardner, Darton and Company in 1901. Clodd recounted the career of the illustrious Dane and the various influences that had shaped his story-writing: precepts of the brothers Grimm, oral folktales abounding in the Odense district, and his own creative fantasy. In spite of Andersen's personal touch, Clodd could yet perceive a law of continuity and unity at work, linking the story traditions of 'widely-sundered

[1] Anonymous, *Folk-Lore Ex Cathedra* (London: Catholic Truth Society, n.d.), pp. 1, 2, 12, 24. [2] Clodd, *Memories,* pp. 212–13.

peoples' and giving evidence of the uniform behaviour of the mind of man.

In the first two decades of the twentieth century Clodd's writings focused on his rationalist views. In these years he brought out memoirs of Grant Allen (1900) and Thomas Henry Huxley (1902), a revised edition (1907) of his *Pioneers of Evolution from Thales to Huxley* which had first appeared ten years earlier, and his frank consideration of *The Question: 'If a man die, shall he live again'? (Job xiv, 14): A Brief History and Examination of Modern Spiritualism* (1917). Clodd's abhorrence of spiritualism, 'the old animism writ large,' and of occultism in general led to his sharp criticisms of Lang's psycho-folklore. One set of superstitions has replaced another, fairies and devils giving way to spirits and mediums.

A final, full-length statement of his folklore and evolutionism thesis appeared in 1920 under the title *Magic in Names and in Other Things.* An extension of *Tom Tit Tot,* it devoted much attention to the Polynesian concept of mana, whereby the magician exerted sway over ordinary persons through his store of power. Again Clodd stated his credo in the psychical as well as the physical unity of man and in Christian assimilation of primitive beliefs and rituals. The Virgin Mary possessed mana in supreme degree; the name of Jesus is powerful with magic.

When Clodd died in his ninth decade, in 1930, his body was cremated and the ashes scattered over the sea, according to his wish.

[6   WILLIAM ALEXANDER CLOUSTON]

'Dear Mr. Nutt,' wrote William Alexander Clouston (1843–1896) from Glasgow on December 11, 1891, 'I am glad the Council have favourably entertained the proposal to re-issue my revised work on the *Squire's Tale*. It's no great matter to me when it can be put to press, if I get the honorarium now, as I'm terribly in want of money, never having got fairly to land since the household wreck last May, though I've been working hard enough.' He would like to see his compensation raised from five to ten guineas. Then he adds a handwritten postscript. '*Entre nous*. I've just got in *last notice* for household taxes &c which must be paid within the next seven days, else there will be trouble and expenses. This I mention as an indication that it would relieve my hand in many ways did I get a cheque very soon!'[1]

[1] This letter is found opposite p. 282 in Clouston's revision copy of *On The Magical Elements in Chaucer's Squire's Tale*, published by the Chaucer Society in 1889. A sub-

Under these pressures did Clouston attempt to persevere in his life work of translating and editing, often in editions limited to a few hundred copies, the story treasures of the Middle East. Born in the Orkneys, he resided during his adult years in Glasgow, eking out his living as newspaper feature writer while publishing, often through Glasgow booksellers, an original corpus of comparative folklore. His intellectual sympathies lay with the diffusionist school of Theodor Benfey and Emmanuel Cosquin, who beheld in India the breeding ground for an original family of Aryan tales that through the centuries had dispersed all over Europe. Clouston did not polemicize but concentrated on making available to English readers the Persian and Arabic tales, jests, and romances found between India and Europe, and placing side by side the similar versions that extended from the Himalayas to the Highlands. Unlike the evolutionists, seeking relics of savagery and barbarism in household tales and customs in quest of the primitive mind, he followed the spoor of individual narratives as they surfaced in Buddhist fables, medieval exempla, Indian and Arabian storybooks, French fabliaux, English chapbooks, and European field collections. A self-taught Arabist, he made his own translations of Middle Eastern stories largely inaccessible and unknown to Englishmen. He delighted in pushing further back in time and further East in space the local legend and magical fiction, but ancient India was his stopping-place, and the tales of Hottentots and Iroquois and Maoris did not enter into his tale histories.

Within the Aryan group of nations Clouston recognized the possibility of survivals from a primitive past, when the nursery tales now found in both Europe and Asia were the possession of one parent people. But for tales of common life, lacking any supernatural element, he credited more recent passages from East to West, through translations, and via travellers, pilgrims, and traders.

The Orkneyman belongs with the Great Team in his sensitivity to the science of folklore, his command of the vast literature, and his development of the work of the earlier English folklorists. In particular he paid his respects to Keightley's *Tales and Popular Fictions* for its pioneering effort, although he considered Keightley overcredulous in accepting independent invention of similar fictions. In view of his Aryan and Indic interests, the Arabist relied upon

sequent letter from Clouston of December 15, 1891 to Nutt indicates that the Council objected to re-publication because of the copyright question. Clouston also refers to the remaindering of his *Flowers from a Persian Garden* by Nutt, the publisher.

Clouston's revision copy is in the library of The Folk-Lore Society, London.

Max Müller and George Cox, but rejected their solar theory as thoroughly as did Lang. When Baring-Gould in turn indulged in solar flights on St. George and the dragon, Clouston refused to take him seriously. If St. George is the sun, his sword the lightning, the maiden the earth, and the monster the storm cloud, what are the persons and beasts whom the dragon first devoured?

All Clouston's folklore writings were crammed into a fifteen-year period. In 1881 he printed, in three hundred small paper copies and seventy large paper copies, *Arabian Poetry for English Readers*. In the Preface he explained, 'I was engaged in collecting material for illustration of the migrations and transformations of Popular European Tales and Fictions, and . . . the idea occurred to me that a reprint would be acceptable to a few personal friends, interested in Asiatic literature.' He adds that it might 'perhaps be thought somewhat strange that a mere English scholar—for my knowledge of Arabic is as "nothing, and less than nothing, and vanity" '— should have attempted this task, but pleads his desire to suit and his ability to judge the taste of intelligent English readers. In 1883 he edited *The Bakhytār Nāma: A Persian Romance*, as translated by Sir William Ouseley. In 1884 he brought out a third limited edition, *The Book of Sindibād: or, The Story of the King, His Son, the Damsel. From the Persian and Arabic*. Besides his usual introduction and notes, Clouston also contributed an appendix of over one hundred and fifty pages. He described the work as 'the first attempt, in this country, to furnish a compendious account of the Eastern and Western groups of romances known respectively under their generic titles of the *Book of Sindibād* and the *Book of the Seven Wise Masters*.'

Meanwhile the Arabist was busy demonstrating parallels. In 1886 he furnished 'Additional Analogues to the Wright's Chaste Wife' for an edition of a fifteenth-century fabliau edited by Frederick J. Furnivall, and in 1887 he supplied Asiatic versions for *The Tale of Beryn*, re-edited by F. J. Furnivall and W. G. Stone. His 'Variants and Analogues of some of the Tales in the Supplemental Nights' of the *Arabian Nights* appeared in 1886–7, and in 1887 he contributed to 'Originals and Analogues of some of Chaucer's Canterbury Tales.'

Also in 1887 he published his best known study, which he had been preparing for years, *Popular Tales and Fictions, Their Migrations and Transformations*. Here he set forth with abundant illustrations his diffusionist theory of the folktale, fitted into the premise that folk romances first sprouted in the fertile seedbed of India and the Middle East. Clouston designed the *Popular Tales and*

Fictions as studies in the history of European folktales and comparative folklore. He did not seek to classify folktales, since that task was being undertaken by The Folk-Lore Society, but to present the genealogies of certain narratives. His method was to assemble versions of the same basic story from his files and link the synopses together in a chain, often stretching from classical India to modern Europe. To some stories he appended notes on themes of special interest threading the tale-cluster. Actually by his chapter divisions Clouston was isolating tale-types of the kind assigned regular numbers today in the Aarne-Thompson index of folktales, while in his occasional notes on the smaller elements in the narratives he was isolating motifs which have found their way into Stith Thompson's *Motif-Index of Folk Literature.* Unlike these skeletal indexes, his essays proffered the full-fleshed stories in their variant garbs.

In the first volume he dealt with magical tales and in the second with realistic tales. Volume One discussed legends of Cupid and Psyche, of bird-maidens and thankful beasts, of contracts with the Evil One, of the race between the hare and the tortoise, of men living inside monstrous fish. The more mundane themes of Volume Two included Dick Whittington and his fortune-bringing cat, Chaucer's 'Pardoner's Tale,' the story behind the proverb 'Don't count your chickens until they are hatched,' and the macabre episode of 'The Lover's Heart' served to his mistress for dinner by her cuckolded husband. In his appended notes he pursued such recurrent folktale incidents as the life-token in external objects, luminous jewels, falling in love through a dream, and the betrayal of husbands by their wives. 'Every popular tale has its history,' he remarked, quoting Baring-Gould, and he endeavoured to construct such histories.[1] His favourite technique, as in his handling of 'The Tailor's Dream,' was to notice an instance close at hand, in this case in an issue of *Chambers' Edinburgh Journal* for 1837, strip off its modern and local features, and trace it back to Europe and ultimately to Asia. Or he would begin with a British tale in the collections of Croker or Campbell of Islay and set his sights for the East.

With his uncanny erudition Clouston was able to point out errors of deduction and gaps of knowledge in the commentaries of his precursors. 'Mr. Thoms does not seem to have been aware, however,' he remarks typically, 'of the incident of sending an inquirer to older and oldest persons being both ancient and common to the

[1] Clouston, *Popular Tales and Fictions, Their Migrations and Transformations* (New York, 1887), II, 25.

folk-lore of most countries.' Clouston was right, and today the tale is classified in the Aarne-Thompson index as Type 726, 'The Oldest on the Farm.' He corrects Douce for associating a fabliau with an Arabian Nights story, raises eyebrows at Baring-Gould's notion that any tales in the *Seven Wise Masters* might derive from the *Fables of Bidpai*, and reproves Campbell for thinking that the legend of Little Fairly reached the Gaelic through Italian, when demonstrably it was brought to the West Highlands by the Norsemen. Again he checks Douce, 'the eminent literary antiquary,' for believing that the German edition of the late medieval *Gesta Romanorum* preceded the English. But he approves Halliwell-Phillipps' observation that witticisms attached to eminent contemporaries are usually old chestnuts, and endorses Sir George Cox's opinion that reasonable men would never accept the independent invention of apologues and stories common to Europe and Asia.[1]

Appreciating Sabine Baring-Gould's *Curious Myths of the Middle Ages* as a pioneer work of storyology, Clouston pushed its researches farther and deeper. Baring-Gould had demonstrated that 'Llewellyn and his Dog Gellert,' the incident of the faithful hound mistakenly killed by his master after saving his child from a wolf, was a travelling legend rather than an actual happening in Wales. Now Clouston followed the fictitious event through the medieval *Book of Sindibād* of the *History of the Seven Wise Masters of Rome*, back to the *Panchatantra*, and forward again to a modern oral version from northwest India involving a snake and a faithful mongoose.[2] Aptly and appropriately Clouston placed the following words of Baring-Gould on the verso of his title page to Volume Two of the *Popular Tales and Fictions*: 'How many uncles, aunts, brothers, sisters, and cousins of all degrees a little story has, and how few of those we hear can lay any claim to originality!'

Collaterally with his major opus Clouston wrote an entertaining and informative treatment of one special story form in *The Book of Noodles: Stories of Simpletons: or, Fools and Their Follies*. (It was scheduled for publication in 1886 but postponed until 1888.) A noodle was a numskull, a dolt, a bumpkin, and his stupidities have provoked mirth through the ages. Clouston was interested in the antiquity of these noodle tales and their common currency among the Aryan peoples. Thoms had once planned for The Folk-Lore Society an annotated edition of the 'Merry Tales of the Mad Men of Gotham'; back in 1837 he had written a paper on 'Early German Comic Romances' dealing with the witless Schildburgers. The

---

[1] *Ibid.*, pp. 98, 343, 183, 263, 333; I, 58, 1–2.
[2] 'Llewellyn and his Dog Gellert,' *ibid.*, pp. 166–86.

proposed work would provide variants lacking in the editions of Halliwell-Phillipps (1840), W. Carew Hazlitt's *The Shakespeare Jest-Books* (three volumes, 1864), and John Ashton's *Chap-Books of the Eighteenth Century* (1882). But the infirmities of age interfered, and Clouston inherited the project. Three of his seven chapters were devoted to 'Gothamite Drolleries,' but he added one chapter on 'Ancient Grecian Noodles' and others on popular simpleton characters in folktales that could usually be traced to Buddhist sources. Captain Richard C. Temple supplied him with some of his Oriental analogues. Clouston thumbed through old English jestbooks for examples of popular tales traceable back to the Far East. On the trail of 'The Three Great Noodles' (Type 1384, 'The Husband Hunts Three Persons as Stupid as His Wife'), he happily tracked it from Italy to Norway and thence to southern India, where he uncovered a variant close to the Norse in Pandit S. M. Natésa Sástrí's *Folk-lore in Southern India*, a work then in course of publication at Bombay. He was pleased to show that the incident known in the droll Scotch song of 'The Barring of the Door' was of Eastern origin, as were various of the Gothamite and similar fooleries. Clouston was the first British folklorist to give comparative treatment to the neglected genre of the fool anecdote.

The Orkneyman's valuable editions and essays continued to appear in rapid succession. He brought out in 1889 in a privately printed edition *A Group of Eastern Romances and Stories from the Persian, Tamil, and Urdu*, with his usual apparatus of Introduction, notes, and appendix. Also in 1889 he wrote for the Chaucer Society *On the Magical Elements in Chaucer's Squire's Tale, with Analogues, as a supplement to John Lane's Continuation of Chaucer's Squire's Tale*. Lane's writing had lain in manuscript for two and a half centuries. Clouston sent a revised edition for re-publication in the series of The Folk-Lore Society, with the letter quoted on p. 257; the marked copy remains in the library of The Folk-Lore Society, the Council having decided against publishing for fear of infringing on the copyright of the Chaucer Society edition. In 1890 Alfred Nutt published his *Flowers from a Persian Garden and Other Papers*. The other papers dealt with Eastern and medieval folk literature: Oriental Wit and Humour; Tales of a Parrot; Rabbinical Legends, Tales, Fables, and Aphorisms; An Arabian Tale of Love; Apocryphal Life of Aesop; Ignorance of the Clergy in the Middle Ages; The Beards of Our Fathers.

A slender volume of eight stories, *Some Persian Tales, from Various Sources*, which he edited with his customary comments and analogues, appeared in 1892. The same year a Glasgow book-

17. ROBERT RANULPH MARETT

18. CHARLOTTE BURNE

seller issued in paper covers another small work of his, *Literary Coincidences; A Bookstall Bargain; and Other Papers*. Two of the four papers involved folklore, 'Ancient Riddles' and 'St. Valentine's Day in the Olden Time,' while the title essay on 'Literary Coincidences and Imitations' dealt on the literary level with a theme he reiterated in his folk studies, the repetitions and grooves channelling the human imagination. A London publisher, Hutchinson, issued his short but well chosen *Book of Wise Sayings, Selected Largely from Eastern Sources* in 1893, a distillation from Hindu, Buddhist, Moslem, Jewish, and Chinese aphorisms. The same year he appended 'Notes on the Folk-Lore of the Raven and the Owl' to a paper on *Birds of Omen in Scotland* by Jessie M. E. Saxby, in which again he showed his vast acquaintance with sources in the Old and New World, from ancient and modern times, and in the East and the West.

Clouston brought within the sphere of folklore science two species of oral narratives in which the anthropological school had shown little interest, not fitting their purposes, the romance of the East and the humble jest. Western students of the folktale have slighted the folk romance, falling as it does somewhere between the literary novel and the conventional *Märchen*. Yet for India and the Arab world it is the staple fare of story entertainment, enchanting generations of listeners and readers with its sequences of heroic adventures and courtships and magical episodes and wondrous journeys and interlocking stories of kings, Brahmans, merchants, beggars, and faithless wives. Clouston traced the intricate appearances and reappearances of these romances in popular literature and tale collections, and demonstrated their folklore elements. Speaking of the *Rose of Bakawali*, he wrote:

> It cannot be said that there is much originality in the romance, most of the incidents being common to the folk-tales of the several countries of India, but they are here woven together with considerable ingenuity, and the interest of the narrative never flags. It may in fact be regarded as a typical Asiatic Tale, in which is embodied much of the folk-lore of the East. Like all fairy tales, it has no particular 'moral,' for the hero achieves all his wonderful enterprises with the aid of superhuman beings and by means of magical fruits, etc. The various and strange transformations which he undergoes in the course of his adventures are still believed to be quite possible by Muslims and Hindús alike.[1]

[1] *A Group of Eastern Romances and Stories* (privately printed, 1889), p. xxxvi.

The romance or 'Asiatic tale' as a genre therefore partakes of characteristics of the *Märchen* and the legend, while its narrative content suggests the heroic epic. One romance of special interest which Clouston introduced to English folklorists was *The Romance of Antar*, a celebrated and interminable chronicle of the pre-Islamite Arabs, filled with details of daily life and luxuriant descriptions, and once thought to rival the *Arabian Nights*. Clouston reprinted selections from Terrick Hamilton's four-volume English translation (1819–20), made from the Syrian version of the forty-five volume work, in his *Arabian Poetry for English Readers*, and he commented in *Popular Tales and Fictions* on the features it shared with other heroic and chivalric romances.[1] Clouston astutely pointed out in *Antar* elements of the Heroic Age patterns later elaborately analysed by the Chadwicks. Antar was an historical hero; his exploits were recited in oral story before they were reduced to writing; he performed precocious feats of valour as a child and engaged in single combat as a man; he possessed a marvellous steed and an unbreakable sword; he boasted of his strength, and rescued imprisoned maidens. In all likelihood, Clouston concludes, *Antar* is a prototype of European chivalric romances.

In the next breath Clouston turns from heroic romance to the lowly joke and discusses its passage from Asia to Europe. 'The same jests,' he observes, 'which amuse the Russian or Norwegian peasant are also well known to the vine-dressers of France and Spain, and to the Italian rustic; to the half-farmer, half-fisherman of Argyllshire; to the wandering Arab; to the luxurious Persian; to the peaceable Hindú; to the crafty Chinese.'[2] And he offers as an example the tale of the Irishman peering over the shoulder of a gentleman in a coffeehouse writing a letter; when the gentleman ended with the words, 'I have much more to say to you but an impudent Irishman is reading every word I write,' the son of Erin exclaimed, 'Upon my sowl, I haven't read a word, sorr!' Many centuries earlier the Persian poet Jámí had related the jest. Clouston went on to multiply such instances of Asian priorities of modern jokes.

The achievement of William Alexander Clouston in rendering visible the network of popular tales and fictions between Asia and Europe has never received proper due, and that field still today remains largely his own.

At the height of their powers, the great team scattered along individual pathways of intellectual exploration. The once solid

[1] *Popular Tales and Fictions*, I, 39–49, 68–71.   [2] *Ibid.*, p. 50.

phalanx of anthropological folklorists had established independent positions. Lang was scarcely recognizable as an evolutionist with his new thesis of a high god among savages and his taste for psychic research. Gomme had added custom and institution to myth and belief, severed the savage from the peasant, taken folklore back into prehistory, staked out Britain as his laboratory, and pushed into pre-Aryan depths. Nutt had blended mythological and anthropological theories in his quest for folktale treasures within medieval Celtic romances, and fought his own battle with the partisans of the high culture theory who saw in folklore only degraded remains of literature. Hartland had plunged more deeply than any into the anthropological study of savages as a prelude to comprehending survivals in peasant folklore. Clodd was embarked on a rationalist campaign to cleanse from Christian ritualism the remnants of pagan superstitions and liberate the Victorian mind from primitive taboo and spell.

And off in the distance Clouston was diligently plotting the relationships between Asiatic and European story forms to buttress the diffusion theory, a theory which would topple Tylor's pyramided stages of the cultural development of man.

VIII   The Society Folklorists

BY ITS VERY EXISTENCE The Folk-Lore Society acted as a catalyst for its subject. Publishing a journal and monographs, holding regular meetings and lectures, appointing committees in the fashion of all such organizations, the new Society touched a centre of interest in numerous Victorians. A vigorous debate ensued in the *Folk-Lore Journal* on the proper goals and boundaries for 'The Science of Folk-Lore.' Laurence Gomme and the council set on foot projects for a bibliography of folklore publications, a dictionary of British folklore, a tabulation of folktales, and a county series reprinting extracts of printed folklore. Excitement and ferment were in the air; the journal grew into a fat and yeasty quarterly, pulling scattered collectors and fledgling folklorists into its pages. Behind the Great Team formed a second rank of devoted enthusiasts, drawn from a variety of fields and occupations, who lent much of their talents and energies to the cause. If Lang and Gomme, Hartland and Nutt and Clodd dominated the scene, they attracted worthy associates and inspired zealous co-workers.

Three illustrious newcomers to the Society joined in a formidable assault on the prevalent theory of survivalism. Joseph Jacobs, the Judaic scholar from Australia, Francis Hindes Groome, the gypsy expert, and Moses Gaster, the Romanian rabbi, found in spite of their divergent backgrounds a common sympathy for the migration hypothesis. Now the conquering evolutionists faced a well-equipped foe within their own gates.

Of all the versatile scholars enlisted by the Great Team in behalf of folklore studies and the Society, none proved more committed than Joseph Jacobs (1854–1916). Born in Sydney, Australia, he was educated at Sydney University, at St. John's College in Cambridge University, and at the University of Berlin. Had he never written a line on folklore he would still be known, as indeed he is principally known, as an historian of the Jews. A series of articles in *The Times* on the persecution of the Jews in Russia first brought him into the public eye. There followed a number of painstaking works: *Bibliotheca Anglo-Judaica, A Bibliographical Guide to Anglo-Jewish History* (1888, with Lucien Wolf), *Studies in Jewish Statistics* (1891), *The Jews of Angevin England* (1893), *Studies in Biblical Archaeology* (1894), *An Inquiry into the Sources of the History of the Jews in Spain* (1894), and *Jewish Ideals, and Other Essays* (1896). In 1896 he began editing *The Jewish Year Book* and in 1900 became revising editor of the *Jewish Encyclopaedia*, a task requiring his removal to New York City for the remainder of his life. There he served on the faculty of the Jewish Theological Seminary of America. Book I of *Jewish Contributions to Civilization* appeared posthumously in 1919. In addition, Jacobs wrote a novel on the life of Christ, *As Others Saw Him* (1895), and many literary reviews for the *Athenaeum* which were later gathered in book form. The Jewish Historical Society of England elected him president in 1898 and 1899.

Yet if Jacobs had confined his labours to folklore his reputation would still have been secure. He served as editor of *Folk-Lore* from 1889 to 1900 during its most brilliant period, working closely with its publisher Alfred Nutt, who also issued various of Jacobs' own writings. Jacobs' interests lay in the popular moralistic literature of fables, apologues, and facetious tales. The fable was his speciality and joy and he traced its devious history in lengthy, learned essays prefaced to English editions. In 1888 he edited, as number three in Nutt's Bibliothèque de Carabas series, *The Earliest English Version of the Fables of Bidpai: or, The Morall Philosophie of Doni*. As he explained, 'I have edited Sir Thomas North's English version of an Italian adaptation of a Spanish translation of a Latin version of a Hebrew translation of an Arabic adaptation of the Pehlevi version of the Indian original. . . .'[1]

This was followed the next year by a handsome two-volume edition of *The Fables of Aesop as first printed by William Caxton in 1484 with those of Avian, Alfonso and Poggio*. Again Nutt was the publisher. Volume one was given over to a *History of the Æsopic Fable*. Jacobs related the 'Beast-Fable' to Greek folklore, explaining the paucity of references in classical Greek literature by the familiarity of Greek youths with these common tales. In only one way was the Aesopic fable unusual:

. . . the Greek Beast-Fable bears the characteristic mark of folk-lore—anonymity. And yet from a certain time it is found connected with the name of a certain personality, that of

---

[1] Joseph Jacobs, *Indian Fairy Tales* (London, 1892), p. 229.

Æsop. Such a conjunction is unique, so far as I am aware. No other department of folk-lore—folk-tales, spells, proverbs, weather-lore, or riddles—is connected with a definite name of a putative author.[1]

Jacobs speculated that Aesop, the slave of Samos who lived about 550 B.C., used jests as a political weapon rather than a source for amusement, and hence they tended, in the manner of anecdotes, to cluster around his name. For a definition of the form which he called at various times Beast-Tale, Beast-Satire, and Beast-Fable, he proposed '. . . a short humorous allegorical tale, in which animals act in such a way as to illustrate a simple moral truth or inculcate a wise maxim.'[2] Only in Greece and India did the folk-fable seem to flourish among the people and rise from folklore into literature. In India where the belief in transmigration generally prevailed, anecdotal stories about men posing as beasts could easily gain currency. In 1894 Jacobs prepared a popular edition, *The Fables of Æsop, Selected, Told Anew, and Their History Traced*, stripped of scholarly apparatus.

In 1895 Jacobs turned to a comparable classic and edited, with an Introduction and full notes, *The Most Delectable History of Reynard the Fox*. Next to Aesop, he wrote, Reynard the Fox was the 'best known of the tales in which animals play the chief part . . . [and] shares with Æsop the distinction of being a piece of folklore raised into literature. . . .'[3] Jacob Grimm's nationalist theory, in *Reinhart Fuchs* (1834), that the story derived from a primitive Teutonic beast epic, was now exploded and a French origin accepted. Jacobs lost no opportunity to plump for migration. Commenting on the well-known folktale of the wolf who lost its tail fishing through the ice, a story reported 171 times by the Finnish folklorist Kaarle Krohn, he pointed out that it was first written down in *Reynard the Fox*. Therefore 'we must assume that the Iced Wolf's Tail has lived among the Folk for over a thousand years, and that it was from the Folk that the French satirist first adopted it.'[4] So the animal tale must have wandered and not arisen independently, because it is found in tropical lands where ice does not form.

Also in 1895 Jacobs wrote a lengthy introduction to the Edward William Lane translation of *The One Thousand and One Nights* in which he once more unravelled an intricate history of a literary classic strongly permeated with folklore. The stories added in 1709

[1] Jacobs, *The Fables of Æsop* (London, 1889), I, 30–1.   [2] *Ibid.*, p. 204.
[3] Jacobs, *The Most Delectable History of Reynard the Fox* (London, 1895), pp. viii–ix.
[4] *Ibid.*, p. xvi.

by the Frenchman Antoine Galland to the narrations first arranged in sixth-century Persia were, Jacobs felt, European folktales in Oriental dress.

He returned to the question of resemblances in European and Indian tales the following year, 1896, in an edition of *Barlaam and Josaphat, English Lives of Buddha*, which Nutt published as Volume ten of the Bibliothèque de Carabas. Speaking of the similar legends attached to Buddha and to Christian saints, Jacobs declared that the enigma of their relationship would have to be solved on 'Folklore principles. In other words, till Folklore has become so much of a Science as to be able to discriminate between foreign and independent origin, this question must remain an open one.'[1] That is to say, folklorists would have to deal with the question of migration. Again he introduced a folk-literary form, the parable, a tale with a double meaning, but differing from the fable in having human not animal actors and from the allegory in its greater conciseness. The parables of Buddha had apparently circulated by literary not oral means and hence threw little light on the diffusion of folktales.

Besides these editions of Indian and Near Eastern folk-literary stories, Jacobs initiated a series of folktale books adapted for children which rivalled that of Lang in appeal and exceeded his in scholarship. Five titles appeared within four years, under the imprint of Nutt: *English Fairy Tales* (1890), *Celtic Fairy Tales* (1892), *Indian Fairy Tales* (1892), *More English Fairy Tales* (1894), and *More Celtic Fairy Tales* (1894). Like many of his co-workers on the Continent, Jacobs asserted he was emulating the feat of the brothers Grimm in assembling and polishing the tales of the people. While Jacobs did faithfully list the sources for his composite and adapted texts, today's folklorists will give their attention to the rich comparative notes in the appendixes. For England Jacobs found slim pickings, but in the other volumes he was able to select from an abundance.

In his essays and notes Jacobs championed the diffusionist theory to explain the scatter of folktales and accordingly he belaboured the survivalists. Andrew Lang had merely substituted one false bride for another in replacing mythology by anthropology. Lang and his school held that complicated plots could be re-invented by men in different times and places, but mounting evidence pointed to the movement of a single elaborate tale, like Cinderella, from mouth to mouth and from speech to print and then back to speech. Jacobs contended that Lang and Hartland erred in looking for survivals in tales

[1] Jacobs, *Barlaam and Josaphat* (London, 1896), p. xiv.

instead of looking at the tales themselves. Unlike other divisions of folklore, such as custom and rite, folktales no longer served practical ends of life, say in placating evil spirits, and so the anthropological method was least applicable to tales.[1] In his ingenious exposition of *The Science of Fairy Tales,* Hartland failed to consider adequately whether fairy legends originated in the countries where they were collected. In short, 'the problem of diffusion is of prior urgency to that of origin.'[2] With his emphasis on printed storybooks and social intercourse as the principal explanation for the similarities of far-flung tales, Jacobs was causing increasing discomfort and dismay to the Establishment.

While Joseph Jacobs directed his broad erudition into the wandering theory, Francis Hindes Groome (1851–1902) was reaching the same position from a single-minded, obsessive interest. Gypsies intrigued and eventually possessed him, and it was his delving into gypsy lore and life that led him into The Folk-Lore Society. 'I am no folklorist,' he announced defensively in the Foreword to his authoritative collection of *Gypsy Folk-Tales* (1899). 'But for twenty years I have been trying to interest folklorists in Gypsy folk-tales.' Born in Monk Soham, where his father was rector, he observed closely the modern nomads who camped on the Suffolk greens and found his wife, Esmerelda Lock, among their number. As a young man he 'knew hundreds of Gypsies in most parts of England and Wales.'[3] At first their Romany speech was his overriding concern, and he would return satisfied after a walk or a ride of thirty miles if he had gleaned two or three new words. In 1880 he wrote from his notebooks a rambling, conversational account of these encounters, *In Gypsy Tents,* which already shows his involvement with matters folkloric: glimpses of the fairies, Romany charms, a children's 'sense-riddle' session, bouts of storytelling. Groome inserted a number of folktales, commenting that the Welsh gypsies, such as his prize narrator John Roberts, were much richer in stories than their English cousins. He himself entered into the story-fests under the stars, noting the tale of 'Happy Boz'll,' a favourite of the East Anglian gypsies, and the conversation that followed.

---

[1] Jacobs, 'The Science of Folk-Tales and the Problem of Diffusion,' *The International Folk-Lore Congress, 1891. Papers and Transactions,* ed. J. Jacobs and A. Nutt (London, 1892), pp. 76–86.

[2] Jacobs, review of E. S. Hartland, *The Science of Fairy Tales,* in *Folk-Lore,* II (1891), 124.

[3] Frances Hindes Groome, *Gypsy Folk-Tales* (London, 1899), p. lv. A new edition with a Foreword by Walter Starkie was published in 1963 by Folklore Associates, Philadelphia.

'That's a regular Lucas's tale,' said Dimitri; meaning by Lucas a Romani Munchausen who flourished half a century ago, but is still remembered for his marvellous powers of romancing. And I capped 'Happy Boz'll' with the Gipsy lying-tale from the Bukovina, of the man who clambered up a willow-tree to heaven, and descended by means of a rope of barley-straw, which proving too short, he kept cutting off above and tying on below. Then Dimitri himself recounted the story of 'Dootherum Jimmy,' which deserves preservation only as being singularly wide-spread among our English Gipsies.[1]

Besides setting down tale texts in their milieu according to modern practice, Groome also showed an instinct for comparison and a familiarity with the standard collections such as Campbell's for the Scottish Highlands, Ralston's for the Russian, and of course the Grimms for Germany. He pointed to the close resemblance of the Romanian gypsy text of the master thief with the Gaelic and its divergence from other specimens in Italy, Germany, and Scandinavia. He was prepared to suggest the view that gypsies transported tales from Asia to Europe.

Groome formed acquaintances with several circles of folklorists and gypsy-lorists who helped him shape his major work. While residing at Edinburgh and writing as sub-editor for *Chambers' Encyclopaedia*, he met such Scottish folklorists as the Reverend Thomas Davidson, contributor of 'admirable folklore articles' to the *Encyclopaedia*, William Alexander Clouston, and Lord Archibald Campbell. With John Sampson, librarian of University College, Liverpool, and a noted savant in gipsies, he helped establish the Gypsy Lore Society and its journal in 1888. Groome indeed became the chief link between the Gypsy Lore and The Folk-Lore societies. A good friend in the English group was his Suffolk neighbour Edward Clodd, whose inspiration to construct a book on *Tom Tit Tot* came from the Suffolk tale of that name recorded by Groome in *Ipswich Notes and Queries*. Clodd devoted a section of his *Memories* to Groome, printing a letter from him alluding to his romantic novel of gypsy life, *Kriegspiel*; Lang read it in manuscript and commented, 'Exciting and unsound: only isn't the butter spread rather thick?' When Groome finally put together his great collection of *Gypsy Folk-Tales*, he named on the dedication page 'Mm. Cosquin, Clodd, Jacobs, and Lang and their Fellow-Folklorists.' From Lang and Clodd he learned about folklore and from Cosquin and Jacobs about diffusion.

[1] Groome, *In Gypsy Tents* (London, 1880), p. 161.

A splendid introductory essay reviewed the known information about gypsies and presented data on Groome's tellers and their tales, concluding with his own theory of migration. He regarded the gypsies as, in the phrase of the American gypsyologist Charles Godfrey Leland, the 'Colporteurs of Folklore.'

To recapitulate, my theory, then, is this:—The Gypsies quitted India at an unknown date, probably taking with them some scores of Indian folk-tales, as they certainly took with them many hundreds of Indian words. By way of Persia and Armenia, they arrived in the Greek-speaking Balkan Peninsula, and tarried there for several centuries, probably disseminating their Indian folk-tales, and themselves picking up Greek folk-tales, as they certainly gave Greek the Rómani word *bakht*, 'fortune,' and borrowed from it *paramísi*, 'story,' and about a hundred more terms. From the Balkan Peninsula they have spread since 1417, or possibly earlier, to Siberia, Norway, Scotland, Wales, Spain, Brazil, and the countries between, everywhere probably disseminating the folk-tales they started with and those they picked up by the way, and everywhere probably adding to their store.[1]

Diffusion with a vengeance! For all his diffidence Groome did not hesitate to lock horns with Lang and to criticize the anthropological theory of folklore. What Lang called survivals in German peasant tales were 'living realities in Gypsy tents' whose inmates sell their blood to the devil, see fairies, worship trees, renounce their favourite food, and cease to mention the name of a dead husband or father. Only sixteen years earlier an English gypsy girl had cut the heart out of a white pigeon and flung the live bird on the fire, to avenge herself on her Gentile lover. In gypsy tales these incidents were not relics of antiquity but daily occurrences. As for Lang's objections against diffusion from India in historic times, Groome presented evidence to show that the gypsies accomplished that very feat.

Still, Groome did not overvalue the prospects for his theory. 'From solar myths, savage philosophy, archaean survivals, polyonymy, relics of Druidism, polygamous frameworks, and such-like high-sounding themes, it is a terrible come-down to Gypsies. . . .'[2]

[1] Groome, *Gypsy Folk-Tales*, p. lxxxii. In his 'Prefatory Note,' p. 2, to the new series of the *Journal of the Gypsy Lore Society*, I (July, 1907), David MacRitchie referred to Groome's Introduction as 'a treasury of recondite learning, displaying a combination of scholarship and intimate knowledge of Gypsy character which has never been equalled.'

[2] Groome, *Gypsy Folk-Tales*, p. lxxv.

When his fellow-diffusionist Jacobs became over-zealous, Groome gently rebuked him, declaring that his gypsies offered only one possible channel of circulation. Between 1879, in his forty-three line contribution to the *Encyclopaedia Britannica*, and 1892, in his twenty-two line contribution to *Chambers' Encyclopaedia* on the subject of gypsies, all Groome had claimed was that the gypsies might have carried some Asian tales to Europe, and this was still his position in 1899. He objected too to Jacobs' including three tales from a Welsh gypsy in *English Fairy Tales*. First and foremost Groome was a gypsy man; second, he was a migrationist. He supported the wandering theory only insofar as it bolstered the prestige of his gypsies. But these colporteurs of popular fictions, distributing tales found in the Grimms, in the *Gesta Romanorum*, in distant India, must be reckoned another thorn in the side of the evolutionists.

Another unpredictable figure came to the Society from Romania, the learned Moses Gaster (1856–1934), exiled from his native land for his part in helping settle Sephardic Jews in Palestine. He arrived in England in 1885, already a committed folklorist; two years earlier he had published in Bucharest *Literatura populară romană* (*History of Romanian Popular Literature*). For the rest of his productive life he resided in London, serving as the chief rabbi of the Sephardic community of England and entering fully into the intellectual activities of his new homeland. Within a year of his coming he was invited to deliver the Ilchester Lectures at Oxford. These were published in 1887 as *Ilchester Lectures on Greeko Slavonic Literature and its Relation to the Folk-Lore of Europe during the Middle Ages*, and their appearance made plain that diffusion had gained an impressive new spokesman.

Gaster leaped immediately into the battle front now taking shape. In a summary review of the folklore systems that had held the field, he lumped together the 'prehistorical theory' of the evolutionists, advanced by Lang, with the 'mythological theory' founded by Grimm, since both schools considered that the folklore of all nations stemmed from 'hoar antiquity.' In their place he proposed a 'theory of migration' or 'historical theory.' This new theory of folklore origins would shake the others 'to their foundations if we succeed by a closer inquiry to prove that it is often the result of a long development, that it is relatively modern, and that the similarity between the European and the primitive and tribal folk-lore is a deceptive one. . . .'[1] Accordingly he marshalled his

[1] Moses Gaster, *Ilchester Lectures on Greeko-Slavonic Literature* (London, 1887), pp. 7–8.

intimate knowledge of eastern European literary history to visualize the route from India, through Greece and the Balkans, taken by folktales in their written and spoken forms. In one footnote he praised Max Müller for tracing an Eastern tale through successive literatures until it became Europeanized, and in this sequence lay the nub of his own thesis. Theodor Benfey had first propounded the general theory of the Indic origin and literary dispersion of folk traditions found in Europe, and his investigation of the *Pantchatantra* constituted, in Gaster's view, 'a turning-point in the history of folk-lore.'[1] The Romanian rabbi admired the German scholar's pursuit of the famed storybook from India into Syrian and Arabic translations under the title *Kalila and Dimna*, thence into Greek in 1080, and ultimately into Slavic and other European languages. In this transcontinental migration of printed folktales Gaster found the key to Asiatic and European folktale resemblances. Once planted in the European nations, the storybooks sowed an oral literature among the peasantry. Once upon a time those books had derived from the lips of villagers in India.

Yet Gaster would correct Benfrey on certain important particulars. Benfey overstated the case for India and failed to separate folktales from other kinds of folklore. The survival theory might well hold for custom, ritual, and belief, but folktales, susceptible as they were to literary influences in historical times, should be considered separately. To support his point, Gaster dwelt on various influential story collections of the middle ages, such as *Syntipas*, better known as *The Book of the Seven Wise Masters*; the legendary biography of Buddha, *Life of St. Barlaam and St. Josaphat* (the latter being Buddha); and the *Life of Aesop*. All had made their way from East to West in successive editions and translations and had inspired a modern mythology some time after the tenth century. In particular, the *Life of Alexander the Great* had passed through numerous adjustments and national adaptations and so offered a superb example of the interacting influences of written and oral literature. So too the middle Greek epic of *Digenis*, a chivalric romance of a knight undergoing dangers for his lady love, entered Slavonic translations and affected Russian epic songs.

Religious legends especially appealed to Gaster, who wove into his thesis the apocryphal stories of the Old and the New Testaments and the miracle-filled lives of medieval saints. The phenomenon of Bogomilism, spreading from Bulgaria to other Slavic countries and to western Europe from the eighth century on, introduced a

---

[1] Moses Gaster, *Ilchester Lectures on Greeko-Slavonic Literature* (London, 1887), p. 117.

Manichaean doctrine of Oriental dualism to the serfs, sugar-coated with fantastic tales and vernacular verses. As a consequence, surmised Gaster, 'a whole cycle of popular religious literature arises.'[1] Merlin and Arthur correspond to Solomon and Asmodeus, Satan and Christ represent the Bogomil personifications of good and evil. The rabbi viewed Greek-Slavonic literature, especially its Christian and Buddhist elements, as a great conveyor-belt between the folk literatures of East and West. What India was to Benfey, the Balkans were to Gaster, a breeding ground for a marvellous literature and lore. Gaster conceived of one literary form coalescing into another and emerging as a folk product: the saga or legend, chronicle, knightly adventure, fairy tale, epic, and lyrical song.

The same year that his Ilchester Lectures appeared, Gaster printed in *Folk-Lore* a still more direct attack on the survivalists, 'The Modern Origin of Fairy-Tales.' Boldly he announced, '. . . instead of seeing in fairy tales remnants of old, forgotten mythology, I see in them the *last and modern* development of folk-lore.'[2] Fairy tales do not rest at the base of the pyramid erected from the lore of the folk; rather, they lie at the top of a literary mass of romances, novels, apologues, and religious legends. Introducing in 1893 a group of 'Székely Tales' in *Folk-Lore*, Gaster gleefully commented that the folktales found among this ethnically distinctive race living in Hungarian Transylvania closely matched the tales of the surrounding Saxons, Romanians, Serbians, Bulgarians, Albanians, and Greeks.

Differ among themselves as they might, the Great Team had never considered denying the prehistoric origin of folktales. With their zest for intellectual combat, they nevertheless welcomed Gaster to the fold, and the Society elected him president in 1907 and 1908. In the journal the rabbi printed a sheaf of articles, chiefly illustrating the eastern provenance of legends concerning the Grail, Merlin, Gulliver and the Lilliputians, and the Virgin Mary. To the Publication Series he offered in 1915 *Rumanian Bird and Beast Stories*, in English translation with an extensive Introduction. There he restated and refined his argument that Europe should be regarded as a spiritual unit evolving from a lower state of savagery but with different internal rates of development for different groups of nations. Evolutionists now searched the ends of the earth, among the Australian Bushmen and the American Red Indians, for

---

[1] *Ibid.*, p. 22.
[2] Gaster, 'The Modern Origin of Fairy-Tales,' *Folk-Lore Journal*, V (1887), 339–51. The article is reprinted in Gaster, *Studies and Texts in Folklore, Magic, Medieval Romance, Hebrew Apocrypha and Samaritan Archaeology*, 3 vols. (London, 1925–8), II, 1039–51.

hypothetical lower stages of culture, but better let them examine the less studied peoples of Europe. In these Romanian popular legends, so strikingly in contrast to the fairy tales of western Europe, one can see evidences of the stage when 'marvellous and wonder-working animals' were implicitly accepted as part of the popular faith.[1]

A confidently challenging voice is heard throughout the essay. 'If folk-lore is to become an exact science I venture to think that the problem of survivals will have to undergo a serious re-examination.' Gaster hammers away at his theory of the transmission of a European tale repertoire arising from one definite centre and moving from nation to nation during a great religious movement— that of the Manichaeans and Bogomils—when modern Europe was taking shape. The Arian and Manichaean heresies, particularly as carried by the Goths, helped disperse popular epic ballads and carols among the illiterate Slavic peoples. In the Romanian beast tales appear Manichaean conceptions of a human God, a shrewish Mary, the belief in metempsychosis. Indeed, the 'Rumanian tales are almost a running commentary on Grimm's *German Mythology*. . . .' Paganism and gnosticism mix happily. 'The heathen gods, the Christian saints, God and the devil legends, fairy tales, oriental imagery, mystical traditions and astrological lore are all inextricably blended together.' In a sense the collection is mistitled, for these are actually creation and biblical folk legends in which birds and beasts play a part.[2]

Gaster's scholarly career continued for two decades after the first World War, but his energies became increasingly channelled into Hebraic studies. In 1924 he brought out *The Exempla of the Rabbis*, based on printed and manuscript sources. He collected his scattered journal articles in three volumes between 1925 and 1928 under the title *Studies and Texts in Folklore, Magic, Medieval Romance, Hebrew Apocrypha and Samaritan Archaeology*; twelve articles had appeared in *Folk-Lore* from 1887 to 1923. His edition of *Ma'aseh Book: Book of Jewish Tales and Legends* was issued in the United States in 1934. This learned rabbi, writing with equal fluency in Romanian, English, German, and Hebrew, serving as officer of the Royal Asiatic Society, the Jewish Historical Society, and The Folk-Lore Society, contributed a Balkan tang to the golden period of the English folklore movement.

If the wave of the future lay with the diffusionists, their triumph

---

[1] Gaster, *Rumanian Bird and Beast Stories* (London, 1915), p. 3.
[2] *Ibid.*, pp. 16, 49, 59.

remained uncertain in the decades before the first World War, and the evolutionists too obtained reinforcements. A devoted trio who laboured for the Society and the doctrine of survivals were women, the first of their sex to make reputations in England as folklorists.

Of the influence exerted by the Great Team on one female convert there could be little doubt, for she was Lady Alice Bertha Gomme, the wife of Sir Laurence. While raising a family of seven sons, she succumbed to the magnetism of folklore, discovered a link between her domestic and intellectual concerns, and produced a work on children's games that in later years made her name more memorable than Sir Laurence's. Lady Gomme dedicated *The Traditional Games of England, Scotland, and Ireland* 'To My Husband.' Alfred Nutt published the two bulky volumes in 1894 and 1898. A preliminary title page listed them as part of a larger enterprise: 'A Dictionary of British Folk-Lore, edited by G. Laurence Gomme, Esq., F.S.A., president of the Folk-Lore Society, etc. Part I. Traditional Games.' In her Preface, Alice Gomme explained that her husband had been accumulating materials for the dictionary ever since the organization of The Folk-Lore Society, but because of the problems involved in publishing so vast a mass of materials, they had agreed to issue the games separately, while preserving the alphabetical dictionary form. Laurence Gomme also had a hand in arranging the two classes of descriptive and singing games. His wife called his system of analysing the game-rhymes 'an entirely novel feature in discussing the history of games.'[1]

In her prefaces, comments on the games, and the sixty-page 'Memoir on the Study of Children's Games' appended to the second volume, Alice Gomme faithfully adopted the methods of the anthropological folklorists. Children's games belonged with other folklore survivals, for they too contained practices and ideas once familiar to primitive peoples. Yet antiquaries had largely ignored them. Strutt confined his *Sports and Pastimes* to the formal games of skill played by boys and excluded singing and dialogue games. Now from her own observation and that of her correspondents Lady Gomme spread a bountiful table, adding to the board all the printed variants she could locate. The comparison of variants would help reveal archaic traits in these youthful diversions, a matter not discussed by Strutt, Halliwell, or William Wells Newell in his *Games and Songs of American Children*.

The alphabetical listing of the games camouflaged Lady Gomme's primary intent, to reconstruct the evolutionary ladder of children's

[1] Alice B. Gomme, *The Traditional Games of England, Scotland, and Ireland*, 2 vols. (London, 1894–8), I, ix.

pastimes. This aim is apparent in her 'Memoir' where she provided classifications by incident, such as courtship, lovemaking and marriage, victimizing or penalty, contest, dance, hide and seek, ball games, and games of skill or chance, which would delineate savage ideas and practices.

These games are of interest to the folk-lorists, as showing connection with early custom. We know that playing at games for stakes involving life or death to the winner, or the possession of the loser's magical or valuable property or knowledge, is not only found in another branch of folk-lore, namely, folk-tales, but there is plenty of evidence of the early belief that the possession of a weapon which had, in the hands of a skilful chief, done great execution, would give additional skill and power to the person who succeeded in obtaining it. When I hear of a successful 'conker' or top being preserved and handed down from father to son, and exhibited with tales of its former victories, I believe we have survivals of the form of trans-mission of virtues from one person to another through the means of an acquired object.[1]

Lady Gomme had even heard of a nut whose proud owner claimed it had conquered a thousand inferior nuts.

Among the various categories of games Lady Gomme beheld the shards of savage philosophy. In some versions of 'Tit-Tat-Toe,' an invisible third player received the score in case of a tie. Known as 'Old Nick,' 'Old Tom,' or 'Old Harry,' he recalled the Devil or earth spirit once assigned a portion of land or crops (a notion re-tained by Georgia poor whites in Erskine Caldwell's novel *God's Little Acre*). Ball games played by hand were once divination rites, and ball games played by teams recalled political contests between parish and town. Other skill and chance games revealed traces of funeral and harvest rites, well- and tree-worship, child-stealing, and forfeits.

Turning from games of skill and chance to dramatic games in-volving fixed words spoken or sung and accompanied by panto-mimic actions, Lady Gomme had no trouble finding all manner of ancient customs and beliefs. First she distinguished five methods of playing dramatic games: the line, circle, individual, arch, and winding-up forms. In them she recognized relics of contests, court-ships, village ceremonies, warfare, and animistic worship. After analysing forty-eight texts of 'Sally Water,' which she printed and

[1] Alice B. Gomme, *The Traditional Games of England, Scotland, and Ireland*, 2 vols. (London, 1894–6), I, 471–2.

arranged in tabular form, she conjectured its original meaning as a marriage ceremonial involving water-worship, a feature preserved in the maiden's name and the line 'Sprinkle, sprinkle, daughter [or Sally Water], and you shall have a man.'[1] Hartland in his *Perseus* and F. B. Jevons in his paper at the 1891 congress on 'The Testimony of Folk-Lore to the European or Asiatic Origin of the Aryans' dealt with marriage customs among both Aryan and non-Aryan speaking peoples. Estonian and Hindu brides alike made offerings to a water spirit and sprinkled their grooms. Jevons speculated that the Teutons obtained from the Estonians an element of this custom in which the bride stepped over a vessel of water. Lady Gomme speculated further that the singing game had very likely preserved more of the primitive custom than the Teutonic practice. 'A custom is very low down among the strata of survivals,' she mused, 'when it is only to be recognized as part of a children's singing game. . . .'[2] Hence 'Sally Water' preserved a rite dating back to pre-Celtic Britain and so confirmed Laurence Gomme's thesis, in *Ethnology in Folk-Lore*, of the non-Aryan origin of water-worship.

Thus wrote Lady Gomme, with perfect conjugal accord. Again, in the game of London Bridge she demonstrated her wifely understanding. When children formed a circle and then an arch, under which each ran and was imprisoned by the others, they clearly were perpetuating the idea of a foundation sacrifice. As the prisoner was taken, the arch (bridge) tottered. All over the world human beings were immured in walls to ensure the stability of buildings, and traditions lingered about the stones of London Bridge being spattered with the blood of children. In *Folk-Lore as an Historical Science* Laurence Gomme would devote much attention to legends of London Bridge to prove the importance of London in antiquity.

In keeping with the anthropological argument, Alice Gomme was obliged to seek out dramatic games and dances among contemporary savages, and ended her 'Memoir' with passable examples from the Mandan Indians, the natives of the Torres Straits, and villagers in India. For a closing benediction she invoked Tylor and Lubbock on miming and dancing among primitives.

The chef d'œuvre yielded by-products. In 1900 Alice Gomme published a small-quarto volume on *Old English Singing Games*, with harmonic arrangements of the traditional music and directions for playing the games. With her husband she brought out in 1916 in the National Home-Reading Union Pamphlets, Literature Series number four, a booklet on *British Folk-Lore, Folk-Songs, and*

[1] *Ibid.*, pp. 149–79.   [2] *Ibid.*, p. 177.

Singing Games. Their opening statement lauded folklore as a subject 'generally useful . . . for home reading and home study' in its humanity, philosophy, richness of local associations, and fascinating manner of explaining the past and present. The Gommes went on to discuss collections, sources, and studies. Folklore as a subject now shared the stage with folksongs. Here was the path of destiny leading from survivals to revivals, from the antiquarian studies of The Folk-Lore Society to the eurythmics of the English Folk Dance and Song Society.

Lady Gomme developed her interest in children's games through Charlotte Burne, as a result of curious circumstances. Miss Burne's sister in Derbyshire employed as a nurse a young woman from the music-loving parish of Madeley in Shropshire. This sister had the nurse teach the singing games she knew to village children in Derbyshire for parish festivities. The result was a great success, Miss Burne informed Mrs. Gomme, who in turn began teaching new games to groups of children in her community of Barnes on the outskirts of London. A dubious committee, representing the 1891 congress, went down to Barnes to inspect this performance, finally agreeing to let the children disport at the *conversazione,* and Lady Gomme 'had the success of the Congress.' Miss Burne recounted this incident in her presidential address to The Folk-Lore Society in 1910, an occasion on which one accomplished woman folklorist paid tribute to another.

In her address Miss Burne described herself as the first female president of a learned society in the Old World. She earned the honour as a stalwart contributor to the journal and the architect of two major contributions, the much expanded and influential revision of Gomme's *Handbook of Folklore* and the volume of *Shropshire Folklore* (both discussed in the following chapter). As these works indicate, her interests lay in the gathering of field materials, not for the sake of dilettante collecting but as part of a vigorous, systematic inquiry for the new generation of folklorists. Unhappily, this inquiry was blighted by the Great War before it was fairly launched.

In her persuasive and programmatic presidential addresses of 1910 and 1911 Miss Burne proposed a new look for folklore. She would turn around the 'method of folklore' first devised by Lang and increasingly emphasized by Hartland. Instead of studying savage customs to understand the European peasant, now, thirty years later, the folklorist should concentrate on his own country traditions the better to comprehend the savage. Here lay the answer to the question currently being raised, what should the Society do now that ethnology and culture studies had won their way into the universities and the historic works of folklorists from Brand to Hartland had earned general esteem? Let the folklorists re-inspect in their own backyard the doctrine of survivals, to distinguish the medieval from the totemic species, the local variation from the separate genus. Students of culture have uncovered reasons for the decay of folklore but in so doing have neglected to investigate the causes for continuance. Why do survivals survive? As they surely do—and Burne rattled off instances of primitive ideas kept alive in modern times. Look, for example, at the folklore surrounding the ballad of the 'Bitter Withy,' recently uncovered in Herefordshire and attached to aetiological myths, sympathetic magic, symbolic rites, and proverbial sayings. Because the Virgin Mary had spanked the Child with a willow stick, the willow was an accursed wood. Custom, belief, and practice all blended in these modern survivals and found expression in song, tale, and proverb. Oral literature of the countryside contained the germs of belief and rite surviving in innocent diversions and rustic speech. Gather in these survivals abounding in village life. Only ten years earlier The Folk-Song Society began its quest and within that short span had gleaned a thousand airs from Dorset, while Cecil Sharp singly had reaped a great harvest from Somerset.

Such was Miss Burne's message: collect in order better to comprehend the nature and process of survivals. The rustic differed only in degree from the savage, who too possessed his survivals, though in lesser number. As of 1911, field work in England displayed large gaps; eleven of the forty English counties, including Kent, Hampshire, Somerset, and Warwick, still lay fallow. To buttress and underpin the field collecting, Burne announced that the Society would sponsor an up-to-date edition of Brand, singling out the Calendar Customs for first attention. Ironically, the call for collecting in behalf of survival would be answered in the spirit of revival. The future lay indeed with the followers of Cecil Sharp, whose motives were vocal and social rather than philosophical and historical.

A timid recluse of delicate health, devoting her maiden life to the care of aged parents in London, Marian Roalfe Cox presented a sharp contrast to the bustling, hearty Charlotte Burne, but she too found in The Folk-Lore Society an outlet and a purpose. Its notable scholars accepted her offer of selfless labour and outlined enterprises. In 1895 she wrote *An Introduction to Folk-Lore* dedicated 'To my friend Edward Clodd, who suggested its theme' and faithful to the quasi-official creed of the evolutionists; Burne indeed described the book as an account of the idea of animism. In her Preface

Miss Cox paid tribute to 'Mr. Lang, as the admitted chief' from whom 'must all students of Folk-Lore learn' and on whose writings she had drawn extensively. Miss Cox made no pretences to eclecticism, saying frankly that her book was written as a 'general survey of Folk-Lore from one point of view only—the anthropological.'[1]

Although coming only fourteen years after George Cox's *An Introduction to the Science of Comparative Mythology and Folklore*, Marian Cox's rival *Introduction* seemingly belonged to a different subject. She portrayed folklore as a record of man's beliefs and customs from the first traces of his thought. Current practices of daily life teemed with survivals of prehistoric ideas. Using illustrations from savage races and peasant peoples around the globe, she showed primitive notions recurring universally, such as the beliefs in a separable soul, animal ancestors, ghost-gods, and the magic power in names. Only in her final chapter did she discuss the categories of oral literature, the myths, *Märchen*, legends, ballads, rhymes, riddles, games, dramas, and proverbs, all of which too expressed ancient philosophy. 'Rhyming charms and mystic formulae are employed in *Märchen* to create mist or darkness or dazzling light,' she explained, 'as the savage medicine-man uses incantations when he makes the weather.'[2] In her final sentence she slapped at the diffusionists who accepted the literary passage of tales from Europe to India within historic times, by calling attention to similar tales on Egyptian papyri of 1400 B.C. The *Introduction* reached a second, enlarged edition in 1904, in which she thanked her publisher, Alfred Nutt, for valuable suggestions, primarily a new twenty-four page 'Bibliography of Folk-Lore.'

In spite of her anthropological alliances the fates decreed that Marian Cox's principal work would delight the diffusionists. This was *Cinderella*, published by The Folk-Lore Society in 1893 and undertaken at the suggestion of its council, as a test case of their plans for classifying the incidents in folktales. The subtitle explained that *Cinderella* comprised 'Three Hundred and Forty-five Variants of Cinderella, Catskin, and Cap O'Rushes, Abstracted and Tabulated, with a Discussion of Mediaeval Analogues and Notes.' She did not intend to betray her benefactors. Lang introduced the work, and she thanked him for making 'so noble a godfather.' Hartland gave 'invaluable advice, and every possible encouragement,' besides translating Spanish, Portuguese, and dialect versions; Miss Cox quoted his article in the *Folk-Lore Journal* on 'The Outcast Child,' discussing the King Lear branch of the Cinderella cycle and demonstrating that Shakespeare obtained

[1] Marian Cox, *An Introduction to Folk-Lore* (London, 1895), p. vii.   [2] *Ibid.*, p. 280.

his plot from Geoffrey of Monmouth.[1] Nutt assisted with books, notes, references to medieval legends, and three Gaelic Cinderellas. With the backing of the council, Miss Cox was able to obtain help from numerous folklorists in Britain and on the Continent who sent her variant texts. In the end her trail led exclusively through Aryan collections, although she loyally pointed to parallels of the story 'in genuine savage folk-lore.'[2]

Cinderella, begun innocently as a pilot study in sorting folktales, ended as a beacon for the diffusionists. This, the first comparative study of a complex tale, ushered in the anatomical method that would dominate folktale scholarship in the following century. The abstracting of tale plots, ransacking of printed and archival collections for variants, co-operation with fellow-workers in other lands, and division of the story into central subtypes (Cinderella, Catskin, Cap o' Rushes) would all become standard procedures of tale specialists in another generation, but in Finland rather than in England.

While the Society grew in numbers and lustre, a solitary don trained in the classics was fashioning in his study at Trinity College, Cambridge, a work on magic that seemed to grow magically and threatened to overshadow all other writings on folklore. When James G. Frazer's *The Golden Bough* made its first appearance in 1890 in two volumes, folklorists did not hesitate in claiming it for their shelves. Jacobs coupled the *Bough* with William Robertson Smith's *Lectures on the Religion of the Semites*, which he reviewed together in *Folk-Lore* (with two lesser works) as 'a veritable triumph for folk-lore' in applying the method of survivals to the study of primitive Semitic and Aryan religion. True, he considered Robertson Smith's researches probably the more original and accorded it first attention. The *Bough* seemed to him a more diffuse production, separable into three themes: the tracing of the custom of slaying the divine king; the presenting of Mannhardt's researches on agricultural deities; and the offering up of the author's own hoards of primitive custom and belief, particularly on harvest rituals. These riches frequently led into sizable monographs on a taboo or a conception. Jacobs frankly envied Frazer his labours of compiling and ordering 'the whole literature of folk-lore and savage life.' Nor was Jacobs disturbed by the anthropological approach, for he perceived a harmony with the borrowing theory: customs,

[1] Hartland, 'The Outcast Child,' *Folk-Lore*, IV (1893), 308–49.
[2] Marian Cox, *Cinderella* (London, 1893), pp. lxix, lxx, xliii.

languages, and institutions originated at one time and place and spread by diffusion.[1]

Ten years later, when the *Bough* had spread to three volumes in a second edition, a battery of eight reviewers gave the magnum opus the most extensive treatment ever to be accorded a single work in the Society's journal. The phalanx of reviewers numbered three of the Great Team, Gomme, Lang, and Nutt, as well as Gaster and Miss Burne, who inspected the *Bough* with close care to see how it fit into, or out of, the forward progress of folklore science.[2]

Gomme observed areas of difference between the Cambridge don and his own associates. 'If Mr. Frazer is right and Mr. Lang is wrong, if Mr. Frazer right and Mr. Hartland wrong, then we have this grand study of a great subject left intact to us.'[3] But if Frazer erred, then some aspects of *The Golden Bough* needed amendment. The collaborative critical process would benefit all parties. Gomme's criticism followed his particular theory of separate racial deposits surviving in folk custom; he felt that Frazer had not sufficiently sifted ritual elements belonging to the religion of Imperial Rome and to more archaic layers. Frazer had found no complete parallel in any European tradition to the rites of the priest-slayer at Nemi, probably because he erroneously viewed the rites as a 'homogeneous original.' Recognizing 'imperceptibly' the problem, the Cambridge don sought to correct it with abundant illustrations to press home his comparisons, rendering the work lavishly readable but also unduly inflated. In making this criticism Gomme was anticipating the objections of twentieth-century anthropologists to Frazer's overfree linkage of customs and rites from unlike cultures. Gomme made his case, however, on the grounds that Frazer was juxtaposing customs from dissimilar 'survival-groups.' In conclusion, Gomme called for agreement on the use of the survival doctrine by Lang, Hartland, Clodd, and Frazer and hoped that such accord would yield the chief fruit of *The Golden Bough*.

Nutt chose to emphasize a point in praise of Frazer neglected by reviewers, 'the force and cogency of his appeal to folklorists.' He also stressed Frazer's deep debt to Mannhardt, saying '. . . their names will remain indissolubly linked together in the history of folklore scholarship.'[4] Delightedly Nutt pointed out that the Frazer-Mannhardt hypothesis treating harvest and May-day customs in place of oral story, song, and riddle fit the evolutionist

[1] Joseph Jacobs, 'Recent Research in Comparative Religion,' *Folk-Lore*, I (1890), 384, 394, 395.
[2] *Folk-Lore*, XI (1901), 218–43. The other three reviewers were E. W. Brabrook, A. C. Haddon, and F. B. Jevons.
[3] *Ibid.*, p. 222. [4] Nutt, in *Folk-Lore*, XI (1901), 238.

better than the diffusionist position. These accumulated examples of vegetation rites well supported the concept of the cultural stages and psychic unity of man, who was for ever concerned with the magical and practical control of food production. As a result of this interest and involvement, man employed his dramatic and mimetic faculty to create ritual forms accompanying the magic actions.

Man lives by bread—man does not live by bread alone: these two statements contain in germ the Mannhardt-Frazer hypothesis, the one which I firmly hold to explain most adequately the largest body of those diverse and well-nigh innumerable practices, opinions, and fancyings designated folklore.[1]

Hence the verifiability of the Arician custom of slaying the divine king is a secondary matter. If ultimately unproven, the merit of Frazer's chief hypothesis, namely the central role played by agricultural rite in the life of early man, remains unharmed.

Lang was not so happy. He attacked the key equation connecting the Saturnalia, the feast of Purim, and the Crucifixion of Jesus, whereby Frazer sought to explain the ritual background of a sacrificial death to insure renewed vegetation. The Scot held that Frazer's reasoning was based on conjecture, false analogy, unwarranted surmise, and invalid reference. In *Folk-Lore* Lang delivered only an abbreviated statement, since his *Magic and Religion* dealing with related questions was then in press, and because in the *Fortnightly Review* for February and April, 1901, he had devoted lengthy essay-reviews to *The Golden Bough* and 'Mr. Frazer's Theory of the Crucifixion,' meticulously pouncing on each detail in Frazer's chain of reasoning. First he discredited the hypothesis of a ritual regicide, preferring to think of such acts as a 'rude form of superannuation,' since commanders and professors were easy to pension off while aged kings presented more of a problem. Next, the Scot disagreed with Frazer's assumption of a primitive, godless stage of culture dominated by magical processes; this is the later Lang arguing against Tylorian animism and for high gods, even among Australian aborigines. In his second essay Lang refuted with closely reasoned logic and evidence Frazer's argument connecting the Crucifixion with the priest-slaying in the Arician grove, a theory added to the second edition.[2]

Moses Gaster, in his section of the multiple review in *Folk-Lore*, presented with a furious passion similar historical objections to the Crucifixion thesis, terming it pure fiction. We may surmise that Gaster's indignation stemmed from the slur attached to Purim as

[1] *Ibid.*, p. 239. [2] Lang, *Fortnightly Review*, LXXV–LXXVI (1901), 236–48, 650–62.

a ritual murder by the Jews, while Lang resented the idea, which in his earlier years he would have underscored, that behind the central drama of Christendom lay a barbarous sacrificial rite.

Burne also cavilled at the Crucifixion theory and warned against any all-encompassing monistic solution, whether animism, totemism, the evil eye, or Frazer's agricultural sacrifice, which might well go the way of solar mythology.

Hartland wrote an extended review in *Man*, where it appeared not under 'Folklore,' as did a number of other reviews, but under 'Religion.' Offering the customary plaudits to the author's felicitous learning, he took issue with Frazer's sharp severance of magic and religion. More personally, he tried to appear unwounded by Frazer's refutation in his third volume of Hartland's views on sympathetic magic. Perhaps more than one train of savage reasoning can account for such therapeutic customs as passing a sick child through a split ash-tree. Frazer has a tendency to impute the same motive to outwardly similar rites. Hartland had said that not all European harvest customs involved the slaying of the corn spirit to insure fertility of the fields: rather, they appeared to guarantee the proper reaping of the harvest. Frazer was far too monistic in his interpretations.[1]

All this attention failed to resolve the question whether and to what degree Frazer belonged to the fraternity of folklorists. By the time the third edition emerged in 1914, the *Bough*, now exfoliated to ten serial volumes, had become a recognized landmark, and the Society promptly claimed it and its creator as their own. The president of The Folk-Lore Society, Robert Ranulph Marett (1866–1943), rector of Exeter College, Oxford, Reader in social anthropology, and the biographer of Tylor, who would hold office for five years during the war period, hailed 1914 as a 'wonder-year' casting glory on the Society.

> Sir James Frazer is one of ourselves. He has been a member of this Society for a long time past, has served on the Council, and is actually Vice-President. Besides, he has the entire contents of our manifold publications at his fingers' ends. There is scarcely a page of his encyclopaedic work that does not bear witness to the activity of our Society. Hence his triumph is likewise our triumph. We participate collectively in his supreme achievement. In fact I am almost tempted to describe *The Golden Bough* as the 'external soul' of this Society.[2]

[1] Hartland, in *Man*, I (1901), No. 43, pp. 57–60.
[2] Marett, *Psychology and Folk-Lore* (London, 1920), p. 3

After these encomiums Marett did consider whether the province of *The Golden Bough* fell to folklore or to social anthropology. The two, he felt, were rightfully allied and applied by Sir James 'to illustrate and explain the workings of the human soul.' Really, Frazer was serving the cause of psychology, 'the rightful queen of the historical methods,' declared the Exeter don, grinding his own axe.[1] *The Golden Bough* could truly be called a study of the psychology of the folk.

In other papers and addresses, gathered together in 1920 in *Psychology and Folk-Lore*, Marett returned to the themes of Frazer's artistic scholarship. An essay on 'Magic or Religion?' considered the evolution of *The Golden Bough* and the ultimate position of its author. On its initial appearance the *Bough* had puzzled and antagonized anthropologists, who found its treatment of superstitious savages degrading alongside Tylor's animistic primitives; consequently they disparaged Frazer as a classicist out of his field. Only Robertson Smith, the great historian of Semitic religion, smarting under the blows his work had suffered in Calvinist Scotland, gave support. After a decade, when a basically unaltered second edition came forth, the *Bough* attained respectability and favour. A reading public indifferent to scholarly polemics relished the 'golden treasury of stories for grown-up children' and appreciated learning about the less advanced peoples within the Empire. Meanwhile, a year before the second edition, Spencer and Gillen had published their momentous ethnology, *The Native Tribes of Central Australia,* whose proofs Frazer had seen through the press at the authors' behest, and whose data admirably confirmed Frazer's view of brutish, benighted savages.

By the time of the third edition, anthropologists and university administrators as well as lay readers had capitulated. And now the greatly expanded *Bough* dropped all pretence of tracing the murderous rite of the priest of Nemi and abandoned its endless pages to lyrical descriptions of picturesque savage customs; the *Bough* had become an encyclopaedic anthology of facts surrounding the thought and custom of primitive man. In Frazer's attempted division of these facts into realms of the magical and the religious, however, Marett scented trouble. If the slain god sacrifice belonged to a religious system, how could it evolve from the rite of the slain priest, which occurred within a vegetation-magic system? But in any event the *Bough* had laid out great masses of materials from which a theorist could draw his evidence.

Marett was also enchanted by Frazer's three volumes on *Folk-*

[1] *Ibid.*, p. 4.

Lore in the Old Testament (1918). In his essay on 'The Interpretation of Survivals' the rector used it as a touchstone for a probing re-examination of the survival concept. Sir James had employed the now classical method of folklore study to ferret out relics of savagery 'preserved like fossils' in a later stratum of culture, in this case the Hebrew civilization displayed in the Old Testament. Such survivals of ruder ideas, observed Sir James in his Preface, fall under folklore. Marett criticized the method for confusing the 'historically ancient with the psychologically crude,' a point he made continually; a blurred survival need not descend from a once clear original, but may simply indicate the unclear idea of a lower mentality found at all times in all societies. In the main, Frazer's industry and learning had saved him from this over-simple interpretation of survivals. He was content to point out without attempting to explain the similarities in widespread legends and customs, for instance in myths of man's creation, found alike in Genesis and among many primitive peoples. As Marett observed, and Frazer apparently recognized, only a Cinderella-like study such as Miss Cox's could advance the case for culture-contact through diffusion. Sometimes a survival might be re-adapted, as in sophisticated myths of man's fall which betray irrelevant elements found in savage Just-So stories, or again limited diffusion could take place from several centres of origin, as seemed to be the case with the flood myths. Turning from legends to customs, Marett beheld the fossil-hunter on firmer ground, for customs did constitute a more substantial order of survivals, less subject to diffusion. Yet here too the evolutionist must read warily. Both in ancient Israel and modern Judaea the alleged survivals of polytheistic worship, expressed in offerings to sacred trees, stones, and towers, were actually rampant revivals.

These essays are more revealing of Marett's mind than of Frazer's, affording the rector of Exeter an opportunity to inject his psychological theory of folklore into appraisals of the *Bough* and the *Old Testament*. Both the Cambridge and Oxford dons wrote primarily as Tylorian culture anthropologists with a strong but secondary interest in folklore researches and a primary concern with primitive religion. Frazer properly belongs in the intellectual tradition of the Cambridge anthropologists—Jane Harrison, Francis M. Cornford, Albert Bernard Cook, Jessie Weston—who perceived in Greek religious ritual the seedbed for literary and dramatic expressions of myth. Sir James took little part in the activities of the Society and was unconcerned with the cause of folklore as an independent science.

Marett, on the contrary, did become involved in the Society as its long-term president, but his academic training, lecturing and research were in social anthropology. Actually he inherited one division of Tylor's chair, the area of social anthropology. His own fame dated from an 'epoch-making' paper on pre-animistic religion printed in *Folk-Lore* in 1900 in which he revised Tylor's concept of animism, contending that primitive man imputed life forces rather than spirit powers to inanimate objects.[1] He wrote brief accounts of Lang, Gomme, and Hartland for the *Encyclopaedia of the Social Sciences* and obituaries of Lang and Hartland in *Folk-Lore*. Yet his one work relevant to folklore, *Psychology and Folk-Lore*, simply brought together eleven occasional papers, five of which he had delivered to The Folk-Lore Society as presidential addresses. Marett represents the end of the great burst of intellectual energy that had invigorated the founding generation of the Society, and he himself was a transitional figure, a younger friend but not a member of the Great Team and without their intense commitment to folklore, which he regarded as a domestic department of social anthropology. Still, even the partial application of his speculative mind to folklore theory enriched the movement.

In his chief theoretical argument Marett sought to refine the doctrine of survivals, link them with revivals, and describe a dynamic and continuous rather than a static and moribund process. Echoing Burne's query, why do survivals survive, he suggested heretically that folklorists participate in the traditional customs and games still extant about them, the better to understand the mechanism of selection and adaptation enabling survivals to persist in the midst of modern civilization. This process of selection intrigued the psychologist within him. Marett was no song-and-dance revivalist but a sophisticated social scientist who did not scruple to introduce such terms as 'depragmatization,' referring to a custom whose utility gives way to ornamentation, and 'devulgarization,' for a debased folklore item which rises in social value. He hoped the analysis of culture change would replace the constructing of a 'bloodless typology,' and a true recognition of the interplay of 'survival and revival, degeneration and regeneration' would be achieved. Folklore belongs to the here and now, Marett proclaimed. In place of a science of survivals, he preferred to speak of 'The Transvaluation of Culture,' the title of his 1918 address. In a civilized country

---

[1] The phrase is used by E. O. James in his obituary of Marett in *Folk-Lore*, LIV (1943), 271. Marett's article on 'Pre-Animistic Religion' appeared in *Folk-Lore*, XI (1900), 162–82. A warm account, 'R. R. Marett,' is given by L. H. Dudley Buxton, the editor of *Custom is King, Essays presented to R. R. Marett on his Seventieth Birthday* (London, 1936), pp. 3–8. Buxton alludes to Marett's friendship and controversy with Lang over the Australian High Gods.

folklore is continually migrating up to and down from 'clerk-lore' and thereby changing its status and use. If most goes down, yet some goes up, as in the case of refurbished folktales or the absorption by Hinduism of primitive cult elements. This vertical change of meaning Marett called metataxis. But a horizontal process was also at work, metalepsis, or change of meaning on the same plane, as when a charm against the evil eye becomes a bauble or an outmoded ritual appears in a folktale episode. Perhaps in the reshuffle of values caused by the Great War, the folk themselves would be redistributed and become absorbed in the people. In any event, 'the unconscious art of the folk can develop into art of the conscious and refined order, and must do so if the latter is to be truly national in type.'[1] Thus the complex mechanism of transvaluation may raise up, renew, and reshape a sunken tradition, completing the cycle of change, 'the downward way being compensated by the upward way, the falling rain by the reascending vapour.'[2]

The rector of Exeter College prophesied better than he knew. One species of folklorists in the postwar years did avidly embrace revivals, but these non-folk singers of folksongs and dancers of folk dances showed no passion for problems of metataxis or metalepsis.

In discussing survivals Marett was not so much the critic as the whittler of his predecessors' ideas, and he sought in particular to synthesize the concepts of Tylor and Gomme in a fruitful new union. He wished to locate a 'meeting-place and joint laboratory' for Tylor the anthropologist, employing the psychological or evolutionary method, and for Gomme the folklorist, applying the sociological, ethnological, or historical method. This meeting-ground he believed to exist in the psychical process of culture contact.

> While the historical method will attend chiefly to the assemblage of pre-existing conditions, the evolutionary, which is likewise essentially a psychological, method will be mostly concerned with the spontaneous origination, the live and truly evolutionary movement of spiritual awakening, that ensues upon the fact of cultural contact and cross-fertilization.[3]

For instance, according to Gomme's thesis, when Aryan invaders in Britain borrowed or adapted beliefs of the pre-Aryan natives, they were conforming to a psychological law that required the alien conquerors to placate the sacred powers of their new homeland. Herein psychology affected ethnology. According to Tylor, this process occurred regularly and could be stated as a universal mental law.

[1] Marett, *Psychology and Folk-Lore*, pp. 116–17.   [2] *Loc. cit.*   [3] *Ibid.*, p. 97.

Both systems, Marett contended, depended on the psychological awareness of culture contact.

One can only speculate as to the results if a new generation of fieldworkers had endeavoured, as Marett hoped, to test his theories of cultural dynamics in the green fields of Britain. But no such generation emerged after the war.

Some part-time but talented folklorists were brought within the orbit of the Society through the publication series which the council supported along with the journal. This growing bookshelf reflected the breadth of the British folklore movement in the scope and variety of its titles, which ranged geographically from the Isles to the far continents and topically from field collections to scholarly reprints, monographic treatises, and special reference works. In a sense the series gave an official imprimatur to earlier classic studies by printing Aubrey's unpublished though well-known and well-pilfered *Remains of Judaisme and Gentilisme* (1881) and elaborating Brand's *Popular Antiquities* into a sequence of volumes on Calendar Customs. The Society also reprinted one of the earliest and most useful of the county collections, William Henderson's 1866 edition of *Folk-Lore of the Northern Counties of England and the Borders* (1879).

While Aubrey and Henderson were household names, a third antiquary brought to light by the Society had reached but a limited audience with his pamphlets irregularly issued between 1846 and 1859. Michael Denham was a tradesman in Pierse Bridge in the north country with an instinct for recording unconsidered trifles. He printed his budgets of local sayings, rhymes, slogans, observances, charms, plant lore, and border traditions in newspapers and booklets; one of 1850 appears to be the first separate publication to carry 'folk lore' in its title. Thoms became interested in these fugitive leaflets, some of which found their way into the libraries of the Society of Antiquaries and the British Museum, and arranged for their reprinting through the council of The Folk-Lore Society. Gomme wrote prefaces to the two volumes which appeared in 1891 and 1895 under the title *The Denham Tracts, A Collection of Folklore by Michael Aislabie Denham*, and when the appointed editor, James Hardy, took ill Gomme completed the task of seeing Volume II through the press. In the unadorned, haphazard, but honest compilations of the tradesman, Gomme saw evidences of great value for the ethnic folklorist. 'Mr. Denham's work is like Aubrey's, and Aubrey's is the foundation of English folk lore.'[1]

[1] Michael A. Denham, *The Denham Tracts*, ed. James Hardy (London, 1895), II, viii.

The first volume contained 'local and family traditions and characteristics' and the second 'peasant superstitions and customs.'

Too often nowadays, Gomme believed, the collector and the student of collections crossed the line that properly divided their functions, but not so with unpretentious Denham. From the materials gathered by such as Denham could Frazer and Hartland weave their *Golden Bough* and *Perseus*. Better the present lawless disarray than an artificially reordered catalogue of superstitions, games, and proverbs. Gomme cited for an example the divination practised by servant girls at Wooler who tied their left stocking around their neck when retiring in order to dream of their future husband. Uninformed classifiers would probably have placed this item under superstitions relating to dress, when properly it belonged with the beliefs of the Romans, discussed by Grimm, in the luck of the left rather than of the right. In the Roman wall district of northern Britain people still believed in this notion, but in the Teutonic south the left was unlucky.

Denham had benefited from contacts with the older antiquaries, contributing to Hone's *Every-Day Book* and to Moses Richardson's *Table Book*. In 1846 he prepared for the Percy Society a seventy-three-page 'Collection of Proverbs and Popular Sayings relating to the Seasons, the Weather, and the Agricultural Pursuits, gathered chiefly from Oral Tradition.' Thereafter he pieced together tracts relating to the Isle of Man and the north of England, and in his last year, 1859, printed in an edition of fifty copies his largest compendium, *Folklore: or a Collection of Local Rhymes, Proverbs, Sayings, Prophecies, Slogans, etc., relating to Northumberland, Newcastle-on-Tyne, and Berwick-on-Tweed*. The good merchant also pursued physical antiquities, writing about Roman remains during the construction of the Darlington and Barnard Castle Railway and collecting Roman coins. An old-style antiquary in the pre-Tylor years with a flair for local oddities, Denham and his modest work were appreciated and resurrected by the Society folklorists. In the *Denham Tracts* the scientific folklorist like Gomme believed he could see traces of god-names, ancient clan and family customs, and the primitive worship of rivers, wells, and fires. The old rhymes of Border chieftains preserved for him a culture in transition from clan to village life.

Personal reminiscences occasionally enlivened the *Tracts*. Denham recalled his fear as a child of being snatched into the river Tees by the evil goddess Peg-Powler. His father, who had died in 1843 at the age of seventy-nine, remembered people in his Yorkshire parish of Bowes attempting to cure murrain in cattle by passing them through the smoke of a need-fire made by rubbing dry sticks together. Most of the items, however, came from print; many of the slogans, rhymes, and epithets embodied local and border traditions of the kind gathered by Chambers, whose *Popular Rhymes* Denham greatly admired, saying that 'a more delightful book on popular archaeology was never written.'[1] A sample anecdote giving rise to a north country proverb illustrates the border humour of the *Tracts*.

'Warse! and Warse!' as the Parrot said to the Yorkshireman.

A story is told how, once upon a time, an honest Northern rode into the yard of a hostelry, somewhere in the *sweet south*, and vociferated at the extent of his stentorian voice, 'Wostler! Wostler!' Now it happened that a parrot (which hung in the court-yard of this neglected mansion of the olden time, not being so well acquainted with the dialectic tongues of Britain as a few *ryght lerned* and unfeathered bipeds which I could readily name) mistook the countryman for a native of *the land of cakes*, and said to himself, in a voice sufficiently loud though to be heard by the new-come guest '*Proud Scot! Proud Scot!!*' The traveller, considering himself grossly insulted by the parrot, cast his eyes up at Poll and retorted with, '*Thou'se a d——d leear, for Ize a Yorkshireman.*' 'Worse! and Worse!' quoth the parrot. And so the dialogue ended, to the great chagrin of the 'honest Yorkshire bite.'—*Literary Gazette*, 14 October, 1848, p. 685.[2]

Talking parrot stories have enjoyed a wide vogue from ancient India down to modern America, and here the bird's riposte serves the formula of Border insults.

Still other volumes added to the assets of English folklore. A series within the series brought together fugitive printed traditions and customs of county folklore to provide an inventory of the existing references in local newspapers, annals, memoirs, and periodicals.[3] Gomme's *Handbook of Folklore* served as a guide for ordering

---

[1] Michael A. Denham, *The Denham Tracts*, ed. James Hardy (London, 1895), I, 311.
[2] *Ibid.*, p. 120.
[3] The following districts were covered in the series *County Folklore: Printed Extracts:* Volume I (Publication XXVI, 1895), 1. Gloucestershire, edited by E. S. Hartland; 2. Suffolk, collected and edited by Lady Eveline Camilla Gurdon, with Introduction by Edward Clodd; 3. Leicestershire and Rutland, collected and edited by Charles J. Billson. Volume II (Publication XLV, 1897), North Riding of Yorkshire, York, and the Ainsty, collected and edited by Mrs. Gutch. Volume III (Publication XLIX, 1903), Orkney and Shetland Islands, collected by G. F. Black and edited by Northcote W. Thomas. Volume IV (Publication LIII, 1904), Northumberland, collected by M. C. Balfour and edited by Northcote W. Thomas. Volume V, Lincolnshire

and classifying the extracts. In *Folk-Medicine, A Chapter in the History of Culture* (1883), William George Black drew instances of traditional cures, charms, spells, and remedies largely from the British Isles, with appropriate savage analogies. No mere cataloguist, Black carefully ordered his materials within an evolutionary structure. He challenged Herbert Spencer's theory that primitive man attributed the causes of disease and death to spirits of the dead, substituting instead, as a good Tylorian, the anger of an external spirit found in animate and inanimate nature, and the supernatural powers of a human enemy. Healthy primitive man did not easily succumb to hallucinations, nightmares, and spirit fancies! The Reverend Charles Swainson, rector of Old Charlton, amassed *The Folk Lore and Provincial Names of British Birds* (1886), giving for each wild bird its local and dialectal names, followed by the survivals of popular belief about the bird gleaned from folklore notes and collections. Thus for 'redbreast' Swainson listed such familiar terms as robin, robin ruck, and bob robin. Proceeding to the accumulated lore, he reported an incident from *Notes and Queries* of a young man who shot a robin to test the belief that the family cow would then give bloody milk, which indeed it did. From Chambers and Henderson he added testimonials to the misfortune befalling those who killed a robin or broke its eggs. Other popular legends associated the robin with the Saviour, the Virgin, and the wren, while traditional rhymes hailed the robin as a fire-bringer and a coverer of the unburied dead.

But England occupied only a part of the attention of members of the Society. Scotland was represented with the ample collections of Walter Gregor, *Notes on the Folk-Lore of the North-East of Scotland* (1881), Donald MacInnes' *Folk and Hero Tales* (1890), and R. C. Maclagen's *The Games and Diversions of Argyleshire* (1901). For Europe there were several tale harvests: *Portuguese Folk-Tales*, collected by Consiglieri Pedroso and translated by Henriqueta Monteiro (1882), *The Folk-Tales of the Magyars*, translated and edited by W. Henry Jones and Lewis L. Kropf (1889), and *Rumanian Bird and Beast Stories*, assembled by Moses Gaster (1915). The high Middle Ages had spokesmen in *The Exempla or Illustrative Stories from the Sermones Vulgares of Jacques de Vitry*, edited by the American Thomas F. Crane (1890) and *The First Nine Books of the Danish History of Saxo Grammaticus*, translated by Oliver Elton

---

(Publication LXIII, 1908), collected by Mrs. Gutch and Mabel Peacock. Volume VI, East Riding of Yorkshire (Publication LXIX, 1912), collected by Mrs. Gutch. Volume VII, Fife (Publication LXXXI, 1914), collected by John Ewart Simpkins.

and introduced by Frederick York Powell (1894). Africa was re-
presented with a reprint of an 1870 treatise by Bishop Henry
Callaway, the pioneer collector of Zulu tales, on *Izinyanga Zoku-
bula, or Divination as Existing among the Amazulu* (1884) and R. E.
Dennett's *Notes on the Folklore of the Fjort*, with an introduction by
Mary H. Kingsley (1898). On other continents, the publications
included tale collections of the Ainos of Japan, the Musquakie
Indians of North America, and the Jamaican Negroes of the West
Indies, as well as the popular poetry of the Baloches, an Asiatic
people inhabiting an area from northwest India to Afghanistan and
Persia.

The Great Team too participated in the series. Hartland published his *Primitive Paternity*, Nutt his *Studies on the Legend of the
Holy Grail*, Miss Cox her *Cinderella*, and Gomme and Miss Burne
their editions of the *Handbook of Folk-Lore*. In the years from the
founding of the Society until the Great War the series grew into a
remarkable library of studies, collections, and scholarly aids swell-
ing the resources of the science of folklore.

Not every active folklorist of the period entered The Folk-Lore
Society. Most of the scientific and fully committed professionals
joined and supported its goals, as did a good many interested
amateurs and converts. Gleefully Gomme announced how the zoologist Alfred Cort Haddon had gone on the Torres Straits expedition
in 1888 as a natural scientist and returned an ardent folklorist,
publishing model tale collections in *Folk-Lore* and continuing his
work in Ireland.[1] But occasionally a semiprofessional pursued his
researches in splendid isolation. On reviewing Canon J. A. Mac-
Culloch's *The Childhood of Fiction* (1905) in *Folk-Lore*, William
Crooke remarked that the author of a work expressing so completely the thesis of folklore survivals had not established connections with the Society.[2] Perhaps his remoteness on the Isle of
Skye accounted for this indifference.

In another category fell the popular writers who, then as now,
catered to a public appetite for the occult and the quaint. Such a
marginal figure was the Reverend Sabine Baring-Gould (1834–
1924), the enormously prolific parson from Devonshire, said to
have more books to his credit in the British Museum catalogue
than any man alive. Antiquarian, romancer, country squire, clergyman, hagiographer, song collector, Baring-Gould flirted with folk-

---

[1] Gomme, in *Folk-Lore*, II (1891), 13. Haddon's 'Legends from Torres Straits'
appeared in *Folk-Lore*, I (1890), 47–81, 172–96.
[2] Crooke, in *Folk-Lore*, XVII (1906), 505.

lore in the course of his torrential output of over two hundred volumes. He was attracted to local oddities and strange events, curious characters and survivals of olden times, and his titles reflected these interests. Tylor quoted his *The Book of Were-Wolves* (1865) for modern illustrations of metamorphosis and demon-possession. Everyone quoted *Curious Myths of the Middle Ages* (1866; Second Series, 1868), an alert round-up of legendary traditions circulating throughout the Western world: the Wandering Jew, William Tell, Prester John, the Pied Piper of Hamelin, the man in the moon, the faithful dog Gellert, the Fortunate Isles, tailed men and swan-maidens. These promising early ventures petered out into skimmings and adaptations from literary sources which he used to fill *A Book of Fairy Tales* (1894), *Old English Fairy Tales* (1895), *Fairy Tales from Grimm* (1895), and *A Book of Ghosts* (1904). He poured a miscellany of beliefs about the human spirit and body, marriage and death, brownies and pixies, and the gods of old into *A Book of Folk-Lore* (1913). His one contribution to folklore science was a plan for classifying the elements in folktales, or 'story radicals,' presented in an appendix to William Henderson's *Notes on the Folk Lore of the Northern Counties and the Borders* (1866) and reprinted in abridged form in the *Folk-Lore Record* in 1882.[1] Family relationships gave him one key to plots about husbands and wives, parents and children, and brothers and sisters, subdivided into stories of desertion, abandonment, supernatural kinfolk, and incestuous love. Another group matched men against supernatural beings, other men, and beasts. The *Types of the Folktale* in standard use today contains some of these divisions.

In his writings on folk beliefs, customs, and tales Baring-Gould engaged in little or no fieldwork, but in the realm of folksong he undertook original collecting. A chance dinner conversation in 1888 on the subject of old Devonshire songs connected with hunt suppers, sheep-shearing, and harvest feasts led him into a successful search for the texts and tunes of traditional songs. Although the parson considered it his duty to rectify inadequate texts, still he stimulated the faithful ingathering of folk music with his *Songs and Ballads of the West* (1891), *A Garland of Country Song* (1895), and his six volumes of *English Minstrelsie: A National Monument of English Song* (1895–7), a vast potpourri of art, popular, and folk songs. For his song prizes he tracked down railroad men on the line and farmers in the pubs. But this imaginative fieldwork led him away from the paths of The Folk-Lore Society, which he apparently never

[1] Baring-Gould, in *Folk-Lore Record*, V (1882), under 'Existing Schemes of Classification,' pp. 208–11.

joined, and toward its distant cousin, The Folk-Song Society, which opened its doors in 1899.[1]

Even more perplexing to the scientific folklorists was the popularizer who wrote without regard for their principles and in complete disregard of the movement. The Reverend Thomas Firminger Thiselton-Dyer spewed forth a spate of folklore books during the heyday of the Society: *British Popular Customs* (1871), *English Folk-Lore* (1878), *Domestic Folk-Lore* (1881), *Folk Lore of Shakespeare* (1883), *The Lore of Plants* (1889), *Church-lore Gleanings* (1891), *The Ghost World* (1893), *Folk-Lore of Women as illustrated by legendary and traditionary tales, folk-rhymes, proverbial sayings, superstitions, etc.* (1905). These alike bore the character of scrapbook compilations juxtaposing roughly similar beliefs and customs. In *The Ghost World*, Dyer combed spooky narratives to furnish information on the appearances, habits, and behaviour of ghosts. For *English Folk-Lore* he strung together fancies about animals, birds, and insects, birth, marriage and death, the days, the months, and the weather. Since the clergyman snipped from proper authorities like Aubrey, Grose, Brand, Pennant, Douce, Halliwell, and Tylor, he deserves a higher rating than the sentimental popularizers of today. In brief, polite notices the fathers of the Society observed that these digests of familiar materials might serve to stimulate deeper interest in folklore matters in their readers.[2] In his *The Fairy Mythology of Shakespeare*, however, Nutt tersely commented that Thiselton-Dyer's *Folk Lore of Shakespeare* 'cannot be recommended.'[3]

Among the private antiquaries pursuing folklore labours in solitude, Vincent Stuckey Lean (1820–99) reared the most imposing structure. Four posthumous volumes appeared between 1902 and 1904 under the title *Lean's Collectanea: Collections of Vincent Stuckey Lean of Proverbs (English & Foreign), Folk Lore, and Superstitions, also Compilations towards Dictionaries of Proverbial Phrases and Words, Old and Disused.*[4] Lean was born in Bristol and studied for the law at the Middle Temple but never practised. Instead he indulged his taste for reading and travel, carrying a book in his hand and marking proverbs on his country walks. Eventually he settled

[1] William E. Purcell has written *Onward Christian Soldier, A Life of Sabine Baring-Gould: Parson, Squire, Novelist, Antiquary, 1834–1924* (London, 1957).

[2] Thus the anonymous reviewer of *Domestic Folk-Lore* in the *Folk-Lore Record*, IV (1881), 200. Hartland found some folklore nuggets in his notice of Thiselton-Dyer's *Old English Social Life as Told by the Parish Registers*, in *Folk-Lore*, X (1899), 475–6.

[3] Nutt, *The Fairy Mythology of Shakespeare* (London, 1900), p. 38.

[4] Actually they were issued as Volumes I to IV, with Parts I and II of Volume II being bound separately. A memoir by Julia Lucy Woodward is given in Volume I, ix–xvi.

down to a routine of steady note-taking at the British Museum reading-room, dining at his club and the Temple. Frugal in his habits, he left considerable bequests to libraries and hospitals.

Lean copied into his notebooks all manner of archaic sayings, allusions, and popular notions encountered in his determined browsing. He intended to bring up to date the great work on English proverbs begun by Ray, and had caustic words for William Carew Hazlitt's 'chaotic mass' of *English Proverbs and Proverbial Phrases* (1869). But the *Blason populaire de la France* of Henri Gaidoz and Paul Sébillot evoked his praise for recognizing proverbial slurs. The bachelor barrister amassed curious nuggets of lore in the manner of Aubrey and Brand and fondled books and manuscripts like Douce. He never arranged his materials for publication, and in their printed form they remain a conglomerate of several miscellanies: English local and domestic sayings; beliefs and superstitions of daily life; literary proverbs; similes; a dictionary of archaic expressions; another of English aphorisms. His list of authorities exceeds a hundred pages. All this was compiled in intellectual solitude, save for excursions into the pages of *Notes and Queries*, and the *Collectanea* stand as a monument to antiquarian self-indulgence in the age of the co-operative new science.

The high water mark of the British folklore movement came with the International Folk-Lore Congress held in London the first week of October, 1891. Almost all the stellar names in the Society participated, and other luminaries crossed the English Channel and the Atlantic Ocean to take part. The newspapers and journals gave full coverage, illustrating their feature articles with sketches of Andrew Lang delivering the presidential address at Burlington Hall, Edward Clodd reading a paper on 'Tom Tit Tot,' Alice Gomme's performing youngsters playing 'Oranges and Lemons' and 'Poor Mary sits a' Weeping,' duellers in a scene from 'The Guisers' Play,' a Welsh harper, and a songstress singing 'Sally Gray.' One marvels at the detailed transcripts of weighty addresses and the attentive commentaries in column after column of small type reporting the daily sessions. Even the correspondence departments carried statements and protests by congress participants. Few newspaper readers in the fall of 1891 could have escaped knowing about the controversial theories of folklore and their vigorous proponents.[1]

The *Telegraph* offered a long disquisition on September 28, although the congress did not begin until October 1, on the subject

[1] Mrs. H. A. Lake Barnett, Hon. Treasurer of The Folk-Lore Society, kindly allowed me to see G. L. Gomme's scrapbook of news clippings of the congress.

of a *conversazione* of the congress members to be held October 5 in
Burlington House, Piccadilly, in the rooms of the Society of Antiquaries. A printed announcement of this 'Conversazione and Exhibition' gave details.

An English Mumming Play, Children's Games, Sword Dance,
Savage Music, and Folk Songs will be given during the evening.
It is further proposed to arrange a Loan Exhibition of objects,
for the week of the Congress, connected with and illustrative of
Folk-lore, Portraits of eminent Folk-lorists, Collectors of Tales,
old Chap-books, etc.

Members were urged to contribute curios and money for expenses,
with any surplus going for the acquisition of specimens to form the
nucleus of a Folk-Lore Museum. The *Telegraph* reporter believed
the *conversazione* would prove

quite the most spirited and peculiar enterprise that any society
devoted to antiquarian research has ever attempted. Our Folk-
Lore enthusiasts are not content with surveying the past 'far
as human eye can see,' unearthing strange old customs, superstitions, tales, and songs, but they now intend to impress their
discoveries on the world by means of an object lesson.

Gravely the *Telegraph* writer recommended the practice of a little
'Variety entertainment' at future learned congresses. He also explained the nature of the *conversazione* as talk, principally on
literary subjects, among the invited guests—a kind of panel dis
cussion, with the prospect of light refreshments in the background.

The next day, September 29, the *Daily News* heralded 'The Folk
Lore Congress' and discussed the concept of folklore with knowledge and wit, in the manner of Andrew Lang, whose name is
missing from the authorities cited.

Folk Lore is a science with a new name, but under other
names it has always existed. The old antiquarians were Folk
Lorists without knowing it, and ARISTOTLE himself had that
interest in savages and their queer institutions, which now
marks the children of Mother Goose. It is rather difficult to say
what Folk Lore exactly is. Perhaps it is hardly to be distinguished from anthropology, which is the study of mankind
everywhere, in the sum of their institutions. The peculiarity of
Folk Lore is to approach the whole subject from the side of
ancient practices, beliefs, and rites, surviving either among the
least educated and most stationary classes; or among the
educated who retain or have borrowed their superstitions.

And so on at length, with allusions to Frazer's 'triumph of the method of Folk-Lore' in solving the riddle of the priest-slaying at the temple of Aricia, McLennan's 'invention' of totemism, the conversion of Mannhardt from the solar mythology still supported by Adalbert Kuhn and Max Müller, the lively sympathy of France for folklore, and the awakening interest of the Finns. 'It should be a pacific little Congress,' the article concluded, 'though a squabble or two is only what we must expect among antiquarians . . . maybe solar mythologists will burn wax images of their opponents, or tie the nine witch-knots against them. Such war is fair in Folk Lore.'

On October 2, all the papers carried extensive accounts of the proceedings of the first day. *The Times* devoted five columns to 'The International Folk-Lore Congress,' most of them taken up with the presidential address of Andrew Lang. By way of background *The Times* explained, 'It is the second assembly of the kind that has been held. The first was organized at Paris in 1889, during the time of the great Exhibition.' At the conclusion of the Paris Congress it was determined to hold the next meeting in London, and the American Charles Godfrey Leland was deputed to express the intention to British folklorists, who warmly responded to the request of their French and foreign *confrères*. *The Times* turned to new 1891 business, reporting a telegram sent to the Queen of Romania: 'International Folklore Congress congratulate your Majesty on the progress to recovery of the most exalted of European folklorists.' (Queen Carmen Silva was known as a patroness of the arts, including the folk arts.) Alfred Nutt expressed the hope that the London congress would presage a long and successful series of folklore congresses, and proposed the creation of an international folklore council to regulate such meetings. His motion was acted upon, and seventy-six scholars were nominated to the council.

The *Chronicle* in its two plus columns on October 2 described how folklore had come to be taken seriously. 'No study is more thoroughly international in its aims, for it pertains to that human nature of which it has been said that we all possess so much.' Aubrey and Brand were its prophets, Thoms its baptizer, and Laurence Gomme its present high priest. The English executive was to be congratulated on the brilliant gathering assembled at Burlington House, which had drawn a considerably larger attendance than at the first congress, in spite of the numbers attracted to Paris by the Exhibition. The London congress offered a feast for the eyes, the ears, and even the mouth, for Mrs. Gomme had assembled a collection of traditional cakes from all parts of the country: simnel and parkin from Lancashire, wigs and wake cakes from Shropshire, statue buns from Rutland, brown geordies from Cumberland, fairy rings from Cornwall, shortbread from Scotland, Parliament cakes from Middlesex. The *Daily News* remarked that ladies dominated the audience, but counted among the male foreign delegates Charles Ploix, president of the Societé des Traditions Populaires, and Paul Sébillot, the well-known collector, from France, and William Wells Newell, editor of the American Folklore Society, and Charles God-frey Leland, president of the Gypsy Lore Society, from the United States. *The Times,* which carried two substantial articles on the Congress on October 2, reported Mr. Leland's appeal to the congress to avoid unseemly heat during the discussions between rival theorists. Formidable polemicists were expected to cross swords: Andrew Lang, 'who has done more than any man to systematize folk-lore,' insisted on the value of folklore as a key to the mind of primitive man; Max Müller saw solar myth in nearly every legend and believed that the early Indo-Europeans talked chiefly about the sun; and J. S. Stuart Glennie explained all through racial con-flict and matriarchal origins. (Müller, as it turned out, could not attend.)

All the papers quoted the presidential address of Andrew Lang, who 'rose mid cheers' to deliver the inaugural speech, described as graceful, witty, and instructive. *The Times* printed the text in full, indicating clever sallies that drew laughter. And so the congress commenced, with each symposium receiving respectful attention.

The full galaxy of stars from The Folk-Lore Society had col-laborated to plan the congress. Gomme was chairman of both the executive committee and the organizing committee, the latter in-cluding Tylor, Frazer, Lubbock, Gaster, Rhys, Robert Brown, Miss Cox, Major Temple, and other well-known figures. Clodd was honorable treasurer of the congress and a member of the executive and literary committees. Nutt was honorable secretary of the liter-ary committee and a member of the organizing committee. Hartland was chairman of the folk-tale section and a member of the organ-izing committee. Jacobs was on all three main committees and chairman of one, the literary committee. Lang was president of the congress. Lang, Hartland, Gomme, Nutt, and Jacobs read papers, and Nutt and Jacobs co-edited the congress proceedings for publi-cation. Mrs. Gomme was honorary secretary of the reception and entertainment committee, on which Miss Burne also served.

This high-powered group deliberated the structure of the congress well over a year in advance and carefully co-ordinated the sessions. The congress revolved around the conflicting English theories of folklore science, although a valiant effort was made to enlist

[301]

international participants. Gaston Paris could not come from France to explain his views on ballad diffusion. Cosquin sent a paper but stayed in Paris. Edmund Veckenstedt, editor of the *Zeitschrift für Volkskunde*, was in disgrace, charged with unscrupulous manipulation of Lithuanian folklore texts, and his invitation was publicly rescinded.[1] On behalf of the Empire there were reports for India and Ceylon. Papers were assigned to four sections, folktale, mythological (myth, ritual, and magic), institution and custom, and general theory and classification. 'The Committee recommend that under each section the papers and discussions should be taken, as far as possible, in chronological or logical order, dealing in turn with the relations of the subject—Tales, Myths, or Customs, in their present phases—to those of savage, classical, and mediaeval times and conditions.'[2] Indeed, the entire congress was viewed as an occasion to examine and probe the system of the British anthropological folklorists.

It is suggested that the papers, so far as practicable, should serve to test a conception now widely held, especially among English folk-lorists and anthropologists—the conception, namely, of the homogeneity of contemporary folk-lore with the earliest manifestations of man's activity as embodied in early records of religion (myth and cult), institutions, and art (including literary art).[3]

But the papers provided only part of the evidence for survivals, and various outings and exhibits skilfully reinforced the master thesis while adding to the fellowship and social pleasure. The much publicized *conversazione* was held at Mercers' Hall, Cheapside, 'by kind permission of the master and wardens of the worshipful company of mercers.' Twelve children of Barnes Village School performed their games under the studious eye of Mrs. Gomme, a company of mummers from Staffordshire put on a folk-play, Clodd recited 'Tom Tit Tot' and Hartland 'King John and the Bishop of Canterbury,' and in addition there were Highland sword dancers, Welsh penillion singers, singing blacksmiths and besom-makers—not simply performing but illustrating survivals. There was the trip to Oxford and the Pitt-Rivers Museum whose archaeological specimens were explained by Tylor. And in Burlington House there was the splendid 'Exhibition of Objects connected with Folk-Lore'

[1] Hartland outlined the charges against Veckenstedt in his 'Report on Folk-Tale Research in 1890,' *Folk-Lore*, II (1891), 99–119.
[2] *The International Folk-Lore Congress, 1891. Papers and Transactions*, ed. J. Jacobs and A. Nutt (London, 1892), p. xviii.
[3] *Ibid.*, pp. xviii–xix.

made available by members of the Society. A kern or harvest baby, so central to Frazer's theory of vegetation rituals, was loaned by Charlotte Burne who had it from William Henderson. Tylor's remarks on his collection of charms and sorcerers' instruments were considered an 'epoch-making contribution to the archaeological side of folk-lore'; he dwelt on magical practices yet surviving and visible in English villages.[1] A forked hazel twig used by a Somerset water-finder was presented by Marian Roalfe Cox with a signed testimonial to his powers. From his celebrated expedition to Torres Straits, A. C. Haddon bequeathed a fire-charm and a bull-roarer. The continental traveller-author Rachel Busk loaned saints' head bands from Siena showing hair growing after death, to be used as charms against headaches. And so on, a panorama of amulets, artifacts, photographs, rare editions and manuscripts, drawings, engravings, carvings, and ornaments, all illustrating the continuity of primitive beliefs from the savage to the peasant. In addition, portraits were hung of John Aubrey, Sir Thomas Browne, Robert Burton, Bishop Callaway, Campbell of Islay, James Orchard Halliwell-Phillips, William Henderson, Robert Hunt, W. R. S. Ralston, Sir Walter Scott, William John Thoms, and Thomas Wright, among British folklorists, and Peter Asbjörnsen, Hans Christian Andersen, Wilhelm Bleek, the brothers Grimm, and Charles Perrault for continental folklorists.

To debate the omnipresent theme of savage survivals the congress participants gathered their forces. In his opening address Lang expressed concern as to the intensity of the passions about to be unloosed. He hoped that his challengers, whether solar mythologists or Archaian white racists, migrationists or ethnologists, would joust good-humouredly. The apprehension of violent disagreements was much in the air. Lang then proceeded to restate his own dogmas with his usual felicity.

Since the first use by Thoms, following upon old Aubrey and Brand, when folklore meant the recording of curious customs and relics of heathenism, the study of folklore has expanded to its present position embracing the science of man. Indeed, Lang can scarcely distinguish between folklore and anthropology. The science of folklore has turned upside down the old method of mythology.

The old manner was to begin with the cultivated and literary myths, as we find them in Ovid, or Apollodorus, or Pausanias, and to regard modern rural rites and legends and beliefs as modified descendants of these traditions. But the method of

[1] *Ibid.*, p. xxii; for Tylor's remarks see pp. 378–93.

Folk-lore is to study these rural customs and notions as survivals, relics enduring from a mental condition of antiquity far higher than that of literary Rome or Greece.[1]

All the harmonies and coincidences now uncovered among ancient peoples, barbaric races in remote corners of the modern world, and the unlettered peasants of Europe are explained by the method of folklore as the products of a 'vast common stock of usage, opinion, and myth, everywhere developed alike, by the natural operation of early human thought.'[2] From this reservoir the priests and poets and legislators find the fabrics for their laws, rituals, and epics. So the customs of the blood-feud form the basis of the Athenian law of homicide, the fertility magic of savages develops into the Eleusinian mysteries, the rural festivities of Attica grow into Greek drama, the *Märchen* of the blinded giant, the returned husband, and the lad with the miraculously skilful companions is molded into the Odyssey and the Argonautica. Upon this common stock of ideas, customs, legends, beliefs, the genius of the individual and the race sets to work to polish and refine its creeds and codes and epics, which co-exist among the advanced Aryan and Semitic races along with the old treasures retained by the folk.

Thus the theory of folk-lore in Lang's terms. He regarded primitive man as always seeking a rational explanation of the universe and arriving at a magical answer through false analogies, the doctrine of sympathies, and belief in spirits. The world he gazed upon was harsh and painful, filled with wizards and sorceresses capable of changing men into rabbits and of withering crops, but relieved by resplendent gods of the sea and the sun. Why did early man believe in ghosts and not in some other kind of non-scientific phantasm? Land could only conjecture that possibly there were ghosts.

The unity, the resemblances among the ideas and expression of all peoples, intrigued Lang, but he drew a division between like customs and beliefs, which responded to similar cultural and mental conditions, and parallel myths and stories, which might in part result from transmission in prehistoric and modern times. He could not align himself, however, with those folklorists who would assign one original centre for the dispersion of ideas or myths to India or Central Asia. The germs of the stories are to be found everywhere; their special forms are given by each race.

Hartland rallied swiftly to Lang's side the next day with the opening paper of the section meetings, his address as chairman of the folktale section. He had prepared his defences against the

[1] Lang, in *ibid.*, pp. 5–6. [2] *Ibid.*, p. 6.

coming onslaught from the disseminationists, as he styled them. First he shored up evolutionism by contending that a story could only penetrate a culture ready to accept it, for the 'stage of culture of the transmitting folk and that of the receiving folk must be identical.'[1] Even accepting Franz Boas' arguments for dissemination among Pacific Coast Indians, the tales Boas cites bear witness to the state of civilization of their tribal possessors. Hartland on his part offered examples of African, Burmese, and South American folktales with a strong family likeness but still completely mirroring their separate cultures. Really, the question of dissemination was quite secondary. Nor could it ever be judged precisely. Borrowing may just as well proceed from West to East, as in the case of the story of Ali Baba which had travelled from Europe to India. Then too, the likelihood of separate invention of basic human plots was more plausible than that of foreign importation. Hartland gave recent instances, confirmed by the novelist Walter Besant (a member of the organizing committee), of strikingly parallel literary fictions not possibly subject to plagiarism. In an appended note Hartland quoted A. R. Wright of Her Majesty's Patent Office on the frequency of parallel mechanical and chemical inventions.

In conclusion, the chairman regretted that the English had not more actively prosecuted the scientific study of folk poetry, which would surely illuminate the discussion of transmittal. To England's shame, the American Francis James Child had compiled the English and Scottish popular ballads.

An initial skirmish promptly took place. The American William Wells Newell offered the tale of 'Lady Featherflight' as collected from a cultured lady in Cambridge, Massachusetts. (This is known today as Type 313A, 'The Girl as Helper in the Hero's Flight.') Then tracing its manifold variations, he arrived at the general proposition that dissemination had taken place along the highways of commerce from higher to lower civilizations. Lang, stung to the quick, rose during the discussion to support Hartland and criticize Newell in the strongest terms. 'I regard the whole question of the origin of folk-tales as mysterious, and one which will, perhaps, never be solved at all.'[2] But he remained firm in his position that tales incorporated survivals of barbaric ways, although he would try to keep an open mind during the rest of the congress.

Two hammer blows immediately descended on Lang's redoubt. The paper sent by Emmanuel Cosquin referred to Lang's thesis as untenable and reaffirmed its author's view on the Indian source of related tales found in Europe and the Orient. Cosquin had

[1] Hartland, in *ibid.*, p. 20.   [2] Lang, in *ibid.*, p. 65.

expounded this argument at the First International Folk-Lore Congress in Paris in 1889 in speaking on 'L'Origine des contes populaires europeens et les théories de M. Lang.' Now he happily quoted Jacobs to the effect that the problem of diffusion must take precedence over that of origin.

Jacobs next read his paper on 'The Science of Folk-Tales and the Problem of Diffusion.' How could Lang and Hartland be so sure of the archaeological deposits in folktales when these tales might have been imported from other lands? This demurrer he had voiced earlier that year in his review of Hartland's *The Science of Fairy Tales*.[1] The pressing questions are, Where did the story first appear, and how was it *diffused* to the places where it has also been found? Little point in talking about savage ideas in folktales that may never have thrived among savages. Jacobs would prefer to study the recurrent incidents in tales and for that purpose has provided an appendix tabulating seven hundred such incidents common to European stories, accompanied by a map of 'Folk-Tale Europe' identifying collectors and their areas. He understands that Karl and Julius Krohn in Finland have been working on similar lines, and is pleased that Miss Cox in her forthcoming study of *Cinderella* has prepared a table of tale-incidents at Jacobs' suggestion.

Jacobs did not endorse Cosquin's view of India as the homeland of all the master tales. India may have borrowed as well as loaned. Rather, Jacobs proposed three criteria to determine centres of dispersion: the country with the fullest forms and most complete variants; the country with a distinctive custom crucial to the tale; and the country where the earliest known variant appears. What is true for the diffusion of folktales may also indeed apply to ballad literature, nursery rhymes, folk customs, and the other forms of folklore. By contrast, the casual theory of Lang and Hartland, arguing that similar incidents happen to cling together in Samoa, China, and Peru, disregards the doctrine of probabilities.

In the discussion that followed Alfred Nutt strenuously upheld Lang and Hartland against the 'false principles of Newell and Jacobs,' who looked to the flower rather than to the root. The quest of the diffusionists was foredoomed to failure. Yet Nutt's fellow-Celticist, Professor John Rhys, declared that after listening to both sides without prejudice or prior commitments he found the doctrine of probabilities the most telling argument.

One disseminationist appeared in another section, Frances Hindes Groome delivering his paper on 'The Influence of the Gypsies

[1] Jacobs, in *Folk-Lore*, II (1891), 125.

on the Superstitions of the English Folk' in the institution and custom section. Groome gave instances to show how gypsies transported non-gypsy beliefs and customs from one people to another. An English gypsy had told him how very ignorant were the Scotch. Why, a Scotchman at Abingdon who had lost his missus did not know enough to inform the bees and put crape over the hives, until told he would lose his bees; thereupon he did so gladly. 'But that shows as the Scotch are wery uncultivated.'[1] Again, the post-paper discussion revealed the schism of opinion, Gaster and Leland praising Groome's *colporteur* theory and Nutt denying that Groome's scattered examples of gypsy beliefs in fairies, the devil, the evil eye, and name taboos had any bearing on the theory. Besides, Leland himself had disagreed with Groome on whether the gypsies knew anything about palmistry.

The debate continued after the congress with a nervous intensity spurred by the publication of Miss Cox's *Cinderella* in 1893. The bemused Lang of the Introduction wore a worried air. Clearly on the defensive before the attacks of Cosquin and Jacobs, he concedes that 'a naked and shoeless race could not have invented Cinderella.' The imposing string of variants amassed among the Indo-European peoples and in the lands where they have penetrated gave him a jar. He will accept that some incidents in the *Märchen* kaleidoscope survive and spread more widely than others, but he will insist that many incidents appear to derive from the early mental habits of man. Some ground he yields to diffusion. Where he had asserted that 'much' is due to identity of early fancy and 'something' to transmission, he will now say 'much' in both cases. To Cosquin he retorts that Cinderella offers no features peculiar to India, and to Jacobs he repeats his disbelief that the original homes of fairy tales will ever be found and proclaims his interest in them as literature, as indeed 'the oldest novels, full of grace and charm.'[2]

Through the issues of *Folk-Lore* for 1893 and 1894 the protagonists tilted, with *Cinderella* as their prize. Nutt, Jacobs, and Lang engaged in parry and thrust with every resource of their dialectical armoury, Gomme and Hartland occasionally joining in, so that Jacobs single-handedly engaged nearly the whole anthropological team.

Nutt opened a continuing symposium on Miss Cox's study with 'Cinderella in Britain.' The publisher found heady comfort in an archaic Irish version he was able to communicate to Miss Cox at the last minute. His Celtic and British loyalties battened on the

---

[1] Groome, in *The International Folk-Lore Congress, 1891*, p. 293.
[2] Lang, Introduction to M. Cox, *Cinderella* (London, 1893), p. xxii.

thought that the tale of the cinder-maid might have originated in the British Isles.

Writing on the same topic, Jacobs pressed home his advantage gained at the congress. Only the borrowing theory could explain the similarities of so many Cinderella plots. The possibility of a story of twelve incidents occurring casually in the same sequence in two different places came to once in 479,001,599 times. Lang should disavow the casual theory which could only block the advance of folklore research.

A strangely ill-at-ease Lang replied with 'Cinderella and the Diffusion of Tales,' seeking to clarify his position to himself as well as to his critics. Not since 1872 had he denied borrowing.

> My first writing on the subject was done about 1863, when I was an undergraduate at St. Andrew's. Then I merely published two tales, which I call Scotch, in the *St. Andrew's University Magazine*. I had only read Mr. Max Müller, Perrault, Dasent, and Chambers, and, on the problem as it now stands, had no right to an opinion. But about 1871–72 I wrote an article for *The Fortnightly Review*. There I stated my whole theory. *Märchen* were of extreme antiquity, of savage origin, and were the stuff of the great classical epics.[1]

Since then he had indeed come to appreciate the fact of borrowing. Yet this modification of his youthful views by no means involved their total abandonment in 1893. 'One is not all Transmissionist, however; one still maintains a belief that casual, or independent evolution may account for *some* cases of resemblance.'[2] A little later Lang flatly declares that he is no casualist but a diffusionist—a term he also disliked—when it came to tales, but at the same time he believed too in independent invention and remained an agnostic on the question of determining a central point of origin. *Cinderella* had not altered but confirmed his thinking.

Another round of exchanges followed. Nutt issued a statement, 'Some Recent Utterances of Mr. Newell and Mr. Jacobs. A Criticism,' in which he seized on Jacobs' citing of conventional devices in Cinderella-like tales as a major concession to the anthropological folklorists. Such conventions prove the existence in Europe of a body of folk literature preserving archaic traits. Seeking to turn the shaft of ridicule back on Jacobs, who had scored heavily with his label of 'casual,' Nutt proposed to tar Jacobs with the brush of 'spontaneous generation.' Jacobs failed to recognize that every tale

[1] Lang, in *Folk-Lore*, IV (1893), 419. The article was actually published in 1873 in the *Fortnightly Review*.　　　[2] Lang, in *ibid.*, p. 420.

possessed a prehistory stretching far back beyond its first recorded literary instance. Trained in historical literature, Jacobs and Newell thought too exclusively in terms of literary influences and too little in terms of ancient folk tradition.

The evolutionists closed ranks behind Nutt. Gomme paused in his presidential address of 1894 to praise 'Mr. Nutt's powerful and singularly lucid defence of the anthropological interpretation' as a 'performance of which any society might be proud.'[1] In reviewing Jacobs' *More English Fairy Tales* the same year, Hartland too tossed a bouquet to the publisher, who had 'criticised with destructive power Mr. Jacobs' theories about the curious versions of "The Pied Piper" and "Cinderella".'[2] Both voiced disapproval at Jacobs' practice of maiming folktales. (Gomme jabbed also at the red, blue, and green fairy-book distortions of Lang.) The president sighed that the folktale had lost much of its anthropological charm now that it was become the 'sport of literature.'

To this multiple barrage Jacobs countered with a devastating cross-fire. The argument had now reached its climactic fifth act, by Jacobs' own count, in the polemic with Lang begun at the Congress. In a paper, 'The Problem of Diffusion: Rejoinder,' Jacobs laid down a series of seemingly unassailable propositions. He himself had begun as an anthropologist and still followed Tylor and Lang on the savage origin of unnatural incidents in folktales. This is the process which Jacobs wishes to underscore and which he here describes as the 'survival of the fittest' in folktales. The old savage fairy tales, which Haddon, Abercromby, and Codrington have been making visible in *Folk-Lore*, succumb to the coherence and beauty of better told European tales, just as the literary tales of Perrault and Grimm have obliterated the native English folktales. Jacobs now introduced the concept of lateral as distinct from vertical transmission. Borrowing proceeds laterally, survivals descend vertically. But who can safely distinguish the two processes and be sure that survivals have not been borrowed from outside? Hence Jacobs will stick to the history of specific folktales. He summed up his creed in eight points which persuasively present the case for transmission of complicated tales after their invention by a gifted story-artist.[3]

In a waspish aside aimed at Gomme, Jacobs observed that open-air assemblies and similar archaic village institutions were dull stuff compared to sparkling fairy tales.

The fireworks closed with a brief postlude from Nutt, who

[1] Gomme, in *Folk-Lore*, V (1894), 63.
[2] Hartland, in *ibid.*, p. 75.   [3] Jacobs, in *ibid.*, pp. 129–46.

commended Jacobs' distinction between lateral and vertical transmission. This was a matter of emphasis which united rather than separated the disputants. Nutt's sympathies lay with European rather than with Indian origins and with internal rather than external lines of movement, but each explanation had its place.[1] On this Hegelian note the long-protracted debate reached an uneasy stasis. But the survivalists had yielded unrecoverable ground.

The direct confrontation between the casualists and the disseminationists provided the main show of the congress, but side engagements were also conducted. Proponent of a unique racist theory of the beginnings of civilization, John Stuart Stuart-Glennie, a barrister of the Middle Temple and sometime Arthurian scholar, alone of the congress presented two ponderous papers on 'The Origins of Mythology' and 'The Origins of Institutions.' (His name was spelled with and without the hyphen.) Stuart Glennie postulated a 'Conflict of Higher and Lower Races' in place of Tylor's uniform stages of culture. A pre-Semitic, pre-Aryan white race, whom he called the Archaians, had dispersed originally from central Asia and secondarily from Egypt and Chaldea carrying aloft the higher culture. From them originated the familial institutions and religious mythologies of the ancient world. Hence, as he explained during the discussion period, 'Culture-lore and Folk-lore of a Civilized Society must be conceived as perpetually reacting on each other, as do the Higher and Lower Races, to which these products respectively more especially belong.'[2] By higher and lower Stuart Glennie meant white and black.

A dour, humourless Scot who bored even his friends—so was he remembered by another participant in the congress, the philologist Archibald H. Sayce of Oxford. But for his graceless personality, Stuart Glennie's original and provocative theory would have won more adherents, Sayce mused.[3] The Scot linked his vision closely to folklore, and had indeed already entered into the dialogue over the science of folklore, suggesting the label Koenonosography to designate folklore as a descriptive branch of sociology.[4] More important, he had worked out a classification of folklore according to Cosmical Ideas, Moral Notions, and Historical Memories which he

[1] Nutt, in *ibid.*, pp. 146–7.
[2] Stuart Glennie, *The International Folk-Lore Congress, 1891*, p. 228, discussion of 'The Origins of Mythology.'
[3] A. H. Sayce, *Reminiscences* (London, 1923), p. 33.
[4] J. S. Stuart Glennie, 'The Science of Folk-Lore,' *Archaeological Review*, III (May, 1889), 199. Other articles on 'The Philosophy of Folk-Tales,' 'Folk-lore as the Complement of Culture-Lore in the Study of History,' and 'The Place of the Science of Folk-Lore' appeared in the *Folk-Lore Journal*, IV (1886), 63–79, 213–21, 363–4.

illustrated in tabular form. These 'Conceptions of Folk-Life' corresponded to 'Expressions of Folk-Lore,' namely Customs, Sayings, and Poesies, each with their subheadings. 'In using this Classification the question will be, What does a Custom, or a Saying, or a Poesy chiefly illustrate—a Cosmical Idea, or a Moral Notion, or an Historical Memory. According to the answer will be the *row* of pigeon-holes into which it goes.'[1] This scientific classification of folklore facts would do more to further the subject, Stuart Glennie asserted, than Gomme's empirical and unscientific system.[2]

A plague on both your houses, snorted Stuart Glennie, rejecting out of hand the two competing theories in the centre of the stage. He wholly repudiates the borrowing theory, which he prefers to call the spontaneous development theory. Good stories may be borrowed, true, but not gods. Survivals and borrowings together yield a mixed ethnology that produces a mixed mythology. Hence he will style his system a mixed descent theory. As for the psychic unity of man, this is patently absurd when races exhibit different brains and brain-pans and highly unlike physical, mental, and moral faculties.[3]

In spite of his dual appearance on the Congress programme, Stuart Glennie felt aggrieved at the lack of attention paid his views in the press, and wrote to *The Times* on October 8 to correct the oversight and see that the intelligent public at large knew about the Archaian theory.

'The world,' you truly say, in your leader on the Folk-lore Congress, 'is in no hurry for theories of mythology.' You have not, therefore, reported my theory, nor do I mean to trouble you with one tittle of it now. But the object of my paper was far less to state a theory than to state certain facts, the results of recent research, and then to ask, Do not these facts require a very considerable modification of that evolutionist theory which you have associated with the names of Mr. Lang and Mr. Hartland? May I therefore hope that, with the characteristic many-sidedness and fairness of *The Times*, you will permit me very briefly to indicate the facts to which I called attention?

These were, first, the facts that tend at least utterly to overthrow the common assumption of the equality of human

[1] Stuart Glennie, 'The Science of Folk-Lore,' p. 202.
[2] Gomme presented his classification in 'The Science of Folk-Lore' in the *Folk-Lore Journal*, III (1885), 1–16.
[3] Stuart Glennie, 'The Borrowing Theory,' *Archaeological Review*, IV (October, 1889), 216–22.

races, and, therefore, to require a reconsideration of Mr. Lang's, as of Dr. Tylor's, 'elimination of ethnological differences.' Secondly, the fact that in the origin of every civilization of which we know anything there was a conflict of either racially or culturally higher and lower races, and that, particularly in the primary civilizations of Egypt and Chaldea, this conflict was between white and coloured or black races. And, thirdly, such facts as to migrations, colonizations, trade routes, &c., since the very foundation of these primary civilizations, as appear to be almost, though I would by no means say altogether, sufficient to account for the extraordinary similarities of custom and myth all over the world, and hence to justify curtailment, at least, of that universal application of the theory of psychological similarity which is necessitated by the theoretical 'elimination of ethnological differences.'

Stuart Glennie dealt, of course, only in facts! Unhappily for his readers, he could not boil down his cumbersome sentences into simple assertions that a conflict between an advanced white and a backward black race produced civilization.

A curious collaboration served Stuart Glennie as the instrument to promote his cause. He teamed up with Lucy M. J. Garnett, a translator of Greek and Turkish traditional literature, bounding her texts with prefatory and concluding essays expounding his system. Their first joint production, *Greek Folk-Songs*, appearing in 1885, contained his statement on 'The Survival of Paganism.' To a second edition of 1888 he added as 'Supplement' an essay on 'The Science of Folk-Lore,' a science arising, he asserts, from the survival of paganism. Stuart Glennie frankly admitted that reviewers of the first edition had praised the folk-poems but regarded his Introduction on pagan survivals as out of place; undeterred, he was now 'aggravating the offence,' at a pecuniary sacrifice, in the hope of raising the scientific level of English criticism. Indeed, were the cost not excessive, he would have added 'a classified set of illustrations of Greek and Keltic Folk-Lore Analogies.' *The Women of Turkey and Their Folk-Lore*, published by Nutt, came out in 1890 and 1891, the congress year. To the first volume he contributed 'Introductory Chapters on the Ethnography of Turkey; and Folk-Conceptions of Nature' and to the second 'Concluding Chapters on the Origins of Matriarchy.' Lucy Garnett surveyed the social status and activities, family ceremonies, beliefs and superstitions, and folk-poesy of the women of thirteen ethnic groups. Stuart Glennie then analysed the marriage-lore and deduced his theory of matriarchal origins, controverting the Roman patriarchal theory of Henry Maine, the sexual promiscuity theory of John Fergus MacLennan, and the sexual aversion theory of Edvard A. Westermarck. In their stead he offered his explanation of marriage privileges given to the white women of a superior colonizing race by their inferior black and coloured husbands.

Nutt and Jacobs commented seriatim later that year in *Folk-Lore* in a statement captioned 'Mr. Stuart-Glennie on the Origins of Matriarchy.'[1] They sensed in the Scot a potent new adversary, who had brushed aside Hartland's reading of swan-maidens as survivals of goddesses in favour of his own matriarchs. Now the co-editors of the congress papers each sought to align him on their side. Nutt regarded Stuart Glennie as basically in agreement with Hartland since both used the anthropological method of fitting folklore into a theory of historical progress. The publisher was straining hard here, for a thesis of civilization resulting in one area in one epoch from a merger of high and low races can hardly be accounted evolutionary. Jacobs seems on stronger ground when he acknowledged, 'Personally I have a sneaking regard for a theory of civilization which makes it one huge example of the Borrowing Theory. . . .'[2]

Emboldened by his success in establishing a beachhead, Stuart Glennie read a paper to the Society in June, 1892, which was printed in the September issue, ferociously assailing Tylor's structure. 'Is not the theory of Animism . . ,' he charged, 'one of the most illogical and self-contradictory, and hence the most inimical to clear ideas, that has ever been introduced into, and had a vogue in science?'[3] He proceeded to flail the ghost theory of Tylor and Spencer that savage philosophers all over the world beheld ghosts as a result of dreams, shadows, and fainting spells. They continually misused key terms like ghost, spirit, soul. Tylor failed to take account of the profound distinction between witchcraft and religion, as demonstrated for India by Alfred Lyall. In thus assailing animism, Stuart Glennie was attempting to remove one of the main impediments to his own theory of higher and lower cultures.

In his third partnership with Lucy Garnett, *Greek Folk-Poesy* (1896), Stuart Glennie restated and reiterated his philosophy in a general Preface emblazoned 'New Folklore Researches,' where they still lie embalmed.

One major controversy of the day, worn a little thin by 1891,

---

[1] *Folk-Lore*, II (1891), 367–70 (Nutt); 370–2 (Jacobs).
[2] *Folk-Lore*, II (1891), 370.
[3] Stuart Glennie, 'Queries as to Dr. Tylor's Views on Animism,' *Folk-Lore*, III (1892), 292.

failed of a hearing at the congress since its champion, Max Müller, had gone to the continent. He had returned to Dessau in Anhalt, his native town in Germany, for the unveiling of a national monument in honour of his father Wilhelm Müller. Still he kept in touch and sent *The Times* on October 8 a letter of protest and correction of its report six days earlier on Andrew Lang's inaugural address. According to *The Times* report

> it is stated that 'I see a solar myth in nearly every legend in such wise that our Indo-European ancestors can have had little other topic of conversation than the sun.' Again I have to say that I deeply regret having lost the pleasure of being present at Mr. Andrew Lang's inaugural speech. I heartily agree with most of his sentiments on the value of a careful and truly scholarlike study of folk-lore, but Mr. Andrew Lang knows better than anyone else how strongly opposed I always have been to any attempt to trace 'nearly every legend back to a solar source.' Those few legends in which I think I have succeeded in discovering solar elements form a very small segment of the enormous mass of Greek or Aryan mythology. Their value, such as it is, consists in a critical analysis of certain mythological names in Sanskrit, Greek, and Latin, and I believe that even our president will admit that Sûrya, Savitri, and Pûihan in Sanskrit, like Helios in Greek and Sol in Latin, have something to do with the sun. I should have been proud to accept the invitation of the secretary of the Folk-Lore Congress to read a paper on the proper limits of what is called, rather promiscuously, the Solar Theory, and on the results of Comparative Mythology which may be considered as beyond the reach of doubt. But other and equally delightful duties called me away from Oxford, where I hope to return before the end of October.

Pace the Honourable Friedrich Max! The members of the Congress had little time for solar flights.

Nearly every speaker at the congress advanced his particular theory of origins and survivals. Sir Frederick Pollock, chairing the session on customs and institutions, noted the 'increasing points of contact' between the studies of law and of folklore, a 'young and growing science—aggressive, like all growing powers,' and hoped it would give light on the origin of contract and on the medieval 'Trial by Battle.'[1] David MacRitchie considered the trustworthiness of oral tradition and contended that the popular memory did

[1] Pollock, *The International Folk-Lore Congress, 1891*, p. 262.

indeed retain historical facts. Frank B. Jevons examined the vexing question of European *vs.* Asiatic origin of the Aryans in the light of folklore and pointed to the Finno-Ugrians as a non-Aryan people in contact with pro-ethnic Aryans, thereby tilting the balance toward Europe. Even in treating the magical property of saliva among rustics and savages, James E. Crombie traced the practice of spitting to the primitive belief in saliva as a life principle on the same order as blood.

The brilliance of bold theory and vast learning on display in the name of folklore at the international congress heralded the maturity of the science. But the congress made plain too that time was running out for the evolutionists, whose dominance was threatened by the diffusionists, a threat also posed at the alliance between folklore and anthropology. Before the Great Team retired from the field, their energies would stimulate still other thrusts of the folklore movement.

IX   The County Collectors

THE GENIUS of the English folklore movement lay in daring systems and ingenious speculation conceived at the writing desk and in the library; none of the Great Team ever ventured in the field. Prodigies of field collecting in the British Isles were undertaken not by Englishmen but by Gaelic-speaking field-workers of Scotland and Ireland. Yet the London group perfectly understood the prime importance of systematic field collecting and encouraged collectors in the countryside, who in turn looked for guiding principles and scholarly direction to the leaders of The Folk-Lore Society.

Laurence Gomme prepared a *Handbook of Folklore* for the Society in 1890 which, in its clarity of divisions, simplicity of explanations, and pertinence of questions, proves serviceable today. Various stalwarts of the Society assisted him in compiling the pocket-size volume. Clodd wrote the section on 'Beliefs relating to a Future Life,' Hartland discussed the folktale, and Jacobs contributed his classification of narrative types. Edward W. Brabrook handled the local customs, Frazer was involved in the subsection on agricultural folklore, and Charlotte Burne supervised the part on collecting. Intended as a collector's guide in Britain, the *Handbook* in fact provided for the layman a pithy statement on the content and scope of folklore in the English definition. Chronologically the *Handbook* came after the major county collections and drew upon their findings.

In his opening comment Gomme declared that the 'subjects which make up the body of survivals called Folk-Lore' could be placed under four principal heads. Within 1. Superstitious Belief and Practice fell (*a*) Superstitions connected with great natural objects, (*b*) Tree and plant superstitions, (*c*) Animal superstitions, (*d*) Goblindom, (*e*) Witchcraft, (*f*) Leechcraft, (*g*) Magic and divination, (*h*) Beliefs relating to future life, and (*i*) Superstitions generally. Section 2, Traditional Customs, included (*a*) Festival customs, (b) Ceremonial customs, (c) Games, and (d) Local customs. Section 3, Traditional Narratives, involved (a) Nursery tales or *Märchen*, hero tales, drolls, fables, and apologues, (b) Creation, deluge, fire, and doom myths, (c) Ballads and songs, and (d) Place legends and traditions. Finally, 4. Folk-Sayings covered (a) Jingles, nursery rhymes, riddles, &c., (b) Proverbs, and (c) Nicknames, place rhymes.

These subdivisions each blossomed into a chapter. Two or three introductory pages succinctly explained the form and furnished one or two illustrative examples, which were then followed with a series of pointed queries revolving around the topic. What is the local name for a goblin, how does he behave, who has seen him? The *Handbook* furnished 784 questions for the first two general divisions of Belief and Custom. Sample texts in Sections 3 and 4 served in lieu of questions to prime the pump of oral literature. An initial chapter on 'What Folk-Lore Is' and concluding ones on 'The Way to Collect Folk-Lore' and 'Library Work' rounded off the model handbook. Throughout the emphasis was on accuracy and precision of recording information. The English view of folklore as a body of irrational local beliefs and associated practices, often embedded in oral genres, is evident in the sequence of the sections.

Besides his share in the *Handbook*, Hartland made separate contributions to the literature on collecting. He exhorted the Liverpool Welsh National Society to undertake field explorations, in a paper published as *Welsh Folklore: Its Collection and Study* (Liverpool, 1892); and he prefaced a volume of printed sources of county folklore with 'Suggestions for the Systematic Collection of the Folk-Lore of Gloucestershire' (1895). Among possible agents in collecting he mentioned patriotic and learned societies, universities, students, schoolteachers, ministers, and doctors. For one hefty county collection, *The Folk-Lore of Herefordshire*, by Ella Mary Leather (1912), he wrote an Introduction stressing the cultural diversity of a border county (Herefordshire lies alongside Wales), the social insights afforded by local traditions, and the need for an orderly arrangement of this printed folk museum. Hartland stated forcefully the values for social history in the county folklore book as opposed to the old-style county history.

The old county histories are little more than the story—often amazingly inaccurate—of the pomp, the pedigrees, the pretensions and the downfall of the ruling families. Of the people at large they hardly take account; and when they refer to local customs or traditions, it is with ill-concealed contempt.

. . . If we want to gauge aright the mind of the community . . .
in short, to know the people as it has been and as it is—we must
turn to the oral traditions, the institutions and practices of the
peasant and the labourer.[1]

And he pointed happily to the evidence of sin-eating discovered by
Miss Leather, which supports his thesis on the survival of this
primitive ritual custom.

In publishing a naturalist's handbook for children by Harry
Lowerison, Nutt conceived the idea of inserting a chapter on folk-
lore, and so introducing the young wildlife observer to the pleasures
of detecting and recording traditions. 'How then does one set about
becoming a folk-lorist, a student of folk-lore, in the sense that one
may set about becoming a naturalist or a botanist?' he queried, and
laid down guidelines. 'Accuracy of observation, rigid fidelity of
recording you have, I take it, already learnt from your training in
"natural" science; they are as important in studying folk-lore, nay
more so, precisely because the subject-matter is so fluid, ill-defined,
and subject to variation.'[2]

Among the Society members Charlotte Burne took the greatest
interest in the technical aspects of fieldwork and became herself a
practising collector. In a persuasive paper on 'The Collection of
English Folk-Lore,' printed in the first volume of *Folk-Lore* in 1890
and adapted for the *Handbook* later that year, Miss Burne charted a
course for workers in the vineyard. To allay the fears of the faint-
hearted, she pointed to recent discoveries—a witch's ladder,
rhyming formulas, well-told folktales—as evidence that folklore yet
abounded in merry England. The Society should undertake a
geographical survey of the 'habitats and boundaries' of local
beliefs and customs, along the lines laid down by the English
Dialect Society in its search for folk language. Such a survey should
pay close attention to the mutual influences of folklore and history.
The president recommended as an excellent example of the historical method of collecting folklore, even though in fictional form,
The Scouring of the White Horse (1859) by Thomas Hughes, author
of *Tom Brown's School Days*, who led a London clerk on a vacation
ramble into Berkshire. To give historical depth to a newfound tradition, the collector should endeavour to trace earlier instances in
the printed record; for the forerunner of a Welsh custom he might
consult Pennant's *Tour*, or for an earlier Wiltshire specimen he

[1] Hartland, Introduction to *The Folk-Lore of Herefordshire*, collected by Ella Mary
Leather (Hereford, 1912).
[2] Nutt, in Harry Lowerison, *Field and Folklore. With a Chapter on Folk-Lore by
Alfred Nutt* (London, 1899), p. 70.

could turn to Aubrey's *Remaines*. Not only would collectors reap specific items of lore, but they can and should learn about folk values and folk morality unknown to outsiders. As for the actual methods of inquiry, these have been simplified by the work of the Society in spreading information about folklore. The explorer should first seek out the parish clerk or the sexton and ask about bell-ringing and burial customs. Then he should move on to small employers, who will respond more readily than working people, who are generally suspicious of strangers.

Miss Burne addressed these helpful hints to the leisured country vicar, doctor, squire, and their spouses. Already these Victorian personalities had begun assembling county field books, noting down remarks of servants and tradespeople and occasionally sallying forth for a genteel interview with the village Nestor. Their attitude was much the same as that of the earlier compilers of popular antiquities who interleaved their copy of Brand with relevant clippings, save that now they also interrogated their servants. The same casual, antiquarian, amateur spirit prevailed; the work was done for its own sake, with little sense of urgency or desire to publish.

Indeed, the collectors almost had to be pushed into print. The first of the county fieldworkers, Robert Hunt in Cornwall, began gathering traditions thirty years before he finally placed them inside a book, in 1865. Georgina Jackson never did transfer to print her Shropshire collection, and Charlotte Burne had to edit and amplify her manuscript after her death. Sir Edgar MacCulloch's manuscript on Guernsey bore a Preface dated 1864 but waited for an editor to place it in print in 1903. Similarly, John Symonds Udal attached a 'Fore-say' to his Dorsetshire collection in 1866, which awaited a printer until 1922, by which time so many persons had helped themselves to the materials without acknowledgment that Udal feared he would be accused of plagiarizing others. Wilkinson completed the manuscript of Harland's *Lancashire Legends* five years after Harland's death in 1868. William Henderson tells how he 'lighted on a treasure of exceeding value' in a fifty-year-old manuscript of Border customs, legends and superstitions assembled by a medical student named Wilkie at the behest of Sir Walter Scott, who used it only for two short essays in the *Border Minstrelsy*. Scott procured Wilkie an appointment in India, where he died, and only by chance did Henderson stumble on his collections and incorporate them into one of the earliest and best of the county field books.

As a consequence of this leisurely attitude, less than a dozen collections, based wholly or partly on fieldwork, reached print between 1865 and the outbreak of the first World War. The following titles, some massive, some slender, are representative:

Robert Hunt, *Popular Romances of the West of England; or, The Drolls, Traditions, and Superstitions of Old Cornwall* (First and Second Series, 1865).

William Henderson, *Notes on the Folk Lore of the Northern Counties of England and the Borders, with an Appendix on Household Stories by S. Baring-Gould* (1866). Reprinted by The Folk-Lore Society, 1879.

John Harland and T. T. Wilkinson, *Lancashire Folk-Lore, illustrative of the superstitious beliefs and practices, local customs and usages of the people of the county palatine* (1867).

———, *Lancashire Legends, Traditions, Pageants, Sports, &c., with an appendix containing a rare tract on the Lancashire witches, &c., &c.,* (1873).

Charles Hardwick, *Traditions, Superstitions, and Folk-Lore, (chiefly Lancashire and the North of England:), Their Affinity to others in widely-distributed localities; their Eastern Origin and Mythical Significance* (1872).

Charlotte Sophia Burne, *Shropshire Folk-Lore: A Sheaf of Gleanings,* edited from the collections of Georgina F. Jackson (1883).

William Brockie, *Legends and Superstitions of the County of Durham* (1886).

Rev. Thomas Parkinson, *Yorkshire Legends and Traditions, as told by her ancient chroniclers, her poets and journalists* (1888; Second Series, 1889).

John Nicholson, *Folk Lore of East Yorkshire* (1890).

Sidney Oldall Addy, *Household Tales with Other Traditional Remains. Collected in the Counties of York, Lincoln, Derby and Nottingham* (1895).

Edgar MacCulloch, *Guernsey Folk Lore, A Collection of Popular Superstitions, Legendary Tales, Peculiar Customs, Proverbs, Weather Sayings, Etc., of the People of that Island, from Mss. by the late Sir Edgar MacCulloch,* edited by Edith F. Carey (1903).

Ella Mary Leather, *The Folk-Lore of Herefordshire, collected from oral and printed sources* (1912).

John Symonds Udal, *Dorsetshire Folk-Lore* (1922). Fore-say by the late William Barnes [1886].

The haphazard and random character of English collecting can readily be perceived from this list. Only a third of the counties are represented. The largest, Yorkshire, enters into four of the collections. Henderson, Hardwick, Harland, and Wilkinson collected independently in Lancashire; the latter two joined forces, but only after they had commenced separately. Accordingly the scale is heavily tilted toward the northern counties. None of the collectors set down literal texts, Addy coming the closest but still not attempting to reproduce dialect. Nearly all mixed oral and printed sources, and the marginal works of Parkinson and Nicholson hardly drew upon word-of-mouth communications, but they did seek to transfix the local traditions of county or district that had taken form and gained currency among the villagers and townsfolk. If the compilers presented a paraphrase or a journalistic reporting of a legend, they yet intended to keep faith with the local inhabitants and indignantly denied any suggestion of tampering. When a scientific friend, 'deep in the cold thrall of positivism,' casually remarked to Robert Hunt, as he was correcting the pages of his Cornish drolls for a third edition in 1881, 'I suppose you invented most of these stories,' he accepted the 'humiliating necessity' of assuring his readers that all had been gathered over half a century earlier in the homes of Cornwall. The new point of view is clearly stated by Hardwick in criticizing his predecessor in Lancashire, John Roby. Hardwick singled out for praise one authentic description of a Lancashire boggart or bargaist printed by Roby in his *Traditions of Lancashire* but actually contributed by T. Crofton Croker; with this exception

... the word 'traditions,' as applied to nearly the whole of these stories, is a sad misnomer. The tales might, perhaps with propriety, be termed *nouvelletes*, or little novels; but when put forth as 'traditions,' in the true acceptation of the term, they are worse than useless, for they are calculated equally to mislead both the antiquary and the collector of 'folk lore.'[1]

These county fieldbooks emphasized the trustworthiness and fidelity of their contents although the idea of accuracy did not at this stage require the literal reproduction of the spoken word. In the modern manner the collectors often included particulars about the human carriers of tradition and even occasional extended sketches of gifted talkers. Charlotte Burne spelled out most precisely the nature of her sources and the methods of her presentation. In relating the legends she employed 'simple colloquial language, such

[1] Charles Hardwick, *Traditions, Superstitions, and Folk-Lore* (*chiefly Lancashire and the North of England*) (Manchester and London, 1872), p. 128.

as a nurse might use to a child, or an old parish clerk to an "intelligent foreigner," ' but she spared the reader dialect. At the risk of tedium, she noted the precise locale of each scrap of folk matter, since in a large border county with varied speech patterns and customs such information might ultimately reveal ancient boundaries of race and lineage. Scrupulously she furnished the names of tellers of two or three variants of a legend, but when a matter was common knowledge in a neighbourhood, the question of an 'authority' became superfluous. When she used statements from the files of *Bygones* and *Shreds and Patches*, she took pains to ascertain the name of the correspondent and his source.[1]

While one collection might offer more depth and substance than another, all shared common assumptions and betrayed a strong family likeness. The county, or the tier of adjacent counties, forms the convenient geographical unit. Henderson ranged over the district between the Tweed and the Humber, but concentrated on Northumberland, Durham, and Yorkshire. Hunt followed patterns of Cornish tradition as far west as Exeter in neighbouring Devonshire, but excluded the divining rod as non-Cornish. From southern Cornwall to northern Yorkshire, the findings display considerable similarity; one table of contents fairly matches another. There are chapters on giants and piskies, boggarts and bogles, witchcraft and leechcraft, charms and divinations, holy wells and haunted caverns, harvest festivals and village fêtes, always with a firm emphasis on locality and landscape and unhesitating acceptance of the doctrine of survivals. The common omissions are equally standard: rarely are wonder tales reported; balladry is slight, since ballad-hunting claimed its own devotees; the lore of occupations passes unnoticed, save for the arresting chapters by Hunt on fishermen and miners whose livelihoods could scarcely pass unnoticed by any chronicler of Cornish folk. Drawing on the same authorities, reinforced by each other's findings, guided from the 1880's on by the classifications of The Folk-Lore Society, and responsive to the guidelines of Brand and Thoms, the county collectors naturally enough reveal a sense of fraternity.

Their major intellectual innovation lay in recognizing the value of oral sources, casually and passively perhaps, but still appreciatively. In almost every case, the county chronicler relied on his house servants and neighbourly acquaintances for oral texts, and did nothing so rude as to barge uninvited into the village pub or visit with quayside loungers, threshing farmers, or miners in the

[1] Charlotte Burne, *Shropshire Folk-Lore* (London, Shrewsbury, Chester, 1883), pp. vii–xi.

collieries. A whole monograph could be written on the relationship between the Victorian gentry and their house servants in terms of culture contact. We catch a glimpse of the contact in a letter written to the collector Sidney Addy by his fiancée in 1890. 'Two more for folk lore. Our servant tells me it is the custom in Killa-marsh to wish before tasting, for the first time, the fruits of the season. Also, it is considered good luck when seeing a snail to take it and throw over the shoulder, not looking where it falls.'[1]

The one shining example of field exploration was set by Robert Hunt, who in 1829 embarked on a ten-month walking tour of Cornwall to gather up 'every existing tale of its ancient people.' Hunt unearthed a disappearing species in the droll-teller, an itinerant minstrel specializing in long, rambling, episodic narratives interspersed with song, which he often adapted to local situations. As secretary to the Royal Cornwall Polytechnic Society, Hunt further availed himself of the opportunity to elicit old stories while seated on a three-legged stool near the blazing hearthfire, or resting on a level after climbing from the depths of a mine. In 1862 he even employed a postmaster-poet to collect for him, but in the intervening years the droll-tellers had vanished.[2] These techniques of the protracted field trip and the paid field-collector were not attempted again within England, although they would become standard practice in Scotland and Ireland.

While Hunt was chary of actually naming and introducing his leading informants, he and other collectors did occasionally identify the elderly persons whose knowledge of antiquities they tapped. Miss Burne gave credit to Mrs. Sarah Dudley, a 'charming old dame' of Abbey Cottage, Much Wenlock, who 'in the course of a long life spent at Clee St. Margaret, Bridgnorth, Easthope, and other places in South Shropshire, garnered a vast store of queer old-world stories and ideas, which she poured forth readily for the use of the present work.'[3] Hunt portrayed in detail the droll-teller Uncle Anthony James.[4] Ella Mary Leather set down thumbnail sketches of several of her best informants, such as William Colcombe, who had died in 1911 at Weobley Workhouse, and 'knew upwards of thirty traditional songs and carols, and had a wonderful memory for old tales and riddles, many of which he had learnt in his youth from "Old Powell," the nailmaker, last of his trade in Weobley, with whom he lived for many years.'[5] Colcombe had heard the

---

[1] *A Miscellany: Sidney Oldall Addy and Family*, collected by Mary Golden Addy (Croydon, 1937), p. 65.
[2] Robert Hunt, *Popular Romances of the West of England*, First Series (London, 1865), pp. viii–x.   [3] Burne, *op. cit.*, p. 149 n.
[4] Hunt, *op. cit.*, pp. xv–xvi.   [5] Leather, *op. cit.*, p. xvi.

story of Jack the Giant Killer from an old man of eighty and read it in a chapbook as a boy—a valuable testimony as to how traditions mixed.

The modern companion to the named and described informant is the literal text, and this too sometimes emerges in the county collections. Henderson quoted a young pupil in Sunday School saying of a battle site now named Neville's Cross, '. . . if you walk nine times round the Cross, and then stoop down and lay your head on the turf, you'll hear the noise of the battle and the clash of the armour.' According to Henderson, 'These were the young fellow's exact words.'[1] In describing the legend of the spectral White Lady of Longnor, in Shropshire, Burne reproduced the precise language of the 'parson's man' who had encountered the wraith on a narrow footbridge:

> 'I sid 'er a-cummin, an' I thinks, 'ere's a nice young wench. Well, thinks I, who she be I'll gi'e 'er a fright. I was a young fellow then, yo' know—an' I waited till 'er come close up to me, right i' the middle o' the bridge, an' I stretched out my arms, *so*—an' I clasped 'er in 'em, tight—*so*. An' theer was nothin'!'[2]

This is far more effective than a bald paraphrase.

Still another sign of growing sophistication in field techniques can be found in the awareness of storytelling habits and stimuli. MacCulloch mentioned the custom of Guernsey, the Channel island with its Anglo-French inheritance, of the véillées, when the island women gathered together in the evening to knit around a single hearth, for the sake of sociability and economy, and each in turn related some tale or anecdote.[3] Miss Burne remarked shrewdly, in giving two oral versions of a legend of a sunken city, how they differed according to the storyteller's mind and habits of thought.[4] Miss Leather realized that the collector must strive to re-create the storytelling atmosphere during an interview:

> It is useless for the collector of folk-lore to ask bald leading questions; like travellers of another sort, it is well to *carry samples*, for your old countryman loves to hear a story: having heard, he longs to tell you one as good, or better. Of course it may not be of the kind that is wanted, but it is well to listen

---

[1] William Henderson, *Notes on the Folk Lore of the Northern Counties of England and the Borders* (London, 1866), pp. 265–6.
[2] Burne, *op. cit.*, p. 76.
[3] Sir Edgar MacCulloch, *Guernsey Folk Lore* (London and Guernsey, 1903), chap. 13, 'Story Telling.' [4] Burne, *op. cit.*, p. 66.

patiently. I remember hearing an old grannie at Pembridge relate the history of her large family: it seemed endless and most wearisome. Last of all, she told how her youngest daughter died, of her neighbour's admiration![1]

So the collectors tasted the mysteries and pleasures of lore-hunting. How did they view their hard-won treasures? These were intellectually curious men and women testing pragmatically the concept of popular antiquities and the doctrine of survivals on which they were reared. Their library debts show clearly enough this rearing. Hunt, the earliest, acknowledged his debt to J. O. Halliwell for his *Rambles in Western Cornwall by the Footsteps of the Giants*, and to Thomas Wright, who studied the Cyclopean walls of the promontory beyond Penzance, popularly known as 'The Giant's Hedges.' Their walking tours to survey physical antiquities gave Hunt the idea that a native Cornishman could profitably inquire into the myths surrounding these relics of the giants. He did amass a sheaf of giant and demon legends, placing them in his first volume of prehistoric traditions as distinct from the historic ones in Volume Two. Henderson, who followed next, searched for like-nesses to his north country legends in Brand, the *Choice Notes* of 1859 culled from Thoms' *Notes and Queries*, Benjamin Thorpe's *Mythology and Popular Traditions of Scandinavia*, Walter K. Kelly's *Curiosities of Indo European Tradition and Folk-Lore*, and Moses Richardson's *Local Historian's Table Book*—vade mecums for pre-Tylorian folklorists. Henderson tendered special thanks to the Reverend Baring-Gould for copious annotations on saints' legends, as well as for the appendix on 'Radicals of Household Stories.' Miss Burne listed key works she regularly consulted in up-dated editions, hallowed titles all:

Grimm's *Deutsche Mythologie*, 2nd edition, 1843
Brand's *Popular Antiquities*, edited by W. Carew Hazlitt, 1870
Henderson's *Folk-Lore of the Northern Counties*, 2nd edition (Folk-Lore Society), 1879
Sir Walter Scott's *Letters on Demonology and Witchcraft*, 2nd edition, 1831
T. Crofton Croker's *Fairy Legends and Traditions of the South of Ireland*, edited by Thomas Wright, F.S.A., 1862

Miss Burne dedicated her bulky tome to Henderson 'in grateful recognition of advice and aid.' Hardwick, like the others, paid his respects to Grimm, through the medium of Kelly's *Curiosities*, and

---

[1] Leather, *op. cit.*, p. xvi.

also stated his attraction to the solar mythologists, Adalbert Kuhn, Max Müller, and George W. Cox, on whom he relied in his analyses of the 'mythical significance' of his north country gleanings. In the same vein Harland and Wilkinson singled out the table-books of Hone and the *Notes and Queries* of Thoms for eulogy, with additional thanks to Chambers, Brand, Aubrey, and Jabez Allies. Harland himself had contributed notes and articles on Lancashire to *Notes and Queries* and to Chambers' *The Book of Days*. By 1895, when Addy published his *Household Tales*, he could draw upon the Stallybrass translation of the *Deutsche Mythologie* and Hartland's *The Science of Fairy Tales*, and he was in correspondence with Tylor. The theories of the philologist and anthropologist blend harmoniously in Addy's thought, both pointing backward by different proofs to the pagan origins whose traces Addy found plentifully strewn throughout his household tales and beliefs.

Conspicuous in every collection, the concept of survivals binds together the county traditions in a uniform product. Not every scrap of folklore could be traced back to its murky origins in nature-worship and sacrificial cults and pagan pantheons, but where the evidence looked promising the collectors happily supplied the missing connections. So in the hard-hearted magistrate Tregeagle, doomed to scoop out Dosmery Pool with a limpet shell, Hunt perceived a modern instance of a medieval Devil-servant and of the classical Orestes legend. In Tom Hickathrift, the English strong hero of chapbook and low comedy extravagances, Harland-Wilkinson glimpsed the grander outlines of Hercules. The White Lady of Lewtrenchard, rustling through corridors in various English mansions, at one time, conjectured Henderson, must have been revered as an Anglo-Saxon goddess.[1]

Ella Leather uncovered two prize survivals in Herefordshire. One was an expression of sympathy between husband and wife during childbirth, which she interpreted as 'a last trace, surviving in the higher culture, of the strange custom found among savages in many parts of the world, which has been called the *Couvade*.'[2] Based on a mysterious and magical connection presumed between father and child, the ritual custom demanded the husband suffer the pangs of his wife's childbirth. The other find, which especially delighted Hartland who had written about the practice among primitive peoples and asked Leather to seek it out, was sin-eating. At a country funeral, the farmer pressed a glass of wine on a neigh-

[1] Hunt, *op. cit.*, p. xvi; John Harland and T. T. Wilkinson, *Lancashire Folk-Lore* (London and New York, 1867), p. 5; Henderson, *op. cit.*, p. 283.
[2] Leather, *op. cit.*, pp. 111–12.

bour, urging him to drink, in order to kill the sins of the farmer's deceased sister.[1] Two centuries before, Aubrey had recorded in Herefordshire the practice of sin-eating, in which through ritual eating and drinking a living person took upon himself the sins of the deceased.

As the most professional of the collectors, Miss Burne naturally plucked a rich bouquet of survivals, which she amplified with comparative references. The will-o'-the-wisp, usually reported by collectors without comment, Miss Burne attributed to an ancient folktale. Once the Devil gave a sinner a coal of hell-fire to carry as a torment; its light, flickering through the woods to lure travellers off their path, and called by them will-o'-the-wisp, lingers on as a vestigial belief divorced from the tale.[2] Or a simple folk rhyme might preserve a heathen outlook:

> To *break a branch* was deemed a sin
> A bad-luck job for neighbours,
> For *fire*, sickness, or the like,
> Would mar their honest labours.

Here was a relic of the days when the oak was sacred to Thor, the god of lightning.[3]

In the legend of 'The Man with the Hatchet' Miss Leather uncovered a hoary survival renewed in a modern revival. One of four almshouses in the Bargates, Leominster, displayed a rude carving of a man holding an axe, above an inscription bearing these lines:

> 'He that gives away all before he is dead,
> Let 'em take this hatchet and knock him on ye head.'

A widow named Hester Clark founded the almshouses in 1736, an act giving rise to the tradition that she had to reside in the almshouses herself after giving all her money to this charitable cause. The facts seemed to contradict the tradition, for a counter-inscription states that Hester Clark endowed the almshouses in her will. Miss Leather was pleased to observe 'the way in which a rhyme and folk-tale of great antiquity are as it were brought up to date and started on a new lease of life by being associated with some local hero or person of note,' and referred to Gomme's *Folklore as an Historical Science* for parallel stories. There Gomme concluded that the tale had descended from a savage time when a mallet was used for killing the aged.[4]

---

[1] *Ibid.*, p. 121. Hartland deals with sin-eating in *The Legend of Perseus* (London, 1895), II, 292–4.
[2] Burne, *op. cit.*, pp. 33–8.   [3] *Ibid.*, p. 241.   [4] Leather, *op. cit.*, pp. 171–2.

So everywhere in custom, usage, rhyme, and legend could be discerned the remnants of primitive mythology. If evidence of heathen origins seemed wanting, the collector could presume its existence. The widespread and often noted practice of 'heaving' required a person of one sex to lift a person of the opposite sex who was seated in a chair. No one knew the whence or wherefore, but Miss Burne unhesitatingly dubbed the business a survival, simply because it stood so much at variance with surrounding codes of behaviour. Not often was she at such a loss for conjectures. A characteristic illustration of her powers of reconstruction is seen in the local legend of 'The White Cow of Mitchell's Fold,' told her by a number of Shropshire cottagers. This fairy cow supplied the starving countryside with milk, giving a pailful apiece to all who milked her. But a wicked old woman milked her into a sieve, and the cow ran dry, and people starved. The old woman was turned into a stone, and a farmer who meddled with the stone came to no good afterward. Miss Burne linked this with similar legends from other English counties, sometimes with a giant replacing the witch; then she cited an early Welsh text of a world-travelling cow whose milk made people wise, and a Scandinavian myth of the cow Audumbla who nourished the primeval giant Ymir and licked salt hoarfrost from stones. These analogies satisfied Miss Burne of the geographical spread and early dating of the original form of the legend among the Aryan races and emboldened her to reconstruct that form. Early man viewed the gods anthropomorphically, and hence saw them as cattle raisers. When rain fell to earth, the gods were milking heavenly cows. Witches with sieves appeared in Teutonic mythology as degenerate descendants of ancient goddesses. Add to these ideas the conjecture that the Aryan peoples moved westward as the Caspian Sea dried up, and the early Aryan myth assumed shape.

Long ago, a heavenly milk-white cow used to come and rest morning and evening on the mountain-top above our homes. And her milk refreshed the earth and made it fertile, and all things prospered with us then. But there came a wicked goddess riding on the stormy wind one day, and milked the poor cow through a sieve, so that her milk fell on the earth in torrents, and when it ceased she disappeared. Since that time there has been a great drought, and we have to wander away in search of pasture for our cattle.[1]

Echoes of Max Müller, from an anthropological folklorist! To the village searcher for heathen survivals, Müller as well as Lang

[1] Burne, *op. cit.*, p. 43.

seemed to open windows into the myth-making processes of early man.

Yet all was not clear-cut survival. In the course of their inquiries the collectors unearthed unusual specimens of living lore from unsuspected places. If on one page Miss Burne declared her allegiance to survivalism, saying that the ghost-belief was surely a relic of the heathenism Baring-Gould had discovered still current in popular Christianity, she could on another reject the class division of folk-lore. The rich and well-born often saw ghosts where certain country folk sniffed their disbelief. 'I dunna believe as there's anythin' in it, as the dead come back. If they bin gone to the good place they wouldna want to come back, and if they bin gone to the tother place they wouldna be let to!'[1] Henderson viewed the matter somewhat differently, seeing class versions of the same basic superstition; peasants resort to the wizard or wise woman, while the gentry hie to the spirit-rapper. And he related an instance of a wealthy gentleman who on the advice of his spirit-rapper dug in a garden for stolen wealth, and was reported by a policeman.[2] In another place he alluded to the ghost of a mine overseer whose comrades could even distinguish his Northumbrian burr.[3]

Living, vigorous lore, in contrast to fading survivals, caught the attention of the collectors and doubtless of their readers. Henderson speaks of the superstitions and legendary rites of schoolboys, recalling that 'no boy would commit himself to the Wear without the precaution of an eel-skin tied round his left leg to save him from cramp.'[4] Particularly he remembered the institution of 'cobbing,' in which a group of youths seized an unlucky peer by the hair and chanted these lines:

> All manner of men under threescore and ten,
>   Who don't come to this cobbing match,
> Shall be cobbed over and over again;
> By the high, by the low, by the wings of the crow,
> Salt-fish regnum, buck or a doe.[5]

Traditional rivalries between friendly enemies, drawn from the floating store of anecdotes about simpletons and numskulls, enlivened the field books. Guernseymen related how the people of Alderney, a sister island, sowed needles they found in the wreckage of an East Indiaman cast on their shores, thinking they were garden seeds. In another example, three audacious Jersey mariners, jealous of the good roadstead and port of Guernsey which gave that

[1] *Ibid.*, pp. 129–30.   [2] Henderson, *op. cit.*, p. 199 n.
[3] *Ibid.*, p. 270.   [4] *Ibid.*, p. 17.   [5] *Ibid.*, p. 18.

island a commercial superiority over Jersey, once fastened a hawser from their boat on to a projecting rock on the Guernsey shore and began to steer for home, singing out, 'Hale, Pierre! Hale, Jean! Guernsi s'en vient!' But the hawser snapped before they could drag back their trophy. Guernsey families also regaled themselves with the report of a speech given by the Procureur de la Reine of Jersey, who recommended that the rotting wooden uprights of the gallows be replaced by stone, arguing 'It will last for ever, and serve for us and for our children.'[1]

The same dunces came to light elsewhere. In the Second Series of his *Yorkshire Legends and Traditions*, Parkinson devoted a chapter to 'Humorous Legends and Traditions,' with one section centring on the fools of Austwick, counterparts to the wise men of Gotham. As one of their exploits they were reportedly the first to attempt to wall in the cuckoo; they tried to lift a bull over a gate, and carried a cow up on a thatched roof to graze. In east Yorkshire the natives of Bridlington smarted under the designation 'Bolliton Jackdaws' because they were unable to transport a beam inside their church until they saw jackdaws carry a straw in endways. Likewise in Shropshire the inhabitants of the colliery village of Dawley bore the nickname 'Dawley Oaves' after the performance of an oaf, the Dawley barrow-maker, who built a wheelbarrow inside an outhouse with so small a door that he could not get the barrow out.[2]

In the midlands the Yorkshireman offered a ready target for regional slurs.

> The counties round Yorkshire called the Yorkshireman's Arms a flea, a fly, a magpie, and a flitch of bacon; because a flea will bite anyone, a fly will drink with anyone, a magpie will talk with anyone, and a flitch of bacon is no good till it is hung. More specifically, it was said there was only one honest man in Cranswick, and he stole a saddle.[3]

Occasional instances appear of the jocular anecdotes so widely reported by collectors in the mid-twentieth century. MacCulloch set down a version current on Guernsey of the half-witted fellow who verbally outwits the clever chap. The dunce takes his corn to the mill, and the miller, to ridicule him, asks: 'John, people say that you are a fool and know nothing. Now, tell me what you know and what you don't know?' 'Well!' answered John, 'I know this, that

[1] MacCulloch, *op. cit.*, pp. 428–32.
[2] Rev. Thomas Parkinson, *Yorkshire Legends and Traditions, Second Series* (London, 1889), pp. 190–4; Burne, *op. cit.*, p. 28.
[3] John Nicholson, *Folk Lore of East Yorkshire* (London, Hull, Driffield, 1890), pp. 97–8.

millers have fine horses.' 'That's what you know,' said the miller. 'Now tell me what you don't know.' 'I don't know on whose corn they are fattened,' said John.[1]

Similarly, a Shropshire lad discomfits a gentleman riding past a small mere, Kettlemere, adjoining another named Blackmere. The horseman asked the youth the mere's name. 'Oh, aye, sir,' answered the lad, 'it's Kettle*mar.*' 'How deep is it?' 'Oh, it's no bottom to it, and the tother's deeper till that, sir!'[2]

While the humour of rusticity crept into the field books, the humour of exaggeration and the tall tale remained almost entirely absent. Miss Burne did note the naming of Bristle Bridge in Shropshire for a tall-story teller who bragged of killing a boar so large its bristles resembled pikeavill grains, i.e. pitchfork prongs.[3] But of other tales we are not told, probably because they lacked sufficient local association.

Some reports from the field fall outside the systematic county inventory. In his personal story of *Forty Years in a Moorland Parish* (1891), the Reverend J. C. Atkinson dipped directly into the lives and hidden lore of his parishioners on the bleak Danby moors. His accounts of witchcraft and deviltry bruited among the Danby folk are set in the midst of village life and work and placed on the lips of vividly sketched farmers and farmwives. Ultimately the industrious Society workers swept into their nets the folklore portions of such individual collecting, and indeed Mrs. Eliza Gutch extracted traditions from Atkinson's memoir to arrange in her classified survey of North Riding printed lore.

The bright promise of folklore collecting in England was never fulfilled. But the contagion of the folklore movement brought forth such massive field books as Burne's *Shropshire*, Leather's *Hereford-shire*, and MacCulloch's *Guernsey*, testifying to riches at hand. The English would perform their greatest feats of collecting in faraway lands.

[1] MacCulloch, *op. cit.*, pp. 545–6.
[2] Burne, *op. cit.*, p. 73.   [3] *Ibid.*, p. 99.

X The Overseas Folklorists

'IT IS IN THE BRITISH EMPIRE, which has to so large an extent grown and been consolidated during Her Majesty's reign, and which includes within its bounds countless races of every degree of civilization and mental development, from the lowest to the highest, that the student of folklore has to seek many of the most precious materials of his study.'[1]

So wrote the president of The Folk-Lore Society, Edward W. Brabrook, in a memorial on the death of Queen Victoria in *Folk-Lore* in 1901. Under Her Majesty's rule, the beliefs and customs of all races had been respected, and 'the study of folklore, a science the very existence of which is bounded by Her Majesty's reign, has thus been rendered possible.' These statements followed the lead taken by Hartland, who in his presidential address of 1900 formulated the 'empire theory' of applied folklore. In that address he stressed the practical advantages for the governors, district officers, and judges of an enlightened mother-country in learning through folklore about the cultures of the native peoples under their dominion. Accordingly the council of the Society had presented a memorial to the colonial secretary calling for a 'methodical survey' of the native tribes. 'No ruler who does not understand his subjects can govern them for the best advantage, either theirs or his,' Hartland affirmed.[2] He pointed to the examples set by other nations; in 1898 the German government spent twenty-five thousand pounds on anthropological explorations, while in the United States the Bureau of American Ethnology received a budget of forty thousand dollars for its field studies of Indian tribes. Yet the opportunities available to Germany and the States shrank before the vast possibilities within the British Empire.

The new imperial outlook of the English folklorists found official expression in the much fatter, revised edition of *The Handbook of Folklore* prepared in 1914 by Charlotte Burne, carrying through the

[1] Brabrook, in *Folk-Lore*, XII (1901), 98. [2] Hartland, in *Folk-Lore*, XII (1901), 38.

revision initiated by Hartland. Where Gomme had aimed his 1890 questionary at English gentry in the shires, Burne addressed her manual first to 'missionaries, travellers, settlers, and others whose lot is cast among uncivilized or half civilized populations abroad' and only second to the educated at home living among the uneducated. The large sections on 'Belief and Practice' and 'Customs' dealt chiefly with the world-view of contemporary savages, invoking examples from Zulus and Aruntas, Loango and A-Kikuyu, Bushmen and Yorubas, Nagas and Todas, with much talk of shamans and phratries, totemism and kinship. Folklore of the Isles has indeed yielded to folklore of the Empire.

In this changed emphasis the *Handbook* was not initiating so much as capping an era. The recording of tales, customs, proverbs, and poetry possessed by the dark-skinned races living under the British flag commenced in the second half of the nineteenth century and gathered exciting momentum in the three decades preceding the Great War. Two powerful motives impelled the overseas folklorists: a desire to test in a living laboratory the new anthropological hypotheses of Tylor concerning primitive man, and a wish to improve colonial government through a sympathetic knowledge of subject peoples. Intellectual and administrative ends thus happily coincided, with fortuitous results for folklore collecting. More and more the pages of *Folk-Lore* and the independent books of folklore materials reflected the concerns of Empire, as British civil servants, military officers, church missionaries, and company traders, and their wives and daughters, turned to the experts of The Folk-Lore Society for advice in processing their hard-won harvests from the field. The new sciences of mythology and folklore gave their work importance and direction, while their protracted residence enabled them to become participant observers in strategic listening posts. Predictably these officials of State and Church, sharing the broad curiosity of their fellow Victorians and Edwardians, would undertake ethnographic surveys, compile dialect and proverb dictionaries, and capture specimens of oral literature in their enforced sojourn abroad. India and Africa especially proved inexhaustible treasure houses of native traditions.

INDIA

Unlike Australia and Africa, the homes of savages, India offered the special charm of an ancient high culture lurking behind the nineteenth-century realities of Hindu village castes and aboriginal hill tribes. Both Max Müller with his revelation of the Vedas and Tylor with his reconstruction of the primitive mind had sharpened the zest of English passengers to India. And, too, the thesis of Benfey and Cosquin and Clouston that the master-tales had originated in India, could be tested. Here was the ideal proving-ground to examine both survivals and diffusion.

Credit for the first field-collected storybook of Indian folktales belongs to the daughter of the governor of Bombay. In 1868 Mary Frere brought out *Old Deccan Days, or Hindoo Fairy Legends current in southern India*. On a tour through Mahratta with her father, the Right Honourable Sir Bartle Frere, and his staff, Mary found the time hanging heavy. Turning to her sole female companion, her ayah, Anna Liberata de Souza, a daughter of Christian converts who belonged to the Lingaet caste of the Mahratta country, Mary one day asked Anna to tell her a story. Anna protested that she knew none. Mary pointed out, 'You have children and grandchildren, surely you tell them stories to amuse them sometimes?'[1] Anna pondered and stretched her memory back to her childhood when, as a girl of eleven, she had listened to wonderful adventures told by her grandmother. So the ayah recalled a story that turned out to be 'Punchkin,' and then others, sitting cross-legged on the floor while Mary took notes and then read back the narratives to Anna for correction.

The governor's daughter realized the deeper implications in her pastime and sought the guidance of Max Müller. Happily the Oxford don informed her that he had chanced on a Sanskrit original of one of Anna's tales and that her version read like a direct translation of the ancient Sanskrit. In her appended notes to a new edition, Mary paid homage to 'the recently published work of Professor Max Müller, which might, without exaggeration, be described as a storehouse of new facts connected with the religion and literature of the East, rather than by its modest title of *Chips from a German Workshop*.'[2]

For a pioneer work the Englishwoman set high standards in presenting these twenty-four tales of rajahs and brahmans, jackals and tigers—although, to her surprise, none of elephants. She strove for fidelity to the spoken word and gave meritorious attention to her teller, even to including a preamble on 'The Narrator's Narrative,' while her father supplied informative notes glossing culture traits and popular practices referred to in the stories. Anna's conversational autobiography admirably disclosed the mind and rearing of

[1] Mary Frere, *Old Deccan Days*, 3rd ed. (London, 1881), p. xi.   [2] *Ibid.*, p. 222.

the storyteller. On the first job she took after her husband's death, Anna apologized to her employer for her poor English, and although she knew 'our Calicut language, and Portuguese, and Hindostani, and Mahratti well enough,' she felt herself 'stupid, like a Coolie-woman.'[1] Eventually, however, Anna learned English well enough to relate the 'Hindoo fairy legends' in her mistress's tongue. On the minus side, a collection recorded in Government House in Bombay could scarcely be accounted a genuine field inquiry, and the governor's daughter was in effect continuing the method of the Victorian gentlewoman who peered into a subterranean culture through the eyes of her house servant. Her father the governor contributed a characteristic Introduction, stating how desirable it was for resident observers to obtain the 'popular non-Brahminical superstitions of the lower orders' so greatly at variance with upper-caste Hinduism. As a boy living on the Welsh border he had heard of huge-nosed goblins called Pwccas [sic], which reminded him of the demoniacal and ghoulish Rakshas of the present legends.

Mary Frere's book enjoyed considerable success. In a Preface to the third edition in 1881, she reported that it had been translated into German, Hungarian, and Danish and retranslated into Mahratti, Hindustani, and Guzerati. Inevitably it inspired emulators.

The second collection to appear, the loosely titled *Indian Fairy Tales*, was also obtained by an Englishwoman, Maìve S. H. Stokes, from her house servants. In this case she acted both as collector and translator. Printed in 1879 in an edition of one hundred copies, the new work set the same commendable standards of text fidelity as *Old Deccan Days* and in addition opened up comparative studies with sixty pages of meaty notes. Young Miss Stokes secured her first twenty-five stories at Calcutta and Simla from two ayahs and a manservant in Hindustani, which she understood. The last five were told her mother by one of the ayahs. Her mother served up the ample notes, and her father prepared a useful index of folklore themes.[2] Maìve's father was the celebrated Celtic scholar Whitley Stokes, who spent the years from 1864 to 1882 as a civil servant in India.

A London edition (1880) contained a judicious introduction by W. R. S. Ralston, a founding member of The Folk-Lore Society and a specialist in Russian folklore. Praising the work for proffering 'faithful transcripts of Indian thought,' he declared that it perfectly complemented Frere's collection from a Christian native, since Miss

---

[1] *Old Deccan Days* (London, 1868), p. xxxii.
[2] Maìve S. H. Stokes, *Indian Fairy Tales* (Calcutta, 1879), pp. 237–95.

Stokes had quarried from two Hindu ayahs and a Mohammedan manservant. Europe was now 'well collected,' but peasant tales could still come from Asia, especially India, to clarify the mythological ideas left unexplained in European *Märchen*. Ralston cited fictions from Stokes' larder at variance with Western fairy tales. The great sitting powers of King Buntal, who for twelve years never budged from his jungle seat, would scarcely commend themselves to nations addicted to active exercise. Indian tales explained how gods were transformed into mortals or animals, in consonance with the folk religion of ancient and modern India, while European *Märchen* volunteered no explanations beyond simple magic. In their older forms the *Märchen* might have relied on the doctrine of the transmigration of souls.

Two noted folktale authorities, Campbell of Islay, the collector of Highland stories, and Charles H. Tawney, the editor of the *Ocean of Story*, perused a number of the tales in manuscript and proffered comments which found their way into the notes. The notes ranged widely over Tylor's savages, Bleek's Hottentots, Rink's Eskimos, Grey's Maoris, European collections from Germany, Russia, Hungary, Scandinavia, and Sicily, the English field books of Hunt and Henderson, and for India, besides *Old Deccan Days*, the numbers of the *Indian Antiquary*, initiated in 1872 at Bombay. Eclectic and tolerant, the comparative references deferred both to Tylor and Müller. The doctrine of survivals is appeased with references to external souls and relics of stone worship, but solar theory too is comforted with sunny backgrounds of Indian folklore heroes apparent in their golden hair and white skin.

These two worthy volumes of the Misses Frere and Stokes opened the floodgates, and the decade of the 1880's witnessed a string of substantial collections of tales, poems, and proverbs. In 1880 Thomas William Rhys-David, an occasional contributor to the *Folk-Lore Journal*, translated *Buddhist Birth Stories, or Jataka Tales*, as edited from the original Pāli by Michael Viggo Fausböll. The subtitle announced 'The Oldest Collection of Folk-Lore Extant,' and in his monographic Introduction Rhys-David underscored the idea that the book of birth stories was '*the oldest, most complete, and most important Collection of Folk-Lore extant.*' For in the Jatakas the modern reader could behold 'the social life and customs and popular beliefs of the common people of Aryan tribes,' passing through the first stage of civilization.[1] Reading these

[1] *Buddhist Birth Stories; or, Jataka Tales. The Oldest Collection of Folk-Lore Extant, being the Jatakallhavannanā, for the first time edited in the original Pāli*, by V. Fausböll, and translated by T. W. Rhys Davids. Vol. I (London, 1880), pp. iv, lxxxvi.

moralistic and comical tales told long ago by the Buddha and by others about him enhanced the excitement Victorians felt in the nineteenth-century oral stories of peasants simultaneously being offered them.

The close friend of Clodd and a distinguished colonial administrator, Sir Alfred C. Lyall, published *Asiatic Studies* in 1882, a work filled with comment on the interaction of Brahmanic and popular religious beliefs. Lyall drew a distinction between the religion of high civilization and the superstitious mythology of the peasant.

In 1883, a Bengali Hindu convert to Christianity, the Reverend Lal Behari Day, issued in London his valuable *Folk-tales of Bengal*, dedicated to the soldier-scholar Richard Carnac Temple, who would soon be heard from on his own.

The next year, 1884, was the *annus mirabilis* of the Punjab. Two illustrious names made their debut in Anglo-Indian folklore. The Reverend Charles Swynnerton brought out in Calcutta *The Adventures of the Panjáb Hero Rájá Rasálu and Other Folk-Tales of the Panjáb*. Swynnerton belonged to The Folk-Lore Society and the year before had printed in the *Folk-Lore Journal* four legends of Rájá Rasálu, the Indian King Arthur, as he had heard them from native guides around a blazing log fire. For half a dozen years he had been gathering numerous stories from Panjábìs and Patháns of all ages, and he hoped shortly to make the whole collection available, with an introduction by Laurence Gomme. Temple published two folklore books in the same year. Flora Annie Steel, the wife of an English magistrate, was the co-author of one volume published under the title *Wide-Awake Stories, A Collection of Tales Told by Little Children, between Sunset and Sunrise, in the Punjab and Kashmir*. While the forty-three tales were addressed 'To the Little Reader,' a goodly portion of the volume—Temple's share—was given over to scholarly aids: extensive comparative and explanatory notes, an 'Analysis of the Tales on the Folk-Lore Society's Plan,' a fifty-page 'Survey of the Incidents in Modern Aryan Folk-Tales,' and a copious index. The Preface announced that 'The analysis has been made to strictly conform to the method adopted by the Folk-Lore Society of England, and is intended to form part of their scheme of investigations into general machinery of Folk-tales.'[1] A second book Temple produced independently, *The Legends of the Panjáb*, the first of three volumes (the others coming out in 1885 and 1900) containing bardic poems, or versified legends as he called them, dealing with Rájá Rasálu and other favourite subjects. As

[1] F. A. Steel and R. C. Temple, *Wide-Awake Stories* (Bombay and London, 1884), p. iv.

Old Deccan Days was a first for the oral folktale in English, so *The Legends of the Panjâb* was a first for the oral folk-poem, which Temple considered the older and more valuable form and one more faithful to the popular creed. Hence he considered it 'even more important, from the point of view of the folklorist—to use an Americanism which seems to be steadily gaining ground all the world over—to gather and record accurately the poems than the tales.'[1] Furthermore, folktales flourished still in every village while the bardic verses were beginning to disappear. Old wives' tales were but the memories of recitations of bards. One could see in these discursive prose legends interspersed with verses about Rájá Rasálu the disintegration of the older, purer poems.

Temple was an excellent folklorist. Like Campbell of Islay, he trained local people, *munshîs*, to record. He took infinite pains to print exact renderings of the poems, transcribing the dialects into Roman characters, translating the Romanized text, and then resubmitting transliteration and translation to the *munshîs*. Sensitive to the quality of his informants, he classified them much as he did the tales, separating the professional ballad singer or *mîrâsî* from the untrained villager with the gift of recitation. One bard would sing nothing unless soaked with opium. To prove that the verses contained authentic modern Indian folklore, Temple supplied references linking them with the four major tale collections of Frere, Stokes, Day, and Steel. (He had seen advertisements of Swynnerton's *Rájá Rasálu* but was unable to procure a copy.) Sure enough, the same extraordinary hero and his companions, the same giants and serpents, saints and fakirs appeared in the poems as in the stories. Metamorphosis, emphasized by Temple as an Indian conception in his Introduction to Stokes' *Indian Fairy Tales*, proved a common trait in the verses. Temple also remarked on resemblances between Indian and Slavic bards who alike kept alive the singing of heroic lays. One marvels how the 'hard-worked official,' as he described himself, writing in his spare hours remote from libraries, could have produced so well-informed a collection.

Each year brought its new contribution. The name of the Reverend J. Hinton Knowles entered the lists in 1885 with *A Dictionary of Kashmiri Proverbs and Sayings, Explained and Illustrated from the Rich and Interesting Folklore of the Valley*. Knowles began gathering proverbs soon after his arrival in the Valley of Kashmir, believing them to be 'the real people's speech' and so a useful entry into the language. 'Sometimes the great and learned Pandit instinctively uttered a proverb in my hearing; sometimes I

[1] Richard C. Temple, *The Legends of the Panjab* (Bombay, 1884), p. xxvii.

got the barber to tell me a thing or two, as he polled my head; and
sometimes the poor coolie said something worth knowing, as carrying my load he tramped along before me.'[1] To extract the full
meaning of these sententious sayings, Knowles consulted a circle of
Mohammedan and Hindu friends in Kashmir. For comparisons he
drew upon Swynnerton's *Rájá Rasálu*, Adolf Bastian's German collection of Siamese tales, and Baring-Gould's *The Book of Were-
Wolves*. Another noteworthy figure in Anglo-Indian scholarship, Sir
George Grierson, published in 1885 an ethnological survey of *Bihar
Peasant Life*, described on the title page as a 'discursive catalogue
of the surroundings of the people of that province.' One division
dealt with 'Ceremonies and Superstitions of Rural Life.' (Grierson
modelled his volume on William Crooke's 'admirable' publication of
1879, *Materials for a Rural and Agricultural Glossary of the North-
Western Provinces and Oudh.*) In 1886 Temple edited *A Dictionary
of Hindustani Proverbs* from materials amassed by the late S. W.
Fallon.

Temple commented, '. . . India is a land of proverbial sayings:
their name is legion and their use constant and never ending. The
natixes employ them in their daily intercourse, in their commercial
and social correspondence, in all the many vicissitudes of every day
life, even in the very Courts of Law.'[2] He himself glossed puzzling
proverbs by synopsizing the legends from which they had sprung,
as in the following example.

He went to Kābul, became a Mugal, and so began to speak
  their language.
The water was by his side and he died, crying '*l'eau l'eau.*'

The proverb is founded on the following story. A man, who
had visited Kābul and had learnt Persian there at the sacrifice
of his own mother-tongue, used to flaunt Persian phrases when
he returned home to his native land, and consequently died of
thirst, crying in vain for water in Persian '*āb āb,*' instead of the
common Hindustānī *pānī*, which none of his servants and
relations could understand.[3]

Knowles reappeared in 1888 with sixty-four *Folk-Tales of Kashmir*, naming his narrators and comparing his tales to those in earlier

---

[1] J. Hinton Knowles, *A Dictionary of Kashmiri Proverbs and Sayings* (Bombay,
1885), p. iv.
[2] *A Dictionary of Hindustani Proverbs*, including many Marwari, Panjabi, Maggah,
Bhojpuri and Tirhuti Proverbs, Sayings, Emblems, Aphorisms, Maxims and Similes,
by the late S. W. Fallon, edited and revised by Capt. R. C. Temple assisted by Lala
Faqir Chand (Benares and London, 1886), pp. i–ii.   [3] *Ibid.*, p. 126.

Indian collections and to such European works as *Grimms' Household Stories*, Clodd's *Myths and Dreams*, Benjamin Thorpe's *Northern Mythology*, and Dasent's *Popular Tales from the Norse*. Also in 1888 Joseph Jacobs edited *The Fables of Bidpai* from the earliest English edition of 1570, adding to the ancient legends attached to the Buddha a characteristically learned and witty Introduction, in which he connected a Buddhist birth story with Uncle Remus' tar-baby.

The cause of Indian folklore was now well-established, and the decade of the 1890's proved equally fruitful. To balance the claims for northern India, Mrs. Howard Kingscote, in collaboration with the prolific collector of Tamil lore, Pandit Natêsá Sástrî, brought forth *Tales of the Sun or Folklore of Southern India* (1890). Once more an Englishwoman obtained from her native servants household fictions which she joined with specimens printed by Sástrî in small books or in the *Indian Antiquary*. In cases where Temple and Clouston had annotated tales, she retained their erudite notes as a 'service to students of folklore.' Swynnerton reappeared in 1892 with *Indian Nights' Entertainment*, forty-nine of the eighty-five tales being reprinted from his previous work. But now he classified them according to Baring-Gould's scheme of story radicals recommended by Gomme, then president of The Folk-Lore Society.

By 1892 the story literature from India had grown to such impressive proportions that Joseph Jacobs for the first, and last, time departed from the British Isles to include in his series a volume of *Indian Fairy Tales*. Nutt now proudly advertised the series as 'Folktales of the British Empire.' Conscious of the theoretical as well as aesthetic values in his contents, Jacobs devoted a good part of his Introduction to restating the diffusionist argument with its Indianist emphasis. Benfey in Germany, Cosquin in France, and Clouston in Britain had all assigned the original home of the *Märchen* to India, whence they had been transported to Europe by Crusaders, Jews, gypsies, traders, travellers, and Mongol missionaries. Benfey believed that literary contact had existed between East and West from the time of the Crusades. On his part, Jacobs conjectured a still earlier literary transmission of Buddhist birth-stories, identifying the Buddha with folktale heroes, some two thousand years before the Grimms began to publish their *Märchen*; in the long ago the legends of Buddha, he believed, had influenced the fables of Aesop. Cosquin contended for direct oral transmission from India to Europe. Never dogmatic, Jacobs in his paper at the 1891 congress identified a moderate 250 out of 630 European folktale incidents as common to India. For the *Indian Fairy Tales*,

Jacobs, in his usual manner, furnished an appendix of elaborate comparative notes, relying heavily on Temple's 'remarkable analysis' in *Wide-Awake Stories* of the incidents in the 200 tales available by 1884. 'It is not too much to say that this analysis marks an onward step in the scientific study of the folk-tale. . . .'[1]

Seeing the British audience so receptive to the feast of exotic Indian fictions being tendered them, industrious collectors renewed their offerings. In 1894, Flora Steel and Richard C. Temple once more collaborated to produce *Tales of the Punjab, Told by the People*. Again, Mrs. Steel collected the stories and selected them with a view to youthful tastes while Temple provided the scholarly annotations and appendixes, and once more his 'Analysis and Survey of Incidents' followed the model recommended by The Folk-Lore Society. Temple listed the number of tales in each published collection referred to and for each individual story gave page numbers, title, dramatis personae, plot outline, incidental circumstances, and a statement on the nature of the collection—whether an original or a translated work and the extent of the particulars it vouchsafed on the narrator and his audience.

So far collectors had confined themselves to genres—oral narrative, bardic verses, proverbial sayings. Now a still more ambitious work capped the efforts of the past quarter of a century. William Crooke (1848–1923), a civil servant and active ethnologist, published in 1894 in Allahabad *An Introduction to the Popular Religion and Folklore of Northern India*, seeking to reconstruct the prehistoric pantheon of Indian gods and godlings from the extant rites and fancies of the popular faith. It was reprinted in London in 1896 with some revision and, according to Crooke himself, widely quoted and cited.

Crooke proved to be the central figure in Anglo-Indian folklore relations. Born in Ireland of a long-established English family, he was educated at Trinity College, Dublin, and entered the Indian Civil Service in 1871, eventually serving as district magistrate and collector of revenue in the United Provinces of Agra and Oudh. A prolific writer successfully combining his official duties with detailed ethnographic surveys, he contributed numerous tale and song texts to the *Indian Antiquary, North Indian Notes and Queries* (which he edited) and *Punjab Notes and Queries*. Eventually he printed many of his accumulated materials in *The Tribes and Castes of the North-Western Provinces and Oudh* (four volumes, 1896). With his broad ethnological, linguistic, and historical interests, he was able to transcend the collector's role and produce a

[1] Joseph Jacobs, *Indian Fairy Tales* (London, 1892), p. 231.

comprehensive synthesis on popular religion and folklore. Viewing India with the eyes of a Tylorian folklorist, he found close likenesses between the folk beliefs sprouting lushly in the northern provinces and superstitions still flickering in the British Isles. Later editions removed his wealth of comparative examples and references and so destroyed the original character of the work.

Crooke in effect wrote a *Teutonic Mythology* for India, but with ethnological in place of philological analyses. He assembled a bizarre pantheon of gods and godlings, ogres and demons, ghouls and ghosts, saints and sorcerers, all attached to village legends, propitiatory rites, and the taboos and charms of daily life. In village India the dim survivals of rural Britain came into full focus. The old animism lived yet in the worship of tree spirits, and primeval totemism lingered in the reverence of serpents and cows. Fearsome creatures from the prehistoric past stalked the woods and haunted the nocturnal darkness. Peasants dreaded the destructive Rákshasa:

> He goes about at night, haunts cemeteries, disturbs sacrifices and devout men, animates dead bodies, ensnares and even devours human beings, and is generally hostile to the human race. He is emphatically a devourer of raw flesh, and eats carrion. Some have long arms; some are fat; some thin; some dwarfish; others enormously tall or hump backed. Some have only one eye, others only one ear; some have enormous paunches, projecting teeth, and crooked thighs; others can on occasion assume noble forms and are beautiful to look at. He is the great *Deus ex machiná* of folklore. He can change into almost any form as he pleases, his breath is a roaring wind, he can lengthen his arms to eighty miles, and he can smell out human beings like Giant Blunderbore.[1]

Exotic as these monsters might seem to a rational Victorian, Crooke was ever quick to perceive similarities with beliefs at home. The Rákshasas misled night travellers like the will-o'-the-wisp; they hid treasures of gold and jewels in the earth as did the Irish fairies; they vanished at dawn, in the manner of Hamlet's ghost and the night spirits that ravished Sodom; they abducted ill-protected new babies as did the Hedley Kow in northern England; and their giant fossil bones suggested Orestes' bones in the gigantic coffin described by Herodotus.

Crooke had digested the whole of his own tradition. He quoted Aubrey's *Remaines* in the newly issued Folk-Lore Society edition,

[1] William Crooke, *An Introduction to the Popular Religion and Folklore of Northern India* (Allahabad, 1894), pp. 153–4.

19. MARY HENRIETTA KINGSLEY

20. JOHN FRANCIS CAMPBELL OF ISLAY

cited Brand's *Observations* and Scott's *Letters*, leaned on Lang, Hartland, and Gomme, and invoked Tylor right up to his final sentence. In drawing analogies he depended on the collections of Henderson for northern England, Gregor and Chambers for Scotland, and Lady Wilde for Ireland. Müller and Cox and Kelly entered his notes, but while he accepted their East-West comparisons, he rejected their celestial symbolism. In his concluding chapter, 'Some Rural Festivals and Ceremonies,' he frankly singled out examples illustrating the principles of Frazer, Gomme, and Mannhardt. The district magistrate followed Hartland in treating folktales as a prime source for congealed beliefs, and he employed Lang's 'method of folklore' in comparing English survivals with Indian daily rituals and in examining survivals of primitive mythology and sacrifice. Of the older antiquaries, Robert Burton in his *The Anatomy of Melancholy* served him with references on aerial spirits and talismanic stones.

While a confirmed survivalist, Crooke was also sufficiently an Indianist to espouse some instances of story-incidents diffusing from India to Europe. To document these migrations he found helpful evidence in Jacobs' copious notes to his *Celtic Fairy Tales*. Thus Crooke could point out, following Clouston (see p. 261), that the well-known Welsh legend of the faithful dog Gelert was told at an earlier date in India about a faithful mongoose. So too the story of the ass in the lion's skin had spread westward from India, noted Crooke, referring to Charles II. Tawney's classic edition of *The Kātha Sarit Sāgara*.

Almost every item of folk-religious belief and practice Crooke uncovered in India triggered off in his mind an apt British or European equivalent. The fight between Indra and Ali suggested to him the Scotch account of Froach killing the great serpent at the Ross of Mull. He recognized the taboo, common in villages throughout northern India, against pronouncing names of ill-omened persons or places. 'When we wonder at people suffering bondage of this kind we must not forget that similar beliefs prevail in our own country.'[1] And Crooke thought of family names in Buckie which no fisherman would pronounce. The Kamís customarily set out a dish of the funeral feast in the jungle until a fly, representing the dead man's spirit, alighted on the dish; just so an English lady of Crooke's acquaintance stopped her game of lawn tennis because a butterfly had settled on the court. The ghoulish ghosts known as Bhúts guarded treasure much as did the Irish leprechauns, and one hill Bhút, Airi, closely resembled the Wild Huntsman. Farmers

[1] *Ibid.*, p. 218.

alike in northern India and northern Scotland left patches of ground as preserves for gods or devils.

If the peasants of Europe and Asia shared such conceptions, a vast gulf separated the educated European from the Indian villager. The overseas visitors became themselves objects of folk belief when they set foot on the subcontinent. Natives dreaded being stared at by Europeans whom they suspected of casting the evil eye. They resisted English surgeons, fearing that amputation of limbs would produce malevolent ghosts. Further, they associated doctors with the terrifying *Momiái*, a belief in the magical efficacy of fat, particularly potent when extracted from a fat black boy suspended by his heels over a slow fire after a small hole had been bored through the top of his head.

Crooke's achievement was the more remarkable since, like Temple, he had to snatch time 'in the intervals of the scanty leisure of a District Officer's life in India' at a far remove from libraries. He designed his book to assist fellow officers working with rural classes, to stimulate educated natives to inquire for themselves into these matters, and to inform European scholars who knew well enough the official Hindu religion of the Brahmans but to whom the popular religion of the lower castes remained a terra incognita. Crooke conjectured that the roots of the popular faith lay in a non-Aryan or Dravidian people, whose original system could be recovered from a close scrutiny of nineteenth-century folk ritual and worship.

The district magistrate became increasingly involved in the subject of folklore, both in India and after his return home. Part of the folktale hoard Crooke amassed during his ethnological survey of the Northwest Provinces reached book form in 1899 under the title *The Talking Thrush, and Other Tales from India*, retold for a youthful audience by W. H. D. Rouse, a Council Member of The Folk-Lore Society. Some of these tales Crooke collected himself 'from the lips of the jungle-folk of Mirzápur,' and others he obtained via a circular issued by the Director of Public Instruction to all teachers of village schools in the provinces. In turn, Crooke edited *Folktales from the Indus Valley*, gathered by Major F. McNair and Thomas L. Barlow in 1902, and *Hobson-Jobson, A Glossary of Colloquial Anglo-Indian Words and Phrases*, by Colonel Henry Yule and A. C. Burnell, in 1903. His popular handbook of *Things Indian* (1906) contained a number of folkloristic topics, for instance, amulets, divination, the evil eye, and folktales.

On his return to England Crooke promptly took up an active role in The Folk-Lore Society, serving as president in 1912 and 1913. In his presidential addresses, 'The Scientific Aspects of Folklore' and 'Method of Investigation and Folklore Origins,' the ex-Bengal civil servant picked up the reins of the folklore movement as if he had been in the driver's seat all along. In 1912 he extended congratulations to Tylor, 'the leader of the English school of folklore,' and to Gomme on being knighted. Reviewing the thirty-three-year span of the Society, he observed how the meteorological method of studying folklore had been replaced by the anthropological, and looked forward to the future development of folklore from contact with related sciences—psychology, sociology, and ethnology. In 1913 he mourned the death of Lang and the fact that he had not lived to write his book on the social aspects of folk belief and custom. From 1915 until his death in 1923 Crooke held the key post of editor for the Society.

The career of the bookish administrator exemplifies the happy fusion of islands-and-empire folklore research. Between 1897 and 1923 he contributed nineteen articles to *Folk-Lore* on such matters as Hindu fire, lamps, and autumn festivals; the house in India as a sociological and folkloric phenomenon; legends of Krishna; cults of the mother goddesses; witchcraft and ghost tales in northern India. His scope transcended 'things Indian,' and in an intriguing essay on 'Some Notes on Homeric Folk-Lore' in 1908 he stole a leaf out of Andrew Lang's book by extracting the folkloristic elements strewn through the *Iliad* and the *Odyssey*. The transformation combat in the tale of Proteus moved him to remark on its manifold appearances in traditional story. 'One of the best examples of this incident is the terrible scene in the tale of the "Second Calendar" in the *Arabian Nights*, where oriental fancy reaches the highest pitch of tragedy, as the Ifrit becomes successively a lion, a scorpion, a wolf, and a cock, and finally blazing fire which consumes the unlucky princess.'[1] The author proceeded to cite Hindu, Norse, modern Greek, German peasant, and Highland Scottish versions of transformation combats.

In the last year of his life, 1923, Crooke saw printed a detailed commentary he had written 'On the Folklore in the Stories' to *Hatim's Tales, Kashmiri Stories and Songs*, recorded by Sir Aurel Stein and translated by Sir George Grierson, a book long in process. The impressive repertoire of Hatim, a professional storyteller in the Sind Valley, was first sampled in 1896 by archaeologist Stein, who

---

[1] Crooke, 'Some Notes on Homeric Folk-Lore,' *Folk-Lore*, XIX (1908), 167. The motif in Stith Thompson's *Motif-Index of Folk Literature* is D615. Crooke's book on 'Homeric Folk-Lore' somehow failed to find a publisher. A related article is 'The Wooing of Penelope,' *Folk-Lore*, IX (1898), 98–133.

called him a 'living phonographic machine.' Sixteen years later, Stein again recorded Hatim's tales, finding them meticulously consistent. In 1910 Grierson undertook to translate the texts for publication. Then the war brought further interruption. The finished volume printed the ten tales and two songs in both phonetic transcription of the village dialect and the literary Kashmir language. Crooke discussed comparable themes in the twelve pieces as found in the *Arabian Nights* and Oriental story-literature generally.

In his energetic career spanning two continents, the colonial civil servant and private scholar helped make true his own assertion that 'folklore . . . is gradually coming into its kingdom, and it is no longer compelled, like the priest-king of the Arician grove, to fight periodically for its life.'[1]

Sir Richard Carnac Temple (1850–1931) wrote the obituary of Crooke in *Folk-Lore* in 1924. The same year he also supplied a Preface for a paper of the 'late Dr. Crooke' on 'Marriage Songs in Northern India,' printed in the *Indian Antiquary*. The lives of the two friends, twin giants in Anglo-Indian folklore, often intersected. Temple was born at Allahabad, India, the son of a prominent British administrator, received his education at Harrow and Cambridge, and then entered the military profession, serving in India from 1871 on and participating in the second Afghan War of 1878–1879. His ethnological and historical studies commenced in earnest with his appointment as cantonment magistrate in Punjab after the Afghan campaign. Thoroughly fluent in Urdu and Hindi, the soldier-scholar threw himself into scientific labours that yielded, among many other works, the three volumes of *The Legends of the Panjâb*. The first volume came out in 1884, but the third was delayed until 1900, at which time its author was president of the municipality and port commissioner of Rangoon in Burma, and so turning to studies in Burmese popular religion. Much of his effort went into the editing of the *Indian Antiquary* and the *Panjab Notes and Queries*, which he filled with his own articles, notes, and reviews, many of them on folkloristic topics.

Temple was in touch with The Folk-Lore Society at an early date. In 1883 and 1885 he printed Punjabi and north Indian proverbs in the *Folk-Lore Journal*, and in 1886 he contributed a bibliography of vernacular publications on folklore issued in the Punjab in Arabic, Persian, Urdu, Hindi, Punjabi, Pashto, and Sanskrit. The same year he read a paper to the Society, later printed in its journal, on 'The Science of Folk-Lore,' an earnest and

[1] Crooke, in *Folk-Lore*, XXIII (1912), 31.

weighty manifesto. Temple drew upon his own experience as editor
of *Panjab Notes and Queries* to emphasize the difficulty in cate-
gorizing materials under folklore. Misstatement was not folk legend.
He proposed a taut definition: Folklore as an object of study is the
popular explanation of observed facts and the customs arising
therefrom. The science of folklore should, in keeping with scientific
method, deduce theory from facts and not do as a comparative
mythologist had done two years previously in the *Westminster
Review*, theorize wildly that Rájá Rasálu was a solar hero. From his
own minute researches Temple could prove that Rasálu was an
historical figure.

Folklorists must know their objectives if they would be practical
scientists. As an example of the practical application of folklore,
Temple held up a large manuscript being edited by James M.
Campbell and sponsored by the Bombay Government, *Notes on the
Spirit Basis of Belief and Custom*. Campbell's carefully planned
inquiry into the inner life of the Bombay population was 'by far the
best exposition of Indian Folk-lore that has yet been compiled,' and
would show the natives of India how old and widespread were their
household rites for scaring away spirits. From these investigations
Englishmen would derive great benefits.

> The practices and beliefs included under the general head of
> Folk-lore make up the daily life of the natives of our great
> dependency, control their feelings, and underlie many of their
> actions. We foreigners cannot hope to understand them rightly
> unless we deeply study them, and it must be remembered that
> close acquaintance and a right understanding begets sympathy,
> and sympathy begets a good government . . .[1]

Temple included a folded insert of the table used by Campbell in
arranging his data on Indian spirits.

In 1899 the soldier was back again before the Society, reading a
paper on 'The Machinery of Folktales as exhibited in the Legends of
the Panjab,' heard and discussed by Crooke, Clodd, and Nutt.
Approvingly the lieutenant colonel observed, '. . . I cannot help
feeling how much the special investigations of the Folk-Lore
Society have gone forward since I last had the honour of addressing
it some fourteen years ago. . . .' But he added a demurrer from his
own point of view, suggesting 'it does appear to me that English
students might make more use than they apparently do of the work
of their contemporaries in the British Eastern possessions.'[2] At

[1] Temple, 'The Science of Folk-Lore,' *Folk-Lore Journal*, IV (1886), 193–212. The
quotations are from pp. 197, 208, 209.   [2] Temple, in *Folk-Lore*, X (1899), 384.

the request of the president, Nutt, Temple printed an expanded version of his paper in *Folk-Lore* as 'The Folklore in the Legends of the Panjab.' Here he stated *in extenso* his thesis that the bardic narratives faithfully represented the folklore traits found in folktales and folk beliefs.

> . . . in the *Legends of the Panjab* we have displayed before us practically the whole machinery of popular Indian storytelling. Both the actors and their actions . . . have all shown themselves to be of the same descriptions, and to have the same characteristics as those in Indian folktales generally, whether pure narrative or of set purpose connected with the hagiolatry or demonolatry of the people.[1]

In the volumes of the *Indian Antiquary*, which he founded and commenced editing in 1872, Temple published an enormous amount of folklore. Yet, he told the Society sorrowfully, they scarcely noticed in their journal what in quantity probably surpassed their own output. The soldier's publications number over one hundred entries in the standard *A Bibliography of South Asian Folklore* by Edwin C. Kirkland and range over every aspect of custom and tradition.[2] One entry alone might reflect a major investigation, as did his protracted description of 'The Devil Worship of the Tuluvas,' which ran in a series of seventeen papers in the *Indian Antiquary* between 1894 and 1897.

Other civil servants and military officers stationed in India published collections of folklore and presented papers to The Folk-Lore Society in London,[3] but Crooke and Temple tower above the rest. By the time of the First World War, their untiring efforts and earnest purpose had firmly grounded the science of folklore in India in keeping with the principles of the leading English folklorists, and helped make available a whole library of unwritten traditions.

---

[1] *Folk-Lore*, X (1899), 442–3.
[2] Edwin C. Kirkland, *A Bibliography of South Asian Folklore* (Bloomington, Indiana, 1966), pp. 213–17, items 6260–6379.
[3] E.g., Lieutenant-Colonel J. Shakespear, political agent in Manipur, read a paper June 16, 1909, on 'Folk-Tales of the Lushais and Their Neighbours' (printed in *Folk-Lore*, XX, 1909, 388–420); Major A. J. O'Brien, deputy commissioner of the Panjab Commission, read a paper April 19, 1911, on 'Some Matrimonial Problems of the Western Border of India' (printed in *Folk-Lore*, XXII, 1911, 426–48).
Representative later titles are *Popular Poetry of the Baloches* by Mansel L. Dames, 2 vols., Publications of The Folk-Lore Society, LIX (London, 1905); *Folklore of the Santal Parganas*, trans. by Cecil Henry Bompas of the Indian Civil Service (London, 1909); *Omens and Superstitions of Southern India* by Edgar Thurston, sometime superintendent of the Madras Government Museum (London and Leipsic, 1912).

AFRICA

If India offered comfort to mythologists and diffusionists with her classical antiquity, Africa seemed made to order for Tylorian evolutionists. Here were benighted savages seemingly little different from men of the Bronze Age. For Victorian folklorists they promised exciting revelations of prehistoric thinking and behaving.

Britain had to share Africa with other European colonizers, and German missionaries of linguistic bent first introduced African folklore to English readers. In 1854 the Church Missionary House in London published *African Native Literature, Proverbs, Tales, Fables, & Historical Fragments in the Kanuri or Bornu Language*, by the Reverend Sigismund Wilhelm Koelle. For five years in Sierra Leone the missionary of the United Church of Prussia occupied himself with mastering the grammar, vocabulary, and oral literature of an important but little-known Negro language, Bornu. Now he set down the original texts and English translations of tales told directly in the Kanuri (or Bornu) tongue and purporting to mirror accurately the mind of their speakers. Koelle's claim in his Preface did not turn out to be well-supported by his texts. Not the Negro mind but the missionary mind is revealed in the proverbs, tales, and fables describing God as an omnipresent figure and presenting priests—even priestly jackals—as common characters. Didactic and moral elements permeate the sayings and stories: 'As to what is future, even a bird with a long neck cannot see it, but God only.'[1] Since Islam had penetrated Sierra Leone, the Christian missionary had more than simply the heathen to deal with. The 'Story of a Priest who had a Heathen Friend' illustrates the Christian bias through an unexpected reverse twist. Instead of the Muslim priest, who entered the mosque in Mecca with an unclean heart, it was his heathen companion who received a reward after death.

If a man has a good and white heart, he will obtain heaven; As for reading, thou mayest have read through all the books of the world, but if thine heart is black, thou shalt not obtain heaven. The priest who had a heathen friend, expected, in his heart, that he would obtain heaven, because he was a priest who knew the books, fasted, prayed, killed the Easter-lamb, and gave alms; whereas his heathen friend neither fasted, nor prayed, nor gave alms, but ate carrion, and hog's meat, and monkey-meat, and drank his beer, and made water

---

[1] Sigismund W. Koelle, *African Native Literature* (London, 1854), p. 3.

while standing: and nevertheless our Lord who knew their hearts, made out the priest for the fire and the heathen for heaven.[1]

The archaic English of the translation blended with the hortatory sentiment of the narratives.

In 1864 another London publisher brought out a second African tale collection prepared by a German, but this time the author was aided by a British administrator. Dr. Wilhelm Heinrich Immanuel Bleek, trained in philology at the universities of Berlin and Bonn, published a slender book, *Reynard the Fox in South Africa; or, Hottentot Fables and Tales, chiefly translated from original manuscripts in the Library of His Excellency Sir George Grey, K.C.B.* Bleek addressed his twenty-page Preface in letter form to 'My dear Sir George.' Grey had served as governor of South Australia and of New Zealand before coming to South Africa in 1854 for a seven-year-period as governor of Cape Colony. During the early years of his career he deliberately sought to elevate his administrative rule through personal acquaintance with the language, customs, and oral literature of the subject races. This principle led him to record and publish *Polynesian Mythology and Ancient Traditional History of the New Zealand Race (English and Maori)* in 1855. On arriving in Cape Town he again set about acquiring native traditions. There he met Bleek, one of a number of German settlers shown hospitality by the new governor, and the two entered into happy partnership. Bleek became the custodian of Grey's library, and together they prepared a *Handbook of African, Australian, and Polynesian Philology* through Trübner and Company in London, also the publishers of *Reynard the Fox in South Africa*. Alone, Bleek produced *A Comparative Grammar of South African Languages*.

As a governor Sir George may indeed be best remembered for his sponsorship of linguistic and folkloristic researches. The career that burned brightly in the beginning with hazardous explorations of South Australia and two terms as governor of New Zealand, followed by the prime ministership, ended in relative eclipse and inactivity. Grey lacked the finesse and flexibility necessary for political survival. But he possessed genuine intellectual interest in primitive cultures, even before Tylor's writings caught the English imagination.

At Sir George's suggestion, Bleek wrote in 1861 to various missionaries in South Africa suggesting they collect specimens of the native literature. From the Rhenish missionary at Beersheba in

---

[1] Sigismund W. Koelle, *African Native Literature* (London, 1854), p. 142.

Great Namaqualand, the Reverend G. Krönlein, he received a manuscript of twenty-four fables, tales, and legends, twelve praise songs, thirty-two proverbs, and twelve riddles in Hottentot texts with German translations. This cache formed the basis for *Reynard the Fox in South Africa*. Bleek also reprinted a few Hottentot 'fables' included by Sir James Alexander in his *An Expedition of Discovery into the Interior of Africa* (1838). Although historically important, *Reynard* was a limited performance whose title and treatment reflected the European as well as the Hottentot outlook. Any tale involving animals Bleek called a fable, and he selected chiefly stories about jackals, lions, tortoises, and baboons. He did insert four legends concerning the famous Namaqua sorcerer Heitsi Eilrip and two 'household tales' on the order of the Grimms' *Märchen*. Bleek tailored the brief narrations for the general reader and for children and volunteered no comparisons, although he did recognize the modern and European character of certain tales about the white man, wagons, horses, tailors, and people praying.

On the side of theory, Bleek raised some speculative points suggested by his philological training. The family of 'sex-denoting languages,' to which the Nama Hottentot belonged, personalized objects and so inspired fables and myths humanizing animals and natural phenomena. Fables being simpler in conception might well both precede and outlive myths, and perhaps this is what had happened among the Hottentots. The Kaffirs, who lacked the grammatical distinction of sex, also lacked myths and fables. Bleek's little volume heralded more important work to come from him and other visitors to Africa.

The following year, 1865, Richard Francis Burton (1821–90), the glamorous explorer who in twenty years would contribute to folklore his famed translation of the *Arabian Nights*, produced *Wit and Wisdom from West Africa*, dipping into proverbial rather than narrative riches. The subtitle was 'A Book of Proverbial Philosophy, Idioms, Enigmas, and Laconisms.' Burton modelled his book on a work familiar to him in his Eastern residence, Captain Thomas Roebuck's *A Collection of Proverbs and Proverbial Phrases in the Persian and Hindoostanee Languages* (Calcutta, 1824), which he regarded as 'a kind of manual of Asiatic thought.' In similar fashion, Burton hoped his compilation of 2,268 wise sayings might pierce the mystery of the Negro mind through their own self-delineation and demonstrate to Europeans the possession by Africans of a worthy vernacular literature.

An old hand at exotic languages, the gifted travel author avidly thumbed through grammars of African tongues constructed by missionaries culling the sententious utterances that in Africa often carried the force of legal precedent. Grammars and dictionaries for the Wolof, Kanuri, Oji, Ga (or Accra), Yoruba, Efik, and Mpangwe yielded him the coveted proverbs. For the Kanuri he levied upon Koelle's *African Native Literature*. Certain sayings he enriched with notes, revealing as much of the thought of Burton as of Africa. His Majesty's consul for the Bight of Biafra and Fernando Po made no attempt to suppress his racist opinions. Elucidating a pair of Kanuri proverbs, 'If a woman speaks two words, take one and leave the other,' and 'If thou givest thy heart to a woman, she will kill thee,' he wryly observed how truly Semitic were these sneers against the veracity of the sex. For the most part he attached few explanations to the Wolof and Kanuri saws of Semitic hue, reserving his glosses for the Hamitic and Negro sayings more alien to European thought. African laziness came clearly to the fore in the Oji saying, 'When a slave becomes a free man, he will drink rain-water'—in his estimation a truly African proverb. When the Oji said, 'If another suffers pain, [*to you*] a piece of wood suffers,' Burton perceived the 'practical selfishness and feelinglessness of the wild West African, who, when tamed by slavery, becomes one of the most tender of men.' He deplored a Yoruba proverb about the unclean parrot who refused to offer sacrifice as 'one of those sneers at religion, much affected by Africans, Hindoos, Chinese, and idolaters generally. . . .'[1] Yet Burton could gibe too at the parochialism of his fellow Europeans, as in his observation on the Accra saying, 'The way after [*the people*] Ga, that is the way':

> The Rev. Mr. Zimmermann here remarks, that 'the Ga people consider themselves a leading people.' I should be thankful, as an amateur anthropologist, or comparative-anthropologist, vulgarly called ethnologist, to know the name of the race that does not.[2]

Burton preferred to interpret the cultural meaning of the proverbs rather than to trace comparisons, but he did note some likenesses. The Yoruba, 'If clothes remain long in the bag they rot,' suggested to him the Arab, 'Standing water stinks,' in opposition to the English, 'Rolling stone gathers no moss.' Also the Yoruba, 'He who injures [*or despises*] another, injures [*or despises*] himself,' seemed to have come from the Moslems, who overran the Sudan in the tenth century. In the Accra, 'A good word removes anger,'

---

[1] Richard F. Burton, *Wit and Wisdom from West Africa* (London, 1865), p. 44, no. 10; p. 45, no. 20; p. 113, no. 195; p. 121, no. 226; p. 299, no. 389.
[2] *Ibid.*, p. 156, no. 119.

Burton recognized the European influence which had pervaded the Gold Coast for several centuries, and compared it to Proverbs 15:1.[1] In the *Wit and Wisdom from West Africa*, with its cargo of tongue twisters, allusions, condensed tales, proverbial curses and charms, plays-on-words, euphuisms, and newer japes at the white man, Burton amply documented his thesis that the Africans owned a distinctive oral literature and traditional philosophy.

A second collector taking his place with Bleek as a hallowed name in the history of Anglo-African folklore was the Reverend Canon Callaway, M.D., an English medical missionary and the first bishop for Kaffraria, who published in 1868 in Natal and London *Nursery Tales, Traditions, and Histories of the Zulus, in their own words, with a translation into English, and Notes.* Canon Callaway had arrived in Africa fourteen years earlier and immersed himself in the language, religion, and mythology of the Kaffirs. To this end he took down statements dictated directly by Kaffirs, thus procuring records far more complete and trustworthy than the notes from ordinary conversation. In a letter of 1858 from Spring Vale, Upper Umkomanzi, he reported, '. . . I have been very busy lately writing accounts, from the mouth of different Kaffirs, of their habits, traditions, beliefs, &c.'[2] A superior native, Umpengula, assisted him in collecting Zulu traditions. Callaway explained his method of procuring accurate texts:

> A native is requested to tell a tale; and to tell it exactly as he would tell it to a child or a friend; and what he says is faithfully written down. We have thus placed before us the language as nearly as possible such as it is spoken by the natives in their intercourse with each other. And, further, what has been thus written can be read to the native who dictated it; corrections be made; explanations be obtained; doubtful points be submitted to other natives; and it can be subjected to any amount of analysis the writer may think fit to make.[3]

Beginning with an interest in the language, Callaway soon felt a desire to understand the mind of the people and to 'trace out their connections with other nations by the similarity which might exist in their traditions and myths, their nursery tales and proverbs.'[4] A broad acquaintance with the literature of anthropology and folk-

[1] *Ibid.*, p. 217, no. 11; p. 198, no. 66; p. 136, no. 10.
[2] Marion S. Benham, *Henry Callaway M.D., D.D. First Bishop for Kaffraria, His Life History and Work. A Memoir*, ed. Rev. Canon Benham (London, 1896), p. 76.
[3] Canon Callaway, *Nursery Tales, Traditions, and Histories of the Zulus* (Natal and London, 1868), p. i.
[4] *Ibid.*, p. ii.

lore had equipped him for the task. He had absorbed Tylor's *Researches into the Early History of Mankind,* although intellectually he belonged to the degenerationist school laid low by Tylor, beholding in the Zulu tales the sunken remnants of a once-proud culture. Darwin's theory he considered but a hypothesis, compatible however with Christianity. Without attempting to account for them, he did point out similar features in his Zulu narratives with story elements in Basile's *Il Pentamerone,* Croker's Irish fairy legends, Campbell's Highland tales, Grey's Polynesian myths, Scott's *Lady of the Lake,* Thorpe's Yuletide stories and his Northern mythology, the Grimms' *Home Stories* (!), Dasent's popular tales from the Norse, Longfellow's *Hiawatha,* Weil's biblical legends of the Mussulmans, and of course Bleek's Hottentot fables. As of 1868 this list shows a surprising sophistication in matters folkloric. Callaway cited these collections in discussing such story incidents as speaking trees, the heaven country, men learning bird languages from serpents, the resuscitation of slain warriors, strange monsters, and spells that immobilized their victims. His extended notes, sometimes inserted as appendixes to the tales, fattened his volume into an appetizing feast for the comparative folklorist, who could now include Africa within the domain of storyology. If Callaway did not accept the premise of Tylor's evolutionism he responded enthusiastically to the method of his comparativism.

In seeking to record native oral literature the Bishop of Kaffraria was consciously emulating the motives of Sir George Grey. Administrator and churchman agreed on the values of folklore for imperial policy.

> What Sir George Grey felt was requisite for the rightful government of the people of New Zealand,—not only a thorough knowledge of their language, but also of their traditional lore,—the earnest and intelligent missionary will feel in a tenfold degree as necessary for himself. . . .[1]

Furthermore, the printing of tales in Kaffir as well as in English would stimulate literacy and education, by encouraging Kaffir youths to learn their own written language. This was indeed an effect produced by the publication of the first part of the Zulu traditions in 1866, making all the easier Callaway's subsequent collecting. European scholars were also impressed. Max Müller, reviewing the first instalment of the Zulu tales, expressed his surprise to see so many

---

[1] Canon Callaway, *Nursery Tales, Traditions, and Histories of the Zulus* (Natal and London, 1868), p. iv.

similarities (such as speaking animals and human rogues) with Greek myths and German *Märchen*.[1]

In 1871 Callaway brought out in Natal, Cape Town, and London a volume of dictated narratives titled *Izinyanga Zokubula; or, Divination, as Existing among the Amazulu, in Their Own Words.* Part I dealt with 'Unkulunkulu; or the Tradition of Creation as existing among the Amazulu and other Tribes of South Africa'; Part II, 'Amatongo; or, Ancestor Worship'; Part III, 'Izinyanga Zokubula; or Diviners'; and Part IV, 'Abatakati; or Medical Magic, and Witchcraft.' The author placed an apposite quotation from Burton on his title page: 'I cannot but admire the incuriousness of so many travellers who have visited Dahome and have described its customs without an attempt to master, or at least to explain, the faith that underlies them.' Recognizing the value and fascination of these firsthand statements of Amazulu supernatural beliefs, The Folk-Lore Society reprinted the work in 1884 as Number XV of their Publications.

In place of the conventional assemblage of traditional tales, Callaway laid before the reader the world view of individual Amazulus. Folklore themes permeated their accounts of the first man and creator, Unkulunkulu, of the ancestral spirits, the Amatongo, of medicine men, exorcists, diviners, dreamers, rain-doctors, and other magicians. Indeed, this forbiddingly titled work (a small running head on the title page and on the cover of The Folk-Lore Society edition used the caption *The Religious System of the Amazulu*) scooped out the very heart of the folklore matter as conceived by Tylor, Lang, and the English school. Here were contemporary savages voicing their most intimate ideas about the seen and the unseen world, ideas pervading their origin myths, ancestral and heroic traditions, folktales, magical songs, wise sayings, enigmas, rites, charms, cures, taboos—in short, the whole oral expression of the society. Little wonder The Folk-Lore Society eagerly reprinted the Bishop's unusual source-study. Callaway treated his oral documents with scholarly precision, placing the Amazulu texts and English translations on facing pages and surrounding the native *dicta* with a running commentary of swollen footnotes, tailnotes, and headnotes.

With commendable objectivity Callaway refuted the identification earlier made of Unkulunkulu as the Christian God. Subsequently in the *Handbook of Folklore* Miss Burne cited as proven Callaway's evidence that the Amazulu considered Unkulunkulu a

[1] Max Müller, 'Zulu Nursery Tales,' in *Chips from a German Workshop*, II (New York, 1872), pp. 206–16. This review essay was first printed in March, 1867.

forefather or remote ancestor, who came forth full-grown from a bed of reeds to provision the world of the Amazulu but who received no worship from them.[1] One Christianized native clearly distinguished between the Amazulu culture hero and the Lord of heaven introduced by the white man.[2]

In keeping with the folklore approach, Callaway frequently suggested comparisons to the myths and tales of other peoples. Unkulunkulu's introduction of death to mankind through the lizard brought to his mind Bleek's Hottentot story of the Moon sending man a reprieve of death through the hare, but the message was corrupted by an insect; and the New Zealand legend in Grey's *Polynesian Mythology* of Maui being squeezed to death by the goddess Hine-nui-te-po when he failed to pass through her vagina and out her mouth, with the consequence that people have since died. One native told of Unjikiza, 'a celebrated brave, of great strength, and huge body; all his muscles were prominent and hard; and his head was high above the ground.' Unjikiza's mighty feats, such as killing a leopard as if it were a fly and suffocating his enemies in a cave with the smoke of firewood, led Callaway to remark, 'This modern Samson has all the characteristics of the champions of old legends.'[3] He observed that as Unjikiza gave his death-dealing club a personal name, 'He-who-watches-the-fords,' so had King Arthur called his sword Excalibur, Roland his Durandel, and Charlemagne his Joyeuse. Elsewhere Callaway drew parallels between Amazulu beliefs and Danish exorcism, the Irish fairy creed, ghost-laying in Iceland and Lancashire, and magical phenomena in the Scottish Highlands.

Sandwiched between Callaway's two publications came a third collection of African narratives in English translation, *Swahili Tales as Told by the Natives of Zanzibar*, issued in 1869 by another language-minded missionary, Edward Steere, LL.D. The title page announced him as 'rector of Little Steeping, Lincolnshire, and chaplain to Bishop Tozer.' Since the Swahili were defined as persons of mixed Negro and Arab origins, their tales not unexpectedly reflected the two lineages, and Steere recognized several of the *Arabian Nights* entertainments in his bag. At the same time he caught suggestions of well-known English tales like Cinderella, Puss-in-Boots, and the House that Jack Built. The rector printed the Swahili texts and English translations on facing pages, 'exactly as they were related,' although recognizing some improvisations,

[1] Charlotte Burne, *The Handbook of Folklore* (London, 1914), p. 93.
[2] Canon Callaway, *Izinyanga Zokubula* (London, 1884), p. 121.
[3] *Ibid.*, pp. 165, 169.

such as the substitution of 'church' for 'mosque,' made by the narrators in deference to their auditor. In his short but useful Preface, Steere distinguished several Swahili oral styles, ranging from Arabic court dialect to the pure Zanzibar language, and identified his speakers and their tales according to these styles.

The eighteen Swahili tales pictured a world not of half-naked savages squatting in a kraal but of sultans and vizirs, sheikhs and kings and slaves, along with talking lions and crows and hyenas. The long adventure-filled romances harked back to the fabled East, but certain features followed the story patterns of mainland Africa, notably the insertion of verses within the prose tales:

> The most curious thing in this collection is perhaps the latter part of the tale of 'Sultan Majnún' . . . where every one present joins in singing the verses, if they may be so called, which besides are not in Swahili. . . . But it is a constant characteristic of popular native tales to have a sort of burden, which all join in singing. Frequently the skeleton of the story seems to be contained in these snatches of singing, which the story-teller connects by an extemporized account of the intervening history. Something similar is very common in the songs of the mainland peoples. Thus as Bishop Tozer and myself were descending the Zambesi in a canoe, the boatmen sang a favourite ditty, the burden of which is a wail over the ills caused by the wars of the Portuguese outlaw Mariano, or Matekenya. The chief boatman took up the solo part, and instead of the old verses made new ones on us, our losses, our generosity, and future intentions, of which unfortunately we understood but very little.[1]

The refrain in Sultan Majnún consisted in the hero, a seventh son, chanting repeatedly:

> 'O mother, I have killed
> The Nunda, eater of people,'

after he slays various animals, from a dog to an elephant, to which is answered:

> 'My son, this is not he,
> The Nunda, eater of people.'

In the end the hunter destroys the monstrous beast and sings his claim without denial from his mother.[2]

[1] Edward Steere, *Swahili Tales, as Told by Natives of Zanzibar*, revised by Alice Werner (London, 1922), p. vii.   [2] *Ibid.*, pp. 255–79.

Besides the stories, Steere also included a few proverbs, enigmas (riddles), and an elegiac, a dance, and a religious song.

Wilhelm Bleek died in 1875, but two co-workers carried on a new project he had commenced with the Bushman language and folklore. Turning aside from Hottentot texts and his formidable comparative study of South African grammars, Bleek resolved to devote his remaining time to mastering the Bushman tongue which was in danger of becoming extinct. In this task he was aided by his wife's sister, Lucy Catherine Lloyd (1834–1914). Bleek had entered the English folklore movement not only intellectually through his association with Grey but conjugally with his marriage to the daughter of a Staffordshire rector appointed archdeacon at the Natal colony. Lucy lived with them at Mowbray, Cape Colony, and plunged into the Bushman project, assisting him to record narratives from Bushmen youths whom they housed in their quarters and from convicts released to them by the government. The year of his death Bleek issued as a preliminary register a *Brief Account of Bushman Folk-Lore and other Texts*, and thenceforth the responsibility for completing the publication of the manuscripts fell to Lucy. The growing interest in folklore led to the formation of a South African Folk-Lore Society in 1879, only one year after the founding of The Folk-Lore Society in London, and Miss Lloyd served as its secretary. A journal was issued for two years, which Hartland saw and cited in *Folk-Lore*.

Meanwhile another recruit to the ranks of South African folklorists had emerged in the person of George McCall Theal, who in 1874 began printing Kaffir folktales in local periodicals and brought them together in book form in 1882 under the title *Kaffir Folk-Lore*. The subtitle read, 'A Selection from the Traditional Tales current among the people living on the eastern border of the Cape Colony, with copious explanatory notes.' Theal had previously written *A History of the Colonies and States of South Africa*. Holding positions as a mission teacher and border magistrate he had come to know well the Amaxosa tribe of true Kaffirs. (In general usage Kaffir signified any black native in South Africa not descended from an imported slave.)

The strength of Theal's presentation lay in his relating Kaffir culture traits to the translated folktales. Thus in his opening chapter he discussed the distinction in the Amaxosa click language between the speech of men and women. A taboo prevented women from mentioning the names of any of their husbands' male relatives in the ascending line, or even from saying any words containing the main syllables of such names. Hence in 'The Story of Tangalimlibo'

21. ALEXANDER CARMICHAEL

22. JOHN GREGORSON CAMPBELL

the heroine, who walks only at night, is betrayed by her father-in-law into drawing water from the river during the daytime and is pulled underneath. Tangalimlibo re-emerges during the night to pacify her crying child and sings this lament:

'It is crying, it is crying,
The child of the walker by moonlight.
It was done intentionally by people whose names are
    unmentionable.
They sent her for water during the day.
She tried to dip with the milk-basket, and then it sank.
Tried to dip with the ladle, and then it sank.
Tried to dip with the mantle, and then it sank.'

According to the taboo, Tangalimlibo could not mention the name of her father-in-law, to whom she was obliged to show the greatest deference, even though he had attempted to kill her. In his extended note to the tale, Theal stated that a woman narrator who sang the song of Tangalimlibo for him even changed the word for water, *amanzi*, into a nonsense word, *angoca*, since the syllable *nzi* formed part of her husband's name. Theal further commented on the accurate portrayal in the tale of the Kaffir idea of drowning. The Kaffirs believed that a spirit in the water seized the victim but might accept oxen as ransom, and he gave instances he had observed. So in the story. At first Tangalimlibo's husband hid in the bushes at night by the river and endeavoured to seize her when she emerged, but the river followed her, turning to blood, until she was relinquished. In the end her father sacrificed a fat ox to the river, her mother prepared medicines, and Tangalimlibo came forth safely.[1] In ethnographic notes such as these explaining Kaffir puberty orgies, children's sports, and kinship relations, Theal made clear the culture content of the tales.

The names of Bleek, Lloyd, and Theal all appeared on the title page of the magnum opus that finally reached print in 1911, *Specimens of Bushmen Folklore*. Miss Lloyd had managed to bring out a supplementary index of Bleek's collections in 1889, a *Short Account of Further Bushman Material Collected*, for transmittal to the Cape government, but the disinterest of London publishers and her own illness thwarted the effort to complete a representative selection of Bleek's texts. Theal at length came to her assistance, writing an informative introduction on 'one of the most interesting savage races of the earth' and the part played by Bleek in salvaging the Bushman tongue. A thorough Tylorian, Theal viewed the

---

[1] George McCall Theal, *Kaffir Folk-Lore* (London, 1882), pp. 56–66, 213–16.

vanishing race of pygmies as childlike savages. The *Specimens*, with its original and translated texts of mythology, fables, legends, poetry, and natural and personal history, its photographs of and drawings by Bushmen, and its inclusion of reports and letters by Bleek, is a volume of signal importance, even though lacking in comparative analysis.

The pioneer collectors, notably Bleek and Callaway, furnished raw materials which were eagerly digested by comparative mythologists and folklorists such as Max Müller, Tylor, Farrer, and Lang. In the 1890's firm bonds developed between the collectors in the bush and the theorists in London, and the ensuing publications became more of a collaborative undertaking.

One of the strongest links between the newly opening world of African cultures and the aims of The Folk-Lore Society was forged by an intrepid Victorian lady, Mary Henrietta Kingsley (1862– 1900), who in a brief life captured the imagination of her country with daring travels in Africa and bold interpretations of Africans. She was born into a gifted family, one uncle being the novelist Charles Kingsley, author of *The Water-Babies* and *Westward Ho!* and her father a combination of doctor, traveller, and amateur anthropologist. On his death she launched her own career with a trip to West Africa in 1893, ostensibly to pursue her father's interest in primitive religion and tropical fish. Other trips followed, resulting in two books that made her famous. Her *Travels in West Africa* (1897) 'took the world by storm. . . . The interest in West Africa was awakened, and she found a new power by means of speech and lecture, which she used in making known the trader and the native, their deeds, their spirit, and their true needs.'[1] In *West African Studies* (1899) she continued her firsthand examination of the west coast peoples and particularly her over-riding interest in fetish, the native system of magic and religion. Mary talked over the question of fetish with Tylor and expressed the pleasure of 'a mere drudge like myself to know there is someone who cares for facts, without theories draping them.'[2] These books, immensely readable, combined exotic travel, astute anthropology, personal adventure and hazard, and a wry, colloquial humour. They earned her enemies as well as friends, for she spoke out sharply against the colonial and missionary policies of State and Church.

[1] Lucy Toulmin Smith, in her obituary of Mary Kingsley, in *Folk-Lore*, XI (1900), 349.
[2] Mary Kingsley, *West African Studies*, 3rd ed. with Introduction by John E. Flint (New York, 1964), p. viii.

The Folk-Lore Society was one of the groups requesting a lecture from Mary Kingsley in the acclamation following her first book. She read a paper before them on March 16, 1897, on 'The Fetish View of the Human Soul,' a forthright and compelling analysis printed in *Folk-Lore* the same year. The discussants that evening included Clodd, Gomme, Nutt, Gaster, and Crooke. In his *Memories* Clodd recalled, 'In the first instance, I met Mary Kingsley in the congenial atmosphere of the Folk Lore Society.' Friendship blossomed between the two Huxleyan agnostics; Clodd called her one of the most remarkable women of the time and praised the *Travels in West Africa* as a work that 'at once took a foremost place in anthropology and the study of the folklore and religion of the lower races.' The doughty freethinker found a kindred spirit in the iconoclastic lady who criticized the missionaries for debasing the native African. Mary thanked Clodd for a copy of his *Myths and Dreams*, which intrigued her, and in the same letter referred to a correspondence with Lang who was looking for 'crystal-gazing cannibals. Unfortunately he seems to take it as a matter of course that I sort of believe in ghosts, as he does in a sort of way, whereas I don't.' Clodd called at her London flat at her invitation, and she sent him an educated African, a Dr. Blyden, 'black as the ace of spades,' so that he might see for himself 'a big black man's mind,' not without a qualm as to how the Savile Club might react.[1]

In addressing the Society, Mary Kingsley began with an imaginative proposal that went straight to the heart of their common interests.

> . . . I most sincerely wish that this society could form a special committee for the consideration of African folklore, for I am certain it would do good work for the British Empire. When I had the pleasure of hearing the Presidential Address the other evening here, Mr. Nutt, if I remember right, stated that all poets should join the Folk-Lore Society. If it had an African committee I should have no hesitation in saying that all members of Parliament and officials at the Foreign and Colonial Offices should be compelled to join the Folk-Lore Society; for I am sure that the work it would do in the careful and unprejudiced study of African beliefs and customs would lead to a true knowledge of the Africans, whom we have now to deal with in hundreds of thousands; and there might be hope that by this true knowledge, hundreds of lives, both black and white,

[1] Edward Clodd, *Memories* (London, 1920), pp. 75–82.

would be saved and a sound base established, from which the African could advance to an improved culture-condition.[1]

Here was the Empire thesis of applied folklore in its loftiest form.

In the main argument of her paper, Mary Kingsley examined closely the fetish concept that was being discussed in England with little understanding. She herself had risked life and limb to penetrate the animistic logic of the West African transmitted through the fetish-priest and witch doctor. Now she could explain the system of hierarchical spirits and plural souls and so illuminate the pervasive terror of witchcraft in West Africa. No native could eliminate witchcraft as a possible cause of death—and Miss Kingsley cited a paper by R. E. Dennett, 'Death and Burial of the Fiote,' read the same evening as her own. Dennet told how the death of a Fiote household head had been referred to the Nganga (witchdoctor) to determine whether old age or witchcraft was the cause. Had a younger man died, the Fiote would automatically have blamed a witch.[2] Witchdoctors actually held African society together, she maintained, since they retained sanity and clarity among a throng maddened and terrified by the power of witches and responsive only to the language of fetish. Europeans who branded the African's legal and social institutions as superstitious savagery and sought to erase them would surely bring about the disintegration of West African society. The system of fetish had managed to eliminate the need for asylums, prisons, and work-houses and to accommodate the sick, criminal, and idle.

Miss Kingsley suggested that the folklore experts study fetish under the categories of law, religion, and witchcraft. 'Owing, I fear, to the Folk-Lore Society not having taken the observation of African customs in hand, there has been a good deal of careless reporting of facts done by my fellow travellers and sea-captains. . . .'[3] Investigators must be wary of possible Christian or Mohammedan influences in fetish. They must also hold in check their comparative tendencies, for customs externally similar might respond to entirely different motives. This point, coupled with all-too-likely inaccuracies in the description of customs, undermined the comparative method, she felt, anticipating the modern critics of Frazerian analogy. She warned against following the fashionable theory of the day in England, whether sired by Spencer, Cox, Müller, or Frazer. Only Tylor would she trust. So spoke out

[1] Mary Kingsley, 'The Fetish View of the Human Soul,' *Folk-Lore*, VIII (1897), 138.
[2] Dennett's paper was printed in *Folk-Lore*, VIII (1897), 132–7.
[3] Kingsley, in *Folk-Lore*, VIII (1897), 149.

the sceptical, hardheaded Mary Kingsley, making good sense of folklore.

The next year, 1898, Miss Kingsley performed further service for the Society by seeing through the press Richard E. Dennett's *Notes on the Folklore of the Fjort* and strengthening it with an astute Introduction. In this work The Folk-Lore Society extended an arm deep into the French Congo to gather in the rough manuscript of Dennett and process it as one of their numbered publications. The task fell chiefly to Hartland, who supplied a brief Preface, and Miss Kingsley, who knew the Fjorts (Fiotes) and had met Dennett, an English trader. In her commentary on the cases of fetish and the Fjort tales compiled by Dennett, Miss Kingsley reaffirmed her confidence in African institutions. Challenging Sir Charles Lyall, who in his *Asiatic Studies* had drawn a distinction between the native witchcraft and the religion of civilization, she upheld witchcraft, so-called, as the genuine religious system of the native tribes. Believing that most white commentators on Africa suffered from bias, bigotry, and limited information, she favoured individual white traders like Dennett, a different breed from missionaries, civil servants, and company agents. The traders came from the lower working classes of Manchester, Liverpool, and other industrial cities to the Gold Coast and the Congo for frankly commercial reasons, and they made the best impression on Africans. Miss Kingsley thoroughly understood the difficulties of climate, travel, language, and cultural communications facing the European in the Congo.

When it came to folklore, Miss Kingsley protested she was a collector solely of West African ideas and knew nothing of comparative storyology. Then she proceeded to make knowledgeable comments on Dennett's collection. His recorded tales, along with proverbs, formed the chief element in African literature, for in them the native spoke to his fellow native about his deepest convictions. Riddles and songs, while of interest, contained fewer mental secrets. She divided the twenty-nine narratives in the book into legal, historical, and recreational groups, according to their function in Fjort society. More than other West African peoples, the Fjort indulged in stories of history. Play-stories offered insights into native customs. But it was the legal stories which counted most heavily in supporting the moral code and reinforcing the administration of justice.

You will find them all pointing out the same set of lessons: that it is the duty of a man to honour his elders; to shield and

[363]

sustain those dependent on him, either by force of hand or by craft; that violence, or oppression, or wrong done can be combated with similar weapons; that nothing can free a man from those liabilities which are natural to him; and, finally, that the ideal of law is justice—a cold, hard justice which does not understand the existence of mercy as a thing apart from justice.[1]

This reliance on traditional tales to help determine points of law led to discussions of the actions of hyenas and bush-cats and monkeys during trial proceedings. With her sharp insight Miss Kingsley recognized the importance of the 'law tale' among Africans.

Turning to the religion of the Fjort presented by Dennett, Mary Kingsley ingeniously discussed, both in her Introduction and in an appendix, the mixture of Christian doctrine with the fetish known as Nkissism. In her view, Roman Catholicism at an early date had penetrated Nkissism, only to be encrusted with native beliefs, leaving the Fjort tribesman 'as dependent "on conversing with the Devil" as ever—in short, a very interesting person to the folklorist.' But Nkissism itself had derived from the Mpongwe tribes. In her appended essay Miss Kingsley wove together letters, additional tales, and observations of Dennett on the earth-spirit Nzambi and the Nkissi spirit of medicines with her own interpretation, even to commenting on comments Dennett had written her about her Introduction.

In contrast, Dennett's own opening chapter on 'The Folklore of the Fjort' set down a series of sketchy remarks on Fjort supernatural beliefs and fear of poisoning, and the absence of Fjort creation legends.

Working closely with Mary Kingsley on the Fjort volume, Hartland turned his thoughts increasingly toward Africa and in his presidential address of 1900 considered Lang's and Marett's ideas on animism in the light of South African tribal folklore. First he mourned the sad death of Miss Kingsley and hoped that friends would fulfil her goals. In the course of his address Hartland referred to Callaway's *The Religious System of the Amazulu*, 'honest but confused' in Lang's words, to the first two volumes of the *South African Folk-Lore Journal*, and to various missionary and travel writings on tribes in British territory. Tentatively he suggested that totemism might change into a tribal cult and thence into ancestor-

---

[1] Mary Kingsley, Introduction to R. E. Dennett, *Notes on the Folklore of the Fjort* (London, 1898), p. xi.

worship with the shift from mother right to father right and a patriarchal system. Hartland's main intent was to bring the African evidence, largely ignored by Lang, into the discussion of folklore and primitive religion.

Andrew Lang finally entered the scene in 1910 with an Introduction to *Folk Stories from Southern Nigeria, West Africa,* collected by the district commissioner for that area, Elphinstone Dayrell. The Scot commented on each of the forty tales in turn with remarks of several paragraphs or a sentence. Happily he pointed to affinities the African narratives displayed with old Irish legends, sagas of classical Greece, the English ballad of Lord Bateman, the romance of Sir Gawain, the *Märchen* of Tom-Tit-Tot, and the fables of Aesop and La Fontaine. These resemblances reassured Lang that 'Human nature is much the same everywhere,' and that all peoples told the same Just-So stories to explain animal traits and wonder tales filled with striking incidents.[1] Inevitably he also perceived in the African tales a layer of barbarous institutions and ideas, much as in the stories of Australian tribes. The totemic idea of animal parents and the concept of the Creator as the big chief struck him as marks of the savage mentality. In 'Why Dead People Are Buried' (No. XXIII), the Creator sent a message to the people garbled by the animal carrier, thus originating death, a popular savage myth found also in one of Callaway's Unkulunkulu traditions.

The unusual and cruel Nigerian institutions depicted in the tales engaged Lang's attention as evidence for the primitive and irrational features surviving in *Märchen.* Dayrell's collection was strongly weighted to law tales, or traditions concerned with judicial ordeals by poison, decisions, and judgments, in all of which the feared and powerful Egbo secret societies played a commanding role. Lang saw a counterpart of the Egbo in the Australian bogey presiding over initiation rites, but he recognized also specifically Egbo ideas. Thus 'The Woman, the Ape, and the Child' (No. 10) illustrates Egbo juridicature very powerfully, and is told to account for Nigerian marriage law,' while 'The Cock who caused a Fight' (No. XXI) 'illustrates private war and justice among the natives, and shows the Egbos refusing to admit the principle of a fine in atonement for an offence.'[2] These and other tales dealt with bitter personal disputes that erupted into pitched battles between armed groups, finally ending in palavers, sentences, executions, and the making of a law. These might be laws prohibiting a man slave from

[1] Andrew Lang, Introduction to Elphinstone Dayrell, *Folk Stories from Southern Nigeria* (London, 1910), p. xi.   [2] *Ibid.,* p. xiii.

marrying a woman slave of another house, enjoining a family from keeping an animal pet, or prescribing the ordeal of the poisonous Esere bean for an accused witch.[1]

Still another contact between the African bush and the English Folk-Lore Society was provided by the Reverend John H. Weeks, who in 1882 commenced a lengthy tenure as Baptist missionary in the Congo. From 1901 to 1912 Weeks contributed to *Folk-Lore* a steady stream of papers on rites of passage, fetish practices, and traditional tales. His 'Notes on Some Customs of the Lower Congo People,' amounting to a small monograph, appeared in successive issues of *Folk-Lore* in 1908 and 1909. These 'Notes,' often vivid in their eyewitness immediacy, reported on Congolese attitudes and behaviour toward pregnancy, birth, babies, poisoning, trials by ordeal, death, funerals, and antelope hunting. In particular, Weeks concentrated on the *nganga*, a term which, he wrote, 'may be variously translated as medicine-man, wizard, witch-finder, doctor in the ordinary sense, exorcist, charm-maker. . . .'[2] The *nganga* worked both sides of the fence, on the one hand causing syphilitic sores and deep ulcers to one client's enemy through his fetish image and on the other preparing protective charms to make another client's enemy forget his evil intentions. Weeks distinguished forty-nine roles of *ngangas*, some widespread, some local, some malignant, some benign, and in their totality governing every aspect of native life and action. He explained the *nganga* cults as devices perpetuated by shrewd fellows who dressed up a genuine medicinal recipe with hocus-pocus to awe the rank and file; hence the Congolese resisted the medicines offered without any fuss at the mission. Therefore, reasoned Weeks, the *ngangas* stifled invention and initiative and reinforced witchcraft and ancient ritual. Yet in a separate article Weeks described in close detail a trial by ordeal successfully conducted among the Bangala tribe of the Upper Congo. To settle a dispute over two slaves and a canoe, the plaintiff and defendant chewed portions of the poisonous *nka* bark, until one fell to the ground insensate, showed signs of intoxication, failed to pick up a plantain stalk, and staggered in pain. The spectators shouted, danced, and rubbed ashes and red powder on the face of the winner. Next day accused and accuser walked around companionably with each other.[3] This incident perfectly supported Mary Kingsley's

[1] Andrew Lang, Introduction to Elphinstone Dayrell, *Folk Stories from Southern Nigeria* (London, 1910), pp. 48, 78, 125.
[2] Weeks, in *Folk-Lore*, XX (1909), 182.
[3] Weeks, 'Notes on Some Customs of the Bangala Tribe, Upper Congo,' *Folk-Lore*, XIX (1908), 92–7.

contention that native African institutions resolved explosive and otherwise insoluble situations.

In 1910 Weeks appeared before The Folk-Lore Society to read a paper, subsequently printed in *Folk-Lore*, on 'The Congo Medicine-Man and his Black and White Magic.' Hartland, Tylor, and the African trader-folklorist Dennett were among those present who participated in the discussion, and Weeks exhibited fetish figures and a medicine-man's charm for curing lung diseases.

For a popular audience, Weeks published in 1911 through the Religious Tract Society in London a book on *Congo Life and Folk-lore*, a curious compound of juvenile fiction and bona fide ethnography. In Part I the author presents 'Life on the Congo as described by a brass rod,' the currency used by the Congolese. In Part II he offers 'Thirty-three Native Stories as told round the evening fires' (eight others had been woven into the preceding section). These 'folklore tales' came from the Portuguese and Belgian Lower Congo around San Salvador and Ngombe Lutete; some he had heard himself, others had been written out for him by teachers and boys at the Walthen Mission School. Speculating on the tales, he presses the analogy with the Uncle Remus stories of Joel Chandler Harris, identifying Brer Rabbit as the gazelle, Brer Fox as the leopard, and the Tar-baby as the fetish called *Nkondi*. Congo natives transported to the United States had presumably carried with them these characters. Weeks was on firmer ground when he dealt with the setting and rendition of the narratives from his own direct observation. He called attention to the symbiosis between the everyday maxims and the fireside tales recited by Congo men and to their delight in arguing out the most plausible solutions to their unresolved puzzle or dilemma tales. 'Each fool and each wonder-worker has his adherents, who will argue in his favour. . . .'[1] He caught too the atmosphere of the narrative performance.

> There is no greater treat than to listen to a Congo story told in the original by one of these born story-tellers—the lights and shadows caused by the flickering fire, the swaying body of the narrator, the fixed attention and grunts of approval of the listeners, the great dark beyond, the many mystic sounds issuing from the surrounding brush and forest lend a peculiar weirdness to the story and its teller.[2]

The neglected area of East Africa received attention from Alfred C. Hollis, chief secretary of the East Africa Protectorate, who

---

[1] John H. Weeks, *Congo Life and Folklore* (London, 1911), p. 369.
[2] *Ibid.*, p. 370.

produced two parallel volumes on *The Masai, Their Language and Folklore* (1905) and *The Nandi, Their Language and Folklore* (1909). The Masai and Nandi were isolated, warlike tribes given chiefly to cattle-herding. Hollis acknowledged the assistance of the Church Missionary Society in East Africa for lending him the services of a Christian convert, Justin Ol-omeni, in obtaining the Masai traditions and to Frazer's *Questions on the Customs, Beliefs, and Languages of Savages* (Cambridge, 1907) to effect entry into the Nandi culture. Subsequently he sent a copy of Frazer's questionnaire to all the stations in the East Africa Protectorate. Primarily a language man, Hollis printed interlinear as well as freely rendered texts of Masai and Nandi tales about the hare, myths of the heavens, proverbs, enigmas, and customs. While not attempting comparative notes, Hollis did recognize a Nandi 'House That Jack Built.' A similar work on a related tribe, M. W. H. Bleek's *The Suk, Their Language and Folklore*, was published in 1911.

Within a five year period, 1908–1913, four folklore and language collections were published on the Hausa, numerically one of the largest peoples of West Africa. A missionary, Hermann G. Harris, issued *Hausa Stories and Riddles* in Hausa in 1908 for students of the language, translating only one tale into English. The reviewer in *Folk-Lore*, G. Merrick, translated two more and summarized another, a tale concerning travelling companions. A *mālam* (learned man), an archer, a wrestler, and a courtesan were travelling together until they reached a swollen river; each then relied on the instruments of his trade to cross; the *mālam* placed his trust not in prayer but in the paper on which he wrote it, showing how thin is the veneer of Mohammedanism.[1]

In 1912 Roland S. Fletcher compiled *Hausa Sayings and Folk-Lore, with a Vocabulary of New Words.* His miscellany covered proverbs, riddles, quips, catches, alliterations, songs, street calls, beliefs, gestures, and games.

A Hausa specialist who developed connections with The Folk-Lore Society was Major Arthur John Newman Tremearne (1877–1915). Born in Australia, educated at the universities of Melbourne, Cambridge, and London, with a diploma in anthropology from Cambridge, he served in the South African War of 1899, held civil appointments in West Africa, and became a university lecturer in Hausa at Christ's College, Cambridge. After writing travel books on his African experiences revealing his taste for 'savage and barbaric lore' (Clodd's phrase in a review of *Hausa Superstitions and Customs* in *The Graphic*), he produced a series of substantial works on Hausa

[1] G. Merrick, in *Folk-Lore*, XX (1909), 374–6.

folklore between 1910 and 1914, cut short by his death in action at Loos in 1915. Tremearne printed 'Fifty Hausa Folk-Tales' seriatim in *Folk-Lore* in 1910 and 1911, adapting some of them, with his wife as co-author, in a children's book, *Fables and Fairy Tales for Little Folk, or Uncle Remus in Hausaland* (1910). A major publication, *Hausa Superstitions and Customs, An Introduction to the Folk-Lore and the Folk*, appeared in 1913, followed the next year by a companion volume of Hausa texts, *Hausa Folk-Tales*. Also in 1914 he brought out *The Ban of the Bori: Demons and Demon-Dancing in West and North Africa*, a compendious treatise on classes of spirits and everyday magic. In a future work he hoped to show resemblances between the Hausa Mai-Bori and the English witch.

The *Hausa Superstitions and Customs* shows plainly the influence on its author of British folklore theory. Hartland and Crooke took a special interest in his collections, supplying parallels to the Hausa tales which he acknowledged in his notes with (H) and (C); Hartland chaired a committee of the British Association to arrange for the publication of *Hausa Folk-Tales*. Tremearne made obeisance to 'the classics of Sir E. B. Tylor, Professor Frazer, the late Mr. Andrew Lang, Mr. Hartland,' and cited them regularly in his pages.[1] As a good Lang comparativist, the major could see common survival elements in the narratives of his Hausa and of German peasants. 'This idea of the fiancée serving in the kitchen is well known in Grimms' stories, and since, both in those and in the Hausa parallel, the girl had plenty of opportunities for addressing the prince directly, it would seem that there must have been some tabu against her doing so.'[2] Other survivals involved king-killing, matrilineal descent, and name taboos. Tremearne also indulged in some solar speculation, following Tylor and the German Africanist Leo Frobenius, and mused that the spider's web symbolized the sun's rays. At the same time he accepted the diffusionist claims of Crooke, who considered the Hausa form of address to the unclean dog one borrowing from Islam, and suggested others.

> . . . Mr. Crooke tells me that the Hausa 'Half-Being' probably comes from the Arabic 'Split-Man' (shikk)—who resembles the Persian 'Half-Face' (*Nimchahrah*)—a kind of demon, like a man divided longitudinally, which runs with amazing speed and is very cruel and dangerous. . . .[3]

Thereupon Tremearne mentioned similar split or divided beings,

---

[1] Arthur J. N. Tremearne, *Hausa Superstitions and Customs* (London, 1913), p. 20.
[2] *Ibid.*, p. 143.   [3] *Ibid.*, pp. 123–4.

described by Tylor and Hartland and in Burton's *Arabian Nights*, who apparently had wandered from one society to another.

Equally sympathetic to the doctrine of survivals, Tremearne sniffed out savage beliefs lingering among the English gentry. Recently a society lady of his acquaintance had written down her desire to injure an enemy and had hidden the paper in a drawer, waiting, Hausa-like, for the charm to take effect. Conversely, Tremearne accepted Lang's notion that the seemingly modern phenomena of hypnotism and spiritualism might account for strange incidents in savage folktales. Perhaps the contest between Moses and the sorcerers in Pharaoh's court was explicable as an exercise in hypnotic suggestion.

On one occasion Tremearne directly encountered the Hausa terror of witchcraft. In Amar in Muri Province in 1906, the native police sergeant brought before him three constables who accused their wives of being witches. The wives admitted the charge, and the husbands now threatened to desert them. Tremearne improvised a solution by attaching a galvanic battery to each wife, saying the evil influence would pass directly from their bodies into the battery. The constables rejoined their wives, and all parties were relieved and satisfied. Mary Kingsley would have approved such a solution, for the European accepted rather than ridiculed the African system and assumed the native role of judicial magistrate.

Hausa Superstitions and Customs unfolds a full spread of African traditions. Tremearne discusses signs, riddles, proverbs, puns, and poetry, as well as presenting examples of Hausa fetish belief and oral narratives. Here was an African ethnography focused on folklore, according to the viewpoint of the Empire-minded English folklorists.

Coincidentally, the year 1913 saw another major anthropological study of the same people, R. Sutherland Rattray's two volumes on *Hausa Folk-Lore, Customs, Proverbs, Etc.* Rattray's Oxford tutor Marett, designated on the title page as 'President of the Folk-Lore Society,' furnished a Foreword. Marett graciously indicated that Rattray had come to him as a mature and experienced ethnologist, who in 1907 had already published *Some Folk-Lore Stories and Songs in Chinyanja* through the Christian Knowledge Society in London. 'It is our privilege at Oxford to be visited from time to time by officers of the Public Service, who modestly apply to us for instruction in Anthropology,' wrote Marett, 'more particularly as it bears on the history of the native races of the Empire.'[1] The assist-

[1] R. Sutherland Rattray, *Hausa Folk-Lore, Customs, Proverbs, Etc.*, I (Oxford, 1913), v.

ant district commissioner in Ashanti, West Africa, and the reader in social anthropology at Oxford formed a natural alliance, one the civil servant in the field, the other the theoretical scholar in the library, but each a disciplined anthropologist strongly oriented toward folklore.

In his brief Preface, Marett emphasized the novel turn to the established method of folklore collecting being employed by Rattray. In place of the ill at ease storyteller and the frequently puzzled translator-scribe working in awkward combination, Rattray had relied on a single individual who both knew and could write out his traditions. Among the Hausas such men of learning and folklore existed in the class of *mālams*, trained to write the Arabic script. The government of the Gold Coast placed Mālam Shaihu at the disposal of Rattray, and between 1907 and 1911 the *mālam* amassed hundreds of sheets of manuscript. In its published form, Rattray's work presented the mālam's original script translated from Arabic into Hausa on the right-hand page, a romanized transliteration on the upper half of the left-hand page, and an English translation on the lower half.

As Marett indicated, the Hausa were no backward primitives but a spirited people embracing Mohammedanism and trading with most West African societies, and their narratives reflected their contacts. Rattray made no attempt to explore the tales comparatively, concentrating on their linguistic accuracy. He divided Mālam Shaihu's materials into a traditional history of the Hausa nation, twenty-one 'Stories in which People are the Heroes and Heroines,' nine 'Animal Stories,' a group of proverbs, and a section of 'Customs and Arts' covering such cultural institutions as the marriage ceremony, child-naming, removal of the clitoris, and the sculpting of Benin figures. The carefully patterned folktales began 'A story, a story. Let it go, let it come,' and ended 'That is all. Off with the rat's head.' Mālam Shaihu's repertoire revealed a blend of Islamic and bush elements; so in the tale of 'The doctor who went on a pilgrimage to Mecca on a hyena,' the jackal tricks the hyena into serving as the learned doctor's mount (a Brer Rabbit plot). The world of caravans, traders, and maidens fair overlaps with the world of the clever spider, the foolish lion, and the plucky he-goat.

By 1914, British folklore workers had delved deep into West, South, Central and East Africa and made visible a mountain of texts, with promise of many more discoveries to come. Folklore seemed a happy partner with anthropological and language studies, and the incorporation of African savages into evolutionist theory appeared to be only a matter of time.

[371]

AUSTRALIA, OCEANIA, THE FAR EAST
(EXCEPT INDIA)

In the smaller units of the Empire, notable individual efforts contributed to the world-wide scope of the English folklore movement.

Less than a decade after Thoms coined the term 'folklore,' Sir George Grey delivered an eloquent and persuasive plea for Crown officials overseas to absorb the mythology and traditions—it was still too early to use 'folklore'—of the subject races. Suddenly appointed governor-in-chief of New Zealand in 1845, he set about the task of ruling an alien and turbulent people with whom he could not communicate. Interpreters helped little, for they could not always be on hand, and in time Grey discovered that no one could explain to him the sentiments of some of the most powerful Maori chiefs.

To my surprise, however, I found that these chiefs, either in their speeches to me or in their letters, frequently quoted, in explanation of their views and intentions, fragments of ancient poems or proverbs, or made allusions which rested on an ancient system of mythology; and, although it was clear that the most important parts of their communications were embodied in these figurative forms, the interpreters were quite at fault, they could then rarely (if ever) translate the poems or explain the allusions, and there was no publication in existence which threw any light upon these subjects, or which gave the meaning of the great mass of the words which the natives upon such occasions made use of. . . .

Clearly, however, I could not, as Governor of the country, permit so close a veil to remain drawn between myself and the aged and influential chiefs whom it was my duty to attach to British interests and to the British race, whose regard and confidence, as also that of their tribes, it was my desire to secure, and with whom it was necessary that I should hold the most unrestricted intercourse. Only one thing could under such circumstances be done, and that was to acquaint myself with the ancient language of the country, to collect its traditional poems and legends, to induce their priests to impart to me their mythology, and to study their proverbs. For more than eight years I devoted a great part of my available time to these pursuits.[1]

[1] Sir George Grey, *Polynesian Mythology and Ancient Traditional History of the New*

So the governor travelled around the islands, questioning the natives at every opportunity and building up an archive of materials in Government House. Fire destroyed them once, and he had to begin again. A sense of duty led him not only to record but also to translate and publish Maori legends for the benefit of Europeans who might subsequently have to deal with the New Zealand natives. Many of his priest-informants had already died. Accordingly in 1855 Grey published *Polynesian Mythology and Ancient Traditional History of the New Zealanders, as Furnished by Their Priests and Chiefs*. In the two previous years he had made available original Maori texts of songs, chants, and traditions, and in 1857 he also printed in Maori a volume of ancestral proverbs and popular sayings.

The *Polynesian Mythology* became at once a standard source work for mythologists and folklorists. Tylor opened a correspondence with the governor and resorted to his myths in the *Researches* and *Primitive Culture*. Now the English reader could listen to the priest of a remote, exotic, uncivilized race intone legends filled with strange, mellifluous names and barbarous episodes. The narratives embraced origin myths of the children of heaven and earth, feats of Maui the sun-snarer and famed Polynesian culture hero, recitals of historical expeditions from Hawaii to New Zealand, grisly accounts of individual and group combats and slayings, incidents of magic and sorcery, all told with jagged discontinuity. Grey apologized for the crude and bestial nature of the mythology, although declaring that the Aryan, Semitic, and Dravidian races had doubtless passed through a similar phase.

A later generation of anthropologists has faulted Grey for his over-free translations and inadequate source identifications, but he measured well by the standards of his time.

Max Müller rescued a second major Polynesian collection from possible oblivion by lending his name and support to the Reverend William Wyatt Gill's *Myths and Songs from the South Pacific*, for which he wrote a Preface in 1876. A member of the London Missionary Society, Gill spent twenty-two years on Mangaia of the Hervey Island group discovered by Captain Cook. Looking through his manuscripts, Müller revelled at the creations of a sequestered island people living under the conditions of a mythopoeic age.

Zealanders, as Furnished by Their Priests and Chiefs (London, n.d.), pp. x–xi. Edward Shortland the year before, 1854, had published *Traditions and Superstitions of the New Zealanders* in London with some Maori as well as English texts of chants, charms, spells, and proverbs. Shortland was a physician stationed for several years at Maketu on the Bay of Plenty.

To find ourselves among a people who really believe in gods and heroes and ancestral spirits, who still offer human sacrifices, who in some cases devour their human victims, or, at all events, burn the flesh of animals on their altars, trusting that the scent will be sweet to the nostrils of their gods, is as if the zoologist could spend a few days among the megatheria, or the botanist among the waving ferns of the forests, buried beneath our feet.[1]

In his delight at examining the products of a race who 'still think and speak mythologically,' Müller leaned over backward to present the issues fairly. Something was to be said for the proponents both of human descent and ascent, although he acknowledged his own bias toward some religious sentiment behind the early 'fetishism'— a term he loathed. Again, while stressing the need for students to explore each mythology in its own language, and dallying with the possible Sanskrit-Polynesian equation *Avaiki* (the Mangaian Hades) = Avîki (the Brahman-Buddhist Hades), the professor of comparative philology magnanimously discarded the idea, in view of the Tahitian *Hawai'i* and the New Zealand *Hawaiki*. Leaving aside the disease of language, the Honourable Max saw ready resemblances between the Mangaian sun and moon and storm gods and those of classical Greece and India, pagan Germany, and Incan Peru.

While containing some of the same figures as Grey's volume, notably Maui, Gill's *Myths and Songs* differed considerably from the *Polynesian Mythology*. The missionary paraphrased his texts for greater readability and interlarded them with commentaries explaining the cosmogonical myths, god and hero chronicles, aetiological legends, and ritual practices of the Hervey Islanders, as well as songs, often of recent composition, lamenting and celebrating events narrated by the priests. A gripping chapter on 'Human Sacrifices' recounted the treacheries and cruelties practised by islanders to obtain victims for Rongo, the god of war, to enable them to beat the ceremonial drum of peace. Throughout the volume the voice of the missionary is heard, equating the Polynesian Io with Jehovah and mentioning former practitioners of human sacrifices now happily converted to Christianity.

The samplers of Grey and Gill gave English folklorists a satisfying selection of Polynesian oral prose and poetry, which would in time be supplemented by the collections of Maori, German, French, and American ethnologists.

---

[1] Max Müller, Preface to Rev. William Wyatt Gill, *Myths and Songs from the South Pacific* (London, 1876), pp. vi–vii.

Australia proved the one conspicuous failure for Empire folklore. No early roundup of native traditions appeared to captivate Victorian readers as had the tale harvests of Frere and Stokes in India and Blcek and Callaway in Africa. Rather, it was the anthropologists who first struck pay dirt, beginning with *Kamilaroi and Kurnai* (1880) by Alfred William Howitt and Lorimer Fison, called by Frazer in *Folk-Lore* 'a document of primary importance in the archives of anthropology.'[1] Influenced by this treatise, Baldwin Spencer and F. J. Gillen completed *The Native Tribes of Central Australia* (1899), and even folklorists like Lang and Hartland were drawn into the detailed discussions of the social organization and religious ideas of the Australian aborigines.

Andrew Lang did attempt to stir up interest in Australian folklore by promoting the collections of Mrs. K. Langloh Parker (Catherine Somerville Stow), living on a mission station in New South Wales. He wrote introductions for her *Australian Legendary Tales* (1896) and *More Australian Legendary Tales* (1898), which Nutt published in London. Lang praised the first book as a 'savage edition of the Metamorphoses,' now for the first time authentically presented by Mrs. Parker. Her collected tales exuded primitive elements reflecting the aboriginal culture. These were unpretentious Just-So stories attractive to the savage mind, portraying actors absorbed in the relentless quest for food and water.

In her own Preface to the book of thirty-one tales subtitled 'Folk-Lore of the Noongahburrahs as told to the Picaninnies,' Mrs. Parker twice quotes Max Müller to the effect that the folklore of any country was worth collecting. She hopes that her little parcel of legends from a dying race may assist toward 'a scientific and patient study of the folk-lore throughout Australia.' Diffusionists should have stirred to Mrs. Parker's remark on loan words.

> Many words, too, have been introduced which the blacks think are English, and the English think are native. Such, for example, as piccaninny, and, as far as these outside blacks are concerned, boomerang is regarded as English, their local word being burren; yet nine out of ten people whom you meet think both are local native words.[2]

The stories deal with such affairs as why Dinewan the emu has no wings and Goomblegubbon the bustard lays only two eggs in a season, and how the Weeoombeen brothers became white-throated

---

[1] James G. Frazer, 'Howitt and Fison,' *Folk-Lore*, XX (1909), 151.

[2] Mrs. K. Langloh Parker, *Australian Legendary Tales* (London and Melbourne, 1896), p. x.

birds and their enemy Piggiebillah a porcupine anteater. A reader may question whether the narratives reflect the taste of childlike savages or a child-minded author. At the suggestion of Tylor, the editor and publisher included one specimen of a native text.

Mrs. Parker extended her second volume of twenty-three tales to other tribes besides the Noongahburrahs and this time printed some tales on sacred subjects not intended for the 'black picaninnies.' In his generally sympathetic review in *Folk-Lore*, Hartland rebuked her for failing to identify the tribal sources of individual tales. In the second Preface, Mrs. Parker exhibited a greater confidence in her own folkloric powers, thanks to kind tributes paid her first volume. As a result she had spread a wider net, interrogating 'the Blacks' upon any likely scrap of legend sent her by friends and encouraging her Blacks to inquire from other tribes at their 'walkabouts' or corroborees. She herself had known individuals of eight tribes besides her favourite Euahlayi-speaking Noongahburrahs. Emulating 'Uncle Remus' creator,' she kept the Blacks about her as much as possible to secure casual morsels of folklore, such as the idea that grey moths fluttering around the lamp are sent by the spirits to steal tomahawks, and the belief that fungi growing on trees were bread for ghosts. Walking through the bush, she often heard legends of birds and trees. An old woman in the camp who called up spirits prophesied a rain three days after the death of the oldest woman of the tribe, and three days later a rain did end the drought.

Lang, of course, appreciated this savage spiritualist. 'Anthropology has no reason for neglecting these affairs any more than the countless other things in which savage practice tallies with the mysticisms of civilisation.'[1] In another vein, he contended for the presence of theistic thought among the natives, for instance in 'A Legend of the Flowers,' telling how Byamee went to dwell in the faraway land of rest, leaving the earth desolate until the wirreenuns (wizards or priests) had journeyed to him. The serious mood of religion should be distinguished from the absurdities of mythology resulting from the savage mentality and surviving in civilization. 'Odd stories enough about Our Lord, the Virgin, and the Saints occur in our European folk-lore. . . .'[2] Reviewer Hartland twitted Lang for first repudiating and then invoking 'folklore as an interpreter of savage belief.'[3]

Lang complained that folklorists and anthropologists ignored the legend books of Mrs. Parker while concentrating on tribal organiza-

[1] Andrew Lang, Introduction to *More Australian Legendary Tales* (London and Melbourne, 1898), p. xviii. [2] *Ibid.*, p. xxii. [3] Hartland, in *Folk-Lore*, X (1899), 233.

tion. Yet, as if bowing to the will of the majority, he wrote an Introduction to her next work, on *The Euahlayi Tribe*.

Around the Far East, within and alongside the Empire, the names of Englishmen became attached to standard works of folklore. From Japan, the second secretary of the British Legation, Algernon B. Mitford (Lord Redesdale) brought out in 1871 *Tales of Old Japan*, a pastiche of literary and folkish stories. For China, Nicholas B. Dennys, compiler of a handbook of vernacular Cantonese, published in 1876 *The Folk-Lore of China, and Its Affinities with That of the Aryan and Semitic Races*, the title revealing the premise. Dennys followed the comparative mythology of Jacob Grimm and Max Müller and pressed analogies between East and West at every turn, using chiefly Brand's *Popular Antiquities* and Henderson's *Folk Lore of the Northern Counties* for English examples. Out of Burma came James Gray's *Ancient Proverbs and Maxims from Burmese Sources* (1866). While employed in the civil service of the Federated Malay States, Walter William Skeat wrote *Malay Magic, being an Introduction to the Folklore and Popular Religion of the Malay Peninsula* (1900). Skeat in effect did for the Malay Peninsula what Crooke had done for India, but without stressing East-West comparisons. Comparative folklorists eagerly seized upon his thick treatise on Malay folklore as overlaid with Hindu, Buddhist, and Mohammedan concepts for their own analogies. After living among the Ainu of northern Japan for a quarter of a century, the Reverend John Batchelor issued *The Ainu and Their Folk-Lore* (1901), scattering pertinent legends and beliefs throughout his chapters on Ainu fetishism, magic, exorcism, recreation, and bird, animal, and fish cults. In Ceylon, where he served in the Irrigation Department, Henry Parker amassed the 262 stories he printed in three hefty volumes, *Folk-Tales of Ceylon*, between 1910 and 1914. Parker arranged the tales neatly by castes and regions and added valuable endnotes comparing variants from India and Tibet. He deliberately sought out remote villages untouched by western civilization in order to procure the genuine Singhalese traditions.

Two early volumes of Asian folklore translated from German sources and edited by English folklorists deserve special mention. Rachel H. Busk brought out *Sagas from the Far East; or, Kalmouk and Mongolian Traditionary Tales* (1873), presenting for the first time in English stories told by the dreaded Calmucks of eastern Tibet and the Mongolians whom they regularly pillaged. Miss Busk had read Benfey and knew his theory of the dispersion of Aryan *Märchen* from India into northern Europe carried by the Mongolians to the Slavs and Germans. The flavour of the *Sagas* suggests the literary adornment, marvellous adventures, and interconnected structure of the *Thousand and One Nights*. Each main division, 'The Saga of the Well- and Wise-Walking Khan' and 'The Saga of Ardschi-Bordschi and Vikramâditja's Throne,' serves as a thread for a series of tales-within-the-tale. Conscious of their unchristian and un-European morality, Miss Busk apologizes for the upbringing of the hero Vikramâditja, who was taught to lie and steal. Her serious intent is evident in the appendix of learned notes abstracted from German Indianist and Buddhist scholars.

William R. S. Ralston translated *Tibetan Tales, derived from Indian Sources* from the German of F. Anton von Schiefner in 1882, providing a long analytical Introduction of nearly sixty pages. In earlier books Ralston had traced Russian folklore west to the Slavic countries, but now he looked east to Central Asia. The Russian specialist Von Schiefner had translated into German the legends and romances strewn through the first seven divisions of the Tibetan sacred work known as the *Kah-gyur*, using the two editions of over a hundred volumes each which had found their way to St. Petersburg. In his lengthy Introduction, Ralston first deals with European scholars who had penetrated the Tibetan monasteries, such as the Hungarian Csoma Körösi, who in searching for the origins of his people lived for nine years in a cell in Calcutta with his books and manuscripts. Ralston then turns to a comparison of Eastern and Western folktales.

At first glance the longer legendary romances of the *Kah-gyur* seems to have little in common with European *Märchen*, but Ralston's probing eye lights on resemblances. Unlike the India-centred diffusionists of the Benfey school, Ralston cared less for the movement of whole narratives and more for the passage of ideas. Some concepts in Indian tales make little sense to European raconteurs. 'An Oriental storyteller can describe a self-sacrificing monarch as cutting slices of flesh off his own arms and plunging them into the fire in honour of a deity, and yet not be afraid of exciting anything but a religious thrill among his audience. To European minds such a deed would probably appear grotesque.'[1] In the same class of ideas fall the praise for lower animals and the demerits of men in Indian Buddhistic fictions, an element emerging in European folktales under the notion of grateful animals.

Both Miss Busk and Ralston would make their most notable contributions in European folklore.

[1] Ralston, Introduction to *Tibetan Tales*, trans. F. Anton von Schiefner (London, 1906), p. lvii.

EUROPE

The European mainland as well as colonial possessions in India, Africa, and Oceania attracted English folklorists, although with a difference. Europe signified peasant, not savage, lore and possessed her own knowledgeable folklore scholars, beginning with the brothers Grimm and extending by the end of the nineteenth century to every nation on the continent. The task of the Victorians was to seek out the published stores of authentic tradition and prepare from them useful and reliable English editions. Between 1850 and 1914 English travellers, scholars, and diplomatic officials had fairly well represented the folklore of European countries and contributed works that acquired their own special aura in the British folklore movement. Collections fared much better than theoretical studies, of which only Jacob Grimm's *Teutonic Mythology* appeared in an English translation.

Some countries did exceptionally well at the hands of British folklorists and others unaccountably lagged. Germany and France failed to attract, or perhaps did not really need, English collaborators. Still, an acceptable edition of the Grimm's *Household Tales* had to wait for the authoritative translation of Margaret Hunt in 1884 with the celebrated Introduction of Andrew Lang, and the *Deutsche Sagen* never were rendered into English. The Scandinavian nations and Greece led the rest. In 1851 Benjamin Thorpe published in three volumes *Northern Mythology, comprising the Principal Popular Traditions and Superstitions of Scandinavia, North Germany, and the Netherlands*. While the first volume contained literary legends from the Eddas and Sagas, the second and third opened up a new vein in translating from the abundant local folk legends actively maintained among the peasants. These traditions, firmly anchored in time and place, concerned trolls, *nisse*, changelings, spectres, churches, priests, hidden treasure, the Devil, werewolves, witches, jack o'lanterns, dwarfs, fiddlers, and knights, and furnished a rich spread for the English evolutionists. Thorpe used various legend collections that sprang up in the wake of the Grimms *Deutsche Sagen*, such as Andreas Faye's *Norsk Folk-Sagn* from Norway (1844). Thorpe knew the work of his fellow antiquaries at home and refers in one note, on the legend of the midwife who could see the fairies after rubbing magic ointment on her eye, to Mrs. Bray, Keightley's *Fairy Mythology*, Brand, Joseph Ritson's *Fairy Tales*, and Gervase of Tilbury. On the efficacy of a silver bullet for killing witches, he cites Thoms' *Anecdotes and Traditions*. In 1853

Thorpe brought out a companion volume for the same area, *Yuletide Stories*.

In *Popular Tales from the Norse*, published in 1859, George Webbe Dasent brought into English homes the Norwegian wonder tales originally collected by Peter Asbjörnsen and Jörgen Moe, who emulated the Grimms in assembling a remarkable national repertoire of *Märchen*. Dasent's long essay on the origin and diffusion of popular tales trumpets the racial thesis of the Grimms and gives credit for the master tales to the superior Aryans.

Thorpe's work, particularly his second volume, was brought up to date in 1896 by William A. Craigie, who planned *Scandinavian Folk-Lore, Illustrations of the Traditional Beliefs of the Northern Peoples* to take into account fresh Icelandic and Danish materials. In place of Thorpe's divisions by nations he groups the *Sagen* according to the leading actors: the old gods, trolls and giants, bergfolk and dwarfs, elves or *huldu*-folk, *nisses* or brownies, waterbeings, monsters, ghosts and wraiths, wizards and witches. Craigie well understood the relation between belief and narrative: 'The story is the soul of folk-lore, by which the general concept is made living and interesting.'[1] He himself undertook translations from the Icelandic, Faröese, Danish (Norwegian), and Swedish, feeling that his countrymen had been remiss, even though 'the science of folk-lore owes more to Great Britain than to any other country.'[2] A modern folklorist would object to Craigie's mingling of literary stories with orally collected legends, but *Scandinavian Folk-Lore* still remains one of the few useful collections in English of European *Sagen*.

The achievement of Elias Lönnrot in rescuing the runes and charms from which he wove the Finnish national epic, the *Kalevala*, became best known to English readers through Domenico Comparetti's *The Traditional Poetry of the Finns*, published in London in 1898. In his Introduction, Andrew Lang compares the composition of the Homeric and the Finnish folk epics.

No doubt the lure of classical mythology brought English visitors and trophy hunters to Greece after Byron rediscovered Hellas. The folklorist could choose among a shelf of offerings. Edmund M. Geldart's *Folk-Lore of Modern Greece* (1884) rendered into English the wonder tales first collected and published in German by Johann Georg von Hahn. Sir James Rennell Rodd enriched *The Customs and Lore of Modern Greece* (1892) with his own field observations and interviews with Greek peasants. In similar vein but striving to

---

[1] William A. Craigie, *Scandinavian Folk-Lore* (Paisley and London, 1896), p. vii.
[2] *Ibid.*, p. v.

justify his title was John C. Lawson's *Modern Greek Folklore and Ancient Greek Religion* (1910), subtitled 'A Study in Survivals,' an attempt to establish the continuity of Greek tradition over three thousand years in the manner Nutt had essayed for the Celtic. Nor were folksongs neglected. Lucy Garnett, the partner of Stuart-Glennie, contributed *Greek Folk-Songs from the Ottoman Provinces of Northern Hellas* (1888) and *Greek Folk Poesy* (1896). George F. Abbot of Emmanuel College, Cambridge, added *Songs of Modern Greece* (1900) and in *Macedonian Folklore* (1903) compared customs in the manner of Tylor, Frazer, and Lang. Mary Hamilton directed attention to *Greek Saints and Their Festivals* (1884). Folklore promised a magic carpet from the modern Greek village back to the land of Mount Olympus.

The attachment of English folklorists to countries of Europe may best be appreciated in the work of Rachel Busk and W. R. S. Ralston.

Born in London of well-to-do parents, Rachel Harriette Busk (1831–1907) enjoyed private schools and continental travels, giving her complete fluency in German, Italian, French, and Spanish. Italian became her second tongue. In 1858 she and her four older sisters and younger brother were converts to Roman Catholicism, and from 1862 on she resided chiefly in Rome, numbering Pope Leo XIII (then a cardinal) among her circle of friends. On her frequent excursions by train and coach into the interior villages of Spain, she began accumulating printed and conversational examples of legends and folksongs attached to the land, attracted, as she admitted, by a love for romantic scenery and primitive character. In 1870 she published anonymously *Patrañas: Spanish Tales, Legendary and Traditional* and in 1871 *Household Tales from the Land of Hofer*, both winning pleasant press notices. The *Brighton Guardian* observed, 'Under the homely household word "Patrañas" we have a collection of tales which form a standard addition to our stock of folk-lore,' while the *British Quarterly* called the Tirolese volume the most important tale collection since Dasent's Norse stories.

The role of Miss Busk as romantic lady tourist is evident in her *The Valleys of Tirol, Their Traditions and Customs and How to Visit Them*, appearing under her name in 1874. Her plan was to provide future travellers with a guide to the picturesque routes, landmarks, and villages in the Tyrol enhanced with historic and legendary associations. Since the Germans, unlike the Italians with whom they shared the Tyrol, had extensively collected *Sagen*, legends, myths, *Märchen*, and *Gebräuche*, Miss Busk drew upon twenty-five German folklore collections and local histories for the traditions she strewed throughout her narrative. Once in a while she quoted a flowery oral legend directly from a native. A beggar woman in the chapel at Schwatz told her of the Sunday hunter who missed Mass while ensnaring a beautiful redcapped bird, but never repeated his folly after the bird grew to the limits of the cage and exuded sulphurous fumes. In this Christianized pagan Miss Busk beheld 'a mine for the comparative mythologist.'[1]

Yet Rachel Busk was more than a well-meaning amateur. Her opening pages deal with the value of recording 'traditions, myths, legends' and she regularly quotes mythologists and folklorists like Max Müller, Cox, de Gubernatis, Dasent, and particularly Jacob Grimm. Grimm's thought is plain in her view that England too was filled with 'current folk-lore; and quaint customs and superstitious beliefs affecting the daily life, which are remnants of the ancient creed.'[2] Legends deserve close attention for their mythological information, their influence on art and poetry, their mirror of early manners and customs, their preservation of word of mouth apostolic teachings, and their deification of heroes and saints. And so to the Tyrol. 'Europe possesses in Tirol one little country at least in whose mountain fastnesses a store of these treasures not only lies enshrined, but where we may yet see it on request.' With her instinct for folklore comparisons, she observes how a legend of a young man, dashed to death as he was about to honour a saint by placing an ornament atop his church, cropped up everywhere, even in her own *Patrañas*, and wonders if the comparative mythologist could give the reason.

The original contribution of Rachel Busk to folklore rests on two splendid field collections covering the folktales of Rome and the folksongs of Italy. She completed *The Folk-Lore of Rome, Collected by Word of Mouth from the People* in 1874, the same year as her guidebook, but this was an entirely different work, a result of a lone quest beginning in the bookshops of Rome to see if an Italian Grimm existed.[3] Miss Busk knew, of course, the older collections of Straparola, Basile, Boccaccio, and Sacchetti, 'but these were made for quite different purposes than that of supplying Italy's quota to the study of Comparative Mythology.'[4] Nor did any bookshop have a copy of Straparola's *Le Piacevoli Notti* for her perusal. Aside from the crudely printed, rhymed legends of street vendors, she drew a blank. So Miss Busk began to collect herself. People readily told her

[1] Rachel H. Busk, *The Valleys of Tirol* (London, 1874), pp. 195–7.
[2] *Ibid.*, p. 5.
[3] An American edition was published in Boston in 1877 under the title *Roman Legends, A Collection of the Fables and Folk-Lore of Rome.*
[4] Busk, *The Folk-Lore of Rome* (London, 1874), p. vii n.

legends for their rational and moral content, but they shied at relating children's fairy tales. She recounts incidents of her field experience and lessons painfully learned. In Rome the seeker of tales must observe all the forms of courtesy to establish his contact but might then suffer disappointment from those who half remembered or refused to repeat unhappy stories. She wonders why many persons knew well the traditional myths while others knew not even a trace. In the end she put together a stock of narratives drawn from localities in the Roman state and the city of Rome which did indeed comprise an Italian Grimm. For the scope and variety, colour and accuracy of its firsthand texts, the informativeness of preface and notes, the perceptiveness of its divisions, and the intelligent conception of the whole, *The Folk-Lore of Rome* merits high praise, even were it not a pioneer collection in English of European folktales. Yet it has received little acclaim.

In the course of her collecting, Miss Busk came to comprehend a point little understood by journeymen rewriters of fairy tales, namely that oral prose traditions encompass a number of distinct forms. Fairy tales or *Märchen*, known as *favole* to the Romans, constitute merely one such form. After learning about *esempj*, or religious and saints' legends, and *ciarpe*, the humorous anecdotes of dolts and scapegraces Clouston would call noodle tales, she asked for them by their generic names—as a collector must. Failing to ask, she would have failed to obtain. For ghost stories and family and local traditions no single Italian term existed (nor does one in English), but roundabout questioning unearthed prime examples. These four categories of the book appropriately conform to the distinctions made by the narrators themselves.

While recognizing the widespread popularity of many of her tales, Miss Busk also perceived their special regional and cultural qualities. Roman stories lacked the elements of heroism and chivalry, the bogeydom of monsters, giants, fairies, and dwarfs, the paganism of Russian and Norse religious legends, the fantasy of animal and bird actors. On the whole they were more realistic, rational, plausible. In relating the cycle of legends about Jesus Christ and St. Peter, Roman storytellers accepted the Gospel miracle literally, as good Catholics. In the story of 'Pret' Olivio,' who tendered Jesus hospitality, cheated Death for three hundred years, and then wangled souls from the Devil to take up to Heaven, Miss Busk professed to see less of the pagan than in Dasent's Norse variant of 'Master Smith.' She could not imagine even an illiterate Roman telling tales about witches and pacts with the Devil, such as Ralston found in Russia.

[383]

In these statements about the absence of superstition among the Romans, Miss Busk clearly showed her own religious bias and Achilles' heel as a collector. She quotes a pious woman who scorned the Devil and witch charms practised by her husband after the wretch had abandoned both his wife and the Church. Miss Busk admits that she refused to listen to scandalous stories about Donna Olimpia, sister-in-law to Pope Innocent X, apologizes for the *ciarpe* of the indigent friar who tricked a landlord into giving him a sumptuous repast, and obviously delights in the cautionary tale of 'Giacinta Marescotti,' a proud beauty brought to a sense of her own sinfulness in a nunnery. *The Folk-Lore of Rome* would surely have proved even richer and more macabre had not Rachel Busk been limited by her piety and prudery.

Still, readers could sample an excellent story fare, especially in the realm of the historical and family tradition impregnated with popular exaggeration. Saints and lovers, noblemen and merchants, boobies and wags and misers trooped through the anecdotal legends. Told for true, supported with specific references to familiar streets and named personages, these accounts of murders, courtships, impostures, comeuppances, and frights might at first hearing sound more like kitchen gossip and newspaper sensations than the stuff of myth; indeed, they were both. One favourite plot turned on the wooing by a wealthy Englishman, for to Romans all the English were rich (as Americans would be in twentieth-century variants) of a beauteous but poor young Roman maiden; after years in the land of Protestantism and fogs, she returned to Rome a prematurely aged and withered crone. Instead of a *favole*, Rachel's friend told her one day a '*bell fatto*' about 'The King of Portugal.' Imprisoned and starved by his son-in-law, the king mysteriously maintained his strength and health. On her visits to the cell, his daughter suckled him between the bars. Miss Busk comments dryly that she had heard of stories being localized but not delocalized.

Before the day of the tape recorder, Rachel Busk managed to convey a sense of the narrator's style, the audience's presence, and the tale's immediacy, chiefly through the illuminating notes appended to each tale. These glosses explain the nuances of dialect terms, add comments from the listeners, supply comparative references to the collections of Grimm, Dasent, Campbell, Ralston, and her own previous works, and set down relevant information on Italian history and Roman customs of daily life. So in the notes to the *favole* on 'Filagrante,' Miss Busk glosses her translation of *orca* as 'witch' with a discussion by the narrator showing the complexity of the concept. For 'stink' she explains that Italian lacks a neutral word for smell; *puzzo* means a bad smell, a stink. Even for the little phrase 'On, on, on,' she entered a gloss to point out that all tale-tellers used the original *camminando* (thrice-repeated) as a singsong refrain. In an extended comparative note, Miss Busk says she placed 'Filagrante' first in the collection because it embraces so many traditionary incidents, from the maiden imprisoned in the tower who drops her long tresses to the prince below, as in the Grimms' 'Rapunzel,' to the magic flight, and the lover's kiss that brings forgetfulness. All that was lacking to make her treatment completely modern was the inclusion of tale type and motif numbers, then unavailable to her, and a brief *vita* of the narrator.

A noteworthy instance of Miss Busk's up to date collecting technique is her transcript of a conversation between two believers in ghosts and a nonbeliever. To her chagrin, the vocal nonbeliever finally throttles the prospective storytellers with her own ghost-laying anecdotes, but the record of the conflict of beliefs and the juxtaposition of 'true' and 'false' ghost motifs is of high interest for the folklorist.

Thirteen years after *The Folk-Lore of Rome*, in 1887, Rachel Busk completed another unusual and even more demanding collection, *The Folk-Songs of Italy*. The subtitle adds 'Specimens, with translations and notes, from each province: and prefatory treatise by Miss R. H. Busk.' An additional caption states 'The Specimens of the Canzuni and Ciuri of Sicily have been Selected Expressly for this Work by Dr. Giuseppe Pitrè, of Palermo.' If a volume of Italian folktales collected and translated by an Englishwoman was a *'bell fatto*,' even more so was a volume of folksongs, whose translation into rhymed stanzas, while maintaining fidelity to the original dialect, presented a challenge worthy of a fairy-tale hero. Her accomplishment merits tribute on three counts: for the collecting of traditional songs, for their poetic yet faithful translation, giving the Italian and English texts side by side (as space had prevented her doing for the folktales), and for enlisting the support of Pitrè, 'the most devoted and prolific of Folklorists.'

The bond with Pitrè strengthened Miss Busk's book and built a bridge between English and Italian folklore scholarship. Rachel Busk gave the songs of Sicily first place, in 'gratitude to my indulgent friend Dr. Giuseppe Pitrè, the Sicilian Folklorist, whose kind encouragement in my study of Folklore has fostered my interest in the traditions of Italy during many years past.' Pitrè points out errors in her spelling of dialect words which she enters on a page of '*Corrigenda*,' corrects her attribution of a Neapolitan folksong to a folk-poem, and sends her seventeen Sicilian song texts for her book. Proudly she refers to his newly edited *Novelle Popolari Toscane*, which cites *The Folk-Lore of Rome* as the sole authority for variants in the province of Rome, and happily she mentions his invitation to her to contribute to his new series of *Curiosità Popolari Tradizionali*. Pitrè loaned her a copy of his rare work, *Studio Critico sui Canti Popolari Siciliani* (*Critical Studies on Sicilian Popular Song*), which she praises as 'eminently a work for students of the science of Folklore,' and yet tuned to the passions and poetry of a menacing and lovely land.[1]

If Rachel Busk experienced difficulties in locating tales, the songs fell at her feet. The people's music was everywhere in the air, and during her twenty years in various parts of Italy she gleaned from Italian friends, servants, peasants, and soldiers hundreds and even thousands of songs. They were sung by peasants in the fields and vineyards, men at charcoal-burning, women at silk-spinning or while washing by the river, by city labourers and families living in the crowded, hilly streets of Rome in the Trastevere and Monti districts where she lived for a time, hearing 'a great deal of popular music and singing pass under the windows.'[2]

In selecting from the abundance available—Pitrè told her 7,000 songs had been collected in Sicily alone—she chose those free from excessive dialect, poetically attractive, and suitable for word-for-word translation. Formidable technical problems, which she discusses with candor and authority, faced her in rendering true English likenesses without improving upon the originals. In the end she produced a garland of lyrical *strambotti* and *stornelli*, strikingly different from familiar English and Scottish popular ballads. If the English renditions often seemed forced and arch, allowance must be made for the rigour of the task. Nor did Miss Busk overvalue her efforts, as this comment on her translation of a Sicilian love plaint sent her by Pitrè reveals:

> My English version by itself would give very little idea of the power of the original, but by its means some idea of its energy may be grasped. A whole romance is drawn in those eight lines—the stages by which a man who thinks himself unjustly kept apart from his sweetheart passes from sorrow to desperation. After long debate there is something magnificent in the sudden outburst in the last two lines. For, it must be remembered, it is his own life that he puts at stake, and that seriously.

[1] Busk, *The Folk-Songs of Italy* (London, 1887), pp. 44, 244–5, 66, 4 n., 46.
[2] *Ibid.*, pp. 16, 236 n.

This is her translated text.

> O God! And you, friends, tell, which way to turn.
> A love I have, yet can't obtain a kiss.
> Distraction makes my brain with fire burn;
> No way I find to 'ttain unto my bliss!
> Her father and his son a pact have sworn
> Arm'd watch to keep—to my increased distress.
> Thus, but to bear her off, I nought discern.
> Let arms clash arms, and one or other dies![1]

During her career as traveller, author, and collector, Miss Busk kept in touch with The Folk-Lore Society. She sent in two short notes to the *Folk-Lore Journal* in 1883 on the belief heard in England of peacocks as birds of ill omen, and she wrote on 'Italian Folk-Songs' in *Folk-Lore* in 1890, reviewing three recent collections. Rachel participated in the London Congress of 1891 and donated seventeen items to the exhibit of folklore objects from Costa Rica, Perugia, Naples, Rome, China, and the village of Biddenden. They included cloves blessed at St. John Lateran and popularly used as a toothache remedy; once when suffering from neuralgia, Miss Busk was given these by her footman, who ran home to fetch them from his father, a choirsinger in St. John Lateran.

In contrast to the lady traveller, William Ralston Shedden Ralston (1828–1889) presents the retiring figure of a withdrawn librarian and desk scholar, but he too left a lasting memorial in his exploration of European folklore. A graduate of Trinity College, Cambridge, and a barrister of the Inner Temple, he spent his working life, after the loss of the family fortune through litigation, as an assistant in the printed book department of the British Museum. Since the department needed a Russian specialist, Ralston undertook to learn the language and journeyed to Russia in 1868 and 1870, gathering materials for three books on Russian folklore and history he wrote with considerable grace and learning between 1872 and 1874.

The first of these related publications bore a misleading title, *The Songs of the Russian People, as Illustrative of Slavonic Mythology and Russian Social Life*. Actually the songs play a small part in the total work which sought to do for the Russians and their fellow Slavs what Jacob Grimm had done for the Teutons in his *Deutsche Mythologie*. While less the philologist than Jacob, and cognizant of Müller's solar and Tylor's survival theses, Ralston followed closely Grimm's general scheme of reconstructing from peasant traditions

[1] *Ibid.*, pp. 72–3.

[387]

the pre-Christian pantheon of deities and sorceresses and diabolic creatures of the night. As Jacob took his stand in the German mid-point of Europe and traced mythological connections of Teutonic goblins radiating out to the Scandinavians, Slavs, and Latins, so Ralston fixed his sights on Greater Russia and pursued eastward the Slavonic network of spectres, charms, and rituals. In the Preface to a second edition (May, 1872), he insists on connections between the folk customs of the Slavs and the modern Greeks.

Making only modest claims for his own role, Ralston considered himself largely a translator and interpreter of the Russian folklorists, whom he freely acknowledged, but he used his sources selectively and judiciously. Oral poetry afforded one kind of traditional source, and Ralston from time to time inserted word-for-word translations of laments, heroic songs, love songs, marriage songs, dance songs, and *builínas* (modern *bylina*) or historical songs, powerful and moving in their direct imagery. Yet the songs were not themselves the object of study. Rather they served as documents, with other folklore evidence, to uncover the old Slavonic mythology of demonism and vampirism.

The Songs of the Russian People remains a mine of information for the folklorist unfamiliar with the Russian language and Russian scholarship. One section of special fascination describes the collecting experiences of P. N. Ruibnikof, who in 1859 initiated the inquiries in the Olonets region leading to his recovery of 236 *builínas*, totalling more than 50,000 verses. Beginning with blind psalm-singers driven from a churchyard by the police, he pursued leads, undaunted by the hostility of the common people toward a government official, until chance deposited him on a desolate islet in Lake Onega. During the night he heard the haunting voice of a peasant *builína* singer, storm-tossed on the same shore, and accompanied him back to his remote village, there to meet other epic singers. Ralston sampled the famed *builína* cycles of Kiev and Novgorod, filled with passages of heroic splendours. Here one hero, Ilya Muromets, meets another, Svyatogor, and his witch-wife:

> There comes a hero taller than the standing woods,
> Whose head reaches to the fleeting clouds,
> Bearing on his shoulders a crystal coffer,
> Opens the coffer with a golden key:
> Out comes thence a heroic woman.
> Such a beauty on the whole earth
> Had never been seen, never been heard of.[1]

---

[1] W. R. S. Ralston, *The Songs of the Russian People* (2nd ed.; London, 1872), p. 60.

Besides the excerpts and summaries of heroic epics, a novelty for English readers lay in the grotesque beings resurrected from the ancient Slavonic faith. These degenerated deities included such creatures as the hirsute Domovoy, once a fire god but now a deflated house spirit living behind the stove; the water-sprite known as the Rusálka, a poetic nymph important in harvest rituals; the Vodyany, a naked, bloated old man, patron of beekeepers, fishermen, and sailors; and the Bába Yagá, a hideous old woman riding an iron mortar. Ralston supplemented this demon gallery with the mortal wizards, witches, and werewolves who turned to vampires after their death, and he also enumerated the various spells, charms, and purificatory rites used by the peasants to combat the forces of evil.

In commenting on these traditions, Ralston draws from existing theories but espouses no single one. Discussing the Russian *zagádki*, the mythical-metaphorical riddles once possessing almost a religious character, he appropriates both Tylor's phrase of 'sense riddle' and Müller's 'chips of mythology' to develop the thought that they contain mythological ideas of the old Slavonians. Although a follower of Grimm, the British Museum librarian accepted, and capitalized, Tylor's Survival. For an example he cites the Raskolniks' burial practice of placing small ladders baked from dough beside the corpse to assist the soul on leaving the body in its ascent of the iron (or glass) hill to Paradise—a clear case of Survival from heathen times. Ralston notes that the great Russian collector Afanasiev preferred the nature-mythologists' explanations for the monstrosities of witchcraft to Tylor's doctrine of savage survivals. To Afanasiev, as to Grimm, witches and wizards had descended from the priests and priestesses of an ancient order. Both views, and a third, holding that Russian myths are derived from the Orient, Ralston regards with caution. He closes on a prophetic note. Perhaps the great mass of the Russian people, like the long crippled hero Ilya Muromets, was ready to rise from its lethargy and conquer the world.

In 1873 Ralston brought out *Russian Folk-Tales*, exhibiting the same preoccupation with mythological conceptions of the old Slavonians. Departing from the conventional format of folktale collections, he introduces each tale or group of tales with analytical commentary, so that the *skazki* and *legendi* illustrate and confirm his argument. Ralston selects his narratives chiefly from the collections of Afanasiev to depict deeply rooted characters such as the evil snake, the fearsome Bába Yagá, personifications of fate, the days, and the whirlwind, witches and wizards, the walking dead, vampires, saints, and devils. In his studious notes he considers such ancient ideas embodied in the recitals as the external life-token and the distinction between enchanted corpses and vampires.

Ralston fully recognizes the danger in treating a stock of folktales gathered within a nation's boundaries as a purely national property, and he calls attention to international story plots and episodes from his broad knowledge of the standard collections. In his note on the forbidden chamber he cites German, Neapolitan, Wallachian, Esthonian, Gaelic, Greek, and Indian uses of the theme. But Ralston still believes it possible to isolate the specifically Russian elements of style and matter in oral tales. Slavonic storytellers shone among the European peasantry in their narrative skill, unaffected humour, dramatic talents, and simple yet descriptive speech. In one place he compares a Russian *skazka* with the same story as told in Gaelic to Campbell of Islay. The *skazka* relates how a daughter-in-law outsmarts the dead Moujik in the coffin, who wishes to take his money to the other world with him, by the simple device of wearing her cross. But the Highland tale about a lykewake was murky and cluttered.[1] In making *skazki* and *bulinas* known to his countrymen, Ralston achieved his main purpose.

With the founding of The Folk-Lore Society, in which he played a main role, the reticent librarian found a kindred circle; he served as a vice-president and as council member until his death. For the first volume of the *Folk-Lore Journal* in 1878, he wrote 'Notes on Folk-Tales,' a judicious appraisal of the questions of East-West diffusion and folk-narrative classification. He rued the leanness of folktale collecting in England, the more so in view of Afansiev's 332 Russian stories (Moscow, 1863), Pitrè's 300 from Sicily (Palermo, 1875), and Campbell's 86 in print in 1862 and 791 in manuscript from the Scottish Highlands. Ralston cautiously reviewed the Aryan mythological and Indianist diffusion theories, content to bring forward instances of 'stories now current in different parts of Europe as folk-tales, preserved by oral tradition, which were centuries ago written down in Asia and imbedded in books.'[2] The interpreter of folktale origins must possess exceptional prudence and deep learning, and he did not yet sight such a person.

Classifiers of folktales as well as their interpreters needed Solomon's wisdom. Ralston considered the plan of the Austrian Johann G. von Hahn, later modified by Baring-Gould (see p. 296), but felt that it stressed accidental rather than essential story elements. He considered the mythological and moral bases of folktales the primary keys and applied them to a classification of the Grimm

[1] Ralston, *Russian Folk-Tales* (London, 1873), pp. 288–9.
[2] Ralston, 'Notes on Folk-Tales,' *Folk-Lore Record*, I (1878), 96.

tales. Of the 200, he found 103 to be non-mythological; this group he subdivided into 50 comic and 43 didactic, with various smaller rubrics. The 'far more important mythological division' he arranged into 10 'husk myths' (gods assuming inferior forms), 12 under 'magic and witchcraft,' 13 under 'transformation,' 16 'eclipse myths,' and 31 under 'demon stories,' usually involving some diabolic creature's struggles with mankind. This ingenious breakdown reflects Ralston's view of fairy tales as repositories of primal ideas and emotions.[1]

When The Folk-Lore Society published in 1882 the *Portuguese Folk-Tales* collected by Consiglieri Pedroso (printing 30 of his 500) and translated by Henriqueta Monteiro, Ralston wrote the Introduction. Characteristically he identified story groups centring on deep-rooted themes: the transformation of supernatural wives, the hero's flight from the demon with the aid of the demon's daughter, the unjust suffering of the calumniated wife. Again he stated a favourite thesis, that certain of these *Märchen* contained ideas, such as the incasing of a celestial being in an ugly husk, once meaningful in Buddhist India but now absurd and grotesque in Christian Europe. In place of Müller's disease of language, Ralston in effect suggested a disease of religious understanding.

From each people on the Continent the English visitors sent back samples of living peasant traditions. Yet the most exciting discoveries were to come in their own Isles.

[1] Ralston also published *Early Russian History* (London, 1874).

XI   The Celtic Folklorists

'To the Memory of J. F. Campbell from whom I first learnt
to love Celtic Tradition' (Alfred Nutt, dedication of *Studies on
the Legend of the Holy Grail*, 1888).
'. . . solution in this matter of diffusion is as likely to come
from the study of the Celtic folk-tales of this island as from any
other quarter I can think of' (Joseph Jacobs, *The International
Folk-Lore Congress, 1891*, p. 83).

IN APPROPRIATE CLIMAX, the English seekers came to learn
that fountains of oral folklore bubbled at their very doorstep.
Technically, the glory of discovery and pride of possession belonged
to the Scotch and Irish rather than to the English, but after all the
Gaels were bona fide residents of the British Isles and subjects of
the Queen, as even the shade of Bonnie Prince Charlie must acknowledge. The Great Team of English folklorists encouraged and
prodded the Celtic collectors and hastened to incorporate the new
Gaelic materials into their systems. Nutt in particular played a key
role as publisher and scholar of Celtic folklore. In time, folklore
studies in Scotland, Wales, and Ireland moved from a spirit of local
patriotism toward an attitude of national separatism. Nationalists
asserted their rights to an ancient cultural heritage submerged
under English history, literature, and language; in the case of Ireland, the folklore movement contributed to the goal of political independence. In this respect the course of folklore research was
following a path marked out in many countries where a new or revitalized nationalism drew nourishment from the traditions of the
people.

In the years from 1860, when the well of living Gaelic lore was
first tapped, to the disruption of war in 1914, the Celtic patriots
handsomely served and co-operated with the cause of imperial
folklore. Their spectacular discoveries compensated for the barren
fields of the English shires and helped redirect attention of English

folklorists from the African savage to the island peasant. The thought of early man could be recaptured in the Highlands, the Outer Isles, and the western counties of Erin where a two-thousand-year-old folk tradition still flourished.

SCOTLAND

In 1860, a counterpart to the brothers Grimm, so often heralded and so often found wanting, did emerge in Britain in the person of John Francis Campbell of Islay (1822–1885). That year Campbell published the first two volumes of his classic *Popular Tales of the West Highlands, Orally Collected*. Two more volumes came out in 1862, the fourth volume being given over entirely to essays on mythology and tradition. The connection with the Grimms was more than metaphorical. A close intellectual chain linked the brothers to their earliest emulators, Peter Christian Asbjörnsen and Jörgen Moe in Norway, who inspired the English scholar of Norse antiquities, George Webbe Dasent, to turn to living traditions. Dasent then urged his close friend Campbell to do for the Gaelic-speaking crofter of the Highlands what the Grimms had done for the German peasant and Asbjörnsen and Moe for the Norwegian peasant.

Dasent met Jacob Grimm in Stockholm in 1840, and the Oxford graduate, then on a diplomatic mission, listened to Jacob expound on the values in studying Scandinavian history and mythology. In 1842 Dasent translated the prose Edda and in 1843 he prepared a grammar of Old Norse. In the following years Dasent became assistant editor of the London *Times* and professor of literature and history at King's College, London. Acquaintance with Asbjörnsen and Moe led to his translation of their *Norske Folkeeventyr*, called *Popular Tales from the Norse* (1859), a work quickly reprinted and gaining a public favour surpassed only by the Grimm's *Household Tales*. In an impassioned introductory essay on the 'Origin and Diffusion of Popular Tales,' Dasent restated the Grimms' Aryan thesis in strident racial terms; the dispersion of the superior Aryans had caused the parent language and folktale stock to splinter but had not destroyed the family kinship of prize fictions. Collectors should gather them in from all the peoples of Aryan descent before the sources dried up.

Campbell heeded Dasent's call. The two shared interest in things Scandinavian and travelled together to Norway and Iceland. Asbjörnsen sent him one of his books, and Campbell wrote on the flyleaf, 'Translated by G. W. Dasent, Popular Tales from the Norse, who started me to collect the Popular Tales of the West Highlands.'[1] Growing up on Islay, young Iain had learned Gaelic from a piper, also named John Campbell, and mingled sociably with the crofters and fisherfolk. He walked about with his kilted nurse, worked with the carpenters, played shinny with the farm boys, heard a blind fiddler recite stories. As early as 1847 he began collecting in a desultory way. Now that the two Norwegians had uncovered such a mine of wonder tales from their own peasantry, who enjoyed historic relations with their Scotch counterparts across the North Sea, why might not he, the descendant of Highland chieftains, hope for similar good fortune among his neglected and forsaken people?

Campbell of Islay was an intellectual living in the midst of his own dying folk tradition. Educated at Eton and at Edinburgh University and called to the bar from the Inner Temple, a cousin of the statesman and scientist George Douglas Campbell, eighth Duke of Argyll, who aided Islay in his folklore enterprise, grandson on his mother's side of the Earl of Wemyss, young John stood far apart from the folk. But he had lived physically close to them, talked their despised tongue, and now set out deliberately to enter their lives. The crushing of the '45 at Culloden and the flight of Bonnie Prince Charlie to France had brought as a consequence the crumbling of the Highland clan system, the Gaelic tongue, and all the cherished institutions of Highland culture. Already despairing sons had departed for the States, Canada, Australia, hastening the doom of a dying race. Campbell would have to work rapidly.

The resourceful, talented, and inventive Islay came up with a brilliant idea which would transform field collecting. He employed and trained collectors expert in Gaelic and born in the Highlands and the Western Isles to interview and record the storytellers in their dialects, providing his men with funds and paper stocks, as in a later day they would be equipped with recording machines. Some of the locals thought him a bit touched. By this device he spread a net across the Highlands and western islands that in a remarkably short time captured a whole archive of folktales. He printed 86 in three volumes and announced in his final note at the end of Volume IV in 1862 that his aides had sent him a total of 791 stories; the manuscripts would fill a wheelbarrow, more were coming in all the time, and yet whole districts were still untouched. Once his machinery was smoothly operating, Campbell had little more to do, had he so wished, than to screen the texts pouring in and send the best on to the publishers.

[1] D. Wyn Evan, 'John Francis Campbell, of Islay, (1822–1885) and Norway' in *Med Boken Som Bakgrunn*, Festskrift til Harald L. Tveterås (Oslo, 1964), pp. 52–64.

Curiously, Campbell himself never placed more tales in print and could not even spare time to oversee a second edition, which did not appear until after his death. Two folklore manuscripts rejected by publishers lay among his final papers, although their interest and his reputation would surely have gained their acceptance, had he made further effort. The explanation is that Campbell led other lives wholly unconnected with folklore. As government secretary to the Lighthouse Commission he was completing a lengthy report while assembling the *Popular Tales*, and as secretary of the Coal Commission he prepared similar detailed, voluminous reports. His interests extended to geology, meterology, art, sports, travel, invention, writing, and languages. He devised a recorder to measure the intensity of the sun's rays and a method of converting collodion negatives into positives. His books included *A Short American Tramp in the Fall of 1864* (1865), *Frost and Fire, Natural Engines, Toolmarks and Chips, with Sketches Taken at Home and Abroad* (1865), *My Circular Notes*, 'written while travelling westwards round the world' (1876), and *Thermography* (1883).

Folklorists are content with the *Popular Tales*. In addition to the precious texts and variants of Highland stories in English and Gaelic, the author supplied an absorbing Introduction of well over a hundred pages, copious observations on elements and variations in the tales, and a fourth volume containing a monographic essay on the Ossianic controversy with additional papers on 'Traditions,' 'Mythology,' 'A Plea for Gaelic,' 'Highland Dress,' 'Celtic Art,' and 'Music.' Campbell's thought suffuses the work and raises it above the level of a collection. For the folklorist the Introduction is a delight, setting forth in intimate detail each step of the enterprise and the difficulties to be overcome. First the minister and then the schoolmaster had descended on the Highland and Island villages to stifle the old storytellers. To the east the paraphernalia of modern civilization—railways, roads, newspapers, tourists—had already blotted out the long oral romances. 'Tradition is out of fashion and books are in.'[1] Still Campbell perceptively realized, as later collections would amply prove, that the fairy faith continued vigorously even where the narrative art had withered. The scorn of the intellectual for the rude peasantry was nothing new, and Campbell cited as a case in point *The Journal of a Tour in the Hebrides* of Samuel Johnson, who despised Gaelic as a barbarous tongue and condemned witless traditions.

His quest defined, Campbell set about preparations in a business-

[1] John Francis Campbell, *Popular Tales of the West Highlands, Orally Collected*, (Edinburgh, 1860), I, xxxi.

like way. With a sure instinct he engaged capable assistants who in later years acquired a celebrity of their own: Hector Urquhart, the gamekeeper; Hector MacLean, the schoolmaster, reputed to be a student of black magic; and John Dewar, a woodman whose occupation on his death certificate was listed as 'Collector of Traditions.' Campbell himself made sorties into the field, summering on the islands of Uist, Barra, Lewis, and Harris, where Gaelic was the daily speech and every English word in use had 'a Gaelic head and tail.' His collectors had already made his name known, he could converse in Gaelic, and he 'got on famously' with the shy and sensitive peasants, hearing stories from men and women of all ages in company with children of all sizes. On some islands tale-telling had mysteriously disappeared but on others the master narrators spun their romances through the night. With an artist's eye Campbell portrayed the boulder and peat houses of the islanders and the varied countenances of their inhabitants. Here is his description of Angus MacDonald reciting Ossianic poems in Barra in 1860.

He is a fine intelligent man, with a clear gray eye and smooth dark hair, very fond of the old poetry of his native country, and charmed to recite it to an audience able to take an interest in it. The audience was a numerous one on the 10th of September, and we were highly attentive. One woman was industriously weaving in a corner, another was carding wool, and a girl was spinning dexterously with a distaff made of a rough forked birch-branch, and a spindle which was little better than a splinter of fir. In the warm nook behind the fire sat a girl with one of those strange foreign faces which are occasionally to be seen in the Western Isles, and which are often supposed by their neighbours to mark the descendants of the Spanish crews of the wrecked armada—a face which, at the time, reminded me of the Nineveh sculptures, and of faces seen in St. Sebastian. Her hair was as black as night, and her clear dark eyes glittered through the peat smoke. Her complexion was dark, and her features so unlike those who sat about her, that I asked if she were a native of the island, and learned that she was a Highland girl. Old men and young lads, newly returned from the eastern fishing, sat about on benches fixed to the wall, and smoked and listened; and MacDonald sat on a low stool in the midst, and chanted forth his lays amidst suitable remarks and ejaculations of praise and sympathy. One of the poems was the Lay of Diarmaid, much the same as it appears here; as I had got it from MacLean, who had written it from the dictation of another man elsewhere. 'Och! och!—aw! is not that sad?' said the women when Diarmaid was expiring.[1]

To his credit, Campbell brought to life the tellers and gave them their due. The neat table of contents listed the tale title, storyteller and his occupation, place and date of the telling, and the collector. The stories came from the lips of fishermen, farm servants, sawyers, drovers, labourers, stable boys, crofters, shoemakers, carters, stalkers, tinkers, gardeners, shepherds, tailors, a pauper, and a blind fiddler. An entry in Campbell's diary for August 17, 1870 (for he maintained his enterprise long after the publication of the *Popular Tales*) shows him visiting Paisley on Islay and finding his collector Hector MacLean installed in a small pub with the shoemaker Lachlan MacNeill who had been relating for about a week the narrative of O'Kane's Leg, already consuming 260 pages of foolscap. Both were rather 'screwed.' A photograph taken that day shows the three seated around a small table, Campbell and MacLean on one side, not unlike in appearance with bushy beards, oval features, and well-combed heads of hair, MacLean in the act of writing, Campbell looking intently at the bald little eighty-two-year-old cobbler in work clothes with a white fringe of beard, one arm leaning on the table close by a glass and bottle, a little tense. How many times this scene must have been repeated throughout the Outer Isles and Highlands as a result of Campbell's initiative! Back in Glasgow later that night, Iain wrote in his notes, 'This is a very interesting old fellow, a gentleman in his manners, a good, sober-looking, clean decent old man. If he has time to think over his old stories, he has enough to fill a good-sized volume. . . .'[2]

Besides visiting his collectors on the scene, Campbell gave them counsel and direction through the post. In a letter of 1866 to Dewar, who was experimenting with his collecting methods, Islay instructed him to search out both sides of the clan feuds and to inquire for remembrances of Bannockburn, Flodden, and Culloden. 'Don't let us make ourselves out to be worse savages than we are, but let us tell the truth and shame the deil.' Next year he was enjoining Dewar to write dialogue:

. . . for I know that these stories are always told as if the people mentioned were talking, and it is far better to write in the same way, thus: then Mackenzie stretched out his hand and said, 'There is the hand that slew thy father.' With this which is genuine and vigorous and dramatic, compare that narrative

[1] Campbell, *Popular Tales of the West Highlands* (Edinburgh, 1862), III, 144–5.
[2] James H. Delargy, 'Three Men of Islay,' *Scottish Studies*, IV, Pt. 2 (1960), 128.

style into which you are apt to fall when you write, viz.: then Mackenzie stretched out his hand and told him that that was the hand with which he had killed his father. One is powerful and good, the other is poor and tame and Sassanach to boot.[1]

Such injunctions show Campbell's alertness to the true Gaelic idiom in contrast to the pale English (Sassanach) imitation. The fruits of his advice finally came to view in the magnificent collection of local traditions published in 1964 as *The Dewar Manuscripts*.

In addition to his skills as collector and organizer, Campbell also manifested a shrewd sense of the nature of his materials and arranged them under nine rubrics, although for some he lacked modern terms. His taste shaped largely by the Grimms and Dasent, he favoured the 'romantic popular tales' or *Märchen*, but he had acquired also archaic and bizarre hero tales and songs of the Finn cycle, distorted popular history, personal anecdotes of weird beings, children's stories, riddles and puzzles, proverbs in prose and verse, and numerous songs with wild and peculiar tunes. In the Fenian legends surrounding the third century warrior-hunter-wizard Fionn or Finn, the Scotch and Irish collectors would reap their greatest triumph. Campbell printed the texts with professional care. 'I have endeavoured to show how, when, and where I got the stories; each has its own separate pedigree, and I have given the original Gaelic, with the closest translation which I was able to make.'[2] Alert to the possibility of literary influences, he pointed happily to a manuscript of Gaelic tales much like Dasent's from the Norse but collected before 1859, thereby removing the chance of the Scotch storytellers having learned the plots from Dasent's book. Next to Dasent, the Highland tales showed likenesses to Grimm and in a few instances to the Arabian Nights. But even where an occasional literary tale had entered the Gaelic repertoire, the crofters had completely assimilated it to their environment. Their archaic romances ignored fine lords and gentle ladies, handsome palaces and radiant fairies, for wild and savage heroes fashioned in the image of clan chieftains. A Gaelic patriot, Campbell was also a widely read, sophisticated traveller who could identify migratory fictions. In his notes he referred to William Grant Stewart, Chambers, Scott, Croker, the Grimms, Dasent, Boccaccio, Straparola, and Washington Irving. One tale he recognized as companion to Geoffrey of Monmouth's twelfth-century version of King Arthur and Merlin being trans-

---

[1] John MacKechnie, 'John Francis Campbell (Iain og Ile) and His Place in the Literary History of the Highlands,' Introduction to *The Dewar Manuscripts, Scottish West Highland Folk Tales* (Glasgow, 1964), I, 37–8.
[2] Campbell, *Popular Tales*, I, xxxviii.

ported to the Fortunate Island or Island of Apples, and another about swans he linked with a Sanskrit original, following an observation in Max Müller's 1856 essay on 'Comparative Mythology.' To test the oral basis of his collections, Campbell revisited the Western Highlands in August and September, 1860, carrying with him his first two volumes, and had the narrators repeat their tales so that he could compare the spoken with the written words. Knowing narrative styles in Devonshire, Cheshire, the Isle of Man, Ireland, Norway, Sweden, and France, he judged that the Scotch Gael surpassed all of these in the abundance and excellent preservation of his tales. Among the lowland peasantry of Scotland he found few stories, and these seemed to have come from West Highlanders moving south to take work as farm servants, cattle drovers, and city porters. On the Isle of Man, too, he failed to unearth wonder tales and conjectured that the local traditions in Joseph Train's *An Historical and Statistical Account of the Isle of Man* (1845) were now dispersed among the Manxmen. However he had better luck in Ireland, hearing a number of stories from a carman in Waterford in 1861, and he hoped that some Irishman would faithfully collect the goodly stores that must exist. Islay even found traditional tales in the heart of London, as he related to the Ethnological Society of London in 1870 in a paper, subsequently printed in their journal, 'Current British Mythology and Oral Traditions,' making the point that Londoners too could collect folklore. Driving to his London office in a hansom cab in March, 1861, he spied a knife-grinder who seemed a likely prospect, jumped out of his cab, and arranged to meet with the man and his brother the next day. William and Soloman Johns, tinkers and gypsies, duly appeared at the office of the Lighthouse Commission, where Islay had prepared tobacco and long clay pipes, beer and bread and cheese. Eventually he thawed them out and heard 'seven long rigmarol popular tales.'[1] In the Highlands, people like these could be found on every corner.

There were storytellers and storytellers, and Campbell was a keen enough folklorist to perceive their distinctions and specialities.

> . . . each branch of popular lore has its own special votaries, as branches of literature have amongst the learned; that one man is the peasant historian and tells of the battles of the clans; another, a walking peerage, who knows the descent of most of the families in Scotland, and all about his neighbours and their origin; others are romancers, and tell about the giants; others

---

[1] Campbell, 'Current British Mythology and Oral Traditions,' *Journal of the Ethnological Society of London*, N.S. II, No. 26 (1870), 326–40.

are moralists, and prefer the sagacious prose tales, which have a meaning, and might have a moral; a few know the history of the Feni, and are antiquarians. Many despise the whole as frivolities. . . .[1]

In the whole literature of folklore there are few passages as astute as this in discerning the talents and tastes of folk narrators. Campbell broke new ground in focusing attention on the tellers and the way in which they manipulated their texts, where the conventional book of folktales even today conceals the carriers of tradition. Islay noticed that the best Highland raconteurs knew all species of narrations and could stretch out a romance to last the whole night before an appreciative audience. 'The Slim Swarthy Champion' occupied four hours and 'Connall Gulban' three evenings when told by the masters.

Although not a system-builder, Campbell was more than an imaginative and creative collector. He sought to fit his bricks into some symmetrical structure, and dallied with what propositions were available to him. In his essay on mythology he reviewed his intellectual turnings. First he had accepted the idea that the similar minds of men bred similar weeds. Then he moved to the view, voiced throughout the 1860 volumes, that wise men of the East had composed oral novelettes which had spread westward in written form. By the time of his second two volumes in 1862, he had come to espouse the Grimm thesis that folktales represented the fragments of early Aryan myths and religions. Accordingly, the mythologist should be able to discern the debris of an ancient Celtic creed in the Highland tales, and Islay believed he could detect 'an astronomical pantheon at war with meteorological, aqueous, and terrestrial powers.'[2] Signs of these Celtic divinities and demons appeared in the seals who turned out to be men and women visiting the world from their home in the West, in the water-bull that haunted lochs, and in the Fàchan monster having 'one hand out of the ridge of his chest, and one tuft out of the top of his head, [and] it were easier to take a mountain from the root than to bend that tuft.'[3]

Reviewers of the 1860 volumes, reading the fabulous tale of 'Osean after the Feen' (No. 31), pressed Campbell to investigate the question of Ossian, and in Volume IV he surveyed the published evidence while polling his own collectors. Islay concluded that the question of James Macpherson's alleged translations of Ossianic poems in 1760 had degenerated into a dispute between Irish and

[1] Campbell, *Popular Tales*, I, lv–lvi.
[2] *Ibid.*, IV, 314.   [3] *Ibid.*, p. 327. A cut of the Fàchan is on p. 326.

Scotch claimants to Ossian (Oisin) as their own hero. In his view the Ossianic poems were fictions founded upon facts, mainly old Scotch facts, but Macpherson had forfeited his hope for Homeric distinction by attempting to deceive.

Theoretical folklorists eagerly seized on Campbell's texts for evidence to support their theses but largely ignored his fertile ideas scattered through the *Popular Tales*. Had his manuscript on 'Oral Mythology,' dealing with Scoto-Irish ancient heroes, found a publisher in 1870, it would, Alfred Nutt believed, have greatly assisted the development of folklore science. Addressing the London Society of Ethnology in 1870, Islay stressed the values in the study of popular traditions as a record of human thought, history, manners, customs, and laws, and urged the Society 'to take up this withered branch of ethnology, and treat it on scientific grounds, to see if it will grow.'[1] Islay came on the scene too early to join forces with the anthropological folklorists, but he served them admirably. Tylor relied extensively upon the *Popular Tales* for such matters as the external life index, and indeed everyone, mythologists and diffusionists as well, fattened upon the splendid array of Highland texts. Müller included a review of the *Popular Tales* in his *Chips* and had no trouble in seeing the frog king as a solar hero traceable back to the Sanskrit, even though Campbell himself thought the story of Gaelic origin since the enchanted frog's Gaelic utterances sounded like the 'gurgling and quarking' of real frogs in springtime.[2]

Of all the Great Team, Alfred Nutt found the greatest inspiration from Campbell. Examining the trove of his unpublished manuscripts in the Advocate's Library in Edinburgh in 1890, Nutt rued their unavailability in print. Besides the 'Oral Mythology' there lay a second volume of the valuable 'Leabhar na Feinne (Heroic Gaelic Ballads),' a fellow to the volume published in 1872, in which Campbell intended to analyse comparatively the structures of Breton, Sanskrit, Scotch, Irish, and Norse sagas. And too, there was the study of 'The Celtic Dragon Myth,' which finally found its way into print in 1911, stripped of scholarly analysis.[3] Still another skeletal project called for a synthetic narrative of the heroic traditions

---

[1] Campbell, 'Current British Mythology and Oral Traditions,' p. 339. Campbell did make contact with Ralston, a co-founder of The Folk-Lore Society, and attended his lectures in London on Russian folktales. Ralston wrote his obituary in the *Athenaeum*, I (1885), 250.

[2] Max Müller, 'Tales of the West Highlands, 1861,' in *Chips from a German Workshop*, (New York, 1872), II, 237–47; Campbell, *Popular Tales*, II, 134.

[3] *The Celtic Dragon Myth* (Edinburgh, 1911) was prepared for the press by George Henderson, who quotes Campbell as saying: 'It treats of water, egg, mermaid, sea-dragon, tree, beasts, birds, fish, metals, weapons, and men mysteriously produced

about Fionn, a project dropped by Campbell for fear Irish readers would resent these rough peasant legends of their idealized heroes. Nutt did not share the fear. Along with these book manuscripts rested hundreds of unpublished tales and Campbell's own diaries filled with incisive jottings. Nutt hoped the tales would enter print and the unpublished works find scholarly readers in the Advocate's Library even though their day had passed.[1] Best, however, that no one attempt to complete the retelling of the Fenian saga, 'The unrivalled combination of knowledge, critical power, and instinctive racial sympathy which gave its owner his unique position in the study of folk-lore can hardly be expected from any other man.'[2]

One other man, one of Campbell's collaborators, came close to earning this tribute. Alexander Carmichael (1832–1912) contributed to the *Popular Tales* and accompanied Islay on collecting trips. In September, 1871, they went to visit an illiterate cotter named Hector MacIsaac in South Uist. The cotter's hut, built of turf walls, thatched with reeds, and set in a peat morass, contained nothing 'that the vilest thief in the lowest slum would condescend to steal.' MacIsaac, who spoke only Gaelic and had never left Uist, and Campbell, 'the learned barrister, the world-wide traveller, and the honoured guest of every court in Europe,' conversed easily and courteously. The cotter knew many heroic tales, poems, and ballads, while his wife could recite secular runes, sacred hymns, and fairy songs.[3]

So Carmichael described the winning ways of the master collector. Yet there were those who said that Carmichael surpassed Campbell in his closer intimacy with the crofter and profound sense of the Gaelic soul. Where the one bagged the tales related in public circles, the other coaxed out the hymns, prayers, charms, and blessings sung and intoned secretly and privately. Where the one interested

[1] *More West Highland Tales* (in two volumes) was transcribed and translated from the original Gaelic manuscripts of Campbell of Islay by John G. McKay (Edinburgh and London, 1940, 1960).
[2] Alfred Nutt, 'The Campbell of Islay Mss. at the Advocates' Library, Edinburgh,' *Folk-Lore*, I (1890), 383.
[3] Alexander Carmichael, *Carmina Gadelica, Hymns and Incantations* (Edinburgh and London, 1928), I, xxiv.

---

from sea-gifts. All versions agree in these respects; they are all water myths, and relate to the slaying of water monsters.'

The Campbell Manuscripts in the National Library of Scotland at Edinburgh contain the manuscript of 'The Dragon Myth,' with the following note written in ink on the inside back cover of a paper bound in the volume: 'This paper is a short abstract of a volume still in manuscript November 1, 1882. The Mss. volume called *The Dragon Myth* grew from a story sketched in outline at the meeting March 22, 1870 [of the Ethnological Society of London] more than twelve years ago. That Dragon Myth is a big thing and my Ms. is heavy work.'

himself in the 'science of Storyology' and moved in cosmopolitan circles, the other devoted himself entirely to the welfare of his Highland people.[1]

No one would deny that Carmichael extended and complemented Campbell's labours in the field. Born on the island of Linsmore and educated in Edinburgh, he spent his professional life as a civil servant at various posts in the British Isles but passed the greater part in Uist. For nearly half a century he gathered Gaelic lore of all kinds in the Western Isles and the Highlands, not prejudging the traditions but receiving whatever the folk had to offer. A stately man of imposing presence, he shared the rude lot of the crofters and cotters, crossed perilous fords and channels to reach their homes, and entered into the spirit of their evening *ceilidhs*, gay with all manner of oral poetry, recitations, songs, and dances. He grieved, as all folklorists must grieve, at the heartless suppression of the *ceilidhs* by clergymen and schoolteachers. A famed violin player on Eigg burned his fiddle, made by a pupil of Stradivarius, after the preacher publicly denounced him from the pulpit; grownup schoolgirls in the parish school at Islay recalled with shame being beaten by the master for singing Gaelic songs. The excise officer honoured the wishes of his confidants, and when an islander travelled twenty-six miles afoot to beg Carmichael not to print the unique lament he had dictated the night before, Carmichael promptly burned the manuscript before his eyes.

In 1900 the collector had printed in a handsome two-volume edition of three hundred copies part of his harvest under the title *Carmina Gadelica, Hymns and Incantations, with Illustrative Notes on Words, Rites, and Customs, Dying and Obsolete. Orally Collected in the Highlands and Islands of Scotland.* The *Carmina Gadelica* brought out a hidden body of poetic oral folklore blending magical and religious, pagan and Christian elements and affecting every aspect of the cotter's daily and seasonal round. Carmichael set the Gaelic texts and his own translations of the blessings and charms on facing pages and provided headnotes, often running to several pages of fine type. Written in a lyrical prose matching the mood of the verses, the notes explained the farming, herding, fishing, and weaving techniques and described the calendar celebrations linked to legend, rite, proverb, and rune. Frequently, Carmichael sketched vivid portraits of the singers and chanters. The whole intricate web of traditional custom, belief, and expression in a folk community takes form in the course of the work.

[1] Kenneth MacLeod, 'Our Interpreter,' *Carmina Gadelica* (Edinburgh and London, 1941), IV, xxvii–xl, especially p. xxix.

Carmichael's synthesis of the legends and festivals connected with the cult of Bride can illustrate his treatment. Bride was the 'Mary and the Juno of the Gael,' presiding over fire, art, and beauty, and protecting men. She assisted the birthing mothers of Uist as she had helped the mother of Jesus when Mary and Joseph had come footsore and weary to the inn where Bride was a serving-maid. On Bride's Eve, girls fashioned and decorated a sheaf of corn in the likeness of a woman, calling it Bride, and carried the image to every house, singing songs and collecting gifts for Bride. Afterward they repaired to a house for the feast of Bride, to which young men came to dance and frolic. Older women made ikons of Bride from oats, and young boys brought fighting cocks to school on Bride's Day. On her day, a serpent came down from the hills and the people sang a hymn to appease the creature, or pounded the serpent in effigy. Bride was also connected in saying and song with the seasons, especially spring. In Barra, the men cast lots at the church door on Bride's Day for the choice fishing banks. Dedications to Bride were also common in England and Ireland. After this essay-note, Carmichael offered the text 'Genealogy of Bride.'

> The genealogy of the holy maiden Bride,
> Radiant flame of gold, noble foster-mother of Christ.
> Bride the daughter of Dugall the brown,
> Son of Aodh, son of Art, son of Conn,
> Son of Crearar, son of Cis, son of Carmac, son of Carruin.
>
> Every day and every night
> That I say the genealogy of Bride,
> I shall not be killed, I shall not be harried,
> I shall not be put in cell, I shall not be wounded,
> Neither shall Christ leave me in forgetfulness.
>
> No fire, no sun, no moon shall burn me,
> No lake, no water, nor sea shall drown me,
> No arrow of fairy nor dart of fay shall wound me,
> And I under the protection of my Holy Mary,
> And my gentle foster-mother is my beloved Bride.[1]

Some charms and blessings crossed the Atlantic with the crofters who, evicted from their small holdings, emigrated to Nova Scotia, Prince Edward Island, and Cape Breton, and, occasionally, the men and their traditions came back, altered by their New World experience. A native of the parish of Small Isles, Donald Maclean,

[1] Carmichael, *Carmina Gadelica*, I, 175.

recited a number of poems to Carmichael he had learned from a Uist-born neighbour in Nova Scotia. When Donald left Canada, the neighbour, Clara Clanranald, who at one hundred and two still possessed all her faculties and a deep love of her home soil, tearfully gave Donald, in Gaelic, this charge:

Thou art going away, beloved Donald, and may the great God be between thy two shoulders. Thou thyself wert the good neighbour and the kind friend. If it be that thou reach the land of thy heredity and the country of thy birth, and that thou shouldst have to come back again to the land of thine adoption, I place it upon thee as a vow and as a charge, and as the nine fulfilments of the fairy women, that thou go to the burial-place of Michael at Ormacleit in Uist, and bring to me from there a little earth that shall be placed upon the tablet of my heart the day that I die.

And may Michael kind-white, strong-white, red-white,
Preserve thee, protect thee, provide for thee,
With the might of his hand, with the point of his spear,
Under the shade of his shimmering shield.[1]

This was not itself a traditional text, and Carmichael placed it in a headnote, but the poetic cast of the phrases, the form of the blessing, the combined appeal to God and the fairy women, and Donald's close remembrance of the spoken words, all indicate the forces of tradition governing the thought and expression of the Hebrideans.

Nutt reviewed the first two volumes of *Carmina Gadelica* in *Folk-Lore* in a sensitive and moving appraisal. While recognizing that much of this 'pan-European popular Christian oral literature' was the Gaelic equivalent of European peasant magic poetry, he saw a special flavour in the homage to the two patron saints of the Western Isles, Columba and Bridget (Bride). On the whole the Christian outweighed the pagan elements and took rank with the loftiest oral verses of Christian sentiment uttered anywhere at any time. Nutt compared an 'Invocation of the Graces,' collected and translated by Carmichael, with Cuchulain's wooing of Emer, ten to fifteen centuries earlier, to show the continuous possession of majestic and moving oral verse by the Gaelic-speaking Highlanders and islanders.[2]

[1] *Ibid.*, p. 285, headnote.
[2] Nutt, in *Folk-Lore*, XI (1900), 419–21. A five-volume edition was published by Oliver and Boyd (1928–54).

Besides the *Carmina Gadelica*, Campbell of Islay stimulated another major field effort, the set of five volumes called *Waifs and Strays of Celtic Tradition, Argyllshire Series*, conceived by Lord Archibald Campbell but given its direction by Alfred Nutt, the publisher, who inevitably contributed essays and notes. If some ministers of the kirk had suppressed Gaelic recitals, others now sympathetically set about recording them at the laird's request. The titles in the series follow:

I. *Waifs and Strays of Celtic Tradition, I, Argyllshire Series*. Edited, With Notes on the War Dress of the Celts, by Lord Archibald Campbell. xvi, 98 pages, 1889. [Nutt in his advertisement for the series listed it as *Craignish Tales*. Collected by the Rev. James MacDougall.]

II. *Folk and Hero Tales*. Collected, edited, and translated by the Rev. Donald MacInnes; with a Study on the Development of the Ossianic Saga and Copious Notes by Alfred Nutt. xxiv, 497 pages, 1890.

III. *Folk and Hero Tales*. Collected, edited, translated and annotated by the Rev. James MacDougall; with an Introduction by Alfred Nutt. xxix, 311 pages, 1891.

IV. *The Fians; or, Stories, Poems, and Traditions of Fionn and his Warrior Band*. Collected Entirely from Oral Sources by John Gregorson Campbell (Minister of Tiree); with Introduction and Bibliographical Notes by Alfred Nutt. xxxviii, 292 pages, 1891.

V. *Clan Traditions and Popular Tales of the Western Highlands and Islands*. Collected from Oral Sources by the late Rev. John Gregorson Campbell, selected from the Author's MS. Remains and edited by Jessie Wallace and Duncan MacIsaac, with Introduction by Alfred Nutt. xx, 150 pages, 1895.

The inspiration of Campbell of Islay pervaded the series. His portrait appears in volumes II and IV, a quotation from him on the title page of Volume III, and allusions to him throughout the set. The *Waifs and Strays* carried forward his work with increased emphasis on local and racial rather than international narrative traditions. These are sagas rather than *Märchen*, filled with battles, journeys, and raids, and the enchantments of kings and warriors, related in a bardic style glowing with epithets, runs, and bold metaphors, mixing mythic and modern notions. English readers encountered ancient heroes of Gaelic story and song: Finn Mac-Cumhail and his little dog Bran with the venomous claw, the Son of the Knight of the Green Vesture, the son of the King of Lochlainn (Scandinavia) who as a suckling babe sipped the heart and breast out of his mother and fifty nurses in a row, each with one suck. Chronicles of later vintage deal with clan feuds fought with sword and dirk, leading to slaughters and massacres that bred ever more killings and burnings. One tells of the bitter fight at Kilmartin River between the Campbells and McMartins whose chiefs were brothers-in-law, during which McMartin was pierced by a dirk. Campbell gave McMartin's son, his nephew, to a clansman to rear, the very man who had slain McMartin. One day this man (later known as Macrae from a Gaelic pun) went to the lake to wash a leather hide and laid his dirk upon the shore; the seven-year-old boy picked up his foster-father's dirk and began to brandish it excitedly. 'My little fellow, if you were a man what would you do with that dirk?' asked Macrae. 'I would drive it into the man who killed my father.' Macrae seized the dirk, slew the boy, and threw his body into the lake, ever after known as McMartin's Lake, then fled the country. A sheaf of place and family names commemorate incidents in this bloody chain of events, and the Campbells and Macraes preserve opposite versions of the affair.[1] This kind of folk annal was a far remove from the *Märchen* of the Grimms and Dasent.

The ministers proved diligent collectors and successfully unearthed prime narrators. James MacDougall, minister of Duror, Ballachulish, obtained the *Craignish Tales* from the McLarty family whose ancestors in the eighteenth century were famed for their recitals of Ossianic poems, and he wrote down all the ten Finn legends that filled Volume III from the delivery of Alexander Cameron, a roadman in his district. The Reverend Donald MacInnes procured nine of his dozen *Folk and Hero Tales* from the shoemaker Archibald MacTavish of Oban in 1881–82, too late to send Campbell of Islay. The best known of the clerical folklorists, John Gregorson Campbell, minister of Tiree, gathered a great variety of Gaelic tales, songs, and beliefs over a thirty-year period, enough to fill two other, posthumous volumes in addition to his two contributions to the *Waifs and Strays*. A book of folk narratives was also edited from the manuscripts left by MacDougall.

For volumes II through V of the *Waifs and Strays*, Nutt wrote

---

[1] 'A Craignish Fence,' in *Waifs and Strays of Celtic Tradition, I, Argyllshire Series,* Lord Archibald Campbell (ed.), (London, 1889), pp. 14–24.

substantial essays furthering the study of Celtic folklore. While Volume I alone did not carry the name of Alfred Nutt on the title page, he did attach three useful notes to the slender collection, pointing out a Faustian parallel for the Scotch magician Michael Scott and Campbell variants to a detailed fairy legend and riddling questions posed to Fionn.

To the *Folk and Hero Tales* of MacInnes, containing heroic legends of the Feunn MacCuail [*sic*] cycle, Nutt appended a close examination of the 'Development of the Fenian or Ossianic Saga.' Here the publisher considered the theories of William F. Skene and David MacRitchie who held that the 'Fayn' were a non-Celtic race preceding the Scots, corresponding to the small-statured Picts of history, and identified in the peasant mind with the Tuatha de Danaan, the ancient Celtic gods reduced to fairy status. After a detailed scrutiny of the medieval manuscripts and their several modes of handling the Fionn saga, Nutt concluded that the Fenians were Gaels and rejected claims for an historical basis to the fairy belief.

> The tales of Finn and his fellow-warriors are Gaelic variants of tales common to all Celtic, to all Aryan, indeed, to the great majority of all human races. They are essentially Gaelic, being found wherever there is a Gaelic population, and practically only where there is a Gaelic population.[1]

The whole intricate and complex question involved the relations of Scotch to Irish Gaels, of literary to popular forms, and of successive reactions and revisions, with all their accretions and alterations, to each other. Summarizing, Nutt declared that the past century of oral tradition in Scotland offered 'the most instructive object-lesson with which I am acquainted to the student of traditional diffusion and transmission.'[2] He would award the palm to the Irish for the earlier genesis and chief moulding of the saga and to the Scotch for its better oral preservation. In spite of the mythic elements in the Fenian saga, leading some to claim that it represented the Gaelic folk-fancy of ten centuries earlier, Nutt viewed the oral legends as essentially modern.

The publisher dismissed Macpherson in a note, saying his poems were worthless to the student of Celtic myth and saga but had given a spark to the romantic movement of the nineteenth century.

In his meaty introduction to MacDougall's *Folk and Hero Tales*, Nutt placed Celtic traditions in the broadest context of folklore

---

[1] Nutt, in Donald MacInnes, *Folk and Hero Tales* (London, 1890), p. 425.
[2] Nutt, in *ibid.*, pp. 429–30.

science. The available facts must be continually subject to renewed inspection, as Professor Heinrich Zimmer, author of *Keltische Studien* (1881), had done in his debatable study, contending that Finn was no third-century Irishman but a ninth-century Ersified Norseman. This issue involved the specific Celtic question of the Fenian saga, but the larger folklore question turned on the debate between proponents of cultural growth on the one hand and cultural decay on the other. Celtic legend and custom afforded the best ground for testing these rival theories, by virtue of the Gael's isolation from the central arena of European life. Nutt himself completely espoused the theory of cultural growth, plain to his eyes at the sight of the beauty, vividness, and creative artistry in Celtic poetry and saga. He had joined Lord Archibald Campbell and the ministers as a fellow worker seeking to trace the historical evolution of Celtic beliefs and practices through their written and oral records. This was a task not simply for a disinterested scholar but for the patriotic Briton:

> So much for the import of Celtic folk-lore (using the word in its widest sense) to the student of man's past. May I claim that it is of equal import to the present-day Briton? However much it may be regretted in certain quarters, the Celt is an abiding element in the imperial life of the British race.[1]

The Celt, the Teuton, and other race elements must co-operate cordially with each other to ensure the growth of their common British civilization. But to know the Celt one must know a 'vast body of anonymous and traditional legend which has at all times faithfully reflected folk-beliefs and folk-aspirations.'[2] So Nutt made his plea for Celtic folklore both in the name of science and in the cause of imperial unity.

Once more in introducing *The Fians*, Nutt restated his faith in the individuality of Gaelic folktales. Among the scholars who imputed common European origins to so-called Gaelic folktales, the American, William Wells Newell, chiefly drew Nutt's fire. Newell's argument that early collections had been printed in Italy, France, and Germany did not determine their priority over Gaelic traditions. Now the disclosure of oral heroic sagas in Scotland strengthened the case for long-lived folktales.

Nutt also returned to the Zimmer thesis of Norse influence on the Fenian cycle, presenting at length the counter-arguments of Whitley Stokes and d'Arbois de Jubainville. After a closely reasoned

[1] Nutt, in James MacDougall, *Folk and Hero Tales* (London, 1891), p. xxviii.
[2] Nutt, in *ibid.*, p. xxix.

résumé, he uttered a plea for native scholars of Scotland to address themselves to these perplexing questions of their own birthright on which German professors had written with such ingenuity. When Lord Archibald Campbell called for assistants to help him preserve Scotch race-traditions, he had to turn to 'hard-working ministers of religion; characteristic also that the most extensive, the most important, the most valuable series of researches which have appeared in Scotland in this department of study are due to a country gentleman, Campbell of Islay.' Contrast the valiant efforts of the Finns in preserving their own heroic epic, the *Kalevala*, with the indifference of the Scots. Let the first task of the newly organized Scotch Gaelic society be the critical study 'of the one living hero-cycle of Western Europe, the tales of Finn MacCumhail and the Fian band.'[1]

Besides his several essays, Nutt strengthened the twelve long *Folk and Hero Tales* of MacInnes with magnificent notes running to nearly one hundred pages. (He adds much briefer notes to *The Fians*.) His declared principles in these notes are to probe relationships between the current folktales and the older Gaelic literature and to examine surviving traces in the tales of early Celtic belief and custom. For greater coherence, he restricts his discussion of variants to those found on Celtic soil but discussed them in depth. To control the Irish evidence, he depends on close correspondence with Douglas Hyde, whose *Beside the Fire* he would publish the same year. Commenting on the folktale incident of the aged man with a hale father, Hyde wrote the publisher that the day before receiving Nutt's proofs he had heard a doctor from County Sligo recount the same anecdote as fact. The doctor 'told me he had seen a very old man putting screws [divots] on a house, and he said to him: "How old are you?" and the man said "Ninety-six." "You're a great old man to be working like that," said the doctor. "No, but if you were to see my father, you'd say he was the great old man." Then father came out, apparently as hale and hearty as the son, and he was 115 years old.'[2] Nutt accepted this secondhand story as another evidence against borrowing, although it is clearly the same folktale (Type 726, 'The Oldest on the Farm,' collected 161 times in Ireland).

In the notes, Nutt first lists references to 'similars' and 'semi-similars' for each tale as a whole and then discusses, often at considerable length, special incidents of the tales. With a sure instinct, he singles out elements today classified as international folktale motifs, such as the 'Infallible Sword,' the 'Recognition of the Hero,'

[1] Nutt, in John Gregorson Campbell, *The Fians* (London, 1891), pp. xxxvii, xxxviii.
[2] Nutt, in MacInnes, *Folk and Hero Tales*, p. 460.

the 'Three Tasks,' the 'Escaping Couple and the Magic Flight,' and the 'Skilful Companions.' After referring to variants in Campbell and other sources, Nutt frequently points out the processes of folk-tale intrusion into heroic saga and the adaptation of heroic legend to changed historical circumstances. In this manner he identifies various motifs in 'Lod, the Farmer's Son' and decides it must be a folktale reworked into the Cuchulain saga. In the last two narratives of battle he perceives a transition from mythic strife between mortals and immortals to a legendary struggle between Fenians and Lochlanners and, finally, to an historical war between Gaels and Norsemen. Kings had taken on the guise of clan chiefs and the epic struggle assumed the character of a Highland clan raid. In sum, 'the older, purely mythic, features have become almost entirely lost in their passage through the heroic stage, so that when the story comes back to the folk, and gradually turns again into a folk-tale, it is no longer a mythic (fairy) tale, but a semi-historic anecdote.'[1] Elsewhere he contrasts the modernized 'accidental' or external properties in folktales with the 'essential' or supernatural properties preserving an older culture, a position counter to Gaster's theory of the modern origin of folktales.[2] The blood-drops incident in 'The Son of the King of Eirin' constitutes such an essential property, traceable on Celtic soil for a thousand years; twelfth-century romances told of a hunter looking at a raven's blood and imagining a beautiful woman with raven-black hair and blood red cheeks.[3] Conversely, the tendency of modern narrators to rationalize marvellous adventures could be seen in 'The Ship That Went to America.' Nutt also comments on stylistic elements such as the 'runs' or conventional rhythmic passages designed as stepping-stones for the oral romancer. Indeed he provides an index of runs in addition to a valuable index of incidents.

In different vein, the publisher wrote a 'Memoir of the late John Gregorson Campbell,' collector-author of the *Clan Traditions and Popular Tales of the West Highlands*, to introduce that volume, and so furnishes a vignette of the clergyman-folklorist type who succeeded Campbell of Islay. John Gregorson Campbell (1836–91) was born in Argyllshire and sent to school in Glasgow at the age of ten, the only Highland boy in his class. After attending Glasgow University and reading law, he changed direction and in 1858 was licensed by the presbytery of Glasgow. Two years later, he accepted an appointment by the Duke of Argyll to the parishes of Tiree and

[1] Nutt, in *ibid.*, pp. 491–2.
[2] Nutt, in *ibid.*, p. 463, referring to pp. 458, 473, and 480.
[3] Nutt, in *ibid.*, p. 431.

Coll. From that vantage point he corresponded with Campbell of Islay and interviewed his parishioners for Gaelic lore in response to the duke's request. Nutt describes him as 'tall and fair, with deep blue eyes full of life and vivacity.' The four volumes bearing the name of John Gregorson Campbell, three published after his death and two after Nutt wrote his memoir, entitle him to a front rank among Celtic folklorists.

In assessing his work, Nutt did not hesitate to compare the minister of Tiree with his great namesake, and even credited the clergyman with a broader range for covering semi-historic traditions. He praised too the minister's skilful translations as equal to the expert Gaelicized English of Islay's *Popular Tales.*

> Readers of this volume cannot fail to note the exceeding skill with which the pithy, imaginative turns of thought, so plentiful in the original, are rendered into English. The reader is at once taken out of nineteenth century civilisation, and, which is surely the first thing required from the translator, by the mere sound and look of the words carried back into an older, wilder, simpler and yet, in some ways, more artificially complex life. The difficulty of rendering Gaelic into English does not lie in the fact of its possessing a rude simplicity which the more sophisticated language is incapable of reproducing, but rather in that, whilst the emotions and conceptions are close to the primitive passions of nature in a degree that our civilisation has long forsworn, the mode of expression has the richness of colour and elaborate artificiality of a pattern in the Book of Kells.[1]

This masterful statement measures the achievement of the leading collectors of Gaelic folktales, Irish and Scotch both, in their dual role as fieldworkers and library translators.

Yet for all his pleasure at the minister of Tiree's good work, Nutt betrayed an uneasiness. With his own literary taste in folklore, he could not hide his disappointment at the failure of the Gaelic storytellers to develop their rude chronicles of clan warfare into artistic histories on the order of the Icelandic sagas. Surely the models of their own mythological and heroic cycles should have equipped the Highland narrators with examples of conventions and formulas in the epic manner. But where they did structure their local traditions, they followed the rustic folktale rather than the heroic epos. In-

[1] Nutt, 'Memoir of the late John Gregorson Campbell,' in John G. Campbell, *Clan Traditions and Popular Tales of the Western Highlands and Islands* (London, 1895), pp. xv–xvi.

structive examples could be spied of 'the action and reaction upon each other of folk-life and oral narrative legend.'[1] But why was their so little literary outcome? What explained this curious Gaelic lapse? Nutt posed these questions to the fraternity of Celtic scholars. One suspects that the publisher was here revealing a chink in his folklore erudition, in lack of sympathy for the oral folk history enjoying its own form and style, wholly dissimilar to the grand flourish of epic poems and chronicles.

Without the essays and notes of Nutt, the *Waifs and Strays* would have remained a parochial series of local collections, valuable in content but amateurish in format. Nutt gave the materials intellectual significance, bringing them into the orbit of international scholarship, indicating their values for the cultural historian of the Celt, defining the enigmatic problems they presented. An Englishman, he sounded a trumpet call to Scottish nationalists to repossess their heritage, forget the silly distraction of the Ossianic controversy, and concentrate on the genuine oral riches at their disposal. The often naïve prefaces and observations of the well-intentioned clergymen—Campbell ended *The Fians* with acclaim for Macpherson—faded into the background before the broad learning of Nutt, whom no one could accuse of narrow Highland filiopietism.

As Campbell of Islay had noted, the tellers of romance lingered only in the western Highlands and islands but the bearers of the fairy creed could be found throughout Scotland. They divulged their beliefs in conversational asides and personal anecdotes lacking in stylistic pattern but falling into a connected system. Dalyell had surveyed these ideas in *The Darker Superstitions of Scotland*, working from the records of the witchcraft trials and older theological writings. Now a new spate of books peered into the hidden world of bogeydom. The desire to purge unchristian observances receded before the folkloristic interest in pre-Christian conceptions while the hortatory words of the author gave way to the spoken words of farmers and fisherfolk.

A transitional work, *Folk Lore: or, Superstitious Beliefs in the West of Scotland within this Century*, was written by the antiquary James Napier and published in Paisley in 1879. For a definition of superstition Napier proposed 'Beliefs and practices founded upon erroneous ideas of God and nature.'[2] His interest lay in the pagan retentions discernible among the preceding generations, misled by what

---

[1] Nutt, in *ibid.*, p. xviii.
[2] James Napier, *Folk Lore: or, Superstitious Beliefs in the West of Scotland within this Century* (Paisley, 1879), p. 4.

[413]

he called Romish and Protestant 'churchmanship.' Still, he made obeisance to the newly formed Folk-Lore Society and hoped that his instances noted in the district west of Glasgow might spur comparative studies of beliefs concerning birth, childhood, marriage, death, animals, plants, witchcraft, second-sight, the Black Art, charms, and divination. Napier presented his case histories in an impersonal, admonitory prose, but occasionally an incident he witnessed comes to life. He himself had been treated in youth for the evil eye. Taken with a mysterious affliction called a *dwining*, he was inspected by a nearby 'skilly' who recognized the aftereffects of 'a blink of an ill e'e.' The skilly placed the lad on a chair before a burning fire in the grate, filled a tablespoon with water, dipped into it a sixpence covered with salt, stirred the salt with her finger until it dissolved, bathed the soles of Napier's feet and the palms of his hands three times with the solution and had him taste it three times, then drew her wet forefinger across his brow. This last act was known as '*scoring aboon the breath.*' The skilly then cast the remaining contents of the spoon into the back of the fire, saying, '*Guid preserve frae a' skaith.*' The boy was then put to bed and duly recovered. Forty years later he diagnosed the 'superstition' as a relic of an ancient form of fire-worship.[1]

'Epoch-making' was the term applied by a sober scholar half a century after its publication to the Reverend Walter Gregor's *Notes on the Folk-Lore of the North-East of Scotland.*[2] The Folk-Lore Society issued Gregor's work in 1881 as their first published field collection. While hardly an epochal achievement, since Gregor covered much the same ground as Napier, the minister from Aberdeenshire did move much closer to oral sources and order his materials more clearly and fully. Throughout his pages he inserts dialect texts of charms, riddles, rhymes of places, animals and birds, formulas, holiday songs, sayings, and counting-out rhymes. In chapters on 'Farming' and 'Boats and Fishing,' he demonstrates how folk custom permeated the livelihoods of the villagers. Continuing the vein opened up by Chambers, the minister from Aberdeenshire sets down local and family legends embalmed in prophetic verses.

> At Gight three men a violent death shall dee,
> And after that the land shall lie in lea.

[1] James Napier, *Folk Lore: or, Superstitious Beliefs in the West of Scotland within this Century* (Paisley, 1879), pp. 36–7.
[2] J. M. McPherson, *Primitive Beliefs in the North-East of Scotland* (London, New York, Toronto, 1929), p. v.

23. JOHN RHYS

24. DOUGLAS HYDE

Lord Haddo fell to his death from his horse on the 'Green of Gight' in the year 1791. A farm servant died violently some years later. When the home farm was being turned into lea, a workman remarked that the third death had not yet occurred. Shortly a wall fell upon him, fulfilling the prophecy.[1]

In a brief but vivid chapter, 'Evenings at the Fireside,' Gregor sketches the physical setting in which the family circle regaled themselves with songs, stories, and riddles by the light of fir candles or eely dollies (iron oil lamps) before a blazing peat fire. 'The story was for the most of the supernatural—of fairies and their doings, of waterkelpie, of ghosts, of witches and their deeds, of compacts with the Devil, and what befell those who made such compacts, of men skilled in *black airt*, and the strange things they were able to do.'[2] These were the themes pursued by Gregor. He remained primarily the local collector, citing a few references to the first three volumes of the *Folk-Lore Record*, Henderson, and *Choice Notes*, and for Europe, Ralston and De Gubernatis.

An unconventional work adding to the published store of north Scottish lore resulted from the chance visit of Oxford's Bodleian librarian to scenic Golspie. When Edward W. B. Nicholson was journeying in a holiday mood along the northeast coast, he lighted upon the hospitable village, put up at the Sutherland Arms, walked past girls playing a ring game, wrote up a proposal for a prize competition, and a folklore book was born. The plan conceived in 1891 bore fruit in 1897, under the Nutt imprint, as *Golspie, Contributions to Its Folklore*. Nicholson placed the names of seven pupils in the Golspie school along with his own as co-authors, and printed in italics their essays on folklore.[3] Commenting upon them at length, he hoped 'by explanation and illustration to make a substantial contribution of my own to the study of British folklore.'[4] For his comparative references the librarian listed half a dozen books he had chiefly consulted, starring those he felt belonged in every British library. These prized titles included Gregor, Henderson, Burne-Jackson's *Shropshire Folk-Lore*, the Scotch rhymes of Chambers and English rhymes of Halliwell and G. F. Northall, and the games of Mrs. Gomme and Newell. Napier he relegated to the unstarred

[1] Walter Gregor, *Notes on the Folk-Lore of the North-East of Scotland* (London, 1881), p. 111. [2] *Ibid.*, p. 56.
[3] The full title page reads *Golspie, Contributions to its Folklore*, by Annie and Bella Cumming, Jane Stuart, Willie W. Munro, Andrew Gunn, Henri J. MacLean, and Minnie Sutherland (when pupils of Golspie School). Collected and edited, with a chapter on 'The Place and its Peopling,' by Edward W. B. Nicholson, M.A., Bodley's Librarian in the University of Oxford (London, 1897).
[4] *Ibid.*, p. 4.

group. Since Lady Gomme's second volume of *The Traditional Games of England, Scotland, and Ireland* had not appeared in 1896, he wrote her requesting proof sheets, with which she kindly obliged him, down to 'Sally Waters,' the point they had reached. Nicholson also drew upon his own collateral study, *The Vernacular Inscriptions of the Ancient Kingdom of Albano* (1896), unravelling the Pictish inscriptions of Scotland, Orkney, and Shetland.

Nicholson acknowledged that before his trip to Golspie he had merely browsed in folklore. He knew of The Folk-Lore Society and its journal and 'priceless' Handbook, only regretting that a copy of the 1890 publication had taken three years to reach the Bodleian, else in 1891 he could have put many more questions to the students. This is an interesting commentary on the blocks to intellectual communication in the period, and one wonders why the Bodleian's librarian could not have learned of the work on his own and purchased it for the half a crown he thought so cheap. At any rate, he volunteered astute suggestions to the Society. Instead of being just a London organization, let it initiate branches in every town and village and undertake collecting in the primary and secondary schools, as a means of reaching the adult carriers of tradition. Look what one lone collector had accomplished in this way in the far north! Let the branch societies offer prizes for the folklore, the old songs, the dialect vocabularies, the accounts of history and antiquities.

The contents offers a sampler of folklore genres, from goblin legends to ghost tales, superstitions, games, rhymes, songs, and similes. Only a modicum of stories came to light, although Nicholson believed more could be found among the Gaelic-speaking fishermen. Still, under 'Celtic Stories' he is able to place several reports of water-kelpies.

Nicholson's definition of superstition as personal belief in irrational and motiveless action by invisible beings is an advance over Napier's equation of superstition with false religion. Lang evinced interest in the Golspie project. The border Scot wrote Nicholson, who had sent him a ghost story, that over a forty-year period he had never heard of a ghost in Morrvich House, although he had stayed there several times. And he sent the librarian an obscure reference to the rhyme of 'Poor Tom.'

Nicholson's ideas would be put into practice with useful results in later times and other places. There is irony in an outsider to the British folklore movement advancing proposals which could have greatly strengthened the movement at its weakest point, systematic field collecting in the counties.

[416]

As Gregor advanced over Napier, so John Gregorson Campbell advanced over Gregor in *Superstitions of the Highlands and Islands of Scotland* (1900) by printing texts of narratives embodying beliefs rather than simply enumerating the bare beliefs. In this respect the mistitled *Superstitions* resembled the *Fairy Legends* of Croker, save that Campbell properly gave the exact words of the tellers. The minister of Tiree declared in his Preface that he had procured every account by word of mouth from Gaelic speakers, even excluding information sent by correspondents. Previous writers thinking in English had, he added, misinterpreted Gaelic expressions and modes of thought. Campbell's own favourite term, 'popular tales,' failed to denote the personal reports of supernatural experiences assembled in his collection. The *Superstitions* spread before the reader a full table of fairy anecdotes relating the behaviour and actions of the elfin people as they came in contact with human beings. In two cases Highlanders fled to America to escape fairy mistresses who pursued them thither. The Glaistig, a human being with a fairy nature, described as 'a thin grey little woman, with long yellow hair reaching to her heels, dressed in green,' haunted houses and castles and, like the fairies, was given to midnight meddling and could render herself invisible.[1] A strong man named MacCuarie in Lochaber once met a Glaistig by a stream, carried her to his house, and kept her until she built a large barn, all in one night. She left him with a blessing and a curse, that the MacCuaries would grow like rushes but wither like ferns. And so they did; his children grew up tall, straight, and handsome and then in their prime wasted away.

Increasingly the collectors became absorbed in the human possessors of occult powers, the casters of the evil eye, the second-sighted, the men and women of magic. In 1899, Alexander Mackenzie resurrected *The Prophecies of the Brahan Seer*, with an introduction by Andrew Lang on 'The Brahan Seer and Second Sight.' Lang pointed out that the seventeenth-century seer, Kenneth Mackenzie, belonged with the crystal-gazers. A tenth edition of the little book was in print forty-three years later. In 1901, another work from John Gregorson Campbell's manuscripts, *Witchcraft and Second Sight in the West Highlands*, gave oral accounts of witches and seers. In 1902, Robert C. MacLagan devoted a whole volume, published by Nutt, to cases and treatments of the *Evil Eye in the Western Highlands*. (The year before MacLagan had published *The Games and Diversions of Argyleshire* through The Folk-Lore Society.)[2] A book

---

[1] John Gregorson Campbell, *Superstitions of the Highlands and Islands of Scotland* (Glasgow, 1900), p. 155.
[2] Other relevant writings of Robert Craig MacLagan are *Scottish Myths, Notes on*

of writings on *Highland Second-Sight*, edited by Norman Macrae with an 'introductory study' by the Reverend William Morrison, was locally printed in Dingwall in 1908. The editor began with these bold words: 'In the Folk-Lore of the Scottish Highlanders there is no chapter more extraordinary or interesting in its way than that which deals with the stories of the Second-Sight—a "gift," notwithstanding the ridicule of the unbelieving, that to the present day, in one or another of its manifestations, is not uncommon among the Highland people.' Macrae brought together selections from noted travellers and authors, excerpting from Martin Martin's *Description of the Western Islands of Scotland*, Aubrey's *Miscellanies*, Pepys' correspondence, Boswell's and Johnson's accounts of their Hebridean journey, and in the customary climax, the prophetic utterances of the Brahan seer.

A kind of leftover volume from the *Waifs and Strays* was edited in 1910 by the Reverend George Calder from the manuscripts of the Reverend James MacDougall under the title *Folk Tales and Fairy Lore in Gaelic and English, Collected from Oral Tradition*. MacDougall, minister of Duror, had contributed twice to the *Waifs and Strays*. This final selection from his trove presented eight wonder tales of kings and smiths, sailors and dragons, and a larger store of 'Tales about Fairies, Fairy-Men, Fairy-Knollers, Little Men, or Good People' and solitary creatures such as the Glaistig and the Urisk.

By 1914 a substantial shelf of books exposed the folk traditions of the Scottish Gaels. Campbell of Islay's initial quest had yielded bounteous harvests, not only of oral narratives but also of oral poetry and proverbial lore. Carmichael contributed many Gaelic proverbs for the new edition by George Henderson (compiler of *The Popular Rhymes, Sayings and Proverbs of the County of Berwick*, 1856), of Sheriff Alexander Nicholson's *A Collection of Gaelic Proverbs and Familiar Phrases*, first printed in 1881. The compilations of Henderson, Nicholson, and other proverb and rhyme collectors assisted Andrew Cheviot in preparing *Proverbs, Proverbial Expressions, and Popular Rhymes of Scotland* in 1896. Cheviot argued the point, through notes and parallel phrases, that Scotland possessed numerous sayings distinct from England. Few would have denied in the second decade of the twentieth century that Gaelic Scotland, at any rate, owned an ample and absorbing body of folklore.

Scottish History and Tradition (Edinburgh, 1882); *The Perth Incident of 1396 from a Folk-Lore Point of View* (Edinburgh and London, 1905); and *Our Ancestors, Scots, Picts, & Cymry, and What Their Traditions Tell Us* (London and Edinburgh, 1913).

WALES

In a long look at Welsh stories in the last volume of his *Popular Tales,* Campbell compared adventurous episodes in the fifteenth-century manuscript of the *Mabinogion,* as translated by Lady Charlotte Guest, and the nineteenth-century Highland tales he had collected and found them strikingly similar. Incident after incident matched up: of knights slaying giants and monsters, of formidable tasks performed by heroes with the aid of supernatural helpers, of King Arthur and Fionn each hunting after a magic boar. One long tale of enchantments centring on a falsely substituted queen bride was collected by John Dewar in the Highlands in 1862 much as it had been written down in Wales four centuries earlier, and Campbell recognized it as the romance of Cupid and Psyche found sixteen centuries before that in Apuleius' *Golden Ass* and again in the Arabian Nights. So the Welsh and Scotch popular tales joined with medieval and Eastern romances and Norse mythology and European peasant fictions in a world-wide community of Aryan story.

Enticing and mysterious prospects beckoned in Wales. Linked with the Gaelic tongue of Scotland and Ireland, yet separate in her own Brythonic speech, secure in her heritage of medieval romance, Wales could await with confidence the inspections of a modern folklorist.

The cause of Welsh folklore found its most eminent spokesman in the Right Honourable Sir John Rhys (1840–1916), a distinguished philologist who served as active member and vice-president of The Folk-Lore Society. Born in Cardiganshire of yeoman farmer stock, he remained ever a firm Welsh patriot in the midst of English academic honours and renown. Rhys became the first professor of Celtic at Oxford in the chair established in consequence of the Celtic Revival inspired by Matthew Arnold, was elected principal of Jesus College, knighted in 1907, and appointed to the Privy Council in 1911. His scholarly writings include *Lectures on Welsh Philology* (1877), *Celtic Britain* (1882), *Lectures on the Origin and Growth of Religion as illustrated by Celtic Heathendom* (1888), and *Studies in the Arthurian Legend* (1891). The Welshman's broad intellectual interests in archaeology, history, and comparative philology eventually extended to folklore and brought him into the London circle of folklorists. He enjoyed close relations with Nutt and Hartland.

In 1901, Rhys brought together the scattered researches of

thirty years in two thick volumes titled *Celtic Folklore, Welsh and Manx.* Stimulated by the work of Campbell of Islay, he had begun searching for popular tales and bardic romancers in Wales, but he turned up only 'bits of stories.' From time to time he had printed his fragmentary findings in *Folk-Lore* and *Y Cymmrodor.* Now he reprinted them with digests of earlier collections and his own philosophizings in what he himself recognized as a discursive, loose-jointed affair. Originally he had planned to present Welsh fairy traditions in the first part and analyse them in the second, but the two parts tended to leak into each other, and rather than abandon the work and unwilling to subject it to complete revision he chose to issue the manuscript as it stood.

After the overflowing abundance revealed by the Scotch collectors, *Celtic Folklore* makes a sorry showing. Where Campbell and Carmichael had displayed before the world the unsuspected reservoirs of Gaelic lore, Rhys makes plain the unexpected poverty of the Welsh oral tradition, and his chief accomplishment appears to be the spinning out of seven hundred pages to make the point. In his anxiety for bona fide, fully developed oral texts, he resorts, in one instance, to a Scotch variant from Chambers to piece out his Welsh fragment, in another to a florid version written out for him by a novelist, and in yet another to a hypothetical tradition based upon a chance conversation in a railway station. While waiting at the Abbey Dore station, the eager collector queried an elderly couple about the fairies. The wife, a Mrs. Elizabeth Williams, remembered that the lady of the house where she once worked told servant girls to tidy everything up before going to bed or the little people—'the fairies, she thinks she called them'—would come and pinch them. As a leading question, the don asked if the fairies might leave presents, like a shilling, for neat servants; Mrs. Williams thought so, and 'her way of answering me suggested that this was not the first time she had heard of the shilling.'[1] This feeble utterance is a far cry from a night-long Fenian saga. In the usual plaint of folklorists, Rhys regrets that he has not commenced his collecting earlier, when a young village schoolmaster on the island of Anglesey. At every opportunity he deviates from his repetitive fairy legends to trace out etymologies of Welsh words and names.

Celtic Folklore emerges as a cross between a country field book and a mythological treatise. Its author alternates between the roles of gentleman interviewer courteously interrogating the peasantry and scholarly don applying the most recently approved theories to his texts. A country vicar would have confined his efforts to a

[1] John Rhys, *Celtic Folklore, Welsh and Manx,* 2 vols. (Oxford, 1901), I, 192–3.

straightforward inventory of water nymphs, fairies, changelings, and spirits abiding in lakes, wells, and caves. Gomme or Hartland would have analysed the primitive mentality and racial deposits concealed in the folklore documents. Rhys tries to do both.

The Oxford don did ferret out and strew through his opus a number of legendary traditions, some with the original Welsh texts, dealing with fairydom. Correspondents captured samples for him, friends took him calling on the rustics, he combed the literary records from medieval chroniclers to nineteenth-century annalists, and from 1881 on, when he began writing his book, he questioned the natives on his rambles through the Welsh counties and the Isle of Man. If the results follow the well-established patterns of fairy encounters with mortals and related folklore themes, they serve Rhys as a springboard for learned speculations.

Dwellers on the Isle of Man call the first male to cross the family threshold on New Year's day the *qualtagh* or 'first-foot.' The family regards him as a harbinger of good luck and treat him hospitably, unless perchance he should be *spaagagh* or splay-footed. Rhys muses on this usage. Perhaps the non-Aryan aborigines as a small nimble people moved more agilely than their slower Aryan conquerors, whom they accordingly nicknamed 'the flat-footed.' Rhys himself had found English shoes too low for him in the instep, and once when speaking to Welsh undergraduates found they agreed with him, with the one exception of a tall, powerful football player of suspiciously light colouring. Karl Blind had complained as a German about English bootmakers in *Folk-Lore* in 1892, conjecturing that he as a south German from hilly country might have a higher instep than dwellers in flat countries.[1] The same reasoning might apply to Celts. So the *qualtagh* might not after all be associated with race.[2]

While visiting Llandeilo Llwydarth in north Pembrokeshire in search of inscriptions, Rhys heard from a local landlady that water given from St. Teilo's well in the skull of St. Teilo would cure a patient suffering from whooping cough. She showed him the skull. Later, he heard a brief legend saying the saint had instructed his serving-maid to use his skull at the well for therapeutic purposes. The principal of Jesus surmised that Christian missionaries had chosen the well as a church site because it was already considered

---

[1] Karl Blind, in *Folk-Lore*, III (1892), 89, in a 'Discussion' printed following the paper by Rhys on 'Manx Folk-Lore and Superstitions, II.' Gomme and Nutt also participated in the discussion, and a concluding note requested that further information be addressed to J. Jacobs and the envelope marked 'First-foot' in the left-hand corner. Karl Blind wrote in a correction of his misquoted views on 'The Flat-Foot Question' in the same volume, pp. 429–32. [2] Rhys, *Celtic Folklore*, I, 342.

sacred by the aborigines. Now the well paganism had annexed the saint, and while the church had fallen into decay, the ritual of well and skull persisted, pointing back to 'an ancient priesthood of a sacred spring.'[1]

Visiting the Isle of Man, Rhys listened to stories about the fenodyree, a hairy, clumsy chap who helped friendly farmers. One such anecdote told how the fenodyree rounded up a farmer's wethers but had to chase a little ram three times around Snaefell before he caught up with him. On checking his herd, the farmer found the ram to be a hare. Rhys recognized the folktale from its appearance in the *Mabinogion* and in versions of the Great Fool cited by Nutt in his *Studies on the Legend of the Holy Grail*. (The tale has travelled to the American West where it is attached to a tenderfoot cowboy herding jack rabbits.) Yet when Rhys visited Glen Rushen, supposedly the home of the fenodyree, he could find no one who knew of the goblin, and rued that he had departed before the inroads of the English tongue and culture.

Such were the wisps with which Rhys had to content himself and assuage his readers. One wonders how successfully the Oxford don established rapport with the folk. Interrogating an old soldier on the Isle of Man, he explained that Welsh contained four terms for the Devil, the use of which immediately fixed the social status of the speaker, while the Greek source was limited to one word. Over-awed, the Manxman could not recall any matters connected with the fairies or the fenodyree.

In his theorizing, the Welsh philologist uses the guidelines laid down by Tylor and Hartland, Gomme and Clodd, whose names recur regularly throughout his pages. Rhys presented several papers to The Folk-Lore Society, one on the spirits of wells to a joint meeting with the Cymmrodorion Society in 1893, and these, subsequently printed in *Folk-Lore*, stirred up further contributions of which he availed himself in the final book. A three-way discussion developed between Rhys, Gomme, and Hartland in the pages of *Folk-Lore* in 1892 and 1893 on the subject of pin-wells and rag-bushes. Sir John believed the rag tied to the well tree was anciently regarded as the receptacle of the disease and the pin, bead, button, or coin thrown into the well was intended as an offering to the spirit of the well. Gomme gave evidence to show that both the button and the bit of clothing were treated as an offering. Hartland then in a searching paper lumped rag and pin together as equal instances of the belief in sympathetic magic; as these objects acquired the effluence of divinity through contact with the well spirit, the dis-

[1] Rhys, *Celtic Folklore*, I, p. 400.

ease left their owner. Rhys accordingly revised his view to consider the article thrown into the well as a special means of connecting with the spirit, and gave several supporting examples from Wales.[1]

In three long closing chapters, Rhys presents his scattered reflections on folklore problems. Before 'Folklore Philosophy' he places a quotation from Clodd on the inconsistency yet inner logic of savage thought, and to introduce his final chapter on 'Race in Folklore and Myth' he quotes Lang in criticism of philological mythology. (The chapter preceding these two, on 'The Difficulties of the Folklorist,' quotes at its head Dryden on the priestly banishment of goblins.) The fluid and evanescent nature of oral traditions bothered the philologist, who remarks on the shifting line between myth and history in the minds of the speakers. Considering the origins of the fairy belief, he favours the thesis of racial memories harking back to a 'swarthy population of short stumpy men occupying the most inaccessible districts of our country.'[2] The conquering people around them regarded the thieving aborigines in their midst as auspicious personages and powerful magicians. Earlier, Rhys had mentioned as other possible origins the popular awe of ancestral ghosts and the popular reverence for demons and divinities of lakes, streams, and bays. The unnamed reviewer in *Folk-Lore*—probably Hartland—queried why the fairy belief could not just as well have inspired the notion of a dwarfish, pre-Celtic race. He also took Rhys to task for reworking his address at the 1891 Congress into his final chapter without warning his readers they were reading 'Chips from a Welsh Workshop.'[3] In that address and chapter, Rhys advocates a marriage between mythology and 'glottology,' as he called comparative philology. The affinity between Latin and Celtic presupposes a similarity of rites and customs, so that light on the relationship of words could well throw light on mythological matters. Although a comrade in arms of the anthropological folklorists, by intellectual predilection Rhys would have favoured the companionship of Max Müller. He did indeed have solar sympathies.

In spite of its diffuse character, *Celtic Folklore* served the cause of Welsh and Manx tradition by capping and to some extent synthesizing the labours of earlier antiquaries and collectors. The extensive lists of references at the beginning of the work, arranged

[1] In addition to comments by Rhys and Gomme printed in *Folk-Lore* in 1892 (see note 1, page 421), Rhys wrote on 'Sacred Wells in Wales' and Hartland on 'Pin-Wells and Rag-Bushes' in *Folk-Lore* in 1893 (IV, 55–77, 451–70); Rhys commented further in *Celtic Folklore*, I, 360 ff.
[2] Rhys, *Celtic Folklore*, II, 668–9.　　　　　[3] *Folk-Lore*, XII (1901), 114–16.

both alphabetically and by counties, covers all the relevant literature up through 1900, and in the book Rhys regularly samples appropriate legends known to his predecessors.

He seems to have missed the first publication on Cambrian folklore with a modern title, *Welsh Legends, A Collection of Popular Oral Tales*, printed in London in 1802 for J. Badcock. The author begins with impressive promises: 'There is hardly any Traveller in Wales, who had not heard, at least, of the titles of some of these ancient traditionary tales, which every grandmother, on a cold winter evening, repeats to her grandchildren, sitting round the blazing hearth.'[1] But he writes up his 'local mythology' in the flowery literary manner of the day.

Rhys did find some value in two books that appeared before Thoms coined the term 'folklore.' Peter Roberts, rector of Llanarmon and vicar of Madeley, wrote in 1815 *The Cambrian Popular Antiquities, or An Account of Some Traditions, Customs, and Superstitions of Wales, with Observations as to their Origin, &c. &c.* The rector drew up his 'tract on Popular Customs and Superstitions of Wales at the request of Mr. Williams, the Bookseller,' who had issued his earlier writings.[2] Roberts finds many of the popular antiquities in Brand common to England and Wales; others, of greater interest, are shared by Scotland and Wales and suggest to him a common Celtic origin. The antiquary notes such matters as corpse candles and fairy kidnappings, which later collectors would amplify, and a strange ceremony practised by the 'lower orders' in north Wales known as 'lifting,' in which a bride is raised aloft in a chair by brawny males. Well-worship arouses his ire as a 'superstition of Paganism' that constitutes a 'disgrace to a Christian country.'[3] Roberts was always more the churchman than the folklorist.

In 1831 William Howells moved closer to oral sources in *Cambrian Superstitions, Comprising Ghosts, Omens, Witchcraft and Traditions, &c.* The youthful author, two years short of his majority, responded to an advertisement in the *Carmarthan Journal* for May 21, 1830, offering a prize of twenty guineas and a medal valued at three guineas 'for the *best printed* English Essay, 8 vo. containing 500 pages, on the Superstitions, Ghosts, Legends, &c. of *all parts* of the Principality, to be delivered *before* Feb. 3, 1831.'[4] A tall order in a short time, but Howells stirred himself to

[1] J. Badcock, *Welsh Legends, A Collection of Popular Oral Tales* (London, 1802), p. iv.
[2] Peter Roberts, *The Cambrian Popular Antiquities* (London, 1815), p. vii.
[3] *Ibid.*, p. 267.
[4] William Howells, *Cambrian Superstitions* (Tipton and London, 1831), p. v.

track down 'pure and unsophisticated' stories and managed to complete a book of one hundred and ninety-four pages, including a few 'Fugitive Pieces.' To guide him he consulted such works as Aubrey's *Miscellanies*, Grose's *Provincial Glossary*, Sir Walter Scott's writings and Cotton Mather's *Magnalia Christi Americana* with its numerous cases of witchcraft and providences.

Young Howells expressed a sense of Welsh folklore patriotism. He regretted that England, Scotland, and Ireland had outdistanced Wales in publishing their legends and traditions, and he singled out folk forms distinctive to Wales. The *bon vivant* was common among the ghosts of Wales in contrast to pallid English ghosts. Corpse candles, the sulphurous blue lights of varying brilliancy veering toward the churchyard where the doomed person would come to rest, 'were universally known to be endemic' to Wales.[1] A bishop of St. David's, while burning at the stake, prayed that the candles might be seen in Wales as a memorial to his martyrdom. People in north Wales became distraught at the sight of corpse candles, not knowing whose death they might portend. Welshmen also witnessed spectral funerals preceding actual ones.

About thirty years ago, there was a rumour which many of the old inhabitants of Carmarthen may recollect, of the singular appearance of three of these funerals *at noon*, near Cwm-dyvran, when several people were reaping in a field not far distant, and one observing them, called out to the rest, when all, to the number of about *twelve*, beheld them for a considerable time moving along; in the course of the week three deaths occurred, and the three funerals passed the way where their forerunners were seen, at the same time. These are a sort of processions that I never heard took place *any* where but in Wales.[2]

Elsewhere Howells remarked how nearly 'every village in Wales formerly had its witch or cunning man, as those of Scotland had their seers, which were esteemed, consulted and revered as much as the oracle of Delphi. . . .'[3] While dismissing saints' legends as so much 'popish blarney,' the youthful collector did relate a number of graphic fairy abduction legends, speculating that the Saxon fairies derived from the Welsh. (Rhys criticized Howells for incorrect transcriptions of Welsh terms but quoted from him freely.)

Another work Rhys invoked necessarily but with a certain reluctance was written by the United States consul for Wales, Wirt Sikes, who in 1880 wrote *British Goblins: Welsh Folk-lore*,

[1] *Ibid.*, p. 59.   [2] *Ibid.*, pp. 55–6.   [3] *Ibid.*, p. 77.

Fairy Mythology, Legends, and Traditions, dedicated to Albert Edward, Prince of Wales. Sikes packed a good deal of information and many illustrative stories into his four sections on 'The Realm of Faerie,' 'The Spirit-World,' 'Quaint Old Customs,' and 'Bells, Wells, Stones, and Dragons.' Sikes exasperated Rhys and fellow folklorists like Hartland because of his insufficient and unsatisfactory statements of sources. The American consul drew from both literary and oral accounts of Welsh goblins. Tarrying at the Huntsman's Rest Inn outside Cardiff, he observed a group of 'humble folk' drinking tankards of ale, smoking long clay pipes, and talking about their dogs and horses, crops and hard times, and prospects of emigrating to America. At this juncture the consul entered the conversation with some suggestions and then steered the talk toward folklore and the fairies, with profitable results later placed in his book. A work confined to narratives obtained in this fashion would have proved a good deal slimmer but far more valuable, but in this respect Sikes resembled all the other Welsh writers on folklore who battened on previous compendiums. In one place Rhys quotes from Sikes who in turn had abstracted from Howells a tradition about fairies from the islands of Pembrokeshire attending the markets at Milford Haven and Laugharne.

Rhys knew personally and worked with a later group of collectors in the 1890's. They included Arthur W. Moore, author of *The Folk-Lore of the Isle of Man, being an Account of Its Myths, Legends, Superstitions, Customs, and Proverbs* (1891); the Reverend Elias Owen, who wrote *Welsh Folk-Lore, A Collection of the Folk-Tales and Legends of North Wales, Being the Prize Essay of the National Eisteddfod in 1887* (1896); and D. E. Jenkins, who edited the manuscripts of William Jones in *Bedd Gelert, Its Facts, Fairies, and Folk-Lore* (1899).

Moore and Rhys travelled together through back roads on the Isle of Man to talk with Manxmen who still feared the evil eye and demons of the night. Moore acknowledged the help of Rhys and his publisher, Alfred Nutt, in shaping his first chapter on 'Myths Connected with the Legendary History of the Isle of Man' and also attributed certain of his stories to Rhys. In turn, Rhys in *Celtic Folklore* thanked the Manx antiquary for informing him that the fairies of Man shot at mortals with bows and arrows and not guns. The better behaved fairies of Wales never shot with any weapon.[1] From Gomme's *Handbook of Folklore* Moore cited the definition of folklore as survivals and gleaned ideas for the arrangement of his topics under such headings as fairies, goblins, magic and witch-

[1] Rhys, *Celtic Folklore,* I, 293 n.

craft, proverbs and sayings, and customs and superstitions of the seasons, the elements, and the ages of man. Moore levied upon the early travellers George Waldron and Joseph Train and on Campbell of Islay who visited the island briefly in 1860 but long enough to assess the state of the traditions. He supplemented their accounts with his own orally collected texts, but regretted that no one had talked with the islanders while Manx was still a living tongue and before tourists had engulfed the Isle of Man.

Just as Howells had written the *Cambrian Superstitions* in 1831 in consequence of a prize competition, so did Elias Owen publish in 1896 a collection of *Welsh Folk-Lore* expanded from a prize-winning essay. Owen dealt with the supernatural traditions of the fairies, mythic animals, ghosts, witches, conjurers, and charms, omens, portents, and spiritualistic beliefs. Rhys cites Owen on the distribution of corpse candles and the sight of phantom funerals in north and south Wales; Welsh traditions of flying snakes turned into winged dragons after drinking milk spilled on the ground by pregnant, breast-heavy women—hence the taboo against such a means of relief; and the legend of the fairy wife who asked the children of her human husband whether they wished a dirty or a clean cow-yard. Those who asked for a clean cow-yard received no gift of cattle.[1]

Sir John Rhys wrote an Introduction for *Bedd Gelert, Its Facts, Fairies, and Folk-Lore* in which he confined his attention to the etymologies of place names. Its author, D. E. Jenkins of Portmadoc, based the work upon articles written by William Jones, who had won a prize at the local Eisteddfod of 1860 with an essay on the antiquities and folklore of Bedd Gelert and its environs. Rhys gave substantial space to Jones and his collection of fairy legends in *Celtic Folklore*, on the basis of personal correspondence and published and unpublished essays. A letter from Jones to Rhys gives a picture of the influences for and against tradition bearing on the life of a Welsh countryman in the middle decades of the nineteenth century.

> I was bred and born in the parish of Bedgelert, one of the most rustic neighbourhoods and least subject to change in the whole country. Some of the old Welsh customs remained within my memory, in spite of the adverse influence of the Calvinistic Reformation, as it is termed, and I have myself witnessed several Knitting Nights and Nuptial Feasts (*Neithiorau*). . . . At these gatherings song and story formed an element of prime

[1] *Ibid.*, p. 275; II, 690; I, 227.

importance in the entertainment at a time when the Reformation alluded to had already blown the blast of extinction on the Merry Nights (*Noswyliau LLawen*) and Saints' Fêtes (*Gŵyliau Mabsant*) before the days of my youth. . . .[1]

Jones went on to say that he had collected many tales from his close-knit kindred in the parishes of Bedgelert and Dolwydelen, mostly small farmers jealous of strangers. His ancestors had enjoyed stories, poetry, and singing, his parents had thought fondly of the past, and the son had grown up with a desire to excel at 'pedigrees and legends.' At his grandfather's house, at the blacksmith's shop, and from travelling storytellers like Twm Ifan Siams, still nimble though over ninety, Jones heard many wonders of water spirits and bogies, mermaids and fairies. Spry little Siams went from house to house reciting tales and pedigrees. One of his narrations closely resembled the tradition reported by the earliest Welsh collector, Edward Llwyd, in 1693, of an afanc enticed from the river Conwy to slumber on the lap of a maiden, with one hand on her breast; awaking to find himself bound in iron chains, he tore off and carried the breast with him in his claw and rushed back to his pool, only to be hauled out again by oxen and men hanging onto the chains. When the peasants began arguing as to who had done most to pull out the afanc, he quieted them by singing,

> Had it not been for the oxen pulling,
> The afanc had never left the pool.[2]

With Jones' manuscripts at his disposal, Jenkins should have brought forth a volume of some interest, but his *Bedd Gelert* amounts to little more than a tourist's guide to scenic spots and historic dwellings decked out with place legends and anecdotes. While Jenkins too refers to the 'merry nights' (he calls them 'pleasant evenings') enlivened by harpers, melodious singers, and popular raconteurs, all he actually delivers are slight accounts of local ghosts, practical jokes, and goblin haunts. But one notorious legend outlasted the Calvinistic Reformation to give Bedd Gelert a certain claim to folklore distinction, and to this legend of Llewellyn and his faithful dog Gelert, Jenkins devotes one curious chapter.

According to the tradition, Llewellyn returned from the hunt to find his babe's cradle overturned and his dog Gelert with jaws dripping blood and wagging his tail in greeting. At once he struck his sword into the greyhound and only then did he lift the cradle

[1] Rhys, *Celtic Folklore*, I, 75–6 (letter translated by Rhys from the Welsh).
[2] *Ibid.*, p. 131.

to find the babe alive and a dead wolf close by. The grief-stricken prince gave Gelert an honourable burial. Hence the Welsh proverbs, 'Before revenge, first know the cause' and 'Reflect twice before striking once.' Jenkins considers in detail the investigations of Baring Gould in *Curious Myths of the Middle Ages* and Joseph Jacobs in *Celtic Fairy Tales*, tracing the far-flung appearances of the story in Asia and Europe. To doubters who might cavil that the episode could have occurred in fact and in more than one place, Jacobs replies that the ever-present moral of warning against a rash action gives the scene its folklore quality. By tricky detective work he claims to have uncovered the path of the legend into Wales, assigning the second edition of Edward Jones' *Musical and Poetical Relicks of the Welsh Bards* (1794) as the point of entry.[1]

Jenkins disparages the arguments of the two comparative folklorists who sought to deprive Bedd Gelert of her prized association. Neither could spell Welsh proper names (Gelert not Gellert, Llewelyn not Llewellyn), but he realizes the futility of expecting English writers to spell Welsh words correctly. In addition, Baring Gould had selected an inferior version and Jacobs had erred in his reconstruction. In point of fact, the antiquary of Bedd Gelert, William Jones, had traced the route of the fiction, which had been brought into town from south Wales in 1793 by the first landlord of the Royal Goat Hotel, David Prichard, a waggish storyteller. So Jenkins concludes his defence with a surprise twist; he concedes the international circulation of the Gelert drama but awards the honours to a hometown antiquary, while still claiming for the community the attraction of a now firmly rooted myth. When townspeople gravely repeat the little saga of Llewelyn and Gelert to inquiring visitors and point out the grave, only a close observer would notice that their eyes are twinkling. According to Jenkins, not the natives but the tourists are gulled.

After Rhys' central study, the course of Welsh folklore turned back from theoretical flights to repetitive collections of local legends and beliefs. Some distinction was given Marie Trevelyan's *Folk-Lore and Folk-Stories of Wales* in 1909 by the helping hand of Sidney Hartland. Hartland's enthusiasm for Welsh folklore extended from his early article of 1888 in the *Archaeological Review* on 'The Physicians of Myddfai,' about the fairy maiden of Van Pool who married a shepherd and taught her sons magical remedies, to his edition, finally printed in 1923, of Walter Map's *De Nugis Curialium*, a twelfth-century manuscript called by Rhys a 'curious

---

[1] Joseph Jacobs, *Celtic Fairy Tales* (London, 1892), pp. 259–64.

miscellany of anecdotes and legends.'[1] Miss Trevelyan acknowledges Hartland's aid in arranging her materials and providing a
brief but trenchant Introduction. In turn, the Gloucester solicitor
applauds the new addition to Cambrian folklore as a volume
worthy to be placed alongside those of Elias Owen and Rhys and
to succeed such memorable medieval chroniclers of Welsh marvels
as Geoffrey of Monmouth, Giraldus Cambrensis, and Walter Map.
Recognizing that he cannot be overly optimistic in encouraging
Welsh folklorists, Hartland chooses to strike a muted note. In the
traditions of Wales he senses a mood of 'sombre mysticism,'
noticeable also in the Celtic population of Scotland and Brittany.
This mood is most evident in the haunting legends of the Cŵn
Annwn or hounds of the underworld who howl and bay while on
the track of their prey, in the recurrent sighting of corpse candles
and spectral funerals, and in the eerie beliefs connected with death
and transformation. Folk stories often deal with Death coming in
person to claim his victim. The transformation theme of the swan
maidens, common in European *Märchen*, takes the form of *Sagen*
on the wild coast of Gower and in Whitmore Bay in Glamorgan,
where young farmers and hunters are said to have captured lovely
young swan wives, only to lose them when their brides find their
swan feathers and fly away as birds. Hartland is particularly struck
by the 'weird story of the Vampire Chair.' A Dissenting minister
visited a farmstead in Glamorgan, converted from an old dower
house splendid with period furniture. After sitting in a quaint old
armchair and sleeping in the handsome bed, he found teethmarks
on his hand and side from which blood flowed, and similar marks
on his grey mare in the stable. The minister explained to his hosts
that the dead owner of the furniture had returned as a vampire to
suck the blood of intruders. 'It has happened to two ministers
before,' said the goodman of the house, 'but not to the ministers'
nags.'[2]

In her Preface, Miss Trevelyan cites Wesley's influence in Wales
and the religious revival of the 1850's as factors inhibiting the old
folklore. In the present volume she deliberately eschewed fairy lore
in order to concentrate on superstitions and rites of the earth and
sky, animal life, and the calendar year.

The transit of Welsh folklore studies from broadly comparative
to local and patriotic concerns is complete in the 1911 publication
Folk-Lore of West and Mid-Wales by Jonathan Ceredig Davies, who
identified himself on the title page as a 'Member of the Folk-Lore

[1] Rhys, *Celtic Folklore*, I, 70.
[2] Marie Trevelyan, *Folk-Lore and Folk-Stories of Wales* (London, 1909), p. 56.

25. LADY ISABEL PERSSE GREGORY

26a. LACHLIN MACNEILL the storyteller dictating to CAMPBELL OF ISLAY and HECTOR MACLEAN the schoolteacher and transcriber on Islay in 1870.

26b. *Below.* DONALD MACPHIE the storyteller of South Uist, drawn by CAMPBELL OF ISLAY who describes him in *Popular Tales of the West Highlands* (see *Peasant Customs and Savage Myths* edited by R. M. Dorson, Vol. II, London and Chicago, 1968, pages 669-70).

Society.' His relative, Alice, Countess Amherst, suggested he compile such a book, and it was printed at the *Welsh Gazette* office in Aberystwyth and financed by subscription. The author, an Anglican churchman who had lived in the Welsh colony in Patagonia and western Australia, visited old men and women in Cardiganshire, Carmarthenshire, and Pembrokeshire to learn their traditions. He heard much about witches, wizards, and death signs but little about the fairies. Davies himself often had portentous dreams and had dreamed in detail of the death of Lady Kensington when she was in India. His anecdotal album covers courting, wedding, and funeral customs, feats of conjurers and charmers, appearances of demons and spirits, and reports of prophecies, curses, and judgments. Such were the common folk fancies with which Welsh folklorists had to rest content after a century of searching for a modern Mabinogion.

IRELAND

The electrifying discoveries in the folklore of the Scottish Gael impelled collectors to seek comparable treasures among the Gaelic-speaking Irish. While the sudden sensation produced by Campbell's efforts in Scotland gradually declined, excitement steadily mounted in Ireland as fieldworkers moved closer to the Gaelic fountainhead. The first climax came with the publication in 1890 of Douglas Hyde's *Beside the Fire, A Collection of Irish Gaelic Folk Stories.* Alfred Nutt was the publisher and not unexpectedly added a 'Postscript' to Hyde's Preface and additional notes to Hyde's notes in felicitous conjunction. Hyde had thoroughly assimilated the work of his predecessors, which he now reviewed in his Preface, appraising their strengths and weaknesses, and he pointed the way for a mature, scientific, and truly national folklore movement in Ireland.

Since Croker's day various hands, not always with proper care, had worked with the multitude of Irish narrative traditions. The Dublin bookseller Patrick Kennedy had opened a window into the treasure house of Irish story with books of tales he had heard growing up in County Wexford in the first two decades of the nineteenth century. In the Pale, many of the Gaelic recitations had slipped over into English, the new tongue of the peasantry. Kennedy placed on record in *Legendary Fictions of the Irish Celts* (1866), *The Fireside Stories of Ireland* (1870), and *The Bardic Stories of Ireland* (1871) a wide range of traditional narratives, from international *Märchen* to ghost stories, saints' legends and, most precious of all, adventures of the Ossianic heroes. But still these remained imperfect English representations of the Gaelic originals.

Another cache was uncovered by Lady Jane Francesca Wilde, the mother of Oscar, noted in her own right as 'Speranza,' a glamorous hostess at literary teas in Dublin's Merrion Square. Speranza brought out in her own idiosyncratic way *Ancient Legends, Mystic Charms, and Superstitions of Ireland* (two volumes, 1887) and *Ancient Cures, Charms and Usages in Ireland* (1890), grab bags of spells, remedies, notions, and invocations. Many of Speranza's materials came from the collections of her husband, the talented Dr. William Wilde. In a little book on *Irish Popular Superstitions* (1852) Dr. Wilde printed a list of 'Queries' on various items of seasonal rite, household custom, and local belief. When Lady Wilde gathered together the responses to these inquiries obtained from Irish and Anglo-Irish peasants, she neglected to identify individuals and localities or to attempt comparative interpretation. Still, Hyde appreciated her charms and usages as intimate disclosures of the Irish folk mind, and William Butler Yeats praised the *Ancient Legends* as the most ample and poetic collection of Irish folklore.

In 1871 an American of Irish ancestry and remarkable linguistic gifts arrived on the scene. Jeremiah Curtin had begun a series of visits to the land of his parents. In 1887 he travelled to the western counties, recording mythic tales from the Gaelic-speaking peasantry, the first time a collector had directly tapped traditions in existence for over a thousand years. Two years later he published twenty long narratives in *Myths and Folk-Lore of Ireland,* unfortunately without naming and locating the storytellers.

This was the stage at which Hyde surveyed the Irish folklore scene. Growing up in Connacht as a member of the Anglo-Irish aristocracy, he was sent to England for his schooling, but illness compelled him to return to Ireland and there, like Campbell of Islay, he learned Gaelic from gamekeepers and workmen. In time Hyde became Ireland's foremost cultural patriot, founder of the Gaelic League to revive and renew Irish speech, song, dance, costume, and nomenclature, professor of Irish at University College, Dublin, historian of Irish literature, playwright and play actor in native Irish dramas, associate of Lady Gregory and Yeats in the Irish Renaissance, and finally the first president of the Republic of Eire. Hyde brought to synthesis the causes of the Irish language, the science of folklore, and the intellectual independence of the Irish people.

Hyde examined the work of previous collectors in the light of his demanding standards. Earlier transcribers and rewriters of Irish lore had failed to give the exact words of the tellers, and even Curtin, who came closest, did not fully capture the folk style and committed some errors because he was dependent upon interpreters. For instance, he mistakenly introduced a stork, a non-Hibernian bird, into one story, confusing the English word with *sturc*, a bullock, or *torc*, a wild boar.

But at least Croker and Kennedy, Lady Wilde and Curtin had recognized the urgent need to scour the land for Irish traditions. They were a handful of exceptions in an apathetic nation. Hyde pointed out unhappily that the *Encyclopaedia Britannica* article on 'Folklore' listed fifty authorities without mentioning a single Irish name. 'We have as yet had no folk-lorist in Ireland who could compare for a moment with such a man as Iain Campbell of Islay, in investigative powers, thoroughness of treatment, and acquaintance with the people, combined with a powerful national sentiment, and, above all, a knowledge of Gaelic.'[1] It was Hyde himself who possessed these qualities, although he did not develop fieldwork on the intensive scale achieved by Campbell. In *Beside the Fire* and its main source book, *Leabhar Sgeulaigheachta* (1889), he strove for accuracy and naturalness of text and completeness of supporting information. His baker's dozen of long tales (six with the Gaelic text) related magical adventures befalling king's sons, wealthy farmers, clever tailors, gentlemen hunters, Finn and his dog Bran, the lad Guloesh Blackfoot who never washed his feet, and Balor with the evil eye. Hyde chose them for their variance from the specimens of Campbell and MacInnes, but there was no mistaking their kinship with Scotch Gaelic narrations.

What was the relationship of the Irish Gaelic tales to both their Scotch counterparts and late medieval Irish manuscripts? Hyde is quick to point out how 'triangulation' on a given problem can solve perplexing questions. On first comparing Irish manuscripts with oral peasant tales, he had concluded that the scribes of an earlier day invented their fictions. In one manuscript he came across a one-eyed, one-handed, one-legged monster more like a devil than a man, which he was prepared to dismiss as a figment of the scribe's imagination, until he recalled the hideous Fàchan in Campbell's West Highland tales. Accordingly he altered his view and posited that both texts derived from a common Gaelic source. After further comparisons, and bearing in mind that the warrior O'Connor Sligo, mentioned in the manuscripts, invaded Munster in 1362, Hyde decided that many such Scoto-Irish compositions had taken their modern form late in the fourteenth or early in the

[1] Douglas Hyde, *Beside the Fire* (London, 1910), p. xvi.

fifteenth centuries on Irish soil and then travelled to the Highlands in the keeping of an Irish bard. Two or three hundred years after the bardic compositions had become stock Gaelic folktales, the Irish scribes wrote them down in still surviving manuscripts. The romance of Conall Gulban, Campbell's longest text and one widely told through Scotland and closely matched in Irish manuscripts, was a case in point. 'Conall Gulban' must date from the fifteenth century, although describing the exploits of a fifth-century chieftain, because the story carried an allusion to the Turkish attack on Constantinople.

Turning from the 'detritus of bardic stories' peculiar to the Gael, Hyde considered the large mass of traditions found outside as well as within Ireland. These traditions comprehended nature myths, Aryan wonder tales, and conversational anecdotes about fairies, ghosts, water horses, and other spectral figures. While Hyde would not go so far as Rhys in identifying Cuchulain with Hercules as a sun god, he had no hesitation in reading into folktales primeval symbols of sun, clouds, rainbows, and lightning. A Czech variant in Wratislaw's *Sixty Folk-Tales from Exclusively Slavonic Sources* gave Hyde the key to the prince's marvellous companions in 'The King of Ireland's Son' in *Beside the Fire*; they personified the rainbow, lightning, and clouds. So the apparently modern Irish story derived from an Aryan source at least three thousand years old.

Hyde closes with a ringing plea to save the Gaelic tongue and Gaelic tales from obliteration by English schoolmasters, the Catholic clergy, and misguided Irish parliamentarians. His remarks on the decay of narrative art, the technical difficulties in translating the oral idiom from Gaelic into English—he checked Campbell on some overly archaic renditions—and the mechanics of collecting are pertinent today. The whole Preface forms a manifesto for Irish folklorists.

In his 'Postscript,' Nutt turns his analytical powers on the vexing questions raised by Hyde. The publisher promptly, and properly, takes exception to the dating of folktales by such slippery internal evidence as references to O'Connor Sligo and Turkish forces who might be merely replacing earlier heroes and ogres. Similarly he cavils at the argument for a common antiquity in the Czech-Irish parallels of the marvellous helpers, recognizing the claim for simple borrowing. Mainly he ponders the relation of the bardic stories to the peasant folktales. How did the folk reciters respond to the compositions of the bards and professional storytellers whom Gaelic chieftains maintained at their courts from the twelfth to the sixteenth centuries? 'This I hold to be the vital lesson the folklorist may learn from considering the relations of Gaelic folk-tale and Gaelic romance . . . that romance, to live and propagate itself among the folk, must follow certain rules, satisfy certain conceptions of life, conform to certain conventions.'[1] Because the Irish bards had remained in tune with their countrymen, their productions proved palatable to the peasantry. Folk reciters recognized the 'older, wilder conceptions' which the bards themselves had originally inherited from the peasantry of an earlier day. What would and would not the folk digest? A voyage from Hakluyt, a novelette from Defoe, George Meredith's literary fairy tale 'The Shaving of Shagpat'? Not the Highland crofters, asserted Nutt, for such writings failed to satisfy the moral and aesthetic conventions of the Highland folk fancy. He proceeded to isolate the formulaic, fatalistic, and animistic conventions governing the various classes of Gaelic oral narrative. Nursery tales and god sagas strike an optimistic note, heroic epos and popular ballads sound the knell of doom. Within the Fenian saga the ballad accounts sing of death and desolation while the prose versions laud the successful deeds of Fionn. Nutt sees myth and epos as nourishing the folklore soil in which they flourished. Irish bardic literature draws upon an earlier, and invigorates a later, folk tradition. Court bards and peasant reciters preserve the same prehistoric conception of the cosmos.

In the illuminating notes at the end, as in their essays in the beginning, Hyde and Nutt join forces to explicate the tales. Most often Hyde laments some Irish institutions extinguished in modern times, such as the *pattern* or festival honouring a patron saint with much revelry, mentioned in 'The Court of Crinnawn.' Usually Nutt looks analytically at the story elements. To him 'The Court of Crinnawn' appears to be a 'curious mixture of common peasant belief about haunted raths and houses, with mythical matter probably derived from books.'[2] Both commentators raise searching questions. Why, Hyde asks, have the nonsense endings so popular in Irish tales all but disappeared in the Scotch? ('They gave me paper stockings and shoes of thick milk. I lost them since.') Had Finn's wife been substituted for the Virgin Mary in 'William of the Tree,' or had the Virgin replaced an older heathen goddess in the German variant, queries Nutt.

In *Beside the Fire*, as in *Waifs and Strays*, a package of Gaelic wonder legends comes wrapped in handsome scholarship, even more impressive in the Irish collection since two powerful minds rather than one are on display. Hyde and Nutt make palpable the

[1] Nutt, in *Beside the Fire*, p. liii. [2] *Ibid.*, p. 192.

historic, literary, and national importance of Irish Gaelic folktales. Their dialogue points up the intricate relationship of oral compositions by the *ollamhs* or court bards to the later bardic manuscripts and to modern Gaelic folktales. Henceforth collectors must record the oral texts of Gaelic-speaking peasant narrators with all the care given any valuable document or manuscript recording the past. *Beside the Fire* and its anticipated sequels would join the *Book of Kells* as precious sources for students of the Irish heritage.

Nutt also adds a Preface to Jeremiah Curtin's *Tales of the Fairies and of the Ghost World Collected from Oral Tradition in South-West Munster* which he published in 1895. In less than five pages he raises the level of the work from a Croker-like collection of fairy legends—although far superior in its accurate recording of conversational narratives in a Dingle farmhouse—to a fresh revelation of the Irish mind. The publisher singles out an anecdote of a man who died in 1847 to show it was actually based on an archaic romance and still retained the name of Lochlin, the 'mythic marvelland.' Again, he points to a narrative in which a wizard-lord merges into the character of St. Martin. These devoutly believed narrations leave questions about the philosophy and outlook of the Gaelic-speaking peasant. Did he distinguish between fairy and ghost? Was the ghost idea the result of Christian influence or did it precede the coming of the Aryan Celts? The fairy mounds mentioned by one teller had signified graves during two thousand years of Gaelic civilization. 'Has the whole fairy belief sprung out of ancestor-worship, and, after passing through a brilliantly romantic form in the minds of poets, is it reverting to its pristine shape in the minds of the peasant?'[1] The publisher ends with the hope that the collector will one day write a treatise resolving these enigmas.

In 1892 Joseph Jacobs turned happily away from the lean pickings in England to the overflowing abundance of Scotland and Ireland for the children's fairy-tale series he enriched with skilful scholarly notes and references. In that year he edited and Nutt published *Celtic Fairy Tales*, followed two years later with a sequel, *More Celtic Fairy Tales*. Finding the pure Gaelic narratives on the mournful side, Jacobs drew also from the English-speaking Pale in Ireland and Scotland where comic Paddy indulged in gay anecdotes. Jacobs sympathized with the unlucky Welsh collectors and congratulated their Gaelic cousins who had uncovered in Finn and Cuchulain cycles of national hero-legends matched only by the Russians. Jacobs calculated that fieldworkers had amassed some

---

[1] Nutt, Preface to Jeremiah Curtin, *Tales of the Fairies and of the Ghost World* (London, 1895), p. viii.

2,000 Celtic folktales, although only 250 were in print. Campbell of Islay counted 1,281 tales in his files. Finland alone exceeded the Celts with a count of 12,000.

In both volumes Jacobs tenders tribute to Nutt, his antagonist in the debate over diffusion. The editor dedicates the first book to his publisher, praises Nutt's writings on the Celtic folktale in the *Celtic Magazine* (Vol. XII), *Waifs and Strays, Beside the Fire,* and the *Studies on the Legend of the Holy Grail,* a work showing the impetus given European romance in the twelfth century by Celtic hero-tales. 'Thanks to Mr. Nutt, Scotland is just now to the fore in the collection and study of the British Folk-Tale.'[1] In the preparation of the twin volumes, the publisher had ever been the editor's mentor and adviser and had even contributed the two orally collected Irish tales of 'Hudden and Dudden and Donald O'Neary' and 'Andrew Coffey.'

Jacobs also sings the praises of the Celtic folktale. It serves the student of literature with its poetic charm, the evolutionist with its traces of thousand-year-old Celtic beliefs, and the diffusionist with its strategic situation at the end of the Indo-European chain of transmission. Admitting he himself is no Celticist, Jacobs hopes that native Celts will continue the noble task of folklore research in their lands, abetted by the 'newly revived local patriotism of Ireland and the Highlands.' Clearly the 'only considerable addition to our folk-lore knowledge in these isles must come from the Gaelic area.'[2] In any other European country some national means of recording this artistic heritage would long since have been adopted, laments Jacobs, pointing to the example of the French Minister of Public Instruction commissioning François-Marie Luzel to collect and report on Breton folktales.

On the score of provenience, the two books give Ireland the nod. All but five of the twenty-six tales in the first selection were known in Ireland. Jacobs did not give a tabulation for the second volume, but a count shows he chose nine from Irish, seven from Scotch, two from Welsh sources, and one from combined Irish and Scotch variants. Ireland clearly offered him the greater variety, with manuscript versions and the collections of Croker, Lover, Griffin, Carleton, Kennedy, Curtin, Lady Wilde, Larminie, and Hyde. For Scotland he relied on Campbell and the *Waifs and Strays* series, and for Wales he had to scrounge isolated literary extracts from the *Mabinogion,* Giraldus Cambrensis, and W. R. Spencer's poem of 1800 on the celebrated legend of Beth [*sic*] Gelert.

---

[1] Joseph Jacobs, *Celtic Fairy Tales* (London, 1892), p. 239.
[2] Jacobs, *More Celtic Fairy Tales* (London, 1894), pp. x, 219.

Folklorists regret Jacobs' mutilation of the tale texts for juvenile consumption, but they respect the 'Parallels' and 'Remarks' he furnishes in appendixes for each tale. Naturally he does not miss the opportunity to demonstrate East-West diffusion. In his commentary on 'Conall Yellowclaw,' a tale from Campbell, he notes that a printed version exists in an Irish chapbook called *Hibernian Tales* and was there read by Thackeray, who abstracted it in his *The Irish Sketch-Book, 1842*, calling it 'The Black Thief' (Conall being the thief), a tale worthy of the Arabian Nights and 'as wild and odd as an Eastern tale.'[1] Jacobs seizes on the comparison and extends it to other examples of the framework device incasing a tale within a tale, a device familiar in the Jatakas, Boccaccio, Chaucer, Queen Margaret, and now in Gaelic variants of Conall Yellowclaw. Was the framework idea independently invented in Ireland? No, thinks Jacobs, it was probably an importation. For instance, the incident of Conall blinding the one-eyed giant and escaping past him clothed in a buck's skin obviously echoes the Polyphemus story in the *Odyssey* and was known in Ireland from perhaps the tenth century.

As a sign of his fairness, Jacobs concedes that the method of survivals would apply to the 'Dream of Owen O'Mulready,' since it is known only in Ireland and centres on the highly primitive notion that spirits cluster around the hearth. A workman places his bed on the hearth to dream and dreams he is taking a letter to America on the back of a crane, then wakes to find himself climbing up the chimney. (Hyde believed the trick of the dream to explain away a visit to the fairies a late development to storytelling.) Jacobs neglects to speculate on the destination of the dreamer before the discovery of America.

This reading was but a sop to the foe. Commenting on Croker's 'The Legend of Knockgrafton,' which he reprints in *More Celtic Fairy Tales*, Jacobs sees 'a problem of diffusion presented in its widest form.'[2] Known in Ireland for two hundred years, the subject of a poem by the great Parnell, and now newly collected in Japan, this story of the good old man whose hump is removed by the demons and the bad old man whose hump is doubled by the demons must be a migratory fiction, and indeed appears to be migrating still. (This is Type 503, *The Gifts of the Little People*.) With examples such as these Jacobs seeks to advance his claim that Gaelic folktales offer the best evidence for the study of diffusion.

[1] Jacobs, *Celtic Fairy Tales*, p. 246; William Makepeace Thackeray, *The Irish Sketch-Book, 1842* (London, 1843), p. 191.
[2] Jacobs, *More Celtic Fairy Tales*, p. 231.

The calls of Nutt and Jacobs for native Irish collectors to set out after their own traditions did not long go unanswered. Hyde himself continued to publish books of folklore both in Gaelic and in English, and in *Love Songs of Connacht* (1893) brought to light a moving lyric strain of Gaelic oral poetry. Hyde's example encouraged William Larminie, a civil servant trained in the classics, who had contributed to *Beside the Fire* the tale of 'Neil O'Carre' told in an unusual, cryptic style, to assemble a superior collection of *West Irish Folk-Tales and Romances* (1893). Meanwhile the towering figure of William Butler Yeats entered the scene, turning over the pages of Irish folktale volumes in the British Museum in London to put together two anthologies, *Fairy and Folk Tales of the Irish Peasantry* (1888) and *Irish Fairy Tales* (1892) with the hope of stimulating Irish poets. His own fancy played upon folk fancies, and he wrote a sketchbook full of folklore reverie in *The Celtic Twilight* (1893). Yeats gibes at scientific folklorists, criticizing Nutt, praising Hyde. Still, when Edward Clodd showed Yeats a sheaf of County Louth traditions, the poet expertly noted County Sligo variations, and *Folk-Lore* printed his comments in 1899.[1] Yeats knew a number of fairy beliefs told him by Sligo relatives and was himself supposed to have been transported by the fairies one night on a four-mile journey.

In her country estate at Coole, Lady Isabella Persse Gregory read *The Love Songs of Connacht* and *The Celtic Twilight* and was stirred to do for her own Galway what Hyde had done for Connacht and Yeats for Sligo. Eventually the widow and the poet traipsed together through Galway's countryside gathering peasant legends in the Gaelicized English that would transform their own literary styles and inflame their imaginations. From this experience Lady Gregory wrote and compiled in the first two decades of the twentieth century memorable books of folklore, cherished and sometimes expanded by Yeats. Hyde often joined their circle at Coole, and the three gave leadership to the cause of casting out the imposed culture of England and reasserting the traditional culture of Ireland. In this cause folklore proved one of their most powerful assets. With their efforts the independent history of the Irish folklore movement begins and the long exciting history of English folklore theory and collection ends in rejection and darkness.[2]

[1] Yeats' notes appeared in *Folk-Lore*, X (1899), 119–22, following Bryan J. Jones' 'Traditions and Superstitions collected at Kilcurry, County Louth, Ireland.'
[2] Further details on the Irish folklore movement are given in my Foreword to *Folktales of Ireland*, ed. Sean O'Sullivan (Chicago and London, 1966).

EPILOGUE

The fading of the British folklore movement may be viewed as one of the collateral tragedies of the Great War. One can simply scan the sharply reduced volumes of *Folk-Lore* from 1918 on to see how the lean years followed the fat ones. But no one can know the loss of human talent due to the attrition of war. Reginald J. E. Tiddy was one clear-cut case of a talented young folklorist killed in wartime who left behind the rough manuscript of a valuable work, published in 1923 as *The Mummers Play*. With the gradual shrinkage of Empire the splendid colonial laboratory of folklore dwindled. The establishment of the Republic of Eire lopped off from the British trunk the most flourishing branch of folklore fieldwork. Professor James Delargy, assistant to Douglas Hyde at University College, Dublin, founded in 1939 an Irish Folklore Commission now housing tens of thousands of oral folktales, and cultivated contacts with Scandinavian folklorists. After the Great War, the brilliant amateur scholar largely passed from the scene. Lang, Nutt, and Gomme had died by 1914, Jacobs had gone to America, and no vigorous younger lights took their places. As scholarship became more and more an academic profession, the university increasingly usurped the role played in the nineteenth entury by the learned society of gifted amateurs. But folklore never gained academic acceptance. Her sister-subject anthropology fared well at Oxford and Cambridge, but the inheritors of Tylor's science concentrated on social organization and turned their backs on fairy tales.

The stirring debates over the mind of early man that had once kept all Victorian England in thrall yielded to the old antiquarianism. An international folklore congress again was held in London in 1928, but this congress lacked a guiding theme or the dramatic clash of philosophies and ended as another congeries of papers. Dutifully, The Folk-Lore Society continued to issue the series of Calendar Customs exfoliating from Brand's *Popular Antiquities*. Where once the vitality of the folklore movement had extended into many adjacent areas and captivated specialists in a host of subjects—philology, archaeology, anthropology, Celtic studies, Scandinavian studies, zoology, the classics, the history of religions, psychical research, law, medicine, political institutions, in fact the cultures and literatures of the world—now other concepts and approaches invaded the diminishing boundaries of the province of folklore. With enthusiasm growing for the performance rather than the study of traditional music and dance, the English Folk Dance

[440]

and Song Society, based at Cecil Sharp House in London, waxed in popularity. Survival gave way to Revival. From museums and institutes a compelling interest developed in the material culture rather than the oral literature of the folk, leading to the creation of a Society for Folk Life Research in 1962, with strong centres at the Welsh Folk Museum in Cardiff and the Ulster Folk Museum in Belfast.

Still all was not lost. Worthy folklorists in the tradition of the private scholar have continued to emerge in England. Peter and Iona Opie received honorary degrees from Oxford University in 1962 for their excellent field investigations of children's folklore, continuing the researches of Halliwell-Phillipps and Lady Gomme and breaking much new ground in *The Oxford Dictionary of Nursery Rhymes* (1951) and *The Lore and Language of Schoolchildren* (1959). The vein of fairy mythology and witchcraft explored by Keightley, Scott, and Hartland was further mined in the notable history of idea studies by Katharine Briggs, *The Anatomy of Puck* (1959), *Pale Hecate's Team* (1962), and *The Fairies in Tradition and Literature* (1967). On the score of field discoveries, the *Tales from the Fens* (1963) and *More Tales from the Fens* (1964) of the articulate and witty Fenman W. H. Barrett revealed a whole new genre of local-history traditions. In Scotland, the collections made by John Lorne Campbell, laird of the Isle of Canna, continued the labours of his famous namesake, and the School of Scottish Studies in the University of Edinburgh began in 1951 a systematic exploration of Scottish oral lore. (High points of the contemporary scene in folklore and folklife studies in Great Britain and Ireland are viewed in a special issue of the *Journal of the Folklore Institute*, II, no. 3. [1965].) Overseas, Verrier Elwin enhanced the splendid achievements of English collectors in India, although it is a sign of changed times that he ultimately became a citizen of India.

Yet in a sense the story that began with Camden's history of Britannia and reached its apogee at the outbreak of the Great War is complete. A firm thread runs from Camden to Lang and holds together a brilliant chapter of intellectual history.

Bibliography

Over the years I have written a number of articles on the British folklorists, and some of these are now incorporated in the present history: 'The First Group of British Folklorists,' *Journal of American Folklore*, LXVIII (1955), 1–8, 333–40 [Croker, Keightley, Wright, Douce]; 'Hugh Miller, Pioneer Scottish Folklorist,' in *Studies in Folklore in Honor of Distinguished Service Professor Stith Thompson*, ed. W. E. Richmond (Bloomington, Indiana, 1957), pp. 92–109; 'Andrew Lang's Folklore Interests as Revealed in "At the Sign of the Ship,"' *Western Folklore*, XI (1952), 1–19; and 'The Eclipse of Solar Mythology,' *Journal of American Folklore*, LXVIII (1955), 394–416. Of 'The Great Team of English Folklorists,' *idem*, LXIV (1951), 1–10, about all that remains is the title.[1]

ABBOT, GEORGE F., ed. *Macedonian Folklore*. Cambridge, 1903.

——— *Songs of Modern Greece*. Cambridge, 1900.

ADDY, MARY GOLDEN. *A Miscellany: Sidney Oldall Addy and Family*. Croydon, 1937.

ADDY, SIDNEY OLDALL. *Household Tales with other Traditional Remains*. London and Sheffield, 1895.

ADLINGTON, WILLIAM, trans. *The Most Pleasant and Delectable Tale of the Marriage of Cupid and Psyche*. With a discourse by Andrew Lang. London, 1887.

ALEXANDER, JAMES. *An Expedition of Discovery into the Interior of Africa*. London, 1838.

ALLEN, GRANT. *The Evolution of the Idea of God*. London, 1897.

ALLIES, JABEZ. *On the Ancient British, Roman and Saxon Antiquities of Worcestershire*. London, 1840. 2nd ed. titled *On the Ancient British, Roman, and Saxon Antiquities and Folk-Lore of Worcestershire*. London and Worcester, 1852.

——— *On the Ignis Fatuus, or Will-o'-the-Wisp, and the Fairies*. London and Worcester, 1846.

ANDERSEN, HANS CHRISTIAN. Fairy Tales from *Hans Andersen*. Introduction by Edward Clodd. London, 1901.

An Essay on the Study of Antiquities. Oxford, 1782.

Anthropological Essays presented to E. B. Tylor in Honour of his 75th Birthday Oct. 2, 1907. Oxford, 1907.

ARNOLD, RICHARD. *Chronicle of the Customs of London*. London, 1521.

ASBJÖRNSEN, PETER, and JORGEN MOE. *Norske Folke-eventyr*. Christiania, 1843.

ASHTON, JOHN. *Chap-Books of the Eighteenth Century*. London, 1882.

ATKINSON, JOHN C. *Forty Years in a Moorland Parish*. 2nd ed., London, 1891.

AUBREY, JOHN. *Brief Lives*. 2 vols., Oxford, 1898. Edited by O. L. Dick; London, 1949.

——— *Miscellanies*. London, 1696; 2nd ed., London, 1721.

——— *Remaines of Gentilisme and Judaisme*. Edited and annotated by James Britten. London, 1881.

[1] So little attention has been given the subject that the Public Records Office and the British Museum Reading Room cannot supply dates of some well published nineteenth- and twentieth-century writers on folklore.

BIBLIOGRAPHY

BARING-GOULD, SABINE. *A Book of Fairy Tales*. London, 1894.
———— *A Book of Folk-Lore*. London and Glasgow, 1913.
———— *A Book of Ghosts*. London, 1904.
———— *The Book of Were-Wolves*. London, 1865.
———— *Curious Myths of the Middle Ages*. London, Oxford, and Cambridge, 1866. 2nd series, London, Oxford, and Cambridge, 1868.
———— *English Minstrelsie: A National Monument of English Song*. 8 vols., Edinburgh, 1895–7.
———— *Fairy Tales from Grimm*. London, 1895.
———— *A Garland of Country Song*. London, 1895.
———— *Old English Fairy Tales*. London, 1895.
———— *Songs and Ballads of the West*. London, 1891.
BARRETT, W. H. *More Tales from the Fens*. London, 1964.
———— *Tales from the Fens*. London, 1963.
BASILE, GIOVANNI. *Il Pentamerone*. Naples, 1674.
BATCHELOR, JOHN. *The Ainu and Their Folk-Lore*. London, 1901.
BAXTER, RICHARD. *The Certainty of Worlds of Spirits*. London, 1691.
BAYNE, PETER, ed. *The Life and Letters of Hugh Miller*. 2 vols., Boston and London, 1871.
BEERS, HENRY A. *A History of English Romanticism in the Eighteenth Century*. London, 1899.
———— *A History of English Romanticism in the Nineteenth Century*. London, 1902.
BENHAM, MARIAN S. *Henry Callaway M.D., D.D. First Bishop for Kaffraria, His Life-History and Work*. London, 1896.
BERNARD, BAYLE. *The Life of Samuel Lover*. 2 vols., London, 1874.
Bibliotheca Brandiana . . . Being the Entire Library of the late Rev. John Brand. London, 1807.
BIRLINGER, ANTON. *Volksthümliches aus Schwaben*. 2 vols., Freiburg, 1861.
BLACK, WILLIAM GEORGE. *Folk-Medicine*. London, 1883.
BLEEK, M. W. H. *The Suk, Their Language and Folklore*. Oxford, 1911.
BLEEK, WILHELM H. I., *Brief Account of Bushman Folk-Lore and Other Texts*. London and Cape Town, 1875.
———— *A Comparative Grammar of South African Languages*. London and Cape Town, 1862.
———— *Reynard the Fox in South Africa*. London, 1864.
BLEEK, WILHELM H. I., and LUCY C. LLOYD. *Specimens of Bushman Folklore*. London, 1911.
BLOUNT, THOMAS. *Fragmenta Antiquitatis, Antient Tenures of Land, and Jocular Customs of Some Mannors*. London, 1679.
BOMPAS, CECIL HENRY, trans. *Folklore of the Santal Parganas*. London, 1909.
BORLASE, WILLIAM. *The Natural History of Cornwall*. Oxford, 1758.
BOSQUET, AMÉLIE. *La Normandie romanesque et merveilleuse*. Paris and Rouen, 1845.
BOSWELL, JAMES. *The Journal of a Tour to the Hebrides, with S. Johnson*. London, 1785.
BOURNE, HENRY. *Antiquitates Vulgares*. Newcastle, 1725.
BRAND, JOHN. *Observations on Popular Antiquities: including the whole of Mr. Bourne's Antiquitates Vulgares*. Newcastle upon Tyne, 1777.
———— *Observations on Popular Antiquities: Chiefly Illustrating the Origin of*

Our Vulgar Customs, Ceremonies, and Superstitions. Arranged and revised, with additions, by Henry Ellis. 2 vols., London, 1813.

BRAY, ANNA. *A Description of the Part of Devonshire Bordering on the Tamar and the Tavy.* 3 vols., London, 1836. Reissued as *The Borders of the Tamar and the Tavy,* 2 vols., London, 1879.

——— *A Peep at the Pixies; or, Legends of the West.* London, 1854.

BRIGGS, KATHARINE M. *The Anatomy of Puck.* London, 1959.

——— *Pale Hecate's Team.* London, 1962.

——— *The Fairies in Tradition and Literature.* London, 1967.

BROCKIE, WILLIAM. *Legends and Superstitions of the County of Durham,* Sunderland, 1886.

BROWN, ROBERT. *Eridanus: River and Constellation.* London, 1883.

——— *The Great Dionysiak Myth.* 2 vols., London, 1877–8.

——— *The Law of Kosmic Order.* London, 1882.

——— *Mr. Gladstone As I Knew Him, and Other Essays.* London and Oxford, 1902.

——— *The Myth of Kirkê.* London, 1883.

——— *The Religion and Mythology of the Aryans of Northern Europe.* London, 1880.

——— *The Religion of Zoroaster.* London, 1879.

——— *Researches into the Origin of the Primitive Constellations of the Greeks, Phoenicians and Babylonians.* 2 vols., London, 1899–1900.

——— *Semitic Influence in Hellenic Mythology.* London, Edinburgh, Oxford, 1898.

——— *The Unicorn: A Mythological Investigation.* London, 1881.

BROWNE, THOMAS. *Pseudodoxia Epidemica: Enquiries into Vulgar and Common Errors.* London, 1646.

BROWNE, WILLIAM. *Britannica's Pastorals.* London, 1613.

BURNE, CHARLOTTE. *The Handbook of Folklore.* Revised ed., London, 1914.

——— ed. from the Collections of Georgina F. Jackson. *Shropshire Folk-Lore: A Sheaf of Gleanings.* London, Shrewsbury, Chester, 1883.

BURTON, RICHARD F., trans. *A Plain and Literal Translation of the Arabian Nights Entertainments.* 10 vols. Benares, 1885–6. *Supplement,* 6 vols., 1886–8.

——— *Wit and Wisdom from West Africa.* London, 1865.

BURTON, ROBERT. *The Anatomy of Melancholy.* Oxford, 1621.

BURTON, ROBERT, or RICHARD. Pseudonym for Nathaniel Crouch.

BUSK, RACHEL H. *The Folk-Lore of Rome.* London, 1874. Retitled *Roman Legends,* Boston, 1877.

——— *The Folk-Songs of Italy.* London, 1887.

——— *Household Stories from the Land of Hofer.* London, 1871.

——— *Patrañas; or Spanish Stories, Legendary and Traditional.* London, 1870.

——— *Sagas from the Far East.* London, 1873.

——— *The Valleys of Tirol.* London, 1874.

CALDER, GEORGE, ed. *Folk Tales and Fairy Lore in Gaelic and English.* From the manuscripts of James MacDougall. Edinburgh, 1910.

CALLAWAY, HENRY. *Nursery Tales, Traditions, and Histories of the Zulus.* Natal and London, 1868.

——— *The Religious System of the Amazulu, Izinyanga Zokubula; or,*

Divination, as Existing Among the Amazulu, in Their Own Words. Natal, Capetown, London, 1870. Reissued London, 1884.

CAMDEN, WILLIAM. *Britannia.* London, 1586.

—— *Remaines of a Greater Worke, concerning Britaine.* London, 1605.

CAMPBELL, ARCHIBALD, ed. *Waifs and Strays of Celtic Tradition, I, Argyll-shire Series.* London, 1889.

CAMPBELL, JAMES M., ed. *Notes on the Spirit Basis of Belief and Custom.* Bombay, 1885.

CAMPBELL, JOHN FRANCIS. *Frost and Fire.* 2 vols., Edinburgh, 1865.

—— *Leabhar na Feinne. (Heroic Gaelic Ballads).* London, 1872.

—— *My Circular Notes.* London, 1876.

—— *Popular Tales of the West Highlands.* 4 vols., Edinburgh, 1860–2. Reissued London, 1890–3.

—— *A Short American Tramp in the Fall of 1864.* Edinburgh, 1865.

—— *The Celtic Dragon Myth.* Edited by George Henderson. Edinburgh, 1911.

CAMPBELL, JOHN GREGORSON. *Clan Traditions and Popular Tales of the Western Highlands and Islands.* Edited by Jessie Wallace and Duncan MacIsaac. London, 1895.

—— *The Fians.* London, 1891.

—— *Superstitions of the Highlands and Islands of Scotland.* Glasgow, 1900.

—— *Witchcraft and Second Sight in the Highlands and Islands of Scotland.* Glasgow, 1902.

CARMICHAEL, ALEXANDER. *Carmina Gadelica, Hymns and Incantations.* 2 vols., Edinburgh, 1900. 2nd ed., 5 vols., Edinburgh and London, 1928–54.

Catalogue of the Greater Part of the Library of the late Thomas Crofton Croker. London, 1854.

Catalogue of the Printed Books and Manuscripts Bequeathed by Francis Douce, Esq. to the Dodleian Library. Oxford, 1840.

Catholic Truth Society. *Folk-Lore Ex Cathedra.* London, 1896.

CHAMBERLAIN, BASIL HALL. *Aino Folk-Tales.* London, 1888.

CHAMBERS, ROBERT. *A Biographical Dictionary of Eminent Scotsmen.* 4 vols., Glasgow, 1835.

—— *Cyclopaedia of English Literature.* 2 vols., London and Edinburgh, 1901–03.

—— ed. *The Book of Days.* 2 vols., London and Edinburgh, 1862–4.

—— *Illustrations of the Author of Waverley.* Edinburgh, 1823; 2nd ed. 1825; 3rd ed., London and Edinburgh, 1884.

—— *Minor Antiquities of Edinburgh.* Edinburgh, 1833.

—— *The Picture of Scotland.* 2 vols., Edinburgh, 1827.

—— *A Picture of Stirling.* Stirling, 1830.

—— ed. *The Poetical Works of Robert Burns.* Edinburgh, 1838.

—— *Popular Rhymes, Fireside Stories, and Amusements of Scotland.* Edinburgh, 1842.

—— *The Popular Rhymes of Scotland.* Edinburgh and London, 1826.

—— ed. *Robert Forbes' Jacobite Memoirs of the Rebellion of 1745.* Edinburgh, 1834.

—— *The Scottish Ballads.* Edinburgh, 1829.

—— *Scottish Jests and Anecdotes.* Edinburgh, 1832.

—— *The Scottish Songs.* 2 vols., Edinburgh, 1829.

—— *Traditions of Edinburgh.* 2 vols., Edinburgh, 1825.

BIBLIOGRAPHY

CHAMBERS, WILLIAM. *The Life and Anecdotes of the Black Dwarf, or David Ritchie.* Edinburgh, 1820.

———— *Memoir of William and Robert Chambers.* 13th ed., Edinburgh and London, 1884.

CHEVIOT, ANDREW. *Proverbs, Proverbial Expressions, and Popular Rhymes of Scotland.* Paisley and London, 1896.

CHRISTIANSEN, REIDAR, ed. *Folktales of Norway.* Chicago and London, 1964.

CLODD, EDWARD. *A Brief History and Examination of Modern Spiritualism.* London, 1917.

———— *The Childhood of the World.* London, 1873.

———— *The Childhood of Religions.* London, 1875.

———— *County Folklore, Printed Extracts. No. 2. Suffolk.* London, 1889.

———— *Magic in Names.* London, 1920.

———— *Memories.* London, 1916.

———— *Myths and Dreams.* London, 1885.

———— *Pioneers of Evolution from Thales to Huxley.* London, 1897. Revised ed., London, 1907.

———— *Tom Tit Tot, an Essay on Savage Philosophy in Folk-Tale.* London, 1898.

CLOUSTON, WILLIAM ALEXANDER, ed. *Arabian Poetry for English Readers.* Glasgow, 1881.

———— ed. *The Bakhtyar Nama.* Trans. William Ouseley. Larkhall, Lanarkshire, 1883.

———— *The Book of Noodles.* London, 1888.

———— *The Book of Sindibad.* Glasgow, 1884.

———— *Book of Wise Sayings.* London, 1893.

———— *Flowers from a Persian Garden.* London, 1890.

———— *A Group of Eastern Romances and Stories.* Glasgow, 1889.

———— *Literary Coincidences.* Glasgow, 1892.

———— *On The Magical Elements in Chaucer's Squire's Tale.* Chaucer Society, 1889.

———— *Popular Tales and Fictions.* 2 vols., New York, Edinburgh, and London, 1887.

———— *Some Persian Tales.* Glasgow, 1892.

COMPARETTI, DOMENICO. *Traditional Poetry of the Finns.* Introduction by Andrew Lang. London, 1898.

COSQUIN, EMMANUEL, ed. *Contes populaires de Lorraine.* 2 vols., Paris, 1886.

COX, GEORGE WILLIAM. *An Introduction to the Science of Comparative Mythology and Folklore.* London, 1881.

———— *A Manual of Mythology, in the Form of Question and Answer.* London, 1867.

———— *The Mythology of the Aryan Nations.* 2 vols., London, 1870; revised ed., 1882.

———— *Poseidôn: A Link Between Semite, Hamite, and Aryan.* London, 1872.

———— *Tales from Greek Mythology.* London, 1861.

———— *Tales of the Gods and Heroes.* London, 1862.

COX, MARIAN ROALFE. *Cinderella.* Introduction by Andrew Lang. London, 1893.

———— *An Introduction to Folk-Lore.* London, 1895.

CRAIGIE, WILLIAM A. *Scandinavian Folk-Lore.* Paisley and London, 1896.

BIBLIOGRAPHY

CRANE, THOMAS F., ed. *The Exempla or Illustrative Stories from the Sermones Vulgares of Jacques de Vitry.* London, 1890.

CROKER, THOMAS CROFTON. *Fairy Legends and Traditions of the South of Ireland.* London, 1825; Parts II and III, 1828. New edition, ed. Thomas Wright, London, 1870.

―――― *The Keen of the South of Ireland.* London, 1844.

―――― *Legends of the Lakes; or, Sayings and Doings at Killarney.* From the collection of R. Adolphus Lynch. 2 vols., London, 1829.

―――― *Researches in the South of Ireland.* London, 1824.

CROMEK, ROBERT H. *Remains of Nithsdale and Galloway Song.* London, 1810; new ed., Paisley, 1880.

CROOKE, WILLIAM, ed. *Folktales from the Indus Valley,* collected by Major F. McNair and Thomas L. Barlow. Bombay, 1902.

―――― ed. *Hobson-Jobson, A Glossary of Colloquial Anglo-Indian Words and Phrases.* By Henry Yule and A. C. Burnell. London, 1903.

―――― *An Introduction to the Popular Religion and Folklore of Northern India.* Allahabad, 1894.

―――― *Things Indian.* London, 1906.

―――― *The Tribes and Castes of the North-Western Provinces and Oudh.* 4 vols., Calcutta, 1896.

CROUCH, NATHANIEL. *Miracles of Art and Nature.* London, 1678. Retitled *The Surprizing Miracles of Nature and Art,* Edinburgh, 1762.

CUNNINGHAM, ALLAN. *Songs: chiefly in the Rural Language of Scotland.* London, 1813.

―――― *Traditional Tales of the English and Scottish Peasantry.* 2 vols., London, 1822.

CURTIN, JEREMIAH. *Myths and Folk-Lore of Ireland.* Boston, 1890.

―――― *Tales of the Fairies and of the Ghost World.* Preface by Alfred Nutt. London, 1895.

DALYELL, JOHN G. *The Darker Superstitions of Scotland.* Edinburgh, 1834; Glasgow, 1835.

DAMES, MANSEL L. *Popular Poetry of the Baloches.* 2 vols., London, 1905.

DASENT, GEORGE WEBBE. *Popular Tales from the Norse.* London and New York, 1859. New ed., Edinburgh, 1912, with Memoir of G. W. Dasent by Arthur I. Dasent.

DAVIDS, THOMAS W. RHYS, trans. *Buddhist Birth Stories; or Jataka Tales.* By V. Fausboll. London, 1880.

DAVIES, EDWARD. *The Mythology and Rites of the British Druids.* London, 1809.

DAVIES, JONATHAN C. *Folk-Lore of West and Mid-Wales.* Aberystwyth, 1911.

DAY, LAL BEHARI. *Folk-tales of Bengal.* London, 1883.

DAYRELL, ELPHINSTONE. *Folk Stories from Southern Nigeria, West Africa.* London, 1910.

DENHAM, MICHAEL AISLABIE. *The Denham Tracts.* Edited by James Hardy. 2 vols., London, 1891–5.

―――― *Folklore: or, a Collection of Local Rhymes, Proverbs, Sayings, Prophecies, Slogans, etc.* Richmond, 1858.

DENNETT, RICHARD E. *Notes on the Folklore of the Fjort.* Introduction by Mary Kingsley. London, 1898.

DENNYS, NICHOLAS B. *The Folk-Lore of China.* London and Hongkong, 1876.

DIBDIN, THOMAS. *Reminiscences of a Literary Life.* London, 1836.

BIBLIOGRAPHY

DODSLEY, ROBERT. *A Select Collection of Old Plays.* London, 1744.

DOUCE, FRANCIS. *Illustrations of Shakespeare, and of Ancient Manners.* 2 vols., London, 1807.

DUGDALE, WILLIAM. *The Antiquities of Warwickshire.* London, 1656.

DOUGLAS, GEORGE, ed. *Scottish Fairy and Folk Tales.* London, 1893.

DOWDALL, MARY, and E. T. CAMPAGNAC, eds. *Lancashire Legends, selected from Roby's 'Traditions of Lancashire'.* London, 1911.

ELTON, OLIVER, trans. *The First Nine Books of the Danish History of Saxo Grammaticus.* Introduction by Frederick York Powell. London, 1894.

FARRER, JAMES ANSON. *Primitive Manners and Customs.* London, 1879.

FAYE, ANDREAS. *Norsk Folke-Sagn.* Christiania, 1844.

FLETCHER, ROLAND S. *Hausa Sayings and Folk-Lore.* London, 1912.

FOSBROKE, THOMAS D. *Encyclopedia of Antiquities.* 2 vols., London, 1825.

FRAZER, JAMES G., *Folk-Lore in the Old Testament.* 3 vols., London, 1918.

—— *The Golden Bough.* 2 vols., London, 1890; 2nd ed., 3 vols., London, 1900; 3rd ed., 12 vols., London, 1907–15.

—— *Questions on the Customs, Beliefs, and Languages of Savages.* Cambridge, 1907.

FRERE, MARY. *Old Deccan Days.* London, 1868. 3rd ed., London, 1881.

FURNIVALL, FREDERICK J., and W. G. STONE, eds. *The Tale of Beryn.* London, 1887.

GAIDOZ, HENRI, and PAUL SÉBILLOT. *Blason populaire de la France.* Paris and Versailles, 1884.

GARNETT, LUCY M. J., and JOHN S. STUART GLENNIE. *Greek Folk Poesy.* 2 vols., Guildford, 1896.

—— *Greek Folk-Songs from the Turkish Provinces of Greece.* London, 1885; 2nd ed., 1888.

—— *The Women of Turkey and Their Folk-Lore.* 2 vols., London, 1890–1.

GASTER, MOSES. *The Exempla of the Rabbis.* London and Leipzig, 1924.

—— *Ilchester Lectures on Greeko-Slavonic Literature.* London, 1887.

—— *Literatura populară romănă.* Bucharest, 1883.

—— *Ma'aseh Book. Book of Jewish Tales and Legends.* Philadelphia, 1934.

—— *Rumanian Bird and Beast Stories.* London, 1915.

—— *Studies and Texts in Folklore, Magic, Medieval Romance, Hebrew Apocrypha and Samaritan Archaeology.* 3 vols., London, 1925–8.

GELDART, EDMUND M., ed. and trans. *Folk-Lore of Modern Greece.* London, 1884.

GIBSON, EDMUND, ed. *Camden's Britannia.* London, 1695.

GILL, WILLIAM WYATT. *Myths and Songs from the South Pacific.* London, 1876.

GLANVILL, JOSEPH. *Saducismus Triumphatus.* London, 1681.

GOMME, ALICE BERTHA. *Old English Singing Games.* London, 1900.

—— *The Traditional Games of England, Scotland, and Ireland.* 2 vols., London, 1894–8.

GOMME, GEORGE LAURENCE. *Ethnology in Folklore.* London, 1892.

—— *Folklore as an Historical Science.* London, 1908.

—— *Folk-Lore Relics of Early Village Life.* London, 1883.

—— ed. The Gentleman's Magazine Library: *Archaeology* (1886), *Architectural Antiquities* (1890–1), *Dialect, Proverbs and Word-Lore* (1884), *Popular Superstitions* (1884), *English Traditional Lore* (1885), *Manners and Customs* (1883), *Romano-British Remains* (1887).

—— *The Governance of London.* London, 1907.

BIBLIOGRAPHY

GOMME, GEORGE LAURENCE. *The Handbook of Folklore.* London, 1890.

——— ed. *The History of Thomas Hickathrift.* London, 1885.

——— *Lectures on the Principles of Local Government.* London, 1897.

——— *The Literature of Local Institutions.* London, 1886.

——— *London.* London, 1914.

——— *The London County Council.* London, 1888.

——— *London in the Reign of Victoria, 1837–97.* London, 1898.

——— *The Making of London.* Oxford, 1912.

——— ed. *Mother Bunch's Closet.* London, 1885.

——— *Primitive Folk-Moots.* London, 1880.

——— *The Village Community.* London, 1890.

GOMME, LAURENCE, and ALICE B. GOMME. *British Folk-Lore, Folk-Songs, and Singing Games.* London, 1916.

GOUGH, RICHARD, ed. *Camden's Britannia.* London, 1789.

GRANT, ANNE MACVICAR. *Essays on the Superstitions of the Highlanders of Scotland.* 2 vols., London, 1811.

GRAY, JAMES. *Ancient Proverbs and Maxims from Burmese Sources.* London, 1866.

GREEN, ROGER LANCELYN, *Andrew Lang: A Critical Biography.* Leicester, England, 1946.

GREGOR, WALTER. *Notes on the Folk-Lore of the North-East of Scotland.* London, 1881.

GREY, GEORGE. *Polynesian Mythology and Ancient Traditional History of the New Zealand Race.* London, 1855.

GRIERSON, GEORGE. *Bihār Peasant Life.* Calcutta, 1885.

——— trans. *Hatim's Tales, Kashmiri Stories and Songs.* Commentary by W. Crooke. London, 1923.

GRIMM, JACOB. *Deutsche Mythologie.* Göttingen, 1835; 2nd ed. 1843. (Trans. as *Teutonic Mythology*; see Stallybrass, James S.).

——— *Reinhart Fuchs.* Berlin, 1834.

GRIMM, JACOB and WILHELM. *Deutsche Sagen.* 2 vols., Berlin, 1816–18.

——— *Grimm's Household Tales*, trans. and ed. by Margaret Hunt. 2 vols., London, 1884. Introduction by Andrew Lang. Reprinted 1910.

——— *Kinder- und Hausmärchen.* 3 vols., Berlin, 1812–22.

GRIMM, WILHELM, trans. *Irische Elfenmärchen.* By T. Crofton Croker. Leipzig, 1826.

GROOME, FRANCIS HINDES. *Gypsy Folk-Tales.* London, 1899.

——— *In Gypsy Tents.* Edinburgh, 1880.

——— *Kriegspiel.* London, 1896.

GROSE, FRANCIS. *The Antiquities of England and Wales.* 6 vols., London, 1773–87.

——— *The Antiquities of Ireland*, edited by Edward Ledwick. 2 vols., London, 1791–5.

——— *The Antiquities of Scotland.* 2 vols., London, 1789–91.

——— *A Classical Dictionary of the Vulgar Tongue.* London, 1785; 2nd ed., 1788.

——— *Military Antiquities Respecting a History of the English Army.* 2 vols., London, 1786–8.

——— *A Provincial Glossary.* London, 1787; 2nd ed., 1790.

GURNEY, EDMUND, F. W. H. MYERS, and F. PODMORE. *Phantasms of the Living.* 2 vols., London, 1886.

[449]

HAKLUYT, RICHARD. *Divers Voyages touching the Discouerie of America.* London, 1582.

HALLIWELL-PHILLIPPS, JAMES ORCHARD, ed. *Ballads and Poems respecting Hugh of Lincoln.* Brixton Hill, 1849.

—— ed. (with THOMAS WRIGHT). *Ancient Ballads and Broadsides published in England in the Sixteenth Century.* London, 1867.

—— *A Dictionary of Archaic and Provincial Words.* 2 vols., London, 1847.

—— ed. *Early Naval Ballads of England;* London, 1841.

—— *Illustrations of the Fairy Mythology of A Midsummer Night's Dream.* Shakespeare Society, 1845.

—— *The Jokes of the Cambridge Coffee-Houses in the Seventeenth Century.* Cambridge and London, 1841.

—— *Notes of Family Excursions in North Wales.* London, 1860.

—— *The Nursery Rhymes of England, Collected principally from Oral Tradition.* 1st ed., Percy Society, 1842; 2nd ed., London, 1843; 4th ed., 1846; 5th ed., 1853.

—— *Popular Rhymes and Nursery Tales.* London, 1849.

—— *Rambles in Western Cornwall by the Footsteps of the Giants.* London, 1861.

—— *The Will of Wit.* London, 1860.

HAMILTON, MARY. *Greek Saints and Their Festivals.* Edinburgh and London, 1884.

HANUSCH, IGNAZ JOHANN. *Die Wissenschaft des Slawischen Mythos im Weitesten.* Lemberg, 1842.

HARDWICK, CHARLES. *Traditions, Superstitions, and Folk-Lore.* Manchester and London, 1872.

HARLAND, JOHN, and T. T. WILKINSON. *Lancashire Legends, Traditions, Pagants, Sports, &c.* Edinburgh and London, 1783.

—— *Lancashire Folk-Lore.* London and New York, 1867.

HARRIS, HERMANN G. *Hausa Stories and Riddles.* Weston-super-Mare, 1908.

HARTLAND, EDWIN SIDNEY, ed. *County Folk-Lore, Printed Extracts. No. 1 Gloucestershire.* London, 1892.

—— *De Nugis Curialium* by Walter Map. London, 1923.

—— ed. *English Fairy and other Folk Tales.* London, 1890.

—— *Folklore: What is It and What is the Good of It?* London, 1899.

—— *The Legend of Perseus.* 3 vols., London, 1894–6.

—— *Mythology and Folktales: Their Relation and Interpretation.* London, 1900.

—— *Primitive Paternity: The Myth of Supernatural Birth in Relation to the History of the Family.* 2 vols., London, 1909.

—— *Primitive Society.* London, 1921.

—— *Ritual and Belief: Studies in the History of Religion.* London, 1914.

—— *The Science of Fairy Tales.* London, 1891.

—— *Welsh Folklore: Its Collection and Study.* Liverpool, 1892.

HASTINGS, JAMES, ed. *Encyclopaedia of Religion and Ethics.* 12 vols., Edinburgh, 1908–15.

HAZLITT, WILLIAM CAREW. *English Proverbs and Proverbial Phrases.* London, 1869.

—— ed. *Popular Antiquities of Great Britain.* Edited from the Materials Collected by John Brand. London, 1870.

—— *The Shakespeare Jest-Books.* 3 vols., London, 1864.

HENDERSON, GEORGE. *The Popular Rhymes, Sayings and Proverbs of the County of Berwick.* Newcastle-on-Tyne, 1856.

HENDERSON, WILLIAM. *Notes on the Folk Lore of the Northern Counties of England and the Borders.* London, 1866; 2nd ed., 1879.

HODGEN, MARGARET T. *The Doctrine of Survivals.* London, 1936.

——— *Early Anthropology in the Sixteenth and Seventeenth Centuries.* Philadelphia, 1964.

HOGG, DAVID. *Life of Allan Cunningham, with Selections from his Works and Correspondence.* Dumfries, 1875.

HOLLIS, ALFRED C. *The Masai, Their Language and Folklore.* Oxford, 1905.

——— *The Nandi, Their Language and Folklore.* Oxford, 1909.

HONE, WILLIAM. *The Every-Day Book and Table Book.* 3 vols., London, 1831.

——— *Every-Day Book.* London, 1826–7.

——— *Table Book.* London, 1827.

——— *Sixty Curious and Authentic Narratives and Anecdotes.* London, 1819.

——— *Year Book.* London, 1832.

HOWELLS, WILLIAM. *Cambrian Superstitions.* Tipton and London, 1831.

HOWITT, ALFRED WILLIAM and LORIMER FISON. *Kamilaroi and Kurnai.* Melbourne, 1880.

HUGHES, THOMAS. *The Scouring of the White Horse.* London, 1859; new ed., 1892.

HUNT, ROBERT. *Popular Romances of the West of England.* 2 vols., London, 1865.

HUXLEY, THOMAS HENRY. *Evidence as to Man's Place in Nature.* London, 1863.

HYDE, DOUGLAS. *Beside the Fire.* Postscript and notes by Alfred Nutt. London, 1890; reprinted 1910.

——— *Leabhar Sgeulaigheachta.* Gill, 1889.

——— *Love Songs of Connacht.* London and Dublin, 1893.

——— *West Irish Folk-Tales and Romances.* London, 1893.

JACOBS, JOSEPH. *As Others Saw Him.* London, 1895.

——— *Barlaam and Josaphat.* London, 1896.

——— ed. *Celtic Fairy Tales.* London, 1892.

——— ed. *English Fairy Tales.* London, 1890.

——— *The Fables of Æsop, Selected, told Anew, and Their History Traced.* London, 1894.

——— ed. *The Fables of Æsop.* 2 vols., London, 1889.

——— ed. *The Earliest English Version of the Fables of Bidpai.* London, 1888.

——— ed. *Indian Fairy Tales.* London, 1892.

——— *Jewish Contributions to Civilization.* Philadelphia, 1919.

——— *Jewish Ideals, and Other Essays.* London, 1896.

——— *The Jews of Angevin England.* London, 1893.

——— *More Celtic Fairy Tales.* London, 1894.

——— *More English Fairy Tales.* London, 1894.

——— ed. *The Most Delectable History of Reynard the Fox.* London, 1895.

——— *An Inquiry into the Sources of the History of the Jews in Spain.* London, 1894.

——— *Studies in Biblical Archaeology.* London, 1894.

——— *Studies in Jewish Statistics.* London, 1891.

JACOBS, JOSEPH and ALFRED NUTT, eds. *The International Folk-Lore Congress, 1891. Papers and Transactions.* London, 1892.

BIBLIOGRAPHY

JACOBS, JOSEPH, and LUCIEN WOLF. *Bibliotheca Anglo-Judaica, A Bibliographical Guide to Anglo-Jewish History.* London, 1888.

JAMES I, KING OF ENGLAND. *Daemonologie.* Edinburgh, 1597.

JAMIESON, JOHN. *An Etymological Dictionary of the Scottish Language.* 2 vols., Edinburgh, 1808.

JENKINS, D. E. *Bedd Gelert, Its Facts, Fairies and Folk-Lore.* Portmadoc, 1899.

JOHNSON, SAMUEL. *A Journey to the Western Islands of Scotland.* London, 1775.

JONES, EDWARD. *Musical and Poetical Relicks of the Welsh Bards.* London, 1784; 2nd ed., 1794.

JONES, W. HENRY, and LAJOS L. KROPF, eds. and trans. *The Folk-Tales of the Magyars.* London, 1889.

Kalilag und Damnag. Alte syrische Übersetzung des indischen Furstenspiegels. Text und deutsche Übersetzung von G. Bickell. Mit einer Einleitung von T. Benfey. Leipzig, 1876.

KEARY, CHARLES FRANCIS. *The Dawn of History: An Introduction to Prehistoric Study.* London, 1878.

——— *Outlines of Primitive Belief among the Indo-European Races.* London, 1882.

KEIGHTLEY, THOMAS. *The Fairy Mythology.* London, 1828; new eds., 1860, 1878.

——— *The Mythology of Ancient Greece and Italy.* London, 1832; 2nd ed., 1834.

——— *Tales and Popular Fictions.* London, 1834.

KELLY, WALTER K. *Curiosities of Indo-European Tradition and Folk-Lore.* London, 1863.

KENNEDY, PATRICK. *The Bardic Stories of Ireland.* Dublin, 1871.

——— *The Fireside Stories of Ireland.* Dublin, 1870.

——— *Legendary Fictions of the Irish Celts.* London, 1866.

KINGSCOTE, MRS. HOWARD, and S. M. NATESA SASTRI. *Tales of the Sun, or, the Folklore of Southern India.* London, 1890.

KINGSLEY, MARY. *Travels in West Africa.* London, 1897. 3rd ed. with introduction by John E. Flint, New York, 1965.

——— *West African Studies.* London, 1899; 3rd ed. with introduction by John E. Flint, New York, 1964.

KIRK, ROBERT. *The Secret Commonwealth of Elves, Fauns, and Fairies.* Comment by Andrew Lang. London, 1893.

KIRKLAND, EDWIN C. *A Bibliography of South Asian Folklore.* Bloomington, Indiana, 1966.

KITTREDGE, GEORGE L. *Witchcraft in Old and New England.* Cambridge, Mass., 1929.

KNOWLES, J. HINTON. *A Dictionary of Kashmiri Proverbs and Sayings.* Bombay, 1885.

——— *Folk-Tales of Kashmir.* London, 1888.

KOEHLER, JOHANN. *Volksbrauch, Aberglauben, Sagen und andre alte Überlieferungen im Voigtlande.* Leipzig, 1867.

KOELLE, SIGISMUND W. *African Native Literature.* London, 1854.

KUHN, ADALBERT. *Die Herabkunft des Feuers und des Göttertranks.* Berlin, 1859.

LANE, EDWARD WILLIAM, trans. *The Thousand and One Nights* (1838–41). Introduction by Joseph Jacobs. 3 vols., London, 1895.

LANG, ANDREW, ed. *The Arabian Nights Entertainment.* London, 1898.

BIBLIOGRAPHY

LANG, ANDREW. *The Book of Dreams and Ghosts.* London, 1897.

———— ed. *Border Ballads.* London, 1895.

———— *Cock Lane and Common-Sense.* London, 1894.

———— ed. *A Collection of Ballads.* London, 1897.

———— *Custom and Myth.* London, 1884.

———— *In the Wrong Paradise, and Other Stories.* London, 1886.

———— *Magic and Religion.* London, 1901.

———— *The Making of Religion.* London, 1898.

———— *Modern Mythology, A Reply to Max Müller.* London, 1897.

———— *Myth, Ritual and Religion.* 2 vols., London, 1887; new ed. 1899; reprinted 1913.

———— ed. *Perrault's Popular Tales.* Edited from the Original Edition, with Introduction, &c. Oxford, 1888.

———— ed. *Sir Walter Scott and the Border Minstrelsy.* London, 1910.

LAWSON, JOHN. *Modern Greek Folklore and Ancient Greek Religion.* Cambridge, 1910.

LEAN, VINCENT STUCKEY, *Lean's Collectanea.* 4 vols., London and Bristol, 1902–4.

LEATHER, ELLA. *The Folk-Lore of Herefordshire.* Hereford and London, 1912.

LOCKHART, J. G. *Memoirs of the Life of Sir Walter Scott, Bart.* 7 vols., Edinburgh and London, 1837–8.

LOOMIS, C. GRANT. *White Magic.* Cambridge, Mass., 1948.

LOVER, SAMUEL. *Legends and Stories of Ireland.* Dublin, 1831; 2nd series, London, 1834.

LOWERISON, HARRY. *Field and Folklore. With a Chapter on Folk-Lore by Alfred Nutt.* London, 1899.

LUBBOCK, JOHN. *The Origin of Civilisation and the Primitive Condition of Man.* London, 1870.

———— *Pre-Historic Times, as illustrated by Ancient Remains, and the Manners and Customs of Modern Savages.* London and Edinburgh, 1865.

LYALL, ALFRED C. *Asiatic Studies.* London, 1882; new ed., 2 vols., London, 1899.

MACCULLOCH, EDGAR. *Guernsey Folk Lore.* London and Guernsey, 1903.

MACCULLOCH, JOHN A. *The Childhood of Fiction.* London, 1905.

MACDOUGALL, JAMES. *Folk and Hero Tales.* London, 1891.

MACGREGOR, ALASDAIR A. *The Peat-Fire Flame. Folk-Tales and Traditions of the Highlands and Islands.* Edinburgh and London, 1937.

MACINNES, DONALD. *Folk and Hero Tales.* London, 1890.

MACKECHNIE, JOHN, ed. *The Dewar Manuscripts.* Vol. 1, *Scottish West Highland Folk Tales.* Glasgow, 1964.

MACKENZIE, ALEXANDER. *The Prophecies of the Brahan Seer.* Introductory chapter by Andrew Lang. Stirling, 1899.

MACKENZIE, WILLIAM M. *Hugh Miller, A Critical Study.* London, 1905.

MACLAGAN, ROBERT C. *Evil Eye in the Western Highlands.* London, 1902.

———— *The Games and Diversions of Argyleshire.* London, 1901.

———— *Our Ancestors, Scots, Picts & Cymry, and What Their Traditions Tell Us.* London and Edinburgh, 1913.

———— *The Perth Incident of 1396 from a Folk-Lore Point of View.* Edinburgh and London, 1905.

———— *Scottish Myths, Notes on Scottish History and Tradition.* Edinburgh, 1882.

MACRAE, NORMAN, ed. *Highland Second-Sight.* Dingwall, 1908.

MACRITCHIE, DAVID. *The Testimony of Tradition.* London, 1890.

MALKIN, BENJAMIN HEATH. *The Scenery, Antiquities and Biography of South Wales, from Materials collected during Two Excursions in the Year 1803.* London, 1804.

MANNHARDT, WILHELM. *Germanische Mythen.* Berlin, 1858.

MARETT, ROBERT R. *Psychology and Folk-Lore.* London, 1920.

—— *Tylor.* London, 1936.

MARTIN, MARTIN. *A Description of the Western Islands of Scotland.* London, 1703.

MAYHEW, HENRY. *London Labour and the London Poor.* 4 vols., London, 1851–62.

MCCABE, JOSEPH. *Edward Clodd, A Memoir.* London, 1932.

MCKAY, JOHN G., ed. *More West Highland Tales.* From the MS. of Campbell of Islay. 2 vols., Edinburgh and London, 1940, 1960.

MCLENNAN, JOHN FERGUSON. *Primitive Marriage.* Edinburgh, 1865.

MCPHERSON, JOSEPH M. *Primitive Beliefs in the North-East of Scotland.* London, New York, Toronto, 1929.

MILLER, HUGH. *Essays, Historical and Biographical, Political and Social, Literary and Scientific.* Edited by Peter Bayne (1862). Boston, 1865.

—— *My Schools and Schoolmasters* (1854). Introduction and Notes by W. M. MacKenzie. Edinburgh, 1907.

—— *The Old Red Sandstone.* Edinburgh, 1841.

—— *Scenes and Legends of the North of Scotland* (1835, new expanded ed. 1850). 8th ed., Edinburgh, 1869.

—— *Tales and Sketches* (1863). 6th ed., Edinburgh, 1872.

—— *The Testimony of the Rocks.* Edinburgh, 1857.

MISSON, HENRI. *Memoirs and Observations in his Travels over England.* Translated by John Ozell from the French edition of 1698. London, 1719.

MITFORD, ALGERNON B. (Lord Redesdale). *Tales of Old Japan.* 2 vols., London, 1871.

MOORE, ARTHUR W. *The Folk-Lore of the Isle of Man.* London, 1891.

Moresinum Depravatae Religionis Orgo et Incrementum. Edinburgh, 1593, 1594.

MÜLLER, GEORGIANA A., ed. *The Life and Letters of the Right Honourable Friedrich Max Müller.* 2 vols., New York, London, and Bombay, 1902.

MÜLLER, MAX. *Anthropological Religion.* London, 1892.

—— *Chips from a German Workshop.* 4 vols., Oxford and London, 1867–1875.

—— *Comparative Mythology, An Essay.* Edited by Abram Smythe Palmer. London and New York, 1909.

—— *Contributions to the Science of Mythology.* 2 vols., London, New York, and Bombay, 1897.

—— *India: What Can it Teach Us? A Course of Lectures delivered before the University of Cambridge.* London and Oxford, 1883.

—— *Introduction to the Science of Religion.* London and Oxford, 1873.

—— *Lectures on the Origin and Growth of Religion as Illustrated by the Religions of India.* London, 1878.

—— *Lectures on the Science of Language, delivered at the Royal Institution of Great Britain.* 2 vols., London, 1861–4.

—— *My Autobiography, A Fragment.* London, 1901.

[454]

BIBLIOGRAPHY

MÜLLER, MAX. *Natural Religion: The Gifford Lectures Delivered before the University of Glasgow in 1888.* London and Oxford, 1889.

—— *Oxford Essays.* Oxford, 1856.

—— *Physical Religion.* *The Gifford Lectures delivered before the University of Glasgow in 1890.* London, 1891.

—— *Selected Essays on Language, Mythology, and Religion.* London, 1881.

MUNBY, ALAN N. L. *The Family of Sir Thomas Phillipps.* Cambridge, 1952.

MUSÄUS, JOHANN C. A. *Volksmährchen der Deutschen.* Gotha, 1787.

MYERS, FREDERIC W. H. *Human Personality and its Survival of Bodily Death.* 2 vols., London, 1903.

NAPIER, JAMES. *Folk Lore: or, Superstitious Beliefs in the West of Scotland within this Century.* Paisley, 1879.

NARES, ROBERT. *A Glossary.* London, 1822. New edition edited by J. O. Halliwell-Phillipps and Thomas Wright. 2 vols., London, 1859.

NEWELL, WILLIAM WELLS. *Games and Songs of American Children.* New York, 1884.

NICHOLSON, ALEXANDER. *A Collection of Gaelic Proverbs and Familiar Phrases.* Edinburgh, 1881.

NICHOLSON, EDWARD W. B. *Golspie, Contributions to Its Folklore.* London, 1897.

—— *The Vernacular Inscriptions of the Ancient Kingdom of Albano.* London, 1896.

NICHOLSON, JOHN. *Folk Lore of East Yorkshire.* London, Hull, Driffield, 1890.

NUTT, ALFRED. *Celtic and Mediaeval Romance.* London, 1899.

—— *Cuchulainn, the Irish Achilles.* London, 1900.

—— *The Fairy Mythology of Shakespeare.* London, 1900.

—— *Ossian and the Ossianic Literature.* London, 1899.

—— *Studies on the Legend of the Holy Grail.* London, 1888.

—— *The Voyage of Bran, Son of Febal, to the Land of the Living; an old Irish saga* now first edited, with translation, notes, and glossary, by Kuno Meyer, with an Essay upon the Irish Vision of the Happy Otherworld, and the Celtic Doctrine of Rebirth. 2 vols., London, 1895–7.

OPIE, PETER and IONA. *The Lore and Language of Schoolchildren.* Oxford, 1959.

—— *The Oxford Dictionary of Nursery Rhymes.* Oxford, 1951.

O'SULLIVAN, SEAN. *Folktales of Ireland.* With a Foreword by Richard M. Dorson. Chicago and London, 1966.

OWEN, ELIAS. *Welsh Folk-Lore, A Collection of the Folk-Tales and Legends of North Wales.* Oswestry and Wrexham, 1896.

PALMER, ABRAM SMYTHE. *Babylonian Influence on the Bible and Popular Beliefs.* London, 1897.

—— *The Folk and Their Word-Lore.* London, 1904.

—— *Folk-Etymology.* London, 1882.

—— *Leaves from a Word-Hunter's Note-Book.* London, 1876.

—— *The Samson-Saga and Its Place in Comparative Religion.* London, 1913.

—— *Some Curios from a Word-Collector's Cabinet.* London, 1907.

PARKER, CATHERINE (MRS. K. LANGLOH). *Australian Legendary Tales.* London and Melbourne, 1896.

—— *The Euahlayi Tribe.* London, 1905.

—— *More Australian Legendary Tales.* London and Melbourne, 1898.

PARKER, HENRY. *Village Folk-Tales of Ceylon.* 3 vols., London, 1910–14.

PARKINSON, THOMAS. *Yorkshire Legends and Traditions*, London, 1888. Second Series, 1889.

PARSONS, COLEMAN O. *Witchcraft and Demonology in Scott's Fiction, with chapters on The Supernatural in Scottish Literature.* Edinburgh and London, 1964.

PEDROSO, CONSIGLIERI. *Portuguese Folk-Tales.* Translated by Henriqueta Monteiro. London, 1882.

PEELE, GEORGE. *The Old Wives Tale.* London, 1595.

PENNANT, THOMAS. *A Tour in Scotland, MDCCLXIX.* Chester, 1771; 2nd ed., London, 1772; 4th ed., 2 vols., Dublin, 1775.

PERCY, THOMAS, trans. *Northern Antiquities* by Paul Henri Mallet. 2 vols., London, 1770.

—— *Reliques of Ancient English Poetry.* 3 vols., London, 1765.

PICKEN, ANDREW. *Traditionary Stories of Old Families, and Legendary Illustrations of Family History.* 2 vols., London, 1833.

PITCAIRN, ROBERT. *Criminal Trials in Scotland.* 3 vols., Edinburgh, 1833.

PITRÈ, GIUSEPPE, ed. *Novelle Popolari Toscane.* Firenze, 1885.

—— *Studio Critico sui Canti Popolari Siciliani.* Palermo, 1868.

PLOT, ROBERT. *The Natural History of Oxford-shire.* Oxford, 1677; 2nd ed. 1705.

—— *The Natural History of Stafford-shire.* Oxford, 1686.

PODMORE, FRANK. *Apparitions and Thought-Transference.* London, 1894.

PURCELL, WILLIAM E. *Onward Christian Soldier, A Life of Sabine Baring-Gould: Parson, Squire, Novelist, Antiquary, 1834–1924.* London, 1957.

RALSTON, WILLIAM R. S. *Russian Folk-Tales.* London, 1873.

—— *The Songs of the Russian People, as Illustrative of Slavonic Mythology and Russian Social Life.* London, 1872.

—— trans., *Tibetan Tales.* From the German of F. Anton von Schiefner. London, 1882; reissued 1906.

RAMSAY, ALLAN. *Poems.* 2 vols., Edinburgh, 1721, 1728.

RATTRAY, R. SUTHERLAND. *Hausa Folk-Lore, Customs, Proverbs, Etc.* Oxford, 1913.

—— *Some Folk-Lore Stories and Songs in Chinyanja.* London, 1907.

RAY, JOHN. *A Collection of English Proverbs.* Cambridge, 1670.

RHYS, JOHN. *Celtic Britain.* London and New York, 1882.

—— *Celtic Folklore, Welsh and Manx.* 2 vols., Oxford, 1901.

—— *Lectures on The Origin and Growth of Religion as illustrated by Celtic Heathendom.* London, 1888.

—— *Lectures on Welsh Philology.* London, 1877.

—— *Studies in the Arthurian Legend.* Oxford, 1891.

RICHARDSON, MOSES A. *The Local Historian's Table Book.* 8 vols., London, 1841–6.

RITSON, JOSEPH. *An Essay on Abstinence from Animal Food as a Moral Duty.* London, 1802.

—— *Fairy Tales.* London, 1831.

ROBERTS, PETER. *The Cambrian Popular Antiquities.* London, 1815.

ROBY, JOHN. *The Legendary and Poetical Remains of John Roby, with a sketch of his literary life and character,* by his widow. London, 1854.

—— *Popular Traditions of England.* London, 1841.

—— *Traditions of Lancashire.* 2 vols., London, 1829. 2nd series, 4 vols.,

London, 1829–31; 3rd ed., 3 vols., London, 1843. Also issued as *Popular Traditions of England—First Series—Lancashire* (1841).

RODD, RENNELL, *The Customs and Lore of Modern Greece*. London, 1892.

ROEBUCK, THOMAS. *A Collection of Proverbs and Proverbial Phrases in the Persian and Hindoostanee Languages*. Calcutta, 1824.

ROSE, HERBERT J. *Andrew Lang, His Place in Anthropology*. Edinburgh, 1951.

ROUSE, WILLIAM H. D. *The Talking Thrush, and Other Tales from India*. Collected by W. Crooke. London and New York, 1899.

SAXBY, JESSIE M. E. *Birds of Omen in Shetland*. With Notes on the Folk-Lore of the Raven and the Owl by W. A. Clouston.

SAYCE, ARCHIBALD H. *Reminiscences*. London, 1923.

SCHIEFNER, F. ANTON VON, trans. *Tibetan Tales*. (*See* W. R. S. Ralston.)

SCOT, REGINALD. *The Discoverie of Witchcraft*. London, 1584.

SCOTT, WALTER. *The Border Antiquities of England and Scotland*. 2 vols., London, 1814–17.

——— *Introductions and Notes and Illustrations to the Novels, Tales, and Romances of the Author of Waverly*. 3 vols., Edinburgh and London, 1833.

——— *Minstrelsy of the Scottish Border*. 3 vols., Kelso, 1802; 2nd ed., 1803. New edition edited by T. F. Henderson, 4 vols., Edinburgh, London, and New York, 1902.

——— *Letters on Demonology and Witchcraft*. London, 1830.

——— *Letters of Sir Walter Scott: Addressed to the Rev. R. Polwhele; D. Gilbert, Esq.; F. Douce, Esq. etc. etc*. London, 1832.

SELDEN, JOHN. *Table-Talk*. London, 1689.

SHORTLAND, EDWARD. *Traditions and Superstitions of the New Zealanders*. London, 1854.

SIKES, WILLIAM WIRT. *British Goblins: Welsh Folk-Lore, Fairy Mythology, Legends, and Traditions*. London, 1880.

SIMPSON, EVE B. *Folk Lore in Lowland Scotland*. London, 1908.

SINCLAIR, JOHN. *The Statistical Account of Scotland*. 21 vols., Edinburgh, 1791–9.

SKEAT, WALTER WILLIAM. *Malay Magic*. London, 1900.

SMITH, CHARLES ROACH. *Retrospections, Social and Archaeological*. 3 vols., London, 1883, 1886, 1891.

SMITH, WILLIAM ROBERTSON. *Lectures on the Religion of the Semites*. 1st Series, Edinburgh, 1889.

SOUTHEY, CHARLES CUTHBERT, ed. *The Life and Correspondence of Robert Southey*. 6 vols., London, 1849–50.

SOUTHEY, ROBERT, trans. *Chronicle of the Cid*. London, 1808.

——— *The Poetical Works of Robert Southey*. Paris, 1829.

SPENCER, W. BALDWIN, and F. J. GILLEN. *The Native Tribes of Central Australia*. London, 1899.

STALLYBRASS, JAMES S., trans. *Teutonic Mythology*. From the 4th edition (3 vols., 1875–8) of Jacob Grimm, *Deutsche Mythologie*. 4 vols., London, 1882–8.

STEEL, FLORA ANNIE. *Tales of the Punjab, Told by the People*. With Notes by R. C. Temple. London, 1894.

——— and R. C. TEMPLE. *Wide-Awake Stories*. Bombay and London, 1884.

STEERE, EDWARD. *Swahili Tales, as Told by Natives of Zanzibar*. London, 1870. Revised by Alice Werner, London, 1922.

STERNBERG, THOMAS. *The Dialect and Folk-Lore of Northamptonshire*. London, 1851.

STEWART, WILLIAM GRANT. *The Popular Superstitions and Festive Amusements of the Highlanders of Scotland*. Edinburgh, 1823. New ed., London, 1851.

STOKES, MAÌVE S. H. *Indian Fairy Tales*. Calcutta, 1879.

STOW, JOHN. *A Survay of London*. London, 1598; 2nd ed., 1603. Edited by William Thoms, London, 1842 [as *Survey*].

STRUTT, JOSEPH. *A Complete View of the Dress and Habits of the People of England from the Establishment of the Saxons in Britain to the Present Time*. 2 vols., London, 1796–9.

—— *The Chronicle of England: from the Arrival of Caesar to the End of the Saxon Heptarchy*. 2 vols., London, 1777–8.

—— *Glig-Gamena Angel-Deod, or the Sports and Pastimes of the People of England*. London, 1801. Edited by William Hone as *The Sports and Pastimes of the People of England*. London, 1830.

—— *Horda-Angel-Cynnan: or a Compleat View of the Manners, Customs, Arms, Habits, etc. of the Inhabitants of England*. 3 vols., London, 1774–6.

—— *The Regal and Ecclesiastical Antiquities of England*. London, 1773.

—— *Queenhoo-Hall, A Romance* [completed by Sir Walter Scott]. 4 vols., London, 1808.

STRUTT, WILLIAM. *A Memoir of the Life of Joseph Strutt, 1749–1802*. London, 1896.

STUART GLENNIE, J. S. *See* Garnett, Lucy M. J.

STRAPAROLA, GIOVANNI. *Le Piacevoli Notti*. 2 vols., Vinegia, 1550–5.

SWAINSON, CHARLES. *The Folk Lore and Provincial Names of British Birds*. London, 1886.

SWYNNERTON, CHARLES. *The Adventures of the Panjáb Hero Rájá Rasálu and Other Folk-Tales of the Panjáb*. Calcutta, 1884.

—— *Indian Nights' Entertainment; or, Folk-Tales from the Upper Indus*. London, 1892.

TAWNEY, CHARLES H., trans. *The Kathā Sarit Sāgara, or Ocean of the Streams of Story*. 2 vols., Calcutta, 1880–4.

TEMPLE, RICHARD C., ed. *A Dictionary of Hindustani Proverbs*, by S. W. Fallon. Benares and London, 1886.

—— *The Legends of the Panjáb*. 3 vols., Bombay, 1884–1900.

THACKERAY, WILLIAM MAKEPEACE. *The Irish Sketch-Book, 1842*. London, 1843.

THEAL, GEORGE MCCALL. *Compendium of the History and Geography of South Africa*. 3rd ed., London and Lovedale, 1878.

—— *Kaffir Folk-Lore*. London, 1882.

THISELTON-DYER, THOMAS FIRMINGER. *British Popular Customs*. London, 1871.

—— *Church-lore Gleanings*. London, 1891.

—— *Domestic Folk-lore*. London, 1881.

—— *English Folk-Lore*. London, 1878.

—— *Folk Lore of Shakespeare*. London and Edinburgh, 1883.

—— *Folk-Lore of Women as illustrated by legendary and traditionary tales, folk-rhymes, proverbial sayings, superstitions, etc.* London, 1905.

BIBLIOGRAPHY

THISELTON-DYER, THOMAS FIRMINGER, *The Ghost World*. London, 1893.
—— *The Folk-Lore of Plants*. London, 1889.
—— *Old English Social Life as Told by the Parish Registers*. London, 1898.
THOMAS, NORTHCOTE W. *Crystal-Gazing, Its History and Practice*. London, 1905.
THOMPSON, STITH. *Motif-Index of Folk Literature*. 6 vols., Bloomington, Indiana, 1955–8.
THOMS, WILLIAM J. *Anecdotes and Traditions*. London, 1839.
—— *The Book of the Court*. London, 1838.
—— ed. *Choice Notes from 'Notes and Queries': Folk Lore*. London, 1859.
—— ed. *A Collection of Early Prose Romances*. 3 vols., London 1828. Reissued as *Early English Prose Romances*, London, 1858.
—— *Gammer Gurton's Famous Histories*. Westminster, 1846.
—— *Gammer Gurton's Pleasant Stories*. Westminster, 1846.
—— *The History of Reynard the Fox*. London, 1844.
—— *Human Longevity, Its Facts and Its Fictions*. London, 1873.
—— ed. *Lays and Legends of Various Nations*. London, 1834. (Individual titles are *Lays and Legends of France; Lays and Legends of Germany; Lays and Legends of Spain; Lays and Legends of Tartary*.)
—— trans. *The Primeval Antiquities of Denmark* by J. J. A. Worsaae. London, 1849.
—— *Three Notelets on Shakespeare*. London, 1865.
THORPE, BENJAMIN, ed. *Ancient Laws and Institutes of England*. London, 1840.
—— *Northern Mythology, Comprising the Principal Popular Traditions and Superstitions of Scandinavia, North Germany and the Netherlands*. 3 vols., London, 1851–2.
—— ed. *Yule-tide Stories. A Collection of Scandinavian and North German Popular Tales and Traditions*. London, 1853.
THURSTON, EDGAR. *Omens and Superstitions of Southern India*. London and Leipsic, 1912.
TIDDY, REGINALD J. E. *The Mummers Play*. Oxford, 1923.
TRAIN, JOSEPH. *An Historical and Statistical Account of the Isle of Man*. 2 vols., Douglas, Isle of Man, 1845.
TREMEARNE, ARTHUR JOHN NEWMAN. *The Ban of the Bori: Demons and Demon-Dancing in West and North Africa*. London, 1914.
—— *Hausa Folk-Tales*. London, 1914.
—— *Hausa Superstitions and Customs*. London, 1913.
TREMEARNE, ARTHUR and MARY. *Fables and Fairy Tales for Little Folk; or, Uncle Remus in Hausaland*. Cambridge and London, 1910.
TREVELYAN, MARIE. *Folk-Lore and Folk-Stories of Wales*. London, 1909.
TURNBULL, A. *William and Robert Chambers 1800–83*. Edinburgh and London, n.d.
TYLOR, EDWARD B. *Primitive Culture*. 2 vols., London, 1871.
—— *Anthropology*. 2 vols., London, 1881.
—— *Researches into the Early History of Mankind and the Development of Civilization*. London, 1865.
UDAL, JOHN SYMONDS. *Dorsetshire Folk-Lore*. Hereford, 1922.
WALDRON, GEORGE. *The History and Description of the Isle of Man*. London, 1744.
WARREN, SAMUEL. *A Popular and Practical Introduction to Law Studies*. 3rd ed., 2 vols., London, 1863.

WARTER, JOHN WOOD, ed. *Selections from the Letters of R. Southey.* 4 vols., London, 1856.

—— *Southey's Common Place Book.* 4 vols., London, 1849–51.

WEEKS, JOHN H. *Congo Life and Folklore.* London, 1911.

Welsh Legends, A Collection of Popular Oral Tales. London, 1802.

WHITE, GILBERT. *The Natural History and Antiquities of Selborne.* London, 1789.

WILDE, JANE F. *Ancient Cures, Charms and Usages in Ireland.* London, 1890.

—— *Ancient Legends, Mystic Charms, and Superstitions of Ireland.* 2 vols., London, 1887.

WILDE, WILLIAM. *Irish Popular Superstitions.* Dublin, 1852.

WILSON, JOHN and ROBERT CHAMBERS. *The Land of Burns.* 2 vols., Glasgow, 1840.

WINSOR, JUSTIN. *Halliwelliana: a Bibliography of the Publications of James Orchard Halliwell-Phillipps.* Cambridge, Mass., 1881.

WODROW [also Woodrow], ROBERT. *Analecta: or Materials for a History of Remarkable Providences.* 4 vols., Glasgow, 1842–3.

WRATISLAW, ALBERT H., trans. *Sixty Folk-Tales from Exclusively Slavonic Sources.* London, 1889.

WRIGHT, THOMAS. *Essays on Archaeological Subjects.* 2 vols., London, 1861.

—— *Essays on Subjects connected with the Literature, Popular Superstitions, and History of England in the Middle Ages.* 2 vols., London, 1846.

—— ed. *Fairy Legends and Traditions of the South of Ireland,* by T. Crofton Croker.

—— *Gualteri Mapes, De Nugis Curialium Distinctiones Quinque.* Camden Society, 1850.

—— *The Historical Works of Giraldus Cambrensis.* London, 1863.

—— *A History of Domestic Manners and Sentiments in England During the Middle Ages.* London, 1862.

—— *History of Ireland.* London, 1854.

—— ed. *Introduction to the Seven Sages.* London, 1846.

—— *Narratives of Sorcery and Magic from the Most Authentic Sources.* 2 vols., London, 1851.

—— *St. Brandan: A Medieval Legend of the Sea, in English Prose and Verse.* London, 1844.

—— *St. Patrick's Purgatory.* London, 1844.

—— ed. *A Selection of Latin Stories.* London, 1842.

—— ed. *The Tale of the Basyn and The Frere and the Boy, Two Early Tales of Magic.* London, 1836.

WUTTKE, CARL FRIEDRICH ADOLF. *Der deutsche Volksaberglaube der Gegenwart.* Hamburg, 1860.

YEATS, WILLIAM B. *The Celtic Twilight.* London, 1893; 2nd ed., London, 1902.

—— *Fairy and Folk Tales of the Irish Peasantry.* London, 1888.

—— *Irish Fairy Tales.* London, 1892.

ZIMMER, HEINRICH. *Keltische Studien.* Berlin and Weimar, 1881.

Index

Note: Since titles are often of great length, they are here given in abbreviated form in many cases, but full details will be found in pages mentioned and the Bibliography. Lists (A) to (F) at the end of general index cover: (A) Fairies and other supernatural beings; (B) Legends, tales, the commoner myths, ballads and other narrations, *blason populaire*, prophecies, motifs; (C) Ghosts; (D) Customs, usages; (E) Rites and ceremonies; (F) Superstitions. As these cannot be mutually exclusive categories, Lists should be consulted one against another.

LIST (A)

Fairies and other supernatural entities (overlapping with legend, e.g., Corpse hounds, Tree fairies). Named individuals will be found in List (B), since transmission of name implies legendary standing

LIST (B)

Legendary figures, both human and supernatural, legends, folktales, fairy-tales, ballads, prophecies; motifs recurring in legends, blason populaire, myths

LIST (C)

Ghosts, spectral sights, revenants

LIST (D)

Customs, Usages

LIST (E)

Rites and Ceremonies

LIST (F)

Superstitions. (Family legends and superstitions of legendary persistence are in List (B).)

337. IS FEAR AN TOIT NA GHAODH A TUADH.
The reek is better than a northern blast.

60. THA SMÙTAIN FEIN AN CEAN GACH FÒID.
It's own reek is in each peat end (head).

367. CHA TIG AS A PHOIT ACH AN TOIT A BHIOS INNTE.
But the reek that is in it can come out of a pot.